ADVERTISING

Fifth Edition

Wright | Winter | Zeigler

yellow only

ADVERTISING

Wright | Winter | Zeigler

black only

ADVERTISING

McGRAW-HILL SERIES IN MARKETING

Consulting Editor
CHARLES SCHEWE
University of Massachusetts

BOWERSOX, COOPER, LAMBERT, and TAYLOR: Management in Marketing Channels
BRITT and BOYD: Marketing Management and Administrative Action
BUSKIRK and BUSKIRK: Retailing
COREY, LOVELOCK, and WARD: Problems in Marketing
DeLOZIER: The Marketing Communications Process
ENGEL: Advertising: The Process and Practice
GUILTINAN and PAUL: Marketing Management: Strategies and Programs
GUILTINAN and PAUL: Readings in Marketing Strategies and Programs
HOWARD: Consumer Behavior: Application of Theory
KINNEAR and TAYLOR: Marketing Research: An Applied Approach
LEE and DOBLER: Purchasing and Materials Management: Text and Cases
LOUDON and DELLA BITTA: Consumer Behavior: Concepts and Applications
MONROE: Pricing: Making Profitable Decisions
REDINBAUGH: Retailing Management: A Planning Approach
REYNOLDS and WELLS: Consumer Behavior
RUSSELL, BEACH, and BUSKIRK: Selling: Principles and Practices
SCHEWE and SMITH: Marketing: Concepts and Applications
SHAPIRO: Sales Program Management: Formulation and Implementation
STANTON: Fundamentals of Marketing
STROH: Managing the Sales Function
WRIGHT, WINTER, and ZEIGLER: Advertising

ADVERTISING

Fifth Edition

John S. Wright
School of Business
Georgia State University

Willis L. Winter, Jr.
School of Journalism
University of Oregon

Sherilyn K. Zeigler
College of Business Administration
University of Hawaii

McGraw-Hill Book Company

New York St. Louis San Francisco Auckland Bogotá Hamburg
Johannesburg London Madrid Mexico Montreal New Delhi Panama Paris
São Paulo Singapore Sydney Tokyo Toronto

ADVERTISING

1 2 3 4 5 6 7 8 9 0 RMRM 8 9 8 7 6 5 4 3 2

ISBN 0-07-072069-X

This book was set in Souvenir Light by Ruttle, Shaw & Wetherill, Inc. The editors were Carol Napier and Peggy Rehberger; the designer was Joseph Gillians; the production supervisor was John Mancia. New drawings were done by Fine Line Illustrations, Inc.
Rand McNally & Company was printer and binder.

Library of Congress Cataloging in Publication Data

Wright, John Sherman, date
Advertising.

(McGraw-Hill series in marketing)
Includes index.
1. Advertising. I. Winter, Willis L.
II. Zeigler, Sherilyn K. III. Title. IV. Series.
HF5823.W7 1982 659.1 81-8408
ISBN 0-07-072069-X AACR2

Contents

Part Four
ADVERTISING MESSAGES

Part Five
PLANNING AND MANAGING THE ADVERTISING CAMPAIGN

Preface

● Come with us on an all-new tour of the exciting world of advertising. More than half a million students have already made the journey, through the first four editions of this bestselling textbook, beginning with Wright and Warner's *Advertising*, in 1962. The solid educational principles presented then remain as the foundation for the fifth edition, as does the skillful blending of marketing and communications viewpoints. Thus, students appreciate advertising's business and socioeconomic involvements, contributions, and responsibilities.

Further, the book ties theoretical background material to practical pedagogy in an interesting, reader-involving manner. In fact, the fifth edition was reorganized and largely rewritten for improved clarity. Its dynamic tone, conversational style, and current illustrations promise an enlightening introduction to all phases of the advertising business.

Every chapter contains new material. For instance, managerial units come to life with graphic examples of how consumer products are advertised to achieve marketing objectives. New cases reflect important advertising developments and trends in a variety of product classes and media institutions. Media chapters give increased attention to cable TV and satellite communication, direct marketing, and mobile billboards, as well as the computer's expanding role in the decision-making process.

Creative areas focus much more specifically on the strategies behind tactical approaches, and on consumer lifestyles. Design and production chapters are more logically presented, and discussions are enhanced by new multimedia ads. Retail advertising receives added emphasis, as does advertising regulation. New, full chapters appear on international advertising, the future of advertising, and advertising careers. Finally, twelve brand new biographical profiles of advertising industry leaders should stimulate readers who aspire to careers in this field.

Newcomers to the book may be pleased to find that its flexible structure permits the rearrangement of units to suit individual teaching styles. And to past adopters the fifth edition should appear as an old friend. Granted, it has changed, but, clearly, age has brought improvements. Ninety percent of the more-than-200 illustrations are new. These, along with a fresh design format, make reading assignments enjoyable as well as educational.

All three authors teach this course on a regular basis. We are, therefore, keenly aware of students' learning environments and of the processes by which concepts are translated into understanding. We pride ourselves in having produced what we believe is the most comprehensive and contemporary textbook in the introductory advertising market. And we address students in a clear, forthright style that respects both their intelligence and their enthusiasm.

May you find the study of *Advertising* as fascinating as the activity itself is in the real world of business.

John S. Wright
Willis L. Winter, Jr.
Sherilyn K. Zeigler

Acknowledgments

Many people over many years have contributed to this book. We wish to call attention to some whose help proved invaluable.

Our own students at Georgia State University, the University of Oregon, and the University of Tennessee at Knoxville and, more recently, at the University of Hawaii at Manoa, added a great deal to the content of *Advertising*. As each of us teach in our classrooms—and we are all teachers of undergraduate students of advertising—we are able to "test market" ideas later to be incorporated in the book.

Many professors have been kind enough over the years to send along suggestions for the improvement of our textbook. At the request of the publisher, or one of the authors, the following advertising instructors and practitioners reviewed either the fourth edition of *Advertising*, the manuscript for the fifth edition, or specific chapters of the new edition. Many useful suggestions for improvement of the "product" resulted from these reviews. The following persons are cited for their contributions, with the understanding, of course, that the authors are responsible for any errors of omission or commission:

Franklin Acito
Indiana University

Keith Adler
Michigan State University

James Brubeck
Illinois State University

Robert Carrell
University of Oklahoma

John Eighmey
Young and Rubicam, New York

James Ferguson
University of Rochester

Alan D. Fletcher
University of Tennessee at Knoxville

Donald Glover
University of Nebraska at Lincoln

Thomas Hitzelberger
Southern Oregon State University

Kenneth Hollander
Kenneth Hollander Associates

Chet Hunt
San Antonio College

Charles B. Jones
Advertising Management Consultant

Harold H. Kassarjian
University of California at Los Angeles

Robert Kopp
Northeastern University

Jay Lindquist
Western Michigan University

Rom J. Markin
Washington State University

Charles Martin
Pepperdine University

Roy Paul Nelson
University of Oregon

Charles H. Patti
Arizona State University

Donald E. Schultz
Northwestern University

Jack Z. Sissors
Northwestern University

Roger Strang
University of Southern California

Peter B. Turk
Syracuse University

Bruce VandenBergh
Michigan State University

Harry Vardis
Tucker Wayne & Co.

Jon Wardrip
Texas Tech University

Nathan Weinstock
Orange County Community College

Sheldon Zwickel
University of Houston Central Campus

The advertising industry has been most gracious in providing the illustrations contained in this book. In most cases, the advertiser is clearly recognized by the mere presence of the firm's ad. The advertising agency behind the advertisement, unfortunately, remains anonymous in most instances.

Publishers of books and periodicals have given permission to quote from their materials.

Finally, each of us received cheerful and dependable assistance from departmental secretarial groups and from student assistants. Without such aid the job would never have been completed.

To all those people, and to those unmentioned, our heartfelt thanks.

Before we begin . . .

Prologue: Why Study Advertising?

● Advertising is a highly visible force in the American society. All of us receive many advertising messages daily. Advertising is essential to the success of business and industry. Furthermore, advertising strategies are employed more and more by nonbusiness organizations such as governments, colleges and universities, public service groups, and charities.

In addition to its usefulness, advertising is inherently interesting—even fascinating—to most people. Your curiosity about how advertising works probably motivated you to study this activity. Additional benefits to formal study of advertising are discussed below.

Social Significance

Informed citizens in the United States realize that advertising is an important institution in our society—a force that helps shape the lives of us all. The way that that force is used is sometimes challenged by social critics, so each of us should understand as much as we can about how advertising does function.

The American historian David M. Potter, in his book *People of Plenty,* highlights the belief that advertising is peculiarly identified with the history of our country. He compares it with "such longstanding institutions as the school and the church in the magnitude of its social influence," and goes on to state that advertising "dominates the media, has vast power in the shaping of popular standards, and it is really one of the very limited group of institutions which exercise social control."*

Another historian, Daniel J. Boorstin, who serves as Librarian of Congress, holds that the United States was the first nation in whose founding advertising played a critical role. Advertising was used to attract settlers and investors to the colonies by carrying the good news of the gospel of American ways of life. Later on, advertising became the symbol of what Boorstin calls "voluntariness" by serving as an educational device to provide opportunities for freedom of choice. There is no need to advertise if there is no opportunity for choice, and its presence is a "clue to the increasing opportunities for choice."†

If you agree with Potter's contention that advertising is an instrument of social influence, you will want to learn as much as you can about how it exerts that influence. Similarly, if you agree with Boorstin's idea that advertising is a vehicle for free choice, you will want to know how that force operates in our economic system.

---

* David M. Potter, *People of Plenty,* The University of Chicago Press, Chicago, 1954, pp. 166–168.

† Daniel J. Boorstin, "The Good News of Advertising," *Advertising Age,* Nov. 13, 1980, p. 20.

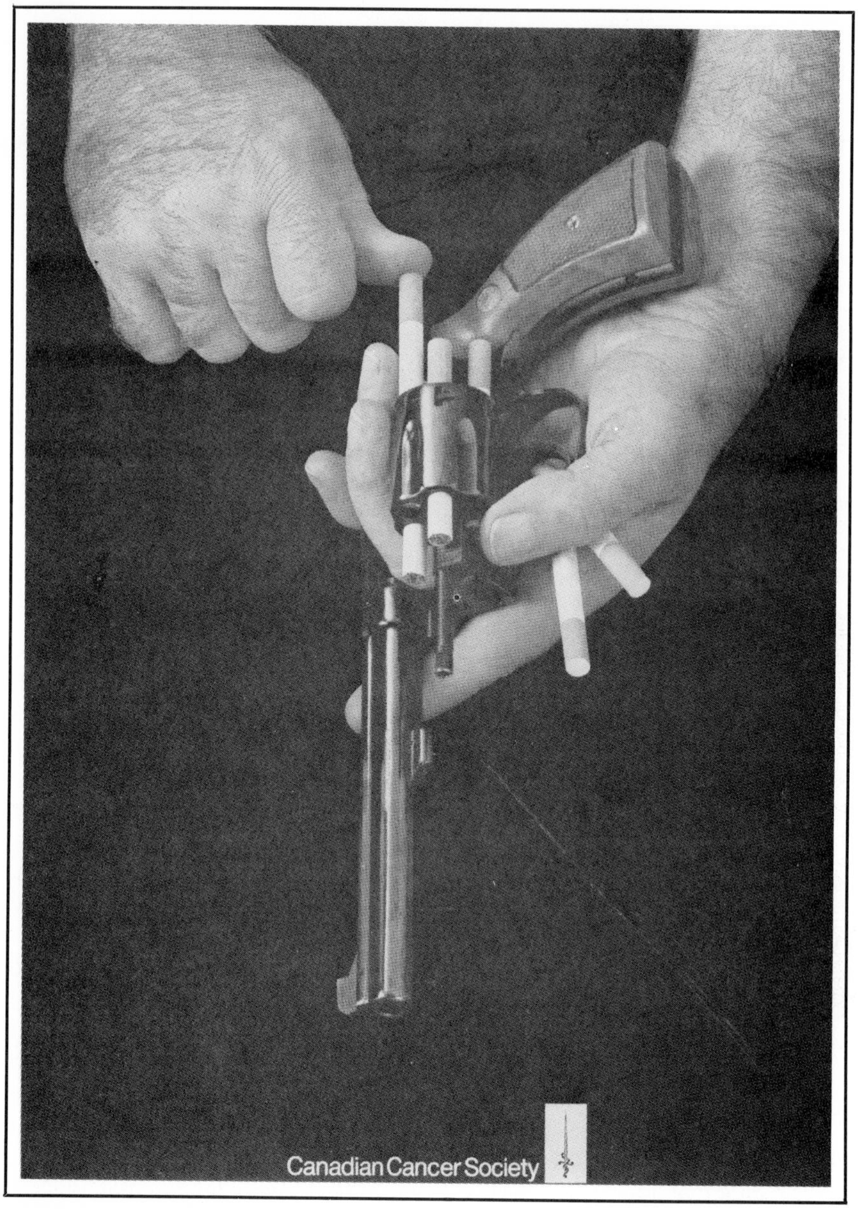

Figure P.1 This public service poster is an example of the use of advertising to persuade people to consider good health factors. [*Courtesy of the Canadian Cancer Society.*]

Practical Value

Each of us is a consumer. In that role, we are the targets of advertising programs. Understanding advertising will help you allocate your limited resources among the choices available in the marketplace, enabling you to become a better-informed buyer whose purchases will be more satisfying. Upon completing this book, you will look at advertising messages with clearer eyes. You should be better able to use advertising as an aid in your pursuit of happiness.

The general public has a poor understanding of advertising as a form of mass communication. This fact is compounded by the many loose comments made about advertising by intellectuals in our society. Knowledge of advertising, which is, or can be, powerfully persuasive and sometimes misused, should help you evaluate both the claims made for advertising and the criticisms of it in order to form your own opinion.

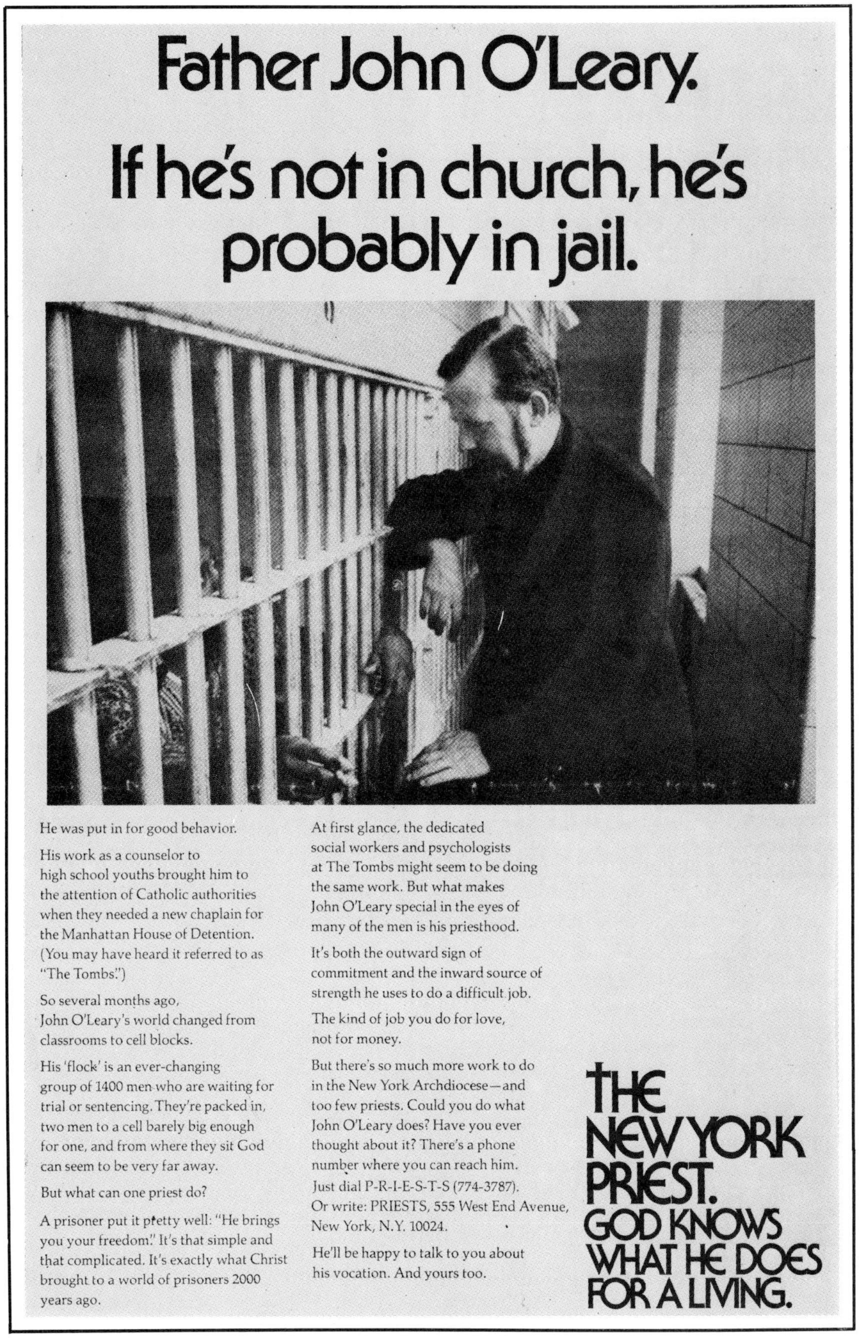

Figure P.2 Advertising is employed to interest young men in becoming priests.

Career Applications

Some of you may have already set advertising as your career goal; others of you may do so after studying it in detail. Marketing people obviously need to possess a thorough comprehension of advertising. Executives in almost every form of business should know the fundamentals of advertising, but this need is crucial in business situations where advertising is highly significant in company success. For

Je unajua?
Gharama ya kufua na Extra Active OMO ni ndogo sana ukilinganisha na sabuni ya kawaida...
...watumia OMO chache tu kwa kung'arisha hata nguo chafu zaidi!
EXTRA ACTIVE
BLUE
OMO
Husafisha na hung'arisha zaidi
Je, umeshajiunga na wanaong'aa? Hao ndio watu wanaosisitiza kutumia Extra Active Omo kila wanapofua nguo zao. Wanajua kwamba hakuna sabuni nyingine ya unga au ya mti iliyo na 'active brightener' maalum kama Omo - na sasa Omo imeongezwa active brightener nyingi zaidi.
Hii ndiyo sababu Omo haigharimu kuliko sabuni ya kawaida.
Watumia Omo chache tu, kwa kusafisha vingi - kwa maji ya moto au baridi. Tumia Extra Active Omo kila mara unapofua kung'arisha nguo zako.
Extra Active OMO hung'arisha hata zaidi–na huonyesha wazi
K OMO 4/SW O&M/1105

Figure P.3 This print ad in Swahili promotes a soap product in Africa much as it is promoted in the United States. American advertising techniques are widely used throughout the world.

example, every chief executive at Procter & Gamble over the past 60 years came up the ladder from early duty in the advertising department.

Business leaders whose interests lie in production must understand advertising methods in order to make goods that can be profitably advertised and sold. Financial officers must know that advertising is an investment essential to maintaining present sales levels and to the development of future business. To achieve a smooth meshing of the parts of the business machinery, each part needs to know how it interacts with the other parts. The basic advertising course helps provide future executives, regardless of their specialization, with the essential perspectives needed for success in a market economy.

Commercial art students should study advertising since most of their creative output will be used in one form of advertising or another. Industrial design students will likewise benefit, for the products they design usually serve also as advertisements for the product.

Students desiring to work in the mass media—whether print or broadcast—should understand the main source of revenue for these media. Practically all income of radio and television stations—and 65 percent of the total revenue of newspapers and magazines—stems from advertising.

In sum, many, if not most, of you will discover that your life work, whatever it may be, is highly dependent on advertising. The more you know about promotional activity, therefore, the better your chances for success.

International Significance

Advertising is indeed an important American institution, as we have already seen. A major development of the twentieth century, however, has been the tremendous expansion of international marketing. Advertising, consequently, has also become an important force in many other nations as people throughout the world have sought to improve their material lot.

The essential techniques of modern advertising came from Britain and Europe when the first printing press was shipped to American shores. These techniques, however, developed to their present levels in the United States because of the presence of surplus goods in our country which, in turn, provided the climate in which advertising prospered by fulfilling an essential need.

As the world changed from colonialism and exploitation to self-determination and economic development, thinking about international trade also changed, and many cartels and prohibitive tariffs gave way to competitive enterprise and customs unions. These changes in the world environment permitted modern advertising to spread beyond the United States—even to the Soviet Union and the emerging African nations.

The economically developing world turned to the United States for instruction and guidance as advertising methods came to be employed. Most large advertising agencies are American in origin; however, their overseas offices now outnumber their branches in our own country. American advertising executives lecture throughout the world, and creative approaches used in the United States are often imitated in other lands.

An understanding of advertising, regardless of our career intentions, should be an integral part of the broad background needed for informed citizenship and for a thorough understanding of the world in which one lives and works.

PART 1

Introduction

Advertising is an exciting, dynamic, and truly challenging enterprise—often misunderstood, but essential to business and industry as we know them today.

What the activity called "advertising" is all about is explained in Chapter 1. This chapter starts with the definition of advertising and continues with a short historical perspective. Six examples of the real-life use of advertising conclude the chapter.

In Chapter 2 the role of advertising in our society is discussed. First, we examine the economic role played by advertising. This discussion is followed by an evaluation of advertising's social effects.

Chapter 1

What Is Advertising?

● Ubiquitous . . . brash . . . pervasive . . . materialistic . . . intrusive . . . dynamic . . . alluring . . . annoying . . . pesky . . . indispensible . . . fascinating. These adjectives are among the many used to describe advertising. The average consumer in the United States is exposed to hundreds of advertisements daily. A carefully designed study revealed that 21 typical Milwaukee residents saw anywhere from 117 to 484 ads per day in four major forms of advertising media.[1] Advertisements are but one part of the advertising process — the tangible part that is alternately praised and criticized. Certainly, anyone living in an economically developed nation knows from personal experience what advertising is. Yet that understanding is often imprecise, and it is characterized by myths and half-truths. This chapter (and for that matter, the entire book) is an explanation of what the advertising process really is and how it functions in the world of business.

Advertising is a powerful communications force and a vital marketing tool — helping to sell goods, services, images, and ideas (or ideals) through channels of information and persuasion. Notice the word "helping" in the last sentence. By itself, advertising almost never "sells" products. Though it is often credited with making cash registers ring or blamed for failing to do so, advertising is, after all, but one part of the marketing and communication processes. The "greatest ad" in all the world cannot sell a product that is not in the store because the distribution system has broken down. Nor will it convince people to buy products that they feel cost too much, are poorly packaged, or in some other way do not live up to their expectations. Even if advertising does help sell such a product once, repeat sales are virtually impossible to obtain; and few advertisers today can survive on one-time sales.

It is crucial to our understanding of advertising, therefore, that we appreciate from the start the dual nature of the process, which draws from both marketing and behavioral science disciplines. It interacts with numerous other marketing concerns, including personal selling, product development and servicing, branding of merchandise, and research. Advertising is also forever intertwined with the social-psychological needs, wants, and backgrounds of consumers.

Advertising Defined

Every occupation, trade, and profession has its own language, nomenclature, and jargon. The practitioners of each field must know and understand the terms their colleagues use. Advertising people must learn its specialized terminology. The obvious starting point is with the hardest term of all to describe adequately: **advertising** itself. The function of advertising can be viewed in two basic ways: as a **tool of marketing** and as a **means of communication.**

The Marketing Point of View

The American Marketing Association (AMA) recommends this definition:

> Advertising is any paid form of nonpersonal presentation and promotion of ideas, goods, and services by an identified sponsor.[2]

Although purists might well point out that the AMA definition actually describes an advertisement, rather than advertising, these words deserve careful scrutiny. Four phrases warrant clarification.

"Paid Form" When products or services are mentioned favorably in the media—newspapers, magazines, radio, or television—the item appears because it is presumed to provide information or entertainment for the audience. This is **publicity,** and no payment is made by the benefited organization. Advertising, on the other hand, is published or broadcast because the advertiser has purchased time or space to tell the story of a certain product or service.

"Nonpersonal Presentation" Personal selling takes place when a personal face-to-face presentation is made. Although advertising complements, or may substitute for, personal selling, it is done in a nonpersonal manner through intermediaries—or **media.**

"Ideas, Goods, and Services" From this phrase we can see that advertising is concerned with much more than the promotion of tangible goods. In recent years the United States has been characterized as a service economy, and banks, insurance companies, airlines, resorts, restaurants, and dry cleaners advertise as aggressively as do the makers of automobiles, detergents, or beer.

Although most advertising is designed to help sell goods and services, it is being used increasingly to further public interest goals.

"An Identified Sponsor" This phrase distinguishes advertising from propaganda. Propaganda attempts to present opinions and ideas in order to influence attitudes and actions. So does advertising. Often the propagandist remains anonymous and the source of the idea is unknown, a condition that makes evaluation difficult. Advertising, on the other hand, discloses or identifies the source of the opinions and ideas it presents. To do otherwise would be a wasteful expenditure of funds.

The Communications Point of View

The phrase "paid form" in the AMA definition is too restricted for many advertising professionals. The phrase was designed to distinguish between advertising, which is delivered through space or time for which the advertiser has paid, and publicity, which is delivered without charge as part of the news or entertainment content of the medium. In 1980 the Advertising Council arranged for more than a half-billion dollars' worth of broadcast time and print media space to be devoted to advertisements for national distribution to promote public service projects such as continuing education, safe driving, and energy conservation. None of this advertising was paid for in the usual sense; various media and advertisers gave the necessary advertising space and time. Furthermore, the creative skill used in writing, illustrating, and producing the advertisements was not paid for either. An even larger dollar volume of public service messages was produced and delivered without cost for local community projects, such as the United Fund and support of symphonies and art galleries. To the media that deliver these messages and to the men and women who create and produce them, they are advertisements just as much as are messages designed to increase the sale of soap.

Information and Persuasion

The words "presentation" and "promotion" in the AMA definition fail to do justice to advertising's role. The words describe an exhibition and an advancement of the featured item. In presenting and promoting an item, the advertiser is engaging in a highly important function of advertising, namely that of *informing* prospective buyers and users of the availability of a product. Advertising, which provides the **communication link** between someone with something to sell and someone who needs something, is often just that simple: the advertiser is providing information to persons who are seeking it. Surely advertising is the most efficient means of reaching people with product information. For example, Coca-

Cola reaches one person with an ad for Coke at a cost of $.002, but the cost of an average personal sales call today exceeds $130.

"Presentation" and "promotion," however, hardly suggest an active attempt to influence people to action or belief by an overt appeal to reason or emotion. **Persuasion,** which is a major objective of modern advertising, is what has just been described.

Clyde R. Miller points out that "all successes in business, in industrial production, in invention, in religious conversion, in education, and in politics depend upon the process of persuasion."[3] Persuasion is the essence of a democratic society. Its opposite is coercion. And in the words of Sir Arthur Quiller-Couch, "Persuasion is the only true intellectual process."[4]

In modern markets, the producer who is content with advertising that merely identifies or informs may soon be occupying a vulnerable competitive position. Moreover, the creator of advertising—unlike the reporter, editor, or commentator—needs to remember that all creative advertising must do more than merely inform or entertain. It must change or reinforce an attitude or a behavior. And the consumer—the average person—should always be aware of the advertiser's persuasive intent, no matter how restrained and informative the message may be.

To avoid restricting the scope of advertising to completely commercial functions, and at the same time to convey adequately its purpose and the creative communication processes required to achieve that purpose, this definition of advertising is recommended:

Advertising is controlled, identifiable information and persuasion by means of mass communications media.

We have already discussed the importance of the words "information" and "persuasion" in this definition of advertising. Let us consider the meaning and purpose of three other key terms.

"Controlled" To the creator of advertising or the advertiser who pays for it, the word "controlled" provides an important distinction between advertising and either personal selling or publicity. The content, time, and direction of an advertising message are controlled by the advertiser. Advertisers say what they want to say—no more and no less. And by careful selection of the medium that delivers the message, it is directed to the people whom they want to receive it. The same cannot be said of personal selling, as almost any sales manager or retail proprietor can verify. The salesperson may tell only part of the story, and may not tell that part clearly or effectively. The message may be wasted on the wrong people or not be delivered at the most advantageous time.

The word "controlled" also distinguishes advertising from publicity. The advertiser cannot control the content, time, or direction of publicity. The story may not be presented as desired, at the time chosen, or to the people selected to be reached. In fact, much publicity material is never presented at all. When the advertiser contracts for advertising space or time, on the other hand, definite results can be expected. The message will be published in the way it was prepared—in the same words and the same pictures—and it will be delivered to the specific audience or group served by the medium, it will be of a certain size or length, and it will appear at a certain time.

"Identifiable" This word is used in preference to such terms as "by an identified sponsor" to indicate that the receiver of the advertising message is able to identify both source and purpose. The source is responsible for the message, and recognizes—or should recognize—that its purpose is to persuade the receiver to accept the ideas or opinions it presents. Publicity or propaganda may not offer these aids to evaluating the message.

"Mass Communications Media" This qualification is designed to separate personal selling and advertising and also to convey the concept of multiple messages delivered to groups of people simultaneously. Basically, there are only two mechanisms of mass communications, and they were developed 500 years apart.

The first of these is the printing press, or, more accurately, the process of **printing from movable type.** With this innovation in the fifteenth century, it was possible for the first time to produce with speed and economy many copies of the same message. Today, by way of the printing press in its modern variations, newspapers, magazines, outdoor posters, direct-mail material, and store displays deliver messages to thousands or millions of people at the same time.

The second basic mechanism of mass communications is the **electronic transmitter**—the radio or television station—which, as we know, did not appear until the first part of the twentieth century, and it made available a means of broadcasting messages simultaneously to many people, even to those who could not read. Radio, of course, makes its impression only through sound; television combines sight with sound.

Many other, less conspicuous methods of delivering advertising messages exist to service specialized needs of advertisers. These will be discussed later, but most modern advertising is delivered through newspapers, magazines, radio, direct mail, and television.

A Brief History of Advertising

Institutions appear when a need for them develops. No mysterious process of self-generation spews forth an institution unless a variety of external forces is present to nourish its development. Similarly, institutions are not assured of immortality. To survive, an institution must be dynamic and adapt to changing conditions. In this section we explore how advertising came to be an institution in our society. We present this information in the belief that the past helps explain the present and provides guides to the future.

Early Advertising

Advertising in ancient and medieval times was crude when measured by present-day standards. Nevertheless, the basic reason for employing the technique was the same then as now: to communicate information and ideas to groups of people in order to change or reinforce an attitude.

Our knowledge of advertising in ancient times naturally is fragmentary. The diggings of archaeologists in the countries rimming the Mediterranean Sea have turned up evidence that the Romans and some of their predecessors knew that "it pays to advertise." Three forms of advertising were used prior to the time the printing press began to open the door to the development of modern mass communication media.

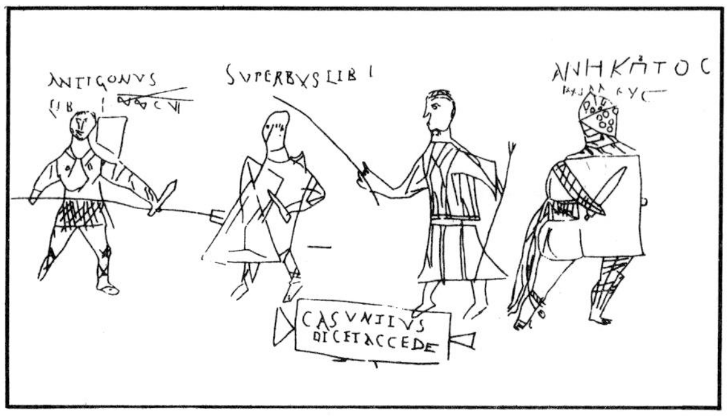

Figure 1.1 Drawings on a wall in Pompeii promoted a gladiatorial contest. Such messages were early forms of advertising. [*Dick Sutphin,* The Mad Old Ads, *McGraw-Hill Book Company, New York, 1966.*]

Trademarks Pride in their skill led early craftsmen to place their individual marks on goods such as pottery. As the reputation of one particular artisan spread by word of mouth, buyers came to look for his distinctive mark just as we look for trademarks and brand names on merchandise today.

The guild system, with its trade monopolies, gave legal protection to those persons permitted to make a certain type of product. Goods could not be sold unless they carried a guild mark, and severe penalties were imposed for placing counterfeit marks on the output of nonguild members. Thus, the trademark has a long history in the world of commerce and still performs its prime functions of protecting (1) consumers by ensuring that they receive the goods they want and (2) manufacturers by preventing inferior goods from being palmed off as their products.

Signs Some traders, like the Phoenicians, painted commercial messages on prominent rocks along trade lanes, much in the fashion of some present-day religious sects. These messages extolled the wares that were for sale and were forerunners of modern outdoor advertising. Excavations at Pompeii reveal that each little shop had an inscription on the wall next to the entrance to tell the passerby whether the shop was a place to buy bread, wine, pottery, or other merchandise.

Town Criers In Greece during its Golden Age, public criers were a civic institution. Men were paid to circulate through the streets of Athens advising the citizens of important news and announcing public events. Later, during the Middle Ages, the only available means of advertising except signs was the spoken word.

Early Printed Advertising

The first known printed advertisement in the English language appeared in 1473. At that time, William Caxton, an English adapter of Gutenberg's idea of movable type, printed and distributed a handbill that called the attention of potential buyers to a book of ecclesiastical rules he had just published. By the middle of the seventeenth century, weekly newspapers, called "mercuries," started to appear in England. The printing press was then used in a fashion that led to the gradual growth and development of advertising by providing a practical, readily available medium to deliver advertising messages to the literate portion of the public. Most early newspaper advertisements were in the form of announcements. Prominent among early advertisers were importers of products new to England. For example, the first offering of coffee was made in a newspaper ad in 1652, followed by an offering of chocolate in 1657, and of tea in 1658.

Evidence of "competitive" advertising, as contrasted with "pioneering" advertising that aims at building acceptance for a previously unknown product, can be found as early as 1710. In that year razor-strap and patent medicine advertisements attempted to convince magazine readers of the advertised product's superiority over similar products. Many of the claims certainly were excessive and, to the more sophisticated reader of today, transparently unbelievable. Printed advertising was in general use by the mid-eighteenth century.

Figure 1.2 Fifteenth-century printers' marks are shown. The mark in the center was used by William Caxton, who printed the first known advertisement in the English language.

The Development of Modern Advertising

Although American advertising has English roots, if any institution other than democracy itself can be said to be synonymous with America, that institution is advertising. For a variety of reasons, however, English and American advertising did not follow parallel paths of development. Of the variety of forces contributing to the difference in advertising's rate of growth in the two countries, a particularly significant obstacle to its expansion in England was the tax imposed by the Crown on both newspapers and their advertisements. The imposition of excise taxes was one of the grievances of American colonists, and when the United States successfully waged its War of Independence, no such taxes were enacted by the government of the new republic.

When the *Boston News-Letter* published its first issue on April 24, 1704, it contained advertisements much like those of contemporaneous English newspapers. But, in addition to the absence of taxes already mentioned, a number of social and economic advances were necessary before American advertising could approach its present stature. The turning point came at approximately the middle of the nineteenth century. While we shall consider each of these socioeconomic advances individually, we should bear in mind that they are closely interrelated.

The Industrial Revolution in the United States

The Industrial Revolution, following Watt's discovery of the principle of steam power, led to expanded manufacturing in England and later on in the United States. The Civil War accelerated the need for and use of mass production methods, and an expanded domestic market provided an outlet for factory-made products. As the Industrial Revolution altered the relationship between the maker and the user of goods, a need for advertising developed.

The Need for Communication

Mechanization turned out goods faster than they could be absorbed in the region of their manufacture. A need arose to extend markets geographically, and manufacturers had to find a way of communicating the value of their products to people who knew nothing of their reputation, as was the case when goods were made to order by local craftsmen. Advertising provided the needed communication vehicle. Later on, it helped raise consumption so that the full use of the machinery was possible, thus bringing about lower per-unit costs of manufacture.

The Need for Transportation

Granted that a high degree of industrialization must precede an advertising system of any magnitude, there are several other important elements in such a development. A comprehensive transportation system must come first. A network of waterways, highways, railroads, and airlines is needed to carry the goods to scattered markets. This same system is needed to carry printed advertising media to prospective buyers living far from the producer.

In the United States the railroads provided this network, and by 1890 the entire country was served by the iron horse. In 1896 the federal government inaugurated rural free delivery (RFD). This system of package delivery to farm homes led to the expansion of markets by the mail-order houses, such as Montgomery Ward and Sears, Roebuck. Slowly, the country became a more homogenized market instead of a series of local and regional markets.

The Need for Education Before the Industrial Revolution and the existence of a transportation system were to have any effect on the need for advertising, people had to be able to read. Until the advent of radio in the 1920s, people could be reached only through the printed word. Our nation was an early believer in the doctrine of compulsory public education, and a high rate of literacy resulted.

The Growth of Newspapers and Magazines

These trends in transportation and education were reflected in the growth of printed media in the United States. The *Boston News-Letter* was the first newspaper of any continuous life in our country. By 1830 there were 1,200 papers in the nation, growing to 3,000 in 1860 and to a high point of 15,000 in 1914. Today, more than 9,800 newspapers serve the reading public of our nation.

In 1741, two magazines were published in Philadelphia. Both failed, but the following century saw

GREAT ENCOURAGEMENT
AMERICAN REVOLUTION
What a Brilliant Prospect does this Event hold out to every Lad of Spirit, who is inclined to try his Fortune in that highly renowned Corps
The Continental Marines
When every Thing that swims the Seas must be a
PRIZE!
Thousands are at this moment endeavoring to get on Board Privateers, where they serve without Pay or Reward of any kind whatsoever; so certain does their Chance appear of enriching themselves by PRIZE MONEY! What an enviable Station then must the CONTINENTAL MARINE hold,—who with far superior Advantages to thefe, has the additional benefit of liberal Pay, and plenty of the best Provisions, with a good and well appointed Ship under him, the Pride and Glory of the Continental Navy; furely every Man of Spirit muft blufh to remain at Home in Inactivity and Indolence, when his Country needs his Assistance.
Where then can he have fuch a fair opportunity of reaping Glory and Riches, as in the Continental Marines, a Corps daily acquiring new Honors, and here, when once embarked in American Fleet, he finds himself in the midft of Honor and Glory, furounded by a fet of fine Fellow, Strangers to Fear, and who ftrike Terror through the Hearts of their Enemies wherever they go.
He has likewise the infpiring idea to know, that while he fcour the Ocean to protect the Liberty of these states, that the Hearts and good Wifhes of the whole American peoples attend him; pray for his succefs, and participate in his Glory!! Lofe no Time then, my Fine Fellows, in embracing the glorious Opportunity that awaits you; YOU WILL RECEIVE
Seventeen Dollars Bounty,
And on your Arrival at Head Quarters, be comfortably and genteely CLOTHED,—And fpirited young BOYS of a promifing Appearance, who are Five Feet Six Inches high, WILL RECEIVE TEN DOLLARS, and equal Advantages of PROVISIONS and CLOTHING with the Men. And thofe who wish only to enlist for a limited Service, fhall receive a Bounty of SEVEN DOLLARS, and Boys FIVE. In Fact, the Advantages which the MARINE poffefses, are too numerous to mention here, but among the many, it may not be amifs to state,—That if he has a WIFE or aged PARENT, he can make them an Allotment of half his PAY; which will be regularly paid without any Trouble to them, or to whomsoever he may directs that being well Clothed and Fed on Board Ship, the Remainder of his PAY and PRIZE MONEY will be clear in Reserve for the Relief of his Family or his own private Purposes. The Single Young Man on his Return to Port, finds himself enabled to cut a Dafh on Shore with his GIRL and his GLASS, that might be envied by a Nobleman.—Take Courage then, seize the Fortune that awaits you, repair to the MARINE RENDEZVOUS, where in a FLOWING BOWL of PUNCH, an Three Times Three, you shall drink
Long Live The United States, and Success to the Marines.
The Daily Allowance of a Marine when embarked, is One Pound of BEEF or PORK.—One Pound of BREAD,—Flour, Raisins, Butter, Cheese, Oatmeal, Molasses, Tea, Sugar, &c. &c. And a Pint of the beft WINE, or Half a Pint of the best RUM or BRANDY; together with a Pint of LEMONADE. They have liberty in warm Countries, a plentiful Allowance of the choicest FRUIT. And what can be more handsome than the Marines' Proportion of PRIZE MONEY, when a Sergeant shares equal with the First Class of Petty Officers, such as Midshipmen, Assistant Surgeons, &c. which is Five Shares each; a Corporal with the Second Class, which is Three Shares each; and the Private with the Able Seamen, one Share and a Half each.
Desiring greater Particulars, and a more full Account of the many Advantages of this invaluable Corps, apply to CAPTAIN MULLAN, at TUN TAVERN, where the Bringer of a Recruit will receive THREE DOLLARS.
January, 1776

Figure 1.3 Marine recruits were sought by this persuasive ad during the Revolutionary War. The crude production of the advertisement reflected the primitive state of printing at the time. [*Courtesy of the U.S. Marine Corps.*]

If you can carry on a tradition...
Marine Corps tradition is one of strength and pride. And, as a Marine, you learn to carry it on. You learn an important job skill from those who know their trade. You sharpen your confidence with tough physical training. And, then, you walk with pride. Because you've earned a part in the tradition of the Corps. Find out more about us. Mail the card or call 800-423-2600, toll free. In California, 800-252-0241.
Maybe you can be one of us.
The Few.
The Proud.
The Marines.

Figure 1.4 Marine recruits are still needed, and contemporary advertising appeals are employed. Note the shift of emphasis to a dominant illustration and short copy. [*Courtesy of the U.S. Marine Corps.*]

many attempts to establish magazine ventures. By 1850 there were some 700 struggling magazines in the United States. The number increased to 1,200 in 1870 and doubled again to 2,400 by 1880. The improvement in levels of education of the population, the expansion of transportation facilities, the benefits of low-cost mailing privileges granted by Congress in 1879, and the development of the rural free delivery system—all of these combined with an increased trend by manufacturers toward national marketing—led to the doubling of the number of magazines in the two decades between 1880 and 1900. Publishers, recognizing that advertising revenues could replace subscription income, lowered prices on their magazines and aggressively promoted advertising sales to fill the revenue gap. Circulations skyrocketed, and today there are more than 9,700 magazines published in the United States.

The Development of the Modern Advertising Agency

For advertising to become an institution, a need for it had to be recognized; its availability had to be communicated to potential users. This information was delivered by the advertising agent, from which the modern advertising agency evolved. Volney Palmer, the first American advertising agent, began business in the early 1840s. The first agents originally were only brokers of space in newspapers and magazines who contracted with publishers for advertising space at bulk rates and resold the space to advertisers at higher rates. They provided none of the creative or planning services that are the primary functions of advertising agencies today. However, in the days when the knowledge of available advertising media was meager at best, and even the basic function of advertising in accelerating distribution was understood by few producers, the limited services of these space-broker agents justified their existence. About 1890, as advertisers became more sophisticated, markets increased in size, advertising budgets grew bigger, and agencies began to add such services as the writing of advertising messages, the creation of illustrations, the choice of typography, and sometimes even market analysis, rudimentary though it was by present standards of marketing research. By the beginning of the twentieth century, agencies had come to assume the role they perform today—the planning, creation, and execution of complete advertising campaigns—in return for commissions paid by media or fees received from advertisers.

The Advent of Radio and Television

Two twentieth-century events gave added impetus to the growth of American advertising, namely, the appearance of radio and television. The invention of the electronic transmission of messages, with its subsequent commercial applications, is second only to the invention of printing in the development of advertising media.

For the first time, except for the minor use of town criers, it became possible to advertise goods and services to people who could not read printed messages. Of course, by the time of the invention and commercial application of radio, nearly everyone in America could read. Still, some advertising messages can be delivered more easily and more quickly through the ear than through the eye. Furthermore, in countries less well developed—in some areas in Latin America, Africa, and the Near East, for example—radio has played a more important role in marketing and mass communication than have newspapers or magazines.

The first wireless message was transmitted by Marconi in 1895. The first broadcasting station established for commercial application of the radio broadcasting principle was by KDKA of East Pittsburgh, Pennsylvania, which carried presidential election returns in 1920. The Federal Communications Commission (FCC) had licensed 30 radio stations by January 1, 1922. Today there are over 7,300. The founding of the National Broadcasting Company (NBC) in 1926 made it possible for all Americans to hear the same program at the same time.

Television, of course, changed the role of radio as TV became the major source of in-home entertainment in the 1950s. Television sets were the fastest-selling appliances in the 1950s, and advertisers switched dollars from radio and print media to take advantage of even larger audiences. For the first time, a medium of mass communication combined the impact of sound with that of sight and motion.

By 1980 there were 708 television stations licensed in the United States alone. The medium was second only to newspapers as a repository of advertising dollars. The addition of color transmissions in the 1960s furthered the growth of television as an advertising medium.

It is difficult to predict what the next major breakthrough will be in the history of advertising. Already we see that videocassette records and computers, now being introduced into many homes, are developments that may well change the practice of advertising. One can safely predict, however, that whatever it is, it will be exciting.

Advertising in a Microcosm

It may be useful at this point to examine several true-life examples of how advertising works, We shall now present six short examples of how advertising operates in the day-to-day world. Four of the cases originated in Atlanta, Georgia, which is quite a distance from "glamorous" Madison Avenue. These campaigns may or may not be considered to be particularly brilliant in their planning or execution, but each was selected as being representative of typical advertising programs used throughout the United States. Furthermore, each campaign was successful in achieving the objectives of its sponsor. Some of the terminology used will be new to the beginner in advertising. All will be clearer by the end of the course. For the present, read these short cases while concentrating on the way advertising is used to meet the goals of the advertiser. The communication objectives of the six campaigns were:

1 To introduce a new product: Mello Yello
2 To sustain an established product in the marketplace: Grease Relief
3 To create floor traffic for a retail store: House of Denmark
4 To secure sales leads: The Medney Organization
5 To demarket a service: Georgia Power Company
6 To promote a public cause: Keep America Beautiful, Inc.

Advertising Helps to Introduce a New Product: Mello Yello

Mello Yello was introduced to the soft-drink market by the Coca-Cola Company in 1979 to compete in the fastest-growing segment of the highly competitive industry: sugar-citrus drinks. Extensive product and market research was conducted to launch this new product successfully.

The Coca-Cola Company considered the following trends when developing Mello Yello:

1 A tremendous change in consumption patterns of beverages had occurred over the past 20 years. The consumption of coffee and milk had dropped and the use of soft drinks and beer had increased significantly.
2 Within major beverage categories, there has been a great deal of growth in products that are actually lighter (fewer calories) than others or that consumers perceive as light.
3 The fastest-growing segment in the soft-drink industry over the past five years had been the sugar-citrus drink.
4 The Coca-Cola Company did not have a product entry in this category, which consisted principally of Mountain Dew, Rondo, and Kickapoo Joy Juice.

With these facts in the background, further research was conducted to determine why the sugar-citrus product, especially Mountain Dew, had tripled its market share in four years. It was discovered that teenagers were the heaviest users of this kind of soft drink, with males consuming 70 percent of the total. It was also determined that the heavy users' education was slightly below the norm for soft-drink users, and that they came from a slightly downscale (lower middle-class) economic background. The prime target for the product was described as a "male blue-collar teenager."

The Coca-Cola Company and its advertising agency, McDonald & Little, studied the lifestyle and needs of this group in order to create an appropriate marketing strategy and to develop an advertising campaign. It was found that teenagers are very active and drink a lot of soft drinks, especially after work or physical activity rather than during meals. Teenagers also drink in big gulps instead of sipping soft drinks. Sugar-citrus drinks are ideally suited to teenage consumption because low carbonation makes it easy to drink fast, the low sugar level appeals to their appearance and weight consciousness, and the citrus flavor satisfies their propensity for things sweet.

A battery of research studies was conducted to develop the right product name and package design. Mello Yello was chosen for several reasons: (1) in taste tests, many people described the drink as "mellow"; (2) it is yellow in color; and (3) the name has an easy, rhyming, memorable quality. The name, combined with strong packaging graphics, enabled the product to stand out on the supermarket shelf and, more important, from the competition.

At this point, an advertising campaign was developed to convert the competition's consumers by building a more desirable product image and to attract new users by demonstrating the unique drinkability of Mello Yello.

An advertising theme, "The World's Fastest Soft Drink," was featured in television commercials, such as shown in Figure 1.5. Each commercial focused on a fast-drinking contest between two well-known athletes. The message conveyed is that Mello Yello has a smooth, mellow taste that is easy to enjoy: the drink is "Chug-a-lug-able."

This well-conceived, thoroughly planned advertising campaign helped Mello Yello become the most successful new-product introduction in soft-drink history. By 1980, Coca Cola advertised to 60 percent of the national market where distribution was established for the brand. The product had achieved an annual market share of 0.6 percent of the $16-billion soft-drink category, or sales of nearly $100 million. Mountain Dew held a share of 2.4 percent at

Figure 1.5 This storyboard shows how one Mello Yello commercial will look once it has been produced in a television studio. The commercial is designed to run for 60 seconds.

the time, so Mello Yello still needs aggressive promotion if the brand is to overtake the leader.

Advertising Helps an Established Product Retain Its Position: Grease relief

Grease relief was developed by Intex in 1973 as a product suitable for use in both the kitchen and the laundry. Ninety percent of the homemakers surveyed thought grease was their most difficult cleaning problem. After considerable additional research, Grease relief was introduced as a "degreaser" for kitchen and laundry. Positioned in this manner, the product competed against Lever Brothers' Wisk for laundry usage, various liquid detergents for dishes, pots, and pans, and all-purpose cleaners for range tops and other surfaces.

A short time after the product was introduced in the Southeast, it was sold to Texize. Texize had national distribution already set up for its other products; thus, it was in a better position to market Grease relief throughout the country.

Liller Neal Weltin, Inc., the brand's advertising agency, developed the creative strategy for Grease relief. The agency consistently integrated all the elements of the product—name, package design, and advertising—to communicate the product's main benefit, an exceptional grease-cleaning ability.

In the years following the initial introduction of the product, Texize, in its efforts to increase market share, conducted research to identify problems in the marketplace and studied ways to provide solutions to these problems. Texize found that the kitchen offers a better opportunity for everyday usage of the product than the laundry does. So the promotional emphasis was modified to position Grease relief as an all-purpose degreaser and cleaner. The goal was to sustain consumer preference for an established brand.

To reflect the new position, the product formula was changed to enhance its all-purpose cleaning abilities. A new package and label were designed for ease of use and eye-catching capabilities. A smaller package was introduced that enabled the product to sell at a lower price. Figures 1.6 and 1.7 show print and television advertising created to broaden the consumer's image of how a grease problem occurs

Figure 1.6
This print advertisement features the Grease relief brand.

texize
"Use Grease relief® Instead"
"Instead" :30
Daughter: Oh sure, Mom used Grease relief . . .
But only on her stove.
She used other cleaners everywhere else.
I said, "Mom, with Grease relief you don't need those other cleaners."
Mother: "But I only get grease on my stove . . ."
Daughter: . . . she said.
"Mom," I said, "when you cook, smoke and grease go everywhere."
Grease relief
There's greasy dirt way over here.
Why buy all those other cleaners?
Grease relief
Use Grease relief instead.
One day she caught me using a special floor cleaner. Know what she said?
Grease relief
Mother: "You oughta' use Grease relief instead."
USE
GREASE
RELIEF
INSTEAD
Grease relief
Grease relief
Announcer: Use Grease relief instead.

Figure 1.7 This photoboard presents a 30-second commercial designed to get consumers to broaden the use of the brand.

and how the product provides a solution to the problem.

Media strategy is aimed at reaching homemakers of all ages, but particularly those in the 29 to 45 age bracket, with three or more family members, whose annual family income is $15,000 or more. About 80 percent of the ad budget is spent on television, which the advertiser feels is the most effective means of communicating with the consumer. The other 20 percent is spent in magazines, such as *Better Homes and Gardens, Woman's Day, Southern Living, McCall's, Good Housekeeping,* and *True Story.* Generally, a one-third page ad is used because the advertiser feels it is the most efficient way to reach the upscale market and the increasing numbers of working women.

By continuing to study changes in the marketplace and incorporating this knowledge in carefully planned campaigns, the advertiser of Grease relief is able to continue the sales growth of the product.

Advertising Helps to Build Retail Traffic: House of Denmark

The House of Denmark is a retail furniture company specializing in imported Scandinavian furniture and accessories. The main store is located in midtown Atlanta, and there is another store in the suburbs several miles away. This store shares a building with the company's warehouse. Merchandise is priced in the medium and upper ranges; the store appearance and mood create a sense of lightness and young sophistication. The House of Denmark sales staff also is young, sophisticated, and college-educated. Sales personnel often have an art-design background. Customers are drawn primarily from young professional singles and married couples.

One Sunday in 1980, the store ran a five-column, 10-inch newspaper advertisement in the *Atlanta Journal and Constitution* (Figure 1.8). This simple, straightforward, informational ad showed no furniture, which usually is an integral part of House of Denmark advertising. The newspaper charged $1,408.25 for the space. The week before the ad ran, the store sent out 11,000 announcement cards, printed with the same selling message, to its mailing list of regular customers. This element of the promotional program cost $101.92 for printing the cards and $1,100 for postage. Along with the newspaper ad, the store advertised on three local radio stations for a 24-hour period starting at Saturday noon prior

Figure 1.8 Sales of more than $70,000 resulted from this small ad in the Sunday newspaper.

to the sale, at a cost of $1,200. From a total advertising expenditure of $3,810.17, the House of Denmark drew large numbers of people to its warehouse-showroom. In a five-hour period, sales totaled more than $70,000, for an acceptable advertising-to-sales ratio of about 5.5 percent.

Advertising Helps to Secure Sales Leads: The Medney Organization, Inc.

J. J. (Jerry) Medney, who is a member of the New York bar, has been selling Florida residential housing to people living some distance from the state for more than 20 years. The publication of his best-selling book *You Don't Have to Be Rich to Make Big Money in Real Estate* in 1973 has enhanced his selling success. Since establishing the Medney

Organization in Long Island, New York, Medney has experimented with such advertising media as TV, radio, telephone, and direct mail. He has found, however, that best results come from advertisements in newspapers similar to the one shown in Figure 1.9. This 5- by 7-inch ad costs about $850 to run in the Long Island newspaper, *Newsday*. The population of Long Island is 2.8 million and the consumer spendable income per household is in the neighborhood of $25,000. Each insertion attracts a sufficient flow of people to the seminars where Jerry makes a presentation for the Florida developments he is currently representing. One out of every ten family units (usually a married couple approaching retirement) attracted to the seminars is converted to making a housing purchase averaging in excess of $60,000. Thus, an effective advertising approach is combined with personal selling to market an expensive consumer durable good.

Figure 1.9 The purpose of this newspaper advertisement is to obtain prospects who may be interested in buying property in Florida.

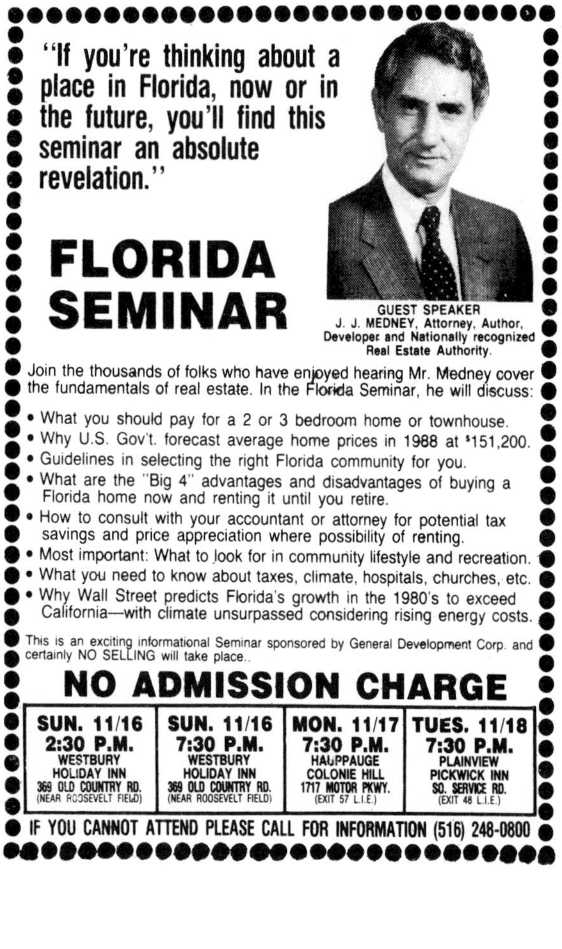

Advertising Helps to Demarket a Product: Georgia Power Company

In the first half of the twentieth century, public utilities, including electric utilities, were urged to produce and distribute their commodities at the lowest price possible so that more people might enjoy their benefits. Increased use of electricity and efficiency in production led to lower prices until electricity became not a luxury but a labor-saving convenience. In such times, public utilities, through advertising, were urging consumers to take advantage of these bargain rates. Figure 1.10 shows a Georgia Power advertisement promoting outdoor lighting service, which, in addition to giving consumers a desired service, added to the company sales volume.

With the onset of nationwide inflation and environmental concern in the late 1960s, however, utilities became hard pressed to maintain low rates. Governmental approval was sought to raise rates to cover higher costs. At this time, it also became prudent to assess the value of product promotion. Thus, instead of stimulating power usage, the objective of electric utility advertising shifted to communicating information about the company to its public: image advertising, if you will.

In the 1970s, inflation continued and a new dimension was added to the picture in the form of fuel shortages and unprecedented costs for the energy industries. Although consumers remained free to impose demands on electric utilities at any time, the utilities began to try to tailor those demands to fit the resources available. They began to take a new marketing approach, called **demarketing,** which is defined as "a state in which demand exceeds the level at which the marketer feels able or motivated to supply it."[5]

Georgia Power is a summer-peak company; heavy use of air conditioning during the summer months places the greatest demands of the entire year on the system. In an attempt to equalize summer and winter demands and to inform customers of increased prices in summer, Georgia Power began an advertising program designed to encourage the wise use of electricity, especially during the air conditioning season. A series of newspaper ads was run suggesting numerous ideas for preventing power waste, including turning thermostats higher during summer months, adding insulation and weatherstripping, and keeping doors and windows closed. Figure 1.11 shows one of the ads in the campaign.

Figure 1.10 A public utility promotes additional uses for its product in the days before America recognized that a shortage of energy existed. The ad appeared in newspapers in the fall of 1968.

Georgia Power continued to emphasize the wise use of energy throughout the 1970s in all its advertising. The results were a drop in total sales of 2.1 percent in 1979 and a drop in residential demand of 4.5 percent. An example of the utility's creative approach showing consumers how they can "budget" their electric costs is shown in Figure 1.12. This campaign ran in local newspapers, and bill stuffers were sent to the company's 1 million residential customers. Nearly 15 percent of these customers requested the free booklet, which was the best response the company had ever received from its advertising efforts.

Although Georgia Power's chief fuel is coal, and there appears to be no immediate shortage of electricity from this fuel source, the company continues its program of conservation information with an increased emphasis on customer service. Many public utilities throughout the nation engage in similar programs.

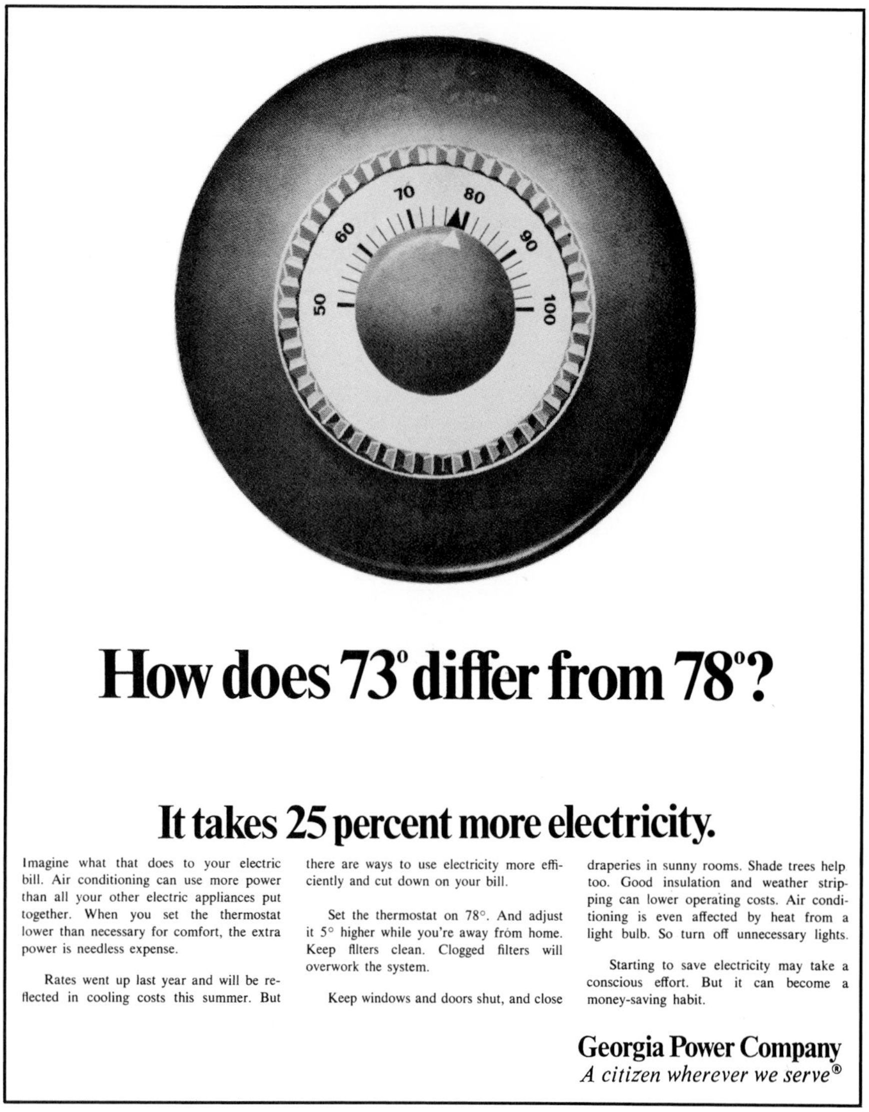

70
80
60
90
50
100
How does 73° differ from 78°?
It takes 25 percent more electricity.
Imagine what that does to your electric bill. Air conditioning can use more power than all your other electric appliances put together. When you set the thermostat lower than necessary for comfort, the extra power is needless expense.
Rates went up last year and will be reflected in cooling costs this summer. But there are ways to use electricity more efficiently and cut down on your bill.
Set the thermostat on 78°. And adjust it 5° higher while you're away from home. Keep filters clean. Clogged filters will overwork the system.
Keep windows and doors shut, and close draperies in sunny rooms. Shade trees help too. Good insulation and weather stripping can lower operating costs. Air conditioning is even affected by heat from a light bulb. So turn off unnecessary lights.
Starting to save electricity may take a conscious effort. But it can become a money-saving habit.
Georgia Power Company
A citizen wherever we serve®

Figure 1.11 By spring of 1972, the same company was showing consumers how to use less of its product. A demarketing strategy was being followed.

Advertising Helps to Promote a Public Cause: Keep America Beautiful

Advertising is becoming important to the success of many charitable, nonprofit organizations. The Advertising Council donates thousands of man-hours creating advertising for several organizations, such as Keep America Beautiful, Inc., which was founded in 1953.

Beginning in 1960, the ads for this organization emphasized the litter problem plaguing our country. Advertising messages appeared in all the major media: magazines, newspapers, radio, television, outdoor, and transit. However, in 1970 a survey showed that people were still unconcerned about environmental pollution.

A new campaign was planned with two goals: to deal with litter control and to attack the larger problem of pollution from municipal, industrial, and individual sources. Marsteller, Inc., the volunteer advertising agency placed in charge of the new campaign, set these objectives: to focus attention on the problem; to increase perception of problem's importance; and, to motivate people to help solve the problem through their own actions. The primary strategy was

YOU CAN BUDGET YOUR ENERGY
THE WAY YOU BUDGET YOUR GROCERIES.
Budgeting. It's something you might do to keep your grocery bills in line. And it's something you ought to do to keep from wasting energy, and money.
To budget energy usage you need, first, to decide how much energy it takes to run your home in a way that's comfortable and convenient to you without being wasteful. Then, if you know the amounts of energy that you're using every week, you can see to it that you stay within your budget by cutting back if your usage begins to be excessive.
To help you do all that, we've prepared a booklet called "How To Budget Your Energy The Way You Budget Your Groceries."
It's yours free for the asking. And it's filled with facts that will help you establish an energy budget, learn how to read your meter, and how to record the readings. So write us or call us today for your free booklet. And get yourself on the right side of the ledger in self-controlling your energy bills.
Georgia Power

Figure 1.12 A 1980 ad tells consumers how to control energy usage and shows an increasing emphasis on customer service.

to convince the public that individuals can act to solve the pollution problem and that individual action was the only way to make progress. This strategy was implemented in the theme, "People start pollution. And people can stop it." The agency also created a symbol that represented respect for the land, a Cherokee Indian named "Iron Eyes" Cody.

Between 1970 and 1980, four different public service commercials featured Iron Eyes. The best-known one shows him paddling a canoe down an unclean river with the fog of air pollution from factories seen in the background. After beaching the canoe, Iron Eyes stands by the side of a road, and a bag of litter is thrown at his feet from a passing car. The spot ends with a close-up of his face showing a tear running from his eye. This spot (shown in Figure 1.13), has been run more than any other commercial in the history of television.

The impact of this message was immediate. Keep American Beautiful sent out more than a half-million copies of the booklet offered in the spot; contributed advertising time and space tripled. Two years after the campaign, a survey showed a 200 percent increase in public awareness of pollution as a major

"Some people have a deep and abiding respect for the natural beauty that was once this country—and some people don't! People start pollution, people can stop it!"
'71 things you can do to stop pollution
Keep America Beautiful
Advertising contributed for the public good.
Help Fight Pollution Campaign
Conducted by THE ADVERTISING COUNCIL
and KEEP AMERICA BEAUTIFUL, INC.
advertising contributed for the public good
ADVERTISING COUNCIL
KEEP AMERICA BEAUTIFUL

Figure 1.13 This photoboard shows the public service television commercial which has been aired more than any other in the history of American television. [*Courtesy of The Advertising Council.*]

problem. Iron Eyes was "linked with the need for personal involvement in environmental improvement" by 94 percent of those interviewed in a survey conducted to check the campaign's effectiveness.

The Advertising Council's work for Keep American Beautiful continues. The 1980 campaign focused on the Clean Community System and cited five cities for becoming cleaner places in which to live: San Diego, for being 29 percent cleaner; Weirton, West Virginia, 35 percent; Texarkana, 69 percent; Indianapolis, 81 percent; and Atlanta, 49 percent. Approximately 200 cities have inquired about the Clean Community System, and the campaign continues to encourage Americans to work together in order to create a better living and working environment.

Profile

David Ogilvy

In the 25 years after World War II, three men influenced advertising creativity to a high degree: William Bernbach, Rosser Reeves, and David Ogilvy.*

David Ogilvy, a Scotsman, was born in 1911 and educated on scholarships at Fettes School and at Oxford University, where he majored in modern history. Upon leaving Oxford, he became a chef at the Hotel Majestic in Paris. The head chef there, M. Pitard, inculcated the principles of discipline and dedication to work into David's personality, an important factor in his success in advertising.

After leaving the kitchen, Ogilvy worked as an associate director of George Gallup's Audience Research Institute and as secretary at the British Embassy in Washington before starting Ogilvy and Mather in 1948.

Ogilvy, beginning with the now classic Hathaway Shirt "Eye-Patch" ad, came to be known as the father of the "image school of advertising." His rather dogmatic ideas were incorporated in *Confessions of an Advertising Man,* which has sold more than 600,000 copies since its publication in 1963. It still serves as a copywriter's bible.

Ogilvy & Mather is now a very large advertising agency, billing over $1.6 billion annually. The organization reflects the dynamism of its founder. In recent years, David Ogilvy is removed from day-to-day management duties, but he still helps the agency attract large advertisers who feel a need for the development of desirable images for their companies and products.

Ogilvy's contributions to the development of the creative function in advertising are unsurpassed. He is often quoted as saying: "I've been in this trade for more than thirty years and written as much advertising as anyone alive. In those thirty years I had nine big ideas. It's not many, is it? But it's more than most people." His accomplishments epitomize the importance of the right idea in successful advertising.

* A profile of Bernbach appears in Chapter 8 and one of Reeves in Chapter 12.

Summary

Advertising should be viewed from both a marketing and a communications perspective. It is undergirded by two forms of mass communication mechanisms—the printing press (printing and movable type) and radio and television stations (electronic transmission). The first was introduced in the fifteenth century, but advertising did not really start in the modern sense until the 1700s, with true growth coming late in the nineteenth century. Commercial broadcasting came in the early 1920s with the introduction. of radio. Its universal success was repeated in the 1950s with the advent of television. Now advertising relies on a blend of print and broadcast media.

Advertising is a well-established institution today, but before it could reach such status, a number of events had to preexist. A primary requisite was the industrialization of the economy, bringing a need for manufacturers to seek markets. This necessitated a means of communicating with prospects who knew nothing of the maker's reputation. Advertising helped to fill that void. Mass transportation facilities and well-developed mass media also were essential. Before the development of broadcast media, a high rate of literacy was needed if advertising messages were to be understood.

Questions for Discussion

1 In the prologue, David Potter gives status to advertising as an American institution. Do you agree with his analysis? Give specific examples when explaining your answer.

2 Why should a newspaper editor or the producer of a television program understand how advertising functions?

3 Is it likely that the less developed nations of Africa will adopt advertising as part of their way of doing business? What conditions will have to be present for them to do so?

4 At least three forms of advertising preceded the development of the movable-type principle. What were these advertising forms? Give examples of their use today.

5 This chapter states that United States advertising developed because there was a need for it. A corollary to this premise is that advertising will disappear if such need no longer exists. Do you foresee such a contingency? Explain your view.

6 How does advertising differ from: (*a*) publicity; (*b*) propaganda; and (*c*) personal selling?

7 Which view of advertising—marketing or communications—is most useful to you as a student of advertising? Why? Why is it important that we recognize the existence of both viewpoints? Discuss.

8 Do you agree that advertising can be classified as persuasive? Is such a classification harmful to the advertiser's position? To that of the general public?

9 Cite current advertising campaigns that are introducing new products (brands) similar to the campaign presenting Mello Yello. List three sustaining campaigns similar to that given for Grease relief.

10 Bring to class a print advertisement that "demarkets" a product such as the one in Figure 1.11 in the Georgia Power case.

For Further Reference

Atwan, Robert, Donald McQuade, and John W. Wright: *Edsels, Luckies, & Frigidaires: Advertising the American Way,* Dell Publishing Co., Inc., New York, 1979.

Foster, G. Allen: *Advertising: Ancient Marketplace to Television,* Criterion Books, Inc., New York, 1967.

Presbrey, Frank S.: *The History and Development of Advertising,* Greenwood Press, New York, 1968.

Peterson, Theodore: *Magazines in the Twentieth Century,* The University of Illinois Press, Urbana, 1964.

Sutphen, Dick: *The Mad Old Ads,* Dick Sutphen Studio, Inc., Minneapolis, 1966.

Wood, James Playsted: *The Story of Advertising,* The Ronald Press Company, New York, 1958.

Wright, John S., and John E. Mertes: *Advertising's Role in Society,* West Publishing Company, St. Paul, Minn., 1974.

End Notes

[1] Steuart Henderson Britt, Stephen C. Adams, and Allan S. Miller, "How Many Advertising Exposures Per Day?" *Journal of Advertising Research,* December 1972, p. 9.

[2] Ralph S. Alexander and the Committee on Definitions, *Marketing Definitions,* American Marketing Association, Chicago, 1963, p. 9.

[3] Clyde R. Miller, *The Process of Persuasion,* Crown Publishers, Inc., New York, 1946, p. 16.

[4] Arthur Quiller-Couch, *On the Art of Writing,* G. P. Putnam's Sons, New York, 1916, p. 161.

[5] Philip Kotler, *Marketing Management,* 3d ed., Prentice-Hall, Inc., Englewood Cliffs, N.J., 1980, p. 11.

Chapter 2

Advertising's Role in Society

As we introduce the various aspects and applications of modern advertising in this book, we most often focus on the management of advertising by a business firm (or nonprofit organization) that uses advertising to achieve its communication objectives with a target group. This is a *micro* view because it treats advertising applications on an individual basis.

If you are to have a complete understanding of advertising, however, you must view the entire field and appreciate the overall role of advertising in modern society. This is the *macro* view of advertising, which is discussed in this chapter. The ideas and concepts that we develop here should be used as a background for understanding the strategies and tactics of individual advertisers as explored in the rest of this book.

In Chapter 1 we observed that advertising is an important institution in the United States, as well as in most other developed nations. Social critics constantly examine society's institutions to see whether they are operating for the general welfare of its members. It is appropriate, therefore, that advertising be placed under such scrutiny if our societal goal is to bring about the greatest good to the largest number of people in our society. James Ferguson, who agrees that advertising is a social institution, observes that its costs and benefits should be evaluated to determine the total impact of advertising in our social welfare:

> The issue is not whether advertising is perfect but whether the benefits of advertising outweigh the costs, so that social welfare is greater with advertising.[1]

We assess the case for advertising as a positive force in our society by first looking at the economic issues that its presence raises. Then, the last half of the chapter is a look at the social issues that may be of concern because advertising is present in our society. We would like, however, first to present an overview of what we believe to be the major contributions that advertising makes to the nation's social welfare. Each is discussed, directly or indirectly, later in the chapter.

Five Contributions of Advertising to Social Welfare

1 Advertising is an efficient source of information for both consumers and industrial purchasers about product quality, new merchandise, new technology, and prices.

2 Advertising reduces distribution costs by making personal selling more effective or by replacing it entirely.

3 Advertising encourages competition by lowering information costs; it also fosters product quality through clear brand identification and producer or distributor accountability.

4 Advertising publicizes the material and cultural incentives of a democratic free enterprise society, and so helps motivate increased productive effort by both management and workers.

5 Advertising enables both print and broadcast media to maintain independence from government, political parties, and other special-interest groups.

Economic Effects of Advertising

The nation's economists are one group with a great deal to say about advertising's role in society. Simply put, economics is the study of the allocation of scarce resources. In the allocation of resources, the normal functioning of a free enterprise economy is based on the idea that the consumer determines resource allocation through free choice: a person can choose one type of job or profession over another and is free to purchase product A instead of product B. Just as our wants differ, so do our abilities to satisfy our wants. The voluntary interaction of individuals in the marketplace, each attempting to satisfy personal wants, tends to maximize social welfare without coercion.

Richard Holton, an economist and former business school dean, describes the traditional critical view of advertising as held by economists in these words:

> . . . advertising leads to distortions in consumption expenditures and reinforces positions of market power, permitting the large firm to extract a higher price from buyers than would be possible if advertising were restricted or prohibited.[2]

Economists who hold this view believe that advertising is a source of market power with high prices to consumers as the inevitable outcome. There is, however, a shift in this conventional view among some economists. Holton goes on to state that economists today feel that "advertising [is] respectable as a subject of scholarly research. And some are prepared to argue that advertising frequently if not generally is pro-competitive and hence desirable."[3] This group thinks that advertising lowers information costs and results in more price competition and consequent lower prices for consumers. In the following section we expand both views of the economic effects of advertising.

Advertising Encourages Economic Growth

Since the Great Depression of the 1930s, with its devastating unemployment of millions of workers, the United States has been dedicated to a policy of full employment for its citizens. Such a policy, of course, requires an expanding economy with more and more jobs. For there to be more jobs, there must be an increased demand for goods and services, and advertising contributes to the accomplishment of that goal. By lowering information costs, advertising assists in the marketing of more and better goods, thus leading to a greater gross national product (GNP) and a higher standard of living.[4] In a statement made as long ago as 1942, Neil Borden, pioneer teacher of advertising at the Harvard Business School, succinctly summarized the point being made here:

> Advertising's chief task from a social standpoint is that of encouraging the development of new products. It offers a means whereby the enterpriser may hope to build a profitable demand for his new and differentiated merchandise which will justify investment. From growing investment has come the increasing flow of material welfare to a level unknown in previous centuries.[5]

Although advertising can play an important role in economic growth, some economists still pose the question, "Is money spent for advertising an undesirable allocation of society's scarce resources?" or, put another way, "Is advertising an economic waste?" Some critics of advertising believe so. It should be noted that advertising expenditures in the United States are currently running at 2 percent of the GNP.

Figure 2.1 This kind of advertising helped to develop the market for California-grown oranges. Notice the health appeals made in the body copy. The campaign is a classic in the history of American marketing. [*Reprinted with permission of Sunkist Growers, Inc.*]

The traditional economic view that advertising is wasteful is based on the assumption that consumers already possess perfect information and can make their choices (allocate resources) without advertising. This assumption is not true in the real world, and many economists now assign a value to information. People do not have complete information and they seek information, a fact that is demonstrated by the growing numbers of subscribers to consumer magazines. Information is an economic good and is subject

Figure 2.2 A modern-day new product introduced to the market through advertising.

to the laws of supply and demand as are other economic goods. Advertising has proved to be a more efficient (less costly) source of information than other sources. If this were not true, then advertised brands would cost more relative to quality, and consumers would choose unadvertised brands. Thus consumers, in buying advertised brands, are allocating some of their resources to advertising; they consider that for obtaining information, advertising is the most efficient use of these resources.

Some people believe that it is not necessary that we be offered a choice of dozens of competing detergents or many brands of after-shave lotion. But when we view this opportunity to select as a manifestation of freedom of choice, which builds from trivial decisions to matters of ultimate concern such as choosing our elective leaders, it takes on new significance. Advertising is sometimes called the "voice of free choice," and certainly manufacturers seeking to serve diverse wants under a system of free choice should have the opportunity to communicate the news about the availability of their products to potential buyers.

When critics state that an excess of advertising messages is being exposed in our print and broadcast media, the principle of free choice can also be invoked. While there may seem to be an overabundance of such messages, especially in some media at certain times, fairness requires that all who wish to advertise be allowed to do so, provided, of course, that their messages are truthful and not misleading. Such abuses of the advertising privilege and the control of misleading advertising are discussed in Chapter 20, which deals with advertising and the law.

Advertising Helps Maintain Competition

Some economists claim that advertising creates the supposition of differences among products that are essentially the same. Consumers then build a brand preference for the advertised good and are willing to pay more for it because they perceive it to be better than an unadvertised but similar product. This tendency limits the competitiveness in the market for the product and gives the advertiser market power. These economists argue further that advertising makes it more difficult for new producers to enter the marketplace by providing a barrier to entry, and, in addition, that its presence reduces competition by bringing about industry concentration and monopoly profits.[6]

Advertising and Monopoly First, let us examine whether advertising does in fact foster monopoly, then look at whether consumers pay more for products because they are advertised.

The argument that advertising reduces competition is based on the assertion that the cost of advertising a new product is prohibitive for any but the "entrenched giants" of industry. In other words, advertising superiority enables large existing producers to block new competition from entering a market and results in the establishment of monopolies with high prices and profits. This situation, the argument continues, leads to more advertising power, and the vicious cycle continues.

One economist states that persons who believe that advertising decreases competition make two basic assumptions: (1) "that advertising by established firms changes consumers' tastes and creates durable brand loyalties," and (2) "that there are increasing returns to advertising."[7] We deal with the first assumption in the next section on advertising as information insofar as its taste-changing capability is concerned. The following quotation sheds light on the brand loyalty issue:

> No proof has yet been offered that it is easier for the first advertiser to win a consumer's patronage than it is for a second advertiser to shift it to him. The fact that the soap companies are constantly bringing out new brands suggests a taste for novelty on the part of the consumer that does not square with the theory of the first advertiser's advantage.[8]

Under the second assumption, it is claimed that monopoly power is increased because increasing returns to advertising bring about the concentration of industry and, furthermore, erect barriers to entry into the industry. After a thorough examination of the studies conducted by the proponents of this point of view, Ferguson found no direct evidence that increasing returns to advertising do in fact exist.[9] Nevertheless, the concentration and barrier-to-entry criticisms are so prevalent in the literature of economics that an additional comment on the subject is in order.

A University of Chicago economist, Lester G. Telser, has closely studied the relationship between advertising and sales concentration in industry. His findings are summarized in these words:

> One measure of competition in an industry, widely accepted by economists, is the concentration of sales among the four leading firms in the industry. The larger the share of the total going to the four leading firms, the less the competition. If advertising reduces competition, then there ought to be high levels of advertising in those industries where the leading firms have small shares. This seems to be true in some industries, for instance, soaps, cigarettes, and breakfast cereals, but it is false in other industries, drugs, and cosmetics. The best way to test the proposition is to examine the data for all consumer-product industries. Such an examination shows a negligible positive association between advertising intensity and concentration. In other words, the exceptions to the hypothesis nearly outweigh the conforming cases. Changes in concentration and advertising intensity ought to move in the same direction according to the hypothesis that advertising lessens competition. The data for the period 1947–57 show, if anything, the opposite relation—an inverse association between changes in advertising intensity and changes in concentration. The weakness of the hypothesis claiming a positive association between advertising and monopoly is shown by another fact. Industries that produce industrial goods hardly advertise and yet may be highly concentrated. Thus if

all manufacturing industries were examined to determine the relations between advertising intensity and the concentration of sales among the leading firms, no systematic pattern would emerge.[10]

Lack of great financial strength does not provide an insurmountable barrier to entering a product field. How Texize, a relatively small company located in South Carolina, competes successfully with the largest of all American advertisers, Procter & Gamble, was explained in Chapter 1. Furthermore, a casual glance at the recent inroads into the markets of such automotive giants as General Motors and Ford by Volkswagen, Datsun, and Toyota provides ample evidence of newcomers successfully competing with entrenched leaders. The communication channels offered by modern mass media are open to all entre-

Figure 2.3 This advertisement employs an interesting appeal as a new market is opened by a relatively small company. The newspaper ad appeared in 20 U.S. markets.

preneurs, and all innovations have a better chance of being accepted now than when communication processes were slower.

Jules Backman sums up the relationship between advertising and monopoly with these words:

> Companies with relatively high advertising-sales ratios tend to have somewhat higher profit rates than less intensive advertisers. These higher profits appear to reflect the larger volume resulting from successful advertising rather than the exercise of market power to charge high monopolistic prices. . . . The relationship between advertising intensity and high economic concentration is nonexistent. There appears to be no link between advertising intensity and price increases. . . . The record shows clearly that advertising is highly competitive, not anti-competitive.[11]

Advertising and Prices Even though the evidence tends to show that advertising does not lead to industry concentration or provide a barrier to entry, we still may wonder whether consumers do not pay more for advertised goods than for unadvertised items. Those who argue that advertising leads to higher consumer prices hold to the idea that "somebody must pay": advertising is a cost of doing business, and as such, must be factored into the price charged for the product.[12] However, this assumption ignores the arguments that lower prices result when advertising is present in the marketplace.

One viewpoint favoring advertising emphasizes that it increases market efficiency with economies of scale; these result from the employment of both mass production and mass distribution methods that are possible only because advertising has expanded demand for the product.[13] Advertising, it is argued, is the cheapest (most efficient) method of (1) communicating with consumers about the product's availability, and (2) obtaining retail distribution for that product. The price of a product obviously reflects its manufacturing and marketing costs, and that price can well be lower when advertising is used instead of less efficient marketing tools. Robert Steiner, in his case study of toy market advertising, illustrates how advertising of a product can lead to lower consumer prices.

Advertising and Toy Prices[14] Historically, toys were advertised in print media and through radio commercials. These media did not reach the primary audience for the toys, which is three- to seven-year-old children. Considerable promotional effort was placed on department-store demonstrations in the 1940s. However, only major outlets were feasible locations for these live demonstrations of toys.

In the 1950s, the growth of television as a mass medium and the development of child-oriented TV programming enabled toy manufacturers to reach their desired target audience with impact and efficiency, and the level of toy advertising increased greatly. In addition to the manufacturer-sponsored television commercials aimed at children, major toy dealers ran ads in local newspapers directed to the secondary toy market—parents. Discount retailers soon learned that ads featuring TV-advertised toys at cut prices were capable of generating major sales results. This new combination of media—TV to reach children and newspapers to reach parents—brought about a large increase of sales from a dollar of advertising. The consequent higher levels of demand for toys permitted substantial economies of large-scale production in toy manufacturing. Increased spending for advertising made the factory salesperson's job easier, thus reducing that form of selling cost.

Two other events of the era—the growth of discount stores and the decline of fair trade laws in the United States—coincided with the increase of television advertising of toys. Discount-store operators learned that the new TV-promoted toy was an ideal vehicle for promotion. The approach brought heavy floor traffic to the store, as well as more toy sales. Retailer margins obviously dropped significantly as a result of this price-cutting. By 1970, strongly advertised toy merchandise enjoyed a distribution margin (markup) nearly 25 percent less than nonadvertised goods, while the overall toy distribution margin as a percentage of retail price fell by one-third, from 49 percent in 1958 to 33 percent in 1970.

The savings resulting from increased manufacturing productivity that reflected greater consumer demand stimulated by advertising were passed on to the retail trade. More effective advertising, along with mass retailing efficiencies, made distribution more productive, and distribution margins and retail prices were reduced. Consumer demand for toys is elastic.

From 1958 to 1970, toy sales increased nearly 80 percent (in constant dollars), and toy makers experienced factory cost savings of 10 percent. Part of the growth in demand was in response to the relative fall in the price of toys that was the result of television, a more efficient advertising medium.

Interestingly, the toy industry of the United Kingdom was not able to duplicate the American success story because retail-price maintenance practices prevented the discounting of toy prices. In France, on the other hand, commercial television advertising of toys was not permitted. So, although discounting of toy prices was prevalent in France, demand remained lower than in the United Kingdom. The strong product identity that TV advertising produces was lacking in the French market. Thus, in sum, the United States consumer has benefited from materially lower toy prices because of their being advertised on TV. When, at long last, the French government allowed toy advertising on TV, the American experience was replicated.

Advertising Informs Customers

Many economists believe that advertisers are interested not so much in fulfilling the desires of consumers as in changing desires to fit that which has been produced. In other words, people's tastes are changed so that they will buy what is manufactured. This criticism in reality is a negation of the concept of consumer sovereignty, which claims that "the free market generates the flow of production along the lines that satisfy consumer tastes; their tastes determine what shall be produced."[15] Producer sovereignty governs the consumer, according to this argument. And argue we could over whether the consumer is king or not. In Chapter 1, we stated flatly that advertising is persuasion and that persuasion can be exercised for good ends. Rather than engage in a long harangue over consumer versus producer sovereignty in the marketplace, we prefer to turn our attention to the question of whether advertising is informative.

Advertising as Information[16] At one time, economists distinguished between "informative" advertising and "competitive" advertising. The latter was designed primarily to shift demand from one brand to another and therefore was called undesirable, uneconomic, and wasteful. Informative advertising, on the other hand, was in favor; examples of informative advertising under this system of classification were classified advertising in newspapers and price-oriented advertisements sponsored by retailers. In a pure sense, only price and terms of sale were classified as information. However, it came to be realized that every ad, if it is to be effective, must contain some elements of information; and identifying advertising as competitive is difficult, if not wholly unrealistic.

Some economists have been devoting considerable thought to this problem and have concluded that all advertising is informative, although different kinds of advertising convey different kinds of information. Nelson postulates: "There are two possible ways by which advertising can increase sales: either advertising changes tastes, or advertising provides information." He rejects the taste-changing role because there is no theory of taste or taste change and therefore no possible empirical test for it. He goes on to develop a theory of advertising as information.

Nelson's theory holds that consumers have far less than perfect information about products and that it costs resources to distribute product information. More important, it costs resources, largely time, to acquire product information. Consumers, furthermore, are acting rationally when they limit expenditures on information acquisition, and they will respond to advertising only if it provides information to them at a *lower* cost than do alternative sources of information. Consumers are not at the complete mercy of sellers; they do have some other sources of information about goods.

Information about product quality can be obtained to some extent through physical inspection; sofas can be viewed in furniture showrooms, and suits can be tried on in clothing stores. Items about which information can be obtained less expensively in this fashion are labeled as **search goods** by Nelson.

Probably more concern over the consumer's relative bargaining strength in the marketplace exists over products whose quality is not so easily ascertained. Such items as toothpaste and canned dog food do not convey much information about their quality through mere physical inspection of their packages, or even the contents thereof. Information about their worth is obtained by experimentation among several brands. Such products are designated

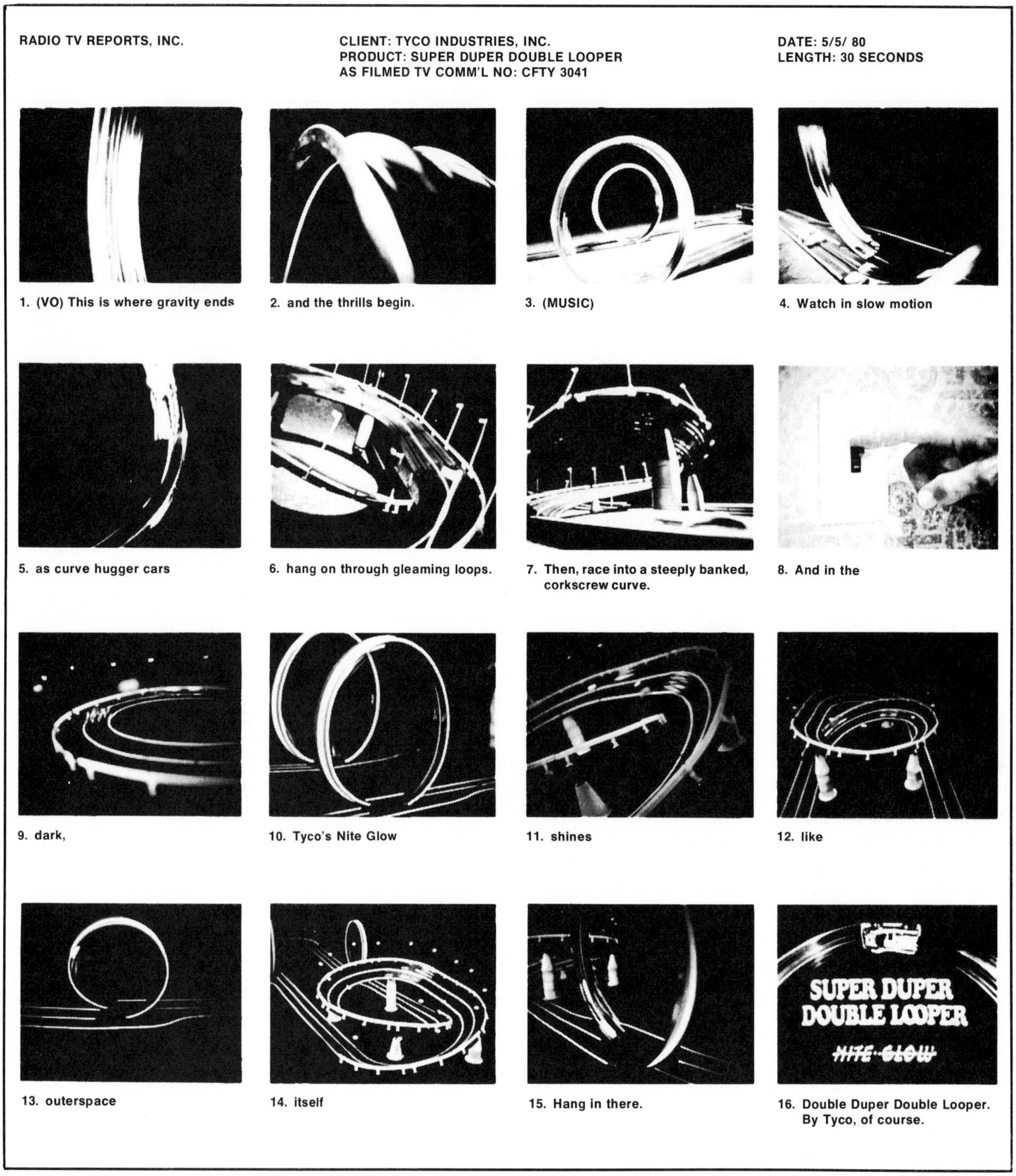
RADIO TV REPORTS, INC.
CLIENT: TYCO INDUSTRIES, INC.
PRODUCT: SUPER DUPER DOUBLE LOOPER
AS FILMED TV COMM'L NO: CFTY 3041
DATE: 5/5/ 80
LENGTH: 30 SECONDS
1. (VO) This is where gravity ends
2. and the thrills begin.
3. (MUSIC)
4. Watch in slow motion
5. as curve hugger cars
6. hang on through gleaming loops.
7. Then, race into a steeply banked, corkscrew curve.
8. And in the
9. dark,
10. Tyco's Nite Glow
11. shines
12. like
13. outerspace
14. itself
15. Hang in there.
SUPER DUPER
DOUBLE LOOPER
16. Double Duper Double Looper. By Tyco, of course.

(*a*)

Figure 2.4 A toy manufacturer promotes one of its products through television commercials (*a*), and a major retailer features the same item in a newspaper ad (*b*) (*opposite.*) Note the stress on price in the retail ad.

2 Big Days.
Tyco's Train & Racing
SILVER STREAK
NITE-GLOW
WITH OPERATING PIGGYBACK LOADER/ UNLOADER & NITE-GLOW WAREHOUSE
• Lighted Alco Century Loco
• Piggyback Loader/Unloader with Truck Depot
• 5 Colorful Freight Cars
• Truck Cab with Trailer
• Nite-Glow Warehouse
• 36" x 45" Oval Track Layout
• Power Pack with Forward and Reverse
29.99
LOCOMOTIVES WITH OPERATING HEADLIGHTS
0-8-0 with smoke 19.99
Alco Century Diesel 14.99
GP-20 Diesel 11.99
FREIGHT CARS
Your choice
1.29 each
9 styles
CLEMENTINE
GOLD MINING COMPANY
NITE-GLOW
WITH OPERATING GOLD MINE, OPERATING DUMP CAR SET & SMOKE
• Lighted 0-8-0 Steam Loco with Smoke and Tender
• Operating Gold Mine
• 6 Colorful Freight Cars
• Ore Dump Car Set with Receiving Bin
• Nite-Glow Sheet
• 36" x 45" Oval Track Layout
• Power Pack with Forward and Reverse
38.99
TRACK & SWITCHES
18" Radius Curve Track (4 pcs.)
1.29
9" Straight Track (4 pcs.)
1.29
Remote Control Switch (right) or (left)
5.79 each
OPERATING ACCESSORIES
Your choice
5.99 each
Cattle Car Set
Nite-Glow Crossing Gate
Remote Control Whistle in Billboard
EASY-TO-ASSEMBLE TYCOKITS
Your choice
2.44 each
6 styles
Snap Together Signal Tower
Arlee Station
Snap-Together Crossover Signal Bridge
Operating Crane Car and Boom Tender
Your choice
6.99 each
Piggyback Loader/Unloader
Howard Johnson's
Three Houses Under Construction
8 styles
Your choice
3.44 each
Ma's Place
DAREDEVIL JUMP
NITE-GLOW
DAREDEVIL JUMP!
18½' OF RACING ACTION IN 2½' x 5½'!
• 2 Lighted CURVEHUGGER HP2 Cars
• 2 Plug-in Hi-Performance Controllers
• Daredevil Jump with Nite-Glow Barrels!
• Nite-Glow Crash Barrier Fence with Flags
• Nite-Glow Decoration Sheet
• Wall Power Pack, U.L. Listed
24.99
SUPER DUPER DOUBLE LOOPER
NITE-GLOW
DOUBLE LOOPS!
20' OF RACING WITH HI-BANKED CORKSCREW IN 2' x 6½'!
• 2 Lighted CURVEHUGGER HP2 Cars
• 2 Plug-in Hi-Performance Controllers
• 2 360° Action Loops
• Hi-Bank Corkscrew Track
• Nite-Glow Crash Barrier Fence with Flags
• Nite-Glow Decoration Sheet
• Wall Power Pack, U.L. Listed
31.99
BIG DETOUR
COMMAND CONTROL
NITE-GLOW
CRASH BARRIER!
19½' OF RACING ACTION IN 3' x 7'!
• 2 Lighted Slotless Passing Cars
• 1 Lighted Obstacle Car with Roof Lights
• 2 Dual Action Command Controllers
• Detour Track with Crash Barrier
• Nite-Glow Fence and Flags
• Nite-Glow Decoration Sheet
• Wall Power Pack, U.L. Listed
44.99
Now, two great ways to charge!
CURVE HUGGERS HP2
SLOTTED RACING CARS WITH OPERATING HEADLIGHTS
Your choice
5.99 each
COMMAND CONTROL
STEER & PASS AT YOUR COMMAND
SLOTLESS RACING CARS WITH OPERATING HEADLIGHTS
Your choice
7.99 each
JCPenney
Sale prices effective through November 24, 1979

(*b*)

CUSTOMER INFORMATION FROM GENERAL MOTORS

HOW TO TELL WHEN YOUR CAR NEEDS A TUNE-UP

AND HOW TO BE SURE YOU DON'T PAY FOR MORE SERVICE THAN YOU NEED.

Remember the old Spring and Fall tune-ups? There was a time when GM cars needed tune-ups every year. But that was a long time ago. Since 1973, we've been building cars that don't need anywhere near as much routine maintenance as they used to.

Now, a lot of people are getting tune-ups they don't really need. Probably out of habit.

Break the habit, and you'll save yourself some money. The maintenance schedule and the owner's manual your GM dealer gives you with your new GM car will tell you exactly what scheduled maintenance is required and when. Some of the newer schedules may surprise you.

For example, spark plugs used to have to be changed every 12,000 miles. Now it's every 22,500 or 30,000, depending on which new GM car you bought. For most drivers that means changing plugs every two years instead of every year.

When you bought your first car, you probably changed oil every 1,000 miles. We upped it to 6,000 a few years ago; and now it's 7,500 on all new GM cars except diesels.

Or take distributor points and condensers. They never need replacing with GM's new high energy ignition system. It doesn't have any points or condensers.

If you do have trouble with your car, just fix what needs fixing. When you take your car in for service, tell the mechanic exactly what's happening. If it's hard to start "hot," but starts okay when it's "cold," say so. If it doesn't perform the way you expected, describe just how and where it doesn't live up to your expectations. Then it'll be easier for the mechanic to pinpoint what's wrong, and he won't have to make unnecessary repairs. That can save you time and money.

Some things have to be watched more carefully, depending on how and where you drive your car. For example, if you do a lot of driving on dry, dusty roads, you may need to change the air cleaner and oil filter more often than the maintenance schedule indicates. Remember, the maintenance schedule that comes with your car is based on average driving conditions.

If you have an older car that still needs an annual tune-up, what should it include? There are some basic things to be checked: spark plugs, points, condensers, idling speed, and drive belts. It can't hurt to check the air cleaner and fuel filter, tire pressure, and brake fluid, either. And when you do take your car in for a tune-up, don't be shy. Find out exactly what you need and what you're getting for your money.

We're trying to make GM cars easier and more economical to service. We've been able to stretch out the maintenance intervals for new GM cars, which should reduce the cost of routine maintenance; and we're working on engineering improvements that should reduce the amount of required maintenance even further. We want to be sure our cars perform well for their entire lifetime, without costing you a lot of time and money in maintenance. That's better for you and better for us.

This advertisement is part of our continuing effort to give customers useful information about their cars and trucks and the company that builds them.

General Motors
People building transportation to serve people

Figure 2.5 The largest car manufacturer in the United States provides highly useful information to all of the nation's car owners as a public service. [*Reprinted with the permission of General Motors Corporation.*]

HOW TO LAND A LORD IN LONDON

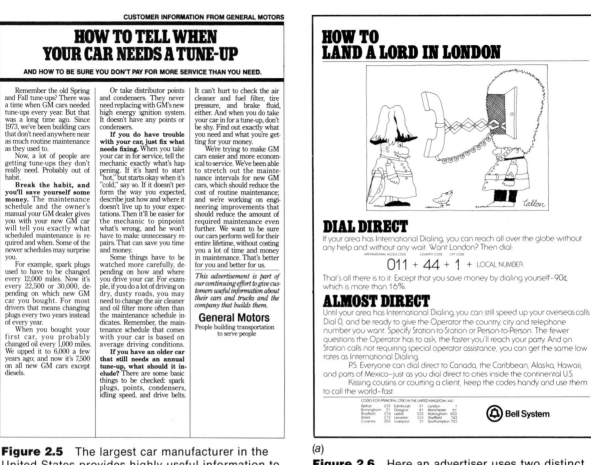

DIAL DIRECT

If your area has International Dialing, you can reach all over the globe without any help and without any wait. Want London? Then dial:

INTERNATIONAL ACCESS CODE		COUNTRY CODE		CITY CODE		
011	+	44	+	1	+	LOCAL NUMBER

That's all there is to it. Except that you save money by dialing yourself–90¢, which is more than 16%.

ALMOST DIRECT

Until your area has International Dialing, you can still speed up your overseas calls Dial 0, and be ready to give the Operator the country, city and telephone number you want. Specify Station-to-Station or Person-to-Person. The fewer questions the Operator has to ask, the faster you'll reach your party. And on Station calls not requiring special operator assistance, you can get the same low rates as International Dialing.

P.S. Everyone can dial direct to Canada, the Caribbean, Alaska, Hawaii, and parts of Mexico–just as you dial direct to cities inside the continental U.S.

Kissing cousins or courting a client, keep the codes handy and use them to call the world–fast.

CODES FOR PRINCIPAL CITIES IN THE UNITED KINGDOM (44)

Belfast	232	Edinburgh	31	London	1
Birmingham	21	Glasgow	41	Manchester	61
Bradford	274	Leeds	532	Nottingham	602
Bristol	272	Leicester	533	Sheffield	742
Coventry	203	Liverpool	51	Southampton	703

Bell System

(*a*)

Figure 2.6 Here an advertiser uses two distinct approaches in appealing to the consumer. The approach shown in (*a*) (*above*) is purely informational. On the other hand, the TV commercial in (*b*) (*opposite*) is highly persuasive in content.

as **experience goods** by Nelson. Through repeat purchases of such products, consumers exercise control over the market for experience goods. Because such experimentation for even relatively inexpensive items is costly, consumers often seek information prior to purchase. Polling friends and relatives or reading articles in newspapers or magazines may well give the needed information. However, these information sources often are not available or are inadequate, and advertising fills the informational gap.

The pertinent question is over the authenticity of the information provided by the advertiser. Nelson states that in the case of search goods, the problem is simple: if the characteristics featured in the advertising are at variance with the product when inspected, no purchase will result. Although the advertisement may attract the prospective customer to the store, it is a waste of money (for the advertisement) and time (of the salesperson) if advertising claims and product qualities aren't equal.

As mentioned earlier, the purchaser of experience goods exercises control through repeat purchases and, to a lesser extent, through recommending or not recommending the product to friends. Because repeat purchase is the goal, the seller wishes the buyer to use the product in such a way that satisfaction will be maximized. Thus, the information in the product advertisements should be geared to the consumer's needs. As Nelson expresses this aim, ". . . advertisements almost always correctly relate brand to function." This is direct information, but most experience goods advertising messages convey only in-

N W Ayer ABH International

CLIENT: AT&T
PRODUCT: LONG LINES
TITLE: "LIKE CATS & DOGS"

COMM'L NO. AXLL 3703
LENGTH: 30 SECONDS

SINGER: Feelings,

nothing more than feelings.
MUSIC FADES FOR VOICEOVER.

ANDY, VO: I have a brother in Los Angeles, that I call.

I enjoy talking to him. He's my only brother.

Just like normal brothers, we used to fight like cats and dogs.

but no one else could hit him but me (LAUGHS). I always maintained that I got the bulk

and he got the brains.

He's just a wonderful guy. And I enjoy calling him.

SINGER: Feelings . . . MUSIC FADES.

(*b*)

direct information to the consumer: namely, that the brand is advertised—that the product has been successful enough to sustain the cost of the advertising program for the brand. Only brands of high quality and high repeat-purchase potential can sustain heavy advertising over a period of time. Consumers are aware of this fact.

Often, market success permits lower prices for the advertised product than for competitive brands, and the consumer benefits from that development. Above all, the indirect information carried in advertisements may aid consumers in making up their minds when confronted with perplexing product choices in the marketplace; it saves their most scarce resource—time. In many instances, consumers want quick, cheap information, and advertising is its purveyor. Otherwise, the consumer may resort to random selection.

That advertising is believed to contribute to the economic welfare of a nation is further illustrated by the fact that controlled economies, such as those of the Soviet Union and its Eastern European satellites, and even of mainland China, employ advertising in varying degrees. In Chapter 21, which is devoted to the international dimension of advertising, we explore this interesting subject.

Social Effects of Advertising

Advertising touches our lives in four significant ways: (1) through its persuasive abilities, (2) by its truthfulness or untruthfulness, (3) through its tastefulness or tastelessness, and (4) by its cultural impact on our values and lifestyles. Advertising's economic roles—its persuasive and informative powers—have been discussed in the first half of this chapter. The question of truth in advertising is examined in Chapter 20, which deals with legal constraints on the practice of advertising. Therefore, we now consider its social effects—taste in advertising and cultural impact.

Advertising and Standards of Good Taste

What constitutes good taste as contrasted with bad taste is a matter of individual perception. Each individual ends up exercising a personal opinion; sometimes an effort is made to project that opinion over the behavior of other individuals. In a sense, this is similar to the criticisms that "advertising makes people want things they shouldn't have." There is no law or universal guideline regarding good and bad taste.

In determining which advertising is in good taste and which fails to meet the test, the primary concern is the *manner* in which the advertising is done rather than its content *matter.*[17] Involved are those ethical, moral, and aesthetic considerations regarding the manner in which advertising is handled. Advertising can be classified as being of questionable taste on four principal scores:

1. Moral concern over the product itself: products such as liquor, cigarettes, contraceptives, and feminine hygiene sprays
2. Inappropriate time or context for the message exposure: laxative advertising at the dinner hour; lingerie ads on early-evening TV
3. Use of objectionable appeals, such as fear or sex
4. Use of objectionable techniques: excessive repetition of messages, loud volume, silliness of presentation[18]

Concern over Product If a person objects to a product itself, it is natural that its advertising will be deemed objectionable and will suffer as a consequence. Advertising is just the most visible part of the total product entity. Rationally, objection to the product should be distinguished from objection to its advertising. The banning of cigarette advertising from the broadcast media illustrates this dilemma. The product has legal sanction; it is subject to special taxation. Some people argue that cigarette processors should have the right to promote the product on television and radio. If cigarettes are believed to be truly harmful to people, they should be banned from sale in interstate commerce. Certainly it is inconsistent to permit their advertising in forms of media other than broadcast. Moral judgments over the use of specific products need to be universally made before the advertising of them should be outlawed. The sounder approach is to ban the sale of such products.

Message Timing and Context Certainly the poor **timing** of advertising for an otherwise acceptable product may show a lack of taste on the advertiser's part, as in the showing of the laxative advertisement at dinnertime. Of course, one might counter that dining and watching television simultaneously is also in bad taste. The clutter of advertising messages on television can be irritating to the viewer. Heavy concentration of advertisements in other media, such as pre-Christmas issues of magazines and newspapers, is tolerated much more readily by the typical consumer. True, one can flip by ads in newspapers and magazines more easily than one can avoid advertising on television. However, in the flood of messages, some may be relevant to part of the audience, and communication value is received by these persons. What messages, if any, should be allowed at times when children listen intensively to television, such as Saturday mornings, is a highly debated question and still is in the process of being resolved.

Objectionable Appeals Opinions on matters of sex are subjective to the utmost degree. Although no advertiser knowingly will use sex appeals in a manner that will offend the majority of the target audience, there is no doubt that such appeals do create interest in advertising messages. "It is not always so much what is in the ad as what the viewer brings to it."[19] What is deemed to be sexy by one person may be bland to another, and we all recognize that the standards of what is socially acceptable are subject to rapid change in our society.

Insofar as the appeal to fear is concerned, this approach has been used to sell products that are of little interest to consumers when so-called rational appeals are employed. Even in cases where the product fulfills a generally recognized need, such as in the case of life insurance, fear appeals are needed to sell policies to some prospects. However, appeals to fear, such as in the case of the cancer hazard in cigarette smoking, are often rejected by receivers of such messages. A more questionable use of the fear appeal is over body odors and the possible effect such odors may have on one's social acceptance. The end result is a fresher-smelling society, but is the advertising in bad taste? Once again, the answer is a subjective one.

Some people object to the appeals being made in advertisements on the grounds that they are too simple-minded, that "they insult a person's intelligence." Part of this criticism is based on the fact that many messages are meant for the mass market and thus are run in the mass media, which, in turn, do address persons in the audience not in the target market for the advertised product. To these people, the messages may seem inane. This is one of the difficult problems that advertisers face.

Objectionable Techniques Techniques of advertising such as repetition of message, use of high volume, sound effects, or the employment of unpleasant people, voices, or music are all part of the intrusive nature of advertising, especially in the television medium. These techniques are used to attract the attention of the audience under circumstances in which such attention may be difficult to obtain. In other words, it is claimed by some advertising people that these tactics are unavoidable if advertising is to carry out its function of communicating with target audiences. On the other hand, some critics firmly believe that their use is a reflection of the bankruptcy of creativity on the part of the advertising community and would not be needed if more time and thought were devoted to advertising message development. However, advertisers spend money and time on testing alternative advertising techniques, and they abandon any that have resulted in decreased brand sales. And for experience goods, the very fact of advertising is the important point, not the content of the advertising message. There is no doubt that some advertising irritates some people, but clearly not most people, or the technique would be found unproductive and would be discontinued. Furthermore, extreme use of such techniques can be counterproductive; for example, the use of excessive repetition can lead to a backlash, a sort of protest, even to the point of consumer rejection of the product featured so frequently.

Conclusion A basic problem is that different people have different standards. At least three problems are present when determining the line between good taste and bad taste in advertising:

1 Ethics, morals, and aesthetics—or general standards of behavior, specific standards of behavior, and artistic standards—are problems involving mores and philosophy that may often differ widely in America's heterogeneous population.
2 Whatever the standards of taste (or tastefulness) are, they change over time.
3 There are semantic problems with the variable called taste.[20]

(*a*)

(*b*)

Figure 2.7 A well-known perfume manufacturer recognizes that women who possess varying lifestyles have different attitudes toward its products. In advertisement (*a*) an appeal is made to women holding traditional values, whereas advertisement (*b*) appeals to women holding modern or "liberated" values. The "Charlie" fragrance ranks first in worldwide sales. [*Courtesy of Revlon.*]

Furthermore, one can argue that the presence of garish, loud advertising is a cost of affluence. Consumers have a scarcity of time, and they seek fast, cheap information about products. In meeting that need, advertisers on occasion may overstep the boundaries of good taste, at least in the view of the more sensitive members of the population.

Advertising, Value Systems, and Lifestyles

A frequently made charge against advertising is "that life tends more and more to be influenced by advertising, and that as a result, the values of our world are not only dominated but even debased by advertising."[21] Jack Sissors, who teaches advertising at Northwestern University, concluded that the evidence to support the charge that advertising has the power to change human values is, at best, scant.[22] He has pointed out that the amount of research delving into the topic is small and too specialized and narrow to ascertain anything about how values are in fact changed by advertising. He does, however, believe:

> . . . that one thing advertising is able to do is to widely disseminate news about the majority's value systems to a huge audience, some of whom, perhaps, are not aware of them. In a sense, then, advertising informs some parts of our culture what the predominant value system is, as reflected through advertising copy and layout.[23]

A social scientist, Ronald Berman, in an examination of the interplay between advertising and the process of social change, arrived at these conclusions:

> A clear distinction has to be made between pragmatic criticism, focused on the truth of advertised claims, and ideological criticism, which derives from particular views of social order. Advertising has been caught up in a situation larger than is generally realized. As the voice of technology, it is associated with many dissatisfactions of the industrial state. As the voice of mass culture, it invites intellectual attack. And as the most visible form of capitalism, it has served as nothing less than a lightning-rod for social criticism.[24]

With these observations by Sissors and Berman as background, we are ready to move on to an examination of those issues that invoke the greatest concern when the impact of advertising on values and lifestyles is scrutinized. We have isolated five areas for special treatment: (1) materialism, instant gratification, and level of consumption; (2) moral, ethical, and aesthetic standards; (3) conformity and diversity; (4) interpersonal and group relationships; and (5) children.[25]

Materialism The desire to possess tangible goods is called "materialism," and the prevalence of this trait among Americans is judged to be undesirable by many intellectuals. People should be interested, the argument runs, in the "finer things of life"—music, poetry, painting—rather than in owning suburban homes, automobiles, snowmobiles, recreation vehicles, motor boats, and the many other symbols of the materialistic life. In characterizing our society as materialistic, a comparison is often made between the amounts of money spent for material goods and for the arts.

Because advertising is used to promote products that satisfy the materialistic requirements of consumers, it is accused of promoting materialism in our population. It is also true, however, that advertising is used to promote "back to nature" items such as natural foods, wood stoves, camping equipment, and denim—all representing a rejection of the materialism of the establishment.

This criticism of materialism has been broadened to include the idea that advertising brought about the "revolution of rising expectations" among our people with the concomitant demand for instant gratification of material desires. The ghetto resident, watching the lifestyles presented on the living room screen, therefore wants the goods that will allow him or her to emulate the manner of living represented on that screen. Many of the most enticing items people see on their TV screens are not in the commercials, of course, but are part of the stage settings used for dramas or are given away as prizes on game shows. Advertising, nevertheless, is often blamed.

The problem with this line of thinking is that advertising, to be effective, reflects the attitudes of its intended audience. It is true that advertising:

> . . . is the chief means of communicating (and reinforcing) to people the range of reasons for which they might want to acquire material objects. It is probable that as long as these reasons are ones which the culture recognizes, e.g., that a given object can indeed be viewed as a symbol of status, it is unlikely that advertising can or will be prevented from appealing to such reasons. If we regard as undesirable these materialistic values in our society, we must look beyond advertising for change.[26]

The conflict existing between the intellectual's view of advertising's role in developing materialistic attitudes and the need for mental satisfactions is clarified in the following quotation, which states that it depends on how one views others in the society:

> Most of the things we want are not material but mental. We want states of mind. The advertiser, beginning with a material object which is to be sold, suggests the states of mind which may be achieved by the purchase. . . . You can either rejoice that human beings have wants, and that other human beings try to satisfy them and be paid for their trouble; or you can deplore the nature of humanity.[27]

Moral, Ethical, and Aesthetic Standards One accusation leveled against advertising is that it is a force for perverting or debasing our aesthetic or cultural standards. Although much advertising certainly is not an artistic triumph (bargain advertising by retail establishments, for instance, does not kindle a spark

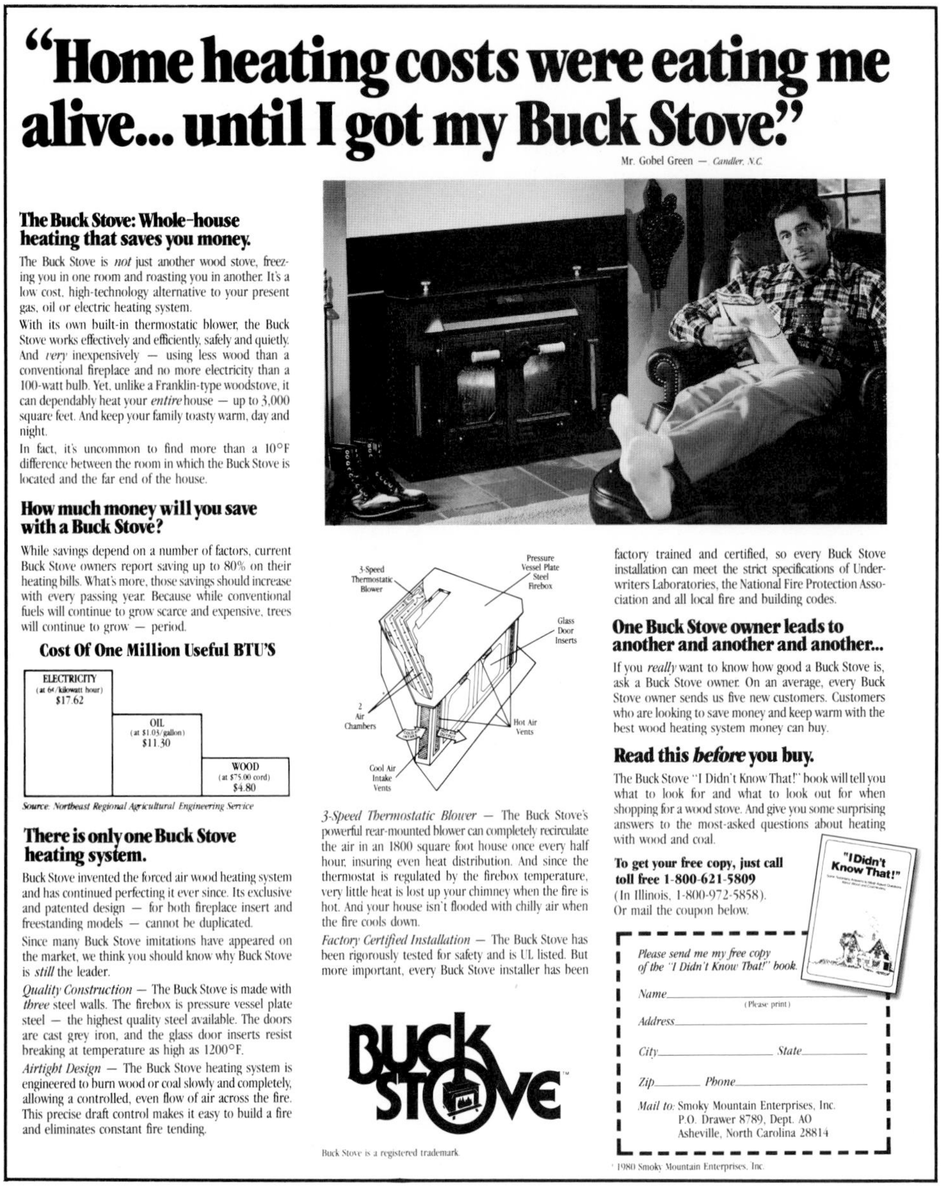

Figure 2.8 Advertising is used to promote a product which is, in a sense, a rejection of materialism as it is normally viewed. The appeal, of course, is to economy, and the ad is informative.

of aesthetic appreciation even in the most uncultured breast), other advertisements with a different purpose may display artwork of the finest illustrators and designers, bringing their creations before the eyes of millions. Artistic satisfaction from drawings, paintings, photographs, music, and drama are as subjective as are other satisfactions. It is unrealistic to assume that advertising has a responsibility to raise or even to maintain cultural standards. Advertising's function is to transmit information from the advertiser to groups of people—to persuade. In attempting to persuade some, it often offends others.

Mass communications media, supported by advertising, are also accused of satiating the public with the most superficial information and entertainment. In doing so, it is said, they have encouraged what is popular rather than what is good, and they have fostered material, rather than spiritual and cultural, values. Television is the medium most frequently cited, and it would be difficult indeed to make a case for the cultural contributions of many TV situation comedies and programs crammed with violence. But can advertising in a free enterprise society be held responsible for the complacency, the erosion of morality, and the cultural lag that may exist in our society? George J. Stigler, professor of economics at the University of Chicago, believes such a position is analogous to "blaming the waiters in restaurants for obesity."[28] He goes on to state that "advertising itself is a completely neutral instrument, and lends itself to the dissemination of highly contradictory desires."[29] Furthermore, he feels that "the intellectuals would gain in candor and in grace if they preached directly to the public instead of using advertising as a whipping boy."[30] It is a historical fact that only a small minority in any society has ever exhibited "good taste," or has been equipped with the capacity and the temperament to prefer the serious over the frivolous. There is no real evidence, moreover, that our cultural standards are lower than they were before modern advertising became an important institution in our society. Enumeration of the amounts spent for symphony concert tickets, lecture series, works of art, books, and other forms of cultural expression belies the claim that our society is completely lacking in what are generally considered to be cultural standards. In fact, advertising is used to promote attendance at and interest in cultural events.

Conformity and Diversity Another criticism revolves around the idea that advertising persuades as many people as possible to buy the featured product, with the end result being conformity in behavior, a homogenous populace. When advertising programs are highly successful and the item is purchased by most of the population, conformity actually results. We know, however, that obtaining universal acceptance of any product is extremely rare. On the other hand, advertising facilitates the introduction of new products and permits the news of their availability to spread rapidly and economically. When this takes place, *diversity*—not conformity—occurs in the society.

Interpersonal and Group Relationships In an urbanized society such as ours, individuals tend to lose their identity, and depersonalization takes place. Relationships among individuals tend to become strained. It is contended that the relationships between people of different races, religions, sexes, income, and age can become tense through the influence of advertising.

The protestations of feminists provide an excellent illustration of this point of view. They feel that the portrayal of women in stereotyped roles, such as homemakers or secretaries, and not in career-oriented roles, leads to the acceptance of these roles as the norm by the population as a whole, and by the young in particular. Thus, women who hope to pursue other careers or lifestyles resent the showing of a stereotyped homemaker ecstatically admiring the floor she has just waxed. They resent the implication that this is all they are capable of. A highly successful campaign, sponsored by National Airlines, that bore the headline "I'm Cheryl. Fly Me!" was protested by NOW (National Organization for Women) on the ground that it cast women in the role of sex objects.

On the other hand, the Boeing ad (Fig. 2.9) which appeared in the late 1970s was lauded by women's rights leaders as showing women in roles comparable with those held by men in our society. The ad was sensitive to the opinions of women. For one thing, women had become buyers of more than household products. Many campaigns, therefore, are now aimed at the career woman. Many other examples could be cited of advertisements that illustrate how the male-female roles in our society have become blurred. Advertising thus reflects changing values.

Similarly, ethnic groups dislike the portrayal of nationalities in a demeaning light, such as in some Frito-Bandito commercials that were aired several years ago. Mexican-Americans, understandably, do not like to be shown as lazy robbers. One active issue has been over the use of black models in advertisements. Once thought to be a concept unacceptable to significant portions of the American public, integrated advertising is now commonplace.

Resolution of this question hinges on whether advertisements should picture society as it really exists, or in some sort of idealistic view of what it should be. Minorities, who are also consumers, certainly have rights that should not be infringed upon, and, of course, pragmatic advertisers, in their own self-interest, avoid confrontation over any portrayal that might be offensive to the public, or a part of it.

Children Because children constitute such a large minority and are viewed as being especially vulnerable to influences, their case warrants special consideration. How advertising, primarily on television, operates in the socialization of children has received considerable attention in recent years. The typical child spends more time in the company of the television set than in reading or being entertained by any traditional medium.

A WOMAN'S WORK IS NEVER DONE.
She had breakfast with the national sales manager, met with the client from 9 to 11, talked at an industry luncheon, raced across town to the plans board meeting and then caught the 8:05 back home. Women are playing a greater role in business. And commercial airlines are helping that come about with Boeing jetliner flights to nearly every major city in the U.S. For women in business, as well as men.
BOEING
Getting people together

Figure 2.9 This ad by a major manufacturer of passenger planes is a good example of advertising that is sensitive to the changing role of women in our society.

Some social critics believe television advertising "corrupts" children by instilling values that are not acceptable in our society. Actually, what is more likely involved is a clash between the values of children and those of their parents. A somewhat acrimonious debate rages over whether the television medium should be held responsible for this conflict of values.

In part because the Federal Trade Commission, in the 1970s, sought the banning of television advertising directed at young children (see Chapter 20 for an expanded discussion), considerable research has been conducted to ascertain the real impact of such advertising on children. One researcher summarizes the situation in these words:

> Against this backdrop of increasing complexity and multidisciplinary involvement, it is surprising to note the emergence of one central age-related issue: the competency of young children to process information (primarily in terms of comprehension) contained in television advertising.[31]

PUT STARS IN HER EYES
with a Questar, for it is a gift that will go on giving. If she is that rare child with a true curiosity, it will help her to discover the nature of things all her life. It will be her own personal contact with the universe, which she will have the excitement of seeing, from her very first glimpse, through the finest of telescopes. Both optically and mechanically, Questar will respond rewardingly to her touch so that she will never know the frustration of an inferior tool. Questar's beauty and versatility will make it a cherished possession and an invaluable companion, whether her main interest becomes the study of the sun, moon, and planets, or an earth-oriented observing of nature close at hand. From her first-hand investigation will come an expanding awareness and continuing enjoyment. And its easy portability will permit her to take it with her wherever she travels.
To open to such a young mind that vast store of knowledge to which she may one day make her own contribution, will be your rare privilege.
© Questar Corporation 1978
The Standard Questar with its beautiful star chart is shown above; at right is the Duplex Questar in the leather carrying case which complements both models.
QUESTAR, THE WORLD'S FINEST, MOST VERSATILE TELESCOPE, IS DESCRIBED IN OUR BOOKLET NOW REVISED WITH NEW PHOTOGRAPHS IN COLOR BY QUESTAR OWNERS, INCLUDING SPECTACULAR DEEP-SKY VIEWS. SEND $2 FOR MAILING COSTS ON THIS CONTINENT; BY AIR TO SOUTH AMERICA, $3.50; EUROPE AND NORTH AFRICA, $4; ELSEWHERE, $4.50.
QUESTAR
Box 20PS, New Hope, PA 18938
204

Figure 2.10 In its December 1980 issue *Ms.* magazine honored this advertisement in its "One Step Forward" section. Periodically ads that "prove change [is] possible" are noted. The magazine has for a long time called attention to messages that run counter to its editorial policy directed to liberated women.

Dr. Seymour Banks, a social scientist employed by the Leo Burnett advertising agency, which includes Kellogg's cereals among its clients, has studied the effects of television advertising carefully. One of his conclusions is:

> . . . children exhibit such variation in viewing behavior that one must conclude that they exhibit a fairly substantial degree of selectivity in what and when they choose to watch television.[32]

Further research into the subject is needed. Normal research methodology, complicated enough when studying adult behavior, is inadequate in the case of children. Bias is a serious problem, and the subjects are not capable of the same degree of cooperation with the researcher. Research findings to date tend to show that children are not helpless victims of television advertising. They do tune out messages under certain circumstances. Some learning, nevertheless, does take place from viewing this form of marketing communication. Efforts for greater government control are therefore predicted unless self-regulations defuse the issue.

Advertising and Freedom of the Press

It has been said that "advertising controls the press." The implication of this criticism is that mass media are at the mercy of their advertisers, who dictate editorial policy and force publishers to kill stories or articles of which the advertiser disapproves. The importance of a free press to a democratic society is so obvious that any attempt to restrict this freedom, whether it comes from advertisers, churches, governments, or any other special-interest group, demands both attention and action.

At the same time, we should keep in mind that freedom is a relative condition rather than an absolute. Inherent in any organizational system, whether commercial, religious, or political, is a person's tendency to respond to power and to anticipate the effect of one's acts on those in the organizational hierarchy. The influence of advertisers on editorial policy and content will naturally vary from medium to medium and generally will run counter to the effectiveness of the medium as a vehicle for advertising messages. The medium that can be "bought" declines in prosperity, in vitality, and in influence. Most media owners value the respect of their audiences too highly to risk destroying it, and most advertisers realize the importance of the medium's influence on the buyers whom they hope to sell.

The exceptions seem to be found most frequently in broadcast media, and especially in television network programming. In television, unlike newspapers and magazines, the advertiser not only pays for the time his commercials are on the air, but also may pay the cost of the entertainment between his commercials. In a sense, he is at the same time both advertiser and publisher, or producer. There is no doubt that, in the past, advertisers have exerted considerable influence on the content of programs they have sponsored and paid for. However, as television costs have mounted, more and more advertisers have turned to the use of spot announcements or joint participation with other advertisers in programs produced and controlled by networks or stations. Advertisers have little or no influence on program content in this situation.

Historically, mass communications media have been notably unsuccessful in attempting to survive on income received solely from readers, listeners, or viewers. The essential financial support has come from political parties, from government, or from advertisers. Unlike governments or political parties, advertisers are rarely interested in the editorial or entertainment policies of media except as they may affect the type or size of audience to whom the advertiser wishes to deliver the sales message. Moreover, the attitude or action sought by one advertiser is frequently the reverse of that sought by another, and the number of different advertisers is legion. Advertising support seems to promise greater freedom of the press than is possible through subsidy by government or political parties.

Summary

Advertising decisions by the business firm are made in a societal setting; advertisements are aimed at members of society. Society is affected by advertising in economic and in social ways. This chapter analyzes the overall effects of advertising on society, as a background for advertising's more specific roles.

Advertising contributes in many ways to our human welfare – economically and socially. It makes three economic contributions: (1) advertising encourages economic growth; (2) it helps maintain competition; and (3) it informs consumers. Economists study the allocation of society's resources. Some economists charge that advertising wastes resources. First of all, they claim that advertising just adds costs to the price of the product. Although advertising is a cost of doing business and must be included in the selling price, it may also bring about substantial reduction in production and distribution costs and result in lower prices paid by consumers. Although much advertising does aim at shifting demand from one brand to another, the process leads to better products for consumers and is not really an inefficient allocation of resources. If advertising made people worse off, they would not respond to it. The idea that advertising makes people want things they don't need and therefore leads to an inefficient use of resources denies the whole concept of freedom of choice underlying our economic order.

Effective advertising is persuasive. It influences people to buy its sponsor's product. But advertising also informs consumers, and therefore has economic value. The critics' model assumes consumers have perfect knowledge (information), but that assumption is not valid in real life. Through advertising, consumers learn of the existence of products, and furthermore, they learn which products are successful from the mere fact that they are advertised. Producers try to determine what people want, make the item, and then advertise its availability. The opposite sequence of trying, through advertising, to get people to want what is being made does not work out. Consumer sovereignty exercises its veto power readily and frequently.

Careful empirical studies have uncovered little evidence that the presence of advertising leads to the concentration of industry or that it erects barriers to entry into industry. In the American toy industry, the availability of television advertising had led to increased sales of the product at lower prices to consumers.

On the social side, we see that advertising touches members of our society in four ways: (1) through its persuasive abilities, (2) by its truthfulness or untruthfulness, (3) through its tastefulness or tastelessness, and (4) by its cultural impact on values and lifestyles. Advertising is persuasive in nature, but there are adequate laws in existence to handle untruthful advertising, which, of course, is not desirable.

Critics say that advertising is often in bad taste. This charge may come about because the product itself is deemed to be undesirable; in such cases, advertising is not at the heart of the problem. Others believe that some advertising messages appear at the wrong time, or that objectionable appeals are made, or that the advertising techniques employed are not acceptable. Each of these three areas is fraught with the hazards of personal subjectivity; what one person thinks is objectionable will not disturb another. Furthermore, standards of taste change over time and the very definition of "taste" poses problems. Errors in judgment may on occasion lead to tasteless advertising, but a generalization to the whole institution of advertising is unwarranted.

Whether advertising has an adverse effect on values and lifestyles is doubtful. It is claimed that advertising breeds materialism, but it is probably more correct to say that advertising reflects people's values. Thus, advertising appeals to the material wants of people rather than creating them.

Similarly, advertising does not debase the moral, ethical, or aesthetic standards of our society. Insofar as values are concerned, advertising is a neutral instrument.

Advertising supports the nation's goal of assuring freedom from government and political controls over editorial matter and programming.

Questions for Discussion

1 What is the essence of the criticism that advertising constitutes economic waste? How can this criticism be answered?

2 Do you believe that advertising is persuasive? Give an example. Do you believe advertising is also informative? Give an example.

3 Goods can be categorized into two main types: search goods and experience goods. Explain how the role of advertising differs in the case of each type. Cite an illustration for each.

4 Does advertising foster monopoly? Or is it conducive to the establishment of a more competitive market? Develop your answer in some detail.

5 What is the interrelationship between the concept of freedom of choice prevalent in our economy and advertising? Explain.

6 Cite an instance from current advertising in which you believe bad taste has been evidenced. Which ways in the fourfold classification of how advertising can be in questionable taste does your case exemplify? How could the advertiser's approach be changed to bring the ad into an acceptable condition?

7 Has advertising affected your personal lifestyle in any fashion? Explain. Has this been undesirable? Worthwhile?

8 "Advertising affects the freedom of the press." Give both sides of this statement.

9 What are some products, other than toys, where the consumer has benefited in relatively lower prices because of their being advertised in efficient mass media?

10 Write a short paragraph giving your opinion of the role of advertising in the establishment of stereotypes in our society.

For Further Reference

Adler, Richard P., et al.: *The Effects of Television Advertising on Children,* Lexington Books, Lexington, Mass., 1980.

Albion, Mark S., and Paul W. Farris: *The Advertising Controversy: Evidence on the Economic Effects of Advertising,* Auburn House, Boston, 1980.

Backman, Jules: *Advertising and Competition,* New York University Press, New York, 1967.

Bloom, Paul N.: *Advertising, Competition, and Public Policy,* Ballinger Publishing Company, Cambridge, Mass., 1976.

Brozen, Yale (ed.): *Advertising and Society,* New York University Press, New York, 1974.

Comanor, William S., and Thomas N. Wilson: *Advertising and Market Power,* Harvard University Press, Cambridge, Mass., 1974.

Courtney, Alice E., and Thomas W. Whipple: *Sex Stereotyping in Advertising: An Annotated Bibliography.* Marketing Science Institute, Cambridge, Mass., 1980.

Crain, Rance: "Twentieth Century Advertising and the Economy of Abundance," *Advertising Age,* Chicago, April 30, 1980.

Ferguson, James M.: *Advertising and Competition: Theory, Measurement, Fact,* Ballinger Publishing Company, Cambridge, Mass., 1975.

Leigh, James H., and Claude R. Martin, Jr.: *Current Issues and Research in Advertising* (two volumes; annual series), University of Michigan Graduate School of Business Administration, Division of Research, Ann Arbor, 1978, 1979.

Pearce, Michael, Scott M. Cunningham, and Avon Miller:*Appraising the Economic and Social Effects of Advertising,* Marketing Science Institute, Cambridge, Mass., 1971.

Schmalensee, R.: *The Economics of Advertising,* North-Holland Publishing Company, Amsterdam, 1972.

Tuercke, David G. (ed.): *Issues in Advertising,* American Enterprise Institute, Washington, D.C., 1978.

Worcester, Jr., Dean A., with Ronald Nesse: *Welfare Gains from Advertising: The Problem of Regulation,* American Enterprise Institute, Washington, D.C., 1978.

Wright, John S., and John E. Mertes: *Advertising's Role in Society,* West Publishing Company, St. Paul, Minn., 1974.

End Notes

[1] James M. Ferguson, "Commentary," in David G. Tuerck (ed.), *Issues in Advertising: The Economics of Persuasion,* American Enterprise Institute, Washington, D.C., 1978, p. 199.

[2] Richard H. Holton, "How Advertising Achieved Respectability Among Economists (Or Anyhow, They've Heard of It)," *Advertising Age,* April 30, 1980, p. 56.

[3] Ibid.

[4] Ibid.

[5] Neil H. Borden, *The Economic Effects of Advertising,* Richard D. Irwin, Inc., Chicago, 1942, p. 881.

[6] James M. Ferguson, *Advertising and Competition: Theory, Measurement, Fact,* Ballinger Publishing Company, Cambridge, Mass., 1974, p. 15.

[7] Ibid., pp. 4–5.

[8] Richard Posner, quoted in U.S. Congress Subcommittee on Monopoly of the Senate Select Committee on Small Business, *Role of the Giant Corporations,* Part I-A, July 1969, p. 923.

[9] Ferguson, op. cit., p. 5.

[10] L. G. Telser, "Some Aspects of the Economics of Advertising," *Journal of Business,* April 1968, as reprinted in John S. Wright and John E. Mertes (eds.), *Advertising's Role in Society,* West Publishing Company, St. Paul, Minn., 1974, pp. 38–39.

[11] Jules Backman, *Advertising and Competition,* New York University Press, New York, 1967, p. 157.

[12] This discussion draws from the thorough analysis reported in Paul W. Farris and Mark S. Albion, "The Impact of Advertising on the Price of Consumer Products," *Journal of Marketing,* Summer 1980, pp. 17–35, especially pp. 31–32.

[13] Loc. cit.

[14] Based on Robert L. Steiner, "Does Advertising Lower Consumer Prices?" *Journal of Marketing,* October 1973, pp. 19–26; as reprinted in John S. Wright and John E. Mertes (eds.), *Advertising's Role in Society,* West Publishing Company, St. Paul, Minn., 1974, pp. 212–225.

[15] Israel M. Kirzner, "Advertising," *The Freeman,* September 1972, p. 516.

[16] This section is based in part on Phillip Nelson, "The Economic Value of Advertising," in Yale Brozen (ed.), *Advertising and Society,* New York University Press, New York, 1974, pp. 43–65.

[17] Stephen A. Greyser, "Advertising: Attacks and Counters," *Harvard Business Review,* March–April 1972, p. 32.

[18] Based on Michael Pearce, Scott M. Cunningham, and Avon Miller, *Appraising the Economic and Social Effects of Advertising,* Marketing Science Institute, Cambridge, Mass., 1971, p. 4.31, and Greyser, op. cit., p. 28.

[19] Pearce et al., p. 4.36.

[20] Ibid., pp. 4.31–4.32.

[21] Walter Taplin, *Advertising—A New Approach,* Little Brown and Co., Boston, 1960, p. 146, as quoted in Jack Z. Sissors, "Another Look at the Question: Does Advertising Affect Values?, *Journal of Advertising,* Summer 1978, p. 26.

[22] Sissors, loc. cit., p. 30.

[23] Ibid.

[24] Ronald Berman, "Advertising and Social Change," *Advertising Age,* April 30, 1980, p. 24.

[25] Pearce, et al., op. cit., p. 4.44.

[26] Raymond A. Bauer and Stephen A. Greyser, *Advertising in America: The Consumer View,* Harvard Business School, Division of Research, Boston, 1968, p. 368.

[27] Taplin, op. cit.

[28] George J. Stigler, *The Intellectual and the Market Place,* The Free Press, New York, 1963, pp. 90–91.

[29] Ibid.

[30] Ibid.

[31] Robert W. Chestnut, "Television Advertising and Young Children: Piaget Reconsidered," *Current Issues and Research in Advertising, 1979,* University of Michigan, 1979, p. 5.

[32] Seymour Banks, "Children's Television Viewing Behavior," *Journal of Marketing,* Spring 1980, p. 52.

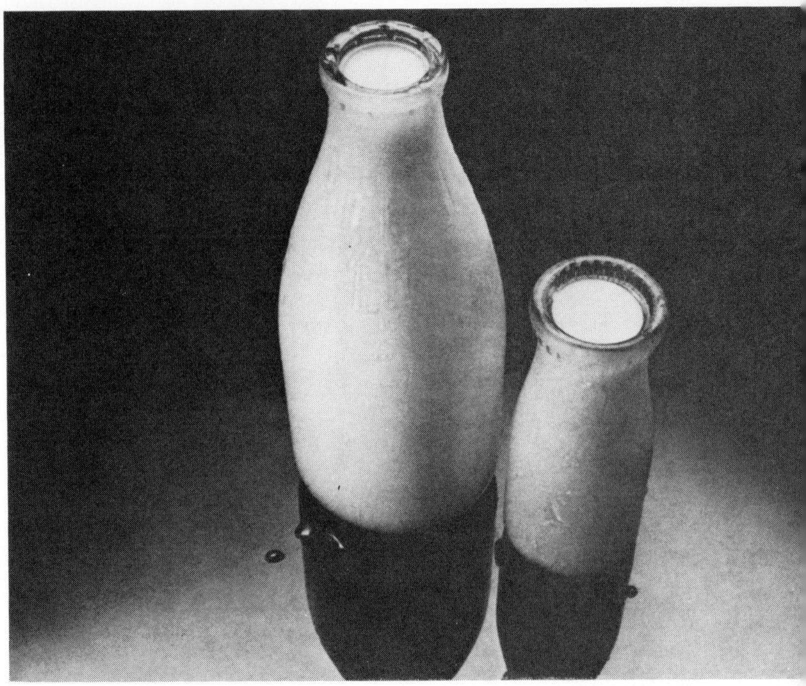

PART 2

Advertising's Role in the World of Business

With some historical, social, and economic perspectives in mind, we now examine the usefulness of advertising to the business firm, particularly in its marketing programs. Advertising enables the selling firm to communicate with prospective buyers to inform them of its products and to persuade them to buy and use them.

To understand the role of advertising, we must recognize its importance in the marketing process. Therefore, Chapter 3 starts by defining marketing and then shows how the qualities of the product are used in advertising it. Included are such components of the

total product as its package, label, brand name, trademark, and trade characters.

Chapter 4 describes how advertising serves the communication needs of business. Both general and specific objectives of advertising are outlined. The various forms of advertising are described. A discussion of the consumer's place in the advertising process concludes the chapter.

Many specialized business enterprises exist to help carry out the advertising process; three major types are described in Chapter 5. First of all, there are the **advertisers** who sponsor advertising. Second, **advertising agencies** create and place advertisements for advertisers. Third, **special-service groups,** such as photographers, engravers, artists, and production studios, help by providing their specialized assistance. The fourth type of business found in advertising—the **media** where ads appear—is handled in detail in Part 3.

Chapter 3

Advertising and the Marketing Process

Production, finance, and marketing are the three main activities of any business firm. The production people create the goods and services offered to consumers. Financial people regulate the resources of the firm. They see that there is enough capital to maintain production and to market the firm's products, and they deal with investors and stockholders to be sure that the firm receives the capital needed to remain profitable. Once sound financial management has enabled the goods to be produced, these goods must be sold. Unsold goods and services are a waste of resources and jeopardize the economic health of the firm. Products made by the firm must reach the homes, offices, and plants where they are consumed. They must be *marketed.*

What Is Marketing?

The **marketing** process entails more than the physical movement of goods from where they are made to where they are consumed. Key marketing functions, in addition to transportation and storage, include buying, selling (including advertising), financing, standardizing and grading, risk bearing, and the gathering of market information. Blended together, these activities constitute modern marketing.

One good definition of marketing is:

> Marketing is a system of business activities designed to plan, price, promote, and distribute something of value—want-satisfying goods and services—to the benefit of the market—present and potential household consumers or industrial users.[1]

In the past decade, business executives tended to focus on the functions of production and finance. This emphasis has switched in recent years to marketing problems, because of the impact of marketing and sales on production and finance. The success of a marketing program will enable the firm's financial managers to attract investors and to reward stockholders with larger dividends. Production can be expanded, offering new jobs and extending the firm's product line. Because of the benefits of marketing success, many observers of the business scene feel that the marketing department is the dominant force in the business enterprise. Peter Drucker, the noted business writer, consultant, and teacher, espouses this philosophy as follows:

> Fifty years ago the typical attitude of American businessmen toward marketing was still: "The sales department will sell whatever the plant produces." Today it is increasingly: "It is our job to produce what the market needs."
>
> Marketing is so basic that it cannot be considered a separate function (i.e., a separate skill or work) within the business, on a par with others such as manufacturing or personnel. Marketing requires separate work and a distinct group of activities. But it is, first, a central dimension of the entire business. It is the whole business seen from the point of view of its final result, that is, from the customer's point of view. Concern and responsibility for marketing must, therefore, permeate all areas of the enterprise.[2]

The central theme in Drucker's second paragraph is known in marketing circles as **customer orientation,** a theme which also permeates this book. Customer orientation is an integral part of all sound marketing programs, for successful marketing means the satisfying of consumer needs and wants.

Advertising and the Marketing Mix

Another concept useful in explaining where advertising fits in the marketing process is the **marketing mix.**[3] To understand the concept of marketing mix, consider the analogy in the procedure followed by the marketing manager and that used by the baker who wishes to make a cake. The baker's first decision is what *kind* of cake to produce—chocolate, angel food, or spice. The necessary ingredients are then assembled and blended into a "mix" to be placed in the oven. If the correct portions of sugar, flour, shortening, and other items are used, the cake will be a success; otherwise, it will fail. On another day, the baker's objective may be a different kind of cake, and different ingredients will be used.

Similarly, the marketing manager has a set of ingredients to blend to accomplish the firm's business objective. The marketing "recipe" is a "mix" of five basic elements, as essential as sugar, flour, and shortening are to baking cake. The elements of the marketing mix are (1) product, (2) price, (3) distribution channels, (4) personal selling, and (5) advertising.

Marketing programs vary widely in the mixture of these ingredients. Some firms omit personal selling and use direct-mail advertising as the sole promotional ingredient; others may omit advertising completely. For example, Hershey's chocolate was long cited as an eminently successful product that did no consumer advertising, standing on product quality and excellent distribution for sales. However, the company's products lost leadership to other candy manufacturers and, finally, in 1969, the firm began advertising to consumers in the United States. By 1971, Hershey's was among the top 100 television advertisers, ranking ninety-sixth on the list, with expenditures of $7.3 million. Total advertising expenditures were $32 million in 1979. The company learned that without advertising it lost ground to competitors such as Mars, Inc.

Marketing executives decide which marketing mix elements to use and the portions to blend into their marketing programs. There is no cookbook to consult for marketing program recipes. Other marketing programs can be consulted for ideas, but, as in baking a cake, any variation in the ingredients will likely produce different results. Right choices determine the executive's success and make for the marketer's reputation.

Most consumer-goods manufacturers, and many makers of industrial products, include advertising in their marketing mixes. Its specific function is *preselling* to present and potential customers. Weir explains this process:

> With an awareness that some kind of communication occurs in every phase of marketing, and that, in the end, the product itself performs the principal and decisive act of communication, management may come to realize that the actual aim of advertising (excluding mail order) is not to "sell" but to induce people to try the product or service offered and to prepare them for satisfaction in its use by "pre-sampling" it verbally.[4]

Products reaching consumers through self-service outlets such as supermarkets are sold largely through display and shelf positions. However, if the consumer knows the brand name and the benefits to be derived from using a product, it is obviously easier to sell that product. Thus, mass retailers prefer that a product have consumer advertising support before agreeing to stock the item on their shelves.

It is clear that advertising is an important function in the marketing programs of most mass-produced, mass-marketed consumer goods. In the marketing of many industrial products, advertising is used to uncover unknown prospects and to help the salesperson obtain a hearing. As the costs of maintaining salespeople in the field continue to rise, this benefit takes on increasing importance. In 1980, the cost of an industrial sales call averaged over $135.

Recently, it has been realized that marketing thinking, approaches, and techniques could be well applied to noncommercial situations. Advertising, of course, has long lent support to noncommercial ventures. Political candidates used banners, pins, outdoor signs, and newspaper advertising in the early days of American politics. Candidates adapted readily to radio and television advertising media. In addition to being employed in political campaigns, advertising is used to help convert people to a particular religious belief, to encourage learning, to secure financial support for charitable causes, and to achieve many other noncommercial objectives.

Although this book deals primarily with the advertising of products and services, bear in mind that the word "idea" usually can be substituted for the word "product." Advertising strategy for selling ideas, such as the conservation of energy, the reduction of drunk driving or litter, and the prevention of forest fires, closely parallels that used for tangible products.

Primacy of the Product

Every element of the marketing mix is vital to marketing success, yet the **product** is paramount. The product is the starting point—the very heart—of every advertising program. An old marketing axiom states that "without a good product, you have nothing." This truism underlies the success of our nation's largest advertiser, Procter & Gamble, as this bit of advice indicates:

> The only way you can succeed in business is with a good product. You can't do it with advertising. It all gets down to the fact that if you've got a good product, you can be successful with a reasonable marketing expenditure, but if you haven't got the product, the surest way to go broke is to pour your money behind it.[5]

No marketing effort can sell a bad product over an extended period of time. Promotional effort may help make initial sales, but long-run success depends on customer satisfaction with the product, which provides the foundation to sound advertising. Product knowledge, therefore, is essential to the practitioner of advertising.

Product Defined

One definition of "product" is:

> A *product* is a set of tangible and intangible attributes, including packaging, color, price manufacturer's prestige, retailer's prestige, and manufacturer's and retailer's services, which the buyer may accept as offering satisfaction of wants and needs.[6]

This definition applies to services as well as to physical products. More than one-half our personal incomes now go toward the purchase of services, including those furnished by banks, hotels, restaurants, real estate firms, stock brokers, and airlines. Such services are, of course, advertised extensively. Just think of the myriad fast-food franchise organizations competing for your away-from-home eating dollars. In this chapter we examine the product in its broad context and explain how product and advertising interrelate.

Product Classification

When products are classified, the most elementary breakdown is between consumer and industrial goods. Those products which satisfy our personal wants and desires, such as food, clothing, and household items, are examples of the **consumer-goods** category. **Industrial goods** are used for a multitude of business purposes and range from blast furnaces,

WE'RE THE NEIGHBORHOOD PROFESSIONALS FOR YOU.
When you're ready to sell your house, it makes sense to call your Neighborhood Professional first.
Whether we're showing off your house to its best advantage, effectively closing the sale or handling the time consuming paper work, we take professional care of more people's real estate needs today than anyone else.
Call, or drop by today for our brochure, "21 Reasons Why CENTURY 21® Should Sell Your House For You." You owe it to yourself to see how our professionalism can work for you.
Century 21®
NKPQRST REALTY
(000) 000-0000 75108 73rd Ave. GardenGrove
WE'RE THE NEIGHBORHOOD PROFESSIONALS.™
© 1978 Century 21 Real Estate Corporation, ® Licensed Trademark of Century 21 Real Estate Corporation, Printed USA, Each office is independently owned and operated. Equal Housing Opportunity
CENTURY 21 "21 Reasons Why" brochure at participating offices.

Figure 3.1 Services as well as products may be advertised. Here a major franchiser of real estate services features the local character of the office operating under the Century 21 designation. Note the line reading, "Each office is independently owned and operated."

pig iron, and forklift trucks to sweeping compounds and typing ribbons.

The distinction is based on the use to which the product is put. Oil used to heat a home is classified as a consumer product: the same item is an industrial good when used to fuel a diesel truck. Thus producers often can sell their products in both the consumer and the industrial markets. For that reason, a company such as Morton Salt has separate advertising directors for its table salt product line and for the hundreds of varieties of salt processed for industrial uses. This distinction in focus reflects different marketing characteristics of consumer and industrial goods and the need for different marketing strategies. The two types of goods do not reach the same market, and they do not require the same advertising. Therefore, every advertiser needs to be aware of where the primary market lies—in the consumer or the industrial area.

Consumer Goods There are three types of consumer goods: convenience, shopping, and specialty.

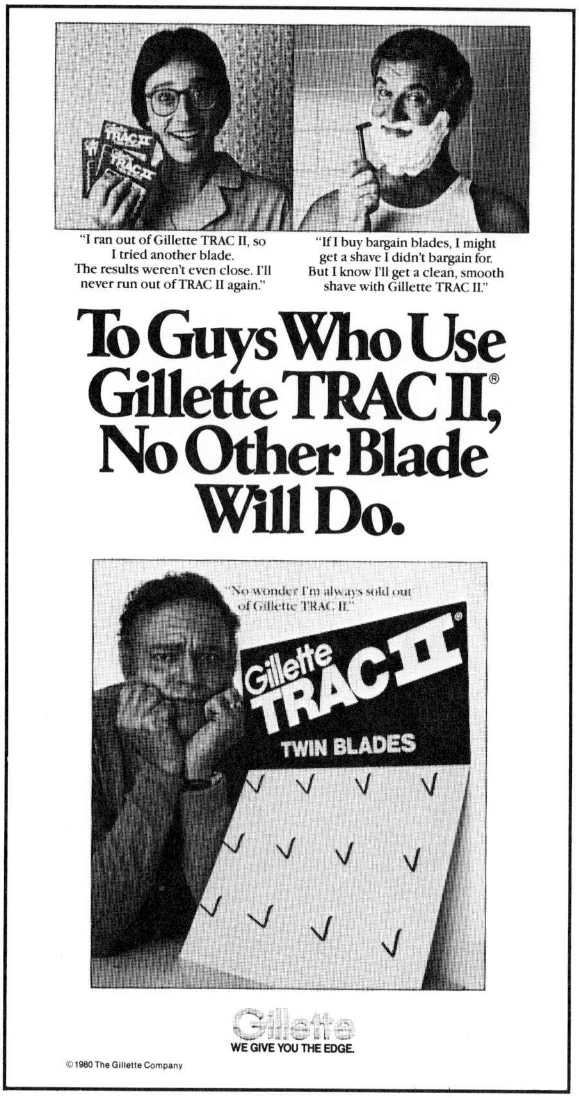

Figure 3.2 Convenience goods are promoted through consumer advertising. [*Reprinted by permission of Gillette Company, Safety Razor Div.*]

Convenience goods are those items that are frequently purchased, are low in cost, and are bought at the most accessible retail outlet shortly after a need for the product is felt. The most desirable marketing strategy for a convenience good is to place the product in every possible retail outlet where a consumer might reasonably look for it. The advertising campaigns of soft-drink, candy-bar, food, disposable razor, and household products provide examples of convenience-goods advertising. The advertising for convenience goods seeks to familiarize the consuming public with the product name and its want-satisfying qualities. The consumer, it is hoped, will recognize the advertised brand and purchase it. At the same time, the manufacturer seeks to persuade retailers, through personal selling and trade advertising, to stock the product.

Products purchased after careful consideration of quality, price, and suitability are classified as **shopping goods.** Style may be an additional factor in the decision. In this case, the product is infrequently purchased and has a high unit price. It is considered to be a major purchase. Family discussions may be held to decide where available discretionary spending power is to be expended. Once a decision to buy is made, the consumer shops a number of retail outlets.

The marketing strategy of the shopping-goods manufacturer calls for placing products in comparatively few outlets. Retail outlets in main shopping centers are preferred, to facilitate comparison shopping by consumers. The decisive factor in the final purchase decision often lies in the store name, because it represents the quality, price, or style sought by the buyers. Thus, much of the advertising responsibility for shopping goods is placed upon the retailer. Dress shops and furniture outlets provide good examples of shopping-goods advertising.

The characteristics of high unit price and infrequent purchase are also present for **specialty goods.** The buying process, however, is quite different. As a guide in purchasing, the buyer relies on brand name and unique product characteristics, instead of shopping. A specialty good is a branded item which the consumer has become convinced is superior to all competitive brands. The retail outlet handling the brand is sought out by the consumer, and substitutes will not be accepted if the preferred brand is not in stock.

Many forces help the consumer develop a favorable attitude toward one brand: recommendations of friends and previous experience with the brand combine to create brand insistence. Advertising, of course, is often important in the picture. The manufacturer of a specialty product stresses the superiority of the firm's brand over competitive offerings. Advertisements for photographic equipment, sporting goods, and men's quality shoes show how specialty-goods manufacturers go about convincing consumers of brand superiority. Figure 3.4 features a

Figure 3.3 Furniture is a shopping good for most consumers. In this example a national chain retailer of furniture advertises in a local newspaper to inform consumers of current offerings. Note that there is no specific reference to brand names, but the ad contains considerable information about store locations and business hours.

piece of consumer electronics equipment. Moreover, the manufacturer makes certain that consumers who are convinced by the claims made for the product can find retail outlets handling the brand without too much difficulty: Yellow Page advertising in the telephone directory is often used; the stores selling the brand may be listed in magazine ads for the brand; or a toll-free phone number through which the prospect can obtain the name and location of the nearest outlet may be provided.

Figure 3.4 Stereo speakers are a good example of specialty goods. Consumers are likely to develop strong brand preferences, and manufacturers advertise to them in an effort to build such preferences, as this ad, which appeared in *Esquire* magazine, shows.

Industrial Goods Industrial goods are classified in five categories: raw materials, fabricating materials and parts, operating supplies, installations, and accessory equipment. Our emphasis in Part 2 is largely consumer-oriented. The special creative problems of industrial advertising are considered in Chapter 12.

Product Positioning

No topic received more attention in advertising circles during the 1970s than **product positioning.** No generally accepted definition has been developed, although the concept can be described in these words: A product's *position* is the image that the product projects in the minds of consumers in relation to, first, other products sold by the company, and, second, to competitive products.[7]

Kraft, Inc., has employed the positioning technique successfully in the marketing of its three brands of premium-priced ice creams. Retailers resisted taking on the Breyers brand, stating that they already stocked Kraft's Sealtest brand; furthermore, all brands, they said, are the same. Kraft realized it was necessary to overcome this credibility gap and to persuade retailers that their maximum profitability depended on offering consumers a *mix* of premium-priced brands and lower-priced private labels (store brands).[8] Kraft's Premium Ice Cream Program evolved and featured products that generated consumer demand for reasons other than price. In other words, each brand was given a distinct position in the market:

Breyers—positioned as "The All Natural Ice Cream"—an ingredient story highlighting the absence of artificial flavoring, coloring, or stabilizers and emulsifiers in the brand

Sealtest—positioned as "The Supermarket Ice Cream with That Ice Cream Parlor Taste"—featuring a flavor story

Light 'n' Lively—positioned as the "Ice Creamy Ice Milk"—offering the absence of fats (and some calories) to weight-conscious consumers

Thus, Kraft created a complete line of packaged frozen desserts, each possessing its own niche in the market. Each brand was distinctly positioned, and the brands did not compete with one another. In the five-year period following 1972, industry sales increased 5 percent while Breyers experienced a 17 percent increase and Sealtest sales jumped 23 percent.

Trout and Ries, operators of a New York City advertising agency, focused on the other variety of positioning, namely, the relating of the product to competitive offerings.[9] The underlying premise of Trout and Ries is that our society suffers from overcommunication; thus, to be successful, an advertiser must create a niche in the prospect's mind. This niche—or "position"—is created not only by the strengths and weaknesses of the product but also by the manner in which the product differs from those of major competitors. Sheer volume of advertising is not sufficient to make a product stand out, because there is a limit to the amount of information that a consumer's mind can absorb and handle. The human mind is selective and filters out information that does not parallel its previous experience. Thus, if RCA advertises "RCA computers are best," most people will respond by rejecting this statement since they believe that IBM, not RCA, holds the number one position in the computer market. Most minds would probably associate RCA with other products, such as TV and radio equipment. For a computer manufacturer to secure a favorable position, IBM must be dislodged (probably an impossibility), or a relationship of his product to IBM must be established.

One example of the implementation of the positioning concept is that of Seven-Up's "un-cola" campaign. Seven-Up was primarily used as a mixer—something to be blended with hard liquor. Although sales were good and steady, the potential was nothing like that available to such soft-drink brands as Coca-Cola and Pepsi-Cola. A great deal more than half the soft-drink product category comprises the cola drinks. In its "un-cola" advertising, Seven-Up says to potential consumers that its product is a good alternative to Coke and Pepsi. Seven-Up sales increased 10 percent in the first year after the new positioning approach, and the product has continued to maintain a healthy brand share.

Johnson & Johnson's baby shampoo, which for years had been positioned as a product for use on children's hair and promoted to young mothers, found its sales potential drying up with the declining

A glorious,
full-color picture of the
Goodrich Blimp.
What? No blimp?
Look again.
Not at the picture, the name.
Goodrich.
Not Goodyear.
Goodrich doesn't have a blimp,
Goodyear does.
We haven't advertised as much as Goodyear, either. So it's not too surprising a lot of people forget our name and remember theirs.
And if you're confused about our blimps, when we don't even have one, just imagine how confused you can get about our tires.
Who knows, you might even go to Goodyear to get them. And that's too bad.
You see, in 1965, Goodrich introduced the first American-made radial tire.
For five years, nationally, we've advertised nothing else.
Not because everybody wanted radials.
But because the radial tire was, and is, the most important innovation in tires in nearly a quarter century.
No conventional tire we've ever made, none, stops as fast, corners as well, and lasts as long as our Goodrich Lifesaver Steel Radial.
It's the result of our company's commitment, for ten years, to make the most advanced radial tire on the road.
Now you watch. You'll probably see Goodyear featuring a steel radial, too.
Along with all their other tires.
It'll be good. But it won't be Goodrich.
And if you still get our names confused, just look up in the sky.
If you see an enormous blimp with somebody's name on it, we're the other guys.
B.F.Goodrich
America's Premier Radial Tire Maker
Lifesaver® Steel Radials.
If you want Goodrich, you'll just have to remember Goodrich.
Cover Date: March 19, 1973—Newsweek—Sports Illustrated-Time—U.S. News & World Report.

Figure 3.5 A tire manufacturer uses a humorous approach to position itself against the industry leader by highlighting the company name.

(*a*)

(*b*)

(*c*)

Figure 3.6 Kraft, Inc., employs positioning to market three premium-priced brands of ice cream: (*a*) Sealtest; (*b*) Breyers; and (*c*) Light 'n' Lively. The first two appeared in magazines and the last in newspapers.

birthrate. Therefore, in the early 1970s, the company sought to shift from that position to one as a general shampoo, serving the needs of every member of the family. Advertising messages were designed which showed virile men and even grandmothers using Johnson & Johnson's baby shampoo. The advertising pointed up the shampoo's performance characteristics as a mild, basic shampoo for use by anyone, changing what had been an appeal to a segmented market to one of universal acceptance and use. The brand replaced Procter & Gamble's brand, Head & Shoulders, as the leading shampoo, despite the retention of a name which previously had provided its own limited positioning as a children's product.

More recently, Luzianne Tea has won considerable market share from Lipton's in the South through its positioning strategy. Luzianne positioned its tea bags as the only brand that results in an iced tea that is not cloudy. Consumers, feeling that clarity is a desirable product attribute, have shifted their buying to the brand.

Advertising and New Products

Products, as well as people, are at the heart of the marketing process, and new products are its lifeblood. The statement "Marketing is dynamic" is dramatized when we look at new-product development and its role in business success. The firm that does not develop new products in its field is likely to fail.

Consumers realize that their lives are changed and enhanced by the many new products constantly being offered by American and international firms. Just contemplate this partial list of new-product successes from the 1970s: Charlie fragrance, L'eggs pantyhose, Miller's Lite Beer, Carefree Gum, Stove Top Stuffing, Dannon Yogurt, Bubble Yum, Perrier mineral water, and Pampers disposable diapers.[10]

The term "new product" conjures up a mental picture of technological breakthroughs and revolutionary ways of doing things. Of course, such events do take place. In marketing, however, the definition of a new product is broadened to include modifications of existing products, imitations of competitive products, and product-line extensions. Thus, if a product is new to the firm, it is viewed as a "new product." As such, the new product carries both stimulating challenges and knotty problems for the marketing executive.

Interest in new products was heightened about 30 years ago when American manufacturers began to emphasize the strategy of **market segmentation.** This approach means that producers seek to modify product offerings in a manner that fits the special needs perceived to exist among a group (segment) of potential buyers.[11]

Advertising, along with other promotional strategies, is then employed to inform members of the market segment that the new product is available. The informational function is dominant. Advertising is used to convince consumers of the product's acceptability. In an interesting new-product development, General Foods introduced nationally its Cycle brand dog food in 1976. The product comes in four varieties, each designed to appeal to owners of dogs that fall into one of the four stages of a dog's life: puppy, adult, overweight adult, and older dog. The Cycle line has captured a large share of the premium dog food market.

An older strategy, **product differentiation,** viewed the marketplace differently. The manufacturer hoped to get consumers to adjust their demands to his product as it existed. Advertising in this context is used to persuade consumers that they should purchase the item instead of competing offerings. Many manufacturers still employ this strategy, especially for products in a mature stage of market development.

Whether a product differentiation or market segmentation strategy is followed, advertising usually bears much of the responsibility for letting the public know about the features of the product. When advertising introduces a new product, its role is crucial, for advertising must gain immediate brand awareness and bring about early trial by consumers. Otherwise, the item will be removed from the retailer's shelves and die from lack of exposure and availability.

The importance of advertising strategy to the success of a new product is shown in the case of Pillsbury's Totino's Crisp Crust Frozen Pizza.[12] In 1976, consumer research revealed that 60 percent of the public disliked the crust of frozen pizza, which many people said tasted like cardboard. After extensive product development, Pillsbury, with its background in dough products, was able to come up with a frozen pizza that was superior to existing entries in the field, including the Totino brand which it had just purchased.

When advertising the new product, the common mistake of promising too much was avoided. Instead of saying, "We're as good as pizzeria pizza," the Pillsbury campaign focused on the idea that Totino's frozen pizza didn't taste like cardboard. Before the new product variety was introduced in August 1978, Totino's held an 18 percent share of the $700 million frozen pizza market; within a year its share stood at 30 percent. The correct advertising message communicated the product's specific consumer advantage.

Without the assistance of advertising, a great deal of the incentive for product development would be missing. The returns from the acceptance of new products would be much slower to materialize. The process of informing the potential buyers of product innovations is speeded through advertising, thus benefiting consumers as well as producers. Despite this useful tool, however, the majority of new-product introductions fail.

The Package

A product's package plays an important role in consumer acceptance of a product. Daniel Boorstin correctly points out that **packaging,** as we know it and distinguish it from packing, is an American phenomenon of the early twentieth century:

> In the Old World, even after the industrial age had arrived, only expensive items were housed in their own box or elegantly wrapped. A watch or jewel would be presented in a carefully crafted container, but the notion that a pound of sugar or a dozen crackers should be encased and offered for purchase in specially designed, attractive material seemed outlandish. Essential to the American Standard of Living were new techniques for clothing objects to make them appealing advertisements for themselves. Industries spent fortunes improving the sales garb of inexpensive objects of daily consumption—a pack of cigarettes or a can of soup.[13]

Packaging, of course, is a concept considerably advanced from product packing. Products were originally packed as a means of protection during transportation and storage. Products still need, and receive, this kind of protection.

Marketing Purposes of Packaging

Our interest is in packaging as a **marketing tool,** rather than as a protective device. Packaging performs four important marketing functions:

The Package as a Means of Identification The package serves as a vehicle for product **identification** by carrying the manufacturer's name, trademark, and the brand name. Information about ingredients and instructions for product use are often provided. These messages are important to sound marketing.

Consumer Desire for Convenience Because consumers look for increased convenience in products they use, manufacturers soon discovered that the package might provide this benefit. In other words, product differentiation was gained through the package. Soda crackers, once sold loose from a cracker-barrel, were first wrapped in family-size containers by the National Biscuit Company in 1899. Now most food is sold in family-size containers. Single-portion can sizes for use by single-person households are a popular trend today.

Package superiority in such areas of convenience as ease in opening is also used to differentiate one brand from competitive ones. Ease in pouring and storability are additional examples of the use of packaging as sales generators.

Packaging designed for convenience in use, such as boil-in-bag vegetables, is probably the most important category. Consumer packaging is a parade of innovations that have included pull-tab cans, unbreakable shampoo bottles, and vacuum-seal plastic lids. Home "displayability" has become a characteristic of containers of such household products as facial tissue, salt, scouring powder, and soap.

Packages may also be designed to have a reuse value, such as a juice glass that holds cream cheese, and are sometimes designed as gift items. Alcoholic beverages are sold at holiday seasons in elegantly designed decanters, for example, and other products are gift-wrapped at the factory.

Competition for Shelf Space Another marketing dimension of packaging is to be found in connection with the intense competition for space on the retailer's shelf. Inasmuch as the revolution in packaging has coincided with the conversion of much of

"Mrs. Butterworth's, I love you."
Mrs. Butter-worth's
The Original Buttered Syrup
THICK 'N RICH
And now, 10¢ off makes loving Mrs. Butterworth's easier than ever.
It's easy to love Mrs. Butterworth's. All it takes is just one taste of her thick, rich syrup poured over a stack of pancakes. Mmmm! Mmmm! Delicious flavor in every thick, rich drop. Invite Mrs. Butterworth's to breakfast and you'll love her, too.
10¢ Mrs. Butterworth's 10¢
STORE COUPON
STORE COUPON
THICK 'N RICH
11115 880020
10¢
10¢

Figure 3.7 Many advertisers display the product package prominently in their advertisements. In the television version of the message, the distinctive bottle "talks" to a child about the product's thick, rich taste. Also note the cents-off coupon in the ad.

America's retailing to the self-service principle, it is clear that a product will not sell easily if it is not visible on the drugstore or supermarket shelf. Thus, the package should be designed so that the important first sale to the retailer is achieved; the retailer must be encouraged to place the product into stock. The large number of new products makes this task more difficult each year. Some retail chains now say, in effect, "When you bring in a new one, tell us which one is to be thrown out." If the product is designed to give the retailer an advantage in stocking the item—in addition to the usual promotional support—the retailer is more inclined to make a decision favorable to the manufacturer. Thus, the two-bulb and the four-bulb packages sold more bulbs and solved the loose light bulb stocking problem, and thus provided a good reason (at that time) for taking on the Sylvania brand.

Packaging as Advertising at the Point of Sale
Retailers profit when stock turns over. Therefore, they favor packaging that stimulates the rate of sale. In addition to brand familiarity and shelf position of the product, the attractiveness of the package itself may influence purchase in the self-service store. Packages with eye appeal stand out on the shelf; some consumers will reach out for the product in the attractive package. Packages must do the work of the

"The new package looks so good on the shelves the customers are leaving it on the shelves."

Figure 3.8 The importance of the package in self-service merchandising is spoofed in this cartoon. [*Reprinted with permission of* Advertising Age.]

fast-vanishing salesperson. For this reason, considerable research and experimentation go on in package design. Such dimensions as color, shape, and size of the package are examined for impact on consumers. The ability of the product to convey status to its possessor may be enhanced by the package. Recognizing the importance of the package, many firms make periodic reviews with packaging updating in mind. Specialized consulting firms and the major packaging manufacturers engage in the activity. The changes made by one company over a period of years are shown in Figure 3.9. The Kellogg Company has updated its package for corn flakes often to keep pace with changing standards of consumer acceptance.

Advertising and Packaging

A close interrelationship exists between the advertising and packaging components of marketing. Many advertisements boldly feature the product in its package. For this reason, there is a need for close coordination between package design and advertising programs. For product categories that possess little physical differentiation (for example, cigarettes and soap powders), the package may serve as an effective device for establishing consumer preferences. In such cases, advertisements obviously will key in on the package.

One way of establishing packaging's importance in modern-day marketing is on the basis of money spent for it. The bill for packages in the United States was $52 billion in 1980.[14] As much money is spent for packaging each year as for advertising. The packaging industry is characterized by continuous changes, some brought about through competition and others resulting from concerns over the environ-

Figure 3.9 Packages need to be modernized if they are to coincide with public ideas of acceptable art styles. Kellogg's has made many changes in the corn flakes package over the past three-quarters of a century.

mental impact of packages. In the latter category are such issues as litter (pull-tabs), solid-waste disposal (plastic containers), and deterioration of the atmosphere (aerosol sprays).

Most marketers realize that "To the consumer, the package *is* the product."[15] Thus, we can observe that packaging is the biggest advertising medium of all. A typical grocery product has been estimated to get more than 15 billion potential exposures to the public in a year. Think what that would cost if conventional media were used.[16]

Although our discussion has been of consumer goods, packaging is becoming increasingly important to the success of industrial-goods manufacturers as well.

Figure 3.10 All three major television networks possess distinctive trademarks that are familiar to every American.

The Brand Name

Once a good product is developed and appropriately packaged, an appealing name is needed. An analogy can be drawn to the naming of a child for identification and communication purposes. We are assuming, at this point, that the manufacturer has already decided to sell the product under his or her name rather than to make it available to others for private labeling or branding.

The Reason for Brands

Manufacturers want consumers to be able to distinguish their product from those made by competitors, hoping to build brand loyalty for their output over a period of time.

A **brand name** is the title given to a product by its manufacturer. Brand names should be distinguished from **trade names,** which are the names of business firms. General Mills, for example, is the trade name of a grocery-products manufacturer that originated as a flour-milling company. Its best flour bears the brand name "Gold Medal."

Names aid communication. Social relationships would be difficult indeed if people did not have names. Similarly, manufacturers use names to speed the communication of ideas about their products. Advertising would be pointless unless attention to the product could be called by a name which is capable of being remembered. The consumer, after seeing the ad and being stimulated to buy the product, may seek out the retailer selling Birkenstock shoes. Matters are simplified, for consumers know their wants and the retailer knows what a consumer is talking about; everyone is satisfied. There has been communication.

When the product is sold through self-service, all communication is impersonal. The name acts as a handy purchasing aid for the consumer and as a promotional vehicle for the manufacturer. Furthermore, the brand name makes the manufacturer accountable for the quality of the product. National advertising would be almost impossible without brand names.

Choosing a Brand Name

Choosing a brand name can be a complex and frustrating activity. When Esso Chemical Company wanted to change its company name, a computer was fed various vowel and consonant combinations and 44,990 four-letter and 500,000 five-letter combinations came out. EXXON was finally chosen because of its distinctiveness and graphic design possibilities. Other firms have created name banks to help in the naming of future products.

In a study of old company and brand names, Leonard Carlton isolated five sources that seem to have dominated the name-choosing process in the past:[17]

1 *The founder.* Procter & Gamble, Borden, and Campbell Soup Company were named after the founders of each firm.
2 *Identification with great events.* The Great Atlantic and Pacific Tea Company (A&P) was named in honor of the opening of the coast-to-coast railroad.
3 *Identification with experience.* Carnation milk was named in honor of President McKinley's ever-present boutonniere.
4 *Coinage.* The classic example is Kodak, which George Eastman named in 1888 because he liked the letter "K" and wanted a name incapable of misspelling.[18]
5 *Remembering the old hometown.* Beatrice Food's namesake is a town in Nebraska, and Oneida Community Plate honors an upstate New York town.

The Appropriateness of a Brand Name The past methods for choosing a brand name are seldom used today. As a general statement, these approaches are the wrong way to go about the job. The overwhelmingly important consideration is **appropriateness.** The manufacturer of a certain brand must first determine what kind of image that brand should project. Along with product quality, recommendations of friends, resellers' opinions, and advertising of the brand name help mold attitudes toward various products. We like some words; others rub us the wrong way. Individual attitudes are colored by past experiences. Once a particular Nancy snubbed us; now we subconsciously reject others bearing that name. Many words are almost universally liked, and others generally disliked. The person picking a brand name must take such factors into consideration.

The marketing implications of such decisions can be found in scores of case examples. One is the share-of-market victory of the Taster's Choice brand of freeze-dried coffee over the Maxim brand.[19] The battle was between two highly successful packaged-goods manufacturers, General Foods and Nestlé. General Foods was first in the field with its Maxim brand and took an early lead in sales. Nevertheless, Nestlé's Taster's Choice garnered a higher brand share in spite of spending appreciably less for promotion. The reasons for this apparent inconsistency are to be found in the areas of name choice and package design. The name "Maxim" was a spin-off of General Foods' highly successful Maxwell House Coffee brand. But, inasmuch as freeze-dried coffee was essentially in a new-product category, the tactic backfired as consumers perceived the brand as a by-product of the established line. Much of Maxim's sales came from the cannibalization of the Maxwell House brand. Nestlé, on the other hand, divorced its new product from its instant coffee, Instant Nescafé. An unusual name—Taster's Choice—was selected to enhance the product's uniqueness and its properties of quality and robust flavor. We are not concerned at this point with the differences in the product packaging of the two products; suffice it to say, the Taster's Choice package was less traditional than that used by Maxim.

The soap manufacturer who desires an image of gentleness for his product would not choose "Grit" as a brand name; "Caress" would be more appropriate. Words and their connotations are much more subtle, of course, than this example. Generally speaking, negative words are seldom desirable in brand names. While the name may merely identify the product, preferably it should hold some attraction for the customer. A name such as A-1 Sauce or Perfection conveys the idea of quality, or is pleasant

(Sunshine), or suggests product composition (Pennzoil), femininity (White Shoulders), or even the benefit resulting from its use (Easy-Off Oven Cleaner).

The brand name should have **graphic possibilities.** How the brand name will look on the package and how it can give something around which a promotional campaign can be built should be weighed. Some brand names lend themselves to use in singing jingles.

Many technical rules surround the choice of a brand name. One is to avoid foreign words, which, although they may connote fashion or prestige, may require the advertiser to spend scarce dollars attempting to teach the elements of, for example, French pronunciation. Other ideas are that brand names be short, unique, accurate, not too imitative, and not capable of unfavorable backward reading or initial-letter reading. How words affect people is the essential knowledge needed when struggling with the creative task of producing a successful brand name.

If a firm wishes to ensure its right to exclusive use of a brand name, it must take affirmative steps to prevent the use of the name by other manufacturers. DuPont lost its right to exclusive use of the name "cellophane" because the public came to think of any and all viscose solidified in thin, transparent, waterproof sheets as "cellophane." Other registered trademarks that have passed into the public domain include aspirin, zipper, and linoleum—now all considered to be generic names for the products. A **generic name** is one used to describe a product category and thus cannot be used exclusively by one manufacturer. More recently, the American Thermos Products Company lost the exclusive right to the name "thermos," and Formica was challenged as the generic name for laminates in 1979. One can think of other products that may be in danger of slipping into the generic name category, such as Kleenex for facial tissue and Baggies for containers for food products.

Trademarks and Trade Characters

Brand names and trademarks are similar in function; both are designed to identify the product of a specific maker. The word "brand" includes both terms within its scope and is defined as "a name, term, sign, symbol, or design, or a combination of them which is intended to identify the goods or services of one seller or group of sellers and to differentiate them from those of competition."[20] The brand name is described as that part of a brand which can be vocalized—the utterable.

One useful definition of a trademark is found in a standard dictionary: "A name, symbol, or other device identifying a product, officially registered and legally restricted to the use of the owner or manufacturer."[21] Although there are a few isolated exceptions (such as service marks for businesses that provide services like dry cleaning and termite control), it is helpful to think of the trademark as a device attached to a product for the purpose of identifying its maker. The trademark may be a distinctive symbol, or it may consist of a special way of writing the brand name. Most manufacturers use both brand names and trademarks.

Trademarks and Advertising

The trademark should appear in every advertisement for the product. The advertiser wants consumers to recall the ad and its featured product when shopping. Thus there is a strong incentive to develop a distinctive and easy-to-remember trademark. Because the trademark is an important factor in the product's brand image, the style or graphic approach in which it is promoted probably should be revised from time to time to keep it contemporary. The Bell System has done this over the last century. Such changes, however, may be expensive. The costs mount for changes in letterheads and everywhere else the trademark appears. The Bell System had to repaint 128,000 vehicles when its trademark was last modernized. The physical representation of the trademark in an ad is usually called the **logo.**

Trade Characters Many sellers use symbols in the form of animals, people, birds, and other animate objects in association with their products. The goal is to enhance the memorability of the products in the consumers' minds. The Jolly Green Giant is an example of the trade character, which is basically a device around which to build promotional programs. The Pillsbury Dough Boy character has touted the company's convenience items and their dairy-case location in the supermarket for many years, and it is believed to be the most popular animated figure in the advertising arena.[22]

The importance of the right name and trade character is illustrated by the Matex Corporation and its trade character, Rusty Jones.[23] In 1972, the company introduced its Thixo-Tex product, a rustproofing chemical to be used on automobile bodies. When advertised as "Body by Thixo-Tex System," sales were good, but they slumped when advertising stopped, for consumers could not remember the name. The firm's advertising agency devised the name "Rusty Jones" in 1975 and advertised the product as seen in Figure 3.11. Retail sales moved from $1.5 million in 1975 to nearly $50 million in 1978 and the company overtook Ziebart as the leading rustproofer.

Figure 3.11 This trade character played an important role in creating awareness for the advertising company after a name change.

The great value of trade characters is to provide continuity to advertising programs, for the public seems able to remember trade characters better than it does brand names, trademarks, or slogans. Nearly everyone in America knows Betty Crocker. And a recent survey determined that Ronald McDonald is better known, among children, than Santa Claus. While an extension not strictly of the product, but rather, of the promotional program, trade characters have a general similarity to trademarks, and when entertainingly presented, enhance brand awareness.

The Label

Another important extension of the product is the label. It is attached physically either to the product or to its package. A label that informs the buyer of the product's brand name and its manufacturer is called a **brand label.** Other kinds of information can appear on the label, for instance, the grade of the product. Some countries, notably Canada, have compulsory grade labeling for some product categories. And, in the United States, certain information may be required by legislation to accompany the product.

The label also can be helpful to buyers when instructions about the proper use and care of the product are placed on it. The consumer movement has resulted in labels with more product information. Thus, imaginative use of the label can forestall aggressive action against the manufacturer by activists. Almost every question about the product which an average consumer might pose can be answered by a skillfully written label. Once again, this information-providing strategy is especially desirable when the product is sold via self-service. Informational labeling possesses a much neglected opportunity for the stimulation of product sales. Since product dissatisfaction often springs from user inefficiency, it is doubly important to make sure that instructions are clear, thus ensuring that the buyers are fully satisfied with their purchases. The purchaser may add word-of-mouth advertising support to the seller's promotional mix. Labels may also reinforce buyers' confidence about the wisdom of a purchase.

As with the other elements found in the product already discussed in this chapter, the label design should be in good taste. It is an integral part of that intangible force that creates a brand image for the product. There is a need for modernizing labels from time to time unless an image of old-fashioned quality is being sought. A change in label, however, must be publicized, or regular buyers may become confused and stop buying the brand.

A recent development in labeling is the Universal Product Code (UPC). Described as the greatest collective change in labeling information in the history of the American food industry, UPC is a voluntary system wherein manufacturers place on all package labels a series of linear bars and a 10-digit number which describes the particular product. Once supermarkets obtain the necessary optical scanning equipment, a computerized checkout system can be used. This speedy checkout process enables store operators to have an almost instant check on inventory levels. What brands are selling, in what sizes, and similar information is at their fingertips.

Once these systems are widespread, the implications for advertising are at least threefold: (1) test-market experiments on advertising campaigns, new products, and size and packaging modifications can be monitored on a day-to-day basis; (2) the success of special promotions, displays, and point-of-purchase advertising can more accurately be assessed; (3) misinterpretation of these data caused by time lag and human error will to a great extent be eliminated.

The Image of the Product and the Brand

The use of the concepts of behaviorial science in the creation of advertisements that will stimulate favorable consumer responses is discussed fully in Chapter 11. Without going into a detailed analysis here, we wish to point out that every phase of marketing can utilize such behaviorial concepts, because what today's consumer buys is not merely the end product of certain raw materials processed to certain specifications. What is wanted, sought, and bought are the benefits, physical and psychological, that the product can deliver to the buyer. One aspect of these benefits is the **image** of a product, which includes all the ideas the consumer possesses about it—the sort of people who make or use it, the kind of stores that sell it, the drama of the ingredients that go into it, the character of the advertising promoting it, the "personality" of the manufacturer. The image of the product is the sum of all the stimuli received by the buyer related to the product.

This bundle of psychological attributes is called the

Is that really Alex Karras hugging a great big banana?
You bet, it's NFL All-pro defensive lineman Alex Karras. And he's hugging that big banana because he loves it.
You'll love it, too. In fact, you may be hugging that great big banana all the way to the bank. Because it's really gonna' sell bananas!
That great big banana is the Dole Banana Buddy. It's 4½ feet tall, inflatable and has a funny face kit. Dole is offering it for $2.95 plus two Dole banana labels. And kids across the country are going to find out about the Dole Banana Buddy on prime time television this spring, (parents, too). They'll also read about the Buddy in the Sunday Comics. So naturally, they're going to want one.
And since you'll have the Dole Banana Buddy display in your produce department, they'll be buying bananas from you!
Let's put that all together—the Dole Banana Buddy, prime time television, comic ads, Banana Buddy display, Dole bananas and your produce department—it all adds up doesn't it?
Dole BANANAS
Dole BANANAS
No one is doing more to help you sell bananas than Dole.
®Castle & Cooke, Inc.

Figure 3.12 Observe how Dole uses a label to distinguish its bananas from those marketed by other producers. This trade ad tells retailers about a consumer promotion that the company is launching.

product image. Most advertisers, however, are more concerned with the **brand image.** The goal is usually not to sell more of the generic product, such as cars or toothpaste, but to sell a particular brand of automobile or toothpaste against competitive brands of the product. When considering the relative inherent interest in two different products, such as sports cars and life insurance, the concept of product image is, of course, useful. Some product categories do intrigue consumers more than others; obviously, it is easier to advertise products successfully if they are interesting and appealing to potential buyers.

The concept of brand image helps to explain why two products that are technically identical are purchased by different people for different reasons. Thus, toilet soap A is preferred by young college

Figure 3.13 The universal product code (UPC) markings shown on the product label help to automate supermarket checkouts.

women, while soap B, which has the same essential ingredients, is preferred by women over forty. When there are many similar products and a large number of brands, development of a distinct brand image is vital to market success. Advertising often contributes a great deal to such brand-image development.

A classic instance of this is the case of Marlboro cigarettes. The Marlboro cigarette had a feminine image until the time when the Leo Burnett agency was awarded the account. Furthermore, attitudinal research showed that all filter cigarettes were thought to be slightly more feminine than masculine. The Burnett and Marlboro people set about trying to revise the image of a filter-tip smoker. The package was redesigned, and the ad campaign featured rugged male models with a tattoo on one hand. A headline reading, "New from Philip Morris . . . the filter that delivers the goods on flavor," was devised to help convey the masculinity of the product. The rest is advertising history; the brand became a best seller, and Marlboro is still projecting essentially the same image, although a cowboy and Marlboro Country have replaced the tattoo as the central visual element in the ads.

Advertising and Channels of Distribution

Earlier in this chapter we saw that marketing includes getting goods and services from where they are produced to where they are consumed. In a craft society, an artisan makes an entire product from start to finish and may even be responsible for finding the component raw materials. When the product is complete, the artisan must meet with the potential customer on a face-to-face basis. However, in a society that relies on mass production to satisfy its demands for goods and services, most products reach the consumer after passing through many steps from raw materials to finished goods, from producer to sales outlet, from retail stores to the ultimate user—the consumer. Those specialists responsible for facilitating this flow of goods are called **middlemen**—wholesalers and retailers—and the paths that products take in moving from producers to ultimate consumers are the **channels of distribution.** In this section, we shall examine the channels of distribution and show how advertising aids middlemen wishing to inform the buying public about the products being sold.

Channels of Distribution

A channel of distribution is a sequence of marketing institutions, principally wholesalers and retailers. Wholesalers buy from producers and sell to retailers or to firms purchasing goods for business purposes. Retailers buy for resale to ultimate consumers for personal use. Marketing acts to close the gap separating producers from consumers; advertising is the important tool in this gap-filling process.

In actuality, there are two parallel systems operating within the channels-of-distribution framework. The obvious one is the **physical distribution** of

Figure 3.14 This cologne ad is an excellent example of an image ad. [*Courtesy of Revlon.*]

goods and involves such activities as transportation and inventory. **Communication** is an equally important part of the channel system, and here the functions of promotion and transaction dominate. Promotion deals with all activities that produce information, including persuasion. In addition to the advertising program, personal selling, sales promotion, and public relations are available for use in the promotional mix. The goal in using the various promotional methods is, of course, to close the perceptual—or knowledge—gap existing between producer and consumer. How advertising functions in closing this gap is more easily understood against a background of channel structure and strategy.

Channel Strategy and Promotional Activity

The choice of the correct channel of distribution is a critical decision for manufacturers, complicated by the large array of alternatives available to them. Some combinations of middlemen are much more

Profile

Jack Trout and Al Ries

Jack Trout (left) and Al Ries (right), president and chairman of Trout & Ries Advertising, Inc.

Jack Trout and Al Ries are the founders and leaders of Trout and Ries Advertising, a New York agency billing more than $25 million annually. Al started the company in 1963 and was joined by Jack Trout in 1968. With previous work experience as advertising managers, both men had spent more than five years at General Electric.

Impressive as their business accomplishments are, Trout and Ries are most widely known for the predictions of where advertising is headed. They might be called the "soothsayers of Madison Avenue." In the June 1969 issue of *Industrial Marketing,* Jack Trout first expressed his ideas on "positioning" and predicted many changes for advertising in the upcoming 1970s. He teamed up with Al to publish a three-part series of articles on positioning in *Advertising Age* in 1972. Requests for more than 120,000 reprints of this classic article were received, and the two men gave more than 50 speeches on the topic in the following year. Finally, their philosophy was presented in a book, *Positioning: The Battle for Your Mind,* published by McGraw-Hill Book Company in 1980. The positioning concept is briefly discussed in Chapter 3.

Now Trout and Ries are plowing new ground. They are examining the concepts of "warfare" as they focus on competitor-directed advertising. Symposiums are given and speeches delivered by both men to advance their ideas, which they have drawn from Clausewitz, the German military strategist of the early 1800s.

Trout and Ries developed useful clues for the better understanding of how advertising works. Their close contact with the advertising industry and with various markets should provide stimulus and direction for their successful predictions in future years.

efficient in tapping potential markets than are others, and the marketplace is ever-changing, thus causing new intermediaries to appear and established ones to disappear. This decision dilemma is complicated further by the tendency for markets to become segmented, with different groups seeking preferred products at different retail outlets. To reach different market segments successfully, a manufacturer may have to use several different trade channels. The proper identification of these market segments requires a knowledge of consumer behavior patterns.

Three useful devices are available to help manufacturers move their products through the channels of distribution: (1) price, (2) personal selling, and (3) advertising. These three devices can be characterized as the lubricants for the machinery of marketing, and to a considerable degree success in marketing depends upon the ability to decide which of these three tools to use and in what combination.

At first blush, price would seem to be the easiest lubricant to use. A low-price approach usually is the quickest way to move goods. But using price as the primary appeal in selling a product has many drawbacks. It may be easy for competitors to meet the low price, thus eroding the initial advantage to the price-cutter; a price war may ensue and eventually force one out of business. Equally serious is the possibility that a product's image of quality will be lost through a drastic reduction in price. When an attempt is made to return to the former higher price, consumer resistance and resentment can be encountered. Product quality may also deteriorate when manufacturers are caught in price wars. Obviously, profits can be reduced below healthy levels if prices are lowered to extremes. Thus, sellers have several good, sound business reasons for trying to minimize price as a key element in their marketing strategies.

Manufacturers and middlemen therefore may emphasize personal selling or advertising, or both, when avoiding a strategy based on price cutting. These promotional activities are designed to substitute persuasion for price as the reason for buying products. Reasons for buying—other than price—are provided to prospective customers, showing the benefits to be derived from the purchase of the product.

Personal selling receives high priority in marketing programs for products needing personal contact and face-to-face presentations to get buyers to make the purchase decision. This is true also when demonstration and detailed explanation of the product are important, when the item being sold is an intangible such as life insurance, or when the purchase is a major one for the consumer, as in the case of cars and homes. Personal selling remains an important mover of goods in the United States, although its relative role has been lessened by the trend toward self-service retailing. Personal selling and advertising often work together in a complementary way, with advertising paving the way for the salesperson's approach, making the sales presentation easier and shorter as the prospect already has some information about the product from advertising.

How advertising lubricates the distributive process is explained in Chapter 4, which is devoted to a discussion of how advertising operates. Now that you have an overview of how advertising fits into the marketing process, a more detailed explanation should be more understandable.

Summary

Advertising is an integral part of most marketing programs. When marketing is characterized as consisting of a "mix" of activities, advertising is one of the five ingredients and works with the rest of the elements of the marketing process.

The product is the core of the advertising program, and is at the heart of the marketing process. The term "product" encompasses more than tangible goods; it includes services and even ideas. Although the needs of both consumers and industrial users are served by products, the emphasis in this book is on consumer products. These can be classified into three groups: convenience, shopping, and specialty. Because each group has a different buying pattern, different advertising strategies are needed for each type.

Product positioning is a strategy involving not only the product's own physical characteristics and its image, but also the way it is perceived by consumers in relation to competitive brands. New products keep individual firms dynamic and competitive and provide challenging opportunities for advertising, which shoulders the task of informing consumers of the availability of the new offering in the marketplace.

In its broader dimension, the product includes the

package, the brand name, trademarks, trade characters, and the product label. All components must be carefully coordinated to ensure a consistent marketing program.

Similarly, the firm's advertising plan must take into account the needs and desires of the channels of distribution. In addition to the physical movement of goods in the channels of distribution, a parallel channel of communication exists to get information about products disseminated in the marketplace.

Questions for Discussion

1. Describe how advertising fits into the marketing process. What is its relationship to the other elements of the marketing mix? Discuss.
2. Explain why it is correct to claim that "the product is paramount." What implications does this truism have for advertising?
3. Bring to class a newspaper or magazine ad for some kind of consumer service, preferably one that traditionally has not been advertisted. Does the ad do a good job of increasing consumer awareness of the service? Discuss.
4. Explain how advertising strategy varies when the featured product is (*a*) a convenience good, (*b*) a shopping good, (*c*) a specialty good.
5. From current advertising campaigns isolate an example of product positioning (*a*) against competitive products, (*b*) in relation to other products in the company's offerings.
6. In a recent issue of *Advertising Age,* find an article about the successful introduction of a new product similar to the success story of Pillsbury's Totino's Crisp Crust Frozen Pizza. Write a brief summary of the article. Can you recommend additional strategies the company might use?
7. What are the four marketing purposes of the product package? Can you think of examples of packages that go beyond protection and identification in serving consumer needs?
8. How are the brand name, trademark, and the trade character for a product interrelated in the marketing function? Is one more important than the others? Explain.
9. What trade character do you believe does the best job for its sponsor? Why?
10. How do the concepts of product image and brand image differ? Cite an example of a product possessing a strong, positive brand image. Explain why you believe the image is strong.

For Further Reference

Barach, Arnold B.: *Famous American Trademarks,* Public Affairs Press, Washington, D.C., 1971.

Dichter, Ernest: *The New World of Packaging,* Cahners Books, Boston, 1975.

Kotler, Philip: *Marketing Management: Analysis, Planning and Control,* 4th ed., Prentice-Hall, Inc., Englewood Cliffs, N.J., 1980.

Neubauer, Robert G.: *Packaging: The Contemporary Media,* Van Nostrand Reinhold Company, New York, 1973.

Ries, Al, and Jack Trout: *Positioning: The Battle for Your Mind,* McGraw-Hill Book Company, New York, 1980.

Schewe, Charles D., and Reuben M. Smith: *Marketing: Concepts and Applications,* McGraw-Hill Book Company, New York, 1980.

Schwartz, David J.: *Marketing Today,* 3d ed., Harcourt Brace Jovanovich, New York, 1981.

Stanton, William J.: *Fundamentals of Marketing,* 6th ed., McGraw-Hill Book Company, New York, 1981.

End Notes

[1] William J. Stanton, *Fundamentals of Marketing,* 6th ed., McGraw-Hill Book Company, New York, 1981, p. 4.

[2] Peter Drucker, *Management: Tasks, Responsibilities, Practices,* Harper & Row, Publishers, Inc., New York, 1973, pp. 61–63.

[3] Neil Borden, "The Concept of the Marketing Mix," *Journal of Advertising Research,* June 1964, pp. 2–7.

[4] Walter Weir, *On the Writing of Advertising,* McGraw-Hill Book Company, New York, 1960, p. 156.

[5] Statement by Howard J. Morgens, former chairman of the board at P&G, undated.

[6] Stanton, op. cit., p. 161.

[7] Stanton, op. cit., p. 180, based on John H. Holmes, "Profitable Product Positioning," *MSU Business Topics,* Spring 1973, pp. 27–32.

[8] Samuel R. Gardner, "Product Positioning: Key to Rising Sales in Ice Cream," *Marketing Times,* November-December 1979, pp. 12–13. Rest of paragraph drawn from this article and personal communication with Samuel Gardner.

[9] This section is based on the work of Jack Trout and Al Ries. See *Advertising Age,* April 24, May 1, and May 8, 1972. Copyrighted by Crain Communications, Inc., and used by special permission. Also see Al Ries and Jack Trout, *Positioning: The Battle for Your Mind,* McGraw-Hill Book Company, New York, 1980.

[10] See "What are the Top Consumer Product Campaigns of the 1970s?", *Marketing Communications,* January 1980, pp. 20–21.

[11] See Wendell R. Smith, "Product Differentiation and Market Segmentation as Alternative Marketing Strategies," *Journal of Marketing,* July 1956, pp. 3–8.

[12] These comments based on Laurence Ingrassia, "There's No Way to Tell If a New Food Product Will Please the Public," *Wall Street Journal,* Feb. 26, 1980, p. 23.

[13] Daniel J. Boorstin, *The Americans: The Democratic Experience,* Vintage Books, Random House, Inc., New York, 1974, p. 434.

[14] *U.S. Industrial Outlook,* 1980, Bureau of Domestic Commerce, U.S. Department of Commerce, Washington, D.C., January 1980, p. 75.

[15] George Weissman, "How Packaging Will Affect Marketing in 1985," *Marketing Times,* March/April 1973, p. 19.

[16] Dik Warren Twedt, "How Much Value Can Be Added Through Packaging," *Journal of Marketing,* January 1968, p. 61.

[17] Leonard Carlton, "The Oldtime Name Game," *Advertising Age,* Nov. 29, 1971, pp. 37–39.

[18] For a fascinating story, see "The Name Game," in *Forbes,* Nov. 15, 1973, pp. 70, 72. The thrust of the article is that businesspeople are superstitious, or "Why else would they need high priests to tell them how to change their companies' names?" The "high priests" are the firms, such as Lippincott & Margulies, that specialize in the design of corporate symbols. The writer goes on to emphasize the apparent appeal of the letter "X" as used in Exxon and in Xerox.

[19] This paragraph was excerpted from Walter P. Margulies, "How Nestlé Beat General Foods in Freeze-Dried Coffee Battle," *Advertising Age,* June 21, 1971, pp. 51–52.

[20] Ralph S. Alexander and the Committee on Definitions, *Marketing Definitions,* American Marketing Association, Chicago, 1963, p. 9.

[21] *The American Heritage Dictionary of the English Language,* Houghton Mifflin Company, Boston, 1969, p. 1360.

[22] Malcolm McNiven, Vice-President of Marketing Services, The Pillsbury Company.

[23] "What's in a Name? Just Ask Rusty Jones," *Marketing News,* Aug. 10, 1979, p. 12.

Chapter 4

How Advertising Works?

Thus far in our study of advertising, we have determined what advertising is, explained how it fits into our society, and also seen that it is part of the marketing process. This chapter extends Chapter 3's discussion of the role of advertising in the marketing mix. Here we zero in on the specific functions of advertising for business firms. We begin the chapter by looking at the objectives that businesses set for advertising. Then we shall discuss the various forms of advertising and see how each operates.

General Business Objectives of Advertising

Business firms serve society by fulfilling the needs of their customers. Any firm that does not do so will fail and economic resources will be wasted, as explained in Chapter 2. In order for a firm to remain economically sound, it must generate sales that yield long-run profits. Advertising may contribute to sales, and each business manager must understand the function of advertising and its effects on sales and profits.

Effect of Advertising on Demand

Advertising can help maximize the demand for goods and services. Demand is often latent within the consumer, waiting to be brought into each person's consciousness through advertising or other forms of stimulation. Although, technically speaking, advertising does not create demand for products, most advertising is designed to stimulate demand.

One way for a firm to obtain more total revenue is to charge a higher price for each unit of its output. By pointing out the advantages of a product or enhancing its image in a way that is of value to some consumers, advertising is a means of convincing prospects that the product is worth the price charged. A more usual alternative is to use advertising to increase the number of units sold. The total sales revenue for the producer is increased in either case.

Some products are more sensitive to increased advertising than are others; that is, more demand can be stimulated for some products than for others. This situation involves the concept of **expansibility of demand,** which exists when the use of advertising and/or personal selling will bring about an increase in the total demand for a product.

Three Ways Advertising Can Stimulate Demand Advertising can stimulate the demand for any product in three basic ways. First, present users may be persuaded to increase present rates of product consumption. No better example can be found than the "take more pictures" strategy followed by Kodak for many decades. Thus, we see in Figure 4.1 that Kodak urges camera owners "to feed your camera this weekend."

Don't forget to feed your camera this weekend.
Kodak 126-20
FILM FOR COLOR PRINTS
126 CARTRIDGE
20 EXPOSURES
Kodacolor-X
Pick up several rolls of your favorite kind of Kodak film at your supermarket. And have a memorable weekend.
Kodak makes your pictures count.

Figure 4.1 The idea behind this ad is that if there is film in the camera, more is likely to be used. Thus, Kodak encourages consumers to stock up.

A second way is to tell present users about new uses for the product. This approach is beautifully illustrated by the Arm & Hammer Baking Soda case. The brand, while synonymous in consumers' minds with its product category, was in a sales slump as home baking declined. When the company hit upon the idea of selling its product as a freshener for the home refrigerator, a single television commercial explaining this product-use concept put the familiar A&H box into 40 million refrigerators. The company further has advocated the use of baking soda in cat litter boxes, for brushing teeth, as a fire extinguisher, in a variety of camping situations, as a rug freshener, and in swimming pools to reduce eye burn from chlorine. Company sales have increased sharply, and a commodity product suddenly has marketing glamour. The television commercial shown in Figure 4.2 is now a classic in advertising circles. In it, the Florida Citrus Commission abandoned an image campaign in the late 1970s for one which promoted the idea that "orange juice isn't only for breakfast." Instead, the drink should be thought of as a refresher throughout the day.

Drawing new users into the market for the product is the third alternative for the firm seeking to increase demand. One approach to the "new users" strategy is shown in Figure 4.3. On the other hand, the airlines have been engaged in a longtime quest for

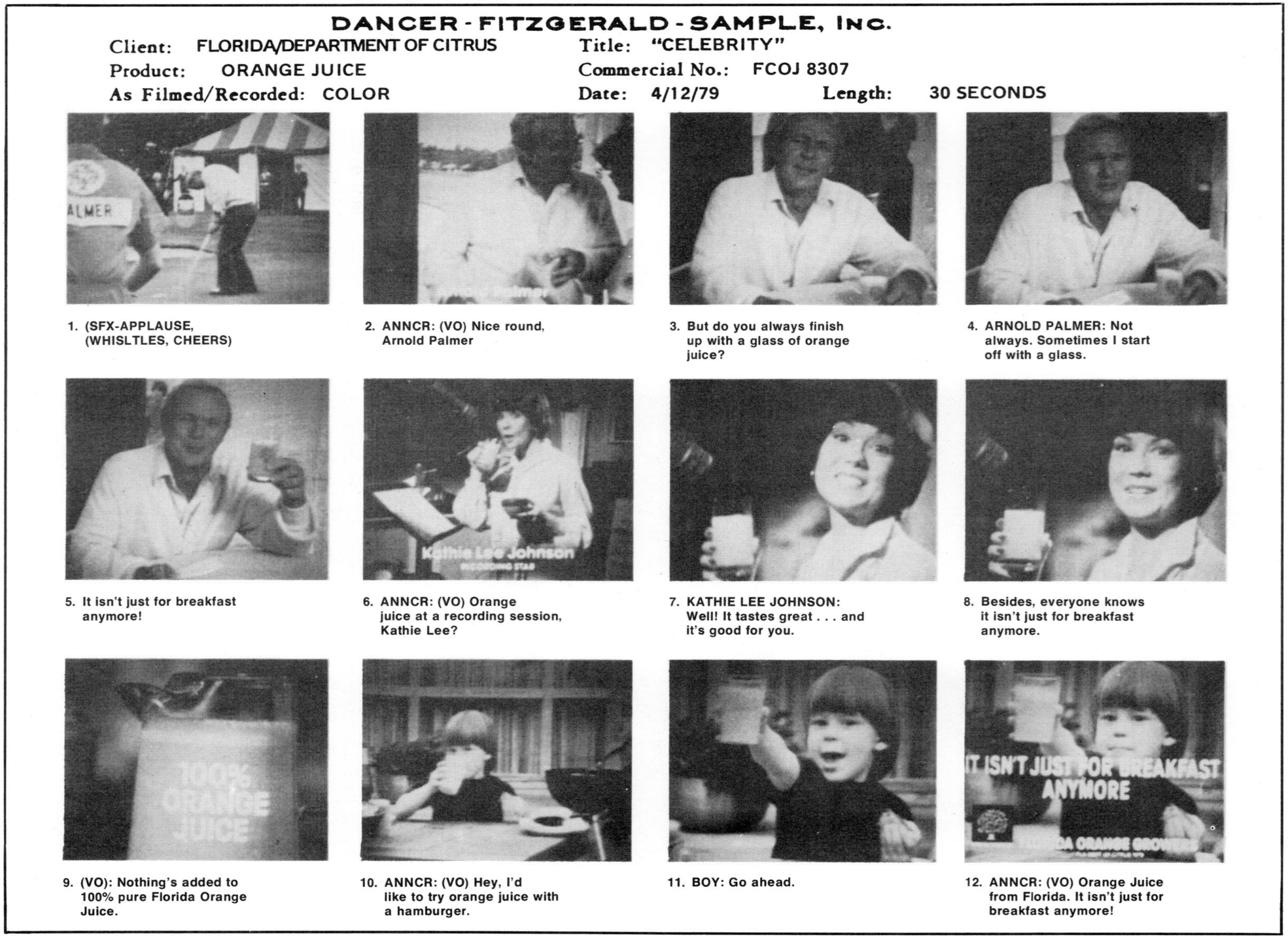

Figure 4.2 The producers of frozen orange juice employ the ''new uses'' strategy in this television commercial, which is now viewed as an advertising classic. In the eight-year period that the ''It Isn't Just for Breakfast Anymore'' concept was first used, total orange juice volume increased nearly 100 percent.

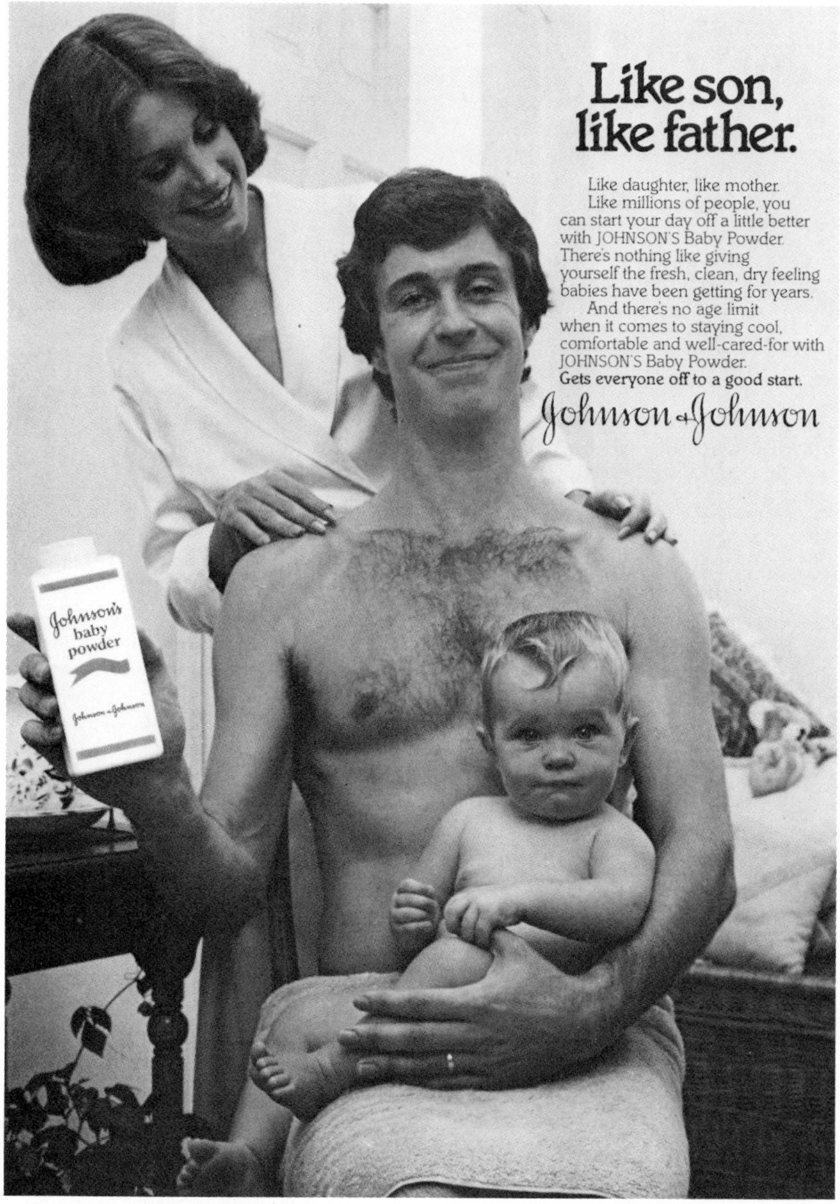

Like son,
like father.
Like daughter, like mother.
Like millions of people, you can start your day off a little better with JOHNSON'S Baby Powder. There's nothing like giving yourself the fresh, clean, dry feeling babies have been getting for years.
And there's no age limit when it comes to staying cool, comfortable and well-cared-for with JOHNSON'S Baby Powder.
Gets everyone off to a good start.
Johnson & Johnson
Johnson's baby powder

Figure 4.3 This ad was developed to convince both men and women to use Johnson's Baby Powder while capitalizing on the brand's acceptance as a product for babies. This ad is an excellent example of the use of advertising to secure new users for an established brand.

"nonfliers." When one realizes that 35 percent of American adults have never flown in a regular passenger airplane, the latent potential for the airlines of America can be readily grasped. However, no airline has been able to develop ads that are able to get large numbers of nonfliers to buy tickets.

Effect of Advertising on Profits

Increased sales are worthless unless they lead to increased profits. Profits may be overlooked in the short run to obtain other worthwhile objectives, such as market penetration; nevertheless, future profits are paramount in the manager's thinking and planning. Advertising may affect the profit performance of a business firm in two important ways.

If advertising does increase sales, the increase may favorably affect **product costs.** If plant capacity is fully utilized and other cost reductions are employed (such as specialization of labor and quantity discounts on raw materials), the per-unit cost of the

California Avocados. Only 17 calories a slice.
Would this body lie to you?
Angie Dickinson

Figure 4.4 This ad, which uses a well-known television personality as a spokesperson, seeks to dispel a misconception that avocados are high in calories.

product will often be lowered. As manufacturing costs are lowered, profits are increased. Advertising similarity may affect **marketing costs.** Less personal selling may be required because of the advertising program. Other marketing costs, such as transportation and storage expenses per unit, may be reduced because of increased sales.

The reduction in manufacturing or marketing costs that can result from advertising must be weighed against the costs of that advertising before we can say that advertising has helped to improve the profits of the firm.

Specific Objectives of Advertising

In their search for productivity gains — more profitable sales — managers must be aware of the potential contribution of advertising. One advertising expert states this philosophy in these words:

> A shockingly large share . . . [of the money] . . . spent annually for advertising is wasted for one fundamental reason: lack of well-defined objectives. In search of profit and growth, corporate management has focused its attention on the technological aspects of business. In the past, here was where the big productivity gains could be made; and here was where top management felt most competent and comfortable. But improved technology is no longer the whole answer. A drug company president tells me: "Advertising has become the second largest item in our corporate budget. The chips are getting so blue that top management can no longer afford to be uninformed — naive, if you will — about advertising."[1]

In the 20 years since Russell Colley made this challenging statement, total advertising expenditures in the United States have grown 6 times as large. His observation is more true today than it ever was.

Despite the ability of advertising to stimulate demand, advertising dollars are often misspent and wasted. Business must understand how to set objectives for advertising programs that will reap the benefits described above.

The technical aspects of setting advertising objectives are discussed in Chapter 15 as part of the advertising-campaign planning process. At this point, we confine our discussion to more theoretical considerations. Although some advertising can be used to produce sales directly, as is done in direct marketing, most national advertisers are less direct in their objectives. For some time now, advertising executives have debated whether a statement of advertising objectives can be couched in sales terms at all.

One view is that advertising goals should be stated in communication terms only, if meaningful measurement of results is to follow.[2] The rationale is that marketing goals depend on the total marketing effort, which includes advertising, but that advertising cannot take full credit when marketing goals, such as sales, are reached.

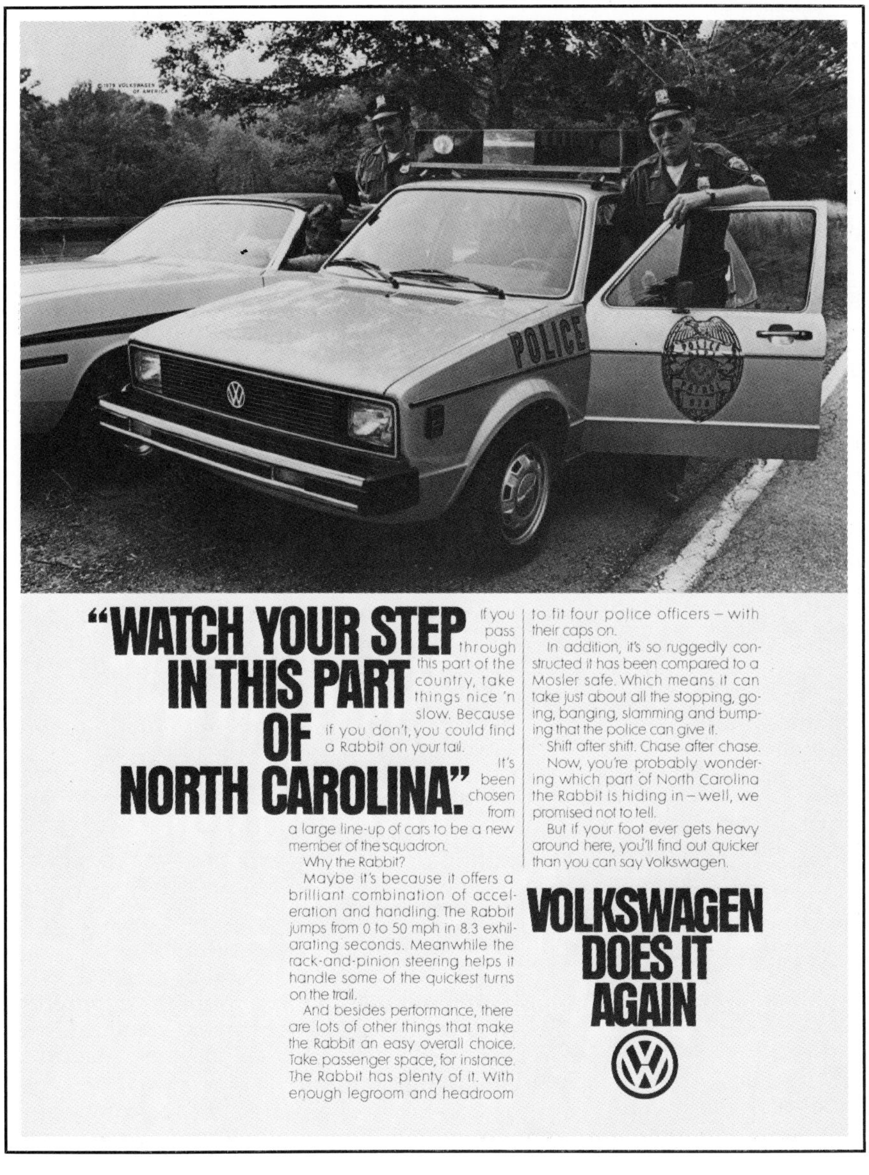

Figure 4.5 This automobile ad, which also appeared in a television version, seeks to dispel the idea that all compact cars are slow. [*Courtesy of Volkswagen of America.*]

In a presentation before The Conference Board, Paul C. Harper, head of one of America's largest advertising agencies, outlined several different ways in which advertising can aid in achieving business productivity. After clearly spelling out the preconditions for advertising success and stressing the need for establishing clear-cut communication goals in advance of advertising, Harper enumerated eight ways that advertising can work for the benefit of the advertiser. To summarize them:[3]

1 *Induce trial.* The introductions of Crest, Polaroid cameras, and Contac II over-the-counter medicine employed advertising to induce maximum trial of these new entries in as short a period as possible.
2 *Intensify usage.* The Arm & Hammer campaign already discussed is a good example of how advertising can get more usage of a product. Advertising brought Accent food-flavor enhancer and V-8 juice off the back of home pantry shelves into

"SURE I CAN GET IT ALL IN. I GOT IT ALL OUT."
Skeptical? You needn't be, you know.
All the assorted paraphernalia that you see in the picture above really did get into a 1980 Volkswagen Rabbit before it came back out again. Because although the outside is definitely all Rabbit, superbly snug-looking and stylishly compact, the inside is all Volkswagen. And you know what that means.
It means that thanks to a fold-down rear-seat, a Rabbit can be terrifically useful whenever you're thinking of transporting things.
Even surprisingly large things.
Like a steamer trunk.
Not to mention your favorite bric-a-brac or knick-a-knack.
But just in case you prefer chauffeuring people to things, we've got some good news in that department, too.
Because, you see, the Rabbit's got ample room to fit four of them comfortably.
And of course, every Rabbit comes replete with front-wheel drive, and the kind of exceptional road-handling that just might spoil you for other cars.
So think about packing you and yours into a 1980 Rabbit.
And remember, when you do, you won't just have a Volkswagen Rabbit.
If you so desire, you'll have a stuffed Rabbit.
VOLKSWAGEN DOES IT AGAIN
© 1980 VOLKSWAGEN OF AMERICA

Figure 4.6 Another ad in Volkswagen's campaign to remove wrong impressions in the public mind is shown. Here, consumers learn that at least one brand of compact car has adequate storage room. [*Courtesy of Volkswagen of America.*]

higher use. V-8 became the best-selling vegetable juice since being promoted aggressively.

3 *Sustain preference.* Long-established brands maintain their lead through advertising. For example, Morton Salt, Parkay margarine, and Marlboro cigarettes have been advertised from 20 to 50 years and are leaders in their product classes.

4 *Confirm imagery.* Cadillac and Mercedes-Benz automobiles, Yves Saint Laurent clothes, and Chivas Regal whiskey are not bought because of advertising; advertising borrows on established imagery and confirms it in the buyer's mind, thus sustaining high sales for these luxury goods.

5 *Change habits.* Clairol helped change American attitudes toward coloring one's hair; Bic taught us it was not wasteful to throw away a pen or cigarette lighter; Volkswagen convinced us that small, albeit ugly, cars are all we really need to get around.

6 *Build line acceptance.* Kraft, Sears, and Levis use advertising to tie together their extensive product lines in the minds of consumers.

Figure 4.7 The communication goal of this magazine ad is to create a mood of ambience for the hotel chain's various facilities.

"I'm holding one terrific reason to open up to Avon. Right now."
The fun begins with this "Open Up To Avon" game card. Your Avon Representative has one for you. It's your ticket to exciting beauty products. Sensational savings of at least $2.50. And maybe even a free gift.
Another terrific reason to open up is Avon's brand new "Open Up To Beauty" brochure. It's filled with all kinds of things to make your spring beautiful.
There's the "Beautiful New You" sweepstakes, too. With a grand total of $100,000 in cash prizes.
You won't want to miss the most exciting four weeks in the history of beauty. Your Representative is on the way with details. So get ready to open up to Avon. Now.
Open up to
AVON
beautiful surprise
©1980 Avon Products, Inc., N.Y., N.Y.
AVON

Figure 4.8 This direct-marketing firm uses consumer advertising to break the ice for its force of salespeople. The appeal is for women to open their door to Avon representatives.

7 *Break the ice.* When the salesperson is the key to the firm's marketing success, advertising can serve as a door opener. The advertising of Xerox, Honda, and Avon (see Figure 4.8) has been highly beneficial to the salesperson when face to face with prospects. These campaigns created familiarity with the product name.

8 *Build ambience.* Advertising can make us feel good about being in the advertiser's establishment. That is the main thought behind the advertising of McDonald's, Household Finance Company, and Barney's clothing store in New York City.

Thus, we have seen how 25 advertisers used advertising to accomplish eight different kinds of communications tasks. Obviously, the list is not exhaustive, only representative. Each advertiser must determine what the specific communication problem is, clearly define the goals, then design advertisements that will get those ideas across in the marketplace.

The Many Forms of Advertising and How They Function

Advertising can be classified according to its function, and each functional classification possesses its own distinctive characteristics. Collectively, these various forms of advertising close the perceptual gap that exists between producers and consumers of goods and services.

National Advertising

A manufacturer who decides to sell under a specific brand name is faced with the need to stimulate consumer demand for the product. Engaging in national advertising is one way to approach this task. **National advertising** is any advertising done by a manufacturer of a consumer product for the purpose of convincing consumers that they will benefit from the purchase and use of the product. It is advertising done by the manufacturer or producer in contrast with that done by a retailer.

The word "national" conveys a picture of mass markets extending from coast to coast and calls to mind such names as Procter & Gamble, General Motors, and Exxon. Such large firms do, of course, employ national advertising in large quantities, but the term also applies to the promotional efforts of companies with limited market coverage. National advertising exists when a trademarked product that has the *potentiality* of being sold throughout the nation, such as a regional beer like Coors, is advertised.

When a new manufacturing firm appears on the business scene, it usually does not seek immediate national distribution; funds are restricted, production capacity is low, personnel are few, and distribution know-how is limited. Management sells its output in the local community, and as conditions warrant, extends market coverage in concentric circles fanning out from the home plant. Well-established companies often introduce new-product items on a limited regional basis, too, through a plan of test markets.

In such situations, embarking upon an advertising campaign in nationally circulated media would be foolish. Potential customers would have little chance of seeing the message. Moreover, much of the advertising would be delivered to people outside the area of product distribution. Therefore, the manufacturer uses media serving the geographic area to be tapped. Local newspapers, local radio and television stations, and local outdoor plants provide appropriate media vehicles. This advertiser, nevertheless, is classified as a national advertiser, because the purpose of the ads is to get customers to purchase the product at any retail outlet that may stock the item.

Retail Advertising

In national advertising, the message says, in effect, "Buy *our brand.*" The manufacturer cares little where the product is purchased. The retail advertiser, on the other hand, has a different goal. His advertising message says, "Buy X brand at *our store.*" *Where* the consumer makes the purchase is more important to the retailer than *whether* a specific brand is purchased.

Not all retail advertisements feature nationally advertised brands. Retailers may place selling messages for unbranded merchandise, as is common in the case of shopping goods, in their advertisements. Large-scale retailers stock private label goods that are promoted in a fashion similar to nationally advertised brands; that is, messages for these products may appear in the mass media. Sears, Roebuck & Co. is the third largest advertiser in the United States, with total national advertising expenditures of $379 million in 1979. Over 90 percent of the company's sales volume is from its own brands, or put another way, less than 10 percent comes from nationally advertised brands. Retail-store advertising by the chain amounted to more than $330 million in the same year. Giant retailers thus employ a combination of national and retail advertising in their promotional mixes, and their private brands become, in effect, national brands that are sold exclusively in their own retail stores.

Retail and national advertising differ in at least five ways: (1) territory covered, (2) customer relationship, (3) target-audience interest, (4) expected response, and (5) use of price. Generally speaking, the retailer works in a more restricted geographic market than does the national advertiser. This proximity to the market means that the retailer's message can be closer to the likes, preferences, prejudices, and buying habits of the intended audience, which is usually more receptive than the national advertising audience. The prospective retail customers, in many instances, seek out the advertisements of their favorite stores. The retail advertiser strives for an immediate response to most of this local advertising, while the national advertiser usually is more interested in establishing long-range favorable attitudes. The retailer frequently stresses price in retail copy; the national advertiser may play down or ignore this inducement, as prices may vary from region to region. The difference between retail and national advertising can be seen in Figures 4.9 and 4.10. Here the Goodyear Tire & Rubber Company wears two advertising hats simultaneously. In its national advertising, Goodyear

Figure 4.9 A brand of tires is featured by means of national advertising over television and in magazines. The emphasis is on the product's ability to perform in all kinds of weather.

is interested in showing the superiority of the Goodyear brand of tire, in its retail ads the goal is to pull bargain hunters into Goodyear outlets.

The Local Advertising Concept

We use the term "retail advertising" in a precise and narrow framework, namely, to describe the advertising done by actual retail establishments for reasons described earlier. As a cursory examination of the local media in any community will reveal, there is an appreciable amount of advertising sponsored by local business firms which falls outside this narrow definition, for example, the advertising done by service institutions such as banks, dry cleaners, beauty salons, and computer schools. The advertiser's aim is to convey the consumer benefits to be derived by the local buying public from the use of the advertised services; brand loyalty, so to speak, must be created for these services. The advertising done by these service establishments is carried in local media. This advertising possesses some of the characteristics of retail advertising and some of national advertising. It should not be classified as retail advertising just because it is run by a local establishment; therefore, we recommend that the special label of **local advertising** be used.

Cooperative Advertising Some manufacturers have a special interest in the advertising efforts of their dealers, particularly in the case of specialty goods. The producer who mounts an extensive program of national advertising for a product doesn't want prospective purchasers to have trouble finding retail outlets that handle the product. Action is often taken to make such store identification easy for the consumer. Street signs and window displays can make a contribution, but the most fruitful means of

Figure 4.10 The same product is displayed locally in newspapers in retail advertising. Now the emphasis is on price instead of product features. Often store locations are added to this material, as created by the manufacturer's advertising department.

identifying the retail outlet selling the manufacturer's product is to advertise over the dealer's name. To facilitate this goal, a procedure known as **cooperative advertising** — a technique that is an important part of the promotional programs of many manufacturers — has developed.

Cooperative ads appear to the general public to be regular retail advertisements of a local store. The featured product is a nationally advertised brand of merchandise, and the signature is that of the local retail store. The brand manufacturer often provides the retailer with the material or guidelines from which the print ads and radio and TV commercials are produced, thus assuring that the message says what the manufacturer wants it to say. The media costs are usually shared. The details of the cooperative advertising arrangement between manufacturer and retailers are discussed thoroughly in Chapter 19.

Business Advertising

Our discussion of the functional forms of advertising up to this point has revolved around consumer products and the interrelationship between their distribution and advertising. From the discussion in Chapter 3, we know that there is another broad category of products identified as industrial goods, which are sold for business use rather than for personal consumption. Manufacturers of industrial products face many problems that are similar to those challenging national advertisers of consumer products. Prospective users must be told of the product's existence, and persuasion often is required before the item is purchased. Advertising is an integral part of the marketing mix of firms producing industrial goods. Advertising designed to communicate with buyers acting in a role of producer rather than consumer has been given many names, including "trade advertising," "industrial advertising," "vocational advertising," and "business advertising." We prefer to use the last-mentioned term and include four specific categories within the broad classification: (1) trade advertising, (2) industrial advertising, (3) farm advertising, and (4) professional advertising.

Trade Advertising Manufacturers use trade advertising to persuade retailers to stock their products, to feature them in their stores, and to tie in with national advertising campaigns in their retail ads. Retailers stock those items that customers will buy, but they are generally limited in shelf space and short of funds for inventory. Therefore, retailers must be convinced that stocking the products of individual manufacturers is to their advantage. Personal selling, by the manufacturer's sales force or by wholesalers, often carries the major responsibility for this job, but trade advertising makes the personal selling task easier.

Direct mail and specialized business publications are the principal media employed in trade advertising. Nearly every retail-business category has one or more specialized magazines or newspapers which circulate among retailers in each kind of specific en-

Texaco's special March and April price allowance is like getting...
"One case free with every twelve. That's a Havoline Supreme Deal."
On top of all that, you get an outstanding $1.00 per case advertising allowance that will help drive customers right to your store.
Talk about a supreme deal! Just look at the package Texaco has put together for you.
First there's the newest Havoline—Havoline Supreme—which gives motorists unbeaten mileage when compared to two leading 10W-40 motor oils advertising extra gasoline mileage.
Then there's Texaco's March and April special price allowance that amounts to one free case (taxes excluded) with every 12 you buy. What's more, there's that $1.00 per case advertising allowance, part of a supreme multi-million dollar advertising program. With a traffic-building program like this, no wonder Havoline Supreme can mean supreme turnover...and supreme profits...for you.
Contact: John P. Wies, Manager, Lubricants & Services, Texaco Inc., 1111 Rusk Ave., Houston, TX 77002, or your local Texaco representative today for all the profitable details.
Act now! This offer good only from March 1 through April 30, 1980.
TEXACO

Figure 4.11 This trade ad features two attractive deals to retailers in order to persuade them to stock the brand. Furthermore, the company's consumer-directed advertising program is mentioned. The woman in the ad served as spokesperson in the company's television advertising.

deavor. Grocery-store operators, for example, may read *Progressive Grocer, Chain Store Age, Supermarketing,* or any number of regional publications aimed specifically at them.

Trade advertising also may be directed to the operators of service establishments and to wholesalers. Some advertising placed in mass consumer media may be directed to retailers or other special groups in order to get the attention of the retailer, industrial user, or professional person when in a relaxed mood. *Vogue,* as an example, carries advertisements by manufacturers of synthetic fabrics, such as Du Pont and Monsanto, aimed not only at consumers but at garment manufacturers and retailers as well. Advertisements meant for retailers are classified as trade advertising; those ads meant for other manufacturers are industrial advertising.

Industrial Advertising A vast array of items, including machinery, equipment, raw materials, semiprocessed materials, parts, and operating supplies, are used by manufacturers and other producers to make products for both the consumer and business markets. The manufacturers of industrial goods sell their products to other producers, and are not concerned with securing retail distribution. Personal selling is significantly more important in the distribution of industrial goods than in the case of consumer products. Prospective buyers are fewer; they tend to be in concentrated geographic locations; and their

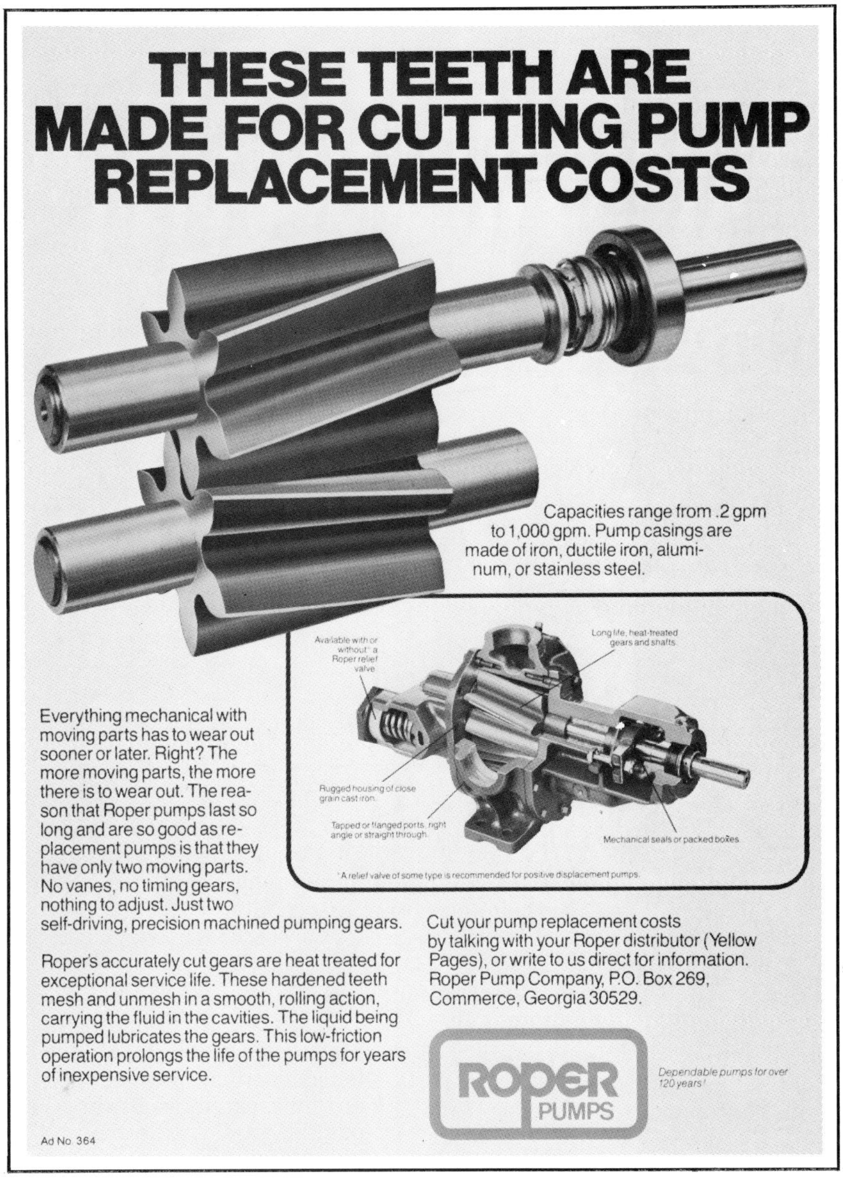

THESE TEETH ARE MADE FOR CUTTING PUMP REPLACEMENT COSTS
Capacities range from .2 gpm to 1,000 gpm. Pump casings are made of iron, ductile iron, aluminum, or stainless steel.
Available with or without* a Roper relief valve.
Long life, heat-treated gears and shafts.
Rugged housing of close grain cast iron.
Tapped or flanged ports, right angle or straight through.
Mechanical seals or packed boxes.
*A relief valve of some type is recommended for positive displacement pumps.
Everything mechanical with moving parts has to wear out sooner or later. Right? The more moving parts, the more there is to wear out. The reason that Roper pumps last so long and are so good as replacement pumps is that they have only two moving parts. No vanes, no timing gears, nothing to adjust. Just two self-driving, precision machined pumping gears.
Roper's accurately cut gears are heat treated for exceptional service life. These hardened teeth mesh and unmesh in a smooth, rolling action, carrying the fluid in the cavities. The liquid being pumped lubricates the gears. This low-friction operation prolongs the life of the pumps for years of inexpensive service.
Cut your pump replacement costs by talking with your Roper distributor (Yellow Pages), or write to us direct for information. Roper Pump Company, P.O. Box 269, Commerce, Georgia 30529.
ROPER PUMPS
Dependable pumps for over 120 years!
Ad No. 364

Figure 4.12 This industrial ad contains detail specifications on how the product can be used.

average purchase is considerably larger. Advertising is used to speed the sales of industrial products, to reduce the costs of personal sales efforts, and to improve sales effectiveness. For example, in one study involving the marketing of heavy electrical equipment to the public utility industry, it was shown that when a client had been called upon by a salesperson and also had been exposed to advertising for the product, brand preference increased 21 percent over instances in which sales calls alone were used.[4]

The list of industrial magazines is long and varied. The advertising messages are designed to show manufacturers how they can benefit from purchase of the advertised products. Appeals of quality, service, durability, and economy are stressed.

Farm Advertising The farm is both a producing and a consuming unit. As a business operation, it produces grain, livestock, poultry, or whatever. As a household, the farm needs household products like any other family. This duality led to the development of specialized media designed to reach farmers and their families. Such publications as *Farm Journal, The Progressive Farmer,* and *Successful Farming*

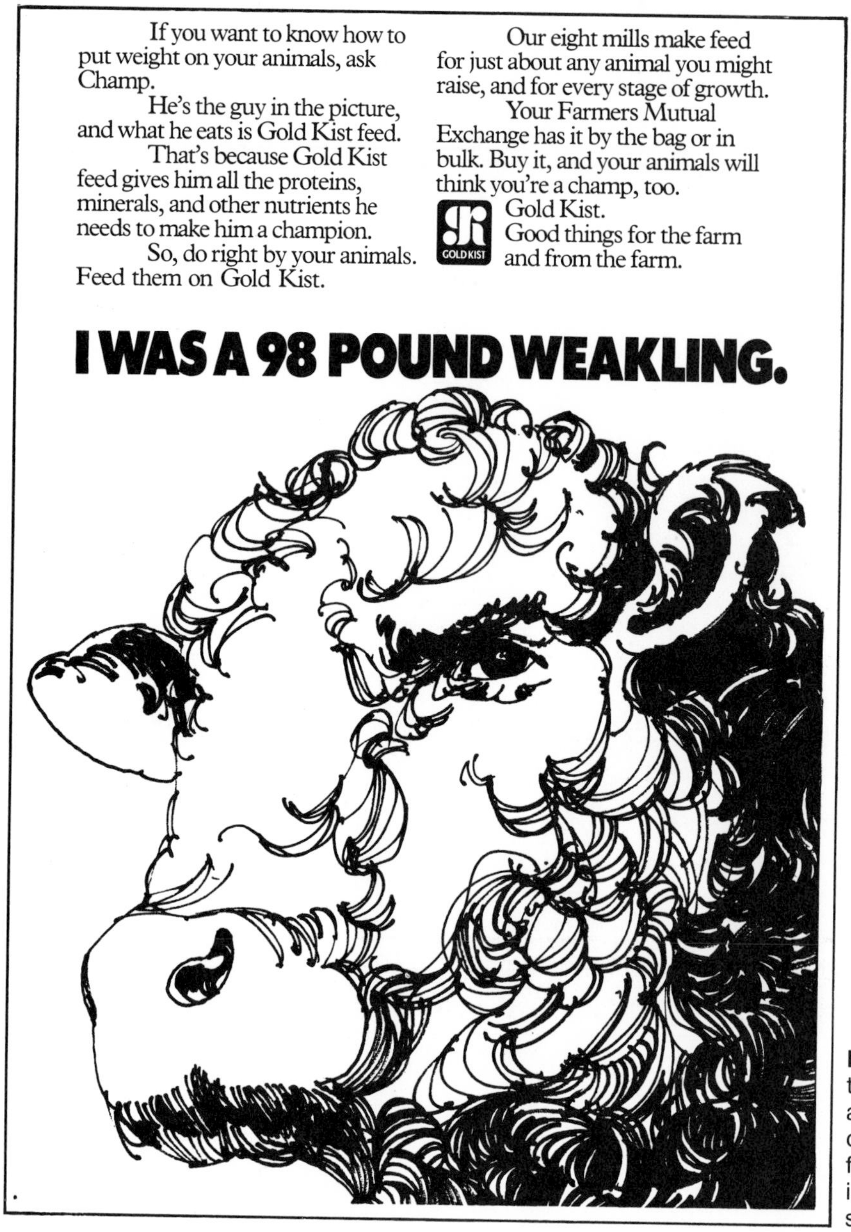

If you want to know how to put weight on your animals, ask Champ.
He's the guy in the picture, and what he eats is Gold Kist feed.
That's because Gold Kist feed gives him all the proteins, minerals, and other nutrients he needs to make him a champion.
So, do right by your animals. Feed them on Gold Kist.
Our eight mills make feed for just about any animal you might raise, and for every stage of growth.
Your Farmers Mutual Exchange has it by the bag or in bulk. Buy it, and your animals will think you're a champ, too.
GOLD KIST
Gold Kist.
Good things for the farm and from the farm.
I WAS A 98 POUND WEAKLING.

Figure 4.13 Promotional strategies used for farm products are similar to those used for industrial products. Yet, this ad for cattle feed employs graphics frequently found in consumer ads.

contain editorial matter aimed at both parts of the farm market, and the advertisements contained in these magazines feature both industrial and consumer goods.

On the one hand, the contents are really industrial in nature, aimed at the farmer as a producer. Feed and fertilizer manufacturers present testimonials indicating how certain farmers profited from giving their cattle brand X feed or how soybean crop yields were improved after spreading brand Y fertilizer on their fields. The profit motive is the basic appeal in this type of farm advertising, as it is in most forms of business advertising. The industrial nature of farming was recognized by the introduction of farm publications appealing only to the business side of farm life. Thus, *Big Farmer* is received by farmers who earn $40,000 or more a year from farming operations. The publication serves 380,000 of the 462,000 farmers earning at least this amount of money.

Advertisers of regular consumer goods add farm publications to their media lists when wishing to sell detergents, cake mixes, electrical appliances, and household furniture to the farm family. The advertising is done in a fashion similar to the way such items are featured in *Good Housekeeping, Better Homes and Gardens,* and *Family Circle.* Thus, farm magazines are now listed in the consumer-magazine edition of *Standard Rate and Data Service* (SRDS), the compilation of advertising rates charged by the various media. The duality still exists and confuses the classification of farm advertising, which accounts for only 0.3 percent of all advertising produced in the United States.

Professional Advertising Historically, professional people, such as doctors, dentists, lawyers, and architects, have been restricted by ethical standards from advertising their desire to obtain clients. This restriction by professional associations has been relaxed, and we now see ads by such individuals going beyond announcements of a new office location or the acquisition of a new partner. This variety of advertising is discussed in Chapter 20. Our concern here, however, is for advertising aimed *at* the professional person, not *by* him or her. This kind of advertising is known as **professional advertising.**

Professional advertising in many ways is similar to trade advertising, except that professionals do not buy goods for the purpose of reselling them to clients; their role is to prescribe or recommend to the client the purchase of certain products. The physician designates specific drugs through the pharmacist, and the dentist recommends a certain toothpaste. The architect specifies a brand of insulation material to be used in the house being built under his or her guidance.

Personal selling also is very important in reaching professional people. Manufacturer's sales representatives, called "detail men," go out into the field and talk about company products to doctors, dentists, and architects. Ads in professional journals, such as *Medical Economics* or *Architectural Record,* tell how the reader's client can benefit from the use of the product. Direct mail and product samples also are important in the promotional mix of such manufacturers. Because the professional's career success depends upon client satisfaction and does not result from the sale of specific goods, it is beneficial to keep abreast of the newest developments in the field. Professional journals and their advertising are must reading.

Other Ways to Classify Advertising

We have classified advertising by the kind of selling task facing the advertiser, and we have studied the essentials of national, retail, and business advertising. These explanations have revolved around *who sponsors the advertising.* Other classification systems emphasize the *strategy behind the advertising,* regardless of sponsorship. Several alternative approaches to advertising, many of which are used in combination by a typical advertiser, will now be discussed.

Primary- and Selective-Demand Advertising

The goal of **primary-demand** advertising is to stimulate a demand for a class or category or product, while **selective-demand** advertising attempts to create a demand for a particular brand in the product category. Per capita consumption of coffee is declining. Americans drank 2.75 cups per person daily in 1960, 2.37 cups in 1970, and only 1.87 cups in 1979. The United States Coffee Association, representing many coffee producers, is concerned about the situation and has sponsored intermittent campaigns to stimulate primary demand for coffee. At the same time, various brands of coffee—Maxwell House, Folgers, Hills Brothers—continue to seek larger shares of coffee sales through *selective-demand* advertising that stresses brand superiority.

The difference between the two kinds of advertising is shown in Figure 4.14 and Color Plate 3 (Kraft cheese). The American Dairy Association mounted a primary-demand stimulation with advertisements similar to the one shown in Figure 4.14; the objective was to increase cheese consumption in the United States regardless of the brand choice. A major processor of cheese, Kraft, tried, on the other hand, to persuade consumers to buy its brand when in the market for cheese.

Primary-demand strategy may be used when a new type of product is introduced. There is no direct competition, and the consuming public needs to be educated about the product's benefits. Mazda's advertising of its Wankel engine in the early 1970s is an example. To get a car with a rotary engine meant buying a Mazda, and so the ads simply stressed the revolutionary engine. More recently, we have experi-

Figure 4.14 Primary-demand stimulation for cheese is sought in this advertisement. The sponsor does not care which brand of cheese is purchased, only that consumption is increased.

enced an increased demand for mineral water as promoted by Perrier, and for food processors from Cuisinart.

In those rare cases in which the brand is heavily dominant in its share of the whole market for the product category, primary-demand appeals may also be featured. Campbell's Soup, with more than 90 percent of all condensed soup sales, stresses the idea of "soup for lunch" in its advertising, fully realizing that if primary demand for soup is thereby stimulated, the Campbell brand will benefit most by the increased sales. Generally speaking, however, the primary-demand stimulation strategy is inappropriate for most manufacturers, as the money spent helps competitors as well as the advertiser who pays the bill.

Product-Reputation and Corporate Advertising

Advertising aimed at promoting the sale of brand-name products is called **product-reputation advertising** and accounts for the bulk of advertising expenditures in the United States. There is, however, another class of advertising, variously called "institutional," "public relations," and "corporate advertising."

The overall objective of **corporate advertising,** as we choose to label it, is to create a favorable attitude, or image, toward the business sponsoring the advertising. One use of this strategy is to enhance the corporate image as a part of a broader public relations program. The many advertisements issued by the oil companies attempting to explain their position in the face of shortages and high profits provide good examples.

Another use of corporate advertising is to enhance the company's image by promoting good causes, as illustrated by the award-winning ad sponsored by Seagram's, the distillery (Figure 4.16). The goal of this advertisement is to show that the firm wants the public to realize that Seagram's, too, wishes its product to be used wisely; in other words, that the company is a good citizen.

The ultimate goal of corporate advertising may be to increase sales, but such diverse objectives as securing favorable legislative treatment, interest in the company by stockholders and investors, better labor relations, or goodwill in communities where plants are located may be sought. In sum, corporate advertising is designed to:

1 Enhance or maintain the company's reputation or goodwill among specific public or business audiences
2 Establish or maintain a level of awareness of the company's name and nature of business
3 Provide a unified and supportive marketing approach (umbrella) for a combination of present and future products and services
4 Educate the audience on subjects of importance to the company's future (for example, profits, free enterprise, economics)
5 Establish the company's concern for environmental or social issues
6 Bring about a change in specific attitudes of the audience toward the company or its products[5]

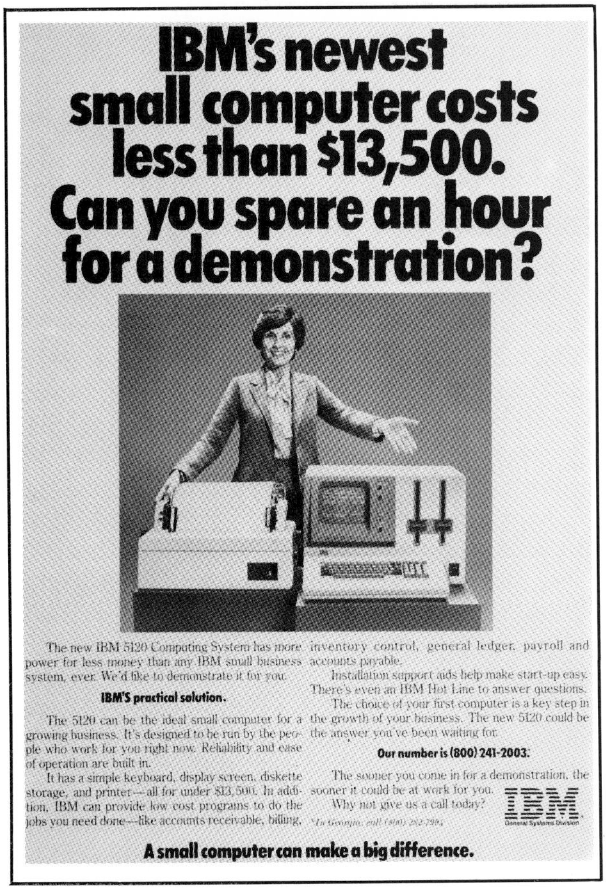

(*a*) (*b*)

Figure 4.15 A leading manufacturer engages in both product reputation and corporate advertising. The ad shown in part (*a*) presents the advantages of the product, while in part (*b*) the strengths of the company are highlighted. [*Courtesy of IBM.*]

Retail establishments may stress the institutional character of the stores, trying to build their store image. Most users of corporate advertising also engage in product-reputation advertising.

Push and Pull Advertising

Push strategy is aimed at middlemen with the goal of getting them to aggressively promote the manufacturer's brand to consumers. It can be used when consumers rely heavily on dealers for advice on product use. Thus, specialty stores often emphasize the push strategy with a lesser emphasis on advertising. The consumer picks a specific sporting-goods store, camera shop, or jeweler because of faith in its reputation and then buys what is stocked.

Pull strategy, in its extreme form, uses advertising to stimulate consumer demand to a sufficient degree to force retailers to stock the brand in order to please their customers. The promotional campaigns of most manufacturers, of course, are a blend of the two approaches. Deciding where to place the emphasis, however, is not always easy; the choice of approach depends on the nature of the product and the buying habits of consumers.

A knowledge of the essential differences between the various kinds of advertising is important. The terminology and the concepts are major communication tools throughout the advertising world.

Your guest is trying to tell you something.
Please listen.
The good host serves more than food and drink. He serves his guest.
By giving him his attention. By making him feel comfortable. By listening to what he wants... and doesn't want.
Next time your guest decides he's had enough, be a good enough host to take him at his word... or his sign. He'll think better of you for it.
Seagram
Distillers Company.

Figure 4.16 Seagram Distillers Company won an award from *Saturday Review* for this public-interest advertisement dealing with the dangers of excessive use of its product, thus showing the firm's good citizenship and public concern.

The Consumer's Role in the Advertising Process

The consumer, who is the receiver of advertising messages, should not be treated as a robot upon which the seller's desires are inflicted without resistance or complaint. Such an attitude is cynical and undesirable from a social point of view, as discussed in Chapter 2. It is also poor business practice, for it results in ineffective advertising.

Advertising is often an important factor in building satisfaction in the consumer's mind. It helps to interpret the want-satisfying characteristics of products in the framework of consumer wants and needs. Consumer orientation is important in all aspects of marketing, including advertising. This subject is examined rather thoroughly in Chapter 11 as a backdrop to the discussion dealing with the creation of advertising. However, we wish to point out, in general terms, how consumers think about ads and advertised products. Such attitudes are influential in the whole marketing communications process. The consumer's role in the distribution process to a large degree depends on how each person perceives and uses advertising.

Consumer View of Advertising

Some people feel that the consumer is a captive for advertising messages—exposed to them because there is no defense available from the onslaught. As the consumer employs the various media in search of entertainment or knowledge, the accompanying advertisements are absorbed through an osmosislike process and the advertising message penetrates the consciousness of the consumer, who then does the bidding of the manufacturer by purchasing the advertised product. Research, however, has shown that this view is not borne out in fact; consumers tend to be inattentive to most advertising and exercise a high degree of **selective perception.** This term describes a psychological pattern which indicates that of the vast amount of advertising being generated daily, consumers pay attention to only that which fits into their personal concerns. The remaining advertising messages are unreceived.

Source of Information On the other hand, the consumer often seeks out advertising in a positive, searching manner. Obvious examples might include newspaper classified advertising, yellow page advertising, fashion ads in women's magazines, and retail grocery advertising. When the consumer is acting as the family buying agent, for example, the market is searched for products that are needed. The real role of advertising in the consumer's life thus emerges as summarized in the following quotation:

> Advertising tells the consumer what's available; offers a parade of suggestions on how she may spend her money; and gives the freedom to accept or reject these options as she wishes.[6]

The consumer thus uses advertising as a **source of information.**

Time-Saver Advertising also can serve as a **time-saver** for the consumer. Once a person knows what he or she wants to buy, where to obtain the item is the next step in the buying process. Retail advertising tells the local source of the product. National advertising itself can save the consumer's time by assisting in the preselection process; instead of shopping every furniture store in the city, the consumer can analyze ads of furniture manufacturers and narrow the choice to two or three brands, which then may be examined in retail-store showrooms. The increasing number of families consisting of two working adults, with the consequent shortening of time available for in-store shopping, should lead to more use of advertising as a time-saver.

Assurance of Quality If a manufacturer invests large sums of money in advertising the quality of the product, it is only logical for the consumer to feel that the product must be of good quality. The surest way to make a product fail quickly is to advertise successfully an inferior product; after being given one trial followed by no repeat purchases, a product will soon be yanked from retailer shelves. When the consumer's choice is between a brand well known because of familiarity through continuous advertising and an unknown product, picking the known product is the natural reaction. Thus, advertising serves the consumer as an **assurance of quality,** which can be an important service when the multiplicity of products and brands is contemplated.

Source of Entertainment Lastly, ads are a **source of entertainment.** In one survey, approximately 20 percent of the population listed entertainment value as a consumer benefit derived from advertising.[7] One frequent comment is that television commercials are better than the programming. Of course, the money spent on a 30-second commercial is usually much greater than the cost of an equal time segment of program material. Although some specific advertising may irritate some consumers, much advertising relies on an entertaining approach to attract consumer attention and interest to the advertising message.

Consumer Attitude toward Products

The consumer's mental attitude toward a product passes through several stages while taking in advertising messages. These possible mental attitudes can be thought of as a hierarchy of effects. The least desirable attitude — other than outright dislike — that a consumer can have toward the manufacturer's brand is one of **ignorance** or unawareness. Awareness of the product is the first rung on the ladder of product success, and a great deal of advertising is aimed at achieving a state of product awareness in the minds of consumers. **Knowledge** is present when consumers possess some facts about the product and its benefits. **Acceptance** is a step higher; now consumers will buy the brand as readily as any other brand offered for sale. **Preference** exists when the brand is desired over other offerings. **Insistence** means that the advertised brand is at the top of the product attitude scale; no substitute brand will be considered.

The advertiser may aim at any one of these levels, depending upon consumers' attitudes toward the product. If it is new, the advertiser may wish to achieve a degree of awareness among the buying public. If the product is quite similar to competitive products, the advertiser's goal may be brand acceptance only. In order to move into the preference and insistence stages, the advertiser aims at product differentiation. Most advertising does not seek direct action; therefore, actual purchase rarely can be attributed to advertising alone. A knowledge of why consumers refer to advertisements and an understanding of the mental processes going on in the consumer's mind cannot be stressed too strongly. The consumer is at the end of the marketing process, and *good advertising must be customer-oriented.*

Summary

Business users of advertising need to understand its impact on the overall performance of their firms. Advertising can favorably affect products by helping to expand the demand for them. Similarly, advertising can affect profits by reducing production expenses and other marketing costs, once demand is increased and the advantages of economies of scale are achieved.

In a more specific way, advertising can help achieve varied communication goals such as:

1 Induce product trial
2 Intensify product usage
3 Sustain brand preference
4 Confirm brand imagery
5 Change consumption habits
6 Build line acceptance
7 Break ice for the salesperson
8 Build ambience for the retail outlet

National advertising familiarizes consumers with the product so that it will be sought, or at least recognized, in the retail store. This class of advertising is sponsored by the manufacturers of branded products. Retail advertising, in contrast, aims at getting consumers to patronize a specific retail store. Retail advertisers emphasize the retail outlet rather than the brand. Local advertising is done by service establishments in a community. The strategy behind local advertising is similar to that of national advertising. A plan to share promotional responsibilities between a manufacturer of a certain brand and the retailer selling that brand is called cooperative advertising.

Business advertising comprises four major subgroups: (1) trade advertising, which attempts to persuade retailers to stock the advertiser's merchandise; (2) industrial advertising, which is aimed at getting other businesses to use the advertiser's products in carrying out their business functions; (3) farm advertising, which communicates with farmers in their roles as producers and consumers; and (4) professional advertising, which seeks to have the advertiser's products recommended by professional people to their clients.

Advertising is used to stimulate primary or selective demand. Most advertising seeks to enhance the reputation of the product, although corporate advertising is used when company reputation is given precedence over the product in the firm's advertising strategy. Promotional programs may stress a push approach or a pull approach.

There are at least four ways in which the consumer uses advertising: (1) as a source of information, (2) as a time-saver, (3) as an assurance of quality, and (4) as a source of entertainment. The advertiser should keep the consumer uppermost in mind when planning advertising.

Questions for Discussion

1 Why do many manufacturers prefer promotional strategies over price concessions as devices to lubricate the channels of distribution?
2 What are the general objectives of advertising? How do they differ from specific objectives of advertising?
3 Bring three magazine advertisements from current issues to class, each illustrating the three different ways that demand for goods and services can be expanded. Write a short statement showing the reasons for your choices.
4 What is the fundamental difference between (*a*) national and retail advertising, (*b*) product reputation and corporate advertising, (*c*) primary-demand stimulation and selective-demand stimulation, (*d*) push and pull strategies?
5 When does a manufacturer use each of the following forms of business advertising: (*a*) trade advertising, (*b*) industrial advertising, (*c*) professional advertising?
6 Keep a log for three days, noting your personal use of advertising in your own purchase behavior. Categorize each example according to the four uses discussed in the chapter.
7 What is cooperative advertising? At whose initiative is a program of this nature started? Why?
8 What is local advertising? Bring a page from your newspaper showing a good example of its use in your city.
9 Paul Harper gives three product examples (pages 787–790) for each of the eight ways that advertising can aid the business when it is communicating with the marketplace. Cite another example for each category.
10 Name an advertising campaign that appears to be striving for awareness among consumers; for preference; for insistence.

For Further Reference

Colley, Russell H.: *Defining Advertising Goals for Measured Advertising Results,* Association of National Advertisers, Inc., New York, 1961.

Darling, Harry L.: *Current Company Objectives and Practices in the Use of Corporate Advertising,* Association of National Advertisers, Inc., New York, 1975.

DeLozier, M. Wayne: *The Marketing Communications Process,* McGraw-Hill Book Company, New York, 1976.

Engel, James F., Martin R. Warshaw, and Thomas C. Kinnear: *Promotional Strategy: Managing the Marketing Communications Process,* 4th ed., Richard D. Irwin, Inc., Homewood, Ill., 1979.

Kotler, Philip: *Marketing Management: Analysis, Planning and Control,* 4th ed., Prentice-Hall, Inc., Englewood Cliffs, N.J., 1980.

Roman, Kenneth, and Jane Maas: *How to Advertise: A Professional Guide for the Advertiser,* St. Martin's Press, New York, 1976.

Schewe, Charles D., and Reuben M. Smith: *Marketing: Concepts and Applications,* McGraw-Hill Book Company, New York, 1980.

Schwartz, David J.: *Marketing Today,* 3d ed., Harcourt Brace Jovanovich, New York, 1981.

Stanton, William J.: *Fundamentals of Marketing,* 6th ed., McGraw-Hill Book Company, New York, 1981.

End Notes

[1] Russell H. Colley, "Squeezing the Waste out of Advertising," *Harvard Business Review,* September-October 1962, p. 76.

[2] Russell H. Colley, *Defining Advertising Goals for Measured Advertising Results,* Association of National Advertisers, Inc., New York, 1961.

[3] Paul C. Harper, "What Advertising Can and Cannot Do," presentation to the 1976 Marketing Conference of The Conference Board, The Conference Board, 1976. Used by permission.

[4] *How Advertising Works in Today's Marketplace,* McGraw-Hill Book Company, New York, 1971, p. 5.

[5] Harry L. Darling, *Current Company Objectives and Practices in the Use of Corporate Advertising,* Association of National Advertisers, Inc., New York, 1975, pp. 6–7.

[6] *What Does Advertising Do for the Consumer?* U.S. Department of Commerce, National Business Council for Consumer Affairs, 1972, p. 8.

[7] Rena Bartos, "The Consumer View of Advertising—1974," talk before the 1975 Annual Meeting of the American Association of Advertising Agencies, March 1975, p. 43.

Chapter 5

The Business of Advertising

● Once an organization decides to advertise, it requires a system to achieve the communication goals set for its advertising program. These goals may be to launch a new product, to increase consumer awareness of the product, or any of the goals discussed in Chapter 4. Top management of the firm will set the budget for the advertising program. Then the firm's advertising department, under the leadership of its manager, takes on the responsibility for following through and creating a program that meets these goals through effective advertising.

The advertising department will often rely on outside experts to perform many of the tasks involved in launching an advertising program. An advertising agency is used to help plan the strategy and prepare advertising copy, art, and commercials. The agency then places the advertising messages in various media, such as magazines, newspapers, radio, TV, or outdoor posters. Other businesses, known as special-service groups, are used in the production of advertising. These include printers, photographers, models, camera operators, and similar specialists. Because the media part of advertising is so diverse and complex, we devote all of Part 3 to an analysis of each major advertising medium. This chapter looks closely at each of the first three subareas of the business of advertising.

The Advertiser: Organizing for Advertising Decision Making

American businesses spend more than $60 billion each year to advertise their products and services. As noted in Chapters 2 and 4, businesses must maintain or increase their sales levels to remain successful in the marketplace. Many firms rely on advertising to keep their products in the public eye, and they are willing to incur the costs that advertising entails because it is an efficient method of communicating with buyers of their product offerings. Because so many individuals are needed to execute an advertising campaign, it is easy to exceed the advertising budget set by upper management. Therefore, it is important to manage an advertising program carefully to prevent cost overruns. Advertising should *contribute* to profits—not waste them.

Figure 5.1 shows where the advertising function is placed within the organizational structure of the typical American manufacturing firm. Advertising is one of the subareas of marketing. This arrangement reflects the policy of specialization of labor, whereby tasks are divided into smaller units in order to get the best possible performance by persons who are best qualified to perform tasks assigned to them.

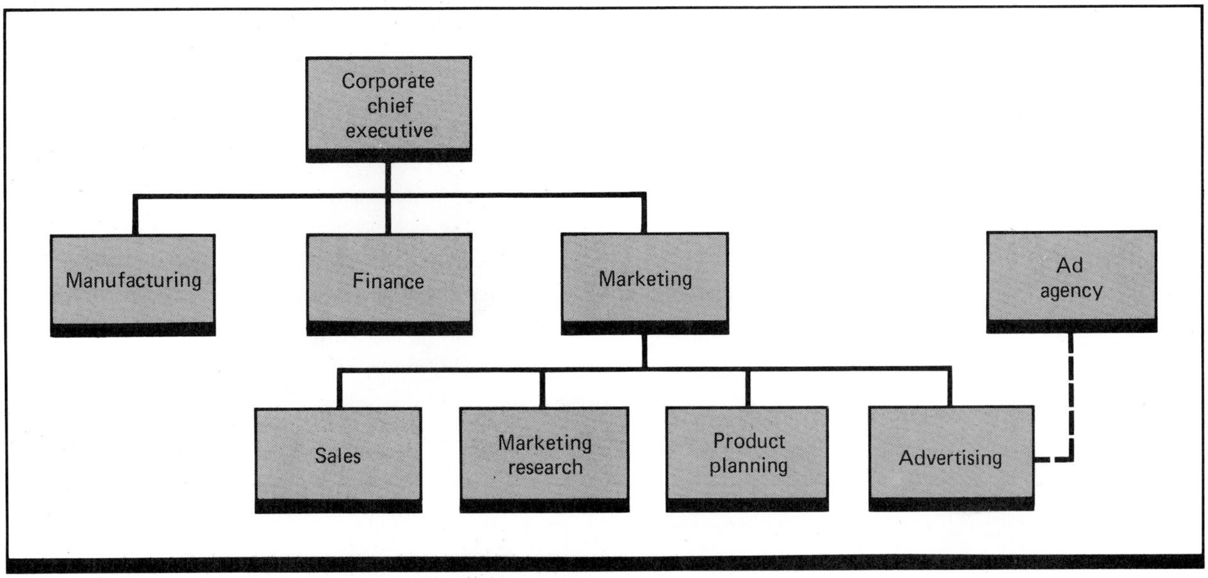

Figure 5.1 Advertising is a part of the marketing function in a typical firm. The dashed line to the advertising agency means that it is not really a part of the company's organizational structure. Nevertheless, the agency is important to the operation of the advertising department.

The Advertising Department

The advertising manager and the department staff perform two main functions: (1) planning the advertising program and (2) maintaining liaison with the advertising agency.

The advertising manager is responsible for the overall planning of the advertising program, including such decisions as which products to advertise, which markets to be reached, and whether to employ an outside agency. The manager also maintains this program within the financial and public relations guidelines set down by corporate management. Corporate management must be advised about advertising policy decisions, since they may affect the corporate image and sales potential of the company.

Most corporate firms hire an advertising agency to provide the communication messages for the advertising program. The firm's advertising manager serves as the liaison person, operating between the corporation that is paying for the advertising and the advertising agency that is creating and placing it. The advertising manager makes certain that the execution of the program, which is the responsibility of the agency, is carried out within company policy and philosophy. He or she is consulted by the agency as advertising messages are being developed and media choices are being made. The manager is responsible to the company management for the progress being made in carrying out the advertising program—that is, for the maintenance of schedules for the appearance of ads. If it is believed that the agency is not doing good work, a change in agency may be recommended to company management.

Creative work may be done within the advertising department, especially point-of-purchase materials, brochures, and other advertising not appearing in established media. Furthermore, some companies do their own media buying. Recently, some advertisers have elected to create more of their own advertising under an in-house arrangement. This development will be discussed after we have explained the operation of the advertising agency.

Internal Structure of the Advertising Department The work performed by the company's advertising department is divided into manageable units so that the advantages of specialization of labor are attained. One commonly used plan of organization is to divide the work according to the **subfunctions** of advertising, with separate departments re-

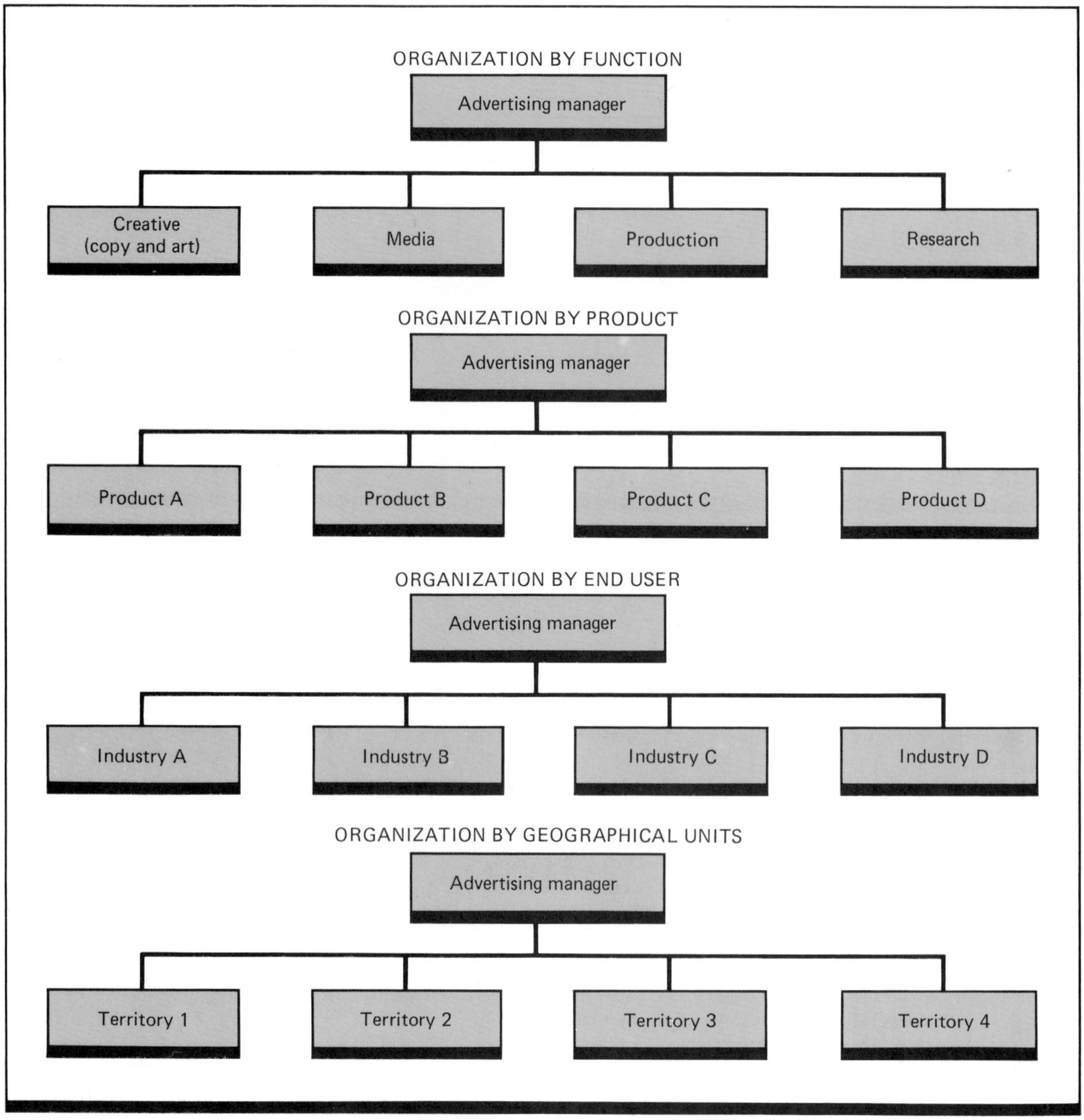

Figure 5.2 The advertising department may be organized by function, product, industry, or territory.

sponsible for ad creation, media selection, research, and advertising production. A similar division can be made by **product.** In multiple-line firms, advertising personnel may be assigned similar responsibilities for specific products or brands that are made by the company.

An alternative organization for a company's internal advertising structure is based on **end users.** One large manufacturer of medical supplies, for example, divides its advertising department into two major groups, one to handle the surgical dressings, tapping medical doctors and hospital users, and the other to handle baby products, reaching consumer markets. This alignment may appear to be a breakdown based on product class, but it is more truly a division by product end user. Major petroleum marketers pro-

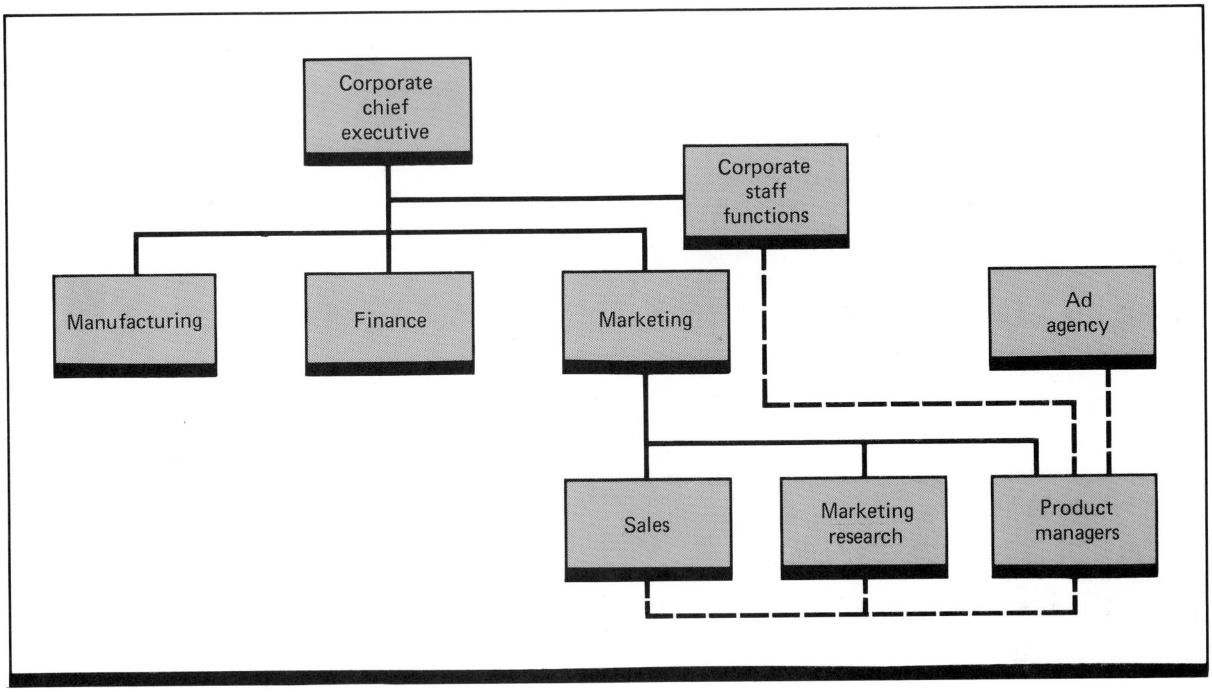

Figure 5.3 How the arrangement shown in Figure 5.1 changes when the firm adopts the product manager system is shown on this chart.

vide another example of organization of advertising by end user. Separate executives, at both the headquarters staff and the regional and divisional-line marketing levels, supervise motor fuels and lubricants sales through retail service stations and to fleet owners, to the commercial aviation market, and to the marine field. Their advertising programs are similarly organized.

Another way of dividing the advertising tasks is on the basis of **geographical units.** A major brewery divides the advertising responsibilities among seven divisional advertising managers. Each manager has the advertising responsibility for one of the firm's seven major sales territories. These organizational patterns are illustrated in Figure 5.2.

Product Managers

The **advertising manager system** just described is not the universal way of organizing the advertising activity. In many firms it has been replaced by the **product manager system** especially when the product line consists of consumer packaged goods such as soap, cigarettes, toothpaste, and soft drinks. The product manager, having particular knowledge of the product (brand), is the executive responsible for all marketing activities pertaining to it, including advertising.

The product manager system came into general use in the 1950s when management experts felt that as companies became larger and produced and sold multiple brands, individual products and brands tended to lose management attention. The system, which was nurtured by Procter & Gamble, became popular with packaged goods manufacturers; by the early 1970s, nearly 90 percent of these firms used this way of managing their advertising programs.[1]

Under the product manager system, the advertising department and the advertising manager are replaced by one or more product managers who "run the brand." The organizational pattern used in a typical situation is shown in Figure 5.3.

Product managers make three kinds of operating decisions. (1) They decide on the advertising strategies needed to achieve the advertising plan's objectives. (2) They make the creative and media decisions to implement this plan. (3) They manage the advertising budget. Policy decisions, on the other hand, that involve issues that affect the public's feelings about a company, its divisions, and brands are made at management levels above the product manager.[2]

Figure 5.4 Product managers meet with advertising agency representatives to discuss advertising strategy. [*Courtesy of General Foods Corporation.*]

The Retail-Store Advertising Department

Both the function and the structure of retail-store advertising departments differ materially from those of the typical manufacturer's advertising department. Most retail firms do not employ the services of an advertising agency. There are many reasons why they do not, but an important one is economic. Since some advertising media do not allow commissions on retail or local advertising, the retail store that wishes to use an agency must pay the agency a fee approximating 20 percent of its advertising expenditure in order to compensate the agency for handling its work. Therefore, many retail firms maintain their own advertising departments, whose functions are considerably broader than those of their counterparts in a manufacturing firm.

The time factor in retailing is also important. Often there is a need for last-minute changes in retail copy. Weather conditions may cause the cancellation of an overcoat sale or call for prompt promotion of swimwear or air conditioners. Special purchases or a delay in the arrival of merchandise may bring about an urgent need for promptness in altering media schedules or advertising content. Processing advertising through a third party such as an advertising agency would reduce the flexibility which retailers who have their own advertising departments enjoy. Moreover, the greater variety of products which many retail stores wish to advertise would place a heavy burden on the personnel of an advertising agency working on the retailer's account. Someone from the agency might well have to stay right on the spot if the needs of the retail advertiser were to be fully served.

Thus, most large retail outlets feel they can do the job more economically—and possibly better—through the use of their own personnel. Retail advertising departments are more heavily involved in the creative function of advertising than departments maintained by national advertisers. Copywriting, artwork, and production are all done internally. The retail-store advertising manager must still plan the advertising program, but has no external liaison function to perform. On the other hand, the manager must maintain close contact with the various selling departments of the store. Good advertising requires a feel for the merchandise being featured, and this comes only from familiarity with the products and the people who sell them.

In a sense, the retail-store advertising department is a company-owned advertising agency serving only one client. Many retail advertising departments are, in fact, bigger than most advertising agencies. The variety of media employed is often more limited, with newspapers holding the dominant position in the media mix. Small retail stores obviously cannot maintain separate advertising departments. Occasionally, the owner or one of the major executives will handle the advertising responsibilities. It is common to turn over the creative function to sales representatives from newspapers and television and radio stations. However, it is becoming increasingly popular for small retailers to hire advertising agencies.

The Advertising Agency

The folklore of glamour and excitement surrounding the advertising agency is more myth than fact and should not cause us to underestimate the agency's very real and important role in modern advertising. A full-service agency has many similarities to a large medical clinic. Each has a variety of specialists operating as a group under business management for profit objectives. In place of internists, orthopedists, radiologists, and the many other professionals found in a clinic, the advertising agency has writers, artists, media experts, researchers, television producers, account executives, and other experts. Agency specialists work together to analyze the advertiser firm's condition in the marketplace and prescribe a course of action designed to keep the business healthy. Advertising specialists, unlike medical doctors, compound their own prescriptions by developing appropriate advertising plans and strategies and by creating advertisements and media plans to carry out those strategies.

Evolution of the Advertising Agency[3]

In our discussion of the advertising department, we have mentioned several times that the advertiser may well utilize the services of the advertising agency. We have noted that the agency then has the responsibility for creating and placing advertising messages and is useful in planning the strategy underlying the advertising campaign. Present-day operations of the advertising agency are better understood, in our opinion, if you know something about how it developed as a business institution. All institutions adapt to their environments, changing as conditions change. This is true in the case of the advertising agency, whose evolution from 1840 to the 1980s is traced in this section.

Space Broker Stage Around 1840 various individuals began to act as sales representatives for out-of-town newspapers in such metropolitan centers as New York and Philadelphia. At first, these people acted as simple agents selling space for their client newspapers on a commission basis. Later on, some would buy a set number of pages from a given newspaper and then resell portions at whatever price could be obtained from advertisers. This has been called the **space broker stage** in the evolution of the modern advertising agency. The arrangement led to price cutting as advertisers sought the lowest possible price. There was little emphasis on advertising planning by the agent, or on the development of the best possible media schedule. Inefficiency characterized advertising at this time.

Standard Services Stage In 1876, the N. W. Ayer & Son agency devised a plan which eventually minimized the dubious practice of brokering advertising space. Ayer entered into agreements with advertisers whereby they promised to place all their advertising through the agency. In return, the agency bought space for its clients only at established rates as published by newspapers and magazines. Thus, the agent became a buyer representing the best interests of the advertiser instead of a seller of space for the publisher.

As this arrangement became adopted generally, agencies, in the competitive struggle for clients, started to take on duties now considered normal—campaign planning, copywriting, artwork, layout, media selection, and research. Before 1900, the Ayer agency had established departments for both copywriting and artwork, and the **standard services stage** in the evolution of the advertising agency had begun. Over the next several decades, advertising agencies improved the quality of their services to clients and added more services.

Agency Recognition Policy One additional change had to take place, however, before the climate for agency development was right. Some agencies were rebating part of their commissions to clients, and in 1901 the Curtis Publishing Company promulgated its **agency recognition policy** to combat the rebate practice. Curtis stated that its magazines would no longer accept advertisements coming from agencies known to be rebating commissions to their clients. All agencies had to charge advertisers the rates prescribed by the publications. The result of this policy was that an advertiser would divert every effort from trying to get a rebate to finding the agency that would provide the most and best services. The cost would be the same. Curtis further stated that commissions would be granted only to recognized agencies. Direct placement of advertising by the advertiser would not be permitted, or at least the advertiser would not be able to collect a commission from the medium. The only sensible course of action for a national advertiser thereafter was to use an advertising agency. The question "*Should* we use an agency?" became "*Which* agency should we use?"

Marketing Services Stage Once these favorable changes had become permanently entrenched, the growth of advertising agencies was rapid. Of course, industrial expansion in the United States was an important factor in this growth. By 1950, agencies were offering more varied and highly skilled services to the client, taking consumer psychology into account when creating ads, as well as furthering the role of advertising in the marketing mix by coordinating it with other marketing procedures. Advertising agencies thus entered into the **marketing services stage** from which evolved the so-called full-service agency, which is representative of most large advertising agencies in the United States today.

Functions of the Full-Service Agency

The overriding function of the advertising agency is to see that its client's advertising leads to greater profits in the long run than could be achieved without the agency. The agency thus plans, prepares, and places advertising to this end. The customer is the key, and the agency supplies an "outside" point of view to aid the advertiser in the firm's efforts to communicate with prospective purchasers of its product. The distinguishing characteristics between various advertising agencies lie in the creative skills of the personnel of each organization and in the philosophies of advertising held by each agency. The agency size may be a significant factor in its effectiveness, as, generally speaking, the larger agency is in a position to offer more services. Smaller agencies argue, however, that they can give more personalized service to their clients.

Advertising Planning As discussed earlier, the advertising manager has the responsibility for planning the advertising program. In effect, a portion of that responsibility is delegated to the advertising agency when one is used. And, of course, in addition to assisting in the development of the advertising plan itself, the agency must do considerable planning in carrying out its own functions of creating and placing advertising. A thorough knowledge of the firm's products, its past advertising history, present market conditions, and the firm's distribution methods is critical if the agency is to do an effective job. The agency also needs to know a great deal about the product—its pluses and minuses—as compared with competitive products. A successful advertising program is built on a good product, and the advertising theme is created in accordance with how the advertiser wishes to position the product in the consumer's mind.

In order to gain the information needed, the agency engages in extensive research into the market for the client's product. Products come and go in the dynamic marketplace of our economy. To market a product successfully, market studies are conducted to ascertain the extent of the market for the product —who buys it, when, where, how, and why. Correct direction and timing of advertising campaigns are aided by such marketing information, as is the advertising message. Competitors' activities are also important.

In planning the advertising for a particular product, the agency analyzes marketing methods and distribution channels used in the past for the product in order to obtain specific information about the business environment in which the advertising message is to operate. The advertising must be relevant to the present (that is, fit conditions as they are) and of such a nature that it is aesthetically acceptable to the consumer and to the trade.

The agency knows the character of each advertising medium, in addition to audience figures and comparative costs. The advertising message must be adapted to the medium in which it is to appear. For example, the product advertisement to be heard on the radio probably will be different from the advertising message with visual impact which appears on television. The print media offer opportunities for longer messages. Different advertising media do have varying impacts on different segments of the market for specific products. The agency knows the physical requirements of each medium and creates ads that fit the space or time requirements of the medium.

From this background of product, market, distribution, and media knowledge, the agency can recommend strategies for presenting the product to prospective buyers. These ideas are submitted to the client for approval. Upon approval of the strategies, the agency is ready to carry them out—to create the ads and place them. In addition, a full-service agency can provide many other marketing services to its clients: for example, it can conduct postadvertising market studies to evaluate the effectiveness of the campaign.

Creation and Execution Media choices are made before the ads are created. Contracts are made with the media selected. Specific advertisements are created. Copy is written; layouts are done; illustrations are drawn or photographed; the advertising messages are prepared in correct mechanical form for running in the selected media; and commercials are produced. Once the messages have been published or aired, the agency verifies the fact, pays the media, and bills the client.

Coordination Before the ad campaign breaks, the agency often works with the client's sales force and distribution network to ensure the long-run success of the advertising program. Maximum sales from the combined efforts of salespersons, distributors, and retailers—all assisted by advertising—are the goal.

Although the agency relieves the client of many details involved in advertising, the client still makes the major decisions, as pointed out earlier. One fundamental decision is whether to advertise or not. Once the decision to advertise is made, the client chooses an advertising agency. Large advertisers may engage a number of different agencies to handle various brands in their product line. Thereafter, decisions are concerned with the strategy to be used in the advertising program. The ideas of the agency are approved, modified, or disapproved. The following section describes the personnel in typical advertising agencies. By looking at agency personnel and their work, we get a more complete idea of what an advertising agency does.

Agency People and Their Work

In large agencies, advertising specialists are assigned to specific tasks in the preparation of ads or the performance of other services. The discussion that follows is designed to help you gain an understanding of these tasks.

Account Management Keeping the client satisfied with the services rendered is of paramount importance to the business success of the advertising agency. This is the primary duty of the account executive, who acts as a liaison between agency and advertising department (advertiser) personnel. The account executive often works on the formulation of the advertising strategy in cooperation with the client. Regardless of the source of the strategy, the account executives must see that the agency keeps to the stated plan. The account executive represents the client by explaining the advertiser's point of view to all agency personnel working on the account, and also represents the agency point of view to the client. The job, therefore, calls for diplomacy and tact. Merely representing the two sides of the agency-client relationship and keeping the channels of communication open in the relationship is not all there is to account management. The account executive is in charge of the administration of the advertising program on the agency side, thus serving as the catalyst in bringing out the best in the agency's creative talent.

The brunt of all misunderstandings arising between the agency and the client is borne by the account executive. If the job of carrying out the advertising plan is mishandled, the account may be lost. Occasionally, an account executive may leave the employment of one agency and take an account along to another agency. One of the qualities which an agency seeks in hiring an account executive, therefore, is loyalty to the agency.[4]

Creative Department Once advertising plans are firm, advertisements are designed by creative personnel to carry out the plan. An agency retains a varied group of creative people, including writers, artists, designers, television producers, and graphic arts specialists. The creative function may be under one department, or it may be divided into several separate departments, such as copy, art, broadcast, and production.

Creativity is not a mechanical technique. It involves a novel or infrequent expression, response, or concept. Creativity in advertising must be oriented to and correlated with the marketing situation and serve as a communication problem solver. Advertising creativity has been described as presenting a product in a way that makes people want to buy it. This creativity often goes beyond the creation of physical properties called advertisements; an agency may recommend new products, different distribution methods, or a distinctive selling idea. The outside point of view shines through in these recommendations. The ideal agency has personnel who can generate new marketing and communication ideas.

Media Selection Another highly specialized agency function is media selection. The goal of media people in the agency is to choose the advertising medium—or combination of media—that will do the most effective job of reaching the client's prospects. Securing the right audience is the most important factor in media choices, but decisions, of course, are affected by costs. From a maze of statistical data concerning rates, circulations, populations, audiences, incomes, and other relevant information, the most productive assortment of advertising media is chosen.

Research A major service performed by advertising agency people is research to support the decisions made in the creative and media areas. The gathering of factual information is often a specialized agency function. Data on the marketplace and consumer buying habits may be gathered and analyzed. The agency may also arrange for copytesting during the creation of ad campaigns and after they have been run.

Internal Control and Other Services Every business must manage its finances, personnel, and office staff. Every advertising agency contains an administrative arm which conducts routine, behind-the-scenes business operations because it is a business enterprise. In addition, it is essential that individual jobs be coordinated and done on time, since deadlines must be met. This function is performed by a specialized traffic department. Furthermore, larger agencies often have a legal department to pass on the advertisements created by the agency; smaller agencies rely on law firms for such advice. Some agencies maintain merchandising departments; others provide public relations services for clients.

Agency Administration

The management of an advertising agency provides true challenges for agency executives. In addition to the usual problems of organizational structure, there are the challenges of securing new business and maintaining relationships with clients.

Organizational Structure Formal organizational structures are needed in any business with multifunctional activities. How large advertising agencies organize their personnel to bring about better delegation of authority and to facilitate coordination of activities is shown in Figure 5.5. Smaller agencies do not have such elaborate organizational structures, but they usually provide the same functions, sometimes through delegation to special-service groups.

The structure of the advertising agency can be arranged in one of two basic ways: on a **departmentalized basis** or on a **group basis.** Under the departmentalized form (typical of small agencies), all major departments, including copy, art, media, production, and research, are available to each account executive to use in carying out each client's ad program. In the group approach (used by most large agencies), specific individuals are assigned to a team, which does the planning, creative work, media buying, and similar activities for client assigned to the group. Other groups, or teams, handle different accounts. In effect, several small agencies are created within the framework of the large agency.

Many agencies maintain plans boards, or review boards, in order to reassure clients that they are receiving the benefit of the best minds in the agencies. A plans board consists of departmental heads, or senior specialists, representing the major departments of the agency. The plans board meets with the account executive to review, criticize, and make suggestions on both the overall strategy and the specific tactics to be used in a client's advertising.

Administrative personnel give direction to departmental operations. Thus, there is a creative (copy) director, art director, research director, media director, office manager, and so forth. The typical agency has a president charged with the responsibility of seeing that the agency operates in a businesslike fashion. A large agency is likely to have a president and a board of directors, and possibly, an executive committee to set policy. Agency stock may be held privately by key executives or sold to the general public.

New Business Our discussion of agency administration so far has dwelled, as it should, on client service. However, top management has another vital duty—to get new business. Agencies grow in two ways: (1) by growing with their present accounts, and (2) by adding new accounts. The first method involves doing good work for the clients and relying on increased business from these accounts. The second method involves acquisition of new advertising programs. The agency management acts as the sales department for the agency.

The importance of adding new accounts to the agency roster is apparent when you consider the

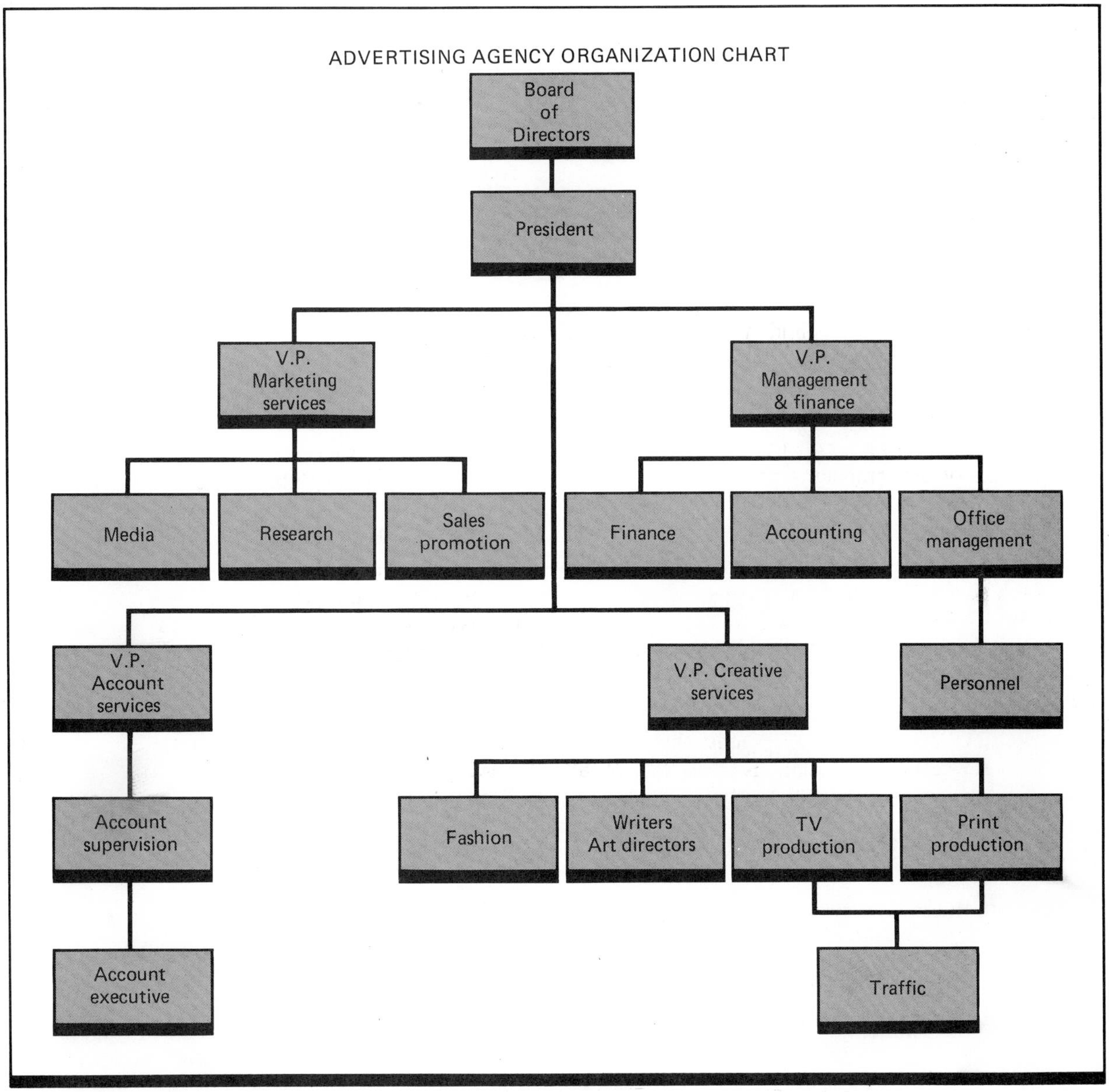

Figure 5.5 An advertising agency divides its work into smaller parts to provide for specialization of labor. [*American Association of Advertising Agencies.*]

turnover of accounts experienced by some agencies. For example, account shifts amount to $500 million in a typical year. Clients change agencies when they feel another agency may do a better job or offer fresh ideas. An agency can become the scapegoat when the client's sales volume falls, regardless of whether advertising is the cause or not. Agencies may resign accounts where there is a lack of compatibility between the advertiser and agency personnel. Furthermore, it is customary in the United States for an agency not to represent competing advertisers; such agency conflicts may lead to an agency's resigning an account in order to take on a larger one in the same product category. On the other hand, many large clients have been with the same agencies for generations. For example, Hammerhill Paper Company has been a client of Batten, Barton, Durstine and Osborn (BBDO) since 1912.

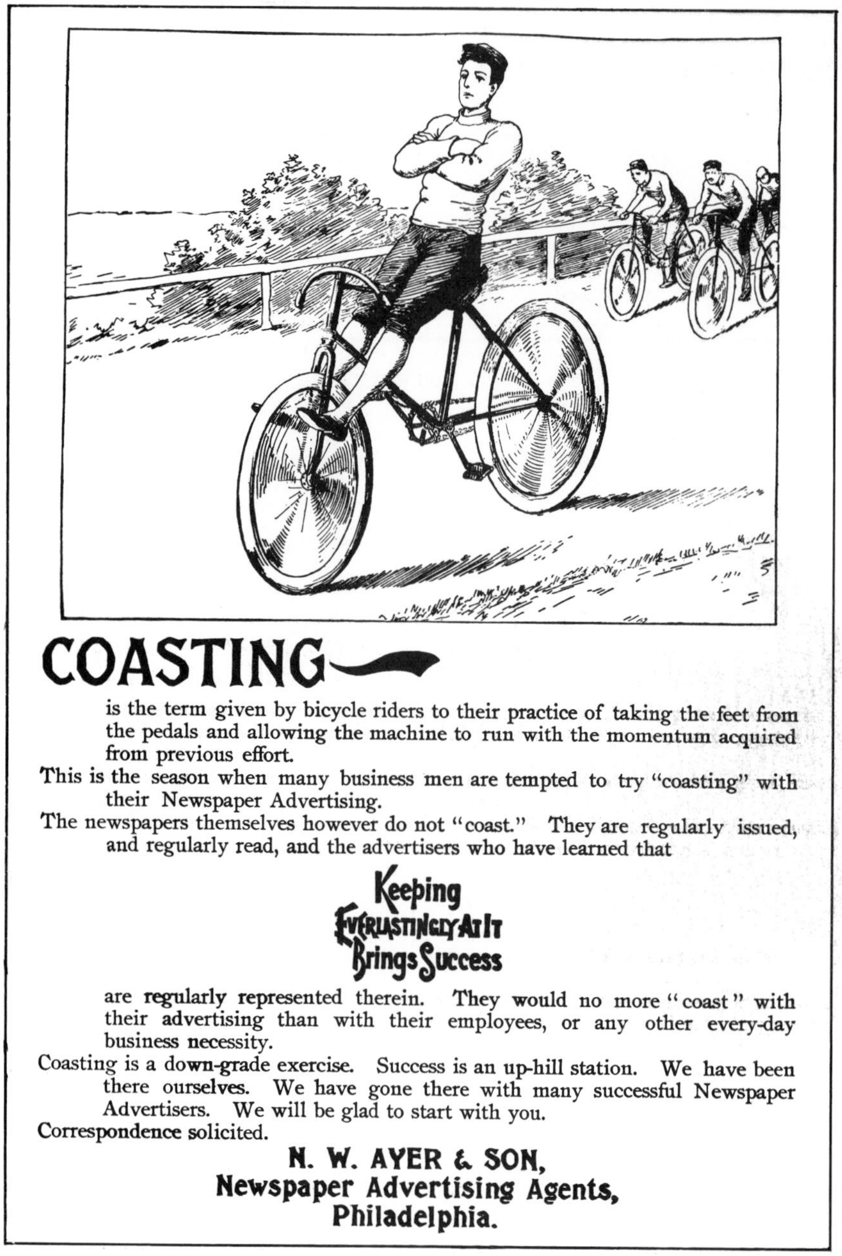
COASTING
is the term given by bicycle riders to their practice of taking the feet from the pedals and allowing the machine to run with the momentum acquired from previous effort.
This is the season when many business men are tempted to try "coasting" with their Newspaper Advertising.
The newspapers themselves however do not "coast." They are regularly issued, and regularly read, and the advertisers who have learned that
Keeping Everlastingly At It Brings Success
are regularly represented therein. They would no more "coast" with their advertising than with their employees, or any other every-day business necessity.
Coasting is a down-grade exercise. Success is an up-hill station. We have been there ourselves. We have gone there with many successful Newspaper Advertisers. We will be glad to start with you.
Correspondence solicited.
N. W. AYER & SON,
Newspaper Advertising Agents,
Philadelphia.

Figure 5.6 Advertising agencies have advertised for many years. This 1893 ad was designed to encourage media buying.

Executives charged with the responsibility of getting business must know the politics of advertising intimately. Knowledge of impending changes in agency-client agreements, awareness of dissatisfactions building up between clients and agencies, and the like provide leads for approaching prospective clients. Some agencies aggressively solicit new business; others discuss the possibility only on invitation. Agencies themselves engage in advertising for new business, as shown in Figures 5.6 and 5.7.

Selling an agency's services to a client involves making a "presentation," which is a description of the agency's personnel, resources, present accounts, and successes. The agency may be making the presentation singly or in competition with other agencies. Often prospective clients require that a "speculative presentation" be made. In these presentations, agency executives show how the account will be handled if it is given to this agency. The costs of such presentations can amount to tens of thou-

Overheard at Intermission.
"Wasn't it magnificent?"
"You mean the flute solo?"
"No, I mean the coup for I.C. Light Beer."
"Ah, yes. The brewer says advertising has put the brand on top in town among the Lights. Local agency, I hear."
"True. But also national. And international. In fact, part of the largest agency in the U.S."
"With a creative staff here?"
"Creative indeed."
"How nice for Pittsburgh."
"How nice for Pittsburgh Brewing."
Marsteller Inc.
ADVERTISING/PUBLIC RELATIONS/MARKETING/SALES PROMOTION
600 GRANT STREET, PITTSBURGH, PA 15219 • (412) 456-2500

Figure 5.7 This house ad for the Pittsburgh office of a major advertising agency appeared in the Pittsburg Symphony and Ballet programs and the Pittsburgh Ad Club directory.

sands of dollars for creative efforts and demonstration materials. Some agency executives feel that advertisers may merely use the device to pick the brains of competing agency personnel. The practice is expensive in time and money, and, as in other business practices, there is no assurance that a competing agency will win the account. Some agencies prefer to stand on their reputation of past performances as the principal means of securing new clients. In any event, the function of getting business must be handled well if an agency is to grow and prosper. The senior executives in the agency, therefore, nearly always are active in this facet of agency operations. Often, the top executive of the agency, having strength in acquiring new business, participates in this endeavor.

Client-Agency Relationship No concept is more sacred to the advertising world than the paramount importance of the client-agency relationship. Carl Spielvogel stated the idea thus: "There is no other industry where the prosperity of a service company, and its future growth, are so closely linked with the success of its clients as in advertising."[5] We have already discussed some of the interdependency of the advertiser and the agency retained to help provide effective advertising as part of the company's marketing effort. A leading advertiser, George Weissman, vice-chairman of Philip Morris, Incorporated, speaking as a client, outlined 10 requirements that a company expects from its advertising agency:

1. We expect excellence in everything you do. We have built a corporate reputation and a corporate success based on outstanding quality of product, advertising, merchandising and—most important of all—people.
2. We expect that your people will know our business almost as well as we do, and that goes from the technical to the marketing, so that if there are potentials for interesting advertising, it will be created.
3. We expect your people to know the industry as well as we do.
4. We expect your people to be with the consumers, the retailers, the wholesalers and in the front lines, where the business is done and the battle is fought.
5. We expect your people to be honest with us and not "yes" us.
6. We expect your people to give us every crazy idea they might have, even though the rate of rejection is high and the work load heavy.
7. We expect your people to stay on your account and not be taken away by competitors. We, as you, have investments in them and, if they are good, we want them.
8. We expect you to have the same corporate affirmative action policy on personnel on our accounts as we do.
9. We expect to be presented with options—good advertising—dependent on mutual creativity.
10. We expect total involvement at all levels of agency management.[6]

Figure 5.8 In this interesting advertisement, a major advertising agency uses print media to promote its services by using one of its success stories for a client. [*Courtesy of Needham, Harper & Steers.*]

Agency Compensation[7]

All businesses need operating revenues to survive. Advertising agency revenues come from two sources: (1) commissions from advertising media; and (2) client fees. The billing-based compensation system, frequently labeled the "commission system," provides the agency with money from the advertising medium. The commission is a percentage based on the medium's charge for the advertising space or time used by the advertiser. With the cost-based compensation system, often called the "fee system," the agency receives fixed fees for services given to the clients with media commissions offset against those fees. The typical agency today receives about two-thirds of its revenues from media commissions.

The Billings-Based, or Commission, System The usual rate of commission granted by media to agencies is 15 percent of the rate charged for media space or time. Outdoor advertising firms allow commissions of 16⅔ percent, and some trade publications allow 20 percent. Although 15 percent is almost universal in the United States, commissions vary widely throughout the world.

A hypothetical example will demonstrate how the commission system works. An agency places a full-page advertisement in a magazine as part of the client's advertising program. A full-page ad in the magazine sells for $20,000. After the advertisement has run, the magazine bills the agency for $17,000 ($20,000 less 15 percent, or $3,000). The agency then bills the client for the regular media rate charge of $20,000, leaving $3,000 in the agency's operating funds. For this $3,000, the agency must pay the costs of creating and placing the advertisement, as well as make a contribution to overhead expenses and to profits. A cash discount of 2 percent is given by most media if payment is made within 10 days of the billing date. This discount usually is passed along to the client in return for prompt payment.

The commission system has the sanction of long usage. The system simplifies the task of the media greatly, as the agency is responsible for payment of media charges. Therefore, the agency's financial responsibility is all the medium needs to ascertain. The system also has stimulated a high level of productivity from agencies; competition for accounts is keen under the commission system.

A potential disadvantage of the system to the advertiser lies in its built-in temptation for the agency to recommend an advertising program that calls for extensive use of expensive media or of media that require little in the way of agency services. This argument has minimal validity over a period of time, for loading a client with unneeded advertising or inappropriate media not only would be unethical but would cause client dissatisfaction. Clients must be satisfied with the results of their advertising or they will change agencies.

Agencies are often evaluated on the basis of their billings. Instead of saying that the agency achieved a certain sales volume for the year or had operating revenues equaling so many dollars, the amount of advertising placed by the agency is quoted. If an agency placed $10 million with various media during the year, it "billed" $10 million. Income from this phase of the agency's activities, of course, totaled only $1.5 million.

The Cost-Based, or Fee, System Agency executives sometimes feel that the 15 percent commission yields an insufficient return to the agency in light of its many services to the client. This assertion is often the case when the agency is working with small accounts. On the other hand, advertisers may argue that the commission rate going to the agency is too high. Heavy users of televison are likely to take this position, for once a television commercial is created, it may be used for a long time, with millions of dollars being devoted to media billings upon which the agency continues to receive the 15 percent commission. When the price-value ratio appears unfair, agencies may ask clients to substitute the fee system for the commission system. When advertisers feel abused, they may ask for a change to the fee system, or they may set up an in-house agency.

In 1960, Shell Oil Company entered into an agreement with its advertising agency, Ogilvy & Mather, Inc., whereby agency payment would consist exclusively of service fees which were to be computed on the basis of cost- plus 25 percent. David Ogilvy, arguing for the fee approach to agency compensation, listed these five advantages that fees hold over commissions:

1 The agency can be more objective in its recommendations; or so many clients believe.
2 The agency has adequate incentive to provide noncommissionable services if needed.
3 The agency's income is stabilized. Unforeseen cuts in advertising expenditure do not result in red figures or temporary personnel layoffs.
4 The fee enables the agency to make a fair profit on services rendered. The advertiser, in turn, pays for what he gets—no more, no less.
5 Every fee account pays its own way. Unprofitable accounts do not ride on the coattails of profitable accounts.[8]

Ever since Shell Oil's breakaway from the commission system in 1960, there have been predictions that the fee system will take over in many client-agency compensation arrangements. The rate of change, however, has been slow.

Many variations in the cost-based compensation system have been developed, including the idea of a fixed fee for doing a specific task. Whatever the arrangement, provision must be made to ensure that the agency recoups its direct costs and overhead and derives an adequate profit.

In the 1980s, a new approach, called the "incentive-based compensation system," was initiated. This method of payment "places major emphasis on the agency's ability to produce an advertising effort which can accomplish stated goals in terms of product sales or in terms of target audience attitudes, awareness and/or perception."[9] The agency becomes a business partner of the client.

Other Income Advertising agencies do not rely on commissions and fees as their sole sources of revenue. The client pays for costs incurred in preparing materials for reproduction of advertisements. The client, in other words, pays for artwork, typography, photoengravings, the production of commercials, and the many other special services to be discussed in the next section. In addition to the actual cost of these services, the advertiser also pays a service charge of 17.65 percent more for the work than the agency pays. This service charge, added to the cost of work, is equivalent to the standard 15 percent commission discounted from billings by commissionable media.

Service fees also are charged for certain work on which commissions are not available. Retail advertising, for example, is not granted a commission by some advertising media. Moreover, catalogs, point-of-purchase materials, sales materials, and direct-mail pieces usually do not involve agency discounts. Extra charges may be made when the media budget is so low that commissions do not pay for the work done on the advertising. Finally, developmental work on a client's new products or any other unusual projects are often done on a special fee basis.

Usually a letter of agreement between the agency and the client spells out clearly the areas of responsibility assumed by the agency in return for the 15 percent commission received on advertising placed for the client. Those services for which the client is expected to pay extra and the rates of pay are also included in the agreement. A contract of employment, however, usually does not exist between the agency and the client, for their relationship is similar to that between physician and patient or lawyer and client. Once mutual trust is lacking, the agency no longer can serve the advertiser, and the relationship is broken off.

Alternatives to the Full-Service Agency[10]

Companies are long accustomed to making the classic "make-or-buy" decisions on the manufacture of their products. Advertisers, more recently, have been exercising the same option. The advertiser may continue to buy the advertising services of the full-service agency (as previously described), or the company may have these services done by the in-house agency vehicle. Moreover, a middle-ground course of action is present in the so-called *á la carte* system wherein services are purchased piecemeal in combination with agency or in-house agency services, or both. The choice is exercised in the pursuit of increased efficiency in advertising operations.

In-House Agency This variation probably has had the greatest impact on the full-service agency. The in-house agency, as its name implies, is owned outright by, and operated under the direct supervision of, the advertiser. It performs all the creative and media services provided by the traditional full-service agency. A major goal in adopting this approach is to reduce the total cost of advertising, for the in-house agency receives the media commissions. If all the necessary work can be done for less money than the commissions total, the remainder goes directly to the profits of the company. Critics of the in-house agency claim that the outside point of view is lost as the creative personnel are working on only one account or product line and tend to become stale over time. Furthermore, a certain independence of thought is lost in the consequent hierarchical relationship of which the in-house agency is a part. Nevertheless, the form appears to be gaining popularity, especially among heavy users of television advertising. Thus, such companies as J. B. Williams, Norton Simon, Quaker Oats Company, Scott Paper Company, and General Electric are users of in-house agencies for at least some of their advertising.

The Á La Carte Agency. Two major kinds of advertising services may be purchased directly by the advertiser: (1) creative work and (2) media buying. In the 1960s, creativity was the byword of the advertising world. Clients wanted assurance that the best creative people available were working on their accounts. Many star copywriters and art directors were motivated to leave full-service agencies and strike out for themselves by establishing their own shops. These creative-service specialists came to be known as "creative boutiques." Many of the successful ones have developed in turn into full-service agencies, but most have failed. However, there are many places an advertiser can still turn to buy creative services on an á la carte basis. The boutique, according to one advertising executive, is "especially adept at revitalizing tired advertising, adding sparkle to new product images, acting as a creative consultant to agencies and . . . developing expertise in specialized media or product categories."[11]

Media-buying services, the other major á la carte service utilized by advertisers, are discussed in Chapter 18. Such services as market research, package design, publicity, and sales promotion are also subject to the make-or-buy choice.

Special-Service Groups

Any keen observer of the business world cannot help but be impressed by the presence of alert entrepreneurs who are constantly seeking opportunities to provide services to consumers and to other business enterprises. There is a great multiplicity of firms whose objective is to provide advertisers, advertising agencies, and the advertising media with a host of specialized services. These firms collectively are called **special-service groups,** and they are by far the least-known component of the advertising industry. Knowledge of their availability and function is vital if the structure of the advertising business is to be fully understood.

Use of the print media involves printers, photoengravers, and typographers. Other supplier groups are needed when additional forms of advertising are included in the advertising mix. Broadcast advertising may involve commercial production studios, musicians, actors, recordings, tapes, transcriptions, and packaged television shows from outside organizations.

Free-lance artists, photographers, and copywriters sell their creative output for use in advertisements. The American Express advertisement shown in Figure 5.12 features a photograph furnished by a special-service group known as the Image Bank. Models, package designers, public relations counselors, and independent market research firms are additional examples of the extensive list of special-service activities that are available to serve the needs of advertisers.

Who should bear the responsibility for handling the many highly specialized creative processes and mechanical details that precede the appearance of an advertisement? This is a perplexing managerial question. One of three organizations must take this responsibility. The advertiser can perform the specific task internally. Large retailers adopt this approach, but the typical manufacturer's advertising department is less concerned with the creative aspects of the advertising program than with the planning and coordinating phases.

The advertiser may turn these duties over to the advertising agency. More and more of these jobs are being performed by agency personnel. Many large advertising agencies, for example, have become recognized as specialists in the production of television commercials. Not only may agency personnel originate the script, but they may also direct and shoot the film for the commercial, or they may choose to purchase the service from a production company.

Lastly, the advertising media can perform the creative and production phases of advertising. Many radio and TV commercials are taped or filmed by stations for their advertisers. Newspaper personnel write copy and do artwork for small advertisers in the paper.

Some facet of the job, regardless of who assumes overall responsibility for production of the ad, is likely to be turned over to someone from the special-service group. If the particular need is occasional, the advertiser, the agency, or the media involved will tap the services of specialists. However, when the need is continuous, the decision should be based on where the best job can be done at the lowest cost.

Advertising media, the part of the business of advertising remaining to be discussed, is the topic for Part 3 of this book.

Figure 5.9 The web offset press is used by printers, one of the special-service groups important to the advertising business. [*Courtesy of King Press.*]

Figure 5.10 Research firms provide special services to the advertising world. This photo shows the projection and video room of one such organization. The camera is shooting through the windows of a focus-group discussion area. [*Courtesy of Communications Workshop, Inc.*]

Figure 5.11 Two special-service groups are shown here: photographer and model.

Figure 5.12 The photograph in this travel ad was supplied by another kind of special-service group. The Image Bank, an agency representing many photographers has approximately 2 million photographs in its inventory.

Profile

David Mahoney

David Mahoney, long recognized for his keen marketing "savvy," was born in New York City on May 17, 1923. He achieved notoriety through his marketing philosophy of cool nerves, cold cash, hot products, and creativity.

While still in school, Mahoney began his career with the New York advertising agency, Ruthrauff and Ryan, where he became a vice-president within two years at the age of twenty-five. Three years later, he set up his own advertising agency with such clients as Noxema Chemical and Good Humor Corporation.

A few years later, Mahoney joined Colgate-Palmolive Company as executive vice-president, a post he held until 1966, when he became president and chief executive officer of Canada Dry Corporation.

When Canada Dry was consolidated with Hunt Foods and Industries and McCall Corporation to form Norton Simon, Inc. in 1968, David Mahoney was named president and chief executive officer. He has served as chairman since 1970 and has witnessed the company grow from sales of $1 billion to sales of nearly $4 billion in 1980. To compensate for his guardianship, he receives over $840,000 in salary and bonus.

With his Madison Avenue roots, Mahoney's corporate strategy will continue to concentrate on brand name and high-profit consumer products employing advertising, promotion, and new-product development to ensure future marketplace success for the firm.

The career of David Mahoney shows how a person beginning in an advertising job can rise to a leadership position in a major corporation.

Summary

Advertising is a business, that embraces four major kinds of enterprise: (1) advertisers, (2) advertising agencies, (3) special-service groups, and (4) advertising media.

Most medium to large businesses relying on advertising in their marketing mix maintain a special department to handle the advertising function. The person in charge, often called the advertising manager or advertising director, has two principal duties: (1) to plan the advertising program within budget limitations, and (2) to coordinate its implementation, commonly through the services of an advertising agency. The work of the advertising department may be broken down along functional, product, industry, or territorial lines.

Larger firms with multiproduct lines often adopt the product management system instead of using the advertising manager arrangement. In the former, an individual is placed in charge of all marketing activities for a specific product—an assignment that includes responsibility for the advertising of the product.

Regardless of the system employed, key advertising policy decisions are still reserved for the firm's top management. The advertising—or product—manager makes only operational decisions. The depth of top-management involvement in advertising decision making depends primarily on how important advertising is in the ultimate success of the firm.

The advertising agency is a highly specialized service organization. It has evolved over the past 150 years from simple media space selling to its present status as the supplier of a complete set of services for its advertiser clients. The agency's major functions today include (1) making strategy recommendations; (2) creating advertising messages; and (3) placing them in appropriate media.

To accomplish these objectives, a collection of specialists, including account executives, creative people, media experts, and research personnel, is assembled. These people are organized within the agency structure on either a departmentalized or a group basis. Superimposed on the organization is a hierarchy of managerial people, including top managers who have the generation of new business as a highly important responsibility. Such alternatives to the full-service agency as the creative boutique and the in-house agency have recently grown in importance.

Agencies are paid either by media commissions or by client fees. The commission system originated from the space-selling background of the advertising agency and usually is figured at 15 percent of the advertising billings placed in the traditional advertising media. Clients may agree to pay specified fees for work done by the agency instead of using the commission system, but the latter still accounts for about two-thirds of all agency compensation.

Special-service groups are specialized businesses that furnish a variety of necessary products and services to the advertising industry. An important decision in advertising is who should do specific tasks—the advertiser, the agency, or the media. All three tap special-service groups when carrying out an assignment.

Questions for Discussion

1 Explain the various types of business that participate in the business of advertising.
2 Who has the prime responsibility for advertising in the typical manufacturing firm's organizational structure? What are the person's principal duties?
3 List some advantages to a product manager system. Contrast the use of the product manager system with other types of market organizations.
4 Name the two major kinds of advertising decisions. Who is responsible for making each kind and why?
5 Why are advertising agencies paid commissions by advertising media? What are the shortcomings of this system of compensation? What alternative is available? When is it used?

6 Describe the operation of the full-service advertising agency. What alternatives to it have emerged recently? Why?

7 How is the work of the full-service advertising agency organized? What services may it provide to clients?

8 Why is new-business generation so important to the advertising agency? Who has the major responsibility for this activity?

9 Explain what we mean by special-service groups. How do they fit into the business of advertising? Is their importance growing or waning?

10 Interview an executive engaged in any one of the forms of advertising business described in this chapter, and write a description of the person's specific job.

For Further Reference

Aaker, David A., and John G. Myers: *Advertising Management,* Prentice-Hall, Inc., Englewood Cliffs, N.J., 1975.

Agency Compensation: A Guidebook, Association of National Advertisers, Inc., New York, 1979.

Barton, Roger (ed.): *Handbook of Advertising Management,* McGraw-Hill Book Company, New York, 1970.

Buell, Victor P.: *Changing Practices in Advertising Decision-Making and Control,* Association of National Advertisers, Inc.: New York, 1973.

———: *Evaluating Agency Performance,* Association of National Advertisers, Inc., New York, 1979.

Ogilvy, David: *Confessions of an Advertising Man,* Atheneum Publishers, New York, 1963.

Pulver, Robert E.: *Advertising Services: Full-Service Agency, A La Carte, or In-House?* Association of National Advertisers, Inc., New York, 1979.

Reeves, Rosser: *Reality in Advertising,* Alfred A. Knopf, Inc., New York, 1961.

Simon, Julian L.: *The Management of Advertising,* Prentice-Hall, Inc., Englewood Cliffs, N.J., 1971.

End Notes

[1] Victor P. Buell, "Where Advertising Decisions Should Be Made," *Journal of Advertising Research,* Vol. 15, No. 3, June 1975, p. 8.

[2] Ibid.

[3] This section was drawn in part, from Gordon E. Miracle and Bernard M. Bullard, "Evolution of Advertising Agencies," in Leonard W. Lanfranco (ed.), *Making Advertising Relevant: Proceedings of the 1975 American Academy of Advertising,* Columbia, S.C., 1976, pp. 125–127.

[4] For more information on the account management function, see "What Every Young Account Representative Should Know about Account Management," American Association of Advertising Agencies, New York, 1978.

[5] Carl Spielvogel, "There Are No Successful Advertising Agencies – Without Successful Clients," a talk presented before the ANA Advertising Financial Management Workshop, April 23, 1978.

[6] Ibid. Useful insights may also be obtained from Herbert Zellner, "Client-Agency Relations 'Satisfactory,' but Both Sides Point to Storm Warnings," *Advertising Age,* Feb. 12, 1979, pp. 3, 43–45, 48.

[7] Based in part on *Agency Compensation: A Guidebook,* Association of National Advertisers, Inc., 1979.

[8] David Ogilvy, *Principles of Management,* privately published by Ogilvy & Mather, Inc., New York, undated.

[9] *Agency Compensation,* op. cit., p. 41.

[10] Based in part on Robert E. Pulver, *Advertising Services: Full-Service Agency, A La Carte, or In-House?* Association of National Advertisers, Inc., New York, 1979.

[11] Ibid., p. 14.

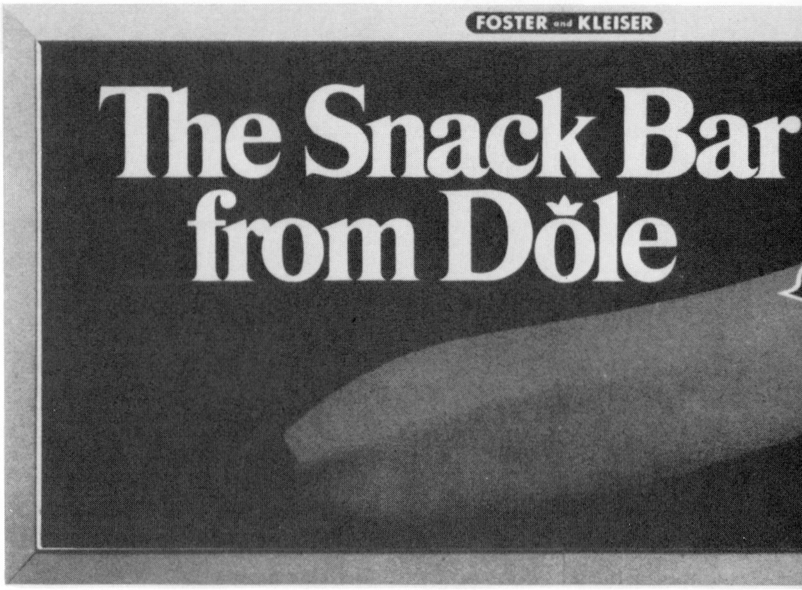

PART 3

Advertising Media

Media, the means by which advertisers reach their prospective customers with advertising messages, were introduced in Chapter 5 as the fourth category of businesses that constitute the advertising industry.

Except for advertisers themselves, more people in the advertising industry work in media than in any other division. Furthermore, of all the dollars spent in the planning and execution of advertising programs and campaigns, approximately two-thirds go to media.

Whether one is involved in planning marketing programs, devising advertising strategy, or creating and producing advertising itself, a knowledge of the basics of each medium is indispensable.

In this section, we shall first present a broad overview of media and then, in subsequent chapters, investigate television and radio, print media, direct mail, out-of-home media, and other collateral media that play important roles in many advertising campaigns.

Chapter 6

The World of Media: An Overview

We have spent a significant portion of our lives being entertained and informed by mass media—television, radio, newspapers, magazines, and direct mail, to name a few. To an advertiser, however, the media are vehicles that carry messages to large groups of prospects and thereby aid in closing the gap between producer and consumer, as described in Chapter 4. But there is still another perspective from which media can be viewed.

Media owners and managers see their companies as manufacturing or service organizations bent on fulfilling a need among consumers for entertainment and information. Television and radio stations program their broadcast fare in a manner designed to attract large segments of the public. In the same manner, newspapers and magazines build their circulations among readers who are drawn to the type of material they publish, be it local news, national news, or some specialized category of interest such as psychology, home decorating, or cross-country skiing.

Once a medium has established itself and has built a significant audience, it is in a position to attract advertisers who are willing to pay for the privilege of reaching that audience with their advertising messages.

Some media, such as outdoor signs, direct mail, or the posters we see in retail stores, offer consumers only the information contained in the advertising itself. They provide advertisers, however, with a channel through which they can reach potential buyers at the ideal place and time to stimulate sales. Regardless of the basis on which media secure their audiences, they constitute, collectively, one of the four categories of businesses (along with advertisers, agencies, and special-service groups) that make up the advertising industry.

In this chapter, we present an overview of media as conveyors of advertising. We shall examine the range of media competing for advertisers' dollars, the theory behind media charges, the institutions supporting the media we see and hear, and the characteristics that make media attractive or unattractive in meeting advertising objectives.

The Evolution of Media into Advertising Vehicles

In the nineteenth century, newspaper and magazine publishers found that subscription and newsstand sales were drastically insufficient in covering writing and production costs. Some were threatened with business failure until they discovered that the secret to success lay not in raising prices, but in lowering them. This action resulted in huge increases in circulation and enhanced the media's desirability as channels through which advertisers might reach prospective buyers.

Everyone seemed to benefit. Publishers increased their audiences and spheres of influence, and the advertising not only subsidized production costs, but often provided a handsome profit. Manufacturers and retailers welcomed the chance to present messages in media whose reach went far beyond the potential of word-of-mouth or street-sign advertising they had used before. The general public benefited from lower-priced magazines and newspapers and from the many advantages inherent in exposure to advertising, as discussed in Chapter 2.

In more recent years, advertising has been a primary source of media revenue. Thus, almost every medium in the country today includes one

Figure 6.1 New Jersey newspaper appeals to prospective advertisers through this ad run in an advertising trade publication. [*Courtesy of* The Star Ledger *and Reichstein Advertising.*]

Figure 6.2 A specialized TV station in Los Angeles appeals to prospective advertisers through this ad run in a broadcasting trade publication.

department, or several, dedicated to selling advertising time or space and to planning and creating advertising messages. A **promotion department** may also work to build audiences or circulations and may be responsible for helping to enhance the image of a medium through public service and other public relations activities.

Types of Media

To a media buyer, there is a seemingly endless variety of advertising media, ranging from skywriting and banners flown over stadiums to television networks and magazines. Some salespeople may offer in their catalogs more than a thousand different "specialty" items to meet advertisers' needs (such as calendars, pens, matchbooks, and the like). Although we shall restrict our analysis of media to the major forms, it is important to note that many other types will be encountered in the advertising world. A few of the fundamental media competing for advertisers' dollars, and some of their key characteristics as advertising vehicles, are shown in Table 6.1 on pp. 130–131.

Each media category consists of hundreds or even thousands of competing businesses. The money any advertiser appropriates for buying media space or time is limited, and media sellers work to convince buyers that the media they represent will meet advertiser needs more efficiently and more effectively than any other medium. Figures 6.1 and 6.2 show how two media try to sell themselves to advertisers.

Media Expenditures

One way to determine the popularity of media as advertising vehicles is to count the advertising dollars spent on each of them. Table 6.2 provides a breakdown of advertising expenditures during 1979 and 1980. As you can see, newspapers claimed the larg-

Table 6.1
Media Characteristics
Important Information on the Strengths and Weaknesses of Media as Advertising Vehicles

	Newspapers	Consumer Magazines	Radio	Television
Features	Broad information and entertainment, plus highly localized news of community activities.	Concentrated coverage of trendy, social events. Slick but uneven in quality.	Highly varied from hard rock to all news, easy listening to country and western. A flexible medium.	Mass audience. Highly visible. Ubiquitous medium for instant exposure of pictures and ideas.
Audience	69% of all adults read yesterday's paper. Stronger among better educated (82% of college grads), older, more affluent consumers.	Selective, from hobbyists to investors, athletes to cooks.	Varies by station. High among youth, also those over 55.	Broad, whole family. Varies by time of day but reaches almost everyone.
Location	Mainly in populous counties. Heavy exposure in northeast and central U.S. Many suburban papers, too.	Most large and medium-sized cities. Better magazines concentrate in major cities.	All markets. Major urban centers have up to 30 or 40 stations. Smallest cities have a handful.	At least three TV stations in most cities. Many have more.
Cost	Cost to cover major city with ¼ page ad in each newspaper: $5,000–$25,000. Medium city: $500–$1,000. Small city: $300–$800.	Extreme variations. Several hundred dollars a page to tens of thousands.	Inexpensive on station-by-station basis. $20,000–$50,000 to cover major markets effectively. $1,000–$7,500 in smaller cities.	Very expensive. $100,000 for schedule in medium-sized market. Up to $1 million for larger markets.
Best way to use	Wide coverage of markets when more than name identification is needed. Good for conveying information on products and companies, and for tie-ins with local store promotions.	Adds a touch of class, develops awareness among trend-setters.	Highly selective exposure among pinpointed audiences. Name identification, musical tie-ins, on-air personalities.	Broad exposure. Product demonstration. Name identity.
Disadvantages	Rising cost. Nonselective audience. Limited appeal to young; reading patterns spotty.	Varies by market. Some are strong, some weak. Advertising clutter in slick publications.	Fragmented audience. Limited information-delivering capacity. Advertising clutter.	Cost may be prohibitive. Difficult to break through threshold of awareness.

est share of advertising dollars. Newspapers are powerful competitors for local and retail advertising dollars, since many are monopolies in their cities of origin. They provide retailers with an effective, sales-generating medium for daily communication with prospective customers at a relatively low cost. In addition, classified advertising is an important source of newspaper income, since many advertisers have no significant alternative when seeking to sell a used car, find a baby-sitter, or hire an experienced machinist.

Although television is the newest of the major media, having arrived on the scene only 40 years ago, it now captures over $11 billion, or almost 21 percent of total advertising dollars annually. It is a surprise to some that direct mail places a strong third, ahead of both radio and magazines, but part of its

Outdoor	Direct mail	Cable TV	Yellow pages
Highly visible mass medium. Obtrusive. Limited applications for many companies.	Increasingly popular (now third largest medium). Highly selective and personal.	Developing rapidly. Much potential. Highly localized. Repeats existing TV fare and originates new programming.	Mass medium reaching most users and owners of telephones. Strongly supported by phone company advertising.
Anyone who goes outside. Age, income, sex vary by location, but it's used to "cover the world."	Completely controlled. Direct-mail lists available to cover almost every conceivable market.	Generally upper income, but is spreading fast by interest groups (sports, movies).	Almost everyone who's a prospect.
Anywhere there are cars and highways. Concentrated on major arteries and around large cities.	Controlled by the mailer.	Concentrated in rural markets but has penetrated major cities. 25% of all homes are wired for cable.	There is a yellow-pages directory in every market, plus specialized editions.
For a strong showing, reaching 89% of the people: average of 14 could cost $5,000–$25,000 per month.	Average cost to rent 1,000 names is $40. Cost of the whole mailing can run $300–$600 per 1,000.	Much cheaper than commercial television. Costs vary widely across the country.	Directories are published by different phone companies in different markets with varying standards and rates. A 2-inch in-column listing may run $400–$1,200 per year.
Name and image identification. Broad awareness.	Personalized, pinpointed marketing.	A highly localized medium, especially suited to pinpoint geographic marketing.	Primary usefulness is in catching consumers when they are looking to buy.
Limited ability to convey product information. Inability to narrow audience. Some local regulatory restrictions.	No editorial environment to attract audience. Low response rate.	Very uneven penetration and viewership from market to market.	Not a dynamic selling medium. Has to be thought of differently. Must give full-service details in ad to maximize value.

strength stems from its universal application. It is a rare company, large or small, that cannot find some advantage in communicating with potential customers through the mail. The large miscellaneous figure in Table 6.2 represents an estimate of the expenditures in collateral media: in-store posters and signs, weekly newspapers, advertising specialties, and others too numerous to mention.

Media as Advertising Centers

Tens of thousands of advertising men and women are employed in the production and sale of advertising media. Some of the businesses for which they work are familiar, such as companies that publish

Table 6.2
Advertising Volume in the United States in 1979 and 1980

Medium	1979 $ millions	Percent of total	1980 $ millions	Percent of total	Percent change
Newspapers					
Total	14,493	29.3	15,615	28.5	+ 7.7
National	2,085	4.2	2,335	4.3	+12.0
Local	12,408	25.1	13,280	24.2	+ 7.0
Magazines					
Total	2,932	5.9	3,225	5.9	+10.0
Weeklies	1,327	2.7	1,440	2.6	+ 8.5
Women's	730	1.5	795	1.5	+ 9.0
Monthlies	875	1.7	990	1.8	+13.0
Farm Publications	120	0.3	135	0.3	+12.0
Television					
Total	10,154	20.5	11,330	20.7	+11.6
Network	4,599	9.3	5,105	9.3	+11.0
Spot	2,873	5.8	3,260	6.0	+13.5
Local	2,682	5.4	2,965	5.4	+10.5
Radio					
Total	3,277	6.6	3,690	6.7	+12.6
Network	161	0.3	185	0.3	+15.0
Spot	659	1.3	750	1.4	+14.0
Local	2,457	5.0	2,755	5.0	+12.0
Direct Mail	6,653	13.4	7,655	14.0	+15.0
Business Publications	1,575	3.2	1,695	3.1	+ 7.5
Outdoor					
Total	540	1.1	610	1.1	+12.8
National	355	0.7	400	0.7	+13.0
Local	185	0.4	210	0.4	+12.5
Miscellaneous					
Total	9,776	19.7	10,795	19.7	+10.5
National	5,063	10.2	5,690	10.4	+12.4
Local	4,713	9.5	5,105	9.3	+ 8.3
Total					
National	27,075	54.7	30,435	55.6	+12.4
Local	22,445	45.3	24,315	44.4	+ 8.3
Grand Total	49,520	100.0	54,750	100.0	+10.6

SOURCE: *Advertising Age,* Jan. 5, 1981.

newspapers and magazines. Direct-mail advertising, on the other hand, is commonly produced by specialized firms that may contract with advertisers or agencies to handle particular assignments. Or, a client or an advertising agency may do all the planning and preparation of a direct-mail campaign and then turn the project over to a printing company for final production. Working in conjunction with direct-mail houses and printers is a subindustry of firms that specialize in compiling mailing lists to aid advertisers in reaching the most desirable groups of prospects.

Out-of-Home Media

Everyone is familiar with out-of-home signs and

posters, but few people have ever been inside a sign-painting company or the basic institution of outdoor advertising—an **outdoor plant.** These businesses vary in size from small local organizations to large national companies, such as Foster & Kleiser, that sell outdoor advertising in many cities. Men and women who work in local offices sell advertising to prospective clients and produce local outdoor ads. When posters or signs are displayed in great numbers, independent printing companies are often hired to prepare them.

Radio and Television

Most national and some local advertising on radio and television is prepared by advertising agencies for their clients. Much local advertising, however, is created by (1) advertising personnel at the broadcast stations themselves, or (2) local advertisers who work closely with the stations' sales staffs in scheduling air time for the finished commercials.

Media salespeople are the lifeline of the broadcast business because their success or failure in selling time is fundamental to their stations' survival.

The Media Representative Firm

The national sales staffs at most radio and television stations, as well as at magazines and newspapers, are interested in selling time or space to advertisers in large business centers such as New York, Detroit, Chicago, Atlanta, and Los Angeles. But it would be too expensive for each individual medium to hire salespeople to visit advertisers and agencies in every major city. Out of this need to economize has grown another advertising sales arm of the media business—the **media representative firm.** A typical office employs a number of salespeople, commonly called "reps," who represent various noncompetitive media: a group of radio stations *or* newspapers, for example, in well-separated cities, or a collection of TV *and* radio stations, also in widely spaced (and hence, noncompetitive) areas. Each firm handles only one station or publication per market, and retains exclusive rights to sell its own clients' time or space.

In return for their services, media reps receive commissions from each medium amounting to about 10 percent of the cost of the advertising time or space sold. For example, the Katz Company represents more than six dozen TV stations across the country. If it sells $20,000 worth of commercial time to Dole Pineapple (through Dole's advertising agency) on each of three different television stations (one in San Francisco, one in Denver, and one in Boston), Katz would collect $2,000 from each station. The stations, in turn, would be spared the task of having to solicit Dole's business individually.

Although the primary role of reps is to sell national advertising for stations or publishers, they also provide advertisers and agency media buyers with current information concerning their media and markets. For example, suppose an agency media director in St. Louis wishes to buy time on one TV station in Indianapolis. Which station should she buy if she's unfamiliar with that city? In this case, the reps for all prospective stations can provide her with audience demographic characteristics for their respective media, as well as station track records (advertising "success stores") and program ratings. Or, if only *one* rep calls on this particular media director, he will undoubtedly give her information on his area's *other* stations, too, to help her make up her mind.

Figure 6.3 shows an advertisement designed for this same media buyer. Clearly, the regional rep's firm knows Indiana radio, and is offering its expertise to help solve a media-buying problem. And, if our media director contacts this company, she may very well wind up buying time on stations outside Indianapolis as well.

Networks

Networks such as ABC, CBS, and NBC are major elements in the broadcasting business, providing programming for their own stations and for affiliated stations across the country. An important arm of each network is the sales division, dedicated to selling time for commercials run in conjunction with network programs as well as advertising that originates from local affiliates. In the latter role, they operate very much like the reps described above. (Chapter 7 will discuss network-affiliated stations in detail.)

Advertising Specialties

When retail or national advertisers present you with a key chain, letter opener, thermometer, or some more elaborate gift marked with a company or brand name, you are the target of **specialty advertising,** sometimes called **remembrance advertising.** Nearly every medium to large city has one or more firms called **specialty distributors** that engage in this busi-

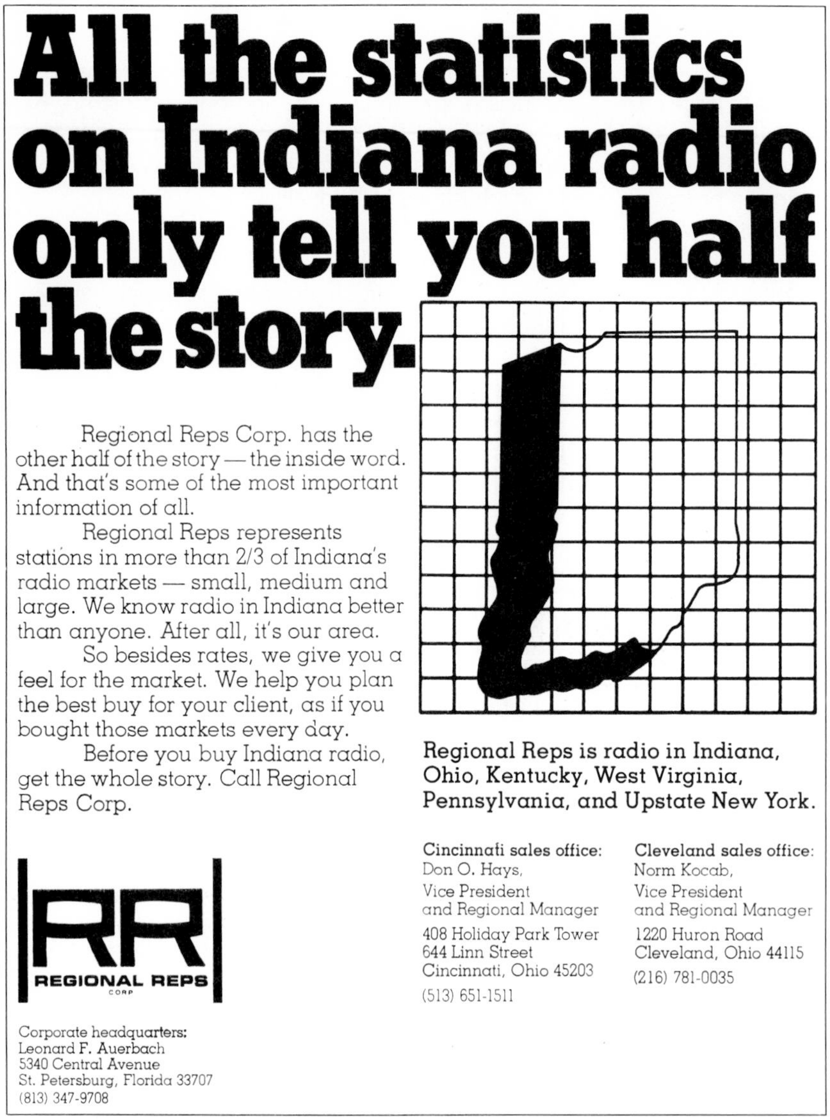
All the statistics on Indiana radio only tell you half the story.
Regional Reps Corp. has the other half of the story — the inside word. And that's some of the most important information of all.
Regional Reps represents stations in more than 2/3 of Indiana's radio markets — small, medium and large. We know radio in Indiana better than anyone. After all, it's our area.
So besides rates, we give you a feel for the market. We help you plan the best buy for your client, as if you bought those markets every day.
Before you buy Indiana radio, get the whole story. Call Regional Reps Corp.
Regional Reps is radio in Indiana, Ohio, Kentucky, West Virginia, Pennsylvania, and Upstate New York.
Cincinnati sales office: Don O. Hays, Vice President and Regional Manager 408 Holiday Park Tower 644 Linn Street Cincinnati, Ohio 45203 (513) 651-1511
Cleveland sales office: Norm Kocab, Vice President and Regional Manager 1220 Huron Road Cleveland, Ohio 44115 (216) 781-0035
RR REGIONAL REPS CORP
Corporate headquarters: Leonard F. Auerbach 5340 Central Avenue St. Petersburg, Florida 33707 (813) 347-9708

Figure 6.3 This advertisement for a representative firm demonstrates how media reps serve the advertising business with information about media and markets. It promotes the entire Indiana radio market in a single message.

ness. Behind them are manufacturers who provide the specialties. Or, giant companies, such as Brown and Bigelow of St. Paul, Minnesota, may have their own sales representatives located throughout the country. These people take pride in their ability to help plan successful specialty campaigns in terms of appropriate and creative tie-ins with their clients' advertising objectives.

It is obvious from the foregoing examples that the variety of institutions and job opportunities—sales, creative planning, production, and promotion—is extensive within the media division of the advertising business.

Media Characteristics

With the wide variety of advertising media available, you might wonder how a seller convinces a buyer that a medium is right for a given campaign. The answer begins with an understanding of the basic characteristics by which media are compared. The following are some important ones.

Selectivity

This quality may be viewed as a medium's ability to reach (1) a specific geographic area such as a city or region, and (2) specific classes of people who possess

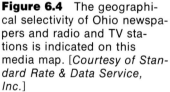

Figure 6.4 The geographical selectivity of Ohio newspapers and radio and TV stations is indicated on this media map. [*Courtesy of Standard Rate & Data Service, Inc.*]

certain common traits. **Geographic selectivity** is obvious. You would not buy advertising in a national magazine to reach the residents of Akron, Ohio, when a local newspaper could do the job directly with little waste circulation. Figure 6.4 illustrates the geographic selectivity of Ohio media.

With **class selectivity,** the objective is not to expose mass markets to an advertising message. Instead, people are classified in a hundred or more different ways, and advertising salespeople study media in terms of specific client needs. Some media may do a better job reaching women than men; *Ms.* magazine, *Glamour,* and *Good Housekeeping* are obvious examples. Another medium, *The Wall Street Journal,* may reach an older, more affluent audience than *Time* magazine or *Esquire.* Although a rock radio station attracts a younger audience than one featuring classical music, each may play an important advertising role depending on campaign objectives.

So far, we've considered class selectivity as applied to **demographic breakdowns** of media audiences in terms of age, sex, income, and other factors. Chapter 11 introduces the concept of **psychographics,** or lifestyle research, which is valuable in the development of advertising creativity —and it is just as helpful in selecting media. Psychographics, as a research procedure, takes quantitative data beyond user/nonuser analysis. For example, we may know that in a certain area 90 percent of the adult residents own cameras (and 10 percent do not). If we were to base a media-buying decision for Kodak film on this demographic finding alone, however, we might well buy television because of the presumed mass audience for our product.

Psychographic research might reveal, though, that only 20 percent of the camera owners accounted for 80 percent of the area's film sales. And those avid picture-takers might also be avid hikers, campers, and fishermen—all loyal readers of a magazine known as *Outdoor Life.* This magazine could easily be a less expensive buy than television, and a more effective one in terms of reaching (and appealing to) prospective customers.

deadlines

Normal Display Advertising
DEADLINES

PUBLICATION DAY	AD DEADLINE	
For SUNDAY	Wednesday	4:00 p.m.
For MONDAY	Thursday	4:00 p.m.
For TUESDAY	Friday	4:00 p.m.
For WEDNESDAY	Friday	4:00 p.m.
For THURSDAY	Monday	4:00 p.m.
For FRIDAY	Tuesday	4:00 p.m.
For SATURDAY	Tuesday	4:00 p.m.

ADVANCED DEADLINES

1. Double trucks and color ads 24 hours in advance of normal deadlines, complete with artwork.
2. Holiday deadlines will be distributed as necessary throughout the year.

TABLOID and REGULAR SECTIONS

accepted for publication under special deadlines arranged with advertising representative.

TV WEEK

Space reservation must be made two (2) weeks prior to publication with complete copy in the shop no less than 10 days prior to publication.

Figure 6.5 The flexibility of newspaper advertising is shown in this portion of a rate card. Other media may require weeks or even months of lead time in the placement of advertisements. [*Courtesy of* Eugene Register-Guard.]

Penetration and Coverage

Penetration describes the size of audience claimed by a particular medium. For example, if there are 80 million households in the United States, and 78.5 million of them have television sets, the penetration of TV is 98.1 percent. **Coverage,** a closely related term, is used to assess the ability of a medium to reach a certain percentage of homes in a given area, or to reach persons within a specific market segment. Thus, a local newspaper with a circulation of 600,000, in a market where there are 2.5 million households, has a coverage of 24 percent.

Flexibility

Another basis for comparing advertising media is **scheduling flexibility.** Newspapers and radio stations afford advertisers relatively short ad-placement deadlines—a big value to media buyers trying to meet a competitive challenge, make an unexpected announcement, or react to a timely news event. The sudden onset of cold or rainy weather, for example, might impel a retail store to run a special on coats, scarves, or umbrellas. Flexibility is also important when, for some reason, an advertiser is forced to withdraw an ad shortly before it is scheduled to appear. Sometimes, merchandise shipments are delayed or stores may be forced to close temporarily because of fire or flood damage. Figure 6.5 illustrates one form of newspaper flexibility.

Politicians know the importance of reserving outdoor advertising space as long as a year before an election; otherwise, it may not be available. In the case of local magazines, or the rotogravure sections of Sunday newspapers, advertising must be placed weeks ahead of the date on which it will actually appear. Retailers using the media must therefore do some advance planning in order to coordinate merchandise on hand with advertising publication dates. Generally speaking, newspapers, radio, and direct mail are considered relatively flexible media. Magazines, network television, point-of-purchase, advertising specialties, and out-of-home media are not.

Obviously, media competition for an advertiser's business exists not only within a given media class (say, radio station A against radio station B), but also between classes (radio versus newspapers). Media trade associations, such as the American Newspaper Publishers Association (ANPA), the Magazine Publishers Association (MPA), the Radio Advertising Bureau (RAB), and the Television Bureau of Adver-

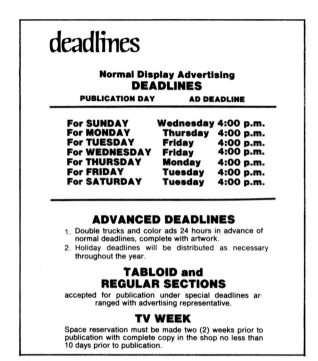

It would take eighteen 30-second TV commercials to tell you what's on this page... and other reasons why I like print.

By Al Hampel
Executive Vice President and Director of Creative Services,
Benton & Bowles, Inc.

When I was a kid, I sold magazines door to door. I didn't do it for the money because they paid you in prizes. I did it because it was the only way I could get to read the magazines.

Of all of them I liked Liberty the best. Before there was Evelyn Wood, there was Liberty magazine. Liberty gave you the reading time for every article.

You have now read about 65 words of this ad or about 30 seconds of TV copy—and, see, we have only just begun.

I will not deny that writing TV commercials can be exciting and producing them can be glamorous, sometimes even fun. But for me there's still no kick to compare with filling a page with copy—even though I find it more difficult to do than TV.

Without the benefit of motion and bedazzling optical effects, without the impact of music and sound, I know copywriters who become paralyzed with fear at the thought of writing a print ad. Can you blame them? They are part of the generation of TV baby copywriters whose experience with print is limited to an occasional trade ad or a cents-off promotion. The shortage of good print writers is acute and so is the shortage of good print ads.

Print–the amazing new medium.

I sometimes wonder what would have happened if print had followed TV as an advertising medium. Think of print as a *brand-new* medium and the possibilities become astounding. Imagine a new form of advertising that lets you stretch out and sell your product in ways that no 30- or 60-second time span could possibly handle. For example, if you sell toothpaste for cavity prevention on TV, in print you can reveal ten ways you can get children to brush with your toothpaste—a story too long to be squeezed into a TV commercial.

Even in less than single-page units you can often say more than you can in a TV commercial. Grab your prospect with a provocative headline and an interesting visual, write bright informative copy, make it easy to read, and smaller space becomes no obstacle to good print advertising.

Great recipe for selling.

It may look like just another ad to you, but to the woman of the house it's tonight's dessert—or Saturday night's dinner. Any food or beverage advertiser who doesn't consider print for recipes or serving suggestions does so at his own risk.

And in print the recipes aren't limited to food or drink. Learn how to select a mattress or a fine vintage wine. Get a crash course in make-up or how to insulate a house. Cut along the dotted line and file an airline schedule in your wallet. Find a new color for a rug and take it to the store when you shop. No TV set can convey color as accurately as four-color print. There are as many variations of hues on TV as there are sets in use.

And only in print: The information in an ad is yours to keep and refer to as long as the paper lasts.

Coupons–the choicest cut of all.

If you've been at a supermarket checkout counter lately, you'll know the family scissors have been working overtime. The person who invented the cents-off coupon must have loved manufacturers, retailers, and consumers alike. There is scarcely a more useful promotion tool in all of marketing.

A recent issue of a popular magazine contained coupons worth $52.39.

Overnight response.

If you have a son or daughter who wants to be a copywriter, encourage him or her to get a job in a department store. It's the best training they could get. When you write retail print copy, you can expect response to your ad at the point of sale the day after it runs. The buyer of ladies' ready-to-wear will tell you within days how good a copywriter you are. You won't need research to tell you.

Print vs. the subliminal address.

In print, when you invite someone to write for something, your address is available forever. Like this:

Free! Handsome button containing the immortal words:
IT'S NOT CREATIVE UNLESS IT SELLS.
Send to: Free Button Offer
P.O. Box 5035, F.D.R. Post Office Station
New York, N.Y. 10022

Name________________
Address________________
City________ State______ Zip______

Could you have remembered that address or copied it from a TV screen in three seconds?

Aubrey Joel, President of Southam Business Publications in Canada, says: "One of print's primary advantages is its ability to free time. A page in a magazine can hold a reader five, ten, fifteen minutes, long enough to fill out a coupon, write a check, make a phone call, or take some other action. And isn't action the ultimate purpose of advertising?"

MAIN IDEA and secondary ideas.

In print you can highlight a main selling idea in your headline. Your secondary selling idea can go in a sub-headline. Other key points can be emphasized with crossheads. And, of course, you can get down to details in the body copy.

This is not as easily done in TV where every word carries as much weight as every other word and it's difficult to communicate more than one major selling idea. Nevertheless, overloaded commercials are very common. They are known as blivots.

Isn't it paradoxical that when TV advertisers want to instill a selling idea they resort to a superimposition of words. In other words, to be remembered it's good to be seen in words—as in print.

Finally, I must mention the seldom used but very titillating print ad that asks you to scratch and sniff the product. I have never resisted becoming involved with this little sensory game and I don't know anybody who has. Unfortunately, there are some ads that smell without scratching.

Those are just some of the reasons why I like print. I speak for no magazine or newspaper, yet I speak for them all. In telling you how great each one of them is numerically, I think they have collectively overlooked the basic virtues they all enjoy.

I could guarantee you this: If somehow print could be viewed as a new medium, you'd see a wave of jaded TV writers and art directors clamoring for print assignments as they once fought for the chance to get into show business via the TV commercial. Print needs that kind of reawakening.

I could write volumes about the effectiveness of TV advertising and maybe someday I will. Call it nostalgia, call it love of the printed word, whatever... this copywriter has seen print go from the most used advertising medium to an underused and misused advertising medium. That bothers me.

Figure 6.6 The intense nature of media competition is revealed in this testimonial on the advantages of magazines by an important agency executive. [*Magazine Publishers Association, Inc.*]

Where else but Family Circle can you get a $7.07 CPM?
Nowhere.
CPM Comparison of 7 Women's Magazines
Family Circle $7.07
Woman's Day 7.47
Better Homes & Gardens 7.85
Ladies' Home Journal 8.11
McCall's 8.42
Redbook 8.97
Good Housekeeping 9.59
Family Circle gives you the lowest CPM of any women's magazine.
And our $7.07 CPM is one of the few things that isn't going up these days. You can count on it through June 1981. We guarantee it.
While our CPM is way down, our total copy sale is way up. At 66.3 million for the first half of 1980, it's way ahead of all the other women's magazines: Good Housekeeping, McCall's, Redbook, Ladies' Home Journal, and Better Homes and Gardens.
Woman's Day, our strongest competitor, doesn't even come close. There's a 13 million difference between us.
And that's not the only difference. Like our CPM, our circulation is guaranteed. Beginning January, 1981 Family Circle guarantees that you will get exactly the circulation you pay for. Should we fall below the level set for each quarter, we'll pay the difference in cash.
Even though our rates are standing still, our magazine is being read faster than ever. In fact, according to IMS Adcume, Family Circle accumulates 53% of its women readers in the first week on sale, and 78% by the end of the second—more than any other women's magazine.
With 17 issues a year, Family Circle lets you reach your target audience closer to your target dates. Ideal timing when you're offering a special promotion or introducing a new product.
Our 17 issue schedule is only one of Family Circle's advertising innovations. Our Advertising Response Guarantee is another. We also offer Brand Discounts, Dollar Volume Discounts and a Special Advertising Section.
With our unique advertising package and our great rates, Family Circle gives your media dollars a chance to really perform.
Family Circle
New ideas every three weeks.

Figure 6.7 Comparative CPMs are used here to promote *Family Circle* magazine as an advertising vehicle.

tising (TvB), spend much of their time promoting the advantages of their respective vehicles to advertisers and their agencies. Figure 6.6 is an example of such an effort on the part of MPA (with a note at the end that a similar piece could easily be written for TV!).

Cost

As you might expect, one of the most important criteria for selecting one medium over another is **cost.** It is helpful to view dollar figures in two ways: (1) as absolute (face) costs, and (2) as costs related to audience size.

Absolute cost is a simple concept. It is the charge for buying a certain amount of time or space in a medium. Since most advertising budgets, once established, are relatively fixed, media costs must be checked for affordability. Regardless of how eager a small advertiser may be to use network television or widely circulated magazines, the tens of thousands of dollars needed may make such purchases impossible.

Relative cost is a comparative cost. It is the absolute cost (just described) related to (or spread over) the size of the audience delivered by the chosen medium. Charges for full-page ads in two different magazines might be exactly the same (say, $30,000 for the space). But if one magazine has a circulation of 3 million and the other has a circulation of 4 million, advertisers choosing the second publication will get considerably more for their money.

Of course, it is vitally important to examine the *quality* of each audience delivered as well as the quantity, and to assess each medium's ability to elicit the desired response from those it reaches. An

Figure 6.8 *The Economist* uses relative cost in terms other than merely "a thousand readers" to make its appeal to advertisers. [*Courtesy of* The Economist.]

audience of 10 million nonsmokers is of little use to a cigarette advertiser, and postcards sent to prospects that fail to accomplish a stated objective are an outright waste of money. On the other hand, a million-dollar investment in magazine advertising that reduces other marketing costs and results in many millions of sales dollars is inexpensive, relatively speaking. Thus, if an advertiser has the money to meet the absolute cost of a media buy, the outlay is not expensive if it does the job intended. By the same token, nothing is cheap if it does not perform its assigned task.

A common term used to evaluate a medium's audience-reaching capacity relative to its advertising rates is "cost per thousand," often abbreviated to CPM. The "thousand" used here may mean a thousand people, a thousand homes, or a thousand persons within a specific group, such as gardeners, hang-glider enthusiasts, or females between eighteen and thirty-four with incomes exceeding $18,000 per year. Figure 6.7 shows how an attractive cost-per-thousand figure is used as a promotional tool for *Family Circle* magazine. And in Figure 6.8, *The Economist* magazine demonstrates the value of using specific audience characteristics instead of just "a thousand readers" in its cost appeal to prospective advertisers.

Although the cost per thousand is important in selling and buying media for an advertising campaign, it is not always the overriding factor. An elegant or esoteric magazine or expensive television program costs advertisers more, relatively speaking, than does a low-quality medium. An exclusive or upper-class audience usually brings higher returns to an advertiser than does a less affluent group. A mailing list of brain surgeons is much more expensive to buy than an equivalent list of taxi drivers because surgeons have more discretionary income to spend.

Figure 6.9 These advertisers capitalized on *Cuisine* magazine's editorial environment in placing this advertisement. [*Courtesy of California Avocado Commission, Holland House Cooking Wines, and SSC&B Inc., Advertising, Los Angeles.*]

Editorial Environment

A big advantage of some media is the nature of the information or entertainment material that surrounds the advertising. This quality, called **editorial environment,** is most obvious in specialized magazines, but, in a sense, it applies to all media.

An advertiser may welcome the chance to place a message in a medium that is prestigious, or authoritative, or respected for its integrity. Naturally, the advertiser believes (or hopes) that some of these qualities will rub off on the product or company advertised. An appropriate advertisement placed in *House Beautiful, Gourmet,* or *Skiing* enjoys many advantages in terms of psychological impact on loyal readers. The advertising often blends in perfectly with the magazine's content and with readers' desires to learn something about the subjects presented. The advertisement shown in Color Plate 1 promotes

Cuisine as an effective advertising vehicle for companies whose products are used in the kitchen. And Figure 6.9 shows an ad which actually ran in *Cuisine* —from two advertisers who believed in the value of this magazine's editorial environment as an aid to sales appeal.

Hallmark greeting cards are advertised in televised dramatic productions developed to blend with the firm's commercial announcements, as well as to attract specific audiences. For example, a family-oriented Thanksgiving show is an excellent backdrop for sales messages designed to help sell Christmas cards.

Advertisements placed in *Barron's,* the *New York Times,* or any other highly reputable newspaper probably enjoy a level of prestige and believability that is higher than the same ads would enjoy in a less respected medium. To a degree, readers seem to equate a trustworthy editorial policy with a trustworthy advertising image.

Production Quality

Traditionally, magazine reps sold advertising space on the strength of their magazines' magnificent color that authentically displayed a product or created a mood in a manner no other medium could match. (For example, take a look at the advertisements for Waterford Crystal and the French National Tourist Office, Color Plates 5 and 7.)

Although the argument has lost some of its impact with the growth of color television, sophisticated newspaper magazine sections, and elaborate direct-mail pamphlets and brochures, magazines are still capable of fine reproduction that can be a strong selling point with some advertisers and media buyers.

At the retail level, radio and television stations that offer excellent local programming and production aids in the creation of commercials have a big advantage over stations that do not. According to the Television Bureau of Advertising, more than half of all TV stations in the United States sell their own commercial production services in competition with businesses that specialize in television and radio production.

Permanence

Some media are more durable than others in the sense that they remain before prospects' eyes or within their grasp for a longer period of time. Painted outdoor bulletins, for example, may continue delivering the same message to the passing public for a year or more. Magazines are often kept around the house for many months, or years, in the case of *National Geographic.* Weekly newspapers are considered current until a new issue arrives, in contrast to daily papers which, characteristically, are read and then discarded. Whatever the case, print media, in general, do offer the reader a chance to study an advertisement or to refer back to it, if desired. Broadcast media, on the other hand, give fleeting impressions which cannot be retrieved at the whim of the listener or viewer.

A degree of permanence, or durability, is important to an advertiser who has a complicated or lengthy message to convey. Retail grocery stores, variety stores, and highly technical industrial companies are examples of advertisers who need a medium that provides some kind of lasting quality. Some readers clip and save ads (especially those for durable goods, or ones that contain coupons, recipes, or other instructions), and then refer back to them before deciding to buy the products advertised.

Trade Acceptability

It is important, when a manufacturer tries to get support for a product along the channels of distribution, that the intermediaries be enthusiastic about the advertising—both the messages and the media that carry them. Without such support from retailers, wholesalers, and others, a campaign will rarely achieve its full impact or move a maximum volume of products.

A cereal manufacturer who has just moved into the production of cookies, for example, may have to convince retail stores that a planned advertising campaign in magazines and newspapers will *deliver customers.* Previously successful cereal campaigns run in these media might be presented—on slides or tapes, or in mailed circulars. Or, trial radio and TV commercials for the new cookies might be played at dealer trade shows to drum up interest. Finally, research findings supplied by the media in question (print readership studies or broadcast ratings) can be important selling tools.

Merchandising Cooperation

Years ago, when newspapers first started to feel the competitive pinch from magazines and radio networks for national advertisers' dollars, they developed a system for helping national clients on the local level. Representatives from newspaper advertising departments visited retailers to urge them (1) to stock up on the nationally advertised products that were running current newspaper campaigns, and (2) to support those campaigns by setting up in-store displays for these products and by featuring the items in the retailers' own newspaper ads. For example, when a manufacturer's product ad and a retailer's ad promoting that same product ran in the same newspaper on the same day, it was felt that communication impact was greatly enhanced. Newspaper sales reps helped build the displays and gradually learned other ways to get and keep retailers enthusiastic about specific products.

Today, this **merchandising cooperation** has become a persuasive addition to the sales presentations of most major media. Some newspapers and broadcast stations help set up contests among store outlets wherein prizes are awarded to dealers who stock and sell the most of a given product. Or, inexpensive flyers containing information about a particular product offering, often at a special price, may be mailed to a store's customers (or handed out at the store).

Advertisers and agency media buyers do consider merchandising activities when choosing between competing media. A danger here is that a buyer may select a medium on the basis of a free or "at cost" merchandising aid, when the decision should be based on the medium's ability to reach the target audience. But when all other aspects appear equal, merchandising cooperation can be the factor that tips the scale in favor of one medium over another.

Summary

Media make up the fourth category of businesses that constitute the advertising industry. Through their ability to inform and entertain both mass and specialized audiences, media provide advertisers with the means to reach potential customers with their messages. Advertising, in turn, subsidizes the cost of producing media by enabling newspaper and magazine publishers to price their media at a cost that is much lower than would be possible without advertising. And advertising permits radio and television stations to provide their services to consumers free of charge.

Because of the importance of advertising to their existence, most media employ staffs that sell time and space to advertisers or their media buyers. They also employ creative people and promotional staffs to expedite the efforts of salespersons.

Each medium has advantages or combinations of characteristics that make it a viable choice for certain advertisers at certain times. Media sales representatives compete with one another for advertisers' business on the basis of these characteristics. Conversely, media buyers, acting on behalf of advertisers, evaluate these characteristics when deciding which media would work together best in a media mix designed to help meet advertising objectives. Some of the most important considerations used to differentiate media are:

1 *Selectivity.* The ability of a medium to reach a particular audience, based either on the audience's geographic location or on unique traits. These traits may be demographic or psychographic.
2 *Coverage.* The size or nature of the audience a medium can reach. Or, more commonly, the degree to which a medium can penetrate a market, such as homes in an area or persons within a specific group.
3 *Flexibility.* The speed and ease with which an ad can be placed in a medium, changed, or deleted.
4 *Cost.* In the absolute sense, the charge imposed for buying a certain amount of time or space. In the relative sense, what the medium yields in terms of audience quality and quantity and results obtained for the money spent.
5 *Editorial environment.* The nature of the information or entertainment material that surrounds a buyer's advertising and its ability to meet the advertiser's objectives.

6 *Production quality.* The ability of a medium to reproduce advertising with great fidelity.
7 *Permanence.* The ability of a medium to keep advertisements before prospects' eyes or within their grasp for an extended period.
8 *Trade acceptability.* The degree of acceptance a medium can generate among an advertiser's intermediaries—retailers, wholesalers, and other persons working within the advertiser's channels of distribution.
9 *Merchandising cooperation.* Services offered by many media that boost retailers' support of and enthusiasm for national advertising campaigns. Examples include creation of in-store displays, promotional mailers, and sales contests among dealers.

Questions for Discussion

1 Describe some of the businesses that make up the media branch of the advertising industry.
2 Explain how media and advertisers depend upon one another for their survival.
3 Discuss several non-cost differences among women's magazines that might make one more appealing than another to a food advertiser.
4 What do we mean by "collateral" media? Can you think of any advertising communication tasks they might fulfill more effectively than the major media?
5 Specifically, what is the job of a media representative firm? How does it differ from the job of a particular medium's sales staff?
6 Name the two types of media selectivity and describe the differences between them.
7 Why is media flexibility important to an advertiser? Give examples of its value.
8 Explain why relative cost is a critical consideration when studying and comparing media advertising rates.

For Further Reference

Barban, Arnold M., Stephen Cristol, and Frank J. Kopec: *Essentials of Media Planning,* Crain Books, Chicago, 1976.
Barban, Arnold M., Donald W. Jugenheimer, and Lee F. Young: *Advertising Media Sourcebook and Workbook,* Grid, Inc., Columbus, Ohio, 1975.
Broadbent, Simon: *Spending Advertising Money,* 2d ed., Business Books Limited, London, 1975.
Sissors, Jack Z., Harry D. Lehew, and William B. Goodrich: *Media Planning Workbook,* Crain Books, Chicago, 1976.
Sissors, Jack Z., and E. Reynold Petray: *Advertising Media Planning,* Crain Books, Chicago, 1976.
Television Factbook, 2 vols.: Stations, and Services, Television Digest, Inc., Washington, D.C., irregular.
World Communications, The UNESCO Press, Essex, England, 1975.

Chapter 7

Television and Radio

In Chapter 6, we noted that the broadcast media distinguish themselves through a sense of immediacy and ubiquity. They transmit instantaneously at the press of a button or the flip of a switch, and they can accompany their owners almost everywhere. They are usually thought of as the most personal of the mass media, too, thanks to their use of the human voice. In fact, they are often used for companionship (at home, in the car, on the job), as background accompaniment to other activities (especially radio), and as a baby-sitter (especially TV). Both are criticized for their advertising clutter, and must cope with a fleeting, perishable quality.

It can be argued, too, that broadcasting is a more competitive business than publishing. Small cities may have only one daily newspaper, but 10 or more radio stations and 2 or 3 television stations. Large metropolitan areas may house 2 to 5 daily newspapers, but 100 or more broadcast stations. Granted, thousands of magazines are published in this country, but only a few are directed to the same target audiences.

All these characteristics, however, separate electronic media from print. Now it is time to look specifically at radio and television, whose stations number more than 10,000 across the nation and claim over one-quarter of annual U.S. advertising dollars. We will examine their similarities and differences as advertising vehicles and discuss the structure of the broadcast industry. Finally, we will look at broadcast advertising strategies in terms of programs, audiences, ratings, and costs.

Radio as an Advertising Medium

Ninety-nine percent of United States homes have radios and the average number of sets per household is six. In addition, 95 percent of the cars on America's roads are radio-equipped.[1] Total listening time averages 3½ hours per day.[2]

Radio has been an important advertising vehicle in the United States for 60 years. Some experts predicted this medium would die after TV's explosive growth in the 1950s. Wise radio programmers, however, changed their formats from drama to music; in some time periods, their audiences actually *increased,* despite the popularity of television. Even FM radio, long considered a distant cousin of AM, by the early 1980s was claiming audiences larger than those of AM in many dayparts. (FM is the common designation for frequency modulation, and AM stands for amplitude modulation.)

Today, Americans buy nearly $3.5 billion worth of radios per year, and an equal sum is spent by radio advertisers for commercial time.[3] Programming is geared to selective audiences and appeals particularly to young adults. (See Figure 7.1.)

Figure 7.1 Radio stations in secondary markets often promote their listenership potential to advertisers through selective audience appeals. [*WJFM Radio; the Fetzer Broadcasting Company.*]

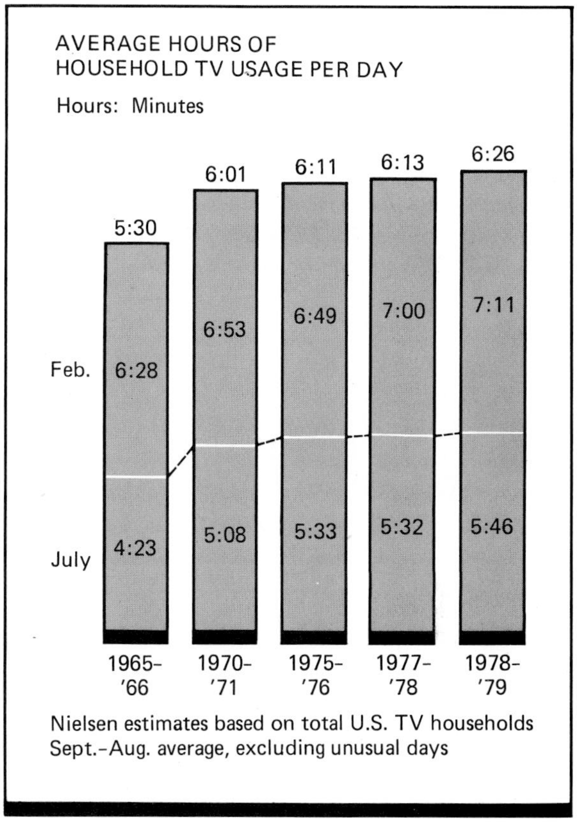

Figure 7.2 TV households, on the average, viewed an estimated 6 hours and 26 minutes a day during the 1978–1979 TV season, the highest season average ever reported. [*Nielsen Media Research.*]

Radio is a relatively low-cost advertising medium, even when commercials are run many times a day in markets across the country. And while its lack of a visual channel may be regarded as a communication drawback, creative people call radio a "theater of the mind," where listeners are free to imagine their own personal pictures of scenes and products.

Television as an Advertising Medium

Ninety-eight percent of United States homes contain TV sets. What is more, half of them have at least two sets and nearly 85 percent have color sets. Average in-home viewing now totals nearly 6½ hours per day.[4] (See Figure 7.2.)

As a significant advertising medium, TV is only about 30 years old. But it has proven itself capable of reaching and holding large audiences comprising (simultaneously) many different demographic groups. In fact, favorite programs often cut across a remarkably wide range of ages. For example, in 1980, the comedy "Three's Company" ranked in the "Top Ten" for children 2 through 11, teens 12 through 17, women 18 and over, men 18 and over, and total United States households.[5]

On an average evening, during prime viewing hours (between 7 and 11 P.M.), close to 60 percent of all American homes watch television—chiefly for entertainment, but also for news and information. TV's realistic communication potential, a combination of sight, sound, motion, and emotion, make it ideal for product demonstration; nearly 90 percent of the nation's leading advertisers place more advertising dollars in TV than in any other medium.[6]

Of course, television is a much more expensive medium than radio, although a number of discounts are available to qualified buyers. These will be discussed later in this chapter. Also, some dayparts—such as 7 A.M. to 1 P.M. and 1 P.M. to 5 P.M.—are less costly than more popular viewing hours, and still draw large enough audiences to make them attractive advertising slots.

national department-store chains are now the largest buyers of local TV advertising time.[7]

National advertisers still contribute the bulk of TV's advertising revenues, but retailers are becoming increasingly involved with television. They are finding inexpensive ways to use this medium, and are learning that effective creative executions need not be complicated. Thus, radio and TV often work hand in hand—nationally, regionally, and locally—to communicate advertisers' sales messages.

Radio and Television Working Together

Table 7.1 shows current and projected broadcast advertising expenditures at both national and local levels. Traditionally, radio has been thought of as a local advertising medium and TV as a national one. Whereas radio's role hasn't changed much, though, some of television's recent sales pitches have been directed to local supermarkets and auto dealers, real estate agents and movie theaters, jewelry stores, clothing stores, restaurants, and banks. In addition,

The Structure of Broadcasting

Before a radio or TV station can be successful as an advertising medium, it must have (1) sound engineering to deliver a usable signal to audiences, and (2) attractive programs to gain and hold their attention and interest. Every station is a functional organization. The activities of each major department—normally engineering, programming, news, sales, and office administration—are closely integrated with those of other units.

Table 7.1
Broadcast Advertising Expenditures
(National and Local Broadcast Advertising Expenditures Projected through the Year 2000)

	1980 expenditures (in millions)	% of total advertising expenditures	Projected expenditures for the year 2000 (in millions)	% of total advertising expenditures
National level				
Television	$8,410	27.5	$46,700	27.0
Radio	980	3.2	5,200	3.0
Local level				
Television	$3,100	12.4	$23,200	16.0
Radio	2,840	11.4	16,000	11.0

SOURCE: Adapted from *Advertising Age*, Nov. 13, 1980, p. 14.

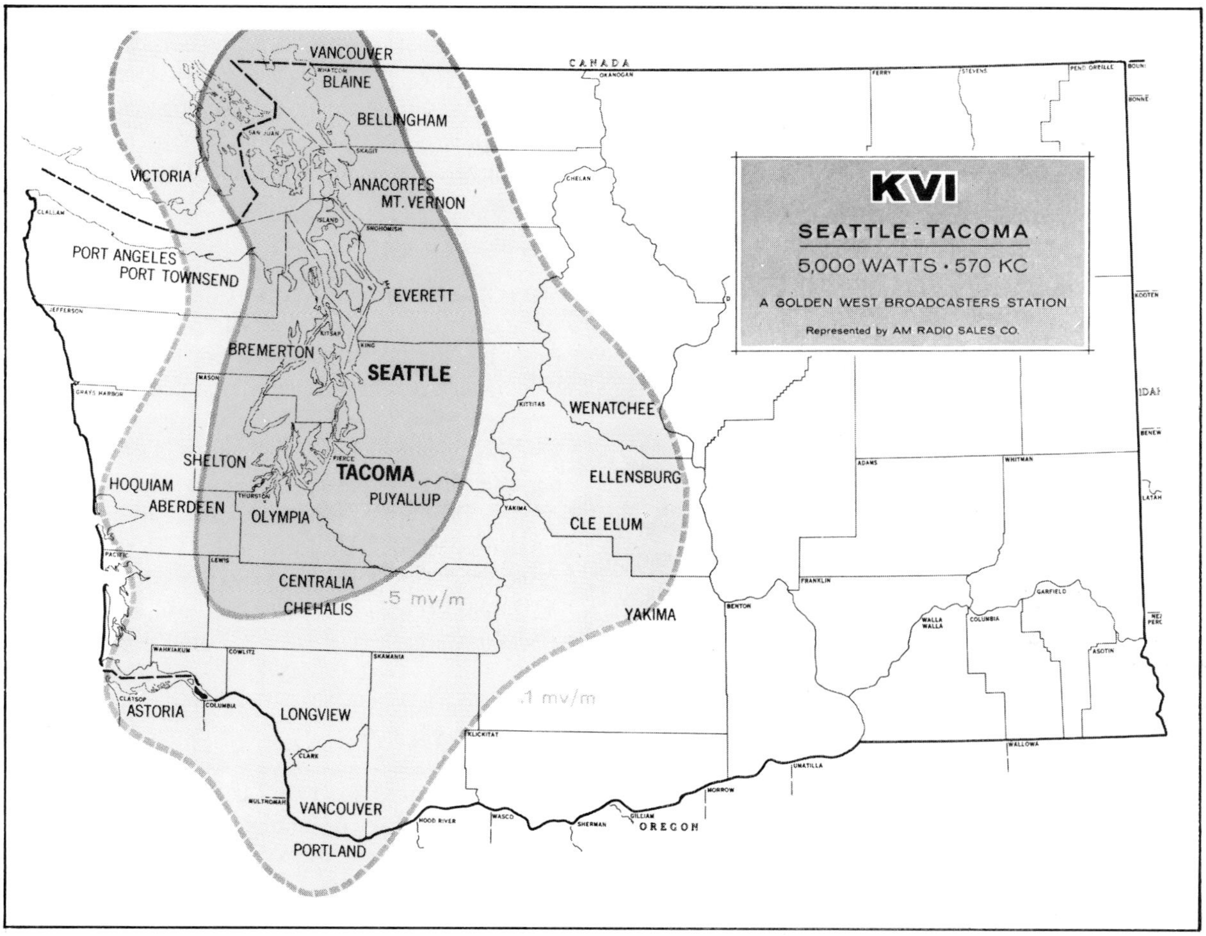

Figure 7.3 The solid line on this radio coverage map indicates the station's best or primary coverage area, and the dotted line indicates the secondary coverage. [*KVI Radio.*]

The Radio Station

The power used in radio signal transmission is important in determining a station's reception area. In addition, the antenna system of the station, its frequency on the dial, and various local conditions are important factors in geographic coverage. Radio coverage maps, such as the one shown in Figure 7.3, indicate where the station may be received with clarity.

On the basis of power, there are essentially three kinds of radio stations. First is the local station, with a receiving range of about 25 miles. Second is the regional station, which may cover an entire state. The least common type is the clear-channel station, with power up to 50,000 watts. It covers a sizable portion of the country, and traditionally it operated on a frequency where no other stations were permitted (at least during evening hours). Today, the Federal Communications Commission has become more lenient in permitting widely separated stations to share these frequencies.

Approximately half of all American radio stations operate on the principle of amplitude modulation (AM), and half operate on frequency modulation (FM).[8] FM's one outstanding advantage over AM is that it is practically distortion-free. On the other hand, obstacles such as large buildings, bridges, or hills affect reception of FM signals. Also, these signals cannot be received over great distances, so FM radio broadcasting has been confined primarily to areas where a concentrated audience is available.

The Television Station

Station designations in television consist of **very high**

frequency (VHF) channels 2 through 13, and **ultra high frequency** (UHF) channels 14 through 83. All TV stations transmit two signals at the same time; video comes via amplitude modulation (AM), and audio uses frequency modulation (FM) broadcasting. Thus, television sound is comparable in fidelity and range with FM radio.

Because station equipment is much more costly in TV than it is in radio, the number of United States television stations will probably never approach the number of radio stations. Rather, the two are expected to remain in about a 9 to 1 ratio for the foreseeable future.

Cable Television

Soon after the advent of television as a popular home-entertainment medium, Community Antenna Television (CATV) systems were established to bring clear reception to viewers who were surrounded by signal-blocking mountains or otherwise isolated from transmitting stations. Broadcast signals were picked up by tall towers and distributed on cables to homes agreeing to pay a monthly subscription fee for the service.

Later, these now-called cable systems became full-scale business operations that either produced or secured their own programs, or used both methods. Thus, subscribers received improved reception of shows carried by regular TV stations plus the chance to view alternative programming (such as sports events, old Hollywood movies, and automated data services such as weather and stock market information). Today, many cable systems also carry commercials, charging advertisers only a small fraction of the figures set by standard VHF and UHF stations. In the early 1980s, 25 percent of all American homes were cable-equipped.

Pay Cable

More than one-third of all cable-subscribing households also participate in a pay-as-you-watch venture known as **pay TV.** In addition to their regular cable-TV programs, these audiences elect to watch special programs distributed over the same cables but in a "scrambled" (distorted, unintelligible) fashion. By paying a monthly charge, in addition to the basic cable subscription rate, viewers receive clear signals. In many respects, this is the same idea as paying to see a particular movie at a theater. The movies shown on pay TV are first-run, unedited, uninterrupted (by commercials) feature films, though program suppliers also offer sportscasts and other shows with appeals similar to those carried by regular cable systems.

Superstations

A station that sends its signal to cable-equipped homes by **satellite** is called a superstation. This relatively new operation is a combination of satellite communication (used by regular, free, over-the-air networks, as discussed in the next section of this chapter), and cable TV (available to paying subscribers). The pioneer superstation in the United States was WTCG-TV (now WTSB-TV) in Atlanta. Today it solicits advertising at rates reflecting the more-than-10 million households it reaches outside its home market.

Networks

In business terms, a network is an organization that provides a variety of programs to affiliated stations in local markets throughout the nation. In technical terms, radio networks traditionally used leased telephone wires to send program material to their affiliates, and TV networks used coaxial cables and microwave relay stations. Today, both radio and television have added satellite communication to their other station-connection systems. For example, one satellite, in orbit some 20,000 miles above the earth, feeds NBC's popular "Tonight Show" from its production center in Burbank, California, to New York. Others are responsible for delivering live telecasts of events from all corners of the world—and from outer space and the moon.

By furnishing quality news and entertainment fare, networks help radio and television stations fill programming needs. Advertisers who can benefit from national coverage then have a chance to tie their commercials into network program offerings.

Radio Networks

Before the advent of television, network radio was a prosperous national advertising medium, bringing

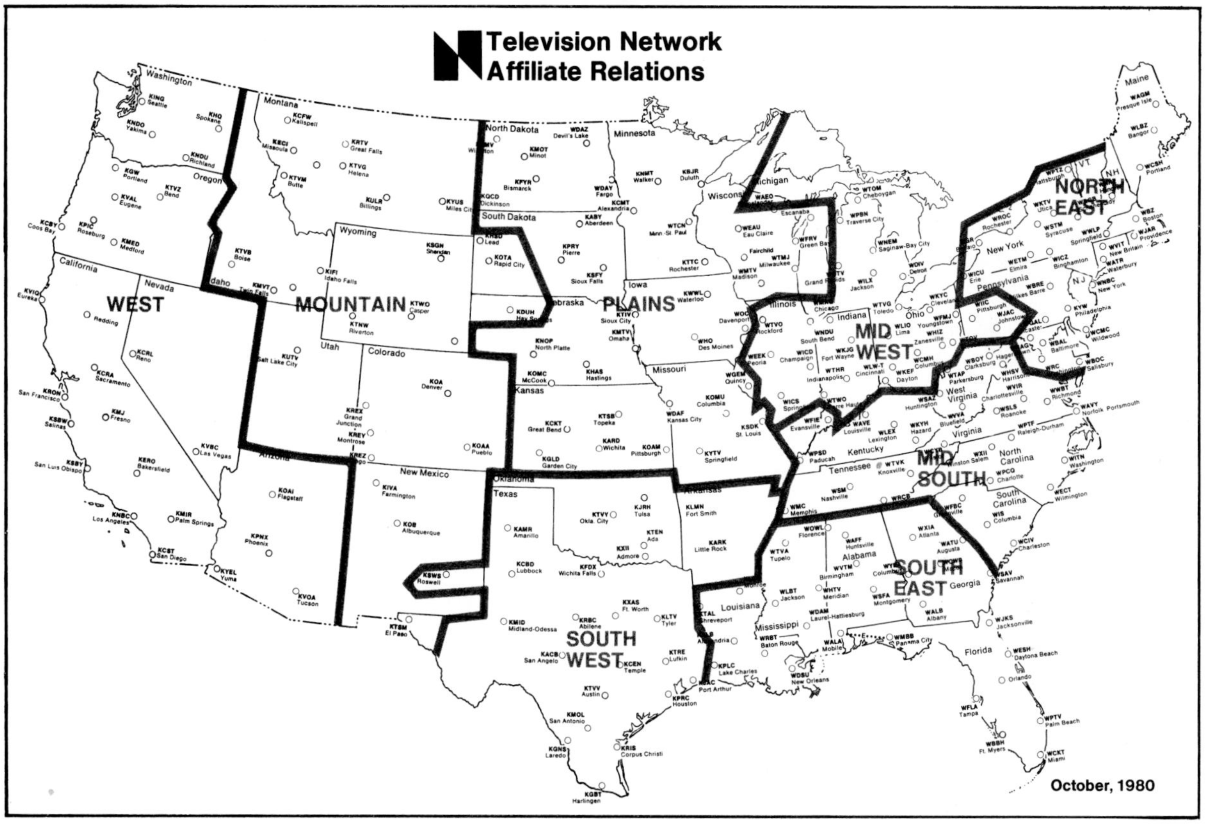

Figure 7.4 The many stations affiliated with the NBC Television Network provide an advertiser with national coverage from a single commercial. [*National Broadcasting Company.*]

American listeners a cherished form of family entertainment. Today, TV has taken over this function and network radio sales account for less than 5 percent of that medium's total advertising revenue.[9]

National radio networks, such as CBS, NBC, and the Mutual Broadcasting System, still do provide news for their affiliates, and they staged a kind of programming comeback a few years ago when they returned dramatic shows to the air (TV had driven them off in the 1950s). Audiences responded enthusiastically to the CBS "Radio Mystery Theater," and Sears, Roebuck launched the "Sears Radio Theater" five nights per week. Other national advertisers have sponsored major radio sportscasts. For example, Hart Schaffner & Marx sponsors the Masters Golf Tournament and Budweiser sponsors National Football League games. The Mutual Broadcasting System is a national sports network for radio only.

Smaller, subsidiary networks also supply program fare to stations. For example, ABC has divided itself into the American Contemporary Radio Network, the American Entertainment Radio Network, the American FM Radio Network, and the American Information Network. The Keystone Broadcasting System is a **transcription network**—a series of stations joined together by tape recordings, so there are no wire costs.

Classifications of Television Networks

National television networks are thriving in the 1980s. Annual TV time sales total over $9 billion, of which more than 47 percent is network advertising.[10] In fact, the most common type of TV network is the **national network:** ABC, CBS, and NBC. When advertisers wish to expose messages to the whole country, they buy time on an entire network. Figure 7.4 shows how thoroughly a network system covers the nation.

Regional networks concentrate on one area, such as New England or the Southeastern states, and

Figure 7.5 Behind the scenes in television and radio stations are housed the complex and expensive pieces of electronic equipment that make effective program and commerical production and transmission possible. [*Photo courtesy of Ampex Corporation.*]

cater to specialized tastes and preferences. Every region of the country is interested in its own news and weather developments, and the regional loyalties of football, baseball, basketball, and hockey fans are legendary.

The time differential between the East and West coasts is another reason for the existence of regional networks. A program aired at 9 P.M. in New York City would be received on the West Coast at 6 P.M.—hardly an equivalent viewing time. So, Pacific Coast affiliates videotape Eastern programs and air them at hours more convenient for their audiences. Since videotape allows immediate playback, the program can be aired the same day. A filmed version would require many hours, even days, to process.

There are no local networks. Instead, a third classification is the **tailor-made network,** in which either a few or many stations join temporarily to broadcast a special program or series. Then the network goes out of existence, although it may be re-formed again later. Tailor-made networks are especially popular for sports events, such as professional football or high school basketball tournaments, because interest in various teams is selective by area.

Although this kind of network often has trouble clearing regularly scheduled time slots and must also overcome engineering problems, it permits advertisers to pinpoint messages to the markets they want to reach without much wasted coverage. Nevertheless, the tailor-made network is the least used type.

The Relationship between Network and Affiliate

Both the network and the local affiliate benefit from the relationship they share. The network enjoys the station's market outlet for airing programs and commercials; the greater the audience for network material, the higher the price for commercial time. The station gets high-quality programming without incurring any production costs. In addition, the station receives compensation from the network—normally, 30 percent of the hourly rate that the station would otherwise charge an advertiser who bought the same time as a program sponsor. The other 70 percent is regarded as station reimbursement to the network for the cost of delivering the program (by means of microwave, satellite, or other method).

Even with the 30 percent payment, the station still comes out ahead—for two reasons. First, it is freed from the time, effort, and cost of not only *producing* or otherwise securing its own programming, but also *selling* it to advertisers. Second, although network programs come complete with commercials, the local station may sell advertising both immediately before and after a network program and during station-break periods within the show. These commercial slots boast higher prices than they would if no network programs were present, because advertisers are willing to pay for the prestige of being close to network-level programming.

The Federal Communications Commission

Without some form of federal control, broadcasting in the United States would be chaotic. Station signals would overlap, and unscrupulous opportunists would wreak havoc on what is now a fairly orderly system. Still, many broadcasters resent the governmental interference imposed on broadcasting that is not matched in the newspaper and magazine businesses, protected as they are by the First Amendment to the Constitution.

Since 1934, broadcasting in the United States has been under the control of the Federal Communications Commission. The FCC not only makes the rules under which broadcasters operate, but also is responsible for licensing each station. These licenses are subject to renewal every three years, and it is this requirement that gives the FCC its muscle.

Before the FCC decides to grant or reject a new station application, it takes into account the commitments made by the owner. Will the station operate in response to public interests and needs? The applicant, whether or not it is a network affiliate, must pledge a certain amount of public service broadcasting. Normally, the station must agree to carry public service advertising as well. Once a license has been granted, the FCC bases renewal decisions on how effectively the broadcaster has carried out original pledges. In addition, the public is always informed of renewal proceedings and asked to testify for or against the application.

A 1972 FCC ruling established the Prime Time Access Rule (PTAR), which requires that network-affiliated TV stations in the top 50 markets air a maximum of three hours of current network programming or syndicated programs formerly shown on the networks, during prime-time evening hours. As a result, many of these stations have lengthened their nightly newscasts, have turned to independent production companies for programs to fill the early evening time slots, or have done both.

Beyond FCC regulations, broadcasters have additional self-imposed restrictions in the form of the Radio and Television Codes of the National Association of Broadcasters (NAB). These ethical codes have helped minimize broadcaster abuses in both programming and advertising, and cover such issues as advertising to children, good taste in presentation, and the number of commercial minutes allowed per broadcast hour. Figure 7.6 shows a page from an NAB code book.

Many broadcasters feel obligated to abide by NAB codes, even though they carry no legal sanction; before granting a license renewal, the FCC checks to see how well the station applicant has met the standards set up by its own industry.

Types of Broadcast Advertising

A national advertiser who uses the broadcast media has a number of decisions to make. This section deals with available alternatives and criteria used in determining campaign strategies.

The Network Strategy

Advertisers often turn to radio or TV networks when they wish to cover either the entire country or a large section of it:

1 A network buy offers the chance to air messages through hundreds of local stations at a lower cost than buying the same stations individually.
2 It is much simpler, administratively, to place advertising through one network than on hundreds

IX. General Advertising Standards

1. This Code establishes basic standards for all television broadcasting. The principles of acceptability and good taste within the Program Standards section govern the presentation of advertising where applicable. In addition, the Code establishes in this section special standards which apply to television advertising.

2. A commercial television broadcaster makes his facilities available for the advertising of products and services and accepts commercial presentations for such advertising. However, a television broadcaster should, in recognition of his responsibility to the public, refuse the facilities of his station to an advertiser where he has good reason to doubt the integrity of the advertiser, the truth of the advertising representations, or the compliance of the advertiser with the spirit and purpose of all applicable legal requirements.

3. Identification of sponsorship must be made in all sponsored programs in accordance with the requirements of the Communications Act of 1934, as amended, and the Rules and Regulations of the Federal Communications Commission.

4. Representations which disregard normal safety precautions shall be avoided.

Children shall not be represented, except under proper adult supervision, as being in contact with, or demonstrating a product recognized as potentially dangerous to them.

5. In consideration of the customs and attitudes of the communities served, each television broadcaster should refuse his facilities to the advertisement of products and services, or the use of advertising scripts, which the station has good reason to believe would be objectionable to a substantial and responsible segment of the community. These standards should be applied with judgment and flexibility, taking into consideration the characteristics of the medium, its home and family audience, and the form and content of the particular presentation.

6. The advertising of hard liquor (distilled spirits) is not acceptable.

Figure 7.6 A page from the *Television Code of the National Association of Broadcasters.*

of individual stations; networks provide a single billing for all stations covered.

3 Networks can provide simultaneous coverage across the country, with excellent control over the placement of commercials within each network's own programming. (Of course, some shows are seen on a tape-delayed basis, as noted earlier, in order to suit different time zones.)

The Spot Broadcasting Strategy

National advertisers seeking geographic flexibility may run a spot broadcasting campaign. There is often some confusion about the term "spot," because it is used in two different ways. A short radio or TV announcement or commercial is commonly called a spot. **Spot broadcasting,** on the other hand, is the placement of commercials in specific markets, on specific stations within those markets, at specific times. It is an alternative to network advertising for achieving national coverage:

1 A spot buy is recommended for advertisers with incomplete national product distribution, limited advertising budgets, or fluctuating regional sales patterns. Electric heaters fall in the third category because their heavy sales are concentrated in areas with cold seasons.

2 Spot campaigns deliver varying amounts of advertising in individual markets selected by the advertiser, and changes in emphasis can be made periodically.

3 Spot broadcasting allows alterations in copy appeals and production to suit local market needs. For example, a youth-oriented radio commercial could be presented by the outstanding disc jockey in each market covered.

Network versus Spot: A Comparison

Network broadcasting may be compared with national magazine advertising. It delivers approximately the same amount of advertising pressure everywhere it goes. It originates from, and is controlled at, one point—usually New York or Los Angeles. Spot broadcasting, however, is analogous to advertising in local newspapers. The advertiser determines how much advertising to place in each market, the stations on which the advertising will run, how long it will last, and the time periods in which it will appear.

Some campaigns involve both network and spot buys, and one supplements the other very effectively.

In 1980, national television advertisers spent approximately $3.3 billion on spot broadcasting buys and $5.1 billion on network. In radio, the difference was more dramatic. National advertisers invested only about $185 million in network radio, but over 4 times that amount, $750 million, in spot.[11]

Program Sponsorship

Evening network television in the 1950s was dominated by big-name advertisers and the weekly programs they sponsored, such as the "Ford Theater" and "Texaco Star Theater," and later, Perry Como's "Kraft Music Hall." In fact, during the early years of TV, 89 percent of evening network broadcasts were paid for by individual advertisers. By the late 1950s, that figure had dropped to 46 percent as advertisers sought compatible cosponsors to share the mounting costs of program sponsorship. Nearly half the programs in this period had two or more sponsors.

In 1963–1964, only 16 percent of the prime evening programs enjoyed the luxury of a single sponsor such as Chevrolet's "Bonanza," and 31 percent were cosponsored. By 1975, regular program sponsorship was almost unheard of. Even cosponsorship is now rare. In the 1980s, some major advertisers, like Kraft, Hallmark, and IBM, still sponsor specials during appropriate seasons of the year, but the vast majority of network advertisers have turned to "participations."

Participation Shows

A **participation show** is one in which a variety of sponsors place commercials within the body of the program: after the introduction of the show, during breaks, and at the program's conclusion. The "participation" here has nothing to do with whether or not members of a studio audience participate in contests or exchange dialogue with a master of ceremonies. Rather, the term describes advertisers who participate in paying for a program, though they have nothing to do with the show's production. This growing trend in network television has been referred to as the "magazine concept." Advertisers buy into network programs as they would buy into magazines, placing commercials (ads) in appropriate programs (issues) with no responsibility for details of the program (editorial) content. In either case they are concerned, primarily, with the size and buying habits of the audiences that certain programs or magazines will attract. "As the World Turns" obviously draws a very different audience than "Wide World of Sports" or "M*A*S*H*."

Another concern in program selection is compatibility. How well does the mood or tone of a show coincide with the image of the product an advertiser is trying to sell? Cosmetic advertising blends well with the "Miss America Pageant," and Kodak and Campbell's soup with "Little House on the Prairie." Conversely, when a network runs a series episode dealing with a fatal plane or car crash, an airline or automotive company that has regularly advertised in that particular program series may well ask that its commercials be withdrawn.

The same thing happens if a program involves a controversial subject (such as abortion, physical violence, or religious discrimination) with which the advertiser chooses not to be associated.

Announcement Campaigns

Announcement campaigns are a form of local advertising or spot broadcasting. The fundamental difference between commercials here and those within network programs is that these are (1) sold only by local stations or their representatives; and (2) aired *between network programs,* rather than within them, and *in* or *between local programs.* There is little chance to identify a product with a show since the commercial announcements placed between programs are isolated from the shows themselves. Still, these time slots are relatively inexpensive, and some advertisers enjoy buying them in large quantities (for the added value that sheer frequency may give to a campaign).

The break between programs is usually longer than breaks within shows, and many commercials, station and network identifications, promotional spots for coming programs, and public service announcements compete for audience attention. But announcement campaigns do have built-in flexibility. Since there are no extended commitments or long lead-times, commercial schedules can be changed or canceled on very short notice.

Radio and TV Programs and their Audiences

Millions of Americans enjoy the companionship of radio or television throughout the day and night. The stations and programs that attract specific audiences are a key concern of broadcast time buyers and sellers.

Radio Audiences

The thousands of United States radio stations vying for advertising dollars compete primarily on the basis of audiences attracted to particular types of music and on-air personalities. This station loyalty is in direct contrast to the situation in television where most viewers select *programs*, regardless of which stations carry them.

There are at least 12 dozen different radio formats today—2 dozen in the field of country music alone—and many stations claim several.[12] The most common ones, however, are known as "Top 40," "Beautiful Music." "Adult Contemporary," "Album Oriented Rock" (AOR), "Middle-of-the-Road" (MOR), and "Country-Western," along with news/sports/talk (more than 150 stations are "all news") and ethnic-oriented formats (such as those appealing directly to blacks or Spanish-speaking persons).

The most popular consumer age bracket sought by radio advertisers today is 18-to-49, although the 25-to-54 group is important in a lot of markets. In addition, radio has proven an excellent way to attract the on-the-go teenage audience.

Although media buyers are vitally interested in audience types and sizes, they are also concerned with **availabilities.** These are the time periods ("slots") that stations have not yet sold; therefore, they are available to carry commercials. Radio listenership tends to peak in morning and evening "drive-time" hours, and to fall off markedly later in the evening. Since commercial time rates are based largely on audience size, many stations divide their days into four periods: class AAA time, from 6 to 10 A.M.; class AA time, from 3 to 7 P.M.; class A time, from 10 A.M. to 3 P.M.; and class B time, from 7 P.M. to midnight. Other arrangements may cover early morning and weekend time periods, and sometimes classes are combined, so a station has only two or three different rate categories covering its entire broadcast spectrum.

Television Audiences

In television, programs (rather than stations) determine the type of people attracted during specific time periods. Network TV advertisers, like radio advertisers, are interested in commercial time availabilities that will deliver large numbers of persons within their target markets. A national beer manufacturer, for example, might advertise on World Series telecasts to reach a significant percentage of males eighteen to thirty-nine years old—the heart of the beer-drinking public.

Suppose, however, that another advertiser is interested in this same audience (say, a sports apparel firm), but (1) has only regional distribution, so does not need national program coverage, and (2) cannot afford World Series program costs anyway. This advertiser might buy spot announcements on only a few of the stations carrying this telecast—during station-break time when these stations are free to run locally sold spots (before returning to the network). Such time slots are known as "adjacencies" because they fall next to (immediately before or after) a program or program segment.

Like radio listening, television viewing follows definite patterns. Figure 7.7 finds the TV audience building fairly steadily throughout the day, and peaking during the evening hours. As the chart reveals, more than 3 times as many people watch television at 10 P.M. as watch at 10 A.M. Furthermore, mornings and early afternoons are heavily skewed toward full-time homemakers and others at home at that time, while late-afternoon hours and Saturday mornings are popular with children. (See Figure 7.8.) Working men and women, of course, do most of their viewing at night.

As human beings, audiences are creatures of habit. So, an increasingly popular TV programming strategy known as **stripping** is pursued in a deliberate attempt to establish and maintain habitual viewing patterns. To "strip" is to run episodes of the same series at the same time, five or six days a week. This practice clearly bypasses the expense and headaches involved with finding different shows to fill daily slots with a "checkerboard" lineup. A majority of the top 50 market stations are now stripping programs—especially in late afternoon and late night hours, as well as during the early evening period right before prime time (known as "early fringe" time or prime-time access).[13]

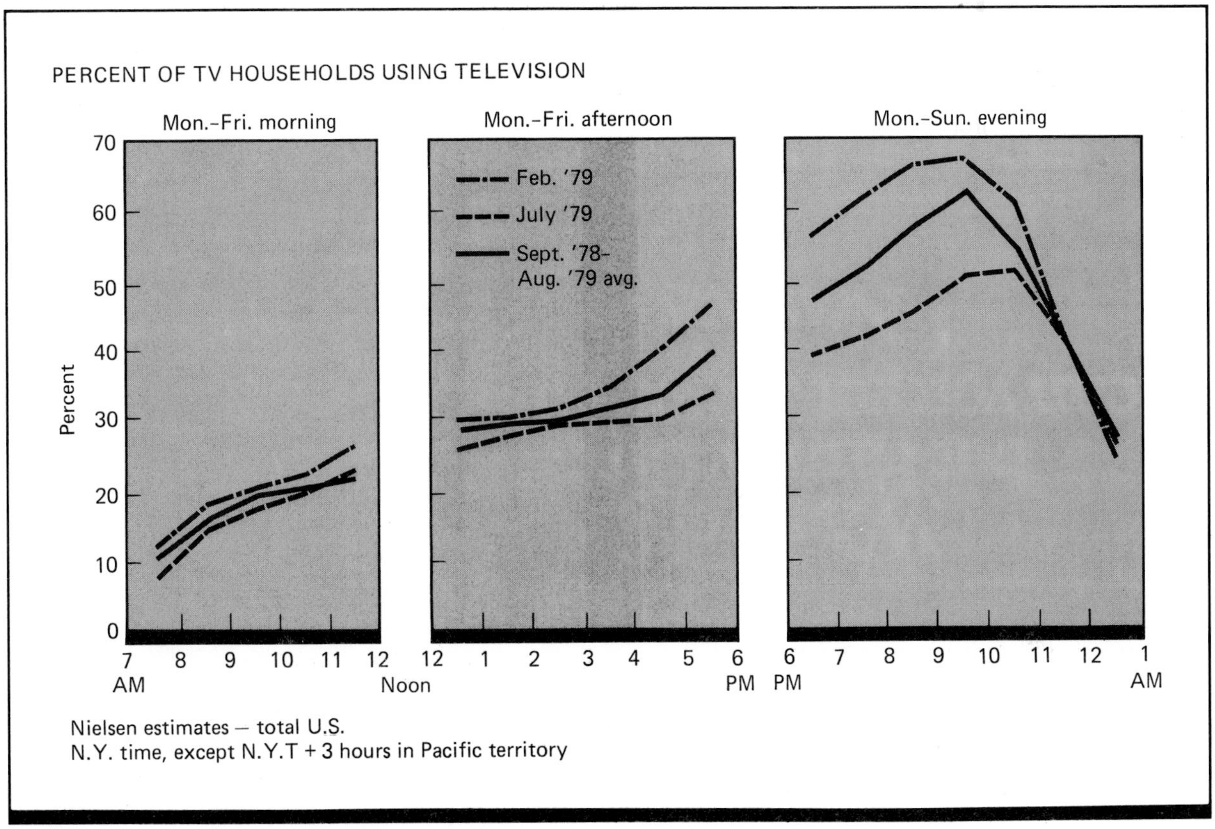

Figure 7.7 TV viewing peaks between 8 P.M. and 10 P.M. each day. Thereafter, a sharp decline sets in as people go to bed. [*Nielsen Media Research.*]

Types of Programs

The FCC divides programs into eight categories: (1) entertainment, (2) religious, (3) agricultural, (4) educational, (5) news, (6) discussion, (7) talk, and (8) miscellaneous. Subtypes of the entertainment category, of greatest interest to advertisers, are programs such as children's daytime shows, variety programs, dramatic performances, audience-participation shows, music, and sports.

A firm that decides to sponsor a **special** may have to justify the expenditure of $1 million or more on a one-time show. Or, as noted previously, advertisers with heavy holiday sales may sponsor intermittent specials to boost their selling efforts or to improve the environment in which they conduct business.

Sources of Programs

There was a time when advertisers and agencies were highly influential in the development of TV shows. Since full-program sponsorship no longer exists on a regular basis, however, networks and local stations decide almost exclusively what goes on the air and when. Once in a while, though, an advertiser-produced offering is bartered (traded) for free advertising time. The stations carrying the program sell only part of the commercial time within it, and give the rest to the advertiser and agency providing the show.

Network and Station Programs Most programs come from a few main sources: networks or stations, feature-film producers, and outside packagers. Networks produce newscasts, athletic competitions, and documentaries like *CBS Reports.* Local stations produce their own newscasts, and often some children's programming and talk and discussion shows.

Feature Films Hollywood motion pictures are available to broadcasters after they have run in local

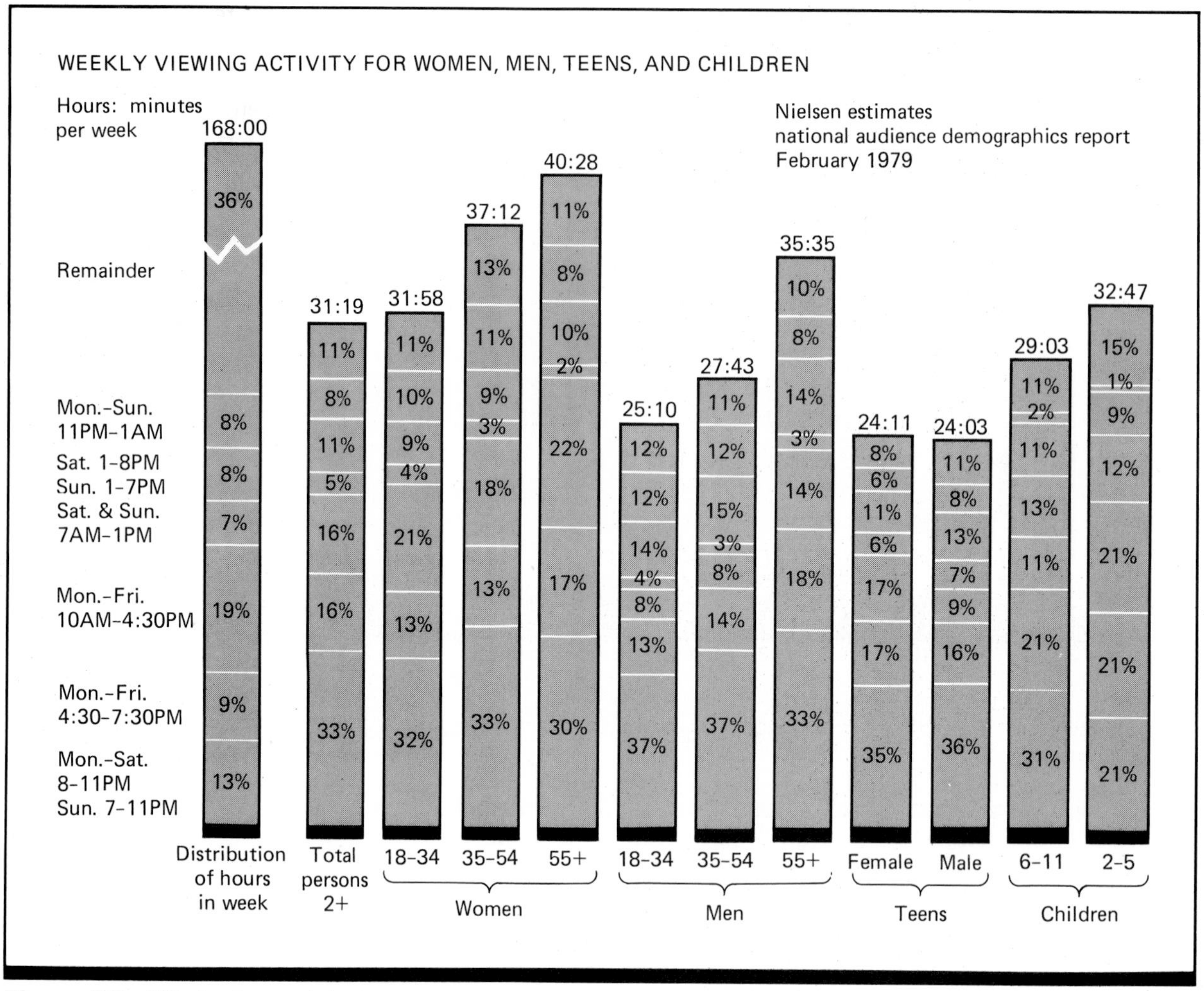

Figure 7.8 TV viewing activity is distributed disproportionately throughout the day, reflecting the relative availability of each age group. [*Nielsen Media Research.*]

theaters. They are usually offered first to the networks, and later to local stations, to be shown a number of times on a rerun basis. Some stations contract with a motion-picture production company such as Paramount or 20th Century Fox for a group of 50 films, to be run at the station's convenience over a three-year period. "Made-for-television" movies may be bought by a network outright, run several times, and then made available to affiliated stations for local rebroadcasting.

Syndicated Programs Syndication takes one of two forms. First, it is the practice of distributing a series of previously successful network TV programs to local stations for use as reruns. These shows fill the hours not covered by current network programming. In the case of independent (nonnetwork-affiliated) stations, syndicated programs often make up the bulk of each broadcast day. Familiar examples of syndicated shows include "All in the Family," the "Streets of San Francisco," and the "Mary Tyler Moore Show." Stations contract for these programs in 13-, 26-, or 39-week blocks and sell advertising time in and around them to local and national advertisers.

In its second form, syndication is the distribution of programs developed by independent producers to interested stations. Today, three or four hundred United States companies package and sell radio programs, both music and commentary, and twice as many are involved in TV. Some of these shows do not appear first on the networks, but go directly to local stations. When the "Merv Griffin Show" lost its TV network slot, it was produced in syndication and now enjoys large audiences in hundreds of cities across America. The same is true of the "Lawrence Welk Show." Formerly a network program, it is now produced independently and sold to individual stations for presentation to local markets.

In the case of radio, one of the largest syndicated shows in the industry is a one-hour country music program entitled "Live from the Lone Star Café." Aired on some 160 stations, it is coproduced by the Clayton Webster Corporation and New York's Lone Star Café. Syndicated programs are very appealing to stations because they provide an excellent source of revenue (since the shows have already proven successful), and, of course, they require no station production costs or efforts.

Broadcast Ratings

Broadcast ratings, describing the numbers and kinds of people who view or listen to particular programs, are used to establish the rates charged advertisers for commercial time. Ratings also determine to a large extent which TV shows remain on the air and which ones are canceled. In radio, they help station managers decide which formats and on-air personalities are most popular.

A well-known method for obtaining national TV ratings is A. C. Nielsen's Instantaneous Audimeter. This electronic device is placed on TV sets in cooperating homes and wired to a central tabulating headquarters. The data collected, coupled with additional information obtained from viewer diaries, are available to subscribing broadcast and advertising industry personnel on a daily, weekly, and monthly basis.

Similar research is conducted by the Arbitron Company, which also works with radio. Figure 7.9 shows a portion of a page from an Arbitron TV rating book covering the St. Louis market. Critical numbers here are the RTG (program rating) and SHR (share of audience) percentages, both of which will be discussed shortly. Figure 7.10 shows findings from an Arbitron radio study in Corpus Christi. A "cume" is simply the accumulated total of all persons in a given demographic group who were reached by a particular station during the period of time under study (often four weeks). Notice that cumes are provided in this example for five different age groups. Some research organizations gather radio ratings by telephone—among them Audits & Surveys, Burke, and Mediastat.

Ratings are calculated in several ways and serve several purposes. The following sections describe some of them.

Homes-Using-Radio and Homes-Using-Television Ratings

All ratings are percentages—but the figures on which they are based vary depending on the kind of rating being computed. Probably the simplest type to understand is called the "Homes-Using-Radio" (HUR) or "Homes-Using-Television" (HUT) rating. Sometimes the term "Sets-In-Use" (SIU) is used for radio. This rating shows the percentage of all radio or TV homes in a given area that have a set turned on (or "in use") during a particular time period, with no concern for the station or program to which each set is tuned. The highest possible rating here would be 100 percent, indicating that all American homes possessing a radio or TV set had the set on when measured. (And, since nearly every American home does have both radio and TV, the 100 percent designation would closely approximate the total number of households in the area being studied.) Never in the history of the rating services, however, has an HUR or HUT rating ever been 100 percent. Nightly television averages are in the neighborhood of 60 percent, although special telecasts may raise this total considerably.

This type of rating may be most useful to advertisers who are considering the use of television or radio in a campaign (as opposed, say, to magazines or newspapers). Or, they may use the HUT/HUR rating to help determine how much emphasis to put on television or radio in a multimedia campaign. If, for example, this rating is very low in a particular advertiser's market, print media may prove more efficient carriers of advertising messages.

Program Ratings

The most prominent of broadcast research concepts, the **program rating,** refers to the percentage of area

8.30P KTVI																						
TUE TAXI	4	8	22	35	23	36	222	167	116	47	75	85	94	114	56	129	93	73	68	73	67	29
THU SOAP	3	6	18	28	19	32	177	132	107	45	82	76	79	93	40	120	92	68	70	76	55	26
KMOX																						
MON WKRP IN CINN	3	6	22	31	23	33	226	183	144	45	97	109	117	129	60	130	98	75	69	73	49	19
SUN JEFFERSONS	3	6	24	35	25	37	238	237	129	54	70	87	115	148	80	164	87	52	58	73	51	25
KSDK																						
WED HELLO LARRY	2	4	15	24	15	24	154	121	57	12	28	51	71	93	46	73	42	28	40	41	48	12.
KPLR																						
MON *CROSS-WITS	3	6	7	10	6	9	85	84	14	4	6	11	14	35	12	54	8	1	8	9	2	2
TUE *CROSS-WITS	3	6	7	11	6	10	79	79	14	3	5	12	17	30	10	46	9	3	9	11	3	2
WED *CROSS-WITS	4	8	8	13	8	12	99	101	18	3	3	17	22	42	13	62	10	4	8	10	6	4
THU *CROSS-WITS	3	6	9	14	8	12	106	105	18	2	6	16	20	36	10	59	8	3	6	9	3	1
FRI *CROSS-WITS	4	8	6	10	6	10	78	73	6	1	1	6	9	25	6	46	7	3	6	7	3	2
SAT COUNTRY ROAD	4	8	6	10	5	9	74	70	15	2	6	14	17	35	10	53	11	3	10	14	3	2
AVG CROSS-WITS		34	8	12	7	11	89	88	14	2	4	13	17	34	10	53	8	3	7	9	4	2
9.00P KTVI																						
TUE HART TO HART	3	12	20	31	21	33	202	175	129	44	85	98	112	131	61	121	90	66	70	73	39	21
WED VEGA$	3	12	18	28	18	27	190	158	90	25	53	75	90	116	49	118	69	44	57	73	36	16
THU *20/20	3	12	20	34	22	38	198	180	123	35	89	93	103	128	51	136	98	64	84	88	35	11
SAT FANTSY ISLND	4	16	19	33	21	37	191	162	89	25	57	71	87	108	51	97	63	44	48	55	49	24
AVG 20/20		16	20	34	23	38	203	179	121	35	88	91	101	127	54	137	99	66	84	87	32	12
KMOX																						
MON LOU GRANT	3	12	23	31	24	33	225	202	146	32	92	123	.134	153	65	128	95	65	71	73	32	14
THU BARNBY JONES	2	8	18	28	18	29	182	156	72	26	36	55	77	111	62	108	64	38	45	49	33	21
FRI DALLAS	4	20	30	48	31	49	304	291	181	64	105	136	162	193	89	160	101	68	74	90	67	38
SUN TRAPPER JOHN	2	8	26	45	29	47	261	246	145	68	89	91	117	147	82	162	89	54	64	80	56	29
KSDK																						
WED BST SAT LIVE	3	14	16	24	18	26	163	123	105	57	86	59	66	74	53	99	80	60	61	64	57	18
THU KATE LV MYST	3	12	12	21	11	19	123	94	64	25	37	48	52	68	25	73	50	34	36	37	28	13
FRI EISCHIED	2	8	11	18	13	20	115	84	41	5	25	38	44	63	29	84	46	26	41	43	13	4
SAT MAN SLOANE	2	8	12	21	12	21	122	80	49	22	27	32	45	52	30	75	45	28	34	47	24	10
SUN PRIME TME SU	2	8	12	18	13	19	121	99	56	14	29	42	49	70	28	97	62	39	49	56	15	3
KPLR																						
MON *JOKERS WILD	4	8	9	12	7	10	108	117	12	3	5	9	14	37	14	66	4	1	4	7	1	1
TUE *JOKERS WILD	4	8	10	15	8	13	113	114	21	6	8	18	23	46	16	71	13	7	13	16	5	3
WED *JOKERS WILD	4	8	11	16	10	15	132	141	24	1	7	23	31	59	18	81	9	3	8	10	3	3
THU *JOKERS WILD	4	8	9	16	9	14	113	112	17	1	5	17	23	44	16	68	16	10	11	14	3	2
FRI *JOKERS WILD	4	8	9	13	9	13	104	99	17	4	5	15	20	39	13	66	15	7	11	15	5	4
SAT POP GO CNTRY	4	8	7	12	6	10	80	81	23	4	9	20	23	41	14	55	13	3	11	15	4	2
SUN NEWSWATCH 4	4	8	5	8	4	6	63	65	8	1	2	7	7	23	7	40	8	5	6	7		
AVG JOKERS WILD		40	10	14	9	13	114	117	18	4	6	16	22	45	16	71	12	6	10	13	4	3
KDNL																						
SUN ERNST ANGLEY	3	12			1	1	5	5	2			2	3	3		4	2	1	1	1		
			1	2	3	4	5	10	11	12	13	14	15	56	16	17	18	19	20	21	22	23

Figure 7.9 This excerpt from an Arbitron rating book covering the St. Louis market shows the ratings and shares of various TV programs as well as demographic data on the audiences viewing those programs. Such rating information is vital in the selling and buying of TV time. [*Arbitron Television.*]

homes tuned to a specific show. When you read that "60 Minutes" or the "Dukes of Hazzard" led the ratings parade during a particular week, you will find that a "winning" rating is about 30. In other words, 30 percent of the TV homes in America watched that specific program. When you consider that large cities may have as many as 10 stations competing for viewer attention, it is understandable that broadcast executives would be pleased with such a showing.

Again, the highest percentage possible here is 100. This never-yet-achieved program rating is considered even more rare than a 100 percent HUT or HUR rating, because it would mean that every TV or radio home not only had a set on, but had it tuned to the same channel or station at the same time.

Program ratings are used to determine the cost of commercial advertising time within and around each show in a station's lineup. Each program rating point represents 1 percent of the total TV or radio homes in an area, and every market area in the country sets its own cost per rating point. This figure is usually based on (1) the area's population, and (2) the popularity of TV time to advertisers (which varies with the time of year). As an example, suppose that New York is charging $400 per rating point and Seattle is charging $100 per rating point. Therefore, running a commercial within a program such as "Dallas," which claims a rating of, say, 27 in both markets, would cost an advertiser $10,800 in New York and $2,700 in Seattle.

Cume Listening Estimates

CUME PERSONS—TOTAL SURVEY AREA, IN HUNDREDS												STATION CALL LETTERS	CUME PERSONS—METRO SURVEY AREA IN HUNDREDS												STATION CALL LETTERS
TOT. PERS. 12+	MEN					WOMEN					TNS. 12-17		TOT. PERS. 12+	MEN					WOMEN					TNS. 12-17	
	18-24	25-34	35-44	45-54	55-64	18-24	25-34	35-44	45-54	55-64				18-24	25-34	35-44	45-54	55-64	18-24	25-34	35-44	45-54	55-64		
381	60	60		22	13	45	82	23	10	31	17	KCCT	258	38	60		9	13	22	57	14	6	22	17	KCCT
815	101	74	12	20	9	109	116	55	24		285	KEYS	630	58	64	5	20		79	93	46	16		239	KEYS
258	11	45	41	31	16	17	6	19	7	24	17	KIKN	224	11	37	41	25	16	17	6	10	3	24	17	KIKN
437		29	37	35	42	5	20	59	90	37	12	KIOU	320		9	22	29	23	5	14	51	62	29	12	KIOU
364	109	50		16	4	40	22	4	14	3	102	KNCN	299	69	50		16	4	34	22	4	14	3	83	KNCN
319	19	37	5	33	4	29	34	37	28	17	64	KOUL	247	19	37	5	28	4	22	34	22	21	17	33	KOUL
108			23		28		12		19	10		KROB	64			16		19				11	10		KROB
68			8	7	6	3		12	8	3	11	KROB FM	55				7	6	3		12	3	3	11	KROB FM
175			31	7	34	3	12	12	26	13	11	TOTAL	118			16	7	24	3		12	14	13	11	TOTAL
603	79	60	17	13		70	84	54	21	11	176	KRYS	442	36	31	17	13		49	67	45	16	11	139	KRYS
166			8	10	20	5	14	9	23	14	12	KSIX	109			8	5	12	5	3	9	15	14	12	KSIX
335	47	34	27	30	22	8	39	49	29	22	6	KUNO	270	24	34	27	17	13	8	32	40	25	22	6	KUNO
528	113	31	4	7		104	21	26	16		201	KZFM	508	93	31	4	7		104	21	26	16		201	KZFM
89			15	5	6		5		19	18		KTRH	53			8		6				16	10		KTRH
420	66	27	15	12		49	50	20	8	7	157	KTSA	96	26	18				14	16	4			18	KTSA
121				14	6		14		5	24		WOAI	74				14	6		9		5	16		WOAI
												TOTAL LISTENING IN METRO SURVEY AREA	2047	188	208	107	116	87	194	207	149	144	122	373	

Figure 7.10 Radio stations prosper or fail on the basis of radio audience statistics like these taken from an Arbitron study of the Corpus Christi market. [*Arbitron Radio.*]

Share-of-Audience Ratings

A **share-of-audience rating,** sometimes called a **share rating,** is the percentage of homes *with sets turned on and tuned to a specific show.* Note that this rating is based only on homes with sets in use, and that it measures how each station rates against its competitors.

Returning to our look at "60 Minutes," we might find that the same episode of this show that drew a "30" program rating also claimed a 50 percent share of the viewing audience. Further, suppose that 60 percent of all American TV homes had their sets on at this particular time—and, to keep the numbers easy to work with, assume a total of 80 million U.S. households. Now, you can do the math:

HUT rating: 60 percent of 80 million = 48 million homes with sets on

Share rating: 50 percent of 48 million = 24 million homes watching "60 Minutes" (this figure can be compared with competing shows on other channels, which, among them, must divide up the remaining 50 percent share of the audience)

Program rating: 30 percent of 80 million = 24 million homes watching "60 Minutes"

The same 24 million homes are watching "60 Minutes," of course, whether we compute share ratings or program ratings. As noted, however, the cost of commercial time in this show is based on the 30 percent program rating and not on the 50 percent share of audience.

Ratings and Campaign Planning

No rating can indicate which audience members are most likely to respond to certain types of advertising messages. Thus, ratings are much more valuable when they are supplemented by lifestyle and product usage information. **Audience composition** data describe the kinds of people who constitute various audiences. Viewers and listeners are categorized by age, sex, race, income level, and, in some instances, buying habits and psychographic data.

Even with this added information, however, advertisers and their agencies would be hard pressed to specify the exact number of commercial airings needed to achieve campaign goals. So they order, instead, a certain number of **gross rating points** (GRPs)—usually on a per-week basis. Recall that one program rating point is equal to 1 percent of an area's home population. If a Monday-through-Friday afternoon soap opera has a program rating of 8, then 8 percent of the area's TV homes are watching it. In a week, therefore, the *added* rating points (referred to as gross rating points) for this show will equal 40. But that 40 can mean a number of different things: (1) that 40 percent of the area's homes tuned in *once;* or (2) that 20 percent of the homes tuned in *twice;* or (3) that 10 percent of the homes tuned in *four times* . . . and so on.

Advertisers who want to reach this soap opera audience, and who decide that 40 GRPs per week provide a suitable campaign emphasis (based on past experience and available funds), can never be sure which of the above options they are getting. Still, each advertiser is assured of *one* of them, and research shows that in almost all cases, GRPs include audience *duplication* (that is, either option 2 or option 3). Most buys include a number of different programs. For example, a buy of 150 weekly GRPs might involve ten shows with ratings of 15, or five with ratings of 10 and five with ratings of 20. In either case, though, the advertiser would be paying to reach (1) every home 1.5 times; or (2) three-fourths of the homes 2 times; or (3) one-half of the homes 3 times; and so on.

Broadcast Rate Structures

Station owners establish their advertising rates with an eye toward (1) covering operating costs and providing a return on their investments, and (2) reflecting the value of their audiences and remaining competitive with other stations. An advertiser makes a station buy with the hope of reaching a larger portion of the desired target market than can be reached with another station or some other medium.

Media rate structures can be extremely complicated, but they are generally based on **inventories** (that is, the extent of unsold, or "available" time), on the **size** and **quality of the audience** delivered, and on the **quantity of time** purchased. First, since time is a perishable commodity, it gets cheaper as its (still unsold) air time approaches; also, as is true in any supply-and-demand situation, even time purchased well ahead of schedule may be less expensive if it has not had many bidders or is part of a generally unpopular segment of hours.

Second, a station that delivers a commercial to 3 million homes can and will charge more than the station that delivers the same message to 1 million homes. Third, some programs appeal to a more sophisticated audience than others. Some stations schedule a large amount of quality programming in an attempt to secure and maintain a well-educated audience—one that often claims a high income and level of buying power. For example, a broadcast of the U.S. Open Golf Tournament draws an audience comprising a high percentage of top business executives. So, the charge for advertising on this program is greater than the charge for advertising to an equivalent audience attracted to a wrestling match.

Finally, once basic rates have been set for a radio time period or TV program, certain variations occur. The first has to do with the quantity of advertising time a client buys. Just as you buy apples cheaper by the bushel, you can buy spot announcements cheaper in quantity than in small groups. In addition, because media owners prefer to stretch their advertising incomes over long periods of time, both radio and TV stations allow discounts to advertisers who buy blocks of commercials spread over many weeks or months. Such discounts are often referred to as **bulk** (quantity) and **frequency** rates.

It is common among many media to charge national advertisers higher rates than retail advertisers. Some say they do so because a national advertiser has more to gain; that is, Procter & Gamble can make more money from an ad for Tide detergent than Sam's Shoe Repair Shop can make from one of its

KCBS
1909
SAN FRANCISCO
CBS Owned

Represented by **CBS RADIO SPOT SALES**

All News & Information

NAB RAB

Subscriber to the NAB Radio Code
Media Code 4 205 7410 5.00
CBS Radio, a division of CBS, Inc. One Embarcadero Center, San Francisco, Calif. 94111. Phone 415-765-4101.
Send all program and advertising copy to the Continuity Editor

STATION'S PROGRAMMING DESCRIPTION
KCBS: Continuous news & information format. Local, reg'l, nat'l & internat'l reports & features. Network news & programs. Emphasis on traffic, business, sports & weather. 50 newscasters, 4 mobile units. Tele/talk M-F 1-3 pm. Call-in gardening Sun 10 am-noon. SPORTS: play-by-play univ & pro football, conference & super bowl contests; baseball all star game, playoffs, World Series; master's golf; local horse race track stretch calls, nat'l derby's. Contact Representative for further details. Rec'd 8/4/80.

1. PERSONNEL
Vice-Pres. & Gen'l Mgr.—Ray Barnett.
General Sales Manager—Jack Sweeney.
National Sales Manager—Vikki Weber.

2. REPRESENTATIVES
CBS Radio Spot Sales.

3. FACILITIES
50,000 w.; 740 kc. Directional—separate patterns day and night.
Operating schedule: 24 hours daily. PST.

4. AGENCY COMMISSION
15% time only.

5. GENERAL ADVERTISING See coded regulations
General: 1b, 2a, 2b, 3a, 3b, 3d, 4a, 4d, 5, 6b, 7b, 8.
Rate Protection: 15b.
Basic Rates: 20a, 21b, 21c, 21d, 22a, 23b, 24b, 24c, 25a, 27, 28b, 28c, 30.
Contracts: 40b, 41, 44b, 45, 46, 48, 51b, 51c.
Comb.; Cont. Discounts: 60i, 60j, 61b, 62d.
Cancellation: 70a, 70c, 71a, 72, 73b.
Prod. Services: 80, 81, 82.
Affiliated with CBS.

TIME RATES
NATIONAL AND LOCAL RATES SAME
No. 24 Eff 5/5/80—Rec'd 8/4/80.
AA—Mon thru Sat 5-10 am.
A—Mon thru Fri 3-8 pm.
B—Mon thru Fri 10 am-3 pm; Sat 10 am-8 pm; Sun 6 am-8 pm.
C—Mon thru Sun 8 pm-midnight; Sun 5-6 am.
D—Tues thru Sun midnight-5 am.

6. SPOT ANNOUNCEMENTS

GRID:	High Range 1 min	High Range 30 sec	Low Range 1 min	Low Range 30 sec
AA	270	216	190	152
A	180	144	120	96
B	110	88	80	64
C	70	56	50	40
D	24	19	10	3

10. SPECIAL FEATURES

GRID:	High Range 1 min	High Range 30 sec	Low Range 1 min	Low Range 30 sec
AA	500	400	350	280
A	250	200	190	152
B	150	120	120	96
C	100	80	70	56
D	40	32	30	24

Limited scheduling.

Figure 7.11 A portion of a San Francisco station's listing in *Standard Rate & Data Service.* Note the varying charges for 60-second and 30-second spots. [*Standard Rate & Data Service, Inc.*]

ads. Others say that since agencies deduct 15 percent from media charges and media representatives deduct another 10 percent, the media have to charge a higher rate to come out as well on national as they do on local advertising. National advertisers have complained bitterly about this situation, and some media have now moved to a single-rate structure.

The basic unit for broadcast time sales is the minute or a portion thereof. In both radio and television, commercial lengths tend to follow general patterns, although stations sometimes differ in what they will accept. The most common lengths for spot announcements are 10, 30, and 60 seconds. Whereas radio has remained fairly constant in this regard, television has exhibited some important trends. The 60-second spot, once the mainstay of network advertising, now accounts for only about 5 percent of the advertising time. Meanwhile, the 30-second announcement has become the workhorse and is used nearly 85 percent of the time. Likewise, in nonnetwork advertising, the vast majority of spot announcements are of the 30-second variety, with 10- and 60-second commercials following far behind.

A close examination of Figure 7.11, reprinted from spot radio's Standard Rate & Data Service (SRDS), gives you an insight into the rate structure of a typical radio station and a clue to some of the complexities involved. This listing covers spot-announcement charges for CBS affiliate KCBS in San Francisco. Station management has divided the day into time periods AA, A, B, C, and D, and the charge for each period reflects the size of the potential audience an advertiser may expect to reach. The high and low price ranges indicate differing degrees of **preemptibility.** If an advertiser buys a *fixed* time on a station for a commercial, it cannot be "bumped" by that of another advertiser. But preemptible spots are subject to removal if the station receives a more attractive offer from another advertiser. The shorter *notice* that an advertiser is willing to be given that a scheduled commercial is being replaced, the less expensive the cost of the time.

Now look at Figure 7.12, reprinted from spot television's Standard Rate & Data Service. This listing shows rates for NBC affiliate KMIR-TV in Palm Springs, California. Notice the little key near the bottom which indicates that "F" and "I" designations stand for preemptible situations—from "FI" (fixed, or not preemptible), through "I2" (preemptible without any advance notice). The differences in costs are considerable.

People unfamiliar with the economies of broadcast advertising are appalled by the fact that a 30-second

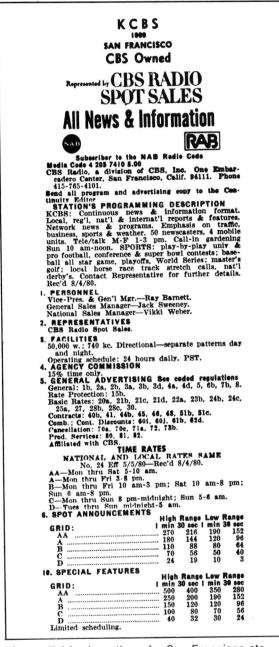

KMIR-TV
PALM SPRINGS
(Airdate October 26, 1968)

NBC Television Network

Katz Continental

NAB

Subscriber to the NAB Television Code
Media Code 6 205 1335 8.00

Desert Empire Television Corp.,72920 Park View Dr., Palm Desert, Calif. 92260. Phone 714-568-3636.
Mailing Address: Box 1506, Palm Springs, Calif. 92263.

1. PERSONNEL
General Manager—John Conte.
Program Director—Bill Secrist.
General Sales Manager—Jeff Massnick.

2. REPRESENTATIVES
Katz Television, Continental.

3. FACILITIES
Video 547,000 w., audio 32,800 w.; ch 36.
Antenna ht.: 680 ft. above average terrain.
Operating schedule: 7-1:30 am.

4. AGENCY COMMISSION
15% to recognized advertising agencies on station time. Bills due and payable when rendered.

5. GENERAL ADVERTISING See coded regulations
General: 1a, 1b, 2a, 2b, 3a, 3b, 3c, 3d, 4a, 5, 6a, 7b, 8.
Rate Protection: 10e, 11a, 12a, 13e, 14a, 16, 16a.
Contracts: 20a, 21, 22a, 22c, 23, 24a, 24b, 25, 27a, 28, 30, 31a, 31b, 31c, 32a, 32b, 32c, 33, 34.
Basic Rates: 40a, 40b, 41a, 41c, 41d, 42, 43a, 43b, 44a, 45a, 46, 48, 49, 50, 51.
Comb.; Cont. Discounts: 60b, 60d, 61a, 61b, 61c, 62a, 62c.
Cancellation: 70b, 70d, 70f, 71, 72, 73a, 73b.
Prod. Services: 80, 82, 83, 84, 85, 86, 87b, 87c.
Affiliated with NBC Television Network.

6. TIME RATES
No. 3A Ann rates eff 9/1/80—Rec'd 9/29/80.
No. P1 Prog rates eff 12/17/79—Rec'd 12/31/79.

7. SPOT ANNOUNCEMENTS

DAYTIME & FRINGE
30 SECONDS

MON THRU FRI:	F1	F2	F3	I1	I2
7-9 am, Today Show	55	45	40	35	30
9 am-3 pm, Daytime Rotation	55	45	35	30	25
PM:					
3-4:30, Mike Douglas Show	55	45	35	30	25
4:30-5, You Bet Your Life	75	65	55	45	30
5-6, John Davidson	75	65	55	45	30
6-6:30, Early News	105	95	85	75	50
6:30-7, John Conte Town Talk	75	65	55	45	30
7-7:30, NBC News adj.	105	95	85	75	70
7:30-8, Let's Make A Deal	105	95	85	75	60
11-11:30, Late News	40	35	30	25	20
11:30 pm-12:30 am, Tonight Show	50	40	35	30	20

PRIME TIME

	F1	F2	F3	F4	F5	F6	F7
8-11 Mon thru Sat; 7-11 Sun	200	170	150	140	120	110	90

60 sec: double the 30 sec.
10 sec: 60% of 30 sec.
F—Fixed.
I—Immediately preemptible.

10. PROGRAM RATES

	1 hr	1/2 hr
7 am-3:30 pm	400	240
3:30-6 pm	500	300
6-8 pm	600	360
8-11 pm	1200	720
11 pm-concl	400	240

Figure 7.12 A portion of a Palm Springs, California, station's listing in *Standard Rate & Data Service.* Check differences in charges based on the length of commercials and programs. [*Standard Rate & Data Service, Inc.*]

commercial on an outstanding network TV attraction may cost $500,000. If the show draws a huge audience, however (in the neighborhood of 40 million households, as a famous episode of the "Dallas" TV series once claimed), the cost per person or home reached is less than the cost of sending a postcard.

It should be noted that many listings in SRDS publications are used for general information and comparative purposes only; stations really expect each media buyer to phone the medium's sales representatives to discuss (and, perhaps, to negotiate) exact costs. Also, especially in radio, some advertisers pay stations a **per inquiry** rate, which isn't listed in any publication. Fees are assessed according to the number of inquiries or actual orders an advertiser receives as a result of commercials run. Obviously, in these cases, the products or services involved must be ones that require a written or telephoned response from potential customers before any sales can be made.

All the costs listed in Figures 7.11 and 7.12 are examples of the *absolute* costs discussed in Chapter 6. They represent what an advertiser must pay in actual dollars. In order to compare them fairly with rates charged by competing stations, however, we would need to compute the *relative* cost presented in Chapter 6 as the cost per thousand.

Future Technology

As we go to press, the Federal Communications Commission (FCC) is seriously considering the creation of thousands of new, low-power TV stations that would offer viewers an increasing number of new program choices. In addition, consumers with home videotape recorders are not only recording material off the air to play back at their convenience, but are also buying prepackaged programs in much the same way they buy records and audiotapes. In fact, the new **videodisc** machines are very similar to record players; they pick up video images on discs and play them back through the TV set (and discs are cheaper than videocassettes).

Another alternative to traditional VHF/UHF programming is the video game, which uses the TV screen as a game board and prevents its simultaneous use for any other purpose. Figure 7.13 shows the predicted growth of these new electronic media through the year 2000.

There are other exciting developments on the horizon, too. In the field of radio, we can look forward

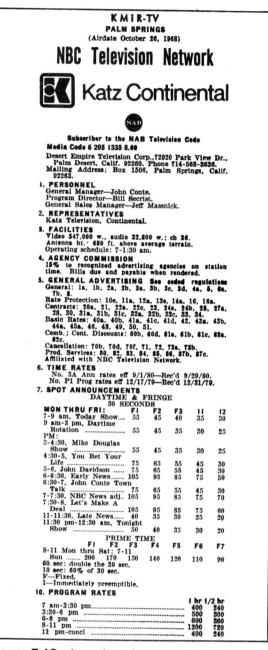

Profile

William Bernbach

William Bernbach is chairman of the executive committee of Doyle Dane Bernbach International Inc., which he cofounded. A native of New York City, he returned to his hometown after serving in the United States Army during World War II and joined Grey Advertising as a copywriter. By 1948, he had advanced to the position of vice president in charge of art and copy at the agency.

Bill, as he is known in the advertising world, worked closely with Ned Doyle, whom he tapped, along with Maxwell Dane, to form their new agency in 1949. Starting with billings of less than $500,000, DDB now bills more than $850 million annually, with offices located throughout the world.

Bill's immortality arises from his genius for creating outstanding advertising. Prior to his influence, advertising's image was generally not very good; many Americans felt that ad agency people were manipulators of society's values and probably not always truthful. Another well-known advertising personality, Tom Dillon, who served with Batten, Barton, Durstine & Osborn for more than 45 years, believed that Bernbach brought to the reader of advertisements a concept of communicating in a truthful, intimate, sympathetic fashion. He instituted the idea of bringing together the artist and writer to create advertising possessing powerful visual imagery, such as his famous work for Volkswagen's "Beetle" when the idea of the compact car was revolutionary in the American marketplace. His philosophy about advertising is summed up in his own words: ". . . the most powerful element of advertising is the truth." He has received many honors, including election to the Advertising Hall of Fame. Along with David Ogilvy and Rosser Reeves, Bill Bernbach changed the practice of advertising, particularly in the realm of creativity.

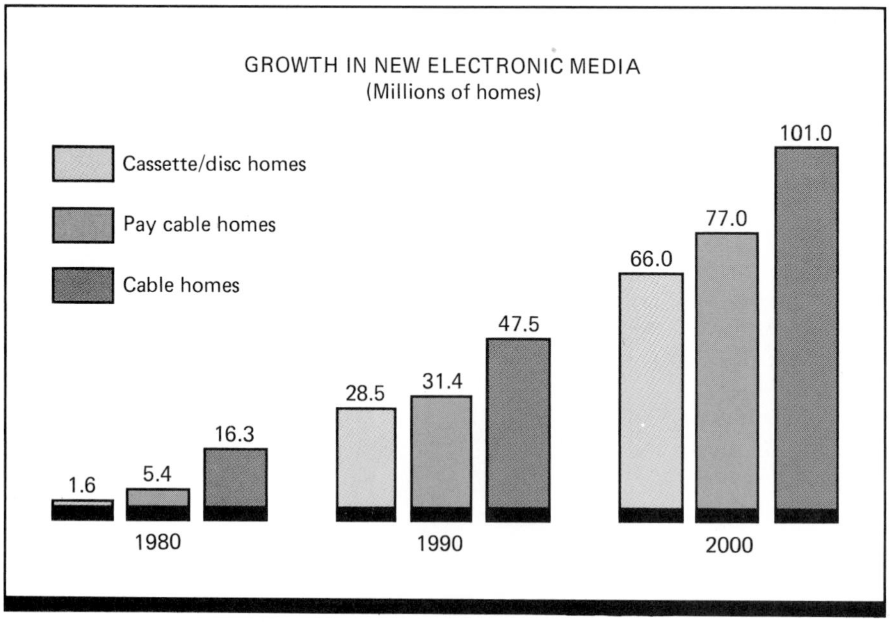

Figure 7.13 Projected growth in new electronic media. [Advertising Age, *Nov. 13, 1980.*]

to more high-fidelity and stereo broadcasts. Technological advancements in television, both in the United States and abroad, are opening doors to a wide range of new services, including retail buying and selling (and comparative pricing), banking activities, and stock transactions. QUBE, a two-way cable system now operating in Columbus, Houston, and Pittsburgh, has featured public opinion polling, and helped advertisers select effective product and premium combinations, commercial appeals, and promotional activities.

The 1980s will see hundreds of millions of dollars spent on experimentation in video technology, pioneered by the British Broadcasting Corporation, that puts pages of printed material (words and graphics) on the TV screen. In effect, the television set may become an information terminal—displaying airline schedules, weather and traffic reports, real estate listings, news updates, and classified ads, to name but a few. "Programming" will come from standard computer terminals and, in some cases, telephones, so viewers can "dial up" the information they want, or simply use the special decoders designed for their TV sets. Television viewers of the future will take courses, shop for products, and vote without leaving their homes.

Summary

Almost every home in the United States contains one or more radio and television sets. Because these media are so pervasive and so personal, they are attractive to advertisers—at national, regional, and local levels.

In order to be successful as advertising vehicles, radio and TV stations must have sound engineering and appealing program fare. Standard AM and FM radio stations and VHF and UHF television stations have been supplemented by cable-TV systems, pay cable, and superstations, all of which provide audiences with an ever-increasing variety of program choices.

Networks supply their affiliates with quality news and entertainment programs and advertisers benefit from national or selective coverage. National advertisers may select a network campaign approach or may choose the spot broadcasting method. Network advertising is simpler to achieve and the cost of attaining national coverage is less than it would be with the nonnetwork strategy. But spot broadcasting is much more flexible and allows advertisers to deliver varying kinds and numbers of messages as needed; here, advertisers select markets and stations independently. This approach is advantageous to an advertiser with spotty distribution or one who wants to concentrate advertising in particular regions because of geographic variations in sales patterns.

As program sponsorship has diminished in TV advertising, participation shows, in which various sponsors place commercials within the body of a program, have increased. Announcement campaigns, on the other hand, place commercials between programs or at station breaks and are sold only by local stations to local and nonnetwork advertisers.

Radio stations attract audiences by developing particular styles or musical formats that will appeal to certain segments of the total radio audience. Television stations generate little loyalty per se, but depend on specific programs to attract viewers. Most of the programs we see are network- or station-produced shows, feature films, and made-for-TV movies, or syndicated programs made by networks or independent packagers.

Broadcast ratings describe the numbers and kinds of people who view or listen to particular programs, and are used to set the rates charged for commercial time. Three widely used ratings are known as the homes-using-radio or homes-using-television rating, the program rating, and the share-of-audience rating. Rating services such as A. C. Nielsen and Arbitron also describe the composition of each station or program audience, usually in demographic terms.

The rates a station charges for commercial time fluctuate according to audience size and quality, the quantity of time purchased, and the amount of unsold, or available, time the station has in its inventory. Most TV spots today are 30 seconds in length, whereas radio's most popular lengths are 30 and 60 seconds.

Technological advancements are gradually turning television sets into information terminals from which consumers may study, shop, and vote, when they do not choose to view on-air programs or prepackaged shows and games.

Questions for Discussion

1 In what sense can it be said that radio and television are unique relative to the other media?
2 What is the major nontechnical difference between standard, over-the-air television and cable TV?
3 Differentiate between three classifications of TV networks.
4 How does an advertiser decide whether to use a network strategy or a spot-broadcasting strategy?
5 In what ways is a participation campaign similar to and different from a program campaign? An announcement campaign?
6 From what sources do radio and TV stations get their programs?
7 Explain what a TV program rating of 25 means to an advertiser. Then explain why a share rating of 25 is different.
8 How do radio and TV stations establish their rates for commercial time?
9 Discuss at least three new technological developments that are expected to affect broadcast advertising significantly between now and the year 2000.

For Further Reference

Abrahams, Howard P.: *Making TV Pay Off,* Fairchild Publications, New York, 1975.

Barnouw, Erik: *Tube of Plenty: A History of Broadcasting in the United States,* Oxford University Press, New York, 1975.

Berger, Arthur Asa: *The TV-Guided American,* Walker Publishing Company, New York, 1976.

Broadcasting and Cable Television, Committee for Economic Development, New York, 1975.

Broadcasting Yearbook, Broadcasting Publications, Inc., Washington, D.C. (annual).

Bunce, Richard: *Television in the Corporate Interest,* Frederick A. Praeger, Publishers, New York, 1976.

Campbell, Robert: *The Golden Years of Broadcasting,* Charles Scribner's Sons, New York, 1976.
Dessart, George (ed.): *Television in the Real World,* Hastings House, New York, 1978.
Radio Facts, Radio Advertising Bureau, New York (annual).
Stanley, Robert H. (ed.): *The Broadcast Industry: An Examination of Major Issues,* Hastings House, New York, 1975.
Television Factbook, vol. 1, *Stations;* vol. 2, *Services,* Television Digest, Inc., Washington, D.C. (irregular).
TV Basics, Television Bureau of Advertising, New York (annual).
Zeigler, Sherilyn K., and Herbert H. Howard: *Broadcast Advertising: A Comprehensive Working Textbook,* Grid Publishing, Inc., Columbus, Ohio, 1978.

End Notes

[1] *Adweek,* Sept. 29, 1980, p. B.R. 46.
[2] *Radio Facts,* Radio Advertising Bureau, New York, 1980, p. 24.
[3] Ibid., pp. 1, 37.
[4] *Nielsen Report on Television 1980,* A. C. Nielsen Company, Northbrook, Ill., p. 6.
[5] Ibid., p. 15.
[6] *Advertising Age,* Sept. 11, 1980, p. 12.
[7] *The Wall Street Journal,* Aug. 14, 1980, p. 21.
[8] *Broadcasting,* Dec. 15, 1980, p. 94.
[9] *Broadcasting,* Aug. 25, 1980, p. 43.
[10] *Advertising Age,* Nov. 24, 1980, p. 56.
[11] *Advertising Age,* Jan. 5, 1981.
[12] *Broadcasting,* Aug. 18, 1980, p. 12.
[13] *Marketing and Media Decisions,* December 1979, p. 40.

Chapter 8

Print Media

● The excitement that is inherent in the producing, selling, and buying of advertising is readily apparent in the world of radio and television. But new, high-speed presses and phototypesetting equipment, along with other factors such as compelling deadlines and the thrill of seeing full-page ads reproduced in high-quality publications, have their own kind of fascination.

Chapter 6 set newspapers and magazines apart from other media through the opportunities they provide for detailed advertising information at reasonable cost. And, when it comes to the ability of media to deliver a quality audience in terms of income, occupation, and education, magazines and newspapers are ranked in first and in second place, respectively.[1]

As the most significant of today's print media, the newspaper and magazine vehicles (sometimes referred to as "publication media") deliver messages, in combination with news, entertainment, or other editorial material, to measurable groups of readers. The degree of a reader's interest in the advertising content of a publication varies from person to person, from vehicle to vehicle, and from ad to ad. Normally, however, the reader's primary focus is on the articles or stories. Thus, a publication's editorial content provides an atmosphere of acceptance for advertisements. In many cases, it attracts the exact audience an advertiser seeks: skin divers, graduate students, business executives, or any other desired group.

Audit Bureau of Circulations

Both newspapers and magazines use circulation figures (1) to determine the rates charged for advertising space, and (2) to promote their respective publications to advertisers (and often in the process, to compare themselves with others). It is very important, therefore, that circulation counts be reported accurately. The Audit Bureau of Circulations (ABC) is a cooperative association of several thousand advertisers, advertising agencies, and publishers that verifies and disseminates circulation and other marketing data on newspapers and periodicals. Every six months, each publication submits an official statement of circulation to ABC for checking, processing, printing, and distributing.

The paid circulation averages included in ABC reports are broken down by subscriptions and single-copy sales and by regional, metro, and demographic editions if applicable. In Figure 8.1, a magazine promotes its audited circulation.

Tear Sheets

It is also important for an advertiser to know for sure that a specific advertisement ran as scheduled in a selected magazine or newspaper. The print media verify the publication of ads through **tear sheets,** or copies of the pages on which ads were printed, cut from the (identified) editions in which they appeared.

Figure 8.1 This magazine plays up its ABC-audited circulation in a trade ad.

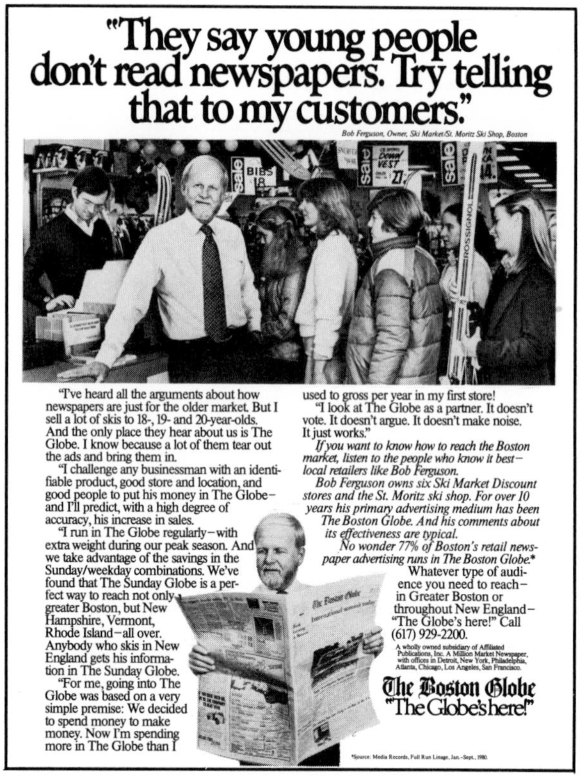

Figure 8.2 The *Boston Globe* makes a good case for reaching young adults through its newspaper ads.

The Medium of Newspapers

A newspaper is typically either a daily or weekly publication that is regarded, with some exceptions, as a local advertising medium. In fact, one of its primary advantages to an advertiser is the intense local coverage or penetration it provides. The word "coverage" in this context describes a medium's ability to reach a certain percentage of homes or prospects in a given area. Because the majority of United States newspapers are virtual monopolies in their cities of publication, they often reach 70 to 80 percent of the homes in their domains. Furthermore, nearly 80 percent of American adults read a newspaper one or more times a week.[2] (See Figure 8.2.) Newspaper coverage may also be regarded as nationwide; approximately 1,770 dailies and 8,000 weeklies effectively blanket the country.

Newspapers normally select their news, features, and editorial subjects with an eye to the wants and needs of people within a particular community. They are usually *geographically* selective. For example, the *San Francisco Chronicle* is published mainly for residents of the San Francisco Bay area—including homemakers, business executives, teenagers, dock workers, sportscar enthusiasts, and electricians. Likewise, as shown in Figure 8.3, the *Atlanta Journal* emphasizes its intensive local coverage.

Magazines, on the other hand, are *qualitatively* selective. They are edited to appeal to the special interests of certain types of people regardless of where they live. A magazine like *Good Housekeeping* is aimed primarily at homemakers, whether they live in San Francisco, St. Louis, or Savannah. Even multimillion-circulation magazines with editorial appeal for both sexes—such as *Reader's Digest*—are more selective qualitatively than newspapers in terms of average income and educational levels.

There are some notable exceptions to this generalization about the geographic, rather than the qualitative, selectivity of newspapers. *The Wall Street Journal,* for example, is a newspaper by format and by frequency of publication. Yet it has a national circulation of approximately 1.8 million and delivers a qualitatively selective audience composed largely of executives in business and finance. So, as an advertising medium, it is more accurately classified as a business publication, along with *Advertising Age* and *Sales Management.* Likewise, religious, ethnic, and foreign-language newspapers appeal to special groups of people rather than to all the residents in a community.

Finally, we should note that some newspapers are introducing lifestyle sections in an attempt to increase daily readership. One such paper, the New York *Daily News,* has also reached out for Manhattan's upscale readers with a special afternoon edition. In Los Angeles, the *Times* reprints features and ads in a "Best of the *Times*" section distributed free to nonsubscribing homes in outer Los Angeles County.[3] In Figure 8.4, the *Buffalo News* promotes a variety of special magazine features.

Figure 8.3 Intense coverage of a specific geographic area is a newspaper's biggest advantage. The *Atlanta Journal* conveys this idea in a competitive advertisement placed in the TV *Standard Rate & Data Book.*

TRUTH IN NUMBERS.

We've got 782,200 adults every Sunday.

Right here in the middle of the broadcast section of SRDS we want to put in a good word for newspapers.

We're convinced, and we think we can prove it with numbers, that any effective buy in Atlanta must include the Atlanta Journal and Constitution.

As a matter of fact we might even be able to help you with your broadcast buy.

Our research department has more information on the Atlanta market, who's who, and who buys what, than any other source in town.

For example: Of the total adults in the 15-county Atlanta area, 58% read our dailies, and 78% of the adults read us at least three days during a five-day period; 71% read our Sunday paper; and 82% read us three out of four Sundays.

Write us and we'll send you the truth in numbers about Atlanta.

Readership: Belden Continuing Audience Study.
Represented by Story & Kelly-Smith, Inc.
Member of the Metropolitan Sunday Newspapers, Inc.

The Atlanta Journal

On-the-go Buffalo won't go without The News.

There are plenty of places to go, lots to do in resurgent, renaissance Buffalo. And our 1.8 million consumers—with their Effective Buying Income of $11 billion a year—aren't just sitting around.

So we give 'em Gusto every Friday, the magazine with guides to Buffalo's best food, shows, listening and entertainment.

Our Sports Magazine on Saturday, with the inside stories on the plays, the players, the teams, standings and schedules.

And our Roto Magazine, great reading about colorful people, issues and the history that surrounds them.

They read us. Our demographics prove it. In fact, our Total Adult Readers in the Buffalo ADI number 656,000 weekdays and 489,000 on Sunday.*

So get your message to Buffalo's active consumer. Put it in The Buffalo News.

For more information, call General Advertising Manager Hugh G. Monaghan at (716) 849-3422.

We deliver. 7 days a week.

*Source: Three Sigma Research Center, Inc., 1980

THE BUFFALO NEWS

One News Plaza
Buffalo, New York 14240
Represented nationally by Story & Kelly-Smith

Figure 8.4 The *Buffalo News* caters to a variety of audience groups with special magazine appeals.

The importance of newspaper advertising is indicated by the amount of money invested in it each year. (See Table 6.2, page 132.) In 1980, expenditures exceeded $15.6 billion—almost 30 percent of the country's total advertising expenditures for the year. The geographic selectivity of newspapers explains in part why more than 85 percent of the dollars invested in newspaper advertising comes from local or retail advertisers.

Classification of Newspapers

In terms of **size,** newspapers are divided into standard and tabloid types. Traditionally, the standard newspaper was approximately 22 inches deep by 8 columns wide, with each column about 2 inches in width. Today, while the number of columns varies from 6 to 9 and page depths run from 18 to 23 inches, 6-column formats are widespread and 8-column pages are declining. The term "standard," therefore, simply refers to a large-page paper, such as the *New York Times, Boston Globe,* and *Chicago Tribune,* whereas "tabloid" papers are only about half that size. Most tabloids are 5 columns wide, and overall pages are 10 by 14 inches, but here, too, there are variations. The page depth of the *Middletown* (New York) *Times Herald-Record,* for example, is 15 inches, whereas two New York City "tabs," the *Daily News* and the *Post,* each have page depths of 14¼ inches. These differences present a problem to the advertiser who wishes to use newspapers in a number of markets; often, printing materials must be adjusted to meet different formats. (See Figure 8.5.)

By **frequency** of publication, newspapers fall into two broad groups, dailies and weeklies. However, a daily may be published five, six, or seven days a week, whereas a weekly may appear once, twice, or three times a week, or only every other week. Generally, frequency is a function of the market in which a paper is printed. *The New York Times* publishes seven days a week, whereas the *Oakridge* (Oregon) *Dead Mountain Echo* appears only once a week. Metropolitan papers often reach homes far beyond their city limits, especially with Sunday editions. For example, the *Los Angeles Times* is sold in Honolulu, and the *Washington Post* in Miami. On the other hand, most small dailies have little circulation beyond their immediate areas.

Small-town and suburban weeklies are even more localized. Their content consists largely of news of the communities they serve; thus, they may enjoy a more thorough reading and longer life than the metropolitan or small-town daily. However, the cost per reader in weekly newspapers is higher than in dailies, and weekly circulation figures are usually small. Increasingly, suburban papers are competing with metropolitan dailies on the strength of their coverage of the affluent fringes of big cities. In retaliation, major dailies may cater to suburbia in special sections. *The New York Times* includes New Jersey and Long Island sections in its Sunday edition.

National advertisers, among them Coca-Cola, Eastern Airlines, General Mills, General Motors, and Mobil Oil, have discovered the value of suburban newspapers (1) as a supplement to major market coverage, and (2) as an aid in product introduction and test marketing.

Newspaper Supplements

A hybrid medium within the newspaper field is the **supplement** delivered as part of the Sunday edition. A familiar one is the comic supplement, sold to advertisers either on an individual market basis or in multiple market combinations known as "comic groups."

In Los Angeles, the Sunday *Times* distributes its own independent comic section, and the *Los Angeles Herald-Examiner* carries "Puck—the Comic Weekly." "Puck" is a nationally syndicated comic and may be purchased only for the Los Angeles market, or it may cover 5 West Coast cities, 4 other regional combinations, or—in a national edition—52 papers in 51 cities.

Another type of Sunday supplement resembles a magazine in both content and format. It is discussed later in this chapter.

Tabloid Inserts

Sometimes, an advertiser provides a newspaper with a tabloid advertising supplement to be inserted into the daily or Sunday paper. Commonly called **tab inserts,** these multipage supplements have become especially popular with discount and variety stores, department stores, and national automobile advertisers. The advertiser is responsible for printing and shipping these sections to the papers included in the media buy. Then, each publisher simply inserts them into the papers as they come off the press.

Newspapers generally charge a flat fee for standard 8-page tabloid inserts—the same charge the advertiser would have paid for the same amount of space at normal black-and-white rates. The use of multiple-page tab inserts is increasing despite the added "clutter factor" that some newspaper subscribers do not appreciate.

The Newspaper Advertising Department

In a typical daily newspaper, the advertising sales department consists of three subdepartments. One handles only **classified** advertising, so called be-

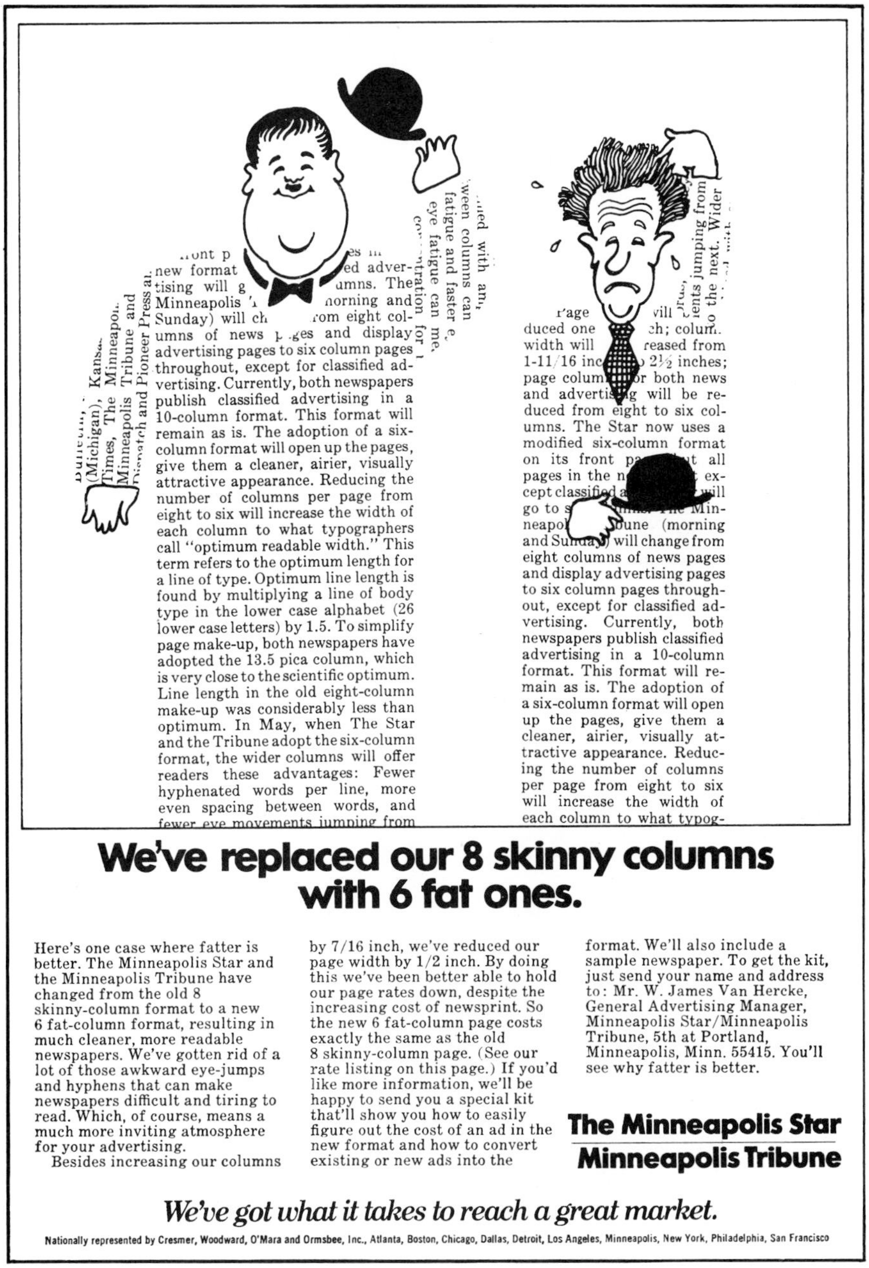
We've replaced our 8 skinny columns with 6 fat ones.
Here's one case where fatter is better. The Minneapolis Star and the Minneapolis Tribune have changed from the old 8 skinny-column format to a new 6 fat-column format, resulting in much cleaner, more readable newspapers. We've gotten rid of a lot of those awkward eye-jumps and hyphens that can make newspapers difficult and tiring to read. Which, of course, means a much more inviting atmosphere for your advertising.
Besides increasing our columns by 7/16 inch, we've reduced our page width by 1/2 inch. By doing this we've been better able to hold our page rates down, despite the increasing cost of newsprint. So the new 6 fat-column page costs exactly the same as the old 8 skinny-column page. (See our rate listing on this page.) If you'd like more information, we'll be happy to send you a special kit that'll show you how to easily figure out the cost of an ad in the new format and how to convert existing or new ads into the format. We'll also include a sample newspaper. To get the kit, just send your name and address to: Mr. W. James Van Hercke, General Advertising Manager, Minneapolis Star/Minneapolis Tribune, 5th at Portland, Minneapolis, Minn. 55415. You'll see why fatter is better.
The Minneapolis Star
Minneapolis Tribune
We've got what it takes to reach a great market.
Nationally represented by Cresmer, Woodward, O'Mara and Ormsbee, Inc., Atlanta, Boston, Chicago, Dallas, Detroit, Los Angeles, Minneapolis, New York, Philadelphia, San Francisco

Figure 8.5 Standardization of newspaper mechanical requirements for the convenience of advertisers wishing to place an ad in many papers has always been a problem. Perhaps the problem will be solved one day if all papers follow the trend to a 6-column page.

cause ads are placed in a special section of the paper and arranged by specific product and service classifications for easy reference, much like the yellow pages of the phone directory. It is a good source of revenue for newspapers, but not so lucrative as display advertising.

Display advertising is placed on news and feature pages throughout the paper, and uses a variety of space sizes, layout designs, type faces and sizes, and illustrative techniques. (Figure 8.6 shows an example.) Some newspapers also offer a third, in-between, form of advertising called **display classified,** which permits the use of limited display techniques in ads published in the classified section.

Two subdepartments work with display advertising. **National,** or **general, display** personnel handle advertisements placed by national and regional advertisers, and **retail,** or **local, display** staffs handle the advertising of retail stores and local service organizations. A national ad emphasizes a product and brand. Retail ads stress a particular store as the place to buy and are usually designed to build store traffic as well as to move merchandise.

Newspaper Rate Structure

Most newspapers quote different rates to national and to local advertisers and base them on different units of space. The local rate is frequently lower than the national one (50 percent lower, in many cases), allows no commission to advertising agencies, and is subject to appreciable discounts for the amount of space used. The basic unit of space is the **column inch,** an area 1 column wide by 1 inch deep. As an example, in Figure 8.7, the standard rate for local advertisers—also called the flat, fixed, or transient rate—is $12.61 per column inch in the Lansing, Michigan, *State Journal.* A local advertiser can, however, through volume discounts, reduce this cost by more than 40 percent. The national or general rate, which is rarely subject to such generous volume discounts, provides for commissions to both the media representative and the advertising agency and is quoted in terms of **agate lines.** There are 14 lines to the column inch. In the case of Lansing's *State Journal,* the national rate is 90 cents per line, and there are no discounts.

Media that employ two different rate scales for local and national advertisers have what is known as a **dual rate structure.** This is common in newspapers and broadcast media, but a single structure is universal with magazines and out-of-home media.

Not all firms that might be considered "local," however, can advertise at the local rate. Many news-

Figure 8.6 Layout and copy for this newspaper ad get a final check before being turned over to compositors for production. [Eugene Register-Guard.]

—

TRANSIENT RATE $12.61

ALL CONTRACTS (EXCEPT STRAIGHT YEARLY BULK) REQUIRE 1 WEEKLY AD MONDAY THRU SUNDAY

YEARLY CONTRACTS

1'' One Time Per Week $8.00

YEARLY BULK CONTRACTS

with weekly minimum

One Time Per Week	Yearly Bulk	Rate
1 Inch	150 Inches	$7.40
3 Inches	300 Inches	7.37
5 Inches	500 Inches	7.29
10 Inches	1,000 Inches	7.25
20 Inches	2,000 Inches	7.19
30 Inches	3,000 Inches	7.17
40 Inches	5,000 Inches	7.12
50 Inches*	7,500 Inches	7.03
100 Inches*	15,000 Inches	6.90
150 Inches*	25,000 Inches	6.76
200 Inches*	40,000 Inches	6.62
300 Inches*	60,000 Inches	6.54
400 Inches*	80,000 Inches	6.45
500 Inches*	100,000 Inches	6.37
750 Inches*	125,000 Inches	6.19
1,000 Inches*	150,000 Inches	6.13

*Cumulative Total each week

YEARLY BULK CONTRACTS

without weekly minimum

SIZE	RATE
250 Inches	$10.31
500 Inches	10.16
1200 Inches	9.97
2600 Inches	9.72
5200 Inches	9.45
10,400 Inches	8.93

SHORT TERM CONTRACTS

May be converted to a longer term contract on or before expiration date to earn lower rate.

13 CONSECUTIVE WEEKS		13 TIMES within 4 weeks (Minimum of 1 ad per week until 13 ads run)	
SIZE	RATE	SIZE	RATE
1 Inch	$8.71	1 Inch	9.65
3 Inches	8.51	3 Inches	9.44
5 Inches	8.39	5 Inches	9.33
10 Inches	8.29	10 Inches	9.27
20 Inches	8.22	20 Inches	9.21
30 Inches	8.16	30 Inches	9.11
40 Inches	8.11	40 Inches	9.07

All Retail Rates Are Non-Commissionable

SPECIAL (TRANSIENT) RATES

Church (services) Civic, Fraternal $8.85
General Tie-In 9.50

COLOR RATES

Charges in addition to regular space rate.

Minimum size — 42 column inches.

Choice of 11 ANPA stock colors; other $20 additional

1 color plus black $185
2 colors plus black 285
3 colors plus black 385

Spectacolor and HI-FI ROLL FED INSERTS

Pre-printed Material Supplied by Advertiser

Roll width 14½''.

SpactaColor Cut Off 23 9/16 Inches Deep.

Repeat Length 23.588-23.596

A. Single Page, One Side — B/W Rate for One Page

B. Single Page, Both Sides, When Publisher Cannot Print on Opposite Side — B/W Rate for Two Pages

GROSS PRESS RUN Confirm with The State Journal, Lansing, Michigan at Time Space Reservation is Made. Accepted Monday, Tuesday, Friday Only. 3-Day Leeway Requested. Rolls must arrive 7-days prior to insertion date.

Sunday Color Comics

1 Page	$1264
⅔ Page	923
½ Page	654
⅓ Page	436
1/6 Page	231

All Insertions, Instructions and Printing Material Should Be Given to The State Journal Advertising Representative or Sent to Greater Buffalo Press, 302 Grote Street, Buffalo, New York 14207 Five Weeks Prior to Insertion Date.

R.O.P. ADVERTISING SECTIONS AND TABLOIDS BY ADVANCE RESERVATION

STANDARD SECTIONS of 8 full pages or more acceptable Wednesday, Thursday and Sunday.

FLAT TABLOIDS (pull-out from regular section) up to 12 pages acceptable daily and Sunday.

SEPARATE TABLOIDS, 16 pages or more acceptable on Wednesday and Thursday.

PREPRINTED INSERTS ACCEPTED DAILY AND SUNDAY

Free Standing	$1902
8 tabloid or 4 full size pages	2578
12 tabloid or 6 full size pages	3169
16 tabloid or 8 full size pages	3815
20 tabloid or 10 full size pages	4241
24 tabloid or 12 full size pages	4614
28 tabloid or 14 full size pages	4983
32 tabloid or 16 full size pages	5357
36 tabloid or 18 full size pages	5777
40 tabloid or 20 full size pages	6200
44 tabloid or 22 full size pages	6605
48 tabloid or 24 full size pages	7004

Discount Available for 30 or more Preprints in One Year.

Zoned Preprint Rates Available on Request

Inserts must be shipped prepaid on pallets in turns of 50 to arrive 7 days prior to insertion date. Page one must carry the following identification: Supplement to The State Journal Preprint linage credited toward total contracted linage but not credited toward earned rebate.

Figure 8.7 This section of a Lansing, Michigan, *State Journal* rate card gives basic rates for retail advertisers. Note that these rates are given in column inches, whereas national rates quoted in the *Standard Rate and Data Service* are given in agate lines. [Lansing State Journal.]

papers apply the national rate to wholesalers or jobbers and to advertisers in automotive, financial, transportation, and other specific product or service classifications. The base or flat rates described here are for black-and-white (b&w) advertisements published **run-of-paper** (ROP)—meaning that the position of the ad in the newspaper will be whatever is convenient for the publisher. Premium rates are charged for advertisements that use color and also for those placed in specified positions.

In some markets where two papers are owned by the same publisher, the advertiser may buy space in both at a single **combination rate.** For example, the only morning paper and the only evening paper in Knoxville, Tennessee, are owned by the same publisher. A national advertiser may buy space in the morning *Journal for* 55 cents a line or in the evening *News-Sentinel* for 68 cents. If the ad runs in both papers, the rate for the combination is only 92 cents —just 37 cents more than for the morning alone.[4] (See Figure 8.8 for another example.)

The Theoretical Milline Rate To compare advertising costs among a number of different newspapers, national advertisers have traditionally used a theoretical figure called the **milline rate.** No advertiser is ever billed at the milline rate; it is merely a common denominator for calculating the relative cost of advertising in newspapers with varying rates and circulations. Specifically, the milline rate is the cost of delivering one line of advertising to an *assumed* 1 million circulation, and it is determined by

The Oregonian\Oregon Journal

DAILY COMBINATION RATES

RATE PROTECTION

It is the condition of rate card that The Oregonian and Oregon Journal reserve the right to revise their advertising rates at any time upon 60 days notice in writing to holders of contracts and contracts are accepted subject to this reservation. First insertion on contract must be made within 30 days of date of contract. No contract made for a period of more than one year. Contracts must start on 1st day of contract month and end on last day of 12th month.

Black and White (ROP)

BULK RATES when covered by Oregonian contract; combined rate daily OREGONIAN and JOURNAL:

Open, Per Line	$1.68	30,000 lines	$1.56
1,000 lines	1.66	50,000 lines	1.54
2,500 lines	1.64	75,000 lines	1.52
5,000 lines	1.62	100,000 lines	1.50
10,000 lines	1.60	150,000 lines	1.48
20,000 lines	1.58	200,000 lines	1.46

To qualify for the above combination rates, advertisements in both newspapers must be identical in dimensions and copy, and must be published within a seven-day period.

Combination rates are based on OREGONIAN contract rate in effect. Advertisements ordered at the combination rate MUST BE COVERED BY ONE ORDER issued to The OREGONIAN and OREGON JOURNAL in combination and specifying insertion dates in each newspaper within the seven-day period.

Sunday Comics (excluding Puck orders) and Northwest Magazine linage may be added to daily and Sunday Oregonian ROP linage to earn more favorable rate.

There are no combination rates between the Sunday OREGONIAN and the daily JOURNAL.

COLOR (ROP)

	Black and 1 color	Black and 2 colors	Black and 3 colors
1000-1499 lines (min. 1000 lines), extra	50%	50%	50%
1500-2240 lines, extra	35%	45%	50%
Full page, extra	25%	40%	50%

*DISCOUNTS

Full page units only, b/w2c. or b/w 3c.:

6 ads per year	2%
13 ads per year	3%
26 ads per year	4%
39 ads per year	5%
52 ads per year	6%

(*) These discounts are in addition to the regular volume rate discounts

Two and three color rates based on standard process colors. Two colors $50.00 min. extra (each paper) for non-standard inks (non-commissionable). Three colors $75.00 min. extra (each paper) for non-standard inks (non-commissionable).

Figure 8.8 This portion of the *Portland Oregonian* and *Oregon Journal* rate card quotes rates for national advertisers wishing to run in both the morning and evening paper simultaneously. It is a much better buy on a cost-per-thousand basis than buying either paper alone. [The Portland Oregonian *and* Oregon Journal.]

multiplying the line rate by 1 million and dividing the result by the paper's actual circulation in this way:

$$\frac{R \times 1{,}000{,}000}{C} = MR$$

where R = actual or published rate

C = actual circulation

MR = milline rate

For example, the *Knoxville Journal* has a line rate of 55 cents and a circulation of 56,908, whereas the *Knoxville News-Sentinel* has a line rate of 68 cents and a circulation of 102,488.[5] Obviously, although the cost per line is greater in the *News-Sentinel,* the relative cost per message delivered is less. Using our formula, we see that the milline rate for the *Journal* is \$9.66, while that for the *News-Sentinel* is \$6.63.

Because line rates are so low, we don't compute comparative costs by circulations measured in thousands (as other major media do). If we did, the small decimal figures would be very difficult to discuss. The above examples, for instance, would be \$.00966 for the *Journal* and \$.00663 for the *News-Sentinel.*

In general, the milline rate goes up as circulation goes down, and the greater the circulation, the lower the milline rate. Overhead and production costs are relatively constant regardless of circulation, but milline rates should be compared only between papers in similar circulation ranges. There is no point in comparing the milline rate of the *Los Angeles Times* with that of the Archbold, Ohio, weekly *Buckeye.*

Both milline and actual rates are purely quantitative measurements, of course. The advertiser should evaluate them in relation to such qualitative factors as editorial interest, coverage patterns, and the income, occupation, and buying habits of readers. One would not select the mass appeal New York *Daily News* over the more sophisticated *New York Times* if the advertising strategy were to aim for a well-educated, élite audience, despite the significantly lower milline rate of the *Daily News.*

Preferred Positions For decades, papers have allowed advertisers to specify sections, pages, or particular locations on pages where they wanted their messages placed, and advertisers have paid a premium rate for this service. But an advertiser who merely suggests a certain position does not pay the extra charge even when the suggestion is followed.

Today, almost all advertising agencies include in newspaper insertion orders some sort of position request, such as placement in a main news, society, or sports section. They often add a request for "well forward" in the paper or section, or "above the fold." (Figure 8.9 shows an insertion order.) Most papers honor these requests to the best of their abilities, but obviously not all advertisements can appear in the front of a given issue, at the beginning of the sports section, or on the upper half of a page.

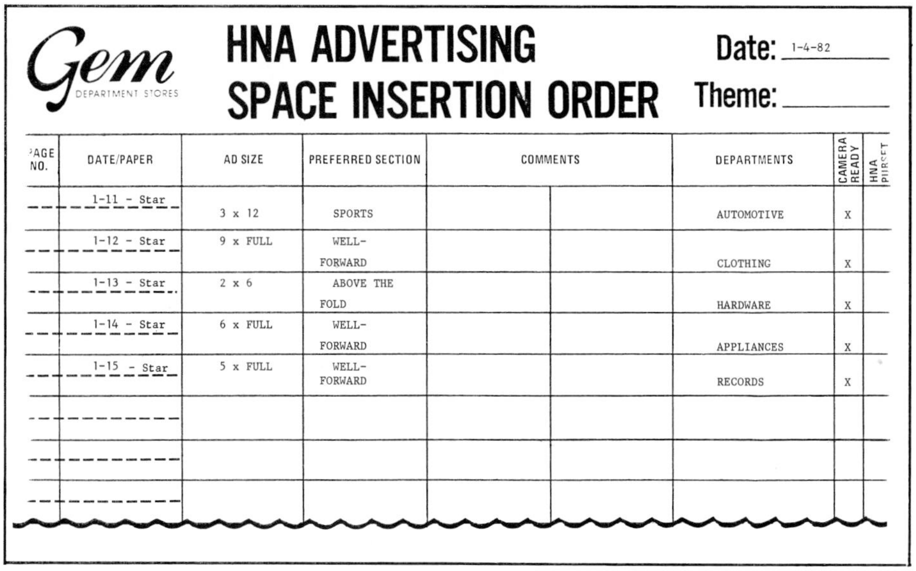

Gem DEPARTMENT STORES

HNA ADVERTISING SPACE INSERTION ORDER

Date: 1-4-82

Theme:

PAGE NO.	DATE/PAPER	AD SIZE	PREFERRED SECTION	COMMENTS	DEPARTMENTS	CAMERA READY	HNA
	1-11 - Star	3 x 12	SPORTS		AUTOMOTIVE	X	
	1-12 - Star	9 x FULL	WELL-FORWARD		CLOTHING	X	
	1-13 - Star	2 x 6	ABOVE THE FOLD		HARDWARE	X	
	1-14 - Star	6 x FULL	WELL-FORWARD		APPLIANCES	X	
	1-15 - Star	5 x FULL	WELL-FORWARD		RECORDS	X	

Figure 8.9 Advertisers use a space insertion order to inform newspapers of their requests for ad placement. [*Gem Department Stores.*]

Color in Newspaper Advertisements Although the great majority of newspaper advertisements appear in black and white, color is available through two methods. **ROP color** is printed by the newspaper on standard newsprint paper as part of its regular press run. The other method, called Hi-Fi or Spectacolor, involves preprinted color inserts, supplied in rolls and fed into the newspaper during a normal run.

Nearly all daily and Sunday papers throughout the nation can print ads either in black and white or in color, and most accept color preprints as well. Only about one-quarter of the country's weekly newspapers, however, offer even one additional ROP color beyond black and white.

The use of both ROP and preprinted color advertising in newspapers is on the rise, even though each additional ROP color increases an ad's space cost. Many newspapers have (varying) restrictions, too, on the minimum amount of space for color advertising. Few papers accept color ads in space units of less than 1,000 lines, and the premiums charged range from 15 to 30 percent, depending on the number of colors used.

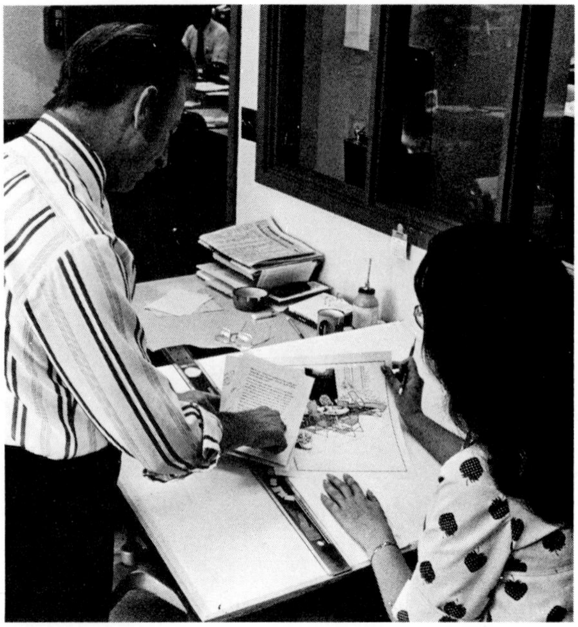

Figure 8.10 Artists and copywriters are as much at home in a modern newspaper as in an advertising agency. Those pictured here work on promotion department projects in addition to performing creative services for advertising salespeople and their clients. [Eugene Register-Guard.]

Split Run in Newspapers Some newspapers will, for a charge, "split" a press run for an advertiser who wants to insert one ad (or version of an ad) in half the copies of a paper and a second ad (or version) in the other half. The purpose is to provide a kind of built-in research situation whereby different readers in a given area are exposed to each of the two ads. Later, when interviews are conducted to determine ad readership and effectiveness, researchers can compare findings to see which advertisement did the better job. Or, response to the two ads might be compared through examination of coupon returns. When each ad includes a coupon keyed with a different box number, it is easy to check the pulling power of the respective ads.

Newspaper Services for Advertisers

To help national advertisers and their agencies plan effectively, many newspapers conduct periodic studies of buying habits, brand preferences, distribution patterns, retail sales, and other indications of the potentials and characteristics of the market areas they serve. They also provide merchandising or sales promotional assistance, such as securing related tie-in advertising from local retailers, encouraging the use of in-store displays, or helping to get adequate distribution. Some do it without charge to advertisers who contract for a specified amount of space; others charge for all assistance except advice.

Most small retailers have no advertising department, and a number of larger ones have staffs too limited to perform all functions necessary in advertising planning and creation. As the retailer's primary advertising medium, newspapers generally provide creative services without charge, although there is a growing trend toward passing some art and production costs to the advertiser. On small papers, the advertising salesperson frequently writes copy, prepares layouts, and suggests illustration material available from syndicated services to which the paper subscribes. (See Figure 8.10.) Most metropolitan dailies maintain advertising departments equipped to furnish complete creative services, including original artwork. These departments are not intended to replace advertisers' own creative departments; rather, they help free newspaper sales personnel to sell more space and to get new accounts. When a retailer uses the newspaper's creative facility too frequently, a fee may be charged for major services.

The Medium of Magazines

Magazines, the second form of print publication advertising, offer the advertiser advantages which in many respects are the opposites of those offered by newspapers. The newspaper appeals to all people in a particular community; the magazine appeals to particular people in all kinds of communities. (Figure 8.11 shows such a magazine.) The life of a daily newspaper ad is short—rarely more than a day. A magazine ad continues to "live" and produce results for a week, a month, or longer, as the periodical is read and reread not only by those who buy it, but by others who come in contact with it (both inside and outside the home).

Although newspapers are limited in the quality of ROP reproduction, most magazines offer high-quality paper and printing. The deadline for newspaper insertions is usually two or three days in advance

Figure 8.11 This magazine appeals to a very specific type of woman, but is not confined to any one part of the country.

of publication, but such flexibility is impossible with a magazine advertisement; few magazine deadlines are as short as three weeks prior to publication date, and some may be as long as two months. (The increased quality that goes into magazine production slows down the insertion process.) The newspaper is primarily a local medium, and the magazine is mainly national.

Regional Coverage by Magazines

Even though we consider the magazine a national medium, the effective use of magazines is not limited to advertisers whose products or services are distributed in all 50 states.

Regional Magazines The circulation of some magazines is restricted to specific regions of the country. For example, *Twin Cities, Gold Coast of Florida,* and *The Pittsburgher Magazine,* all with circulations between 30,000 and 35,000, are edited for, and delivered primarily to, residents of three very different locations: Minneapolis/St. Paul, southeastern Florida, and the Pittsburgh metropolitan area.

Regional Editions Among magazines that once offered only national coverage, there is a strong trend toward making special editions available to manufacturers who advertise different brands in different geographic areas or whose marketing efforts are limited to certain sections of the country. The editorial content of each regional edition remains essentially the same, but the advertisements on some pages vary. *Newsweek,* for example, offers advertisers a choice of 40 metropolitan city editions, 16 regional editions, and a number of editions focusing on specific interest or vocational groups. *Newsweek*'s Los Angeles edition delivers 161,000 circulation and its Detroit edition 81,000. But the availability of regional editions is not limited to magazines with multimillion national circulation figures. *Bride's Magazine,* with about 350,000 circulation, publishes a special edition delivered only to the Northeastern market. *TV Guide* currently offers the maximum in geographic selectivity among magazines with a national circulation of 19 million that can be broken down into 110 different metropolitan editions.[6]

Split-Run Editions When a magazine is not published in regional editions, special arrangements may sometimes be made for split-run insertions. Two or more products with different regional-distribution patterns cooperate in sharing the same space, each advertiser paying for the share of circulation actually delivered into the specified region. Thus, there are two different ways an advertiser can use just part of a publication's total circulation. However, when regional editions are available, advertisers can buy any one edition without including the others; split-run coverage often requires special arrangements with the publisher so that other ads can be found for the portion of the national circulation that the regional marketer cannot use.

The Newspaper Magazine Supplement

The differences between newspapers and magazines help explain the dual nature of the newspaper **magazine supplement.** Some, especially Sunday newspaper supplements, are locally edited. Others, such as *Family Weekly* and *Parade,* are syndicated—produced by a publishing company and distributed as inserts for Sunday newspapers in different cities. (See Figure 8.12.) Some locally edited supplements can be bought as groups of markets; others are sold only individually. Syndicated Sunday magazines are sold only in groups, but the groups have different market profiles. *Parade* is distributed currently in 127 markets and may be bought in 5 regional groups. *Family Weekly* goes into more than 328 smaller markets, such as Klamath Falls, Oregon, and Bowling Green, Kentucky.[7]

Whether locally edited or syndicated, the content and format of magazine supplements resemble magazines more than newspapers. Most enjoy a longer life than newspapers, are printed by the gravure process, and offer greater color fidelity and finer reproduction than the ROP sections of newspapers. Their deadlines for advertising copy are similar to those of magazines. But here the similarity stops. Readers do not select the magazine supplement as they do a regular magazine. The supplement is delivered with the newspaper to a mixture of all types of people in a given community. Hence, its content has a much more general or mass appeal than is true of specialized magazines.

Classification of Magazines

Like newspapers, magazines can be classified by size. Most of them today use a "standard" 8½ by 11-inch page size. The relative visibility or attention value of

Plate 1 The use of color enhances advertising effectiveness. Here a magazine that appeals to food preparation hobbyists portrays food in a mouth-watering fashion. The purpose of the ad is to convince advertisers to use *Cuisine* in their media mixes.

Personalities are for People.
Cuisine's recipes don't come from celebrities, they come from cooks.
They call for interest and involvement, not arcane skills. They're always clear, doable and tested to ensure success.
That's why you'll find Cuisine on many more kitchen tables than coffee tables. After our readers enjoy and absorb our sophisticated editorial, they put it to work.
Put Cuisine to work for you as your number one alternative lifestyle magazine. Because we deliver the audience you need in the '80s—very bright, innovative men and women with money. Let Chuck Colletti startle you with facts and figures about them. (212) 661-2700.
CUISINE
Dinner In Minutes
If you're not in CUISINE, you're not in the kitchen.

Plate 2 Lithographers are important special-service groups who supply the advertising business with needed materials. This high-quality advertisement projects the idea that this lithography company can help advertisers project similar images for their own products. [*Courtesy of Litho Masters, Inc.*]

We separate the cream from the milk
And the milk from the bottle. And the bottle from the background. We do offset color separations. That's all we do. That's why we're the best at what we do. Call us. Write us. We're ready to serve you.
Litho Masters, Inc.
55 Veterans Boulevard
Carlstadt, N.J. 07072
(201) 933-5162 (212) 695-4028
Photo by Al Gommi

Upper crust chicken with down-home flavor.
It's top-notch—the flavor you'll enjoy in this tasty chicken bake. What makes it so good is the creamy richness of KRAFT Real Mayonnaise and the every day freshness of KRAFT Sharp Natural Cheddar Cheese. They're two ingredients to use when you want quality that's above the ordinary.
Upper Crust Chicken
10 white bread slices (day-old)
2 cups chopped cooked chicken
1 cup celery slices
2 cups (8 ozs.) shredded KRAFT Sharp Natural Cheddar Cheese
1 cup KRAFT Real Mayonnaise
2 eggs, slightly beaten
½ teaspoon salt
½ teaspoon poultry seasoning
1½ cups milk
Trim crust from bread, reserving crust. Cut bread slices diagonally into quarters. Cut reserved crust into cubes. Combine bread cubes, chicken, celery and 1¾ cups cheese; mix well. Spoon into 11¾ x 7½-inch baking dish. Arrange bread quarters over chicken mixture. Combine mayonnaise, egg and seasonings, mix well. Gradually add milk, mixing until blended. Pour over bread. Sprinkle with remaining cheese. Cover. Refrigerate several hours or overnight. Bake, uncovered, at 375°, 30 minutes. Garnish with celery leaves, if desired.
8 servings
KRAFT
REAL
Mayonnaise
KRAFT
NATURAL
SHARP CHEDDAR CHEESE
© 1980 Kraft, Inc.

Plate 3 As mentioned in Chapter 4, cheese can be either promoted through primary-demand stimulation advertising, or more likely, through selective-demand advertising. In a classic food recipe ad Kraft not only features its brand of cheese, but also its mayonnaise. If the formula for chicken preparation intrigues the family cook, it is likely that Kraft brands will be used. The ad ran in seven different magazines.

that's
packaging!
Want your product to stand out?
Ask us about packaging that will set your product apart from the rest. Call us today.
Packaging Corporation of America
A Tenneco Company
TENNECO
General Offices • Evanston, Illinois

Plate 4 At first glance this advertisement appears to be featuring a popular variety of vegetables. However, instead it dramatizes the importance of the package to total marketing success, as we explain in Chapter 3. [*Courtesy of the Packaging Corporation of America.*]

WATERFORD®
IN BLOOM.
Illustrated booklet.
Waterford Crystal,
225 Fifth Ave., NY 10010
Photo: Pesin

Plate 5 One should not feel that color is useful only in the advertising of food products. Here high-quality glassware is featured in an ad that is part of a campaign voted to be the most beautiful running in magazines. [*Waterford Crystal. Agency: Pesin, Sidney & Bernard Advertising.*]

Plate 6 Superb workmanship and rare materials are highlighted in this bread board advertisement. The aura of quality is enhanced by the use of caviar. [*Courtesy of Dansk International Designs and James R. Flanagan Advertising Agency.*]

When it looks this good...
it's got to be DANSK
Teak Bread Board
Hand assembled endwood...designed by Jens Quistgaard
Dansk International Designs
Mt. Kisco, New York 10549, Box 248
Write for free color brochure

Plate 7 (Right) The importance of tourism to the economies of many nations is discussed in Chapter 21. France seeks to capture travel dollars through the use of a Van Gogh painting. Only print media are capable of such fine reproduction quality. [*Courtesy of the French Government Tourist Office and Needham, Harper & Steers.*]

SEE THE LANDSCAPE THAT INSPIRED THE LANDSCAPE.

France. Known throughout the world for great artists and great art. And known by great artists for its breathtaking light and magnificent countryside.

For as much as you will appreciate French museums, châteaux, and cathedrals, you'll discover one of the greatest masterpieces in France is the country itself.

On a "Fly-Drive" tour, you can fly to Paris the French way on Air France, and see the treasured works of the masters. Then drive to the country and see the works of nature that inspired them.

Or you can tour the country in the comfort of the French Railroads, without cramping your legs or your wallet.

And you'll see why the world's greatest artists, poets and dreamers made France their home. Or wished that they could.

The French Government Tourist Office, Box 477, New York, N.Y. 10011.

Please send me the information about your "Fly-Drive" tours. Quickly.

Name__________

Street__________

City__________

State______ Zip______

NY

France

Helping you say it right

FTD — FLORISTS' TRANSWORLD DELIVERY — SINCE 1910™

ACCOUNT	FTD-Florist Transworld Delivery
PRODUCT	Tickler
TITLE	"New Toy"
LENGTH	:30-seconds
SCRIPT NO.	FDTB0403-81

1. *ANNCR VO:* When she's finally reached her goal.

2. When she rates some private space.

3. When he launches his new toy.

4. When she's second in a race. This is the time for a little tickle.

5. That's why FTD created the tickler bouquet.

6. It's an inexpensive way to say . . . *SFX:* Wolf whistle.

Plate 8 The medium of television, of course, also uses color in a dramatic fashion as this commercial reveals. Florists have tried for years to expand primary-demand for flowers beyond special occasions, such as weddings and funerals. Here small bouquets for lesser occasions are featured.

7. *ANNCR VO:* You deserve it.

8. Bon Voyage.

9. You're first with me. Now, don't you know someone who deserves a little tickle?

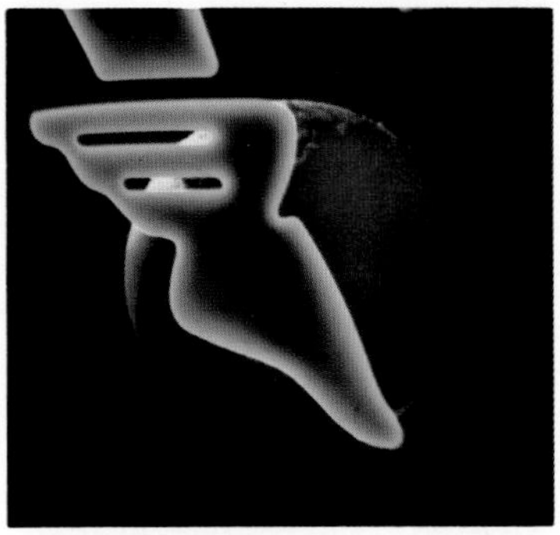

10. Logo Music.

11. Logo Music.

12. Logo Music.

Plate 9 Out-of-home media rely heavily on color to make an impact on passing motorists. This standard billboard presents a popular fruit in its characteristic color along with a catchy five-word slogan.

Plate 10 Although color is used in this painted bulletin, its dramatic effect comes primarily from its real-life portrayal of a shark.

Plate 11 This point-of-purchase display won a POPAI Display-of-the-Year Award in 1981. Note the large number of cans displayed in a small area of floor space. [*Courtesy of the Point-of-Purchase Advertising Institute.*]

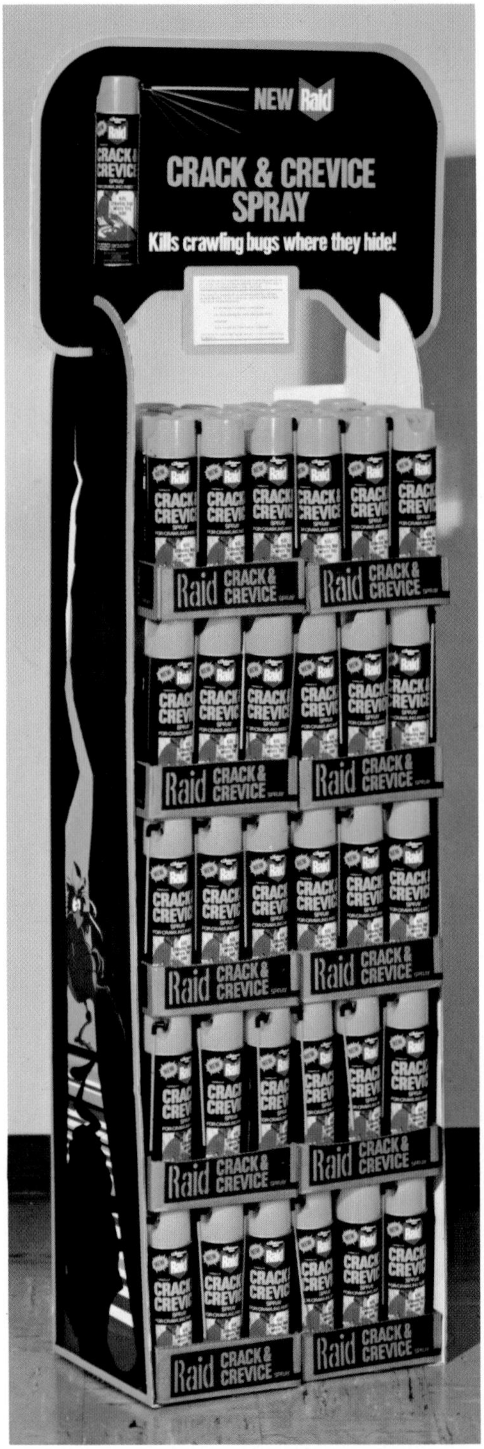

Plate 12 Although sponsored by Chiquita bananas, this point-of-purchase display allows the produce manager of the supermarket to feature many fruits associated with the Christmas holiday season. [*Courtesy of the Point-of-Purchase Advertising Institute.*]

Plate 13 "Take one" is the message implied by this wall box. Note the use of the company's slogan and the request for action by the consumer. [*Courtesy of the Point-of-Purchase Advertising Institute.*]

Plate 14 This display incorporates the capability for demonstration of the product. The unit requires no assembly at the retail store level. [*Courtesy of the Point-of-Purchase Advertising Institute.*]

Real quality has a way of creating its own image.

Images can be fleeting. A shadow. A rippling picture in a pond. Or they can be as lasting as a lifetime. A lifetime of hard work.

As a maker of home appliances, Whirlpool Corporation believes that a lasting quality image is simply the reflection of the people who build and stand behind the product. Special people. Motivated by pride of concept. Of craftsmanship. Of their ability to make things that last.

This is why we take pride in stocking parts for as many years as we do. Why we maintain a toll-free Cool-Line® service number* you can call 24 hours a day. And why we have a nationwide organization of authorized Tech-Care® service companies that are as close to you as your phone book.

You see, at Whirlpool we believe every appliance we build should create its own image of quality. And do it for one person—you.

It's our way of saying this is more than just an appliance. This is our way of life.

Whirlpool
Home Appliances

*800-253-1301. In Alaska and Hawaii 800-253-1121. In Michigan 800-632-2243.

Plate 16 The use of cosmetics is a way of adding color to a woman's presence. Matching nail polish and lipstick are featured in this ad which shows the prospective buyer exactly how the product looks, thus aiding in the purchase decision. [*Courtesy of Christian Dior Perfume, Inc.*]

Plate 15 (Left) Corporate advertising, as we discuss in Chapter 4, is different from product reputation advertising shown in the earlier ads of this section. Here the reader is asked to think favorably toward the manufacturer rather than his specific products. The calm scene and subdued colors evoke the mood or image desired. [*Courtesy of Whirlpool.*]

Plate 17 Perfume is often sold through images as Figure 2.7 in Chapter 2 illustrates. Because of its familiarity among consumers Chanel No. 5 needs only to show the famous package in its advertisements. You will recall that the package has been described as "a product's best form of advertising." [*Courtesy of Chanel, Inc.*]

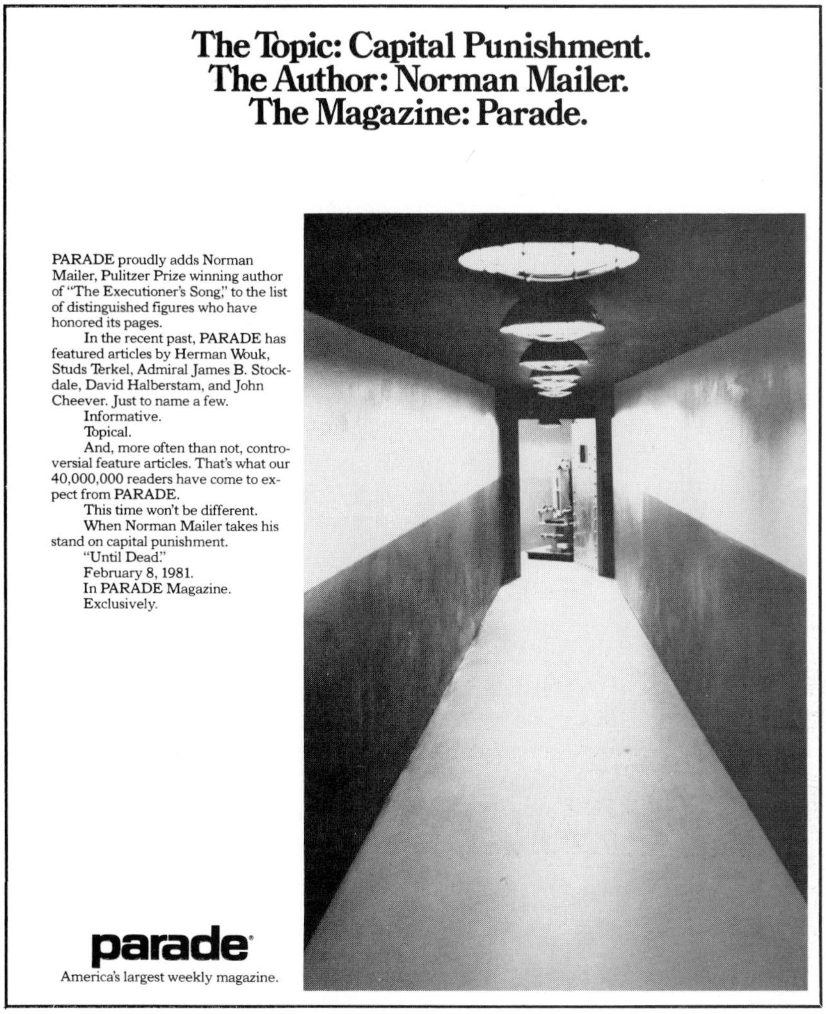

The Topic: Capital Punishment.
The Author: Norman Mailer.
The Magazine: Parade.
PARADE proudly adds Norman Mailer, Pulitzer Prize winning author of "The Executioner's Song," to the list of distinguished figures who have honored its pages.
In the recent past, PARADE has featured articles by Herman Wouk, Studs Terkel, Admiral James B. Stockdale, David Halberstam, and John Cheever. Just to name a few.
Informative.
Topical.
And, more often than not, controversial feature articles. That's what our 40,000,000 readers have come to expect from PARADE.
This time won't be different.
When Norman Mailer takes his stand on capital punishment.
"Until Dead."
February 8, 1981.
In PARADE Magazine.
Exclusively.
parade
America's largest weekly magazine.

Figure 8.12 *Parade* magazine is a popular addition to Sunday newspapers throughout the United States.

a full-page ad, however, is the same whether the page is 10 by 12½ inches ("large"), as it is in *Life*, or 5¼ by 7¼ inches ("small"), as in *TV Guide*. Advertisers who wish to present a message that cannot be accommodated on one small page may use several consecutive pages in the same magazine.

Another way to classify magazines is by frequency of publication: weekly, biweekly, monthly, bimonthly, quarterly, or semiannually. Monthly magazines are by far the largest group, with weeklies second. For advertisers with seasonal product messages, and for those attempting to establish a new product as rapidly as possible, publication frequency may be an important consideration. For example, an advertiser aiming at the Christmas gift market in the field of athletics can deliver 12 ads in *Sports Illustrated* (a weekly) between the first week in October and Christmas, but only 3 ads in *Tennis* or *Runner's World* (monthlies).

Magazines Grouped by Editorial Appeal The most important method of classifying magazines is in terms of their editorial appeal or the type of readership they attract. Here, each of three broad groups—consumer magazines, business publications, and farm publications—is divided into specialized subgroups.

1 Consumer magazines A common division of consumer magazines separates them into general appeal and special-interest appeal. The former type offers readers a diversified editorial content, whereas the latter focuses on more restricted subjects. For example, *Reader's Digest* appeals to both men and women and to many levels of age, occupation, income, and education. (See Figure 8.13.) On the other hand, the special-interest appeals of *Car & Driver* and *Better Homes and Gardens* are indicated by the very names of the magazines.

General magazines have changed considerably over the last two decades. Some weeklies, such as *Life* and the *Saturday Evening Post,* went out of business completely and only recently have been revived as monthlies. Television, it is believed, took over much of the story-telling function of these magazines (with its daily soap operas, for example), as well as the presentation of dramatic photographs and the instant analysis of major sports events. Even weekly news magazines now emphasize features, rather than hard news. Thus, they don't compete with TV's immediacy and worldwide satellite communication, but rather, they provide the background material and depth that television cannot include.

It is noteworthy, however, that some current best-

Figure 8.13 *Reader's Digest*'s huge audience cuts across most demographic lines and interest categories. [*Courtesy of the J. Walter Thompson Company.*]

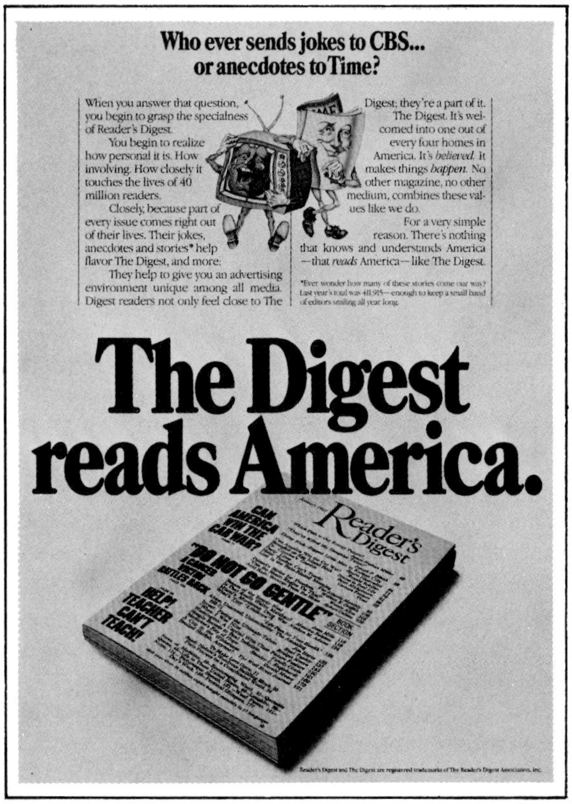

seller magazines have been going strong for 100 years (*Cosmopolitan, Good Housekeeping, Ladies' Home Journal,* and *McCall's*), and others for 50 (*Family Circle, Glamour,* and *Woman's Day*). (See Figure 8.14.)

Special-interest magazines are flourishing today as Americans become better educated and their tastes grow more sophisticated. Despite the increasing costs of magazines, circulation figures are rising, too. Science, money, and sports publications are multiplying, as are city magazines such as *Chicago* and *San Francisco.*[8] In addition, advertisers are paying increased attention to the quarter of the United States population now aged fifty and over. These people have been found to do a great deal of traveling, spending, and reading. So, recent magazine débuts include *50 Plus, Modern Maturity,* and *Prime Time.* (See Figure 8.15.)

The Standard Rate & Data Service publication, *Consumer Magazines and Farm Publications Rates and Data,* lists 51 magazine classifications, ranging alphabetically from "Airline inflight" to "Youth." And these listings are in addition to newspaper supplements, directories, and general-appeal lists. But the effectiveness of magazines as advertising media does not rest entirely on their ability to deliver selective audiences. Editorial content influences readers' moods and their receptivity to advertisements. For example, when a woman reads *Better Homes and Gardens,* her thoughts may be directed toward her home and family. But when she reads *Newsweek,* she concentrates on things outside her home—possibly transportation or entertainment. Similarly, when a man reads *AutoWeek,* his interests are focused on the subject of cars—one that may well play an important role in both his business and his personal life (with results suggested in Figure 8.16).

2 Business publications A business publication appeals to an occupational group or a particular industry. In terms of numbers, both of publications and of advertisers using them, the business magazine group is larger than the consumer and farm groups combined. However, because circulations are usually smaller and page rates lower, the dollar volume of business publication advertising is about 70 percent that of consumer magazines.

The advertiser who wishes to reach, for example, radio and TV personnel on the one hand, and woodworkers on the other, can do so through the

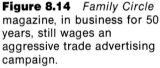

FAMILY CIRCLE AND SPORTS– THE WINNING COMBINATION.
60% of Americans are involved in some athletic activity these days—more than half with other members of their families. And those families are reading Family Circle, the largest selling women's magazine in the world. You can reach millions of these sports-active families with the three big annual sports promotions in Family Circle Magazine.
As sponsor of the $150,000 Family Circle Cup, the annual tennis event televised nationally since 1973, we're proud to encourage participation of women in sports. Our pro tournament attracts top seeded women superstars every April; and millions of viewers,who watch the nationally telecast finals. The media package consists of one four-color page in Family Circle, and two 30-second network commercials, for an estimated reach of over nineteen million readers and nine million viewers. And every participating advertiser receives invitations to attend the tennis spectacular. When it comes to reaching sports-active families in style this one's a put-away!
Soccer is the fastest growing family sport in America, with nearly as many girls playing as boys. And 40% of the fans rooting at the sidelines are women. Millions of American families are finding that soccer is a kick! You can team up with them through category-exclusive participation in the third annual Family Circle/U.S. Soccer Federation promotion, in our July 21, 1981 issue. There'll be a special offer for readers, and a special advertising section. You'll have eye-catching P-O-S materials, and a special soccer logo for displays, packaging and advertising.
Millions of Family Circle families combine football, fun and food in picnics at the stadium or at home by the TV. We've had a football/tailgate promotional program since 1979. Because of enthusiastic advertiser participation, we're currently developing an even bigger, more exciting program built around this market for 1981. You'll be hearing more about this unique marketing opportunity in the near future.
Use these all-star Family Circle advertising promotions to capture the hottest market in the U.S.—the millions and millions of sports-active families.
Family Circle.
New ideas every three weeks.
A New York Times Company
© 1980 The Family Circle, Inc.

Figure 8.14 *Family Circle* magazine, in business for 50 years, still wages an aggressive trade advertising campaign.

pages of *Broadcasting* and *Woodworking & Furniture Digest*, respectively. The Standard Rate & Data Service lists business publications under 159 occupational or industrial classifications, some of which include as many as 20 different magazines.

Readers of business publications are looking for news and information that will help them on the job. As a result, there is a direct correlation of interest between editorial and advertising columns. Subscriptions are often paid by companies instead of individuals, and a single copy is frequently routed to a number of employees.

A large and important group of business publications is composed of **professional magazines,** designed for men and women in recognized professions such as medicine, architecture, education, and

Mom and Pop like simple cooking.
At long last! The only hungry mouths Mom and Pop have to feed now are their own.
And they're indulging in the kinds of foods that extend their new leisure. Frozen entrees. Brown-and-serve baked goods. All the better brands of today's convenience food products.
And it's no more slaving over a hot stove. Our Maturity Magazines readers are turning to convection ovens, microwaves and the other new appliances of the 80's.
Mom and Pop have earned this new kind of lifestyle and they can afford it. A special Simmons Study released in December, 1979, shows that over 2/3 of the readers of Modern Maturity have HH incomes of over $15,000. Dynamic Years subscribers have a median income of $20,554. Bear in mind that this is mostly disposable income.
Mature Americans have $355 billion to spend. Maturity Magazines will give you *the* dominant depth and penetration in this vital market. And at remarkable efficiency. Like a 4/c page in Modern Maturity at a CPM of $2.91.
We'd like to tell you more. Call Jim Sutherland at (212) 599-1880. Or write: Maturity Magazines Group, 420 Lexington Avenue, New York, NY 10170.
MATURITY MAGAZINES
Our prospects are excellent.
Modern Maturity • Dynamic Years • NRTA Journal
AARP News Bulletin • NRTA News Bulletin

Figure 8.15 Magazines have recently begun catering to mature readers in an active and very appealing manner.

law. Examples are the *Journal of the American Medical Association* and *Architectural Forum.* Readers are not primarily interested in ways to cut costs or increase profits, but in new technical developments in their fields. And they do not usually purchase the products and services advertised to them; instead, they recommend them to patients or clients. Figure 8.17 shows the difference between a professional ad and a consumer ad for the same product.

A second subgroup of business publications consists of **trade magazines,** concerned with merchandising or marketing operations. They circulate to dealers, jobbers, and distributors. *Supermarket News* is a trade publication on the food business, and *Men's Wear* is read by wholesalers and retailers of men's clothing.

A third subdivision is **institutional magazines,** with editorial content aimed at the problems of hos-

Figure 8.16 *Autoweek* claims a reading audience of not mere product *users,* but *heavy* users. It backs up its claims with convincing figures, too. [*Courtesy of* AutoWeek *magazine, Division of Crain Communications, Inc., and Earle Bower Associates, Inc.*]

pitals, hotels, and other institutions or service organizations. *Modern Hospital* and *Hotel and Motel Management* are examples.

Fourth, **industrial publications** are edited for the manufacturing and production side of business. *Iron Age* and *Factory* are examples, and advertisers are commonly manufacturing or service organizations selling their products to other companies.

The final classification is the **general business** or **executive magazine,** designed to appeal to men and women in executive or managerial positions in all types of businesses and industries. *Business Week, Fortune,* and *Dun's Review* are general business magazines addressed to specific readers. By editorial content, newspapers like the *Journal of Commerce* and *The Wall Street Journal* clearly belong in this category, too.

Business publications may be either horizontal or

Figure 8.17 In these ads, Sanka is promoted to members of the medical profession and to general consumers.

vertical in coverage and reader interest. The **horizontal** publication attracts readers in similar positions of responsibility in many different businesses. A **vertical** publication, on the other hand, is edited for people at all levels of responsibility within a single industry. *Factory* is horizontal, covering plant managers, engineers, and other supervisory personnel, regardless of whether they manufacture electric motors, automobile tires, or furniture. *Advertising Age* is vertical, edited for all types of persons employed at any level in the advertising business.

3 Farm publications A farm publication is a business magazine, but it may also have family appeal. Agriculture, of course, is a family enterprise as well as a business to be operated for profit, and a farm or ranch is also a home. Many farm families read the same consumer magazines their city cousins read, but the farm publication supplies them with ideas and information they are unlikely to get elsewhere. *Successful Farming* is a national farm magazine with approximately 700,000 circulation whose stated editorial policy is designed "as management guidance for business farmers and their families . . . as practical help in making those decisions which directly affect the profitability of the business and the welfare of the farm."[9]

Gross Impressions

Media planners use the concept of **gross impressions** as one method of comparing the delivery of one magazine or combination of magazines with another, or for adding media weight or emphasis to certain geographic areas that have better sales potential than others. One impression denotes one person reached by a medium. For example, if magazine A reaches 2 million people and magazine B reaches 3.5 million, then magazines A and B together make a total of 5.5 million gross impressions—even if some of magazine A's readers are also readers of magazine B. So gross impressions, like gross rating points in the broadcast media, usually represent duplicated audience totals.

In the example above, suppose a media plan called for magazine A to receive 20 ads during the year, and magazine B 5 ads. Then:

For magazine A: 2 million $\times$ 20 ads =
40.0 million gross impressions

For magazine B: 3.5 million $\times$ 5 ads =
17.5 million gross impressions

Total for magazines A and B =
57.5 million gross impressions

Figure 8.18 illustrates the use of gross impressions in a promotional campaign designed by *Good Housekeeping* to attract new advertisers. One of the problems involved with the use of such figures as decision-making criteria, however, is that there is no precise definition for the term "impressions." Circulation figures reflect magazine subscribers and persons who buy at newsstands, but possessing a copy of a magazine and actually reading its editorial content (much less its advertising) are two different things. Also, any magazine issue may claim some "pass along" readers, too (nonsubscribers who look through the magazine at a neighbor's home or in a doctor's office). Finally, media experts have never

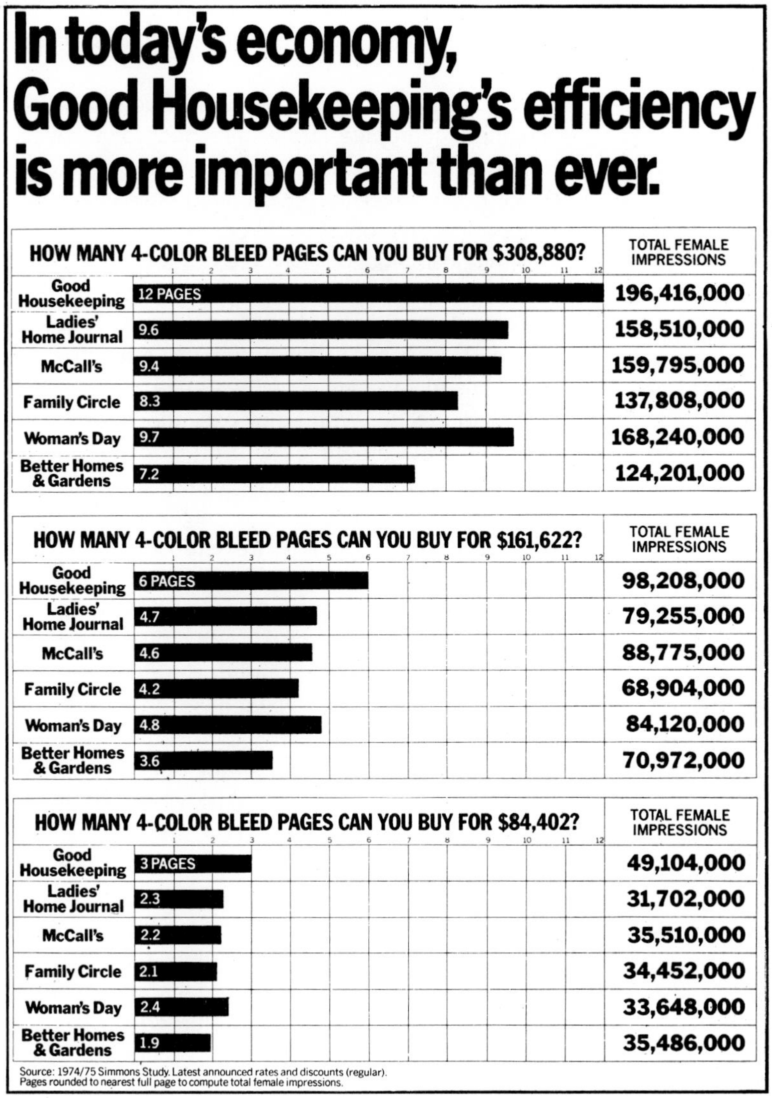

Figure 8.18 *Good Housekeeping* builds a case for itself with a research study showing its advantageous relative cost when compared with competitive women's magazines.

agreed on a method for determining true readership of a medium or an ad. They have different opinions on both the quantity and the quality (depth) of reading required to establish, for example, high, medium, and low reading levels.

Magazine Rate Structures

Magazine advertising rates are quoted in units of pages, partial pages, and agate lines. Most rates include a commission to advertising agencies (15 percent) and to media representatives (10 percent).

Color Premiums Color reproduction is available in almost all leading magazines, including those in the business or farm fields, but the premiums charged are by no means uniform. A two-color page in *Playboy* cost $45,240 in 1980, approximately 25 percent more than a black-and-white page, and a four-color page cost 40 percent more. In *Reader's Digest,* an advertiser could buy a two-color page for $79,000, 6 percent more than for black-and-white, and a four-color page for a premium of 20 percent. In publications with small circulations, four-color reproduction may increase the space cost as much as 70 percent. Minimum space requirements for full color vary also; Woodall's Market Command Group (three camping publications) accepts color in full-page ads only, whereas the Shoppers Section of the *Saturday Evening Post* sells color ad space by the inch.[10] Discounts for volume or frequency of insertions are the rule rather than the exception among magazines of all types.

Magazine Cost per Thousand The standard method for comparing magazine advertising costs relative to circulation is based on the cost of delivering one full-page black-and-white ad to 1,000 homes (or, in the case of business publications, to 1,000 engineers or 1,000 airplane pilots). The formula is:

$$\frac{R \times 1{,}000}{C} = CPM$$

where R = rate for one page, black and white

C = actual circulation

CPM = cost per thousand

Applying this method, a magazine with a basic black-and-white page rate of $11,000 and a circulation of 2 million would have a cost per thousand of $5.50. But a magazine with only 40,000 circulation and a rate of $640 per page would have a CPM of $16. As with the milline rate for newspapers, the cost per thousand for magazines usually goes up as circulation goes down. In many cases, however, an advertiser may be justified in absorbing a higher relative cost because of a magazine's selectivity; that is, waste circulation is minimized. If a product is bought only by artists, advertising funds are invested more wisely in a magazine that reaches 40,000 artists at $16 per thousand than they would be in a publication read by 5 million people of all kinds, even though the ad in the second magazine might reach more artists and the cost per thousand for the latter publication might be as low as $2.83. The key in this case is the cost per thousand *prospects.* (See Figure 8.19.)

A peculiarity of magazine rate structures is the circulation guarantee. Rates are tied to a specific quantity of circulation called the **rate base.** Any excess of copies over the guaranteed base is a bonus for the advertiser, but if the circulation falls below the guarantee, the advertiser receives a refund.

Preferred Positions for Magazine Advertisements Compared with newspapers, magazines are relatively small in size, and they enjoy longer audience reading time. With a few exceptions, therefore, neither the placement of ads on a page nor the location of specific ad pages within a publication is of great importance to the magazine advertiser. Granted, because of its extra exposure, the back cover of a magazine is always considered a *preferred* or *premium position* and commands a higher rate than inside pages. "Inside covers"—that is, the second side of the front cover and the inside of the back cover—are also usually classed as preferred positions, and in most magazines they carry a premium rate somewhat lower than that for outside covers.

The next most important consideration in magazine advertising is probably its compatibility with editorial content. For example, food manufacturers prefer to have their advertisements in the section of a women's magazine devoted to recipes and food preparation. Studies of direct inquiries received from advertisements in national magazines, however, indicate that differences in returns based on location within magazines are moderate except for cover positions.

NOBODY STRETCHES YOUR MEDIA DOLLAR
In 1981, when media dollars have to work even harder than ever, here's a reassuring word from Newsweek.
Efficiency.
Newsweek continues to be more efficient than any other newsweekly at reaching the people who count the most with advertisers.
Whether it's a matter of Total Adult Audience or Household Income of $25,000 or more.
Whether it's College Graduates or those in Professional/Managerial fields.*
Newsweek will deliver more of these critical audiences for your money than any other newsweekly in the coming year.
If you advertise in Newsweek, all this is something to think about. And if you don't, it's really something to think about.
Fall 1980 MRI-Total Adults CPM*
Newsweek Time U.S.News
$1.57 $1.92 $2.10
3.84 4.93 5.19
5.37 6.54 6.56
4.99 6.40 6.66
1980 SMRB-Total Adults CPM*
Newsweek Time U.S.News
$2.25 $2.46 $2.78
4.72 5.19 5.76
7.06 7.54 7.31
6.71 7.53 8.06
* Source: 1980 Fall MRI.
LIKE NEWSWEEK

Figure 8.19 *Newsweek* stresses its efficiency in reaching advertisers' target audiences. [Newsweek, *Dec. 15, 1980.*]

Magazine Services for Advertisers

The fundamental difference in the editorial appeal of newspapers and magazines is reflected in the marketing and merchandising assistance each type of publication offers advertisers. Except in competitive newspaper cities, newspaper market studies concentrate on the buying habits and other characteristics of a heterogeneous group within the geographic area the paper covers; magazine studies tend to focus on the attitudes, opinions, and buying behavior of different income, sex, and occupational groups regardless of geographic location. In addition, many magazine publishers collect market data of special interest to specific advertisers more rapidly and with less expense than other research sources.

Magazines do not supply the elaborate creative services furnished to local advertisers by newspapers, but most have departments that will assist in the preparation of folders, special letters to distributors and retailers, counter cards for stores, and other materials. Few magazines offer any merchandising or promotional services without charge or without a sizable purchase of space; some, however, have merchandising specialists in certain trade or product classifications on their staffs, and they may send representatives to sales meetings to help present advertising plans to wholesalers, retailers, and advertisers' own sales organizations. Finally, magazines may provide advertisers with reprints of their ads that can be used for merchandising purposes at the point of sale and as trade mailers.

Sources of Publication Information

When media buyers seek information on print media, they may turn first to the Standard Rate & Data Service. But, as noted in Chapter 7, the information found in its publications, while valuable, is incomplete. So, a second data source is the publication being considered as an advertising medium. Through salespeople and representatives, information is available ranging from simple rate cards to elaborate brochures detailing both geographic markets and audiences covered by special publications. Often, comparative figures on competitive publications are also included.

The third and most prominent print-media information sources are the private research firms that compile in-depth reports on such matters as advertising linage placed in leading publications and intricately detailed profiles of media audiences. These research organizations include Media Records, Inc., Leading National Advertisers, Inc. (LNA); Simmons Market Research Bureau (SMRB); Mediamark Research Inc. (MRI); and Publishers Information Bureau (PIB).

Through them, a media buyer can get answers to such questions as: What accounts are running how much advertising in which newspapers or magazines? How do the psychographic and demographic profiles of the readers of one newsmagazine differ from those of another? What is the most efficient magazine to buy to reach female skiers between eighteen and thirty-five? Which newspaper in a two-paper market carries the bulk of the retail book advertising? Obviously, advertising has important scientific aspects, and computers are playing an ever-increasing role in the ad agencies' media-buying activities.

Summary

One of the major categories of print media is publication advertising, which includes newspapers and consumer and business periodicals as well as farm magazines.

With few exceptions, newspapers offer advertisers intensive coverage of the homes in a particular geographic area, but little class selectivity. Newspaper advertising costs and deadlines are highly flexible, but ads are short-lived. The bulk of newspaper advertising revenue comes from retail and classified ads, but national advertisers also find newspapers valuable in meeting certain campaign objectives.

Newspaper supplements, such as comic sections, Sunday magazines, and tabloid inserts, broaden the flexibility of newspapers and enhance the medium's value to advertisers.

Newspaper advertising space is usually sold to retailers by the column inch and to national advertisers by the agate line. An agate line is a unit of space 1 column wide and 1/14 inch deep; 14 of these lines equal 1 column inch. At the retail level, newspaper advertising is usually subject to attractive bulk or frequency discounts. Under a single rate system, national advertisers may benefit from similar discounts, but this practice is still relatively rare. Rates may also vary when an advertiser uses color or demands a guaranteed position in the paper.

While a newspaper appeals to all sorts of people within a certain community, a magazine interests particular people in all kinds of communities. It is this ability to reach homogeneous groups that makes magazines so attractive to advertisers. In addition, magazines offer excellent reproduction possibilities and extended exposure of messages.

Although magazines are usually viewed as a national medium, there are also regional magazines, regional editions of national magazines, and split-run possibilities that give the medium geographic flexibility.

Magazines may be classified by page size, by frequency of publication, and by editorial appeal. There are three major groupings by editorial appeal: consumer magazines, business publications, and farm publications. Business publications include professional magazines, trade magazines, general business magazines, institutional magazines, and industrial publications.

Gross impressions help media planners compare the value of certain magazines or magazine combinations. They represent the size of audiences reached by specific magazines, even though there is no widespread agreement as to the quantity or quality of readership required before a person can be called a magazine reader. Gross impressions for a combination of magazines usually include duplicated audiences; that is, some of the same readers may read two or more of the magazines involved in the audience-measurement activity.

Magazine space is generally sold at rates based on pages, partial pages, or agate lines. As in the case of newspapers, premiums may be charged for color or special positions.

The most important sources to which media buyers turn for information on magazines are the Standard Rate & Data Service, the magazines themselves, and private research firms that sell detailed information concerning audiences, advertising linage, and other relevant data.

Questions for Discussion

1 Discuss the main function of the Audit Bureau of Circulations.
2 What are the fundamental differences between newspapers and magazines as they would be viewed by a media buyer?
3 Newspapers continue to dominate the American advertising scene in terms of total advertising dollars invested. Why does this situation exist? Would you expect it to continue in future years?
4 Compare the rate structures of newspapers and magazines.
5 Explain, without using the formula, what the milline rate reveals to a media buyer. How does it differ from the cost-per-thousand concept?
6 Salespeople for newspaper magazine supple-

ments claim they offer an advertiser the best advantages of both media. Why?

7 Both newspapers and magazines are classified by size and by frequency of publication. Explain what each of these classifications entails.

8 Select a particular magazine and discuss why you believe some of its advertisers selected that medium to carry their advertising.

9 How do vertical and horizontal business publications differ? Cite examples of each.

10 Describe some of the services that newspapers and magazines offer to advertisers.

For Further Reference

Gill, Brendan: *Here at the New Yorker,* Random House, Inc., New York, 1975.

Jugenheimer, Donald W., and Peter B. Turk: *Advertising Media,* Grid Publishing, Inc., Columbus, Ohio, 1980.

Lewis, H. Gordon: *How to Make Your Advertising Twice as Effective at Half the Cost,* Nelson-Hall, Chicago, 1979.

Northwestern University, Medill School of Journalism: *Magazine Profiles: Studies of Magazines Today,* Evanston, Ill., 1974.

Van, Karyl, and John Hahn: *Guidelines in Selling Magazine Advertising,* Appleton-Century-Crofts, New York, 1971.

Vanderwarker, James H., and Richard G. Gustafson: *The Complete Guide to Effective Local Advertising, Public Relations, & Sales Promotion,* The Guide Publishing Company, Honolulu, 1978.

Wolseley, Roland E: *The Changing Magazine: Trends in Readership and Management,* Hastings House, Publishers, Inc., New York, 1973.

Wood, James P.: *Magazines in the United States,* The Ronald Press Company, New York, 1971.

End Notes

[1] *Marketing & Media Decisions,* October 1980, p. 104.

[2] *Facts about 1980 Newspapers,* American Newspaper Publishers Association, Washington, D.C.

[3] *Marketing & Media Decisions,* op. cit., p. 195.

[4] *Newspaper Rates and Data,* November 1980.

[5] Ibid.

[6] *Consumer Magazines and Farm Publications Rates and Data,* Oct. 27, 1980.

[7] Ibid.

[8] See *Advertising Age,* Sec. 2, June 16, 1980.

[9] *Consumer Magazines and Farm Publications Rates and Data,* op. cit.

[10] Ibid.

Chapter 9

Direct Advertising, Specialty Advertising, and Point-of-Purchase Advertising

When choosing an advertising medium, an advertiser or a media buyer is like a golfer choosing a club. Each medium, and each club, must be selected in terms of the needs of the situation in which it is to be used. Each is indispensable in its place, regardless of its size. The finest driver is of little value on the green or in a sand trap. By the same token, neither network television nor a multimillion-circulation magazine can substitute for some of the less glamorous but highly effective media available to advertisers involved in the intense competition that characterizes marketing today. These forms of advertising, often called **collateral advertising,** are explained in this chapter and in Chapter 10. Although they are usually employed as supplementary buys to other media in an overall mix, to some advertisers they represent the most important media in their campaigns.

Unlike the media discussed earlier, most of which are measurable in terms of dollar volume, those we now consider do not lend themselves easily to accurate record keeping in this regard.

Direct Advertising

The terms "direct advertising," "direct-mail advertising," and "direct marketing" or "mail-order advertising" are frequently confused. **Direct advertising** includes all forms of printed advertising delivered directly to the prospective customer, instead of indirectly through a newspaper or magazine. It may be handed over the counter of a retail store, distributed from door to door, delivered by messengers, passed out on the street, or sent through the mail. If it reaches consumers by mail, it is **direct-mail advertising.**

On the other hand, **direct marketing,** or **mail-order advertising,** refers to a method of product distribution. When a sale is made without the aid of middlemen or without personal, face-to-face selling it is direct marketing. And if orders are secured by mail, we have mail-order advertising—although orders may also be taken by telephone and soon, as Chapter 7 pointed out, through computerized television systems. The Newspaper Advertising Bureau predicts that by 1990, half of all consumer buying will be accomplished through nonstore means.

Note that any ad or commercial may ask its audience to "order today by writing to . . . ." Thus, a mail-order advertising message is not restricted to the medium of direct mail. It may reach prospects through the channels of direct advertising (mail or other), or it may appear in publications, on radio or TV, or in any other mass-communications medium. (See Figure 9.1.)

More than 10,000 companies currently use mail-order advertising, and over $100 billion worth of business is generated each year through the mail.[1] Even though media costs are rising rapidly, it is prob-

STEREO BREAKTHROUGH

Bone Fone

T.M.

A new concept in sound technology may revolutionize the way we listen to stereo music.

The Bone Fone surrounds your entire body with a sound almost impossible to imagine.

You're standing in an open field. Suddenly there's music from all directions. Your bones resonate as if you're listening to beautiful stereo music in front of a powerful home stereo system.

But there's no radio in sight and nobody else hears what you do. It's an unbelievable experience that will send chills through your body when you first hear it.

AROUND YOU

And nobody will know you're listening to a stereo. The entire sound system is actually draped around you like a scarf and can be hidden under a jacket or worn over clothes.

The Bone Fone is actually an AM/FM stereo multiplex radio with its speakers located near your ears. When you tune in a stereo station, you get the same stereo separation you'd expect from earphones but without the bulk and inconvenience. And you also get something you won't expect.

INNER EAR BONES

The sound will also resonate through your bones—all the way to the sensitive bones of your inner ear. It's like feeling the vibrations of a powerful stereo system or sitting in the first row listening to a symphony orchestra—it's breathtaking.

Now you can listen to beautiful stereo music everywhere—not just in your living room. Imagine walking your dog to beautiful stereo music or roller skating to a strong disco beat.

You can ride a bicycle or motorcycle, jog and even do headstands—the Bone Fone stays on no matter what the activity. The Bone Fone stereo brings beautiful music and convenience to every indoor and outdoor activity without disturbing those around you and without anything covering your ear.

SKI INVENTION

The Bone Fone was invented by an engineer who liked to ski. Every time he took a long lift ride, he noticed other skiers carrying transistor radios and cassette players and wondered if there was a better way to keep your hands free and listen to stereo music.

So he invented the Bone Fone stereo. When he put it around his neck, he couldn't believe his ears. He was not only hearing the music and stereo separation, but the sound was resonating through his bones giving him the sensation of standing in front of a powerful stereo system.

AWARDED PATENT

The inventor took his invention to a friend who also tried it on. His friend couldn't believe what he heard and at first thought someone was playing a trick on him.

The inventor was awarded a patent for his idea and brought it to JS&A. We took the idea and our engineers produced a very sensitive yet powerful AM/FM multiplex radio called the Bone Fone.

The entire battery-powered system is self-contained and uses four integrated circuits and two ceramic filters for high station selectivity. The Bone Fone weighs only 15 ounces, so when worn over your shoulders, the weight is not even a factor.

BUILT TO TAKE IT

The Bone Fone was built to take abuse. The large 70 millimeter speakers are protected in flexible water and crush resistant cases. The case that houses the radio itself is made of rugged ABS plastic with a special reinforcement system. We knew that the Bone Fone stereo may take a great deal of abuse so we designed it with the quality needed to withstand the worst treatment.

The Bone Fone stereo is covered with a sleeve made of Lycra Spandex—the same material used to make expensive swim suits, so it's easily washable. You simply remove the sleeve, dip it in soapy water, rinse and let the sleeve dry. It's just that easy. The entire system is also protected against damage from moisture and sweat making it ideal for jogging or bicycling.

The sleeve comes in brilliant Bone Fone blue—a color designed especially for the system. An optional set of four sleeves in orange, red, green and black is also available for $10. You can design your own sleeve using the pattern supplied free with the optional kit.

YOUR OWN SPACE

Several people could be in a car, each tuned to his own program or bring the Bone Fone to a ball game for the play by play. Cyclists, joggers, roller skaters, sports fans, golfers, housewives, executives—everybody can find a use for the Bone Fone. It's the perfect gift.

Why not order one on our free trial program and let your entire family try it out? Use it outdoors, while you drive, at ball games or while you golf, jog or walk the dog. But most important—compare the Bone Fone with your expensive home stereo system. Only then will you fully appreciate the major breakthrough this product represents.

GET ONE SOON

To order your Bone Fone, simply send your check or money order for **$69.95** plus $2.50 postage and handling to the address shown below. (Illinois residents add 5% sales tax.) Credit card buyers may call our toll-free number below. Add $10 if you wish to also receive the accessory pack of four additional sleeves.

We'll send you the entire Bone Fone stereo complete with four AA cell batteries, instructions, and 90-day limited warranty including our prompt service-by-mail address.

When you receive your unit, use it for two weeks. Take it with you to work, or wear it in your car. Take walks with it, ride your bicycle or roller skate with it. Let your friends try it out. If after our two-week free trial, you do not feel that the Bone Fone is the incredible stereo experience we've described, return it for a prompt and courteous refund, including your $2.50 postage and handling. You can't lose and you'll be the first to discover the greatest new space-age audio product of the year.

Discover the freedom, enjoyment, and quality of the first major breakthrough in portable entertainment since the transistor radio. Order a Bone Fone stereo at no obligation, today.

JS&A

Dept. One JS&A Plaza
Northbrook, Ill. 60062 (312) 564-7000
Call TOLL-FREE 800 323-6400
In Illinois Call .... (312) 564-7000
©JS&A Group, Inc., 1980

Figure 9.1 A mail-order advertising message, asking readers to order the product by writing or calling, appears in the medium of magazines. [*JS&A Group, Inc.*]

able, therefore, that advertisers will continue to run mail-order ads for everything from cosmetics to insurance. In the early 1980s, it cost an advertiser $250,000 to place a mail-order response card in the centerfold of one issue of *TV Guide;* yet, this advertising vehicle remains extremely popular.[2]

The Selectivity of Direct Advertising

The almost universal use of direct advertising, particularly direct-mail advertising, reflects its ability to deliver messages to selected prospects who are difficult to reach economically through other media. For example, a service-station operator may send messages only to car owners who live in the immediate neighborhood. The Ford Motor Company, through its advertising agency, J. Walter Thompson, once created a special direct-mail campaign addressed only to women owners of Plymouth and Chevrolet cars. No other major medium can offer advertisers this degree of both geographic and qualitative selectivity.

The most popular items purchased by direct response are magazines, followed by products such as books and records, garden and hobby supplies, clothing, housewares, and food. Two-thirds of American adults purchase something every year through a direct shopping technique.

The Flexibility of Direct Advertising

Another important advantage of direct advertising is its flexibility—in format, in size, in color, and in cost. Direct advertising may be as simple in form as a leaflet or postcard, or as impressive and comprehensive as a Sears, Roebuck catalog. Letters are the most widely used form because they can personalize every message. Postcards are less expensive and are well suited to short, direct messages such as a retail store's announcement of a sale to its charge customers.

Other commonly used forms of direct advertising are leaflets, broadsides, booklets, brochures, and house organs or company publications. A **leaflet** is a short, simple folder, whereas a **broadside** is a giant one sent as a self-mailer or enclosed in an envelope, and used primarily when the dramatic impact of size seems needed. **Booklets** have pages bound together rather than folded; they carry longer messages than folders and broadsides and are used for reference as catalogs, technical manuals, and price lists. A **brochure** is an elaborate booklet, planned to impress readers with the importance and prestige of an advertiser and the sales story.

House organs or **company publications** may seem to fall outside our definition of direct advertising material since they contain editorial matter—news or entertainment. However, since the advertiser prepares the entire content of these items, they are usually classified as direct advertising. Whether it is an internal house organ (published for employees) or an external house organ (published for dealers, stockholders, or customers), the sole aim of the publication is to further the interests of the company issuing it.

The variety of sizes, shapes, and formats of direct advertising material is limited only by the ingenuity of the advertiser, by the advertising budget, and—in the case of direct mail—by postal regulations.

Direct-Mail Advertising

A widespread advertising myth claims that the general public dislikes direct mail and rarely even opens it. Hope S. Roman, director of the United States Postal Service's Market Research Division and a prominent marketing and advertising research specialist, has stated, however, that almost 80 percent of recipients read their direct-mail advertising.[3] And, according to U.S. Postal Service surveys, close to three-fourths of all adults receiving direct mail have a favorable attitude toward it. Furthermore, prestigious corporations are turning to direct mail as a cost-efficient way to market and sell supplies and services to other businesses as well as to consumers.[4]

Since 1971, the Direct Mail/Marketing Association has operated a Mail Preference Service, through which consumers may have their names added to or removed from advertisers' mailing lists. A surprising 75 percent of all requests every year are for the "add-on" service. Why? Studies suggest that people like the convenience and gas-saving economy of shopping at home, appreciate the relatively unique offers made through direct advertising channels, and have come to trust the companies behind the goods. Successful business in any form is built on customer satisfaction. When corporate giants, such as Exxon, General Motors, IBM, and AT&T, enter and prosper in the field of direct marketing and advertising, they lend it an aura of prestige that many consumers find attractive.[5]

Some 10,000 companies send out mail-order catalogs every year. Moreover, some advertisers use other media to promote their use of direct mail. The *Reader's Digest*, for example, precedes its mass mailings with TV announcements advising viewers to "watch your mailboxes." In 1980, direct mail was the third most popular advertising medium in the United States, behind newspapers and television.[6]

Creative Guidelines

Because direct mail is a more personal, individualized medium than any other, it has its own set of creative advertising guidelines for both the content and the form of sales letters.

Content The first sentence of the mailing piece should serve as a headline, clearly defining the product or service being sold and promising a consumer benefit. Success stories and testimonials make interesting reading and enhance credibility. Personal pronouns and enthusiastic copy lines are essential to keep the selling atmosphere friendly and inviting. Requested action should be simple, specific, and immediate (often within a specified time limit).

Form Colored ink and paper often draw more responses than a black-and-white combination. Indented paragraphs, the underlining of key words, the use of type-matched salutations and hand-signed signatures, and the inclusion of a postscript (P.S.) all help increase results. Finally, an additional illustrated circular and postage-paid reply card raise the value and prestige of the sales letter.

Postal Classes

Postal rates and size regulations, always subject to change, are important to direct-mail advertisers because they affect the cost of delivering messages. There are four postal classes, three of which (first, third, and fourth) may be used for advertising purposes. First-class mail carries the highest rate except airmail parcel post, and it is required for typewritten or handwritten communications. Second class is reserved for newspapers and magazines with paid circulations, and fourth class is parcel post. In 1981 the rate was 63 cents for the first pound, but then decreased considerably (so that 8 pounds cost just $2.15). Parcel post rates are also affected by postal zones across the country.

Third class covers all other mail, and must be so marked on the mailing wrapper, or the mail must be left unsealed to permit postal inspection. Bulk mail is a special classification of third class that qualifies for an even lower rate. It applies to a minimum of 200 identical pieces or 50 pounds of them bundled together. The sender must pay a fee for the permit required to use bulk mail, but the savings are worth the effort when mailings are large and frequent. The current rate is only 8.8 cents if the mail is specially prepared and sorted. For advertisers like Donnelly Marketing, whose Carol Wright cooperative mailings (containing coupons for a wide variety of products) of 21 million go out six times a year, bulk mail obviously represents a tremendous saving.[7] Figure 9.2 shows a fund-raising organization's mailing envelope, complete with its bulk-rate stamp.

Mailing Lists

Both the quantity and the quality of direct-mail circulation are determined by the mailing list the advertiser uses. Ideally, lists should include only those people who are in a position to purchase, or to influence the purchase of, a product or service. Names and titles should be spelled correctly, and addresses must contain proper zip codes. In addition, good mailing lists are free of duplication and "deadwood." People move to different locations, change jobs, get married, raise families, and eventually die. Direct.mail experts estimate that the average turnover, or obsolescence, in mailing lists is as high as 25 percent of the names each year.

Today, more than 75 list brokers work full time assembling names and addresses of likely prospects for specific products and services. Their lists sell for $35 to $100 and more per thousand names.[8] Of course, a list of names and addresses does not necessarily constitute a ready-made source of prospects, because many factors affect a person's desire and ability to buy. Advertisers still face the task of determining who the best prospects are. Some build their own mailing lists, or trade with other advertisers in the same business. Others buy or rent lists from firms, such as Doubleday, that specialize in furnishing names of people classified by occupation, income, product ownership, or special psychographic factors, including the propensity to buy by mail.

Figure 9.2 This direct-mail advertiser has taken advantage of the economical bulk-mail postal class.

Sources for building such lists include rosters of present customers; reports from sales staffs; inquiries from periodical or broadcast advertising; city, business, or professional directories and club rosters; tax lists; auto registrations; and other public records. Standard Rate & Data Service (SRDS) publishes rates and data for direct-mail lists.

Problems of Direct Mail

Two major disadvantages are inherent in the use of direct-mail advertising. First, it has a relatively high cost per recipient, and second, appropriate mailing lists are difficult to secure and maintain. Large-circulation magazines and newspapers deliver full-page advertisements to millions of homes at a cost per reader that is a fraction of the cost of mailing a postcard. The total cost of a direct-mail piece, however, includes the postage plus paper, printing, addressing, and handling charges. On the average, this cost approaches 50 cents per piece, depending on the number mailed. Rates have been escalating severely in recent years, and no end is in sight.

Advertising Specialties[9]

Another form of direct advertising is known as **advertising specialties,** sometimes called **remembrance advertising.** It consists of merchandise that bears the name and address or slogan of a business firm and that is given away free by the advertiser to present and prospective customers. By creating a feeling of goodwill, the advertiser hopes that recipients will do business with the firm in the future, even though items are given on a no-obligation basis. Industry estimates place the annual sales volume for advertising specialties at more than $3 billion.[10] And an A. C. Nielsen study found that firms using specialty advertising enjoy 43 percent more patronage than those who do not.[11]

Specialty advertising has proven to be a good attention-getter in a competitive arena, especially for a new company or store. And, although creative people may not be able to pack the persuasive content of a printed advertisement or TV commercial into a specialty item, it has lasting value in reminding prospects of previous advertising and in reinforcing messages in other media. Since the advertiser's message is exposed every time the item is used, it is hoped that when a need arises for the advertiser's product or service, a sale will result.

Types of Advertising Specialties

The specialty advertising industry classifies its more than 10,000 offerings into four main categories: calendars, novelties, matchbooks, and executive gifts.

Calendars It is estimated that more than one-third of the money spent annually for advertising specialties goes into the purchase of calendars. The number printed annually is said to exceed the population of our country.

The calendar advertiser must make two important decisions. First, a chosen design and illustration must be appropriate and attractive to the target audience. If the intention is to promote a family-oriented product such as pizza or a soft drink, the graphics must fit a home environment. Examples are reproductions of landscapes, animals, children, or humorous situations. Brown and Bigelow, the country's leading calendar producer, reports that sexy calendars now rate low in popularity among male audiences when compared with patriotic themes and nature scenes.

Many calendars omit the illustration in favor of recipes, almanac notations, or space for daily memoranda. Others, like the one shown in Figure 9.3, combine consumer appeal with a solid reminder of the advertiser's sales message.

A second challenge facing calendar advertisers is the matter of physical distribution. If calendars are distributed in the advertiser's place of business, only current customers are reached. They can also be delivered door to door or by mail—a system commonly used by national calendar advertisers—but this procedure can involve considerable expense in terms of mailing lists, postage, and other delivery costs.

Despite the problems involved, however, many business executives continue to favor calendars as part of their advertising programs. Tradition itself is at work here, and customers come to expect a calendar once a year. Fortunately, if they are well designed and efficiently distributed, calendars are an effective, inexpensive way to keep an advertiser's name before the public every day.

Novelties The great variety of advertising novelties is staggering. The pen or pencil many of us use is the gift of some advertiser, as are ashtrays and bottle openers, paperweights and memo pads, rulers and swizzle sticks.

The novelty advertiser faces problems similar to those encountered with calendars. The distribution system must reach *prospects,* and the novelty must be appropriate—not so much in design as in use. The gift should be closely related to the advertiser's business or to the prospect's own interests. Personalized golf balls are hardly an enduring reminder if the prospect isn't a golfer. But an appropriate advertising specialty for a service station may be a key ring, since every time drivers unlock their cars, the name of the station will flash into sight. On the other hand, a key ring might not do a good job for a dairy, while an ice cream scoop should be effective. Or, a fuel oil dealer would find a wall thermometer an appropriate device.

Fads often develop in novelties, and for a while every merchant in town may be giving away ball-point pens. At that time it would be advantageous to switch to felt- or nylon-tipped pens if the price is not prohibitive. If full impact from the use of novelties is to be realized, items selected should be as novel as possible. Figure 9.4 shows two types of personalized novelties.

Matchbooks Although matchbooks are not technically a novelty item, they are another useful advertising specialty. Manufacturers who wish to give wide, repeated exposure to their messages can have them printed on matchbook covers and distributed through retail outlets. The store that gives them away may pay part of the cost of the matchbooks, but ordinarily the advertiser absorbs it all. Many retailers distribute matchbooks containing their own advertising, and hotels often use them to enhance their images.

Calendars, novelties, matchbooks, and other advertising specialties are sold by sales representatives just as other advertising media are. These salespeople work to develop creative approaches that incorporate the use of one or more of their items, and then call on prospective advertisers to try to sell their programs.

Executive Gifts When the potential business to be gained from individual buyers is appreciable, reliance on an inexpensive trinket is replaced by the power of a more costly gift. The principle involved is the same: the item is given in anticipation of future business, although specialty advertising people are quick to point out that it is also a means of expressing friendship during a holiday season or of saying thank you. The difference is a matter of degree. The key ring is supplanted by a genuine leather, personalized key case, or the ball-point pen by a fine desk set. Slogans and advertiser identification may be held to a minimum or eliminated completely. The word "novelty" is no longer fitting, so the industry has coined the phrase "executive gift" to describe the more expensive specialty. Gift lists include jewelry, watches, pen sets, sporting goods, cocktail sets,

Figure 9.3 A national drugstore chain allows local outlets to personalize its calendars by including their own store names and addresses. [*Rexall Corporation.*]

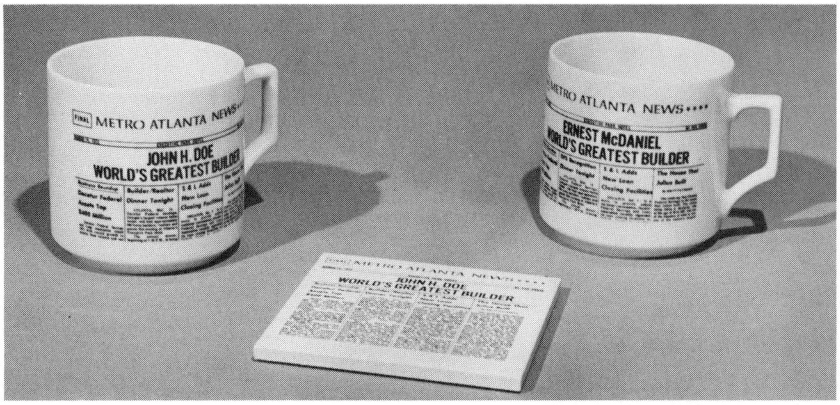

Figure 9.4 Few forms of advertising offer the personal touch represented by these cups and the ceramic trivet that won an award for the *Metro Atlanta News.* [*Specialty Advertising Association.*]

leather goods, luggage, and liquor and food specialities. It has been reported that 70 percent of the companies in the United States give business gifts.

As the potential gain is greater, however, so is the cost. There is no assurance that business will result from a gift. Furthermore, as the value of the gift increases, the line between a simple act of giving and commercial bribery becomes fuzzy. No one can object on moral grounds to the giving of a T-shirt worth $5, since it probably would not influence the recipient to make an unwise purchase of any consequence; but would the receipt of a desk set worth $200 unfairly stimulate a change of attitude? The sense of obligation might be intensified, to say the least.

This matter becomes even more touchy when the gift goes to an executive whose job is to make purchases advantageous to his or her employer. Nothing should be allowed to color buying decisions among competitive offerings. Some corporations even have regulations against the receipt of gifts, as do most governmental agencies. Moreover, the Revenue Act of 1962 removed any gift valued at more than $25 from its status as a tax-deductible business expense, thereby placing a constraint on the practice of executive gift giving.

Point-of-Purchase Advertising

The ultimate purpose of most advertising is to persuade prospects to buy a particular product or service. Print and broadcast media help create a favorable attitude while the prospects are at home, and radio, outdoor, and transit advertising follow when they go out. Finally, when the prospective buyer arrives in the marketplace, the moment of truth has arrived: the customer decides either to buy the advertiser's brand or not to buy it. There is, however, one last chance to influence that decision: **point-of-purchase** (POP) advertising.

In the case of advertisers who sell **impulse items** —those purchased without preplanning—POP represents an opportunity to suggest to people not only that they buy gum, but that they buy *Wrigley's* gum. Recent studies have shown that as many as 65 percent of all supermarket purchases are made on impulse.

Principal Forms of Point-of-Purchase Advertising

"Point of purchase" is used as a collective term to describe a wide range of advertising devices. (Two alternative names are "dealer displays" and "point-of-sale" advertising.) It consists of promotional materials situated in, on, or immediately adjacent to retail distribution points, and is designed to build traffic, register advertising impressions, and help sell merchandise. The variety of POP forms appears infinite, as a trip to any supermarket will reveal. The volume, while officially unmeasurable, is estimated at close to $3 billion per year, according to the Point-of-Purchase (POP) Advertising Institute.

Signs **On-premise signs** are discussed in Chapter 10 along with other forms of outdoor advertising, but they also qualify as point-of-purchase items. They furnish the bridge between external advertising presented outside a store and efforts exerted internally.

In effect, stores say, "Here is a place to buy that brand you saw advertised."

Window Displays In certain types of retailing, store location is extremely important. A site may be selected because it is convenient for consumers or because a sizable volume of pedestrian traffic passes it. Window displays attempt to slow the pace of passing consumers long enough to entice them into the store to look further; thus, the windows, which are in fact advertisements, should be both striking and timely.

Wall Displays Posterlike ads may be affixed to a store's interior walls. Behind the counters of cafés and snack bars, colorful messages may urge the

AZAR NUTS
Azar offers you a professional consultation service that's tailored to your specific market demands.
As America's largest independent nut processor/distributor, Azar stands on a platform of 66 years of experience obtained through the development and implementation of professional marketing programs with major corporations throughout the country.
Indepth Market-Analysis – Azar will work with you to establish a marketing profile of your marketplace, inclusive of present and projected sales trends. Azar will also consult with you on a specific product/package mix, merchandising concepts to capitalize on marketing opportunities, and assist you in preparing short-term and long-term sales objectives.
Retail and Food Service Lines – A product mix that serves all your needs. Azar's retail line offers cans, jars, pegboard cellophane packages, and lay-down packages. And now, Azar's new food service line offers you extensive product/package selections in larger sizes to meet your bakery and deli requirements.
Quality – Azar provides your buyers with the finest quality nut meats in the industry.
Service – When you talk to Azar, you talk directly with top management. In addition, Azar distributes its products through its own trucking system – no common carriers. Azar is proud of the fact that it maintains the lowest short ship percentage in the industry – less than 2%. Your product arrives when and where you want it, the way you ordered it.
Promotional Support – Azar will assist you in the design and implementation of promotional programs throughout the year, not just at peak holiday periods. These programs are supported with extensive point of sale, including nut trees, dump bins, and two-step end-aisle displays. This material can be customized and included in special stretch-wrap pallet configurations, and is delivered to you in a single unit.
Competitive Pricing – Azar's pricing strategy is geared to provide you with the finest quality nut meats at competitive prices. Discounts, case allowances, promotional incentives and co-op programs are offered throughout the year, thus allowing you to take an aggressive position in obtaining new nut purchasers.
When you want more than an order-taker and more than discount prices – you want a **total** professional consulting service. You want Azar.
BRAZILS FILBERTS
AZAR® QUALITY NUTS
6975 Commerce Ave., El Paso, Texas 79915

Figure 9.5 A trade publication ad encourages retailers to talk to this company about setting up in-store displays bearing the advertised product. [*Azar Nut Company.*]

purchase of a particular soda pop. Often such signs carry the same theme as other media—especially outdoor posters. Breweries vie for display space in taverns and retail stores with elaborate, often animated, and illuminated signs.

Display Cards A great deal of point-of-purchase advertising appears on display cards. They may be as elaborate as life-size cutout models that stand on the selling floor, or as simple as reproductions of a magazine advertisement. They may be used as part of a window display, or as **counter cards.** Magazines often provide reprints of ads affixed to display cards for use on store counters; they are offered free, or at cost, as part of a magazine's merchandising cooperation, and may have recipes or coupons attached.

Merchandise Racks and Cases Another effective device is the rack or case. Consumers see both a message about the product and the merchandise itself. An example is the candy rack designed and placed by Life Savers. Its collection of candy offerings fits near the cash register where impulse buying is highest. Likewise, displays of nuts and other snackfood items are often found close to checkout lanes. Figure 9.5 shows a trade ad designed to convince retailers to stock a product—and to display it in specific ways.

Merchandise racks for larger items are placed on the floor. Greeting-card companies place them in retail outlets where cards are displayed attractively, and an ample reserve stock is stored in drawers below. Figure 9.6 shows a display rack that has helped revolutionize the marketing of stretch hosiery.

Pennants, ceiling streamers, mobiles, decals, window banners, and end-aisle displays are among miscellaneous forms of point-of-purchase advertising in common use. Occasionally, retailers—especially department stores—take the initiative in POP advertising by designing and placing displays on the store premises. But usually the manufacturers of nationally advertised brands handle these tasks.

In-Store Commercials The newest form of POP has already been tested in thousands of American stores. On-line Media, Inc., pioneered the suspension of TV sets from ceilings over checkout counters. Six-minute video discs display up to 72 minicommercials to remind shoppers of products they might have forgotten or to stimulate impulse buying.[12]

Figure 9.6 Display racks such as this one for L'eggs are popular in supermarkets and other stores throughout the country.

Point-of-Purchase Advertising Strategy

A manufacturer decides to use **dealer displays** for one or both of two reasons. First, POP advertising promotes buying at the retail level. The goal is to continue the flow of advertising communication right down to the time of purchase. After the consumer learns that a brand is available at a particular store, a reminder is furnished that brings back previous advertising impressions. Thus, when a woman visits her favorite specialty shop in search of the "right" swim-

Profile

Joseph Sugarman

Born and raised in the Chicago area, Joseph Sugarman majored in electrical engineering at the University of Miami (Florida) in the early 1960s. Throughout much of his early life, he knew failure intimately, only to become very successful in recent years.

Joe dropped out of college after three and a half years to spend three years with the Army Intelligence Group in Germany and with the CIA. Upon his return to the United States, he formed a ski-lift sales company. Then he discovered the field of mail-order advertising.

Initially, his efforts were only minimally successful: fewer than 20 percent of his product introductions went well in the marketplace. But, he is a person of perseverance with the ability to learn from his mistakes. Therefore, Joe Sugarman's mail-order business today has annual sales over $12 million, with his product introductions success rate now standing at a whopping 80 percent.

Regarded as a maverick in the mail-order field, Sugarman writes all the copy and designs the layouts for the advertising done by his JS&A Company. Such products as pocket calculators, ion producers, and computer blood-pressure systems are featured in ads that run in male-oriented publications as well as in-flight magazines.

In his autobiography, *Success Forces,* he relates the tempestuous highlights (and low points) of his career. The book also reveals his ideas for success in the world of business. These ideas are shared with people who enroll in his success seminars, for which he charges a fee of $2,000. However, he is best known for his ability to sell new products through the printed word. Joe Sugarman is one of our nation's premier writers of advertising copy. Using that skill, he has opened up the market for a variety of new products through what is now called "direct marketing."

suit, several brand names are probably in her mind, including White Stag, Cole of California, and Jantzen. Although style will be the dominant factor in her choice, attractive displays, by providing evidence of superiority, will help her make a decision and will reassure her that her choice is a wise one.

Second, as noted previously, manufacturers use dealer displays to stimulate unplanned, spur-of-the-moment purchasing, usually called impulse buying. For example, a customer pays a check at a restaurant and takes one of the 5-cent mints displayed near the cash register. Or, the smell of popcorn from a street-corner stand convinces a passerby to buy a bag.

Self-service trends have underscored three principles that are critical for manufacturers. One, packages must stand out attractively against a galaxy of competing brands. In fact, the most important form of point-of-purchase advertising is the package itself. Two, good shelf position—high, low, or hand level—is extremely important. Shoppers are less apt to stretch or bend over to find a particular brand if acceptable substitutes are in easy reach.

Finally, consumers' buying decisions hinge largely on favorable brand attitudes. Prior usage experience is a vital factor, and so is the advice of acquaintances. Advertising plays a key role in preselling, but if attitudes toward several competing brands are approximately the same, the brand that makes the best impression at the point of purchase makes the sale.

Problems in Point-of-Purchase Advertising

The manufacturer who decides to use point-of-purchase advertising faces a number of problems.

Creativity The principal technique used in designing POP materials is simply to adapt ideas and themes from current campaigns in other media. But when the primary purpose of a display is to stimulate impulse buying, the actual product should be incorporated into the display so that consumers can easily help themselves—to magazines, to rolls of film, to greeting cards.

Placement There is only so much window, wall, floor, and counter space in every store, and ordinarily store owners want to use it for stocking and displaying actual merchandise. At this point, two forces come into play. One is trade advertising, wherein the retailer is exposed to arguments for the use of a manufacturer's POP. The other is the display allowance often paid to retailers by manufacturers for permitting the use of in-store displays.

Waste Obviously, manufacturers' sales forces can't check to see that all point-of-purchase advertising is installed in every possible outlet. Hence, many materials may never leave the retail storeroom, and considerable amounts of money, ranging from 30 cents to $30 per item, are wasted. Also, many retailers put displays in out-of-the-way corners that see little traffic. Or, a display may be removed very soon because another manufacturer agrees to pay a higher price for the space. Only a binding contract for a specified time period, accompanied by close policing on the premises, will prevent such actions.

Another source of waste is the improper selection of retail outlets. Stores generating the lowest sales volume are often the most willing to use POP materials, especially if a cash allowance is included.

Summary

Direct advertising and point-of-purchase advertising are vital elements in the campaigns of many manufacturers and retailers despite the fact that these media may not receive a large share of budget allocations. To some advertisers, however, these media represent primary communication channels.

Direct advertising is defined as any printed material delivered directly to potential customers without the use of an intervening medium such as radio or magazines. Direct advertising enjoys broad usage because of two outstanding characteristics. First, it is highly selective, eliminating much of the waste normally connected with broadly based media such as television and newspapers. Second, it is very flexible—in format, color, and cost. Thus, the selection of a direct advertising piece may range from a simple postcard or letter to a huge catalog, calendar, or specialty item.

The most prominent form of direct advertising is direct mail. It is an extremely efficient way to reach prospects without waste circulation, but there often is a problem in securing and maintaining an appropriate mailing list. Also, direct mail is high in terms of cost per thousand persons or homes reached.

Advertising specialties are products of small unit value that carry the names and addresses or slogans of advertisers. The items are given free of charge to present or prospective customers in anticipation of future business. The four main types of specialties are calendars, novelties, matchbooks, and executive gifts, and one or more serve as "remembrance advertising" for many companies.

Point-of-purchase advertising is promotional material located in or near retail establishments. The power of POP lies in its ability to persuade and remind potential customers of a particular product or service at the point of sale. POP is the last opportunity an advertiser has to speak to prospects before a purchase is made. Sometimes, it stimulates impulse buying by reminding shoppers of latent wants and needs; these unplanned purchases are commonplace among such items as greeting cards, stockings, and magazines.

Although POP advertising may be the only medium in a campaign, it is used chiefly to back up national campaigns in print or broadcast media.

Questions for Discussion

1 Most direct advertising is of the direct-mail variety, but a significant share is not. Using the text's definition of direct advertising, list as many examples as you can.

2 Direct mail is described as a medium with almost universal appeal to advertisers. Review its prime attributes and explain how it might be useful to (*a*) a small gift shop; (*b*) a national automobile insurance company.

3 Differentiate among the following: direct advertising, direct-mail advertising, and mail-order advertising.

4 Bring to class two direct-mail advertisements and discuss (*a*) why you think the advertiser included you in the mailing, (*b*) how you got on the mailing list, (*c*) whether you normally open direct-mail advertising (and why).

5 Name an advertising specialty item you have encountered that you feel was an especially good tie-in with the product being sold.

6 What is the strategy behind the sending of executive gifts? Discuss the ethical problems involved.

7 Both direct-mail and specialty advertising campaigns register high cost-per-thousand figures when compared with other mass media. Why do advertisers spend so many dollars in these media when they could reach more people for less money through broadcast or through print media?

8 Why do many package-goods advertisers use point-of-purchase advertising?

9 Name some impulse items other than those listed in this chapter whose sale might be affected by the use of point-of-purchase advertising.

10 What are the basic problems encountered in the use of point-of-purchase advertising?

For Further Reference

Bagley, Dan S., III: *Specialty Advertising: A New Look*, Specialty Advertising Association, Rolling Meadows, Ill., 1979.

Direct Mail Advertising & Selling for Retailers, National Retail Merchants Association, New York, 1978.

DMMA Fact Book on Direct Response Marketing 1979, Direct Mail/Marketing Association, New York, 1979.

Hodgson, Richard S.: *Direct Mail and Mail Order Handbook,* 2d ed., The Dartnell Corporation, Chicago, 1977.

Jain, Chaman L., and Al Migliaro: *An Introduction to Direct Marketing,* AMACOM, New York, 1978.

Kobs, Jim: *Profitable Direct Marketing,* Crain Books, Chicago, 1980.

Stone, Bob: *Successful Direct Marketing Methods,* Crain Books, Chicago, 1979.

End Notes

[1] *Fortune,* April 21, 1980, pp. 110–111.

[2] Ibid., p. 124.

[3] Hope S. Roman, "Do Consumers Love Mailers?" *Direct Marketing,* October 1975, pp. 64, 66.

[4] *The Wall Street Journal,* Nov. 13, 1980, p. 37.

[5] *Advertising Age,* Jan. 21, 1980, pp. S-16, S-22.

[6] Ibid., Jan. 5, 1981, p. 56.

[7] Ibid., Jan. 21, 1980, p. S-6.

[8] *Fortune,* April 21, 1980, p. 112.

[9] Some of the materials for this section were obtained from a pamphlet, *Specialty Advertising,* by Walter A. Gaw, Specialty Advertising Association, Chicago.

[10] *Advertising Age,* Aug. 25, 1980, p. 29.

[11] *Imprint,* Fall 1979, p. 58.

[12] *Marketing News,* Dec. 28, 1979, p. 4.

Chapter 10

Out-of-Home and Other Media

In concluding our survey of media, in this chapter you will learn about a group known as **out-of-home** media, along with a few miscellaneous advertising vehicles which, while less intrusive in our daily lives than major print and broadcast media, are efficient means for reaching certain target audiences.

In Chapter 1, we noted that signs outside a merchant's building and along routes followed by traders of the ancient world were the earliest forms of mass communications. Today, out-of-home media, sometimes called **traffic** or **position media,** represent modern refinements of this method of delivering messages to large groups of people. While other media seek out prospects in their homes or offices, out-of-home media depend on the passage of people, or traffic, past the location of each medium. The unique advantage of this approach is that, when properly placed, it lets the advertiser reach consumers at a critical moment in the pattern of buying behavior—en route to a store or other point where purchase decisions will be made.

Out-of-home media include standardized outdoor advertising in several forms, nonstandardized signs, and transit advertising placed on public and private transit vehicles and in rail, bus, and air terminals. In the analysis of how more than 60 billion advertising dollars are spent each year, there is no specific category for out-of-home media. In Table 6.2 (page 132), however, the organized outdoor industry accounted for approximately $610 million in 1980, while nonstandard signs and transit advertising were lumped together in the big "miscellaneous expenditure" category.

Outdoor Advertising

Among out-of-home media, the dominant subtype is **outdoor advertising,** sometimes called the largest advertising medium in existence (in terms of physical structure). Only in outdoor ads can a car be shown full size or an aspirin tablet 1,000 times its actual size. Supposedly, use of the outdoor medium dates back to 3200 B.C. when Egyptians carved the names of kings on their temples.

Key characteristics of a typical outdoor advertisement are (1) an easy-to-identify advertiser or product name; (2) short, simple, legible copy; and (3) illustrative material that is large, bold, and colorful.

Most people think of outdoor advertising as billboards that dot commercially zoned city streets and appear along highways, advising us of manufacturers' products and of the services of many local businesses. Early uses of this advertising were for the promotion of theatrical performances. "Bills" were placed where passersby could see them on boards, fences, or walls. Thus, the word "billboard" came into use. With the coming of automobiles and high-

Figure 10.1 This effective outdoor ad contains a very simple message. The product is instantly identifiable. Compare this ad with Color Plate 9. [*Foster & Kleiser, Division of Metromedia, Inc.*]

way systems, a natural evolutionary process brought outdoor posters to the roadside.

But not all the posters on American streets and highways are included in the technical definition of outdoor advertising. Only those signs that meet certain standards established by the Outdoor Advertising Association of America (OAAA) are so classified. These requirements deal with the size, design, and method of construction of boards called either **posters** or **painted bulletins.** Roadside and on-premise devices that are not standardized are called **signs.**

Basic Types of Outdoor Advertising

The Poster The workhorse of the standardized outdoor industry is the **poster.** It accounts for more than two-thirds of the national outdoor sales volume. Traditionally, the most popular size has been the 24-sheet poster. A standardized structure is built so the advertising message "posted" on the board fits into a copy area 8 feet 8 inches high and 19 feet 6 inches long. The message is framed by a border that remains part of the structure. The term "24-sheet poster" dates from the time when printing presses could handle only relatively small sheets of paper; thus, 24 individualized sheets were needed to fill the board. With modern presses, larger sheets can be used and more of a message can be printed on one sheet; thus, only 10 sheets have to be pasted on the typical 24-sheet poster today.

The outdoor industry is busy developing new structures; old wooden boards have been replaced with plastic or metal frames. These new construction materials have enabled outdoor advertisers to produce advertising that is attractive to the public, as well as efficient and durable.

Another change in the production of outdoor advertising has been the development and rapid acceptance of the 30-sheet poster. The copy area is 25 percent larger than that of the 24-sheet poster: 9 feet 7 inches high and 21 feet 7 inches long (see Figure 10.2). Faster traffic flows and increased competition for the motorist's attention produced a need for this poster with its greater impact and easier readability. It is replacing the 24-sheet poster as the standard in the industry, and "bleed" posters, which utilize all the space within the poster frame for the creative display (so there is no border) and measure 10 feet 5 inches by 22 feet 8 inches, are gaining popularity. On the other hand, in many markets today we are also seeing a new burst of activity in the development of 8-sheet posters, just 5 feet high and 11 feet wide.

In most cases, the paper used on posters is printed for the advertiser and distributed to outdoor plants where the advertising campaign is scheduled to run. (An outdoor plant is the local business unit in the field of outdoor advertising as the station is in the case of broadcast media.) Poster panels may be illuminated or regular (nonilluminated). Where night traffic is relatively high, it is often desirable to provide light on the poster until around midnight. The need is obviously greatest in metropolitan areas, and the ratio of regular to illuminated posters in a community depends on the nocturnal habits of its residents and visitors.

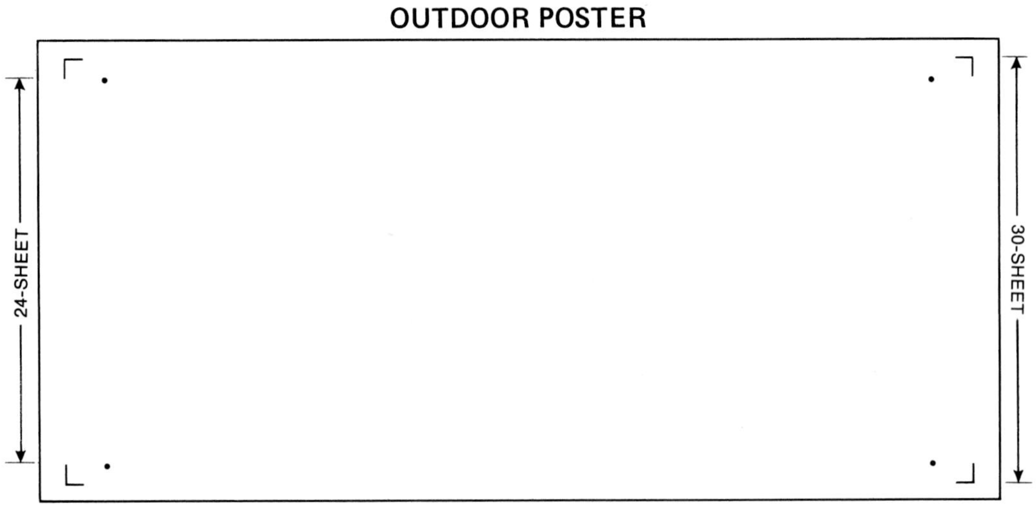

Figure 10.2 This illustration shows the difference in size between a 24-sheet and a 30-sheet poster.

Painted Bulletins **Painted bulletins** ("paints"), the second major form of outdoor advertising, feature messages that are hand-painted by artists at individual outdoor plants. (Figure 10.3 shows an example.) Their structures, which usually measure 14 by 48 feet, are larger and more streamlined than those used for posters. (See Figure 10.4.) Both posters and paints may be embellished with extensions (letters, figures, packages, mechanical devices) that protrude from the top, bottom, or sides. Local market codes limit the extent of these projections, but they are often used, at additional cost, to create dramatic, three-dimensional effects (as illustrated in Color Plate 10). Some paints even feature revolving panels.

Despite our nation's energy shortage, electric billboards are still in evidence. One of the most notable, perhaps, is a giant (20 feet by 40 feet) computer-animated board six stories above New York's Times Square. Designed by Spectacolor, Inc., the flashy display changes as often as every 10 seconds, showing up to six different ads per minute. Clients have included NBC-TV's "Saturday Night Live," Seven-Up, Du Pont, and General Motors, along with record

Figure 10.3 This painted bulletin won an "Outstanding Design of the Month" award for its graphic appeal. [*California Milk Advisory Board.*]

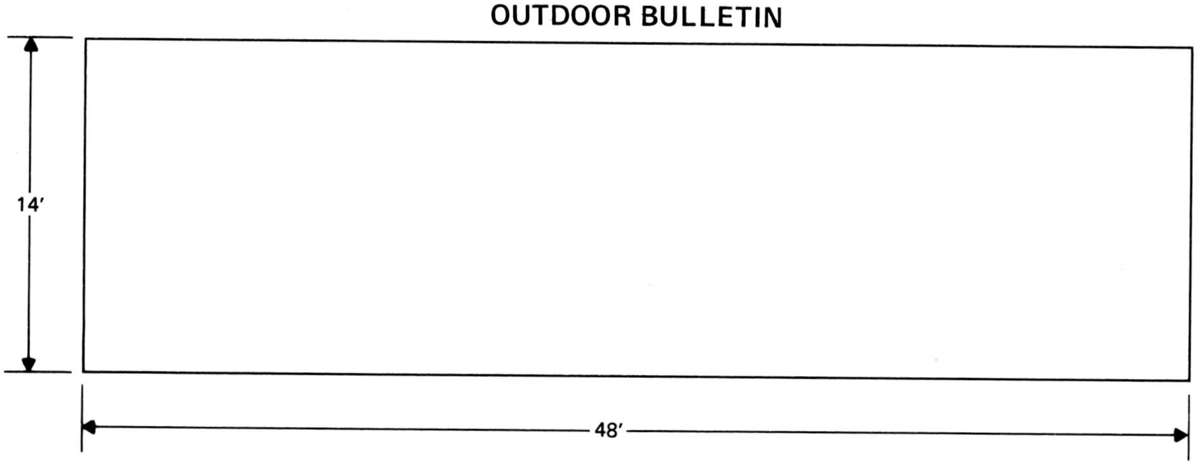

Figure 10.4 An illustration of the dimensions of outdoor bulletins, also known as paints.

and movie companies and theater and concert promoters. Advertising packages cost several thousand dollars a week for 10-second ads run every few minutes.[1]

This Spectacolor creation, however, is but a child next to the granddaddy of all outdoor signs—surely one of the largest in the world—located on a building near New York's Madison Square Garden. The billboard, 325 feet high, took 700 man-hours to paint for its client, Newport cigarettes.

On a smaller scale, back-lighted display spaces in indoor shopping malls have also been selling well in major markets across the country.[2]

Buying Outdoor Posters

In the print media, the unit of purchase is an area of space: a page, a column inch, or an agate line. In broadcasting, advertising sells by the minute or fraction of a minute. Outdoor advertising is purchased through a system that incorporates both space and time. All outdoor plant operators offer advertisers the 24- or 30-sheet panels described earlier, and the standard time period for renting space on boards is a 30-day unit.

Poster panels are sold by the month in packages of **gross rating points** (GRPs). A 100-GRP package in the outdoor business provides enough panels to deliver *in one day* a number of consumer exposure opportunities equal in size to 100 percent of the population of the market in which the panels appear.

Figure 10.5 This rate card shows the number and cost of poster panels in sizes of buying packages ranging from 10 to 150 GRPs. [*Foster & Kleiser, Division of Metromedia, Inc.*]

DALLAS METRO MARKET

Population: 1,559,500

Dallas, Ellis Counties.

SIZE	UNILL. PANELS	ILLUM. PANELS	TOTAL PANELS	COST PER MONTH	DAILY GRP
150	24	168	192	$38,304	
100	16	112	128	25,536	100
95	15	106	121	24,148	
90	14	101	115	22,968	
85	14	95	109	21,720	
80	13	90	103	20,540	
75	12	84	96	19,152	75
70	11	78	89	17,764	
65	10	73	83	16,584	
60	10	67	77	15,336	
55	9	62	71	14,156	
50	8	56	64	12,768	50
45	7	50	57	11,380	
40	6	45	51	10,200	
35	6	39	45	8,952	
30	5	34	39	7,772	
25	4	28	32	6,384	25
20	3	22	25	4,996	
15	2	17	19	3,816	
10	2	11	13	2,568	

Rates and Allotments quoted above are for general coverage showings only. Coverages other than general in composition are available on an individual quotation basis.

Thus, there must be enough posters to reach the entire population once, or half the population twice, or a third of the population three times, and so on. A 50-GRP package delivers just half as many exposure chances, and a 25-GRP buy one-quarter as many.[3]

As with any medium, however, "exposure" does not necessarily mean interest or readership. In the print media, it implies merely an "eye open to a visible advertisement."

Market size determines the cost and number of boards needed to achieve 100 gross rating points. In San Francisco, with a population of approximately 1¼ million, 70 boards are required. In New London, Connecticut, with a population one-fifth the size of San Francisco's, 32 boards deliver 100 GRPs. And in Detroit, a city 2½ times the size of San Francisco, 188 boards are needed.[4] Figure 10.5 shows a rate card for a Texas market.

As a rule, outdoor advertising's cost-per-thousand figures are far below those of other media (often less than $1). Audiences are huge, since almost everyone you can think of passes outdoor ads every time he or she drives anywhere (and then passes them again on the way back, day after day). Discounts are offered for purchases extending over a period of months, especially in cold climates when the somewhat less desirable winter months are included. The message (known as **paper**) on a panel may be changed every month at no extra charge if the buyer provides the new paper. It is the responsibility of the plant operator, however, to see that the paper is in presentable form. If it tears, or if the copy is defaced by vandals, new paper is installed free by the plant owner.

ROTATING PAINTED/PRINT BULLETIN RATES

SPACE RATES

MARKET	UNIT COST PER MONTH PAINTED	UNIT COST PER MONTH PRINTED
CALIFORNIA (SOUTHERN)		
Los Angeles	$2,015	$1,915
San Diego	$1,830	$1,740
CALIFORNIA (NORTHERN)		
San Francisco Bay Area	$1,890	$1,795
Sacramento	$1,565	$1,485
FLORIDA		
Tampa/St. Petersburg	$1,040	$1,040
ILLINOIS		
Chicago	$1,960	$1,860
Chicago Expressway	$3,065	N/A
MARYLAND		
Baltimore	$1,350	$1,280
NEW YORK		
New York	$2,700	$2,565
OHIO		
Cleveland	$1,625	$1,545
Cleveland Airport	$1,900	$1,805
Cincinnati	$1,320	$1,254
Canton	$ 890	$ 890
Akron	$1,070	$1,070
TEXAS		
Dallas/Ft. Worth	$1,225	$1,225
Houston	$1,300	$1,300
San Antonio	$ 900	$ 900
WISCONSIN		
Milwaukee	$1,165	$1,165

Figure 10.6 A rate card for "rotary plan" buying of outdoor painted bulletins. Rotating ads may be painted or preprinted on paper. [*Foster & Kleiser, Division of Metromedia, Inc.*]

Buying Painted Bulletins

The arrangements for advertising on painted bulletins are entirely different. Since paint is much more durable than poster paper and much more costly to apply, the usual length of time for an installation is one year. Because relatively few painted bulletins appear in any community, each position is selected individually, and there is no such thing as a GRP buy. Advertisers do have the option of changing their copy more than once a year at their own expense. The outdoor plant is responsible for the upkeep of existing messages and structures.

Although it is customary to hand-paint bulletins, it is also possible to print larger designs on paper without sacrificing the gloss or reflective quality of paint. Such a procedure saves money for national advertisers and gives them more flexibility in making copy changes at frequent intervals.

An advertiser with limited means may buy one painted bulletin and then have it moved from one spot in a city to others for extended time periods. This plan gives viewers the impression the advertiser has purchased a number of locations, and it also extends message reach.

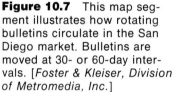

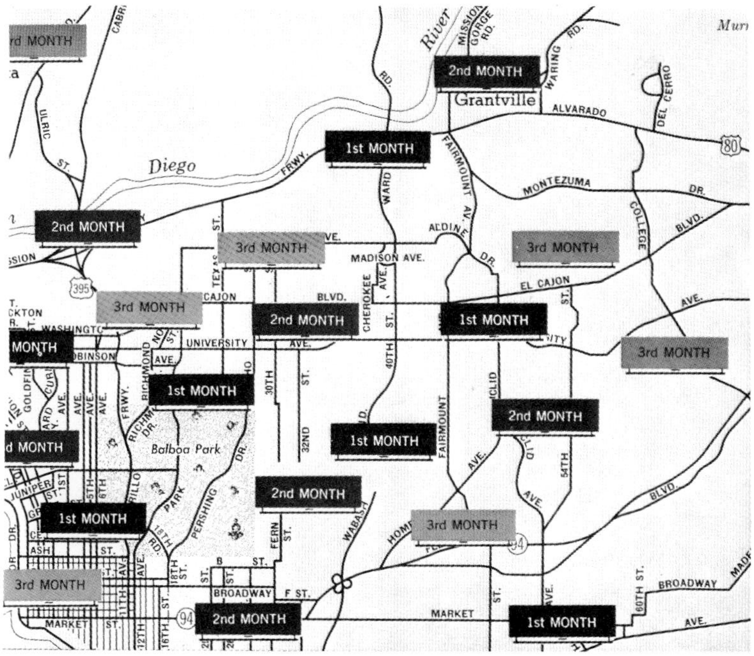

Figure 10.7 This map segment illustrates how rotating bulletins circulate in the San Diego market. Bulletins are moved at 30- or 60-day intervals. [*Foster & Kleiser, Division of Metromedia, Inc.*]

A more common, but expensive, alternative is a "rotary plan." Under this arrangement, a buyer may purchase three painted bulletins in a central city, each featuring a different message. Then, every month or two, bulletin number 1 is moved to site 2, bulletin 2 to site 3, and so on. The painted advertisements are placed on metal panels that can be installed or removed from a bulletin very easily. Figure 10.6 shows rates for rotating bulletin displays in a variety of markets. Figure 10.7 illustrates the actual rotation system in one market.

Despite the high cost of painted bulletins—often thousands of dollars per month—they have proven popular with large local advertisers, and the outdoor industry claims dozens of national advertisers who believe in the value of the medium.

Industry Organization

The outdoor advertising industry is primarily a local business operation. More than 700 individual firms own poster and painted-display locations in some 15,000 American communities. In a few market areas, there are competing firms, but generally it is a monopoly situation. Chain organizations also operate outdoor businesses in several different regions. In the years since 1960, the industry has experienced several mergers and consolidations, particularly in major markets. Today, for example, Foster & Kleiser, originally a Pacific Coast firm, is a division of Metromedia and operates outdoor plants in Illinois, Ohio, Texas, Michigan, and New York, as well as California and the Pacific Northwest.

The most obvious part of the local outdoor plant consists of the structures on which messages are placed. The plant owner erects these structures on land which the company owns or leases; employees see that the messages are posted and changed. Office work and painting are done in the firm's shop, and poster paper is stored there. The sales force works out of this headquarters, as do the crews that keep the boards in good repair and the grounds surrounding them landscaped and neat.

Whereas national advertising provides the bulk of outdoor business, probably one-fourth of the business of a typical plant is derived from local advertis-

Figure 10.8 Fischer's "Bacon-makin' people" slogan, appearing in a number of different media, is reinforced in outdoor. These ads are part of a campaign that has won numerous regional and national advertising and marketing awards. [*Fischer Packing Company.*]

ers—department and specialty stores, hotels, cafés, financial institutions, and the like. As is true for any medium serving local advertisers, the outdoor firm may perform various creative duties (art and copy preparation) for local clients, while advertising agencies do the job for national advertisers.

The advertiser pays the plant operator for message placement and for paper, artwork, and printing. When boards are filled throughout the country, the production cost may be as low as $20 on a per-unit basis; the small firm, however, which uses a limited number of boards, may find the cost per unit 10 times as high in the case of posters. The monthly charge for a painted display includes the cost of painting the bulletin.

In an attempt to save money, the local advertiser often turns to cooperative advertising. With this approach, the national manufacturer furnishes the poster paper and the name of the local retailer is bannered at the bottom of the message. The two then share the cost of board rental on some agreed-upon basis, such as 50-50.

Outdoor Advertising Locations

One of the most intricate phases of outdoor plant operations deals with real estate. Boards must be located in well-traveled places and where they can be seen easily. Plant owners must study areas constantly to catch population shifts, changing traffic patterns, and new road construction. Owners must lease or buy sites for structures that can deliver the exposures their advertiser clients demand.

But what constitutes a good location for a poster or

painted display? The Traffic Audit Bureau (TAB) has been studying this problem since 1934 and has developed useful techniques for measuring the total circulation of a plant and the **space position value** (or visibility) of individual locations. A number of traffic counts are taken, and allowances are made for portions of passing traffic unlikely to see specific posters. Angled panels, for example, can be seen only by traffic flowing in one direction. A site's overall visibility is affected by the following factors:

1 *The length of approach:* The longer the panel is visible, the more effective the location, other things being equal.
2 *The speed of travel:* The slower the traffic passing the spot, the greater the opportunity to see and read the message.
3 *The angle of the panel:* The closer to "head on" the approach is to oncoming traffic, the better the site. The worst location is one parallel to traffic.
4 *The proximity to other panels:* Preferably, a panel should be alone. If joined with others, the one closest to the road has the best chance of being seen. Many panels, very close together, lead to viewer confusion.

TAB gives numerical weights to each of these factors and arrives at an individual rating for every location. Recall that a newspaper or magazine sells total circulation as a reason for advertising in the publication, and a radio or television station sells audience. Outdoor operators must sell circulation of a different kind: namely, the total amount of traffic passing their posters in such a way that the messages can be seen by potential audiences.

Obviously, outdoor circulation and newspaper and magazine circulation are not the same. In outdoor circulation, message exposure is duplicated many times. The poster usually remains unchanged for 30 days, and many a passerby may see it every day. A publication advertisement is seen only when the reader looks at the newspaper or magazine that contains it.

In preparing circulation reports, TAB performs a function for outdoor that is similar to that performed by the Audit Bureau of Circulations for magazines and newspapers. It audits some 100,000 panels per year and is also active in gathering evidence of the value of outdoor advertising as far as total coverage, impact, and effectiveness are concerned.

Industry Associations

The Outdoor Advertising Association of America (OAAA) is the industry trade association that promotes the use of outdoor advertising. It is the driving force behind the standardization of outdoor structures; it represents the industry in legislation; and it handles public relations programs.

The National Outdoor Advertising Bureau (NOAB) is cooperatively owned and used by some 200 advertising agencies. It handles much of the creating, placing, buying, billing, supervising, and checking of outdoor advertising, and thus frees agency staffs for planning activities. NOAB also helps evaluate the performance of individual plants in carrying out their clients' advertising programs. The Institute of Outdoor Advertising (IOA), formed in 1965, is concerned with research, creativity, and information dissemination in outdoor advertising.

The Uses of Outdoor Advertising

Early users of outdoor advertising were manufacturers of automotive, petroleum, tobacco, food, and beverage products. All are still featured on outdoor posters, but many more items have been added to the list. An analysis of the top 100 advertisers in the United States revealed that about half used outdoor in their media mixes. But under what circumstances?

National Advertisers More than likely, a national advertiser uses outdoor as part of a campaign that includes other media. Often a slogan is developed to tie the campaign together, giving prospects something easy to remember; and outdoor boards offer repetition of the slogan frequently and economically. Figure 10.8 provides a good example.

It is common for outdoor advertisers to feature products that are associated with transportation and travel. Oil companies, tire manufacturers, and battery makers are prime examples. Hotels, motels, and restaurants use outdoor boards on traffic routes leading into cities, and airlines buy posters and paints on highway approaches to airports.

Other advertisers who find outdoor useful are the makers of well-known, impulse-purchase products,

Figure 10.9 An example of a neat, well-maintained roadside sign. Rock City promoters had formerly employed painted barns to draw tourists to this attraction. [*Rock City.*]

such as Coca-Cola and Wrigley's gum. Reminder advertising keeps company names before the public. In recent years, advertising has been used to presell customers as well. If a prospect is exposed to advertising just prior to making a purchase, the advertiser has an excellent chance of being remembered. Thus, food manufacturers now try to place outdoor messages near supermarkets. Advertisements for Morton's salt and Del Monte canned fruits are examples.

Product introductions benefit from outdoor's self-merchandising feature, too. Its simultaneous coverage of distributors, retailers, and salespeople, in addition to consumers, gives outdoor advertising a distinct advantage over other media forms.

Local Advertisers Local advertisers usually expect a more immediate response to their advertising than national advertisers do. Their primary goal is to reach people as they move about a community and persuade them to trade at a specific place of business. If the tourist is an important prospect, posters or paints are purchased at the approaches to the city. Restaurants, hotels, motels, shopping centers, garages, and service stations are examples of businesses that benefit here.

Regulation of Out-of-Home Advertising

Few media have been exposed to the critical pressure that out-of-home advertising has endured in recent years. Attacks have been made on grounds of aesthetic and environmental considerations and of traffic safety. The furor has resulted in the removal of thousands of posters and signs from America's roads and highways.

The Federal Aid Highway Act of 1958 and the Highway Beautification Act of 1965 made it financially advantageous for states to limit boards along freeways and primary road systems by providing for federal highway fund bonuses or penalties in connection with construction grants.

Surprisingly, the outdoor advertising industry has been reasonably supportive of these regulations, feeling they were designed to strike primarily at the poorly built and irresponsibly placed signs made by individuals rather than at those built in accordance with the organized industry's guidelines. In fact, it appears that the industry has been strengthened appreciably by the clean-up campaign.

Mobile Billboards

Before leaving this area of outdoor advertising, we need to mention a relatively new concept: the **rolling billboard,** or vehicular advertising. In the early 1970s, a company known as Beetleboards International began covering Volkswagen Beetles with advertising messages; each car served one particular brand of product or service. Effective in reaching specific geographic markets, these custom-painted "Beetleboards" became popular with soft-drink manufacturers, airlines, and radio stations, and today's roster of advertisers includes companies in a multitude of industries. For example, White Stag ski wear has been advertised on cars owned by ski-club members who drive extensively in and around ski resort areas.[5]

Since the VW Beetle is being phased out in the 1980s, thousands of Volkswagen Rabbits now constitute the "Bunnyboard" program. In addition, Ad-Vans Advertising International operates a competing business using all makes of vans throughout the United States, Puerto Rico, Canada, and Mexico.[6]

According to industry figures, vehicular advertising receives an average of 260 visual impressions per mile and is used to complement traditional outdoor campaigns. Sometimes, it is also used to cover markets where legal restraints limit or prevent advertisers' use of stationary billboards.[7]

Nonstandardized Signs

We are all exposed daily to signs that fall outside the organized outdoor advertising framework. Not all are unattractive, but, on the other hand, many are truly repulsive. Some are built by sign companies operating outside the organized industry and others by amateur or itinerant sign painters. Independent businesses may create signs in their back rooms or install those supplied by manufacturers. But, regardless of their source, these signs fall into two main categories: roadside and on-premise signs.

Roadside Signs

Roadside signs are similar in function to regulation posters and paints, but they lack uniformity. They may be placed in a careless, hit-or-miss fashion, and they are seen in abundance on streets and roads leading to tourist traps, such as private "zoos," hot-dog stands, and souvenir shops. On the other hand, as Figure 10.9 illustrates, some types of signs are very acceptable.

Nonstandard signs are largely local. Retailers and service firms, such as gas stations, motels, and restaurants, have regarded them for years as the primary link between their establishments and passing motorists. In light of this need, highway officials have constructed exit signs revealing the location of such tourist necessities as gas, food, and lodging. In some areas, they have even allowed entrepreneurs to place business logos on highway department signs—for a fee, of course. (See Figure 10.10.)

Figure 10.10 Many states now sell listings on signs such as this as a replacement for roadside signs of a more commercial nature.

Figure 10.11 TravelInfo Centers are one means that resort and restaurant owners have to tell tourists of the merits of their establishments. [*TravelInfo Centers of Oregon, Inc.*]

UTAH

15 **ARIZONA STATE LINE To IDAHO STATE LINE**

MILEAGE FROM/TO
UT./AZ. STATE LINE
0 UTAH/ARIZONA STATE LINE
8 St. George

ST. GEORGE. N-13

ATKIN'S SUGAR LOAF CAFE. Varied family menu, popular. AAA. 6 a.m. - 11 p.m. 309 E 100 N. Most cr. cards.

FOUR SEASONS MOTOR INN. Luxury lodging featuring the "Golden Pheasant". Gourmet fare served in your private alcove. Coffee shop, lounge, 2 pools. 1 blk off Exit. Ph. (801) 673-4804. Outstanding!

10 Bus. I-15—St. George—Santa Clara
18 UT. 15—Hurricane

TO HURRICANE. N-13

EL CHAPARRAL BEST WESTERN MOTEL. 30 deluxe rooms with color TV, dd phones, queen & kings. Rest. & coffee shop. Near Zions Park. Res. Ph. Coll. (801) 635-4647.

32 UT.17—Toquerville—Hurricane—Zion Park
51 REST AREA
66 UT. 130—Bus. I-15—Cedar City
68 UT. 14 East—Cedar City &
UT. 56 West—Newcastle

Figure 10.12 A column cut from a Travelaide map book demonstrates how this company has moved to fill the void created when signs are banned from highways.

Information Centers There is a strong movement in states across the country to establish tourist rest facilities to relieve the tedium and discomfort of long-distance driving. For example, TravelInfo Centers, Inc., has secured franchises from state governments to establish travel information centers at rest-stop locations along major highways. (See Figure 10.11.)

These centers, in the form of attractive gazebos, provide the resting tourist with information on local points of interest plus tasteful advertisements for motels, service stations, restaurants, and camping facilities in the surrounding area. This material is presented colorfully on back-lighted panels, easy to read day or night. Advertisers may buy anything from a simple listing to a large display ad, depending on their assessment of the value of such a medium.

Travel Directories A second example of business ingenuity in the face of changing times is National Advertising Company's Travelaide directory and map publication. Along with the government's regulation of roadside signs has come a trend among gasoline companies to abandon the practice of providing free road maps.

Travelaide's response is to provide a group of maps in brochure form covering a particular portion of the country. Integrated with the maps is a directory of establishments whose services may benefit travelers (as shown in Figure 10.12). Rates are charged advertisers according to the amount of space they use and whether or not they have their listings set in contrasting colors. It is assumed that motorists will carry these directories in their cars for easy reference. Therefore, Travelaide directories are classified as out-of-home media.

On-Premise Signs

The open road is not the only place where signs are useful. Nearly every business identifies itself through an on-premise sign. Movie theaters have brilliant marquees, department stores have multistory "skyline" signs, and service stations have signs telling approaching motorists the brand of gasoline they sell.

Since on-premise signs are an integral part of the business image, they should be carefully designed and placed where they can be seen easily by prospective customers. Identification is the primary purpose of these signs, although many may also be used to promote bargains or help convey a store's personality.

Transit Advertising

A third category of out-of-home media is transit advertising. It depends on consumer usage of commercial transportation facilities such as buses, taxis, airlines, subway and commuter trains, and on pedestrians viewing on-street advertising (on bus benches, for example, as well as on passing vehicles). (See Figure 10.13.)

Transit advertising volume is small compared with some other media, but steady increases in recent years suggest the industry is nevertheless healthy. In fact, investments by some national advertisers have

Figure 10.13 A jeweler, a restaurant, and a brewery all find transit advertising beneficial to their sales efforts. [*Washington Transit Advertising.*]

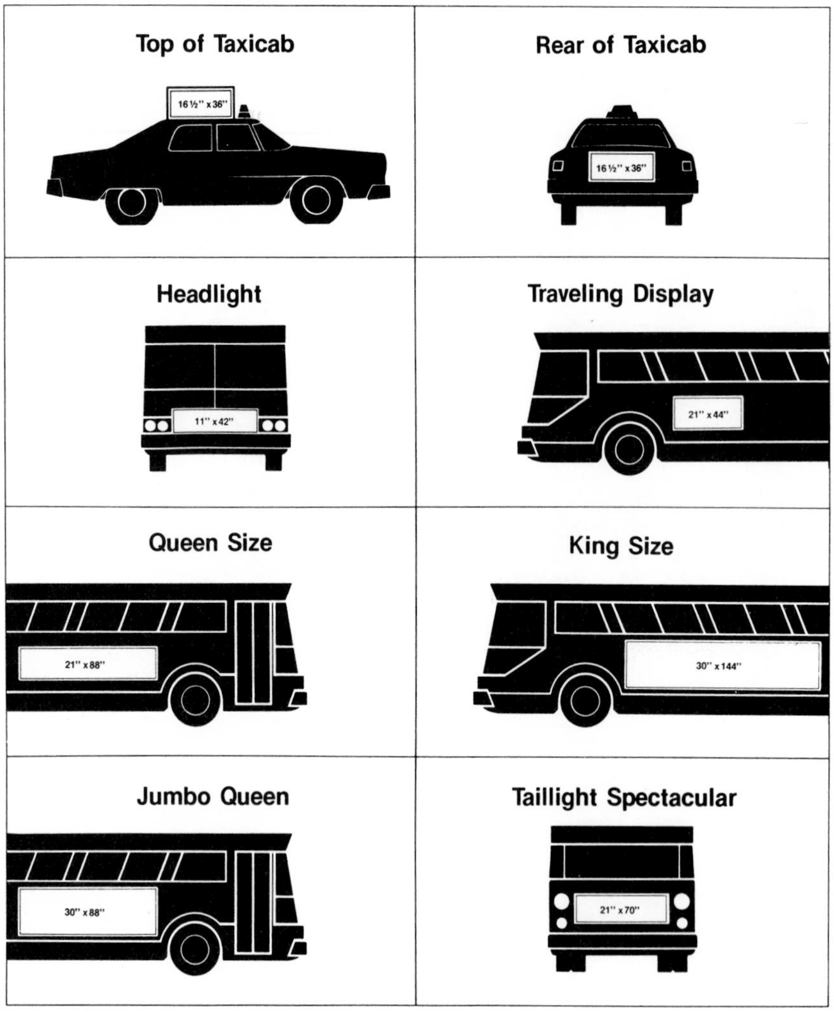

Figure 10.14 Traveling display advertisements are available in many shapes and sizes, as pictured here.

been a strong testimonial to the medium's worth in these days when energy shortages and working women are increasing the number of transit users. Cost-per-thousand figures for transit are extremely low, too, as they are for outdoor. Financial institutions, oil companies, other media, beverages, and food products have been leaders in the use of transit ads.

There are three basic forms of transit advertising: **car cards** (inside a vehicle), **traveling displays** (on the exterior of vehicles), and **station posters and displays.**

Car Cards

Car cards account for only 10 to 15 percent of total transit advertising income and are secondary to the traveling display ads found on the exterior of transit vehicles.

Car cards are the small advertising messages placed in the overhead racks and other interior locations of buses, streetcars, subways, and trains. They are normally 11 inches high by 28 or 56 inches wide, although a 22- by 21-inch interior card is becoming a standard also. Car-card messages are often coordinated with those appearing in an advertiser's other media buys. In this respect, the car card is very much like the outdoor poster; it simply and efficiently provides a reminder to persons who, very often, are on their way to shop. But, since readers are riding public vehicles, the time of exposure is lengthened from an average of 5 seconds to an average of 20 or 30 minutes, and the audience is a captive one in a very real sense.

Some astute advertisers take advantage of the unique nature of transit advertising by adapting their copy directly to the medium. For example, a famous fish restaurant in Hoboken, New Jersey, uses car cards to direct riders to its door—across the street from the last mass-transit stop of the New York-New Jersey PATH line.

Buying Car Cards In the sale of transit advertising, the standard unit is a **full service** or **run.** Here, an advertiser gets one card in every vehicle operated by a given transportation company. Half-service or quarter-service may also be purchased. Cards are placed by a firm similar to the outdoor plant, and the standard time period is 30 days or multiples thereof.

Traveling Displays

This form of transit advertising is really a cross between the car card and the outdoor poster. The message is placed on the outside of buses or streetcars and is seen by motorists and pedestrians as well as persons waiting for public transportation.

The sizes of traveling-display advertisements have, like car cards, been standardized. (Figure 10.14 shows some examples.) The most popular dimensions are 21 inches high and either 44 or 88 inches wide. "King-size" displays measuring 2½ feet by 12 feet are also available in many markets. Rates vary by display size and by the percentage of a transit system's vehicles that carry a particular campaign. Purchases are usually made for 30-day periods.

Station Posters and Displays

Station (terminal) posters are similar to outdoor posters except that they are smaller in size and are found in bus and subway stations and railroad terminals. Their role as advertising media is precisely the same as that of other forms of transit advertising.

Standardized display units are located in dozens of metropolitan rail and bus terminals and more than 100 airports in the United States and abroad.

Some Miscellaneous Media

Alert entrepreneurs have found ways to attach advertising messages to almost everything we see, including garbage cans, tires, motorcycles, T-shirts, blimps, Frisbees, and even shopping bags (as in Figure 10.15). No text could touch on every conceivable medium, but a few deserve mention because, for certain advertisers, they are very important.

Figure 10.15 Plastic shopping bags are an example of the myriad of media available that are not treated in detail in this text. It behooves advertisers to be alert to new ideas and changing modes of communication.

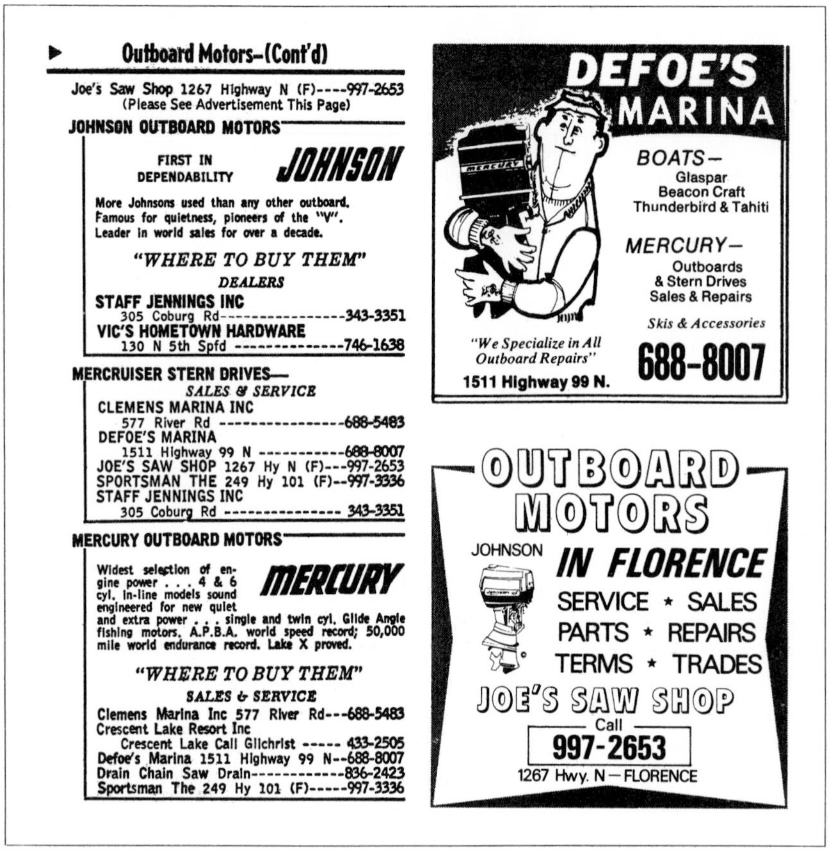
Outboard Motors–(Cont'd)

Joe's Saw Shop 1267 Highway N (F)----997-2653
(Please See Advertisement This Page)

JOHNSON OUTBOARD MOTORS

FIRST IN DEPENDABILITY
JOHNSON
More Johnsons used than any other outboard. Famous for quietness, pioneers of the "V". Leader in world sales for over a decade.
"WHERE TO BUY THEM"
DEALERS
STAFF JENNINGS INC
305 Coburg Rd----------------343-3351
VIC'S HOMETOWN HARDWARE
130 N 5th Spfd --------------746-1638

MERCRUISER STERN DRIVES—
SALES & SERVICE
CLEMENS MARINA INC
577 River Rd ----------------688-5483
DEFOE'S MARINA
1511 Highway 99 N -----------688-8007
JOE'S SAW SHOP 1267 Hy N (F)---997-2653
SPORTSMAN THE 249 Hy 101 (F)--997-3336
STAFF JENNINGS INC
305 Coburg Rd --------------- 343-3351

MERCURY OUTBOARD MOTORS

Widest selection of engine power . . . 4 & 6 cyl. in-line models sound engineered for new quiet and extra power . . . single and twin cyl. Glide Angle fishing motors. A.P.B.A. world speed record; 50,000 mile world endurance record. Lake X proved.
MERCURY
"WHERE TO BUY THEM"
SALES & SERVICE
Clemens Marina Inc 577 River Rd---688-5483
Crescent Lake Resort Inc
Crescent Lake Call Gilchrist ----- 433-2505
Defoe's Marina 1511 Highway 99 N--688-8007
Drain Chain Saw Drain------------836-2423
Sportsman The 249 Hy 101 (F)-----997-3336

Figure 10.16 A portion of a page from a classified telephone directory illustrates three basic types of listings: firm listings, trademark headings, and display advertisements. [*Pacific Northwest Bell Telephone Company.*]

Advertising on Film

Some advertisers produce their own films to meet advertising and public relations objectives. They may be shown in regular movie houses, in advertisers' factories, in dealers' showrooms, or in retail stores by means of closed-circuit television. Only theater or drive-in showings are comparable with those of other advertising media in that a charge is made for showing the film. Nontheatrical showings, such as plant, school, or service club presentations, are public relations activities not included in our discussion here.

In movie theaters and drive-ins, the preview of coming attractions is advertising by the theater itself; we are concerned, however, with the messages of other businesses, sometimes called **trailers.** Ordinarily, they are shown between presentations of the main feature, along with short subjects and previews. They are usually 45 seconds or 1 minute long, and most theaters restrict the number shown consecutively to three.

Though the medium is older than television, the messages are similar to TV commercials in format and style. It is claimed that films are superior to television as an advertising medium because the larger screen and better projection equipment present a more powerful message to the viewer. On the other hand, since the television program comes free to viewers, it is argued that they may have a more tolerant attitude toward the TV ad. It is considered a price of admission, so to speak, whereas movie-goers may feel they paid their money for entertainment and do not want to be part of a captive audience for advertising. Furthermore, it is impossible for theater advertising to approach the potential coverage of TV, so film advertising is most effective in areas where the impact of television has not been great. Thus, theatrical showings are more numerous in other parts of the world than in the United States.

Both local merchants and national manufacturers use the film medium for its geographic and viewer selectivity. Rates are ordinarily based on audience size and ticket prices. Although the rate per exposure is not low, the viewer is almost certain to see the message. Quoted rates are for one-minute messages and the charge is based on an average weekly attendance figure for the past three or six months.

National advertisers can select the specific regions where they want messages placed. Farm-implement firms tap agricultural areas, and ski-equipment manufacturers hit areas near ski resorts. Selection can also be made on the basis of income groups or other classifications. The roster of national users includes food, clothing, and electronic firms, automobile manufacturers, and the makers of beverages and cosmetics. Specialized firms assist these advertisers in selecting theaters and scheduling films.

Local advertisers who place films in movie houses include dealers for automobiles, farm equipment, and similar products. Often their messages appear as part of cooperative advertising programs with manufacturers. Among other local users are jewelry stores, insurance agencies, and dry cleaners, along with those who cater to the after-theater crowd—cafés, pizza parlors, and ice cream shops. We might also note that several major airlines have started running commercials with their in-flight movies in an attempt to counterbalance escalating costs. In-flight entertainment has traditionally proven very unprofitable.

Advertising in Directories

Directories are valuable sources of information for people who wish to locate, with a minimum of effort, a street address, a person's occupation, or the name of a firm that manufactures or sells a certain item. Advertising space is often sold between listings in a directory, so the directory itself can sell for a nominal price. In some instances, it is even given free for the asking. Advertisers here have a unique opportunity to call attention to a product or service at precisely the time of the prospective customer's search for it.

The Yellow Pages

The most familiar directory is the telephone book's yellow pages. About 6,000 classified directories are published annually in the United States; Canada offers about 500 more. Although all business telephones are automatically listed in the classified directory, the telephone company tries to get each business to emphasize its listing by having its name printed in boldface type or by showing a display advertisement (as shown in Figure 10.16). For either of these services, the firm must pay—from a few hundred to several thousand dollars per year, depending on market size.

Whether a local business should request special treatment in telephone directories depends largely on the role the telephone plays in the business. If the need for a particular service is infrequent, a company's name and phone number may not be known. The plumber is a good example. When a pipe springs a leak, the need is sudden and urgent. What could be simpler than to go to the yellow pages and look for the nearest plumber's name?

When the nature of the business is less urgent and the purchase pattern is one of comparing before buying, many people use the phone as a shopping device. By calling all appropriate business outlets, the consumer can decide which stores hold the greatest potential for shopping success. One telephone company survey revealed that 74 percent of the population over twenty years of age uses the yellow pages during a 12-month period. Thus, this form of advertising is an important supplementary medium for the vast majority of local businesses.

Many national advertisers list the names of local dealers in telephone directories in an effort to lessen consumers' brand switching. If print or broadcast ads for a product arouse the interest of a consumer who then turns to the phone book's classified pages for the local dealer's address, sales potential is greatly increased.

In recent years, two separate volumes of the yellow pages have been published in major markets. The traditional consumer-oriented book has been supplemented by a "business-to-business" yellow pages. It includes all the businesses that *other* businesses need to deal with plus an easy-to-use index.

Other Directories Before deciding to use *any* kind of directory, advertisers must consider (1) whether it will have a significant distribution and fill a need for users, and (2) whether that distribution taps a potential market for their business.

Probably the best-known general directory serving the industrial market is the *Thomas Register of American Manufacturers,* which the publisher claims is the most widely used advertising medium in the United States.[8] In addition, *Post's Pulp and Paper Directory* is an example of a vertical directory (confined to one designated industry) whereas *The Data Processing Yearbook* is a functional directory (related to selected technical skills). Figure 10.17 shows copies of a directory of particular importance to advertising personnel: the *Standard Directory of Advertisers.*

SALES BEGIN WITH A KNOCK AT THE RIGHT DOOR
Standard Directory of Advertisers
Standard Directory of Advertisers
Geographical
Standard Directory of Advertisers
Geographical Index
When only reliable information will do, depend on the source the experts do. Top salesmen depend on The Standard Directory of Advertisers to direct them to the right door to make the sale.
"The Advertisers Redbook," published in two editions, Classified and Geographical, provides all necessary data for selling to the 17,000 listed companies and their agencies, doing national and regional advertising. 80,000 executives are listed by title for direct contact. The Classified Edition arranges companies in 51 classifications for contact by line of business. The Geographical Edition shows companies by state and city for territorial contact. A pocket size Geographical Index comes as a cross reference with the Classified Edition. The Monthly Supplement, issued 9 times a year, is a cumulative updating of changes in advertiser companies, advertising agency appointments and newly advertised products.
When making a sale depends on knocking on the right door . . . depend on the Standard Directory of Advertisers to get you there.

Figure 10.17 The *Standard Directory of Advertisers* is one and the *Standard Directory of Advertising Agencies* is another of the basic reference books used by people in the advertising industry. [*National Register Publishing Co.*]

Donation Advertising

Local and national firms alike are approached by organizations who want businesses to advertise in promotional media such as charity-event programs, trade-union newspapers, and even church bulletins. Some of these publications may offer a little advertising value, but in most cases their advertising charges should be considered solely as charitable donations or public relations expenses. Money spent in this area should not be charged to the advertising budget, since such questionable communication ventures do not give advertising a chance to prove its worth.

Theoretically, one might argue that no business firm should participate in these schemes, as they are of little value to the contributor; often, however, pressure is applied by a soliciting organization—through a promise of advertiser goodwill in the community or by implications of boycotts by the sponsoring organization's members. The turndown process, therefore, is a delicate, sometimes time-consuming, one. But once a decision to "advertise" has been made, regardless of the motivation, the job should be taken seriously. The resulting ad may affect the mental picture of the firm held by some segment of the general public.

Summary

Despite the relatively small amounts of money invested in out-of-home media, each one is used as a primary medium by some advertisers who find it useful in meeting specific objectives. Most out-of-home media are used by national advertisers as backup or secondary media to reinforce campaigns that are run in television, magazines, newspapers, and radio.

Out-of-home media include posters, painted bulletins, and on- and off-premise signs of all descriptions. However, posters and paints are the mainstays of the outdoor advertising industry because they are part of a well-organized business that has made giant strides in standardizing its offerings. Advertisers may purchase outdoor space in almost any region of the country, confident that their advertisements, or paper, will fit the panels purchased and that they will receive a fair allocation of boards relative to those assigned to other advertisers.

The standard system includes 24- and 30-sheet posters and the gross rating point (GRP) method of selecting boards. Outdoor plant operators sell boards in packages known as 100 gross rating points, or portions or multiples thereof.

Other signs along roads and highways are primarily individual efforts that, for the most part, follow no standardized specifications. Although some of them are respectable in both concept and design, many are not, and much of the public distaste for outdoor advertising stems from these.

On-premise signs are those located on the property of retail stores or service establishments, and they are used to identify a place of business or the products offered therein.

Out-of-home advertising fills the gap between an advertiser's promotional activities and the location of the actual product sale. Outdoor reminds potential customers of products they may wish to buy and, in some instances, guides them to the point of purchase.

Federal regulations covering the outdoor advertising industry have resulted in the removal of thousands of posters and signs, but they have also strengthened the organized industry by eliminating many disreputable signs.

Transit advertising was developed to accomplish essentially the same functions as outdoor advertising: to reach potential customers on the way to shop. The most important categories of transit advertising are car cards, traveling displays, and station, or terminal, posters and displays.

Car cards are generally, but not always, located above the heads of bus, railroad, or subway-train passengers. They claim many of the benefits of outdoor advertising but offer a much longer period of exposure and therefore may carry a more complex message. Traveling displays appear on the outside of transit vehicles and have much wider (but much shorter) exposure than car cards; again, however, the message must be kept brief. Station posters are small outdoor posters located inside public transit stations. They are confined mainly to major metropolitan cities.

Film is important to advertisers who wish to advertise in motion-picture theaters. Filmed commercials provide maximum impact among a group of viewers who are quite homogeneous. The geographic selectivity here is outstanding, but the cost per thousand limits the use of film either to national advertisers who want to tap audiences located in particular regions or to local retail establishments.

The main vehicle for directory advertising consists of the yellow pages of telephone directories. The great value of directories is that customers tend to turn to them at a time of product need.

Donation advertising is an unwarranted expense in a well-planned advertising budget. It generally involves little-known media with low circulations and high cost-per-thousand figures. Such expenses, if necessary, should be charged instead to public relations.

Questions for Discussion

1 What are the basic underlying needs of advertisers that are fulfilled by out-of-home advertising?

2 Referring to question 1, how might these needs differ for national and for local or retail advertisers?

3 What is the difference between an outdoor poster and a painted bulletin?

4 Explain how a buy of 100 gross rating points might reach all, or only half, the population in a given area.

5 Explain what constitutes a "good location" for an outdoor ad.

6 What are the values of mobile billboards to advertisers? Which of these values are unique to this category of outdoor advertising, and which ones are shared with other specific types?

7 Describe the three forms of transit advertising. Name some advertisers who use each form and explain why you think they find the buy a profitable one.

8 Discuss your uses of the yellow pages, and poll your classmates as to whether they find this type of directory a useful medium to consumers (and why).

9 As the owner of a retail stationery store, you are constantly besieged by individuals trying to sell you advertising in church bulletins, theatrical programs, and lodge publications. How would you handle this situation? Try to be as realistic as possible in your discussion.

10 You have now been exposed, in some depth, to more than a dozen advertising media representing thousands of individual media companies throughout the nation. Discuss the reasons why, in your opinion, these media are able to survive in such a competitive field.

For Further Reference

Advertising in Motion, Transit Ads, Inc., San Francisco, 1975.

Buszik, Budd: *Planning for Out-of-Home Media,* Traffic Audit Bureau, Inc., New York, 1977.

Clarke, George T.: *Transit Advertising.* Transit Advertising Association, New York, 1970.

The First Medium, Institute of Outdoor Advertising, New York, 1974.

Nelson, Roy Paul: *Design of Advertising,* 3d ed., Wm. C. Brown Company Publishers, Dubuque, Iowa, 1977.

Sissors, Jack Z., and E. Reynold Petray: *Advertising Media Planning,* Crain Books, Chicago, 1975.

End Notes

[1] *Forbes Magazine,* Oct. 1, 1979, p. 144.

[2] *Marketing & Media Decisions,* September 1979, pp. 26–27.

[3] *The First Medium,* Institute of Outdoor Advertising, New York, 1974.

[4] *Metro Market Rate Card,* Foster & Kleiser, 1980.

[5] *Advertising Age,* March 10, 1980, p. S-28.

[6] Ibid., p. S-29.

[7] Ibid., p. S-28.

[8] Donald A. Dodge, "The Case for Directory Advertising," *Media/scope,* July 1964, p. 47.

PART 4

Advertising Messages

The advertising media discussed in Part 3 serve as vehicles for carrying advertising messages to customers and prospects. Part 4 explores the creation of these advertising messages. This section deals with the communication aspect of advertising, and each chapter explains ways that advertisers can increase the communication potential of their advertisements.

Chapter 11 reviews how people act in their respective roles as consumers. The fundamentals of consumer behavior are extremely important to the cre-

ator of advertising messages, for ads should convey information and ideas in terms that are readily understood and accepted by their intended receivers. The more ad makers know about the purchase-consumption process, the more effective will be their messages.

Basic techniques employed in writing the words of the advertisement—the activity known as "copywriting"—are given in Chapter 12. Because illustrations, as well as words, communicate information and

the focal point of Chapter 13. A simplified explanation of the mechanical production of both print and broadcast advertisements follows in Chapter 14. Taking these elements—an understanding of consumer behavior, copywriting, art direction, and the production of advertisements—and blending them together should mean that the basic instrument in advertising, the advertisement itself, will be capable of establishing efficient and effective communication between buyer and seller.

Chapter 11

Consumer Behavior and Advertising

● When cultivating markets, the producer seeks consumers who have the ability to pay for the product, who possess the power to make the buying decision, and who are capable of deriving satisfaction from the product. This satisfaction may spring from its personal use or from the purchase for use by others. Mary and Tom Jones get satisfaction from using their microwave oven because it is a time-saver, while the satisfaction they get from buying Wheaties comes from the pleasure its purchase gives their son Billy.

Knowledge of how people derive satisfaction from products is important when manufacturers and advertisers are deciding about the scope of their products or markets in our complex economy. Basically, manufacturers try to satisfy consumer wants and needs. But how can they be sure of what consumers want and how do they know what facets of their product are most appealing? Producers and advertisers need to understand the basic forces that shape human behavior within the context of the marketplace. Many of the social sciences, notably psychology and sociology, provide such basic knowledge about consumer desires. The body of knowledge that has been developed on this topic is called **consumer behavior.** In this chapter, we analyze some of the basic motivations of people as consumers. In real life, these insights concerning consumer behavior are used to construct models that enable marketing people to plan their strategies. After a survey of these ideas, we show how they are used in an advertising campaign.

The Importance of the Behavioral Sciences in Advertising

Any academic discipline that deals with characteristics of human behavior can be labeled a "behavioral science." Some people have claimed that marketing belongs in the behavioral sciences, and it is certainly vitally concerned with buyer behavior. The usually accepted disciplines of behavioral science include anthropology, economics, linguistics, political science, psychology, and sociology. Although all have made important contributions to our knowledge of how and why people act as they do, the two that have provided the most direct assistance to advertisers are sociology, the study of humans in relation to society, and psychology, the study of humans as individuals. Both viewpoints are important and are combined in social psychology. Advertising, like politics and diplomacy, is one of the sociopsychological arts.

Consumer psychologists are interested in the behavior of masses of consumers rather than in the behavior patterns of individuals. Four principal areas of interest are (1) decision making in the marketplace, (2) changes in attitudes and behavior of consumers, (3) influence of time and uncertainty, and (4) studies of group belonging.[1]

Many models, each attempting to explain how humans behave in their role as consumers, have been developed in the last 30 years. In these models of consumer behavior, two extreme positions are held.

At one end of the spectrum is the **stimulus-response model,** as derived from the behaviorist school of psychology. Believers in this model state that "exposure to advertising virtually guarantees that the consumer will respond in a manner desired by the advertiser, even if this is against the consumer's best interests."[2] In other words, the consumer can be manipulated at the will of the seller. We do not believe this to be true today, if it ever was.

At the other extreme, the consumer is believed to be sovereign. Underlying this model of consumer behavior is the assumption that the consumer is "an individual with a highly developed cognitive filter fully capable of admitting only those stimuli which are felt to be pertinent. Non-pertinent stimuli . . . are screened through selective attention, comprehension, retention and response."[3] The advertiser, consequently, "must adapt to the basic dispositions of the consumer, and behavior change results when the basic dispositions are either favorable or at least neutral with respect to the suggested change."[4] In other words, consumers react to the offerings of the marketplace in ways that they believe are in their own best interests. We hold this to be a correct view of marketplace reality—so important that it deserves elaboration in the following sections.

Cognitive Psychology[5]

Cognitive psychology focuses on the human's *desire to know.* The underlying notion is that behavior is a function of **cognitions** (knowings), which are nothing other than ideas, bits of knowledge, values, and beliefs held by the individual. One authority describes cognition as "those processes by which any sensory input is transformed, reduced, elaborated, stored, recovered, or used."[6] Cognitive structures and processes provide two functions: (1) "They are *purposive* in that they serve the individual in his attempt to achieve satisfaction of needs," and (2) they are "*regulatory* in that they determine in large measure the direction taken in the consumer's steps toward his attempt to attain the satisfaction of his initiating needs."[7]

The following quotation sums up nicely the cognitive psychology view of human behavior:

> The human organism, and especially the focus of our inquiry, the consumer, is a sensory-processing and data-gathering organism. His behavior stems from his goal striving and his aspirations. He is not so much driven to acts of choice by his goals and aspirations. Consumers *learn*—they modify their behavior over time. What was sufficient cause or *motivation* for behavior in one situation may for numerous reasons no longer be interpreted or *perceived* as sufficient justification for action or similar action in a subsequent situation. Thus, it can be seen that motivation, learning, and perception lie at the core of the consumer cognitive processes.[8]

In advertising terms, the consumer is looked upon as a thirster for knowledge—for cognition. Producers try to find out more about people and about the products they use or may consider using in their daily lives. The consumer is a solver of problems; to be such a person, information is needed. Advertising is one source of such information, and to be effective, advertising must be presented in proper psychological terms.

Social and Cultural Influences on Consumer Behavior

Human behavior is purposeful. As we experience needs, we seek to satisfy them. The pattern of interrelated motives and attitudes that determine our responses is acquired largely from groups, beginning with our early learning in the primary group of the family. If an advertisement is to reinforce or change a consumer's attitude, the action or response desired must conform to the standards of that person's group. If group approval is lacking, the suggested action is not likely to take place. On the other hand, if strong group approval for a particular action is present, this is the action we are most inclined to choose from many otherwise equally desirable.

Vast numbers of consumer behavior studies have been conducted over the past 30 years. Those studies and concepts most directly related to advertising are reviewed in this chapter. We shall start off with the following behavioral topics:

1. culture and subculture
2. social class
3. reference groups
4. opinion leaders
5. the family
6. lifestyle

Later sections of the chapter discuss such topics as attitude formation, learning theory, product and brand image, the communication process, and information processing.

Culture

Strong influences on consumer behavior come from the culture in which people live. Culture represents the ideas, values, attitudes, artifacts, and symbols governing the behavior of a member of the group; it determines many of the responses that individuals make in given situations.[9] Thorstein Veblen, in his book *The Theory of the Leisure Class,* first aired the idea that social influences can affect how people spend their money.[10] His thesis revolved around the idea of "conspicuous consumption," by which he meant that people of wealth buy products not so much for their utilitarian value, but to impress other people with the purchaser's exclusiveness and individuality. Since Veblen's time, many economists and other observers of American life have studied cultural patterns and offered various explanations on how culture does affect our spending of money—consumer behavior, if you will.

Out of the various cultural influences operating upon us as individuals emerges a personal **value system.** *Values* define what is expected and desired by the consumer; values predispose an individual to certain behavior. Every person goes through a long socialization process wherein "the impact of family, culture and groups shape and affect our personal values of standards."[11] One common value standard observed by Markin is that "Americans in general value goods"; furthermore, "their core values all have, to differing degrees, a consumption orientation."[12] Accepting these generalizations as true, we see that there are other facets of value systems and the effect of culture upon them that need to be known if product and promotional programs are to be designed to fit into consumers' value systems.

The role of materialism and acquisitiveness, as well as the symbolism versus the utilitarianism of goods, as cultural factors in our society has been discussed and debated for a long time. That our society's standards of value are undergoing rapid and drastic change is common knowledge. The marketer must be listening to the right drummer if the marketing and advertising programs are to stay in step with the target market's way of thinking.

In the early 1970s an observer of American lifestyles, Daniel Yankelovich, noted five major social trends then operating in our society, each altering consumption patterns. These trends, along with selected manifestations of each, are:

1 "Psychology of Affluence" trends, including physical self-enhancement; personalization; physical health and well-being; new forms of materialism; social and cultural self-expression; personal creativity; meaningful work.
2 "Quest for Instant Change" trends, including the "New Romanticism," novelty and change; adding beauty to surroundings; sensuousness; mysticism; introspection.
3 "Reaction against Complexity" trends, including life simplification; return to nature; increased ethnicity; increased community involvement; less reliance on technology; away from bigness.

Figure 11.1 This advertiser appeals to the desire of young people to enjoy services often denied to them because of their age. (The credit card offer in the ad may not be in force due to governmental restrictions on credit.)

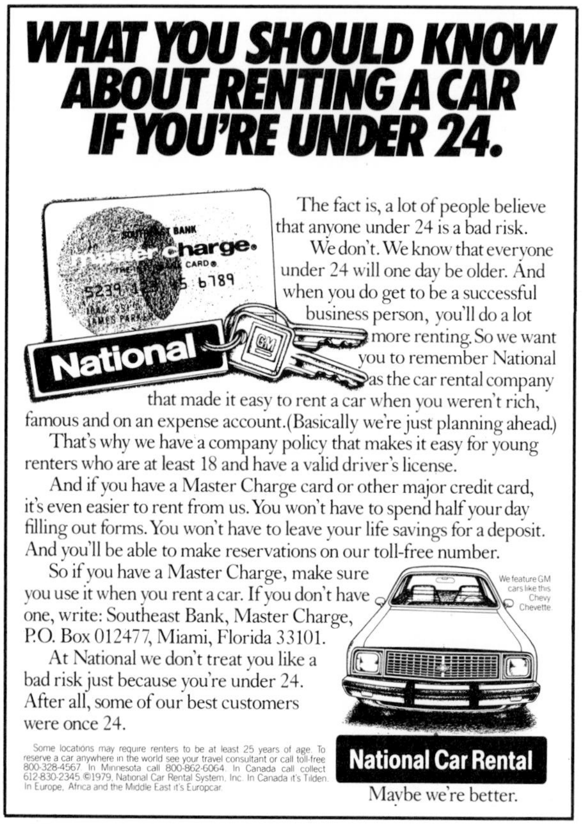

4 "Anti-Puritanical Value System" trends, including pleasure for its own sake; blurring of the sexes; living in the present; more liberal sexual attitudes; acceptance of stimulants and drugs; relaxation of self-improvement standards; individual religions.
5 "Trends Associated with the Emerging Generation," including greater tolerance of chaos and disorder; challenges to authority; rejection of hypocrisy; female careerism; familism.[13]

In the decade after Yankelovich outlined these social trends, great upheavals took place in the United States and throughout the world. The Vietnam war was finally ended, to be followed by the deep business recession of 1974–1975. The OPEC nations then forced up the price of energy to previously unthinkable heights, which materially influenced consumer buying habits. Later on, double-digit inflation hit the economy and inflicted both an economic and a psychological impact on consumer behavior.

A turn to a more conservative outlook then started to take place. For one thing, our population was get-

Alabama the Beautiful
Come to this land where the warm summer sun seems to shine almost all year round on clear clean lakes and sugar-white beaches. Where ante-bellum homes sit like Southern ladies, surrounded by a sweep of green pasture. Where your ears still seem to hear echoes of faint war cries of the Indians who first explored our deep cool caves. Come to where you can disco 'til dawn at a glittering city club or have a toe-tapping good time at a down-home Bluegrass festival.
And where people are friendly and a "How y'all doing?" is genuine. Come show your children this bountiful land . . . rich in history and tradition. And rich too, in what has made America, America.
Alabama the Beautiful.
Alabama Bureau of Publicity and Information
532 South Perry Street, Montgomery, AL 36130
Please send free Alabama Booklet to:
Name
Address
City State Zip
MC-8
Visit the Alabama Exhibit at the Canadian National Exhibition.

Figure 11.2 One way of spending discretionary money is on travel. Many vacation areas try to attract visitors. Here the State of Alabama, in an award-winning magazine advertisement, tells of the state's attractions. Canadian "snowbirds" comprise the target market for this campaign.

THE $60 DIFFERENCE
The Heritage craftsman guides the dowels into place, extends the curve of the arm to the back and sets the basic design. When a chair, or any piece of furniture, takes its shape from its frame and not just the bulge of its padding, only more money can buy it.
You might be able to buy a chair that looks like one from this pair for about $260. But you won't be buying the same chair or one that's even close. As time will tell when the springs go their own way, the fabric pulls away from a welt and your chair loses the comfort and the looks you bought in the showroom.
Upholstered in this elegant cut velvet, one of these Heritage swivel base lounge chairs will cost you about $320. Or $60 more than its look-alike.
Cut to form the basic design of this chair alone, the parts of the frame were carved or cut and locked into one solid unit. The springs it supported were tied to the frame and to one another. Then the Heritage upholsterer stretched, shaped and stitched layer on layer of batting over the lines set down by the frame. By the time the fabric was fitted, the contours of the chair were true to the frame, the final repeat of the basic design.
The higher price on this chair, or any other piece of furniture we make, buys something that only more money can buy. Whether it's our concern for the support that holds the lines and ensures the look of a chair. Or the way we'll take the time to bring a wood to its fullest beauty by hand... because no machine or shortcut method can match it.
When you see work like this, you'll find the Heritage name. Stitched on the platform under the cushions of this pair of Heritage chairs. Burned inside the drawers of a mahogany Heritage lowboy. Stitched under the cushions and swinging on a hangtag from a crushed velvet Heritage sofa.
If you would like to know more about Heritage and see how it could fit into your home, send two dollars for a Heritage catalog collection and room planning kit to Dept. HG-9-67, Heritage Furniture Company, High Point, North Carolina.
HERITAGE®
A division of Drexel Enterprises, Inc.

Figure 11.3 During inflationary periods product quality becomes increasingly important to consumers. A furniture manufacturer appeals to this concern by showing the value of the product.

ting older, but other factors were operating, too. This trend toward conservativism manifested itself in the election of Ronald Reagan and a Republican Senate in 1980. Many of the trends listed above appeared to have been aborted, or at least slowed down. A return to more traditional values, as discussed in Chapter 2, seemed to occur. The work ethic returned, as our nation struggled to meet competition from such nations as Japan and West Germany. Affluence in our society, while still great when compared with that experienced elsewhere in the world, diminished.

Prediction of where our society is headed is not our task at this point; instead, our goal is to dramatize how volatile that society is and how important it is for the advertiser to know what values are held by the consumers with whom communication is desired. Advertising specialists, when operating in their professional capacities, cannot indulge in value judgments on the desirability of cultural changes taking place in our society. The job of the advertising specialist is to recognize these changes in order to plan creative and effective communication with people who accept new values. Trends in our society are further explored in Chapter 22, where we discuss the future of advertising.

Blacks—An Important American Subculture
One principle of good communication is that the audience should be defined as clearly as possible—the "mass" divided into smaller parts so that we don't try to talk with everyone at once. The most elementary way to divide society is to look at American **subcultures.** By far the largest such grouping is our black population, which consists of approximately 26.5 million people who constitute 80 percent of the nation's nonwhite population. Blacks are concentrated in urban areas of the nation, which, in one way, makes communication with them easy. Their cultural heritage is different from many segments of the United States populace; for example, they have different language patterns. Special advertising media exist for marketers who wish to sell to

Figure 11.4 Cosmetics formulated for special needs of black consumers are featured in this print advertisement. The manufacturer specializes in such products and probably is the largest minority business advertiser in the United States.

members of this minority, and sometimes different creative strategies must be implemented.

The following behavior characteristics tend to be present when blacks collect product information:

1 Blacks are more favorable to advertisements with all-black models or to integrated groups, although those under thirty years of age are negative to advertisements with integrated settings.
2 Black consumers appear to respond (in recall and attitude shift) more positively to advertisements than do white consumers.
3 Black consumers appear to be reached more effectively by advertisers appearing in both the black and the white general media and by black-oriented media for products specifically directed to black consumers.
4 Black consumers listen to radio more than whites, particularly in the evenings and on weekends, although blacks listen to FM radio less than whites.
5 Black television viewers dislike programs emphasizing white-oriented subjects such as white families, organizations, and similar topics; they watch more on the weekends, in contrast with whites, who enjoy higher viewing through the week.[14]

Hispanics Another subculture receiving increased attention by advertisers is the Hispanic one. In fact, the 1980s have been described as "the decade of the Hispanics," and predictions are being made that they will supplant blacks as the nation's leading minority by 1990.

How familiar advertising messages are adapted to reach Spanish-speaking people in the United States is shown in Figure 11.5. It should be noted that as blacks and members of other ethnic groups move up the economic scale, typical American middle-class values take over, in which event regular media and appeals are used.

Social Class

A more logical way to divide the population into manageable groupings is found in the concept of social class. A **social class** is a group of the population whose members hold comparable positions in the socioeconomic system and who hold generally similar attitudes, beliefs, and value systems. Warner, in a classic study, broke the population of the United States into six social classes.[15] The accompanying table summarizes each group, along with a short description of its membership and its relative proportion of the total population.

Group	Membership	Percentage
Upper-upper	Aristocracy	0.5
Lower-upper	New rich	1.5
Upper-middle	Professional and managers	10.0
Lower-middle	White-collar workers	33.0
Upper-lower	Blue-collar workers	40.0
Lower-lower	Unskilled workers	15.0

A person's attitudes, beliefs, and value system are influenced by the group, or social class, in which he or she resides. For example, upper-lower-class men

Figure 11.5 A well-known product is promoted to Hispanics. The English translation is the familiar "Nobody can do it like McDonald's can."

prefer baseball as a spectator sport, while hockey is patronized by the upper-middle and higher classes. Furthermore, each class sets different priorities for the spending of its discretionary income, with blue-collar workers opting for pickup trucks, snowmobiles, and guns, and white-collar workers preferring more intellectual items, including books, records, and theater tickets. These preferences are not so much a result of differing levels of income, for the two groups may receive the same size paychecks; it is a matter of how each group wishes to spend its money. In the early 1970s, union wages and the recession caused the earnings of blue-collar and white-collar workers to become equivalent, but buying patterns still remain quite distinct in the 1980s. Spending income for "appropriate" purposes results in the class members' receiving acceptance by their peer group; deviation from acceptable norms may lead to rejection by the group. Obviously, advertisers can benefit greatly in their communication efforts if the social class of target markets is known.

Because an important belief in our society is that of egalitarianism—that everyone is equal—the concept of social class is repugnant to many of us. We prefer to associate the concept with medieval days of nobles and serfs. With social mobility a relatively common phenomenon in our society, families are not necessarily locked into one social class from generation to generation, and people in one class aspire to moving to a higher status group and may even emulate the consumption patterns of that group.

Since social classes encompass groups of people who share similar lifestyles, market segmentation is highly useful in advertising planning.

Sidney Levy states that media are used in contrasting as well as similar ways by different class groups. Television studies made in the early 1970s have shown that members of the upper-middle-class prefer the NBC channels while lower-middle-class viewers favor CBS. Lower-class families spend more time watching TV than upper-class families. They enjoy quiz shows, variety shows, and late movies, while middle-class families like drama, prime-time movies, and late-night talk shows.

Levy's studies show that lower-class people are more receptive to advertising that depicts activity, on-going work, and solutions to practical problems in daily life and social relationships. Upper-middle-class families generally are more critical of advertising and more suspicious of emotional appeals, and they prefer advertisements that are witty, sophisticated, and stylish.[16]

Some media-usage studies have shown that lower-class people are less likely to subscribe to newspapers than middle-class people. Another study discovered that lower-class people prefer *Reader's Digest* and *Ladies' Home Journal,* whereas upper-class readers identify with *Time, Sports Illustrated, The New Yorker,* and *Saturday Review.*[17]

Reference Groups

Remember that it is quite natural for individuals to act in a manner associated with their status in life, or with a status to which they aspire. This self-awareness leads us to identify ourselves with certain reference groups. A **reference group** is any collection of people that helps to shape the attitudes and behavior of an individual. These groups can be formal in nature, as found in church, fraternal, and social organizations, or informal, such as friendships. Such groups usually adopt certain objects as symbols. Therefore, these objects become desired by group members. The advertiser might find the opposite situation equally important—how to reject identification with individuals or groups of lower status and the symbols that represent them. Our choice of a college, a profession, an automobile, or a restaurant can be strongly influenced positively or negatively by status and prestige identification.

Reference groups help in the socialization of individuals—the process by which a new member learns society's value system, the norms and the required behavior patterns of the society and its organizations, or of the group that the person is entering. There is high interest among consumer researchers in understanding the socialization processes of children. Their behavior both as family members and as users of the media, especially television, is being studied.

In a rather extensive and elaborate study, George Moschis has researched the influences; of family, television, peers, and school on the development of selected consumer skills of adolescent consumers. His studies reveal that mass media and peers are more influential than family or the school in developing these skills. Upper-class adolescents possess the abilities cognitively to filter puffery in advertising and to differentiate advertising stimuli.[18]

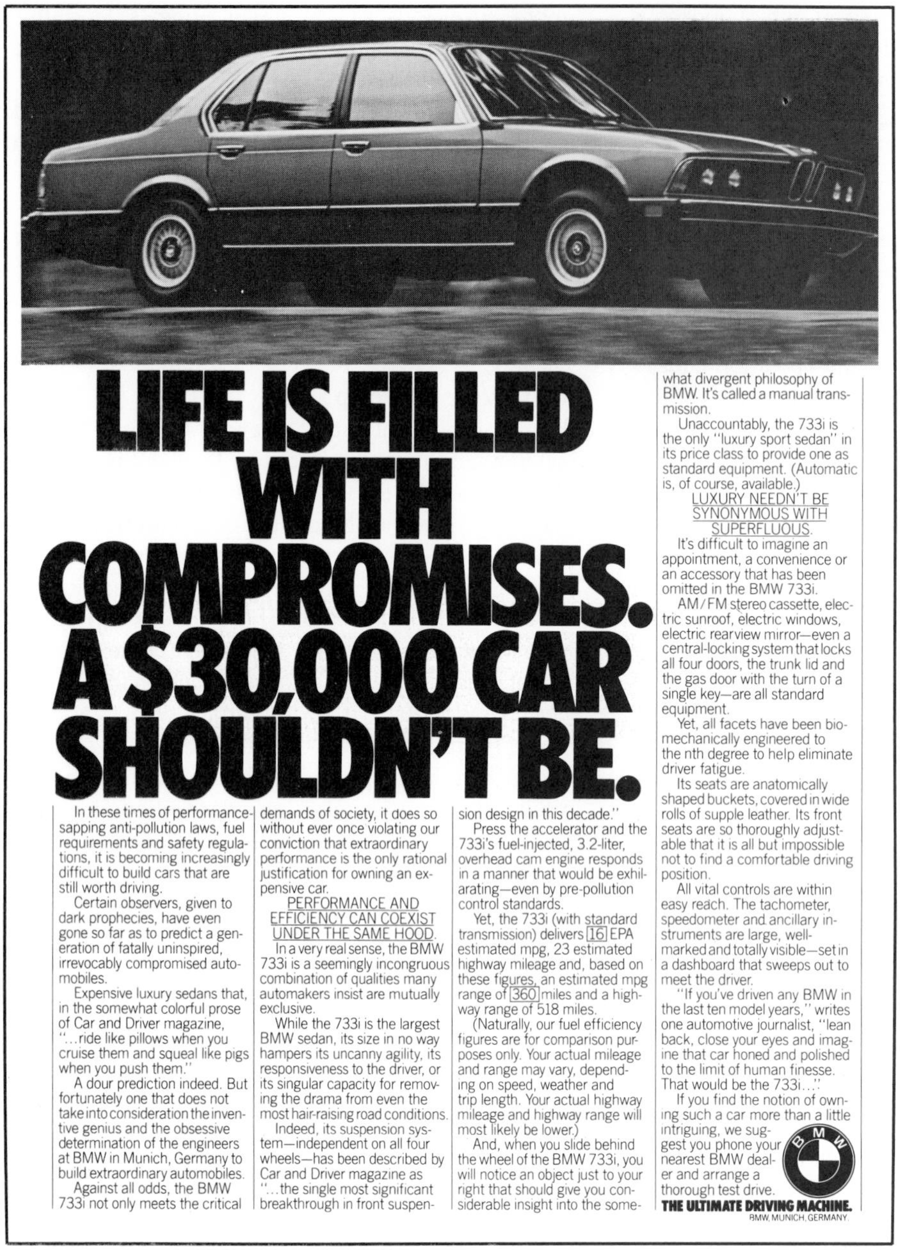

Figure 11.6 This magazine advertisement appeals directly to high-income consumers. The message is a rational justification of the automobile's high price.

Opinion Leaders

Katz and Lazarsfeld developed a concept dealing with the role of opinion leaders.[19] Their theory contends that an opinion leader can influence other consumers in making buying decisions about products. They believe that opinion leaders exist at all levels of society and function in a two-step flow of communications where the opinion leader gets the information from the media, including advertising, and passes it along to the opinion followers in the leader's sphere of influence. A practical problem in putting the theory into action is that it is very difficult to locate opinion leaders, and the leader for one product category often is not influential for another one. For example, Joe Smith, a fullback on the football team, is an authority on rock music, whereas Ed Jones, captain of the chess team, is an expert on stereo equipment or movies. Furthermore, restaurants become the "in" place in a city because celebrities patronize them. Isolating appropriate media vehi-

"Nobody ever returned a diamond for being a size too large." Lauren Bacall
As you might suspect, Lauren Bacall's gift list is a bit larger than most. Which is one reason she can't be bothered remembering things like sizes.
The solution, of course, is a set of monogrammed gold cufflinks instead of a monogrammed shirt. A quartz watch instead of silk pajamas. And, maybe an opal and gold ring instead of gloves.
And since you can select all your gifts from row upon row of diamonds and precious gems, aisles of gold jewelry, tiers of watches, walls of silverware and pewter and centuries of antiques, you might even find a little something for yourself.
A. 14 karat gold bracelet with a buckle of 85 diamonds totaling over 4.5 carats. $6000.
B. Emeralds and diamonds set in an 18 karat gold ring. $2500.
C. A heart of 20 marquise-shaped diamonds, totaling over 2 carats, set in a 14 karat gold pendant/pin. $2900.
fortunoff on fifth
fortunoff on fifth
A
B
C
681 FIFTH AVENUE at 54th STREET: Monday-Friday 10AM to 6:30PM, Thursday to 8:30PM, Saturday to 6PM, Sunday from Noon to 5PM. Call (212) 758-6660. Out of New York State call toll-free (800) 223-2326. Also in WESTBURY, L.I. on Old Country Road and PARAMUS, N.J. at Paramus Park Mall. We honor the American Express Card.
Fortunoff, the source, on fifth.
NEW YORK WESTBURY, L.I. PARAMUS, N.J.

Figure 11.7 A famous entertainment personality acts as an opinion leader for people interested in high-fashion jewelry.

cles to reach opinion leaders is difficult. More research is needed on the subject before the theory can be widely adopted in the development of advertising strategy.

The Family

Most of our personal attitudes were developed within the context of our immediate family. Attitudes are formed by parents and other family members not only toward God, country, motherhood, sex, and politics, but also toward products, brands, and retail outlets. Certainly, the influence of each family member is important when products for family use are being purchased. The relative influence of each spouse in the purchase of various consumer durables, such as homes and automobiles, has received much attention. Advertisers need to be aware of these influences when disseminating information about their products. For example, it is quite possible that automobile manufacturers have underestimated the importance of the woman's influence when a new car is being chosen. Certainly, the changing status of women in society has had an impact on such decisions. Where once the decision of buying a new car was wholly the prerogative of the man, the woman, who now drives the automobile and may well be making the payments for it, will have a strong voice in the decision.

Lifestyle Another important influence on consumer behavior is **lifestyle.** Whereas social class, reference groups, and opinion leadership come out of cultural and nonfamily group relationships, this concept is largely derived from the influence of the family, and it is still in the process of being defined. In many ways, it is closely akin to individual differences; yet whole families adopt lifestyles, and family influence in their creation is high. The term describes a distinctive mode of living or, to turn the phrase around, a "style of living." The concept goes beyond the broad characterizations that result from a person's social class. Lifestyle variables describe how people go about their daily routines. Some authorities put the emphasis on how people allocate their time, rather than how they spend their money, although the two are interrelated in many instances. What is important to individuals is reflected in their actions. Thus, we may see two people who are in the same social class and who possess the same demographic characteristics, yet lead very different lives. Such popular descriptions as "swinger" and "straight" cover widely divergent lifestyles.

"Psychographics" is a term closely related to the concept of lifestyle and is often confused with it. One definition of the term is:

> Psychographics is a quantitative research procedure which seeks to explain why people behave as they do and why they hold their current attitudes. It seeks to take quantitative research beyond demographic, socioeconomic and user/non-user analysis, but also employs these variables in the research. Psychographics looks into three classes of variables, of which life-style is one. The others are psychological and product benefits.[20]

Psychographics, or lifestyle research, can be extremely useful in the development of advertising strategy and copy. It provides data beyond dealing with such demographic variables as age, sex, and income or studies of consumer attitudes about the product and its use. Psychographics gives creative people in advertising a feel for the lifestyles pursued by members of the target market for the product. When Schlitz Beer felt there was a need to freshen its advertising campaign in 1968, lifestyle research found that the heavy beer drinker could be described as

> . . . a dreamer, a wisher, a hero worshiper. He goes to the tavern and has six or seven beers with the boys. . . . To talk with this man where he lives, in terms he respects and can identify with, we must find for him a believable kind of beer he inwardly admires. The major life style patterns that emerged indicated that the heavy beer drinker was a risk taker and a pleasure seeker, at least in fantasy. . . . More than the nonuser, the heavy user tended to have a preference for a physical and male-oriented existence . . . the life style data showed . . . an enjoyment of drinking, especially beer, which was seen as a real man's drink.[21]

Schlitz built a campaign around the imagery of the sea to dramatize the adventure of one of the last frontiers. The focus was on the lifestyle of the men of the sea, men who lived their lives with "Gusto." The campaign communicated with members of the target market in terms of their lifestyles as related to the product category of beer. Schlitz's share of the beer market increased, and the "Gusto" theme was continued until 1976.

In sum, the advertising strategist attempts to learn as much as possible about the social and cultural influences playing upon the members of the target market. These insights combine to permit better communications.

Attitude Formation and Change through Persuasive Communication

Attitude was the single most important variable in the literature of social psychology until the 1970s. Attitude is defined as *a neutral mental state of readiness to respond, which is organized through experience and exerts a directive or dynamic influence on behavior.*[22] From the outset of attitude research, it was believed that a change in attitude will be followed by a change in behavior. The entire theory of persuasion is based on this assumption. In an advertising context, several factors are commonly employed to create a favorable attitude, or to change an unfavorable one, toward the advertised brand. These factors include fear appeals, humor, source credibility, conclusion-drawing, one-sided versus two-sided messages, and repetition.

Fear Appeals One classic study indicated that a message stressing the unfavorable physical consequences of not taking a suggested course of action can have an adverse effect on attitude if this fear appeal is too intense.[23] Campaigns designed to induce cigarette smokers to quit because of the fear of lung cancer are usually unsuccessful. More recent re-

Figure 11.8 The classic Schlitz "Gusto—You Only Go Around Once" campaign is shown. Television was the dominant medium used for the total campaign.

search into the subject has been inconclusive, and many advertisers are employing fear appeals in advertising messages. For example, Chevrolet dealers may use a picture of a horrible automobile wreck accompanied by the headline, "But it got 43 mpg!" The point of the ad was that even though American-made autos may not give as many miles per gallon (mpg) of gas as imports do, there are other reasons for buying them instead of the imported car shown in the ad.[24]

Humor Appeal Research shows that humorous messages excell in attracting attention. Furthermore, humor can enhance source credibility. The risk is that prospects will remember the humor and not the product message. A classic example of this occurred some time ago when Alka-Seltzer's funny television commercials were the talk of the nation, yet the brand lost market share. The humor appeal is most effective when the brand is identified in the opening 10 seconds of the commercial, and when the humor is relevant to the brand.[25]

Source Credibility Typically, there is a positive relationship between source credibility and attitude change. Consumers seem to place greater confidence in a trustworthy source and hence are more receptive to what is said, even when there is a substantial deviation from their own position. Similarly, there is a substantially reduced tendency to accept a discrepant message when the source is of moderate or low credibility. This suggests that it is quite difficult to make an advertisement credible when the intention of the message is very obviously to persuade.

Conclusion-drawing In recent years, growing use has been made of what some now call "cool commercials." A cool message is unstructured; viewers are told a fragment of the story so that each person must fill in from imagination. The "hot message" on the other hand, is structured, logical, and sequential. The cool commercial is more appropriate to build a long-range image, when the basic product is emotional (for example, perfume, makeup, or designer jeans), or when a product has no apparent differential advantage compared with competitors' brands.

One-Sided versus Two-Sided Messages In a large number of studies undertaken in a nonbusiness setting, it has been found that a two-sided message (that is, favorable *and* unfavorable information on the issue) results in more attitude change than a one-sided appeal.[26]

Similar findings are reported by Faison in his study of automobiles, ranges, and floor waxes.[27] He presented both favorable and unfavorable product attributes in advertisements for these three products. The influence of the two-sided message was significantly higher than the one-sided message. However, in practice it can be difficult to convince an advertiser to advertise positive and negative values of the product.

Repetition The effects of repetition of advertising on attitudes have their theoretical foundations in learning theory, which will be discussed in the following section.

Learning Theories and Advertising

Steuart Henderson Britt claimed "that learning theorists and experimentalists have contributed practical and testable methods of behavior-influence that are relevant to marketing communications."[28] For example, he indicated that "a dichotomy exists between *intentional learning* and *incidental learning,*" with the latter having important implications in the promotional aspects of marketing, for "most advertising messages are presented to people who either are doing something or relaxing."[29] This fact obviously has significance for the writer of advertising copy.

There is some general agreement on how people learn, regardless of whether what they are learning is "a concept, a message, information about a brand, or even such things as typing and bicycle riding."[30] **Learning** is slow at first, but with repetition it increases rapidly until a plateau is reached, after which it slows down again. With more repetition, a new plateau may be reached.[31] Thus, an important question for the media planner is how many exposures the target audience should receive. Research into the matter is inconclusive, but Kassarjian believes that "the massive repetition of an advertisement may be sufficient to induce the consumer to buy the product advertised."[32] This introduces the

Figure 11.9 Learning involves an association between a stimulus and a response.

opposite side of learning, **forgetting,** and the intriguing question of the **decay of advertising effects.** If the earlier learning involved reinforcement or rewards, the fact would have an effect on the decay rate. There is evidence that after several repetitions, or fewer if the ad is memorable, forgetting is not complete for many years and even many decades.[33] Sometimes a so-called **sleeper effect** takes place wherein there is actually a lack of decay of a learned response after an advertising campaign has ended and the consumer is no longer exposed to the message.[34] The effects of advertising messages may be difficult to eradicate; passage of time alone is not sufficient. The argument for corrective advertising, discussed in Chapter 20, is based upon this premise.

Research on repetition suggests the following:[35]

1 Repetition can result in increased liking for the repeated stimulus.
2 Increases in the number of outside cues available to a subject and in the monotony of the repeated exposure are likely to lead to zero or negative effects on attitudes.
3 The effects of repetition seem to be less on measures of behavior, such as purchasing action, than on measures of affect such as brand evaluation or intention to purchase.
4 The effects of repetition in advertising depend upon the given advertising situation. These effects are likely to be influenced by factors such as the type of product or brand, the appeal and format of the ad, and the media frequency schedule.

Directly related to the concept of repetition is the issue of **clutter.** Clutter describes the situation where the amount of nonprogram material aired over television is excessive, thereby diluting the effectiveness of the messages reaching listeners. Limited research shows that consumers learn to pinpoint the timing of commercials and to avoid them effectively.[36] If broadcasters and advertisers want to eliminate the negative effects of clutter, they should vary the patterns used in airing commercials instead of sticking to the common schedule of three breaks of four commercials or six breaks of two commerdials. Another alternative is to shift advertising funds from television to other media. However, newspapers and magazines face the same problem of clutter when ads become disproportionate to editorial material. The problem in the print media, however, is less severe than on television.[37]

The Image of the Product and the Brand

What makes a consumer prefer one brand of soft drink over another? Soft drinks are most often similar products—99 percent physically alike—so the differences in their consumption must result from people's perceiving one brand as somehow different from others. A consumer's perception of a brand's image—the kind of people who buy the product, the quality of the product—does affect the purchasing process. Part of the image comes from ways in which the product is advertised. But we should not make the mistake of thinking of behavior as activated by a single motive; more often than not, the individual is driven by a combination of several motives. The behavior we describe as marriage may be traced to a combination of such motives as the biological sex urge, a desire for comfort, and a desire for social approval, to name only a few possibilities. The purchase of a new auto might well involve the urge to be superior, the need for social approval, and the desire for more comfort or convenience.

It should be clear that not every signal or cue sent out by an advertiser is fully and accurately received or digested. There is a great deal of selectivity going on in the process of perception. A popular word in the lexicon of the consumer behaviorist is **selective perception.** This means that the "human mind is highly selective with regard to what signals are allowed to contribute to the learning process."[38] Three kinds of selectivity occur:

1 *Selective exposure.* The customer attempts to encounter only those media and messages that are important to him and consistent with his deeply held values and beliefs.
2 *Selective perception.* The customer will "see" or "hear" certain signals and not see or hear others.
3 *Selective retention.* The retention and forgetting rates will differ among incoming signals.[39]

In other words, the advertiser must design a message that consumers will be willing to receive, or else they will use the filter that each individual possesses to avoid the message's impact.

Product Image

The behavioral concepts that we have discussed are not only important to the creation of advertising messages that will stimulate favorable rather than unfavorable responses from consumers. Any phase of marketing can utilize them, because what the modern consumer buys is more than the end product of certain raw materials processed to certain specifications. What the consumer wants and buys is a package of symbols appropriate to the person's self-image. This package of symbols is known as the **image** of the product, and it is considerably broader than the physical combination of many ingredients. The image of a product includes not only the picture the consumer has of the intrinsic qualities of the product, but also all the ideas relating to it—the sort of people who use it, the kind of stores that sell it, the character of the advertisements about it, the "personality" of the firms that make it—in other words, the total of all the stimuli received by the buyer that are related to the product. This bundle of product attributes is called the **product image.** We measure the worth of a product to us in terms of values that result fundamentally from the interraction of perception, learning, and motivation. We may see a book on advertising that is a bargain and can be a useful supplement to our study, but if added knowledge of advertising is an unimportant goal, we may buy a couple of T-shirts or a stereo album instead.

Brand Image

Most advertisers and marketers are more concerned with **brand image** than with product image. Their basic problem is not to increase the sales for a generic product, such as neckties or toothpaste, but to sell a particular brand of necktie or toothpaste in competition with other brands of the same type of product. The concept of product image is useful when considering the relative inherent interest two different products, such as automobiles and dishwashers or television sets and life insurance, offer consumers. The concept of brand image helps explain why two products that are technically identical are purchased by different types of people for different reasons: why, for example, soap A is preferred by young college women, while soap B, which has the same essential ingredients, is preferred by women over forty. Economist John K. Galbraith says that there is no such phenomenon as identical products, or the "undifferentiated market," in the modern economy of monopolistic competition:

> If the number of sellers is small, they will always be identified as distinct personalities to the buyer. And although their products may be identical, their personalities will not and cannot be. There is always, accordingly, a degree of product differentiation.[40]

This economist's viewpoint is underscored by advertising practitioners. A large advertising agency cautions advertisers with these words:

Because of the great and growing similarity of products and multiplicity of strong brands, it is vital to build a distinct brand personality and engrave a sharply defined brand image on the consumer's consciousness.[41]

Building meaningful product and brand images for consumer goods involves the use of the concepts of consumer behavior. Certainly the images appeal to the consumer's desire for information, and attitudes and beliefs about products are useful bits of information. Advertising is a vehicle for building bridges between the consumer's self-image or self-perception and product and brand images. Purchase and consumption activities are generally nothing more than an exercise in matching images.

One technique used in image measurement that has received considerable attention in recent years is multidimensional scaling (MDS). Unlike many other methods, MDS rejects the notion that consumer perception about a product can be combined into a single score. Instead, multidimensional scaling attempts to locate products within the framework of an "attribute space" based on consumer perceptions of similarities and differences among products. A classic use of the technique is shown in Figure 11.10. Eleven brands of cars were examined in 1968 as to consumer perceptions of two attributes: sportiness and luxuriousness. The Ford Falcon (5) was perceived as neither luxurious nor sporty, and the Jaguar Sedan (7) was perceived as a sporty car but not as a very luxurious one.

Multidimensional scaling represents one of the few attempts to apply quantitative models and computers to the problems of product positioning, using consumer perceptions as input data.

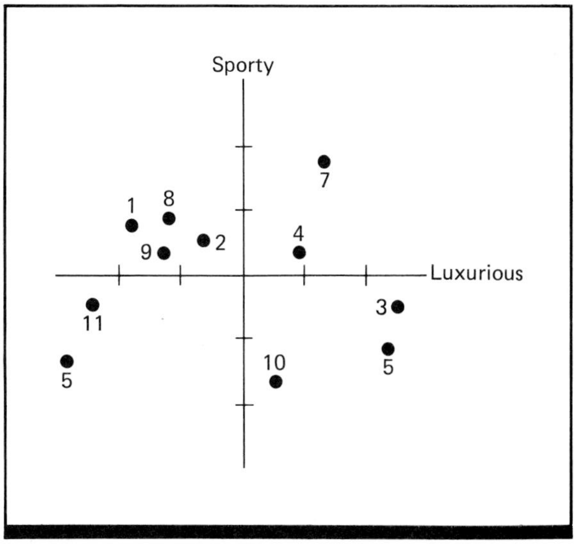

Figure 11.10 This perceptual map shows the findings made in a classic study. Conducted in 1968, the survey asked consumers to evaluate eleven car models on the characteristics of sportiness and luxuriousness. Key for the various car brands is:

1. Ford Mustang 6
2. Mercury Cougar V8
3. Lincoln Continental V8
4. Ford Thunderbird V8
5. Ford Falcon 6
6. Chrysler Imperial V8
7. Jaguar Sedan
8. AMC Javelin V8
9. Plymouth Barracuda V8
10. Buick Le Sabre V8
11. Chevrolet Corvair

[*Adapted from: P. E. Green and F. J. Carmone,* Multidimensional Scaling and Related Techniques in Marketing Analysis, (*Boston, Mass: Allyn & Bacon, 1970*), *p. 53.*]

Consumer Behavior and the Communication Process

Basic Elements in Mass Communications

When the consumer is viewed as an information-processing, decision-making entity, it is important to understand how needed information reaches this entity. In other words, how does the information communicated reach the consumer? We have seen how the behavioral sciences help producers and advertisers to understand buying behavior. Psychological theories are equally valuable in analyzing advertising as a form of mass communications. Essentially, the process of communication includes three elements: a source; a message; and a destination, or receiver, for the message. In personal or direct communications, (see Figure 11.11), the source is an individual; the message may be a speech, a gesture, or some other sign or signal; the receiver may be either another individual or a group—students in a classroom, a lecture audience, or the other 10 members of a football team. In mass communications, however, the source is not in direct contact with the receiver, and the receiver is always a group—or more precisely, an *aggregation*—rather than another individual. Thus, mass communications require a fourth element—a

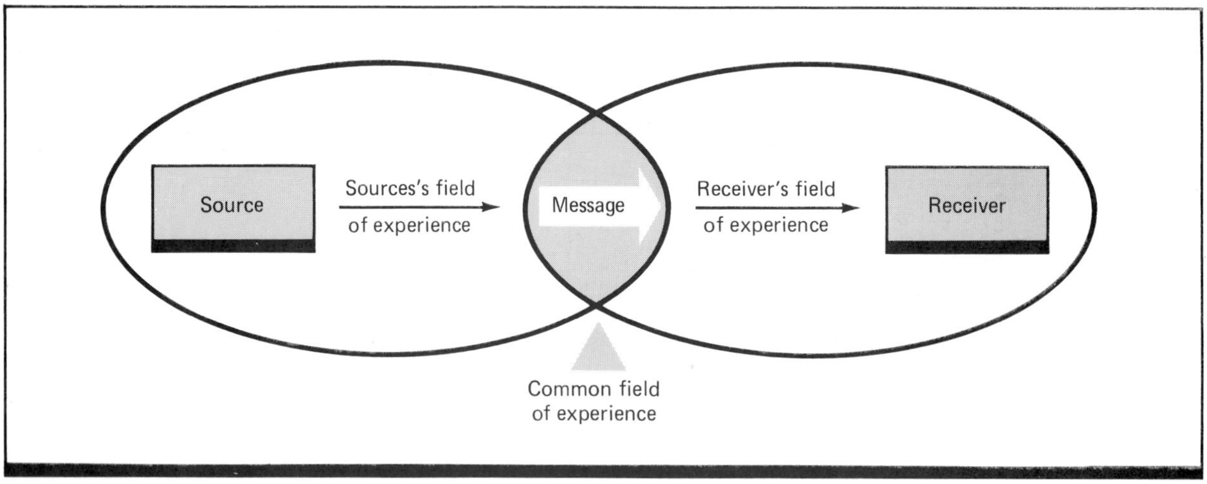

Figure 11.11 Effective communication requires a field of experience common to both sender and receiver. Advertisers must translate product information into the language of the customer.

mechanism or medium, such as a newspaper, magazine, outdoor poster, or broadcast station—to deliver the message simultaneously to many persons. The message may take the form of ink on paper, motion-picture film, electronic impulses, or paint on metal.

As we shall see later, it is important to visualize the real receiver of mass communications as the individual member of the group reached by the mass medium—the reader of a particular newspaper, the motorist who passes a certain outdoor poster, someone listening to a radio newscast or watching a television program. In advertising communication, the message becomes a stimulus designed to obtain a certain response from the receiver—the purchase of a product or the acceptance of an idea.

Special Problems of the Advertiser

This elementary source-medium-message-receiver analysis is inadequate, however, if we are to understand some of the basic problems of mass communications that are of particular significance to the advertiser. Even in direct or personal communications, the source or sender must be capable of transmitting signals that the receiver is able to receive. There is obviously little or no communication if the students in the back of the room cannot hear the instructor's voice. But it is not enough for receivers to be able to see or hear the message. Their reception must be psychological as well as physical. The receivers must perceive and be able to understand what is seen or heard.

In certain personal situations, communication can be quite complete with a soundless gesture. The symphony director's baton says "*fortissimo*" (very loud) to the members of the orchestra as effectively as if the word appeared on a screen in 4-foot letters. Although the new recruit will not understand the sergeant's arm signal, the trained soldier will. In both examples, a field of experience common to both sender and receiver assures understanding of the message. But the advertiser and the consumer do not have this close relationship. One of the primary problems in the creation of advertising is the **translation** of news and information about the product from the language of the advertiser into the language of the consumer.

Another problem the advertiser must face, which is not inherent in all types of communication, is **lack of feedback.** When we talk with a person face to face, or even when we address a group, it is possible to get an impression of how successfully our message is being delivered. The receivers may ask questions about points that are not clear to them and even though they do not talk back, their actions or expressions can indicate whether the message is being received. A yawn from the audience, for example, is a signal that the information is not getting through. In this way, interpersonal communication is usually a two-way process.

Most advertising, however, is one-way communication. The prospect, or the receiver of the message, has no opportunity to ask questions or even to indicate to the advertiser whether the message has been received. Instead of feeding back reactions, the prospect turns the page or changes the channel. The advertiser may subsequently find through research or through sales reports that all too few people received the message, but this fact was not known at the time the advertiser was actually trying to communicate. The nonpersonal nature of the presentation through mass communications media prevents two-way communication. To overcome this obstacle, the advertiser must attempt to anticipate the audience's reaction when exposed to the message.

Interference is another problem the advertiser must cope with. To a degree, interference is present in all forms of communication; even when two completely sympathetic friends are conversing in a soundproof room, distractions or interruptions will be present—a fly speck on the wall or the squeak of a chair under shifting weight. Interference to advertising messages can come from many sources. The phone rings while we are reading the newspaper. The traffic light turns red when we are listening to the car radio. The baby cries, and the mother leaves the television set. But the greatest interference to advertising is not external interference, but internal interference that is inherent in all the media of mass communications. This internal interference takes the form of other messages competing for the attention of the reader, the listener, or the viewer—not only news and entertainment, but advertising messages being transmitted by other advertisers.

Three Requisites for Effective Communication

Lack of feedback, interference, and translation of advertiser language into consumer language are important problems in advertising, but they do not alter the basic requirements for successful advertising. For any idea to be transmitted effectively from source to receiver, whether the source is personal or nonpersonal, the message must meet these three qualifications:

1 It must be so designed and delivered as to gain the attention of the receiver.
2 It must use signals that are understood in the same way by both source and receiver.
3 It must arouse awareness of needs in the receiver and suggest some way of satisfying these needs that is appropriate to the receiver's group situation when moved to make the desired response.[42]

These three requirements are often combined to form the first rule of effective communication: *Know your audience.* This rule applies equally to direct or personal communications and to indirect or mass communications. It applies equally to residents of the white, middle-class American suburb and to the growing black and Hispanic inner-city audiences in urban areas. A lecture that will hold the attention and interest of graduate students in marketing is not likely to hold the attention and interest of sophomore English majors or the members of the Eastlake Garden Club. In the same way, an advertisement designed to stimulate increased use of long-distance telephone service among business executives is unlikely to be an efficient means of increasing long-distance telephoning among families or for personal reasons.

In personal, face-to-face communications, the fundamental rule, "Know your audience," may be comparatively easy to apply, although in a surprising number of instances it seems to be ignored, and the members of the Eastlake Garden Club get the same lecture as the graduate students in marketing. For the advertiser, who never enjoys the luxury of a captive audience like the marketing class or the garden club, the task is both more difficult and more important.

Consider for a moment the advertiser's problem in gaining the audience's attention. Unlike the marketing students and members of the garden club, the advertiser's audience is not conveniently gathered in a room waiting for the message. All the advertiser can do is make the message available through newspapers, television, or some other mass medium, and hope that prospects will select it from the vast volume of other advertisements, entertainment, and information competing for their attention. None of us can possibly receive all the communications to which we are exposed. The ones we select are those that quickly provide a cue—an illustration or a headline, for example—that relates to our needs and interests at the time of exposure.

Obviously, signs that are not meaningful to the intended receiver provide no such cue, nor will they hold interest long enough to complete the balance of the message unless the sender is in tune with the receiver. This is one of the problems faced by the advertiser who tries to communicate with prospects whose culture is unfamiliar. Even when the language is the same, the meaning of words may be quite different. In England, for example, the "hood" of a car means the top, and what we call the hood is the "bonnet." We should also realize that the meaning of a message is not merely the combined meanings of the words used. In an oral communication, such as a brief radio announcement, meaning is conveyed by the timing, the pattern of emphasis, the intonations and the quality of the announcer's voice. Even when viewing a purely verbal printed mass communication, such as a newspaper advertisement without illustrations, the reader derives meaning from the size of the ad, the size and design of the type, the position of the ad on the page, and the page within the paper. So we should, as Schramm says, "visualize the typical channel of communication, not as a simple telegraph circuit, in which current does or does not flow, but rather as a sort of coaxial cable in which many signals flow in parallel from source toward destination."[43]

Particularly significant for the advertiser is the third requirement of effective communication—suggesting need or *want* satisfaction that is appropriate to the group situation of the receiver.

Another Communication Model

Many models, in addition to the Schramm model, have been designed to help clarify the communication process. The best known, and the most frequently used, is the "Hierarchy of Effects" model. Lavidge and Steiner, in a classic study, think of advertising as a force that must move people up a series of steps,[44] starting from their being unaware of the product's existence, on to their actual purchase of it. The positive steps in the model are shown in Table 11.1.

The first two positive steps in the chain, "awareness and knowledge, relate to *information* or *ideas.*" The next two steps, "liking and preference, have to do with favorable *attitudes* or *feelings* toward the product," while the final two steps, "conviction and purchase, are to produce *action*—the acquisition of the product." These three advertising functions compare to the classic psychological model that divides behavior into three dimensions: (1) cognitive—intellectual, mental, or "rational" state; (2) affective—"emotional" or "feeling" state; (3) conative or motivational—"striving" state, treating objects as positive or negative goals. The point is made that "the

Table 11.1
Lavidge and Steiner's "Hierarchy of Effects" Model

Related behavioral dimensions	Movement toward purchase	Examples of types of promotion or advertising relevant to various steps
Conative: The realm of motives. Ads stimulate or direct desires.	Purchase ↑ Conviction	Point-of-purchase Retail store ads Deals "Last-chance" offers Price appeals Testimonials
Affective: The realm of emotions. Ads change attitudes and feelings.	↑ Preference ↑ Liking	Competitive ads Argumentative copy "Image" ads Status, glamour appeals
Cognitive: The realm of thoughts. Ads provide information and facts.	↑ Knowledge ↑ Awareness	Announcements Descriptive copy Classified ads Slogans Jingles Sky writing Teaser campaigns

SOURCE: Robert J. Lavidge and Gary A. Steiner, "A Model for Predictive Measurements of Advertising Effectiveness," *Journal of Marketing,* October, 1961, p. 61.

Profile

Barbara Proctor

It all started for Barbara Proctor at a young age. Born in Asheville, North Carolina, Barbara spent much of her childhood with her grandmother, who instilled the principles of dedication and hard work in the child. One product of this discipline was two bachelor degrees—in education and psychology—from Talladega College, in Alabama. This training prepared her well for a career in communications.

Soon after completing college, Barbara became a successful writer for *Downbeat,* a popular jazz magazine. This assignment provided her with media experience and exposure to advertising professionals. Many were impressed by her talent.

With these personal and human resources available to her, Barbara Proctor changed the bent of advertising history by becoming, on May 5, 1970, the first female to open a full-service advertising agency specializing in marketing to the black community of our nation.

As a noted lecturer on the communications industry, women's rights, and the minority consumer market, Proctor has addressed audiences in the nation's key colleges and universities, the White House, and other distinguished groups. She holds the distinction of being the first woman to serve on various boards of directors, including that of the Illinois State Chamber of Commerce.

In addition to her success within the political arena, Barbara Proctor's agency now employs more than 25 people and bills around $12 million a year in advertising. She ranks in the millionaire class, a fact often minimized to facilitate business dealings.

Proctor's career highlights the fact that through hard work and dedication, she has broken through the white, male-dominated barriers to leadership status in the business of advertising.

actions that need to be taken to stimulate or channel motivation may be quite different'' depending on whether knowledge is being produced or favorable attitudes are being created.

The ''Hierarchy of Effects'' model attempts to show that advertising moves people along a kind of continuum, starting them with an inoculation of basic information, moving them through the process of creating interest in and favorable attitude toward products, ending ultimately in a stage of commitment or action. As shown in our discussion of copywriting and art direction in Chapters 12 and 13, there is no one ''right'' model.

Figure 11.12 Hair care products involve consumers to a high degree. Here a serious appeal is made to mature women, a demographic group that tends to be concerned about their physical appearance. [*Reprinted with permission of the copyright owner, © 1981, Clairol Inc. All rights reserved.*]

© 1978-80 Clairol Inc.
FREE, GRAY AND 51.
I'm not 29 anymore. I've done a lot since then. And I'm proud of my gray hair that proves it. That's why I show off my gray with Silk & Silver® from Clairol. It's the gentle haircolor lotion – without peroxide or ammonia. I just shampoo it in and for a whole month that yellow tinge is gone. My gray is full of silvery highlights. And the built-in conditioners make my hair so soft. I love the way I look. You know, I wouldn't be 29 again for the world!
SILK & SILVER
GIVES YOUR GRAY THE SPUNK NATURE LEFT OUT.
Silk & Silver

The Effects of Involvement

Several studies done over the last decade have suggested that applicability of the ''Hierarchy of Effects'' model is limited to conditions of high involvement on the part of consumers. Krugman was the first person to advance the notion that involvement with the product or the message acts as a moderator variable in the communication process.[45] According to this theory, individuals process advertising in one of two ways. One process, called ''high-involvement hierarchy,'' corresponds to the ''Hierarchy of Effects'' model. A highly involving communication creates some cognitive change, which gives rise to a change in affect and finally a change in behavior. The second process represents a different sequence. The ''low-involvement hierarchy'' begins with a cognitive change followed by a change in behavior, then a change in affect. The two hierarchy models are diagrammed thus:

HIGH INVOLVEMENT	LOW INVOLVEMENT
Exposure	Exposure
Cognition	Cognition
Affect	Behavior
Behavior	Affect

The high-involvement model assumes that people behave according to their prior attitudes and that they sometimes act to rationalize their attitudes. The low-involvement model, on the other hand, assumes that people are passive learners and that their behavior is not preceded by strong beliefs about the product. It is claimed that the product involvement is affected by the degree of consumer commitment, the importance of and familiarity with a product on the consumer's part, and the degree of differentiation in the product. The role of advertising in the high-involvement case is to create attitudes favorable toward the product or brand. The use of print media, little repetition of messages, and clear-cut advertising themes are recommended. In the low-involvement case, advertising should aim to create awareness. The use of a short message and a frequent-repetition strategy in broadcast media are recommended.[46, 47]

Information Processing

Many researchers studying consumer behavior have conducted projects to determine how consumers process information that reaches them through advertising and how this information alters their buying decisions. Much of this research has shown that more frequent messages do not produce a positive response (that is, purchase of the product or service).[48]

The research directed toward the problem of how people simplify the task of choosing competitive products has shown that consumers process information by attributes rather than by brands.[49] Drawing on these studies, an advertiser who wishes to reach consumers will use comparative advertising. These ads will stress the superiority of the advertised brand versus competitors' brands on a specific set of attributes, rather than vaguely suggesting that brand X is better than brand Y.

Consumers' information acquisition patterns are strongly determined by the format in which the information is available.[50] Thus, information must be both available and processable. For example, supermarket shelves are organized by brands. Consumers selecting a supermarket product will process information by brands rather than by attributes.

Finally, information processing is easier and more effective when the advertisement is novel and placed in a prominent position. In a magazine, for example, it should appear in the first 10 percent of the pages, on the cover, or next to compatible editorial features.[51]

Figure 11.13 Writing instruments are an example of low-involvement products. In this ad, humor is used to attract the customer's attention.

Summary

Planning effective advertising requires a knowledge of the behavioral sciences. The insights of psychology and sociology provide an explanation for the communication process between the advertiser and the consumer and for the reasons why consumers will favor one product over another or make their buying decisions. What makes humans think and act is a complex question; therefore, the advertiser should know the basic principles guiding people in their roles as consumers, which are best explained by psychological and sociological research and theories.

All humans have a desire to know, and in the role of consumer, an individual is actually an information processor who uses accumulated data to assist in problem solving.

Social and individual influences determine consumer behavior. Culture provides a significant influence upon such actions, for it leads to the development of personal value systems, which in turn determine how people view products. The social class to which individuals belong also affects the symbolic value that products may possess for each of them. Reference groups, opinion leaders, and especially the family are other sources of group influence upon a person's behavior. Within the family, its own life cycle and its lifestyle are additional influencing forces. Anyone designing mass communications messages needs to know as much as possible about these social and cultural influences upon members of the target audience. If the message does not fit into the audience's collective value system, there will be no communication. Furthermore, products and brands have images that must be matched with the self-images of consumers.

Different types of appeals, message positioning, and repetition factors are important in creating favorable or changing unfavorable attitudes toward the advertiser's brand. The research on information processing is useful in planning the format and quantity of information to be provided to consumers.

Questions for Discussion

1 What aspects of the behavioral sciences help advertisers in creating messages and placing advertisements? Support your answer with examples from current campaigns.

2 How does television influence the socialization of children? Why should advertisers be interested in this issue?

3 What is a lifestyle? Cite specific examples where advertisers appear to be employing the concept in their advertising strategies.

4 What is an attitude? What are the different ways of achieving an attitude change via mass communication? Are there other ways of changing attitudes?

5 What is selective perception? Cite a personal example of its operation from your own experience.

6 What are the implications of involvement for advertisers?

7 If you were planning an advertisement for an automobile, what concepts of consumer behavior do you think would be useful to you? Why?

8 In a current magazine, locate an advertisement that appears to be appealing to a subculture in our society. If possible, clip the ad and bring it to class with a statement on what seems to be its underlying strategy.

9 Basing your judgment on your observation of current advertising, list two or three persons who are being employed as opinion leaders; write a paragraph describing why each of these persons is entitled to play this role.

10 Collect two print ads for similar products: one ad using a one-sided message, and the other a two-sided message. Write an analysis of each ad's potential effectiveness.

For Further Reference

Berelson, Bernard, and Gary A. Steiner: *Human Behavior: An Inventory of Scientific Findings,* Harcourt, Brace & World, New York, 1964.

Bettman, James R.: *An Information Processing Theory of Consumer Choice,* Addison-Wesley, Cambridge, Mass., 1978.

Boone, Louis E.: *Classics in Consumer Behavior,* Petroleum Publishing Company, Tulsa, Okla., 1977.

Engel, James F., David T. Kollat, and Roger D. Blackwell: *Consumer Behavior,* 3d ed., Holt, Rinehart and Winston, New York, 1978.

Kassarjian, Harold H., and Thomas S. Robertson: *Perspectives in Consumer Behavior,* rev. ed., Scott, Foresman and Company, Glenview, Ill., 1973.

Katona, George: *Psychological Economics,* Elsevier, New York, 1975.

Markin, Jr., Rom J.: *Consumer Behavior: A Cognitive Orientation,* The Macmillan Company, New York, 1974.

Petty, Richard, Thomas Ostrom, and Timothy Brock (eds.): *Cognitive Response in Persuasion,* McGraw-Hill Book Company, New York, 1978.

Wells, William D. (ed.): *Life Style and Psychographics,* American Marketing Association, Chicago, 1974.

Woodside, Arch G., Jagdish N. Sheth, and Peter D. Bennett (eds.): *Consumer and Industrial Buying Behavior,* North-Holland Publishing Company, New York, 1977.

End Notes

[1] Carl M. Larson, Robert E. Weigand, and John S. Wright, *Basic Retailing,* Prentice-Hall, Inc., Englewood Cliffs, N.J., 1976, p. 57.

[2] James F. Engel, "Advertising and the Consumer," *Journal of Advertising,* no. 3, 1974, pp. 6–7.

[3] Ibid., p. 7.

[4] Ibid.

[5] Based in part on Rom J. Markin, Jr., *Consumer Behavior,* The Macmillan Company, New York, 1974, pp. 110–113.

[6] U. Neisser, *Cognitive Psychology,* Appleton-Century-Crofts, New York, 1967, p. 10.

[7] Markin, op. cit., p. 112.

[8] Ibid., p. 113.

[9] Larson, op. cit., p. 78.

[10] Thorstein Veblen, *The Theory of the Leisure Class,* The Macmillan Company, New York, 1899.

[11] Markin, op. cit., p. 120.

[12] Ibid., pp. 120–121.

[13] Daniel Yankelovich, "What New Life Styles Mean to Market Planners," *Marketing/Communications,* June 1971, pp. 38–45, as excerpted from David J. Schwartz, *Marketing Today,* Harcourt Brace Jovanovich, Inc., New York, 1973, pp. 170–171.

[14] James F. Engel, Roger D. Blackwell, David T. Kollat, *Consumer Behavior,* 3d ed., The Dryden Press, Hinsdale, Ill., 1978, pp. 100–102.

[15] W. L. Warner et al., *Social Class in America,* Harper & Row, Publishers, Inc., New York, 1960.

[16] Sidney J. Levy, "Social Class and Consumer Behavior," in John A. Howard and Lynn E. Ostlund (eds.), *Buyer Behavior,* Alfred A. Knopf, Inc., New York, 1973.

[17] Harold M. Hodges, "Peninsula People: Social Stratification in a Metropolitan Complex," in W. Claton Lang (ed.), *Permanance and Change in Social Class,* Schenkman Publishing Co., Cambridge, Mass., 1968, p. 15.

[18] George P. Moschis, "Acquisition of the Consumer Role by Adolescents," Research Monograph 82, Georgia State University, College of Business Administration, Atlanta, 1978, pp. 110–115.

[19] Elihu Katz and Paul F. Lazarsfeld, *Personal Influence,* The Free Press of Glencoe, Ill., Chicago, 1955.

[20] Emanuel Demby, "Psychographics and from Whence It Came," in William D. Wells (ed.), *Life Style and Psychographics,* American Marketing Association, Chicago, 1974, p. 28.

[21] Joseph Plummer, "Applications of Life Style Research to the Creation of Advertising Campaigns," in Wells, op. cit., pp. 164–165.

[22] G. Allport, "Attitudes," in C. Murchison (ed.), *Handbook of Social Psychology,* Clark University Press, Worcester, Mass., 1935, pp. 798–884.

[23] I. L. Janis and S. Feshbach, "Effects of Fear-Arousing Communication," *Journal of Abnormal and Social Psychology,* vol. 48, 1953, pp. 78–92.

[24] *Wall Street Journal,* Dec. 16, 1980, p. 35.

[25] Brian Sternthal and C. Samuel Craig, "Humor in Advertising," *Journal of Marketing,* vol. 37, October 1973, pp. 12–18.

[26] C. I. Hovland, A. A. Lumsdaine, and F. D. Sheffield, *Experiments on Mass Communication,* vol. 3, Princeton University Press, Princeton, N.J., 1948.

[27] E. W. Faison, "Effectiveness of One-Sided and Two-Sided Communications in Advertising, *Public Opinion Quarterly,* vol. 25, 1961, pp. 468–469.

[28] S. H. Britt, "Applying Learning Principles to Marketing," *MSU Business Topics,* Spring 1975, p. 5.

[29] Ibid., pp. 5–6.

[30] Harold H. Kassarjian, "Applications of Consumer Behavior to the Field of Advertising," *Journal of Advertising,* vol. 3, no. 3 (1974), p. 11.

[31] Loc. cit.

[32] Ibid., p. 12.

[33] Loc. cit.

[34] Loc. cit.

[35] Alan G. Sawyer, "The Effects of Repetition: Conclusions and Suggestions about Experimental Laboratory Research," in G. David Hughes and Michael L. Ray (eds.), *Buyer/Consumer Information Processing,* The University of North Carolina Press, Chapel Hill, 1974, pp. 190–219.

[36] Michael L. Ray and Peter Webb, "Experimental Research on the Effects of TV Clutter: Dealing with a Difficult Media Environment," Report No. 76–102, Marketing Science Institute, Cambridge, Mass., April 1976.

[37] Ibid.

[38] Larson et al., op. cit., p. 73.

[39] Ibid.

[40] John K. Galbraith, *American Capitalism,* Houghton Mifflin Company, Boston, 1956, p. 43.

[41] *Grey Matter,* Grey Advertising, Inc., New York, November 1968, p. 8.

[42] Adapted from Wilber Schramm (ed.), *The Process and Effects of Mass Communications,* The University of Illinois Press, Urbana, 1954, p. 13.

[43] Ibid., p. 10.

[44] Robert J. Lavidge and Gary A. Steiner, "A Model for Predictive Measurements of Advertising Effectiveness," *Journal of Marketing,* October 1961, pp. 59–62. All quotes in the paragraph are from this source.

[45] Herbert E. Krugman, "The Impact of Television Advertising: Learning without Involvement," *Public Opinion Quarterly,* vol. 29, 1965, pp. 349–356.

[46] Michael Ray, "Marketing Communication and the Hierarchy of Effects," in R. Clarke (ed.), *New Models of Mass Communication Research,* Sage Publications, Beverly Hills, Calif.

[47] Thomas Robertson, "Low Commitment Consumer Behavior," *Journal of Advertising Research,* vol. 16, 1976, pp. 19–24.

[48] Jacob Jacoby, Donald E. Speller, and Carol A. Kohn, "Brand Choice Behavior as a Function of Information Load," *Journal of Marketing Research,* vol. 11, 1974, pp. 63–64.

[49] James R. Bettman, "Issues in Designing Consumer Information Environments," *Journal of Consumer Research,* vol. 2, 1975, pp. 169–177.

[50] James R. Bettman and Pradeep Kakkar, "Effects of Information Presentation Format on Consumer Information Acquisition Strategies," *Journal of Consumer Research,* vol. 3, 1977, pp. 233–240.

[51] James F. Engel, Roger D. Blackwell, and David T. Kollat, *Consumer Behavior,* 3d ed., The Dryden Press, Hinsdale, Ill., 1978, pp. 345–349.

Chapter 12

Advertising Creativity and the Copywriter

● The most widely known, discussed, enjoyed, and criticized parts of the advertising process are the ads and commercials. They appear daily, by the millions, in print and on the air throughout the United States. The business of conceiving, writing, designing, and producing these messages is called advertising creativity; the key wordsmith is called a **copywriter** (or sometimes copy chief or copy supervisor). Before we examine this person's specific job, however, we must see how *advertising* creativity differs from other types.

The creative writer—poet, novelist, playwright—takes well-known ideas, words, and phrases and relates them in a fresh, often brilliant manner. Thus, a household pet, plus a hazy weather condition, in the hands of a Carl Sandburg turns into the classic: "Fog comes on little cat feet . . . ." And while anyone who so desires may write about revolution, there is only one Charles Dickens and one *Tale of Two Cities*. Creativity also is expressed through painting and music. Even a child can draw a picture of a smiling woman, but Leonardo da Vinci's artistic talents produced the *Mona Lisa;* likewise, the creative genius of Anton Dvořák displayed simple impressions of America in the masterpiece we know as the *New World Symphony*.

In each of these cases, the creator's purpose was self-expression. Similarly, when a student is assigned a creative writing or art project, he or she gives imagination free rein and lets ideas come together as they will. The purpose is to achieve a tangible representation of what the mind's eye can already see; and in most cases, the author aims to create in others an understanding of and appreciation for his or her artistic output. By translating ideas and impressions into poems, pictures, or other words, each composer gains personal satisfaction and creates enjoyment for those who come in contact with the results.

Disciplined Creativity

Creativity in advertising most assuredly draws on "pure" writing talents, but, as should be obvious by now, the nature of the business demands a certain kind of discipline not found in creative writing circles. Granted, writers in every field should be adept at spelling, grammar, and punctuation, and familiar with current idiomatic expressions. Successful advertising, however, requires knowledge of overall marketing environments and awareness of consumer learning abilities and selective processes; creativity in advertising, therefore, must be *disciplined* creativity.

The advertising copywriter still writes with a purpose, but now the purpose is to achieve *clients'* objectives instead of the writer's. Self-expression gives way to expression of features or attributes of particular products and services, which are presented in terms of consumer benefits and in the language most appropriate to defined target audiences. As noted in Chapter 5, advertising messages present merchandise in ways that interest people in buying. Print ads and broadcast commercials portray products as problem solvers or methods whereby wants and needs may be fulfilled.

In this case, creativity is really the opposite of pure freedom of imagination. When creating, the copywriter builds messages according to specific plans, to fulfill specific objectives. In the words of research practitioner Alfred Politz:

> [Advertising creativity] has to follow rules which are guided by a well-defined purpose, by an analysis of the thoughts supplied by imagination, by a selection of the useful ones which meet the purpose.[1]

The copywriter's starting point for every ad and commercial, therefore, should be a creative strategy statement, sometimes called a copy platform or blueprint.

Creative Strategy

Although there is no one set form for such statements, most incorporate the following:

1 The Advertising Objective

First, as pointed out repeatedly in this text, although marketing's function is to *sell,* advertising's purpose is to *aid* the selling process through communication with prospective customers. Most advertisements both inform and persuade. Some are designed to help establish attitudes and buying behaviors. Still others strive to reinforce or to change existing shopping habits, brand images, and usage patterns.

The advertising objective expresses the desired *positioning* of the product or service in question by describing the image the advertiser wishes to communicate to consumers. For example, consider a proposed advertising message for Simplicity sewing patterns. The objective might be stated as follows:

> To position Simplicity patterns as the solution to fashion problems faced by today's woman: high prices, changing styles, limited size and color availabilities, and poor quality construction. To convince active women that sewing with Simplicity is a quick-and-easy way to get the clothes they want, and to allay doubts of those who haven't had experience with home sewing.

2 The Target Audience

Second, the copywriter needs a description of the demographic and psychographic makeup of the specific target audience for whom the ad is being created. Quantitative data (such as age, sex, marital status, occupation, income, education, place of residence) must be supplemented by information on consumer attitudes (related to the advertised product and its competitors, as well as to the types of creative claims being considered for the message), on relevant media, shopping, and buying habits, and on product usage.

For example, the target audience for the Simplicity campaign might be:

> Women, 18 to 34, college-educated, with limited budgets. Both single and married, they have part-time or full-time out-of-home careers. These are women on the go, both socially and professionally. They're very interested in their looks and have definite opinions as to fashions that are right for them. Quality is important, but since both time and money are in short supply, clothing needs tend to be a source of frustration. These women may or may not be experienced with a sewing machine, but they're willing to try new things if they are assured of a personal benefit. They take pride in personal achievement.

3 The Creative Promise

Next comes a statement of the exact product value that the ad will communicate to potential consumers. The heart of the creative message is presented as a clearly defined brand advantage or benefit—one that is important enough to the target audience to serve as the power base around which the entire ad will develop:

Simplicity patterns end the difficulties of searching for fashionable outfits that are affordable. Clothes made with Simplicity patterns are the right size, color, and style, and are still durable enough to keep up with an active lifestyle. So, the customer can "stop taking it" (the frustration), and "start making it" (her own wardrobe).

4 The Backup Claim

In order to establish credibility for our promise, we need to support it with facts and with satisfactions derived:

Simplicity patterns are so easy to follow that even a beginner can make a dress in a few hours. The cost of materials is far below that of comparable store-bought outfits. Satisfied customers have made the Simplicity pattern catalog the hottest fashion publication around.

5 The Creative Style

Finally, every copy strategy must describe the intended mood or tone of the forthcoming ad or commercial: cheerful, dramatic, businesslike, or whatever. Successful messages all have distinct personalities that are expressed both through copy (printed or spoken words) and through graphics and aural effects (printed and moving visual effects plus sound effects and music). The most effective ads are also those that are all but overlooked *as ads.* If they call attention to *themselves,* we have a condition known as "adiness." Message receivers may remember creative gimmicks of the ad in question but forget the product and sales promise completely.[2]

To keep our Simplicity advertisement on target here, we call for:

A lively, dynamic, exciting mood and a no-nonsense approach that talks with the audience very directly, very personally, and very emphatically. The message should be focused on results and directed (both verbally and graphically) toward a single goal—action.

Figure 12.1 shows four Simplicity advertisements that ran in *The New York Times Magazine.* Notice that they are all variations on the theme called for in our creative strategy. Interestingly enough, they ran on consecutive right-hand pages of the same issue so that if readers missed the first ad, they were bound to see one of the others.

Sources of Creative Ideas

It is important to point out that although imagination is an innate human quality, truly creative ideas are not easy to find. Advertising copywriters must be doers as well as thinkers. They must participate in life, soaking up as much of it as they possibly can, for their work demands a heavy reliance on prior experiences. They must be familiar with current trends and culture, such as popular novels, plays, and symphonies; hit movies, TV shows, and records; comic strips, gossip columns, and sports features. They must travel, too. It need not be around the country or the world, but often, just across town to museums and parks, to taverns and hospitals, to courtrooms, airports, and bus depots. They must talk to cab drivers and truckers, clerks and mechanics, salesmen, waitresses, and teachers, while keeping up to date on fads and fashions in clothing and cars.

Finally, copywriters make it a point to study products—their own and those of competitors. They scrutinize intended audiences (wants and needs, likes and dislikes) and the competition (products and ads) in painstaking detail. They read and watch, listen and remember, analyze and experiment until they find the right words to express the theme, or concept, or idea that is the beginning of a message or series of messages.

Advertising creativity, then, is almost always based on a systematic, logical accumulation of *facts* that forms the foundation on which insight and ingenuity can build. Both heredity and environment do contribute to creative talent, but effort and motivation

Figure 12.1 Four ads for the same product running in the same publication. They illustrate four variations of an identical creative theme and are tied together with a common slogan-line at the bottom. [*Courtesy of Simplicity Pattern Co. and DKG Advertising.*]

are important forces in its cultivation. In creating, we associate known facts (or factors: people, objects, issues, events) with one another in order to develop unique relationships. Or, as veteran advertising man James Webb Young has long maintained, creativity is the combination of existing elements in new and unexpected ways.[3] John Matthews, former chairman of the Plans Board of Draper Daniels, notes:

> Many times the most creative thing you can do in your advertising is not to create something new—but to utilize something so old you may have forgotten you had it. Not to discover, but to uncover; not to innovate, but to renovate; not to seek new horizons but to capitalize on an element which is right under your nose waiting for you to recognize its potential.[4]

Remember, though, that no matter how original an advertising idea may be, it must help solve a consumer problem (convey a benefit) if it is to be successful. So, fact gathering must precede all copywriting pursuits.

Digging for Facts

According to Webster, a fact is something that exists: an occurrence or an event. It is a fact that you are reading this book. It is a fact that the book was published by McGraw-Hill Book Company. These are *absolute* facts, one of several kinds with which copywriters work. Is a product priced at $6.95 or $7.95? Is the fabric Dacron or nylon? Does an engine deliver 105 or 150 horsepower at 3,000 rpm?

Other facts are not so easy to substantiate by observation or test. Is it really a fact today, for example, that the initial impetus for the purchase of an automobile comes from the husband in two out of three families? A study conducted 25 years ago showed that it did—but what about now?[5] In some cases, companies demand updated research reports prior to the launching of a new advertising campaign. Often, however, both time and funds run short, and copywriters must make use of existing information. On the other hand, research does not necessarily provide the copywriter with a campaign theme. It reduces the probability of error, but cannot substitute entirely for educated judgment or knowledge gained from past experience.

Fact-gathering activities can be complex, involving extensive market and psychological research procedures. On the other hand, they may be quite simple. In retail advertising for a department store, for example, the copywriter is usually given a merchandise "fact sheet" by the buyer. Frequently, this information, along with firsthand examination of the merchandise, gives the copywriter enough data to prepare effective retail copy. (See Figure 12.2.)

caa commercial art associates

ADVERTISING & SIGN REQUEST FORM

USE SEPARATE SHEET FOR EACH ITEM-ILLEGIBLE OR INCOMPLETE FORMS WILL BE RETURNED!

DEPT. NAME: SPORTS EQUIPMENT

DATE ADVERTISEMENT TO RUN IN PAPER, ETC.: SUN., March 22, 1981

☐ FEATURE ☐ BLOCK BUSTER
☐ BOX NO ART ☐ COUPON
☐ LINER

ABOUT THE MERCH.
Your merchandise is due at advertising along with this sheet filled with utmost care.

☐ NEWSPAPER
☐ TABLOID
☐ ELECTRONIC

SIZE OF AD: FULL PAGE
COLOR: GREEN

ITEM	TYPE		ADV. PRICE	REG. PRICE	COMP. PRICE	NO. OF UNITS AVAILABLE
TENNIS RACQUETS			25% off			60
TENNIS BALLS			25% off			200 cans
(at The Tennis Stop/Shop)						

DESCRIPTION: (List selling points in order of importance):

Wide variety of styles to choose from (all 25% off our already regular low prices!) A racquet for every member of the family. Balls in optic yellow and orange, 3 per can, all popular brands. Sale runs Sunday through Tuesday only. Sorry: no phone orders accepted. Location: Fairfield Mall.

MERCHANDISE ATTACHED ☐

GLOSSY ATTACHED xxx

ARTWORK COSTS MONEY! DO NOT REQUEST NEW ART WORK UNTIL YOU HAVE CHECKED YOUR ADS FOR OLD ART. ATTACH ANY MANUFACTURER'S ART OR LITERATURE THAT WILL HELP

INSTRUCTIONS TO AD. DEPT. Client requests "Swing Into Spring Savings" headline.

DATE OF PICK-UP OF ART ___/___/___

Figure 12.2 A merchandise fact sheet for a department store, giving copywriters information needed to prepare advertisements.

In any case, the answers to certain basic questions provide valuable copywriting information for almost any form of advertising. The following list is not exhaustive, but it will give you an idea of the kind of data copywriters need to create advertisements.

Figure 12.3 A familiar ad from a well-known company illustrating the functional use of a product. The message is simple and convincing, and the selling theme is credible and clear. [*Eastman Kodak Company.*]

Background Information

First, the copywriter must study the company behind the proposed advertising. What is the reputation of the manufacturer, service organization, or store involved? How does it affect prospective customers? Is there, for example, a long-standing company philosophy of service with a smile or of putting the customer first? Is there a history of success stories, technological advances, or contributions to public service activities? Have there been recent laboratory tests, audience research studies, industry or government inspections for safety or cleanliness around which an advertising campaign might be based? Can expanded company facilities and distribution outlets, changes in employee hiring and training procedures, or improvements in packaging, pricing, and service or warranty arrangements be promoted favorably?

Although all these questions may appear to characterize the *advertiser* rather than the product or service, the copywriter must evaluate the answers for their influence on potential customers. If information about the advertiser is not of value to consumers in solving problems or making decisions in the marketplace, the copywriter must move on.

Functional Information

The next area a copywriter studies is the in-use operation of a product, service, or store. The research may require both observation and participation. Is there something about a cooking or cleaning procedure, a preventive or protective activity, or a developing or dissolving process that is noteworthy? Perhaps the product's speed, efficiency, simplicity, or reliability sets it apart from competitors. (See Figure 12.3.) Or,one brand of product may be able to win a comparison test with other brands (or survive a torture test).

An advertisement for a retail outlet might feature express checkout lanes, a free delivery service, special courtesy cards, or a noteworthy exchange or refund policy. Banks may have automatic tellers, Christmas savings clubs, and special loan programs. Airlines offer excursion rates, convenient check-in systems, and in-flight services designed for extra comfort.

Result-of-Use Information

Additional information may come from studying the results of using a product, patronizing a store, or partaking of a service. It takes time for the effects of some weight-loss, skin-care, and hair-treatment products to be seen, but the results influence buying behavior much more than does the manner in which these items are used.

Likewise, the act of placing money in a savings

plan isn't nearly so stimulating as seeing its accrued interest figures add up as the months go by (or spending the money saved for some special occasion). A consumer's repeated visits to a particular store can result in (1) a collection of redeemable stamps or cash register tapes; (2) friendships with store personnel and a valuable credit reputation; and (3) a feeling of confidence and satisfaction as charges prove reasonable, merchandise is dependable, and special requests are honored.

The facial and verbal reactions of family, friends, and business associates to a person's continued use of a particular item may also motivate new buyers to switch brands. Finally, the effects of time- and work-saving devices or of personal grooming aids can provide convincing reasons for buying. (See Figure 12.4.)

Incidental Information

Often as a last resort, when none of the above three categories of information seems appropriate, copywriters may dig for material incidental to product development and use. For example, attention might focus on one of the characters discussed in earlier chapters of this book, such as Aunt Jemima, Betty Crocker, or Charlie the Tuna, or on a symbol such as Prudential Insurance's Rock of Gibraltar.

In other cases, a special price, a combination offer, or a new package size or color may be enough to win

Figure 12.4 An advertisement illustrating the results of using a product over time. [*The Procter & Gamble Company.*]

consumer acceptance. On rare occasions, the only thing noteworthy about an advertisement or commercial is the relationship between the product and a new spokesperson, jingle, or slogan.

In every one of these four situations, the copywriter must combine knowledge of the advertiser with insights into the behavior of intended customers. Product characteristics must be viewed in the light of consumer wants and needs as well as of unique media capabilities. A full-page magazine ad, for instance, is quite different from a 10-second television commercial. Each medium has its own way of involving audiences with the sight, sound, smell, taste, and touch of products advertised. In all cases, however, each audience must be addressed in its own kind of language (verbal expressions, color schemes, background music) and, as Chapter 11 made clear, current lifestyles must be the stage setting of every advertising message. Some examples are discussed below.

Working Women More than 50 percent of American women are now employed outside their homes. To advertise to these consumers, a copywriter must be aware of their special needs and desires. For example, many ads appeal to working women by depicting female executives, athletes, and scientists. On the other hand, Dad may be shown fixing dinner, diapering the baby, or shopping for groceries. Working women need products such as life insurance, luggage, and clothing for office wear more than their homemaker counterparts. To promote these products adequately, a copywriter must understand the demands of this segment of the female market.

Small Families Today's relatively small families affect consumer demands in different ways. On one hand, with fewer mouths to feed and fewer bodies to clothe, parents may choose to spend more on personal luxuries and on activities that involve all members of the household. On the other hand, the children in some one- and two-child families may ask for and receive larger portions of each dollar earned than would be possible if there were more siblings. Moreover, senior citizens are now seen as active family members: riding to work with their sons and daughters, exercising with their grandchildren, and even flirting with one another.

Leisure Time Today many Americans are interested in sports—both as spectators and as participants. Men and women, children and teenagers, and youngsters barely able to walk engage in swimming, tennis, jogging, and calisthenics. Also, television ratings reports confirm that sportscasts remain very high on viewers' program preference lists. Even advertisers of so-called health foods, although not selling athletic gear, jump on the bandwagon here by using sports terms: "Jog on over to your favorite store"; "After the game, serve your tennis star a refresher"; "The dessert that's sure to score with your little sluggers."

Attitudes toward Shopping and Buying Today's educated consumers make remarkably sophisticated purchasing decisions. They are concerned about inflationary prices and have definite attitudes regarding generic, private, and national product brands. They are aware of suspected cancer-causing elements and ingredients, and some take the time to read labels before they buy. Recent research studies conducted by Yankelovich, Skelly, and White have found that as many as 70 percent of Americans are worried about distortion and exaggeration in advertising. The copywriter's job is indeed challenging.

Societal Interests In addition to inflation, the energy shortage ranks high on the list of consumer concerns. Advertisements that can truthfully (and credibly) relate conservation to a particular brand of merchandise may help position and sell products effectively.

Americans are generally in favor of some form of medical and housing assistance to needy fellow citizens, and they expect governmental and private social responsibility programs. Some advertisers run periodic corporate campaigns stressing their public service contributions, and others add an occasional public relations line to regular brand-item advertisements.

Personal Priorities and Values Self-fulfillment remains a key objective in the lives of most of us, so advertising messages often advise audiences: "You're worth it" (L'Oréal's expensive hair-color treatment), and "You'll feed good about yourself" (when you drink Diet Pepsi). Status symbols are sought and flaunted, too, in such areas as transportation (flashy cars), attire (designer outfits), and travel (luxury cruises and flights to exotic islands).[6]

If an advertisement does not communicate how a product or service answers the prime prospect's problem, it is like an automobile with square wheels. It may be beautiful, entrancing, memorable, and a triumph of creative skills . . . but it will not function![7]

Analysis of Selling Points and Benefits

Once a copywriter has collected all possible data about the product and the people who buy and use it, his or her role changes from fact gatherer to analyst. The next step is to develop from these facts a set of selling points and benefits.

A selling point for a product is a characteristic of the product itself that can contribute to the satisfaction of a need or desire of the buyer. A benefit, then, becomes the satisfaction received from purchase or use. *However, from a creative point of view, any relevant factor may form the basis of a selling point or benefit.* It is up to the copywriter to match an important product feature or quality with its resulting value to the consumer. For instance, suppose ingredient X is a detergent's most outstanding property. If it is used as a selling point, the idea might become: "Because this detergent has ingredient X (selling point), you get the satisfaction of whiter, brighter clothes (benefit)."

Or, if it is used as a benefit, we might have: "Because of the extra time and special effort that went into this detergent's research and development (selling point), it now gives you the cleaning properties of ingredient X (benefit)." It all depends on how the copywriter chooses to present the sales message.

How are specific advertising appeals (selling points *and* benefits) selected from the (often long) list of potentials? First, the copywriter must remember that one of the most important functions that must be performed for an advertiser is the creation of campaigns from the outside in—looking at the product through the eyes of *prospects* and seeing it as something they may willingly buy, rather than as something the advertiser must sell. Second, the copywriter notes that people are not interested in the advertiser's product per se; they are interested in the *rewards* the product promises—the values it holds in terms of want or need fulfillment. Tom Dillon, president and chief executive officer of Batten, Barton, Durstine & Osborn, maintains that:

David Malickson and John Nason, two highly successful advertising practitioners, have set up a three-pronged approach to the determination and selection of key selling points and benefits for a given creative campaign:

1. First, they suggest, examine physical, tangible attributes of a product or service—and, we would add, *do so through the eyes of prospective customers*. Does the shape, color, flavor, fragrance, texture, or form of a product make it especially attractive, satisfying, and useful to consumers? (For example, a solid air freshener is neater than a spray.) Does a repair service come with a warranty that relieves buying worries? Or has a print shop installed the most modern and elaborate equipment available, so that jobs are done quickly and with professional flair?

Perhaps a specific product ingredient (bleach), a component (adhesive backing), or an attachment (protective shield) eases the user's workload or makes a job safer. (NOTE: Consumers might also view favorably the absence of particular ingredients, such as chemical preservatives.)

2. Second, these authors recommend studying advantages resulting from the manufacture of an item. Individually (and uniquely) wrapped packages, a variety of product sizes, and economical quantities within packages (for example, "more towels per roll") may appeal to consumers' desires to save money, trips to the store, and storage space.

A production process such as freeze-drying or encapsulating in timed-release form may deliver improved taste, comfort, or convenience, and thus make customers more contented, healthier, or more efficient. A fast-food operation might offer short-order lines, special children's menus, and facilities for both large groups and small families, all so that customers can relax and enjoy an evening away from home and kitchen.

3. Third, we're advised to check advantages connected to an overall marketing strategy.[8] Personal

bankers, stockbrokers, and travel consultants, as well as exclusive club membership privileges and free legal advice, may all appeal to a person's need for attention, recognition, and information. We can regard the premiums or games included in many promotional packages as direct attempts to relieve customers' anxieties over today's high costs (by offering them chances for free gifts or prizes).

Many products promise more than one benefit, and many advertisements offer more than one basic appeal. A new reading lamp may (1) make the buyer more comfortable by providing better light, (2) add some distinction to the home and its owner, and (3) appeal as a bargain because of its relatively low price. However, the copywriter must analyze product selling points and the benefits they support and focus the message on one or two that are stronger than others in order to provide a central selling idea for the advertisement.

Unique Selling Proposition

Development of this central idea, or what is often called a **unique selling proposition,** is one of the copywriter's most important and difficult tasks. The USP (as it is often abbreviated) originated at the Ted Bates advertising agency in the early 1940s. As its famous originator, author, and agency vice-president, Rosser Reeves, has stated, however, it has been picked up by hundreds of agencies and has spread from country to country. Unfortunately, it has also become a very **misused** concept. Frequently, it is applied loosely and without understanding to slogans, clever phrases, unusual pictures, or sound combinations—in short, to almost anything deemed "different" in copy, layout, or production. We believe our interpretation of the USP comes close to the one intended by Rosser Reeves, but every student of advertising creativity must ultimately develop his or her own.

A USP, Reeves claims, gives leverage to an advertising campaign—that extra tug that pulls consumers over the line of indecision or confusion to specific product preference, and then to brand loyalty. Now consider the three words individually.

"Unique"

"Unique" describes a feature that only the brand itself possesses (for example, only V-8 has this unique combination of eight vegetables in one juice) or a claim not currently being made by competing brands (even though they could make it if they so desired). Klear floor wax provides an example of the latter with its long-used claim: "Dries clear as glass, never yellows." Note that Bravo floor wax does not yellow floors either. We shall come back to this example shortly.

It is important to point out that today's Federal Trade Commission does require substantiation of advertising claims, and may take issue with anything presented as unique. Some copywriters feel that regulation tends to stifle advertising creativity. In any case, the challenge to create effectively despite such laws is often monumental.

"Selling"

"Selling" refers to sales value. The claim—whatever it is—must be strong enough, important enough, relevant enough, believable enough to convince consumers that it is in their own best interests to try the brand in question. Consider vegetable juice again, and suppose that V-8 had been developed by a person named Vladimir Van Vaulkenburg. Unique? Certainly—but the consumer's reaction will merely be: "So what? Who cares?"

There is no *sales value* in the name Vladimir Van Vaulkenburg. Even if he represented a well-known company, it is doubtful in this day and age that consumers would buy his juice without some idea of its taste and/or nutritional value. On the other hand, Chapter 11 discussed a number of factors that do motivate consumers today, such as health, convenience, and the desire to care for loved ones; these are the kinds of appeals that copywriters in the food and beverage lines should latch onto and develop.

"Proposition"

"Proposition" is a promise. The consumer who buys a certain product with the unique feature or claim attached (selling point) will receive a specific benefit. In other words, the USP *matches a selling point with a consumer benefit, and does so in a unique way.*[9]

Now let us return to the floor-wax example. It is a fact that neither Klear nor Bravo (both made by Johnson Wax) will yellow floors. Also, both dry "as clear as glass." But *only* Klear has made that claim in that specific way. Klear's ability to dry clear (selling point) is matched with the benefit of worry-free, yellow-free floors, and the "glass" idea helps express the promise in a unique fashion. Advertisements for many years (in both magazines and television) have featured shining glass and sparkling décor along with the Klear sales message—a beauty theme for the homemaker interested in entertaining.

Conversely, advertising positioned Bravo floor wax quite differently. Research showed that working women with large families needed shiny floors that were easy to care for—floors that would not require a rewax job every time a child spilled a glass of milk (especially since Mother was tired after a long day away from home). So Bravo took durability as its selling point, ease of maintenance as its benefit theme, and the unique expression became: "So tough, you can wash it with detergent, and it comes up shining."

The point is, again, that Klear is tough, too. It withstands detergent, too. But Bravo capitalized on the claim *as a USP,* while Klear stayed with the beauty treatment. The products became positioned (thanks to advertising) in consumers' minds as floor waxes that fulfilled two different needs. One was primarily for beauty, and the other was primarily for ease of maintenance, although it was well known that Bravo gave a pretty shine and Klear was not hard to care for (secondarily). Here is an excellent example of advertising which caters to the divergent lifestyles discussed in Chapter 11. On the basis of physical composition alone, either Klear or Bravo would have been suitable for either group. Each of the two USPs, however, catered to a separate set of audience wants and needs for a specific kind of floor wax.

By now, you should begin to appreciate the complexity of this creative tool. USPs are difficult to grasp and apply, but they make or break most advertising campaigns. They are really so crucial to creative (and overall communicative) success that they should pretty well *fill* their respective advertisements. A maxim for copywriters is: "one solid USP per ad"—and if additional selling points and benefits are included, they had best be few in number and relatively minor in importance. (Otherwise, they overpower the USP.)

We may also think of the USP as the heart of the positioning effort that was discussed in the earlier section on creative strategy. Suppose the USP in an advertisement for a new Star automobile is as follows:

Superior craftsmanship with every known test for safety and durability (*selling point*) promises you many years of trouble-free driving and an impressive mpg rating (*benefit*). So "sign up the Star—for your next road show" (*unique expression*).

Clearly, this car is to be positioned as the best engineered, highest-performance car in its class.

The two ads in Figure 12.5 are part of a long-running campaign for Lawry's salt. Note that the selling point is the same in both cases (the special blend), as is the unique expression ("cook's best friend"). The benefit, however, changes ever so slightly from enhancing the flavor of beef to adding zest to fish. Notice, too, the subtle change in audience appeal revealed by the difference in hands.

Copy Defined

Only in a restricted sense does the word "copy" refer to typewritten material or spoken dialogue. Granted, copywriters are often thought of as people who write the words for advertising messages. Today, however, except for the classified columns of newspapers, few advertisements rely on words alone to deliver their sales stories. Print ads make impressions through words and pictures that support and supplement each other. Radio uses sound effects and music as well as words. Television combines the elements of both printed advertising and radio and adds motion—both actions and reactions.

A broader meaning of the word "copy" includes all the elements in an advertising message. In this sense, copy for a newspaper advertisement includes not only the reading matter—headlines, subheads, picture captions, slogans, and body copy—but also pictures, trademarks, borders, and other illustrations or visual symbols. Copy for a TV commercial includes not only the words to be spoken by the characters in the script but also sounds and music, graphic material, and movements, along with camera cues.

When we think of copy in this manner, the function of the copywriter and the techniques of writing advertising appear in proper perspective. Whether the plan for a particular advertisement starts with a visual idea that is explained or amplified by words, or with an idea expressed in words that are dramatized

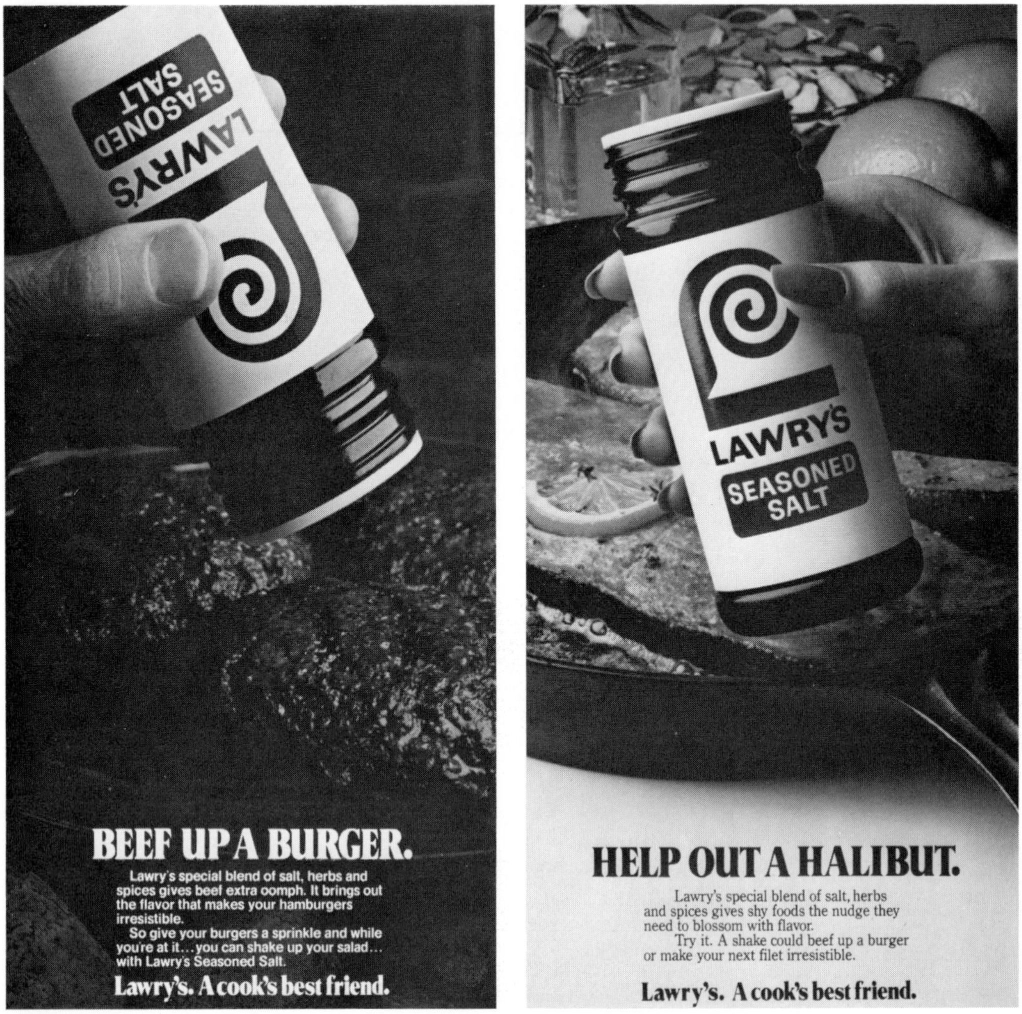

Figure 12.5 Two ads from the same campaign. The USP is basically the same in both cases, but is presented in slightly different ways so reader interest is maintained. [*Lawry's Foods, Inc.*]

and supported by illustration, the copywriter is responsible for every element that appears in the finished message.

The Copywriter as a Visualizer

In most cases, advertising messages are created by two-person teams consisting of a copywriter and an art director. But copywriters who think in terms of pictures, sounds, and movements as well as words, and who visualize advertisements in final form as they write the copy, help ensure effective results.

Visualization and Layout

The term "visualization" is an elusive one. Writers, artists, and production personnel all visualize when creating an advertisement, but visualization often is confused with layout in the print media. True visualization, however, embodies the *creation* of an idea, whereas layout involves the *arrangement* of the various elements—headlines, illustrations, trademarks, company names, and main text or body copy—to deliver the idea effectively. In suggesting the composition, or the situation for the key illustration of the ad, the artist is visualizing. In arranging this illustration with supporting illustrations and verbal elements in the form of the finished ad, the artist is making a layout—a blueprint for the printer. Visualization is a step that must precede the design step of layout, and must either precede the actual writing of the words or take place simultaneously.

Some copywriters work simultaneously with typewriter and sketch pad, writing to develop the theme and drawing "rough-roughs" or "thought sketches" to help convey ideas to the artist.

Visualization and Commercials

In visualizing for radio, the copywriter uses two methods to stimulate the listener to evoke personal images: scene-setting and word-painting. In scene-setting, familiar sounds or remarks immediately create the scene in the listener's mind. The ping of the pump-island bell and the sound of an automobile engine stopping, for example, create a filling station scene. Word-painting is a subtle and exacting art in which the writer relies on both the literal meaning and the emotional connotations of words to evoke mental images.

While radio communicates by sound alone, television is primarily a visual medium. In fact, the real test of an effective TV message is whether the video alone can deliver the story. If the full impact of this unique combination of sight, sound, and motion is to be realized, however, the creation of a television commercial calls for a greater variety of skills than does the creation of any other type of advertisement. TV copywriters must not only visualize pictures but also think in terms of movement. An understanding of both the stage and motion-picture studio and the techniques of television production is even more important than a knowledge of graphic arts processes is to the print copywriter.

Chapter 13 covers the graphic side of advertising in detail.

How Copy Communicates

Returning to the "Hierarchy of Effects" Model presented in Chapter 11, we can chart the progress of advertising copy communication through six stages:

Awareness: Gaining prospects' attention to the product and its sales message

Knowledge: Presenting the USP in a clear and interesting manner so that prospects will understand and accept it

Liking: Relating the message to prospects' own lifestyles, making it relevant and believable

Preference: Developing a desire for the specific brand advertised, promising physical or sensual, mental or intellectual, emotional or social rewards or benefits

Conviction: Persuading prospects that buying the product is in their own best interests, perhaps because it will alleviate a discomfort or fear, a state of drudgery or boredom, or a potential risk or embarrassment[10]

Purchase: Motivating prospects to act in the manner intended by the advertiser—physically, in some cases, and mentally or emotionally in others, because the "sale" is sometimes acceptance of an idea rather than a product.

Although there will probably never be any pat formula for ideal copy, these six steps constitute a handy guide for the copywriter. They provide a convenient means of orienting a message toward its prospects and of identifying the responses that it should stimulate.

Of course, not all advertisements require a detailed inclusion of all six parts. Some ads and commercials accomplish their objectives with a very simple structure because the product, the desires it satisfies, and the pattern of distribution and purchase are simple. A 10-second television spot for a soft drink, for example, may contain only the first and last parts (awareness and motivation to purchase), combined into a single sentence or slogan.

How Print Ads Communicate

At this point, the copywriter faced with creation of a newspaper or magazine advertisement can concentrate on ways of meeting the model's requirements. And usually, though not always, the most important copy element is the headline idea; for, if it fails in its function to attract prospects to the message and product, the remaining parts of the ad are wasted (rarely seen). Creative personnel who place great importance on the illustrations in printed ads may take exception to this statement, claiming that the reader's eye is more often caught by a picture than by the words above or below it. But any argument over words versus pictures as attention-getting devices in advertisements is fruitless and overlooks the correct viewpoint toward advertising copy—the broad concept that copy consists of verbal and graphic symbols working together. The headline idea is not limited to the words in large type that appear above or below the main illustration. In some effective advertisements, a dramatic or provocative photograph provides the "grabber," unaccompanied by a verbal headline. But most advertisements rely on both words and illustrations for the primary attention-getting device. (See Figure 12.6.)

Figure 12.6 In this ad, the headline and illustration work together to deliver the sales message. [*Quaker Oats Co.*]

The fact that a simple change in the wording of a headline can increase the efficiency of an advertisement by several hundred percentage points clearly illustrates the importance of the headline idea. For example, the following two headlines were compared in a split-run test in which all other elements in the two advertisements remained the same:

1 NEW JOBS ARE OFFERED IN TELEVISION STATIONS
2 TELEVISION COURSES FOR $11.50 PER WEEK

Headline (1) returned 6 times as many orders as headline (2), or 6 times the value for an identical investment in advertising space.

Headlines Perhaps the most important element of content in the headline area is **selectivity.** The headline must serve to signal or "cue" those who are dieting that a low-calorie dessert message is directed specifically to them. That example may seem obvious, but it is not so easy to understand why an ad for a product used by everyone (such as soap or toothpaste) should not strive to attract everyone's attention. As John Caples, former vice-president of Batten, Barton, Durstine & Osborn, has said: If your attention-getting device tries to appeal to everybody by simply shouting "Hey, everybody!" you may fail to attract the very people who might be interested in buying your product. Copywriters must not inflate readership or listening or viewing audiences by attracting curiosity seekers at the expense of losing customers.[11]

In certain instances, a *question* may make an effective headline: "Need a cleanser that shines without scratching?" Or perhaps: "Have you checked your energy IQ today?" At other times, an *invitation* is more on target: "Treat yourself to convenience and rich flavor."

In addition to selecting key prospects, the headline idea should make them aware of the promise Samuel Johnson described as "the soul of an advertisement." Sometimes it is in the form of a *command:* "Don't miss your chance to save!" while a simple statement of fact also has merit: "Eight essential vitamins in each crunchy serving."

Finally, "news flashes" may be just as important in advertising as they are in a purely journalistic sense:

"Introducing a delicious one-step cake and frosting mix" (which could be exactly what key prospects have been waiting for).

There are no right or wrong words, lengths, or forms for effective headlines. Copywriters must take care, however, to avoid calling attention to their ads per se, instead of to their products and real sales messages. (How many times have you described an ad or commercial to a friend—and found you had forgotten the brand advertised?) Each headline must relate clearly and specifically to the intended audience *and* to the rest of the advertisement.

Subheadlines If a headline clearly suggests a product's value to the consumer, no subheadline, or subordinate backup headline, may be needed. Sometimes, however, subheads (as well as picture captions) may help convert reader interest into product knowledge by expanding or amplifying the main headline idea. For example, the headline in an advertisement for General Foods proclaimed: "Sweet Savings!" A subheadline then explained that readers could "Make these delicious desserts and save up to $2.00."

Subheads form a kind of transitional bridge between the headline and body copy and may be valuable when the headline does not contain any sales message but merely a *teaser* line: "Don't read this ad. . . ." In this case, the subhead might be: "unless you'd enjoy having younger-looking skin." At other times, a subheadline may provide an answer to the question posed in the main headline. Chevrolet recently ran an ad whose headline queried: "Need a family wagon and don't know which way to go?" The subhead countered with: "You could go the mid-size way. Chevy Malibu."

Finally, subheads may break up long blocks of body copy and thus ease the reading task. An ad from General Motors Parts Division, telling "why it's good to know Mr. Goodwrench," featured 160 words of copy. Three separate copy blocks divided the copy into groups of 76, 37, and 47 words respectively, and each one began with a bold-type subheadline:

1 He puts his name on the line.
2 Mr. Goodwrench has GM parts.
3 He's trained by GM to understand GM cars.

Body Copy In stimulating liking and preference for a given product, body copy must *develop* the benefit-promise, *explain* product features and values, and *support* claims logically and convincingly. Most effective advertisements use a combination of two basic types of writing: the *emotional* reason why and the *rational* reason why. The first is mainly subjective and the second mainly objective, but both must provide compelling reasons why the consumer should spend hard-earned dollars for the advertised product (brand). For example, this copy from an ad for Lord Calvert Canadian Whisky is mainly emotional:

> Right from the start, its Canadian spirit stands out from the others. What puts it in a class by itself? Super lightness. Superb taste. If that's your goal, step up to Lord Calvert Canadian.

The copy from an ad for Bulova Accuquartz Watches, however, is mainly rational:

> These watches are as accurate as miniature computerized quartz crystal movements can make them. They are as dependable as *we* are (and *we've* stood the test of time for 100 years now). They can be seen in a variety of styles, from $150 to $2500, at fine jewelry and department stores.

Proof of claims, to enhance conviction, may come from (1) descriptions of how a product works or is made, (2) test results, (3) performance case histories, (4) testimonials or quotations from experts, and (5) sales records and guarantees. Or the proof may take the form of sensory appeals and challenges to the reader to "see for yourself" or "try it for a week and feel the difference."[12]

The extent to which rational or emotional appeals should be used varies with the type of product and the buying motives of prospects. More stress is usually placed on emotional appeals in consumer advertising than in industrial, trade, and professional advertising. Copy for convenience items makes greater use of emotional appeals than copy for durable goods, such as lawn mowers, refrigerators, or water heaters. But emotional appeals need to be handled with care; if overdone, they destroy the credibility of the entire message.

The Closing Idea All efforts to establish product awareness, knowledge, liking, preference, and conviction are designed for the sole purpose of persuading readers to act. If they accept an idea, change an attitude, agree with a proposition, visit a store, ask for a brand name, or react in any of a host of other ways, they have taken a big step toward ultimate purchase of the product advertised.

Because an advertisement, unlike a personal sales call, is one-way communication, its closing efforts must supply all information, directions, and motivation necessary for the buyer to take action. In addition, it must make that action appear as easy as possible, and present a final stimulus as well. Interest in the product may be keen and the desire for attainment of benefits intense, but if the ultimate action required is too difficult a process, the consumer will rarely make the effort.

Generally, there are two types of "calls to action" in advertising copy. The first asks potential customers to "buy now," "do it today," or "come in this weekend," and is known as **hard-sell** (or direct-action) advertising. Unfortunately, because so many direct-action advertisements feature a fast talker or supersalesperson, the term "hard sell" is often erroneously associated with anything loud or pushy.

The second call to action is known as *soft sell* (or indirect action), and asks readers to "remember a name," "ask your family," or "plan to visit" sometime in the future. Often, this form of ad closing is judged preferable by consumers asked to choose between the two. Just as often, though, people like (and identify with) the advertisements that speak to their own needs and predispositions, regardless of the directed nature of the call to action.

In any case, examples of ways to ease readers into action include (1) providing a coupon (to reduce cost); (2) emphasizing convenient accessibility (available at a nearby location—address or directions supplied); (3) urging immediate compliance (to take advantage of limited quantities or short-lived sales); (4) offering early-bird shopper specials; (5) noting easy buying terms (possibly even mail and phone orders with clear addresses and telephone numbers included); and (6) reminding readers of special reasons for buying (birthdays, anniversaries, graduations, and the like).

In some cases, ads seem to end with "no sell." That is, no specific command is given to the audience. Usually, however, the desired action is at least implied. Consider, for example, the E. F. Hutton & Company campaign, featuring TV commercials with the memorable closing line: "When E. F. Hutton talks, people listen." The suggestion is, of course, that *because* this company is worth listening to, viewers should make E. F. Hutton their stockbroker.

Similarly, for many years the final line of Zenith appliance advertisements has been: "Where the quality goes in before the name goes on." The clearly intended meaning, however, is: *Remember* Zenith quality when you are ready to buy that special gift.

How Broadcast Commercials Communicate

Commercial messages on radio—combinations of voices, words, music, and sound effects—can develop "mind pictures" bounded only by the extent of listeners' imaginations. Radio gives the copywriter complete freedom of time and place, and unlimited forms and amounts of physical activity. Television combines sight, sound, and motion to approximate face-to-face selling better than any other medium. The TV advertiser can, in effect, come into a viewer's home, chat with the viewer personally, display products actively over a musical background, and stimulate sales by demonstrating ease of purchase.

On the other hand, both radio and television, as entertainment media, present advertising copywriters with the challenge of keeping the urge to entertain under control. It must always be secondary to the application of sound selling principles and to the development of a solid USP.

In broadcast, unlike print, the copywriter controls the direction of attention. There is no page to scan, no chance to reread selected lines or to spend extra time studying a given caption or illustration. Once the listener or viewer has chosen to "tune in" or "become aware," the copywriter can focus attention exactly where the advertiser wants it. A problem here, however, is that *listening* and *watching* usually require less effort than reading. So we tend to get careless in our listening and viewing habits—to take them for granted. We hear with only half an ear and watch without really seeing or comprehending. Our attention to these media is often divided (while we are busy working or cleaning, cooking or eating, even talking, writing, or paging through a magazine or newspaper).

Awareness Broadcast copywriters, therefore, have to work *extra* hard to gain attention. Unexpected words or actions sometimes prove effective stoppers: "When was the last time you *dyed* . . . with bright, color-fast results in clothing or bedspreads?" Or picture an animated soda-pop can that "flips its lid" and begins a furious fizzing action as its contents fill a frosty glass. The copy warns: "*Watch out!* for the new, sparkly soda pop that keeps on fizzing."

Some broadcast writers argue for an establishing shot or sound at the beginning of a commercial—a scene-setter that orients viewers or listeners to the environment of the forthcoming message. Indeed, if attention can be snagged in the first few seconds with material that sets the stage for USP development, there is no need to jump immediately into the sales pitch.

Another school of thought, however, maintains that the USP may begin effectively in the opening moments—in a suspenseful atmosphere, for instance, which motivates the audience to stay with it. Again, no one rule applies in every case, and a careful analysis of the product and sales message, audience, competition, and available media resources must precede creative decisions. Gaining awareness is as vital in one medium as another, for once the audience gets up to visit the refrigerator or decides to switch channels, it rarely comes back.

Knowledge and Liking Simple commercials generally hold interest best. Long lists of items or sets of figures bore radio audiences, and TV scenes whose actions do not exactly parallel copy lines prove confusing. (Research has shown that maximum recall is obtained when audio and visual elements say and show the same thing at the same time).[13]

Repetition of both product name and USP is essential in commercials since messages are perishable (*and* very short). Studies have also shown that repetition *with variation* enhances both retention and interest.[14] Thus, copywriters need to concentrate on saying and showing the same thing in different ways not only at different times within a message, but also in different messages, so that audiences do not become bored by redundancy.

Developing Preference and Conviction As is true in print, both rational and emotional reasons are used in commercials to prove that claims are true, valuable, and relevant to selected audiences. Radio commercials assume any of the following six basic formats in developing the desire for a particular product or service:[15]

The Straight Sell: This is a clear, simple presentation of product benefits with emphasis on product differentiation. Usually it is spoken by a single announcer.

The Educational Appeal: More rational than emotional, this format is frequently used for corporate or institutional messages. These commercials sometimes utilize an exchange between an informed person and someone unaware of a product or company.

The Testimonial: Credibility is important here. The endorser may be a celebrity or an unknown person with whom the viewer can easily identify. A case history normally unfolds.

The Humorous Approach: Humor is entertainment, and it holds audiences. It is also both elusive and fragile, however. A humorous commercial contains comic material that helps position and sell a product. It must be delivered by someone who knows how to be funny.

The Musical Spot: This format may include instrumental background music with a spoken message, or it may be a singing commercial.

The Dramatization: A narrative technique is particularly effective in presenting a problem that can be solved by the product. An example might be a type of "stain-in, detergent-applied, stain-out" sequence.

These six formats also might be applied to television, but the visual, rather than the aural, character of TV requires different, though somewhat overlapping, classifications. The straight sell, dramatization, and testimonial formats are visual interpretations of the same arrangements in radio. A "personality" format emphasizes the fame and following of a star who presents the product message in a well-known visual and verbal style.

Two additional formats unique to television are the song-and-dance commercial and the demonstration technique. Song-and-dance productions are really visual presentations of radio's musical format, requiring peak professional performances in both visual and aural areas; they are usually feasible only for advertisers with large budgets.

Creative advertising professionals agree that the demonstration format is the one that best utilizes TV's unusual potential. But Charles Wainwright also stresses the importance of *simplicity* with this warning:

> Commercials can be so loaded with frills that the message becomes buried under the glitter and glamour of a tiny motion picture epic. A true selling commercial requires the writer to have a logical, disciplined, orderly mind. He must think first of the problem and eventually determine the solution.[16]

Demonstration can, of course, be combined with dramatization, testimonial, personality, and even song-and-dance formats. If the product lends itself to demonstration, failure to make use of such an opportunity is difficult to justify.

Purchase Both hard-sell and soft-sell calls to action are used in commercials, although radio tends to feature hard sell more often than television does. The reason is usually that radio is more locally oriented and commercials are more apt to stress hurry-up sales, limited offers, and other time considerations.

Copywriters should avoid using lengthy addresses and telephone numbers on radio and, to some extent, on TV. Although the visual channel is helpful in this regard, messages are so short that it is questionable whether viewers really have time to take notes. Some possible alternatives to giving actual numbers might be: "Check yellow pages for the store nearest you"; "Located on the corner of Elm and Main Street"; or "Across from the Varsity Theater."

Building Blocks of Style

Advertising copy style is different from editorial writing or formal English composition style. Learning to write effective advertising requires more than an understanding of the techniques involved. It demands practice and constructive criticism, just as learning to play the violin or piano does. Writing advertising is a difficult art. Aldous Huxley said it calls for more skill than any other form of creative writing.

A well-written ad, however, like a fine wine, can even improve with age. McGraw-Hill's Laboratory of Advertising Research has shown increased levels of readership through as many as 41 insertions of the same advertisement (over a period of years).

Although this chapter cannot teach anyone how to write, a brief discussion of style in advertising copy will help ensure a practical understanding of the copywriting business. It should also be useful to persons who do not plan careers in advertising but whose positions may require appraisals of creative advertising efforts.

Emphasis

Many a copywriter has said it, but the advice is all too frequently ignored: To emphasize everything is to emphasize nothing. If a message incorporates multiple USPs, it tends to become a kind of fact sheet; a run-on list of features and claims is easily misconstrued and quickly forgotten. Credibility suffers in such cases, too, since the advertised item seems to promise everything. This approach is bound to make consumers wary.

On the other hand, consider an extreme example in word emphasis. The simple headline, "I didn't buy that tennis outfit," might precede a message for any of *six* different advertisers: an automated buying service, a department store, a bank, a clothing boutique, a sporting goods store, and a tennis shop. It all depends on which word is emphasized:

(*a*) "*I* didn't buy that tennis outfit." (An automated buying service bought it for me.)
(*b*) "I *didn't* buy that tennis outfit." (Fortunately, however, the department store's sale has been extended.)
(*c*) "I didn't *buy* that tennis outfit." (I got it free for opening a new account at my bank.)
(*d*) "I didn't buy *that* tennis outfit." (But my favorite clothing boutique always has a large variety to choose from.)
(*e*) "I didn't buy that *tennis* outfit." (But this sporting goods store sells terrific jogging suits, too.)
(*f*) "I didn't buy that tennis *outfit*." (But the tennis shop gave me a great deal on a new racquet.)

Specificity

When advertising recall and value are tested, facts are almost always remembered better than generalizations. Copywriter Aesop Glim called vague, overused terms in advertising copy "weasel words." These are undependable words, he claimed, because they describe anything or nothing. They cannot differentiate products, services, or stores from one another because no one has a clear mind's-eye picture for them. Thus, consumers do not associate them with specific advertisers. Wise copywriters strive to avoid them (although, admittedly, doing so is not always possible or necessary).

We have added a few of our own choices to Glim's list below, and perhaps you have some favorites, too:[17]

best	high standards
better	highest quality
dependable job	ideal
extra special	perfect
for every need	real bargain
good	superb job
great	superior performance
greater	top-notch
greatest	top quality
guaranteed satisfaction	variety of uses

Now, see if you can improve on these words by incorporating a *specific* meaning for each one in a potential advertising claim. For example, instead of saying the relish "tastes good," say it has a "tangy, invigorating taste . . . one that leaves bland relishes sitting in their jars."

Or, instead of a "casserole topping of highest quality," try: "The thick, creamy texture promises you a rich cheese flavor throughout."

Truth and Believability

Despite careful adherence to disciplined creativity, occasionally a copywriter's claims for a household cleaning agent may appear to be mere product puffery. Homemakers need try the product only once, however, before discovering the ad's exaggeration, and ensuing copy for the same item—though highly creative in nature—falls by the wayside as far as potential customers are concerned. On the other hand, advertising that is accurate to the last detail is of little value if it is not believable. Even if a medication is someday discovered for instant cure of the common cold, advertising creative strategy will have to follow some very clearly laid persuasive tracks; otherwise, consumers' deep-rooted skepticism regarding cold remedies may prevent acceptance of the advertising message.

We should be aware, however, that *literal* truth or falsity is not much of an issue in advertising today; the rise of consumerism and resulting government regulations have pretty well taken care of that problem. What we are concerned with is truth *as perceived by the consumer* (often called believability). Without it, advertisements have no chance for successful communication. William Blake's famous warning still holds: "A truth that's told with bad intent, beats all the lies you can invent!"

A special tip to broadcasters is to be wary of putting too much of a sales message in the mouths of characters engaged in dialogue. Somehow, it all seems to come out sounding artificial unless handled by *very* experienced writers and acting talent. Believability is often best served by letting an announcer or TV commercial presenter handle the technical aspects of the sales story.

Readability

More than 65 years ago, Arthur Quiller-Couch lectured his students at Cambridge on the importance of making their writing readable:

> All reading demands an effort. The energy, the goodwill which a reader brings to a book is, and must be, partly expended in the labor of reading. . . . The more difficulties, then, we authors obtrude on him by obscure or careless writing, the more we blunt the edge of his attention.[18]

People buy books to read what the authors have written. But people do not buy advertisements at all, much less buy them to read what some copywriter has written. Easy reading is of greater importance in advertising than in business reports, news articles, editorials, or literature. With the tremendous increase in mass communications media, the competition for the reader's attention is many times as great as it was when Quiller-Couch stressed the importance of writing that is easy to read.

We can extend "readability" to include "listenability" and "viewability," too. A conglomeration of voices, sound effects, and musical fanfare can make a radio commercial impossible to comprehend; and televised scenes that are too "busy" block understanding and lose viewers. Readable ads and viewable commercials speak to consumers on their own levels and in their own terms. They make liberal use of the "you" attitude—because people like to be addressed in the second person (you, your(s), and you're).

John O'Toole, president of Foote, Cone & Belding, put it very well when he said:

> Advertising isn't about products, it's about a person's life and how a product can fit into that life to make it better. This is advertising designed to get into someone's heart, not under his skin.[19]

Readable copy is also enthusiastic copy. The late Leo Burnett, chairman of the board of his own agency, once noted that there are no dull subjects, only dull writers. Headache remedy and cold-relief messages may seem tedious or boring to some recipients, but if they tell a specific, credible, welcome sales story to those who need the product advertised, they are as successful as we could ask them to be.

Simplicity and Human Interest

Reduced to its essence, the readability of copy depends on simplicity and human interest. The extent of each varies according to the audience and product involved, but any writing is more readable when it uses familiar, personal words and short, uncomplicated sentences.

Contemporary readability experts like Flesch and Gunning emphasize the importance of simple, colloquial language, but so did Thomas Wilson, in 1560, in his *Arte of Rhetoricke,* and the Apostle Paul, in biblical times. Paul said:

> Except ye utter by the tongue words easy to understand, how shall it be known what is spoken? For ye shall speak into the air.[20]

Ideally, copy should contain no words that stop the reader's flow of thought. The word "obtrude" in the earlier quotation from Quiller-Couch is an example. Perhaps "obtrude" was a familiar word to students of literature at Cambridge in 1916, but it is hardly a word to use in a message to American business executives, homemakers, or students in the 1980s. Granted, unfamiliar or complex words are sometimes necessary, because they describe a new ingredient, a new process, or a new design. But if they are readily explained in simple terms, they need not hinder the communication process. If, for instance, the word "obtrude" *had* to appear in an advertisement, a skilled copywriter would say something like: "The more responsibilities your job obtrudes, or forces, on you, the more you need . . . ."

The use of familiar words is particularly important in connection with technical terms which may be everyday language to a product manufacturer, but which would make reading difficult for the public. Most major kitchen appliances have vitreous finishes. But ask your friends what "vitreous" means, and you'll see why advertising copy will be more effective if it describes the finish as having a "surface hard as glass." The latter is not only easier to read, but also clearer, more graphic, and more persuasive.

In short, good style in advertising copy relies on concrete words that correspond to the experiences of the audiences it wants to interest and motivate to act. Sometimes humor is appropriate, but only if it relates directly to a product message. The appeal selected must enhance the selling story and brand image created and stimulate favorable audience recall of both.

According to H. Gordon Lewis, however, we are now living in an age of skepticism, and clever salespeople are successful only if they make the buyer feel clever.[21] That's not an easy assignment to fulfill, but once in a while an advertiser can use a frivolous approach successfully. (See Figure 12.7.)

Clichés and Superlatives

In a critical study of advertising messages published in 1952, William H. Whyte, Jr., pointed out that the effectiveness of much advertising copy is greatly reduced by the use of clichés and superlatives because they block communication in much the same way that abstract and general terms do.[22] We have al-

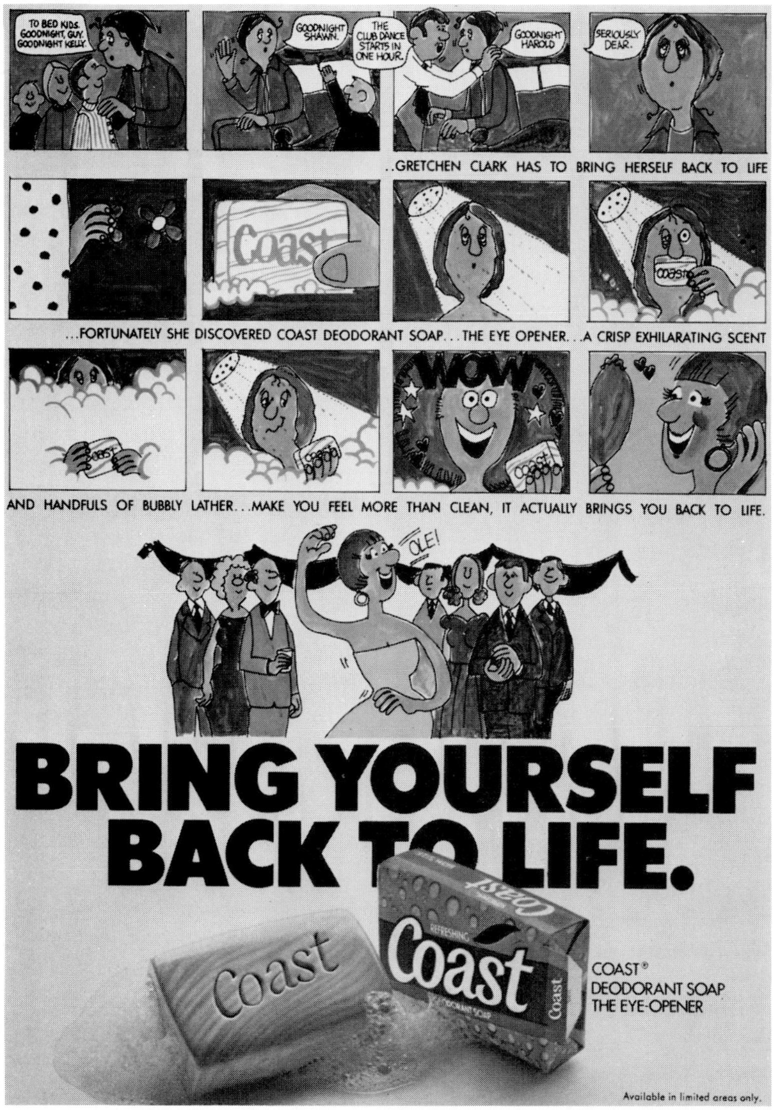

Figure 12.7 Sometimes, a light, humorous approach conveys an advertiser's message most effectively. Here, Coast makes its point simply and memorably. [*The Procter & Gamble Company.*]

ready discussed the problem of "weasel words" (also called stock expressions), but we didn't note that the use of superlatives ("world's strongest") and comparatives ("cleans whiter and brighter") may result in Federal Trade Commission rulings of "false and misleading."

At any rate, these claims are probably unbelievable, as is the case with clichés: quick as a wink, sharp as a tack, hard as a rock. In addition, these expressions may sound so dated and boring in an advertisement that they convey those same impressions of their products. (See Figure 12.8.)

In 1969, the Grey advertising agency published this comment on clichés and superlatives:

. . . people today are wary of advertising which assumes the consumer is gullible. Shopworn gimmicks are rapidly losing their power to persuade. . . . A growing number of consumers in our affluent society have more realistic, mature attitudes about the role of material things in life. . . . Thus, effective advertising reflects a new, more modest attitude about products and portrays with greater candor the role they play in people's lives. The superlatives once

Lord & Thomas Creeds

No. 1. Exaggeration

Men whose opinions are effective are men of moderation.

Instinct discounts superlatives. And the discount often goes too far—to the article's injustice.

Adjectives callous credulity.

Blatancy does not command respect.

Over-statement, in reaction, creates commensurate resistance.

Some things may be the best of their kind in the world. But it is pretty hard for finite minds to know it. And harder still for cynical minds to believe it.

Modesty, by its very rarity, commands attention. And by its fascination wins.

Too much effort makes men think that your selling task is hard.

Remember how the expression "Morgan & Wright Tires are Good Tires" stood out amidst the bombast of its time.

What advertising phrase was ever more effective than the simple words "It Floats"?

Figure 12.8 Advertising professionals have long recognized the danger of using superlatives in advertising copy. This is one of a series of ads published more than 70 years ago by Lord & Thomas, predecessor to the Foote, Cone & Belding advertising agency.

thought essential to the lexicon of salesmanship are being replaced in good advertising copy by a more colloquial tone of voice even to the point of engaging in understatement.[23]

But it is easy to overgeneralize. A cliché becomes a cliché to begin with because it is a useful tool with which to communicate. However, not all stock expressions are clichés. Some retain interest and emotional appeal long after their novelty has worn off. The purchases men and women make every day illustrate perhaps better than readership studies the interest people have in things that are new, easy, economical, reliable, or safe. Sometimes, too, the cliché can't be avoided any more than the abstraction can. Attempts to replace it with fresher words may end in confusion or awkward wordiness. A clear stereotype is better than an obscure image, no matter how fresh the wording of the latter.

Still, copywriters must beware the tendency to beat a clever expression to death. A decade ago, "write on" was deemed a superb pen-company application of the currently popular slogan "Right on!" But it has pretty well outlived its usefulness by now, since "right on" is rarely used as a colloquial expression today. The same may be said of the play on words "sell-a-bration." On the other hand, the Bell Telephone System found a very appropriate way to tie a selling theme into a campaign promoting low-cost weekend calling. Advertising headlines proclaimed: "The U.S.A. is on sale—all day Saturday and Sunday."

The Importance of Connotation

As an interpreter, the advertising copywriter must be aware of both the denotation, or literal meaning, and the connotation, or indirect implication, of words. A word can produce a positive or negative response quite apart from its literal meaning, and different people may associate different meanings with the same word. "Substitute" is an example of a word with a negative connotation to most people. Literally, this noun describes a person or thing acting or being used in place of another. But the idea that it has been used to express most often—the "substitute quarterback" and "avoid substitutes"—has given the word a connotation of inferiority or cheapness. To the college professor, a *theory* is a systematic statement of principles; to the lay person, it is a guess or an impractical idea.

Every Word Should Work

Good advertising writing is tight writing. It contains no stuffing, no padding, no empty words or phrases. It does not say "in terms of the maintenance of the plant, BXB is able to save . . . ." It says "in plant maintenance BXB saves . . . ." In *The Elements of Style,* William Strunk and E. B. White maintain that:

Vigorous writing is concise. A sentence should contain no unnecessary words, a paragraph no unnecessary sentences, for the same reason a drawing should contain no unnecessary lines and a machine no unnecessary parts. This requires not that the writer should make all his sentences short, or that he should avoid all detail and treat his subjects only in outline, but that he make every word tell.[24]

Note that conciseness should not be confused with brevity. Although increased competition for a prospect's attention emphasizes the need for greater use of graphic symbols as well as tightly written copy, people *do* read long copy. Length is a matter of structure rather than style, assuming the writer knows how to use words effectively. Three important factors are involved here. First is the character of the unique selling proposition—the simplicity or complexity of the message itself. Second is the objective of the advertisement. Third is the consumer interest inherent in the product.

Short copy is more likely to be effective when a brand of product or service has low inherent interest and little differentiation, and when the advertiser is primarily seeking favorable brand awareness. Package goods like facial tissues, snacks, and soft drinks are examples, as is the Eastern Airlines' delivery service advertised in Figure 12.9. When the product or service is one that will be bought thoughtfully or cautiously, long copy is often necessary to build confidence, present believable advantages, and persuade prospects to buy.

Special Creative Problems

Before leaving the topic of creativity, we must consider a few special copywriting problems at the local level. Recall that, in Chapter 4, the objectives of retail advertising were explained, and true retail advertising was distinguished from local advertising. Now we need to examine the creative problems of both.

Retail versus Local Advertising

The true retail advertisement for a department store, a specialty shop, or a supermarket is part of a continuing series that presents a parade of different products. Retail ads in newspapers enjoy a degree of directed readership not unlike the yellow pages of the telephone directory. People shop the advertisements of department stores and food chains to see

WHY SETTLE FOR NEXT-DAY SERVICE?
EASTERN
Sprint
SAME-DAY PACKAGE SERVICE
SAME-DAY PACKAGE SERVICE IS OUR BAG.
Your urgent small package gets there *today* with Sprint—Eastern's same-day package service.
Get your package to our airport passenger counter and we'll put it on the next flight out. So it arrives that very same day. Guaranteed. (Unless the specific flight is scheduled to arrive after midnight.) We have same-day Sprint service to more than 90 cities nationwide on over 1,500 daily flights.
Eastern can also Sprint your small packages to Canada, Mexico and other international destinations. For rates and flight information, call Eastern. For pickup and delivery in the U.S., call 800-336-0336, toll-free.
EASTERN

Figure 12.9 An example of an ad in which short copy tells the sales story most effectively. [*Eastern Airlines.*]

what new merchandise is offered and what bargains they can find. On the other hand, a national advertisement has no such preconditioned audience to search it out; it must create its own attention.

When local advertising is not this kind of continuing series, its creative problems are closer to those of national than those of retail advertising. Fuel dealers, hotels and motels, restaurants, insurance agents, firms handling building supplies or office equipment, and banks are examples of local advertisers who do not have a ready-made audience with advance interest in what their advertisements will say. Generally, people do not shop bank ads, since most banks offer essentially the same services at the same rates. So, each ad must reach out and stop the reader, listener, or viewer by promising to tell an interesting story. (NOTE: Some bank ads today feature special incentives, such as gifts for opening new accounts, so that people *will* begin to shop and compare.)

The retail advertiser can count on a logotype, new merchandise, or a price appeal to bring intended readers into an ad and, thus, into the store. A mere photograph or drawing of the product, which is often a weak method of visualization for the national advertiser, is one of the more effective forms for retail advertising and may play a major communicative role.

Some stores, especially large department stores, create much of their own advertising art. Others rely mainly on material furnished by manufacturers or on monthly books of seasonally timed illustrations that are provided to advertisers and newspapers by organizations ("mat services"). Both these latter sources can save the advertiser time and money, but the material rarely carries any exclusive right of use. It is unlikely, therefore, to be as relevant or as distinctive as artwork created for a specific advertising message or a particular store personality.

Essentials of Retail Copy Since retail copy is basically information about what a store has for sale, the message should be simple, direct, and specific. Advertisements should describe products, give prices, and tell readers where and how to buy. The buying directions should include not only the store name and address, but also the location of the department in which each item can be found—such as the "Young Modern's Shop, Fourth Floor." If the store has more than one location, the advertisement should indicate at which ones the merchandise is available. If mail or phone orders will be accepted, the advertisement should say so, and give mail-order addresses or coupons and phone numbers to call.

There is no excuse, however, for dull, trite retail advertisements. Every ad tells two important stories: the story of the merchandise and the story of the store. Even the most direct-selling retail copy will, intentionally or not, reflect the store's personality and should be as personal, friendly, and helpful as the institution itself strives to be. Research has shown that shoppers become rather expert in evaluating the character of department stores from the physical appearance of their advertising, even in the case of an unfamiliar store in a strange city.

Conveying Store Image Clearly, then, retail advertising should strive, by choice of words, illustrations, and layout designs, to establish a distinctive style that identifies the store and reinforces its image in the minds of customers. Advertisements jam-packed with items are symbolic of bargain basements that attract all kinds of people with inexpensive merchandise. As the appeal shifts from price to prestige, and to people with higher levels of taste and income, layouts have increased white space and present a more orderly and more sophisticated appearance.

The headline and text treatment of retail advertising should expand on the impression created by the overall design. Body copy, however, need not necessarily supply all the information that prospects need to arrive at buying decisions. In its simplest concept, retail advertising says, "Buy this item at my store." But the primary objective of retail advertising, whether direct selling or institutional, is to build store traffic, to get customers into the store to buy what is advertised along with other merchandise.

Retail USPs With the above thoughts in mind, we can examine a few retail USPs. They share the same three features that national product ads have, but are naturally a little different in content. For example:

1 If you buy now, we'll install your new [brand name] air conditioner free. Don't miss *a cool deal on a hot item.*
2 See, smell, and taste before you buy. Let this special in-store demonstration convince you the proof *is* in the [brand name] pudding.
3 Join the fun—and see if you've won! The [store name] tent sale (or after-inventory clearance) features a carnival of entertainment and chances to win valuable merchandise by matching your family's birthdates with our list of winning numbers.

Profile

Rosser Reeves

Rosser Reeves, one of advertising's great copywriters, once said, "Any profession—if you're going to be good at it—will swallow up your life; advertising swallowed up my life completely." Born in 1910 in Danville, Virginia, Reeves graduated from the University of Virginia and first worked for the *Richmond Times-Union.*

After graduation in 1930, Rosser became the advertising manager of the Morris Plan Bank, where he stayed for three years before moving on to New York to begin his advertising agency career. He joined Ted Bates and Company in 1938 and rose from copy chief to partner, then to vice chairman, and finally to chairman in 1955, a position he held until his resignation in 1966.

Reeves is one of the founders of the "hard sell" school of television advertising. Using his "Unique Selling Proposition" formula, the Bates agency mounted such famous campaigns as Anacin's "Fast, Fast, Fast Relief," M&M Candy's "They Melt in Your Mouth, Not in Your Hand," and Bic Pen's "It writes the first time, every time." His advertising philosophy is contained in a best-selling book, *Reality in Advertising,* which was published in 1961. The book still stands as a sound description of the "product approach" to advertising copywriting.

Reeves sat outside the practice of advertising for a decade because of a no-competition clause in the contract selling his interest in Ted Bates and Company. Returning in 1977 to form his own agency, he was described as the "man who returned." However, in 1980, after publishing a novel, he retired once again to write fiction and manage his investments, as he had done during his ten-year sabbatical from advertising. He remains, nevertheless, famous in the advertising industry as a person who did much to help the business make the transition from print media to television.

Fashion Advertising

The word "fashion," like the word "propaganda," has negative as well as positive connotations. It is still associated with concepts of "conspicuous consumption" developed by Thorstein Veblen more than 75 years ago. Although fashions are both transitory and emotional, they provide a foundation from which customs emerge. Later students of society, like Max Lerner, have noted that fashions are an index, and sometimes an instigator, of social change.

Most fashion advertising is definitely feminine. Despite the success in the apparel field of such male couturiers as Bill Blass, Christian Dior, and Yves Saint Laurent, many retailers still believe it takes a woman to buy, sell, or advertise fashion merchandise. There are probably no more male fashion copywriters than there are female sportswriters.

The broad objective of fashion advertising is the same as that of any other retail advertising: to create store traffic. But there are two quite different types of fashion advertising: the high-style or high-fashion advertising most often seen in magazines like *Vogue* and *The New Yorker,* and the volume-fashion advertising of department stores and apparel shops. High-fashion advertising aims at people who feel they are making or establishing style, and the primary appeal is prestige. Volume-fashion advertising reaches people who want assurance that they are good judges of fashion, and who wish to be in style rather than ahead of it. In a way, high-fashion copy stimulates primary demand, as for "the slim, shaped-line suit," while volume-fashion copy stimulates selective demand for a specific suit at a specific store. Mention of price and details of color, fabric, and workmanship are definitely secondary in high-fashion copy, and may even be omitted completely. Volume-fashion copy should include this information and answer questions that may be in the prospect's mind, such as those dealing with washability or durability. Both types of fashion copy should have a light, cheerful tone, rely heavily on illustration to convey mood as well as design, and carefully avoid overworked adjectives and words or phrases prospects might consider passé. Fashion must be fresh and new to be fashion.

Local Copy Calls for Local Flavor

Even retail copy outside the fashion classification can be written in a sprightly manner that will add much to the stimulation of interest and desire. Close relationships between stores and customers make it easier to inject a personal tone into retail than into national copy. Copywriters who live in the same community as their readers should understand the local point of view and write with a local flavor for either true retail or local advertisements.

A proprietor who is well known and respected in the trading area, for example, might personally sign an occasional advertisement to reassure prospective customers that the boss (owner, manager, or designer) will stand behind each sale made. At times, this approach proves an excellent way to communicate knowledge and expertise.[25]

In another area, Robert L. Emerson, author of *Fast Food: The Endless Shakeout,* reported results of a recent survey of fast-food customer complaints. The following problems were listed (in descending order of frequency):

Too crowded at mealtimes

Too much ice in soft drinks

Condiments not given unless requested

Hamburgers too thin

Take-out packaging doesn't keep food warm

Advertising oriented too heavily toward children

Tables too small for large groups

It is probable, however, that the order of importance of these complaints might differ from community to community and even according to the time of day and day of the week. An "on-the-way-to-work breakfast" advertisement or commercial, therefore, might well focus on different issues than would a message for a "tired shopper's lunch," a student's "after-class pick-me-up," or a couple's "after-movie snack."

We have discussed special creative problems in retail and local advertising for the newspaper medium. In fact, newspapers do receive the major portion of local or retail advertising budgets. More than half the nation's food chains, however, use local radio to deliver repeated messages to consumers at low cost, and retailers of all types are increasing their use of both radio and television, while outdoor, direct mail, and transit media are also used successfully.

Summary

Advertising creativity is disciplined creativity, channeled in such a way that the advertiser's communication objectives are achieved through mass media messages. Copywriters work with ideas, which come from carefully gathered and analyzed facts about products and prospects.

The starting point for every ad and commercial is a *strategy statement,* which includes discussion of a proposed message's objective, target audience, creative promise and backup, and overall style.

Copywriters must participate in a wide variety of real-life experiences, and study products, services, stores, and prospective customers and media audiences very carefully in order to develop effective selling messages. Categories of information sought include background data on a company, in-use details of products, result-of-use material, and incidental information—all in terms of consumers' wants, needs, and lifestyles.

One of the copywriter's most difficult but important tasks is the development of a unique selling proposition—the unique matching of selling point and customer benefit. Only after that task is accomplished can real ad development take place, since the USP lies at the very heart of product positioning (strategy).

The term "copy" includes all the elements in an advertising message, and the copywriter's job includes writing words *and* visualizing pictures, sound effects, and music for radio and televised action. Successful ads and commercials are often built around the "Hierarchy of Effects" model, but may be presented in a variety of formats.

Effective copy *style* calls for both literal truth and believability in advertisements, and for words and graphics that are "readable" in print and easily understood in radio and TV. Specifically, simplicity, along with human interest, is an important requirement in all media, but clichés and exaggerations tend to block effective communication. An appreciation for the connotation of words is also valuable, since different audiences may perceive different meanings from the same message.

Special creative problems are found in retail and local advertising as well as advertising in the fashion area. The concepts of store image and the nonproduct USP deserve additional emphasis in a copywriter's program of study.

Questions for Discussion

1. Disciplined creativity lies behind all successful advertisements. What does that term mean to the copywriter? What disciplines other than those mentioned in this chapter appear important to you?
2. Name the five major components of an advertising strategy statement. Then, select an ad and discuss the information which you believe preceded its creation in terms of its creative strategy.
3. Explain how ideas are formed and what kinds of factual materials are most helpful, calling on your own experiences for reference.
4. Consider a recent purchase you have made. Who and what led you to make that purchase? Name as many different people and stimuli as you can remember.
5. Find an ad in a popular magazine. First, identify its USP, and then explain how the "Hierarchy of Effects" model was applied to copy and layout.
6. Name several ways radio and TV commercials gain attention and call for action. Which ways do you think are the most effective? Why?
7. Describe the elements that make up a sound piece of selling copy. Do they differ between print and broadcast media? Why or why not?
8. Why do you think believability is often hard to achieve in advertisements?
9. Give an example illustrating how different connotations for the same word might lead to legal difficulties in advertising.
10. Differentiate clearly between local and retail advertising. Then explain how local and retail USPs differ from brand-name product USPs.

For Further Reference

Aiki, Judy Y.: *Retail Advertising Copy: The How, the What, the Why,* National Retail Merchants Association, New York, 1977.

Burton, Philip Ward: *Advertising Copywriting,* 4th ed., Grid Publishing, Inc., Columbus, Ohio, 1978.

Hafer, W. Keith, and Gordon E. White: *Advertising Writing,* West Publishing Company, New York, 1977.

Hilliard, Robert L.: *Writing for Television and Radio,* 3d ed., Hastings House, Publishers, Inc., New York, 1976.

Hopkins, Claude: *Scientific Advertising,* Chelsea House Publishers, New York, 1980.

Lewis, H. Gordon: *How to Make Your Advertising Twice as Effective at Half the Cost,* Nelson-Hall, Chicago, 1979.

Malickson, David L., and John W. Nason: *Advertising—How to Write the Kind That Works,* Charles Scribner's Sons, New York, 1977.

Orlik, Peter B.: *Broadcast Copywriting,* Holbrook Press, Boston, 1978.

Peck, William A.: *Anatomy of Local Radio-TV Copy,* 4th ed., Tab Books, Blue Ridge Summit, Pa., 1976.

Pei, Mario Andrew: *Weasel Words: The Art of Saying What You Don't Mean,* Harper & Row, Publishers, Inc., New York, 1978.

Schick, C. Dennis, and Albert C. Book: *Fundamentals of Creative Advertising,* Crain Books, Chicago, 1979.

Schwab, Vic: *How to Write a Good Advertisement,* 3d ed., Marsteller, Inc., New York, 1976.

Zeigler, Sherilyn K., and J. Douglas Johnson: *Creative Strategy and Tactics in Advertising,* Grid Publishing, Inc., Columbus, Ohio, 1981.

End Notes

[1] Alfred Politz, "Creativeness and Imagination," *Journal of Advertising,* vol. 4, no. 3 (Summer 1975), p. 14.

[2] See also Ken Roman and Joel Raphaelson, "5 Subjects a Sound Creative Strategy Should Cover," in *How to Write Better: The Ogilvy Mather Guide to Writing Effective Memos, Letters, Reports, Plans and Strategies,* Ogilvy Mather, Inc., New York, 1978.

[3] James Webb Young, *A Technique for Producing Ideas,* Crain Communications, Inc., Chicago, 1960, pp. 25–41.

[4] John E. Matthews, "A Two-Course Survey of 'Creative Country'," *Journal of Advertising,* vol. 4, no. 2 (Spring 1975), p. 15.

[5] Daniel Starch et al., *Male vs. Female, An Exploratory Depth Interview Study,* Fawcett Publications, Inc., New York, 1958, p. 108.

[6] See also Florence R. Skelly, "Emerging Attitudes and Life Styles," mimeographed paper, American Association of Advertising Agencies, 1979 Annual Meeting, May 16–19, White Sulphur Springs, W. Va.

[7] Tom Dillon, "The Triumph of Creativity over Communication," *Journal of Advertising,* vol. 4, no. 3, (Summer 1975), p. 10

[8] David L. Malickson and John W. Nason, *Advertising—How to Write the Kind that Works,* Charles Scribner's Sons, New York, 1977, pp. 70–72.

[9] Rosser Reeves, *Reality in Advertising,* Alfred A. Knopf, Inc., New York, 1961, pp. 46–49.

[10] See also Vic Schwab, *How to Write a Good Advertisement,* 3d ed., Marsteller, Inc., New York, 1976, pp. 17–18.

[11] John Caples, *Making Ads Pay,* Harper & Row, Publishers, Inc., New York, 1957, pp. 3–4.

[12] See also Vic Schwab, op. cit., pp. 28–29.

[13] Thomas Fredrick Baldwin, "Redundancy in Simultaneously Presented Audio-Visual Message Elements as a Determinant of Recall," unpublished Ph.D. dissertation, Michigan State University, 1966.

[14] Carl I. Hovland, Irving L. Janis, and Harold H. Kelley, *Communication and Persuasion,* Yale University Press, New Haven, Conn., 1953, p. 247.

[15] Adapted from Robert L. Hilliard, *Writing for Television and Radio,* Hastings House, Publishers, Inc., New York, 1962, chap. 3. See also 2d ed., 1967, pp. 73–83.

[16] Charles Anthony Wainwright, *The Television Copywriter,* Communications Arts Books, Hastings House, Publishers, Inc., New York, 1966, p. 90.

[17] See also H. Gordon Lewis, *How to Make Your Advertising Twice as Effective at Half the Cost,* Nelson-Hall, Chicago, 1979, pp. 23–24, 148.

[18] Arthur Quiller-Couch, *On the Art of Writing,* G. P. Putnam's Sons, New York, 1916, p. 292.

[19] John E. O'Toole, "Are Grace Slick and Tricia Nixon Cox the Same Person?" *Journal of Advertising,* vol. 2, no. 2 (1973), p. 34.

[20] I Corinthians 14:9.

[21] H. Gordon Lewis, op. cit., p. 2.

[22] William H. Whyte, Jr., "The Language of Advertising," *Fortune,* September 1952.

[23] *Grey Matter,* Grey Advertising, Inc., New York, June 1969, pp. 1–2.

[24] William Strunk, Jr., and E. B. White, *The Elements of Style,* 3d ed., The Macmillan Company, New York, 1979.

[25] See also "The Budd Gore Retail Marketing Sourcebook," Budd Gore, Inc., Austin, Texas.

Chapter 13

Advertising Visualization and Design

Although we emphasized verbal communication in Chapter 12, we should not underestimate the role of graphic elements in advertising messages. Drawings, paintings, photographs, and moving pictures can often convey ideas more quickly than words. Moreover, the arrangement of such elements in combination with verbal symbols—the *design* of a total advertisement—can seriously affect message responses.

If the basic appeal of a message is bargains, for example, both copy and graphics must convey that theme. Draper Daniels, chairman of the board of his own advertising agency, defined the precept well when he noted that:

> The best advertising is a combination of words that make pictures in the mind and pictures that make words in the mind. . . . strong, simple words and arresting obvious art combined in a fresh and surprising manner.[1]

Figure 13.1 is an example of a well-designed bargain ad that ran in the newspaper. Notice how the "stacks" of products suggest stacks of savings (supported by the copy). Prices are featured, of course, but they don't overpower the illustrations (pictures that help communicate quality and value along with the theme of savings).

While copywriters visualize in a general way how advertisements will ultimately appear, art directors prepare the physical advertising layouts. They decide on the specific nature and placement of layout elements and are responsible for securing final artwork (normally produced outside the advertising agency). It is not necessary to be an artist, however, in order to understand the basic principles of design and visual communication. Likewise, you can learn to evaluate advertising graphics without being a connoisseur of fine art.

Design and Layout

When used as a noun, design means both an arrangement of parts and the plan behind the arrangement that produces a desired unit or structure. Used as a verb, design applies to any activity that organizes, arranges, and displays elements to achieve some specific purpose.[2]

The word "layout" is also used as both a noun and a verb and is more or less synonymous with design, but in a narrower sense. As an advertising colloquialism, "layout" is a condensed way of saying "laying out the elements of an advertisement within specific space limitations." The term is most specifically applied to the design of a newspaper, magazine, outdoor, or transit advertisement. In direct and point-of-purchase advertising, which usually require a

Figure 13.1 A newspaper ad stressing savings in both copy and layout design. [*Gem Department Stores.*]

three-dimensional presentation of the message, the layout is called a **dummy.** In the creation of television commercials, the layout is known as a **storyboard,** which is a series of pictures or frames that coincides with the audio or sound script. In each case, however, we are talking about drawings or graphic representations of some kind that simulate finished advertisements.

As noted in Chapter 12, an ad layout is a blueprint. Its function is to assemble the different parts of an advertisement—illustrations, headlines, body text, the advertiser's signature, and perhaps borders and other graphic materials—into a unified presentation of the sales message. In all but the very simplest form, layouts present these elements in the same size, shape, position, and proportion as desired in the final ad. Hence, the layout gives both those who have created the advertisement (copywriter and artist) and the one who will pay for it (the advertiser) a good idea of how the finished ad will appear.

Like an architect's drawing, the layout offers an opportunity for modification by creative teams and approval by agency management and advertiser representatives before actual construction or production begins. Finally, the layout provides specifications for estimating costs, and it is a guide for engravers, typographers, and other craftworkers to follow in producing the ad.

Layout Stages

Some designers begin with **thumbnail** layouts—miniature sketches (even doodles) often only one-quarter the size of the proposed ad. From such preliminaries may come the one design that is worthy of further development.

The second stage (or the first if thumbnails are omitted) is the **rough** layout (often shortened to "rough"). This is an actual-size layout in which headlines and subheads are lettered in (and type styles approximated), artwork and photographs are drawn or provided, and the position and extent of copy are indicated with ruled parallel lines. As the rough presentations become more true to their ultimate form, the layout stage may be called **finished,** although it is far from ready for publication. Students in advertising layout classes, as well as many retail advertisers, direct-mail users, and even clients of advertising agencies, work somewhere in the rough-to-finished area.

A **comprehensive** layout (or "comp") gets additional polish. In fact, it is considered perfect in every detail. Important clients paying thousands of dollars for magazine ads usually demand comps before giving approval. Photographs are pasted in and copy is set. If a printing plate for an entire ad is required for production, a **paste-up** or **mechanical** is prepared (camera-ready work); this stage, however, is actually a step beyond our discussion of layout.[3]

Principles of Design

As we saw in Chapter 12, headline ideas do not necessarily require verbal headlines; nor do all advertisements utilize graphic elements or art. In fact, *all* layout elements (headlines and subheads, picture captions and blurbs, illustrations and product packages, body copy and coupons, trademarks and advertiser logotypes) appear in today's ads with varying degrees of frequency.

Basic design principles, however, should be followed regardless of the number of specific design elements in an ad. All must, in the end, form a single effective communication message. (Recall Chapter 12's admonition that "to emphasize everything is to emphasize nothing.") The following five principles of good composition are important to anyone who creates or evaluates advertisements.

Balance

Designers point out that balance is a fundamental law of nature. It occurs when equal weights or forces are equidistant from a reference point, or when a light weight is placed at a greater distance from the

Figure 13.2 An attractive, formally balanced ad whose optical center falls two-thirds of the distance up from the bottom. [*Stokely-Van Camp, Inc.*]

reference point than a heavy weight. A familiar example of the principle is the child's teeter-totter or seesaw. The board will stabilize in a horizontal position when two children of equal weight are equidistant from the fulcrum, or when a light child is farther from the fulcrum than a heavy one.

In a layout, the reference point or fulcrum is the optical center of the advertisement. The artist always begins with a given area—a magazine page 7 inches wide by 10 3/16 inches deep, for example. All the elements must be kept within this space. The optical center of the ad is often a point approximately two-thirds of the distance from the bottom; it is the reference point that determines the balance of the layout. In Figure 13.2, the reader's gaze is drawn naturally to the eyes of the two children—and they are placed exactly two-thirds of the way up from the bottom of the ad.

The weight of a layout element is affected by both size and intensity of color or tone. Two units have the same weight if both the size and the color value are equal; a small element may be equal in weight to a large one of lighter tone or less intense color value.

When the weight of all elements on both sides of the vertical center line is equal, the layout has formal or symmetrical balance. (See again Figure 13.2.) When the equilibrium is the result of placing elements of different weights at unequal distances from the optical center, the layout has informal or asymmetrical balance. Most of the ads displayed in this book have this characteristic. Formally balanced layouts with nothing unusual or unexpected about them may be less interesting than the more dynamic, informally balanced compositions, but they certainly need not be dull. Some artists suggest that the primary value of formal balance lies in its suggestion of dignity, conservatism, and dependability—attributes desirable in the creation of corporate images for financial institutions, for example. While the lively pattern of informal balance may prove exciting and provide an opportunity for effective display of a number of different elements, there is much to be said for the direct simplicity of formal balance when an inviting illustration helps deliver the headline idea.

Proportion

Proportion is closely related to balance, since it refers to the division of space among layout elements for a pleasing optical effect. Good proportion in an advertisement also requires placing a specific (and varied) emphasis on each element in terms of size and position. For example, if USP communication depends on an unusual illustration, this element should be relatively large and prominently placed so the reader's eyes will focus on it. If the major appeal is a product's price, then this dollar figure should receive key display space.

As a rule, *unequal* dimensions help create lively advertising design. Conversely, when distances separating elements (headlines, subheads, pictures, and logotype) are equal or when the layout is exactly half copy and half illustration, the layout may appear monotonous. Figure 13.3 shows two different ads with the same message for the same product line. Both are attractively and informally balanced, but the proportions (as well as the sizes) are different. The one with the woman is about 75 percent illustration and 25 percent copy, whereas the one with the man is about 85 percent illustration and 15 percent copy. Notice that the first one seems to call more attention to the product (it is underlined in the headline with the word "fruit" added, and it is displayed in a cluster in the lower insert). The second one, however, places more emphasis on the consumer benefit (eating enjoyment).

Contrast

Contrast means variety. It gives life to a layout and adds emphasis to selected elements. Advertisers want their ads to stand out from the competition. In an ad with good contrast, the most important elements attract the most attention.

Variations in the size, shape, and color of layout elements create contrast. The varying directions of design elements (vertical trees, horizontal pavements, arched rainbows) add contrast, too. There must be a sales communication purpose behind every layout decision made, however, or "adiness" is apt to result. In Figure 13.4, the product itself is shown in contrasting movement patterns, all of which help demonstrate the ease-of-use sales message.

Eye Movement

Eye movement is the design principle that carries the reader's gaze from element to element. An effective

Figure 13.3 Two highly similar ads illustrating different proportions between illustration and copy. [*Del Monte Corporation.*]

ad uses movement to lead its reading audience from initial message awareness, through product knowledge and brand preference, to ultimate action (intent to purchase). Mechanical eye direction may be created by devices such as pointing fingers, lines, arrows, or even a bouncing ball that moves from unit to unit. Planned eye movements should take advantage of established reading patterns, too, such as the tendency to start at the top left corner of a page and read through to the lower right corner. The eye also moves naturally from large items to small, from dark units to light, and from color to noncolor. (See Figure 13.5.)

A more subtle type of movement is suggestive direction. The curve of a model's figure, for example, may lead the eye from headline to body copy, or the direction in which the model is looking may cause the reader to look the same way. Also, if a sales story is told in comic-strip sequence, readers will follow it in the intended order. The designer should be careful not to direct readers' eyes out of the advertisement, of course, or into adjacent ads.

Unity

Some artists consider unity, or harmony, the most important of all design principles. Although it is necessary to consider each element as a separate unit in striving for balance, proportion, contrast, and eye movement, the complete layout should appear as a

single unified composition. To use the comparison with architecture again, a reader's attention should not be attracted to doors, windows, or chimneys. Rather, these structural details should blend into one harmonious impression of the complete building. Common methods of securing unity in layouts are (1) use of a consistent typographical design, (2) repetition of the same shapes or motifs, (3) the overlapping of elements, (4) use of a border to hold elements together, and (5) avoidance of too much white space between elements.

Two questions generally arise here. First, do the demands for unity and contrast conflict with each other? Although they may appear to operate at cross-purposes, they can actually function quite smoothly together—if the artist strives for "balance" here, too, as well as in the layout overall. Unity contributes orderliness to elements—a state of coherence or of belonging together. And if they are properly placed, contrasting sizes, shapes, colors, and directions can flow together beautifully.

A second question concerns white space and its role in a layout. Sheer nothingness (blank space) can be a very significant part of an overall pattern. It can lend prestige to a product (setting it off from the rest of the ad), give any illustration more prominence, and make blocks of copy easier to read. Conversely, too much white space (or white space at the wrong spot) can throw a layout off balance or detract from a claim of low-cost items or bargain-basement sales.

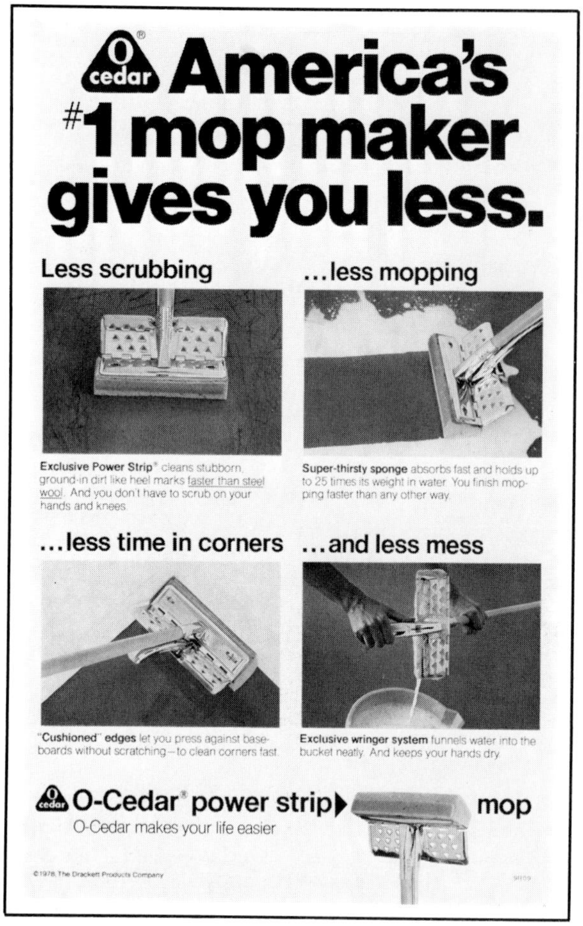

Figure 13.4 A simple but effective demonstration layout utilizing contrasts in direction. [*The Drackett Products Company.*]

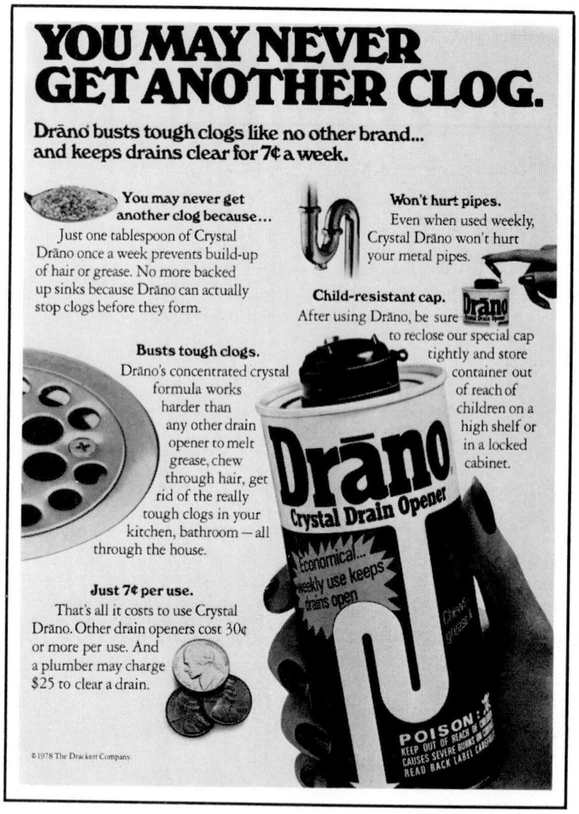

Figure 13.5 An example of a hard-working sales message with excellent pointing devices to direct eye movement. The product-package is at the focal point. [*The Drackett Products Company.*]

Designing for Television

Because TV's visual messages are *moving* pictures, we cannot apply the print media's static design principles to them. There are some parallels we can consider, however.

First, there is the idea of **emphasis.** Television is primarily an entertainment medium, and commercial copywriters may be tempted to focus on such attention-grabbers as children and pets, celebrities and humorous situations, and dramatic or special effects. As should be clear by now, though, unless a selling message dominates the frivolity, the advertiser's dollars are wasted. For example, ask yourself whether it is necessary to show a classroom full of students talking, laughing, and toying with notebooks, when it is the *pens* in their *hands* that are being compared.

Second, numerous research studies have found that TV viewers' eyes follow on-screen **motion.** Hence, a word to the wise: Keep your product and USP active and make sure that movements irrelevant to them do not compete for viewer attention.

Third, the concept of **unity** is critical in television because of the limited time span. Thirty seconds, the standard length of TV commercials, barely provides enough time to get one benefit message across, let alone multiple messages.

Contributions of Visual Elements

Some pictures—still shots in print and moving pictures in TV—communicate an idea so quickly and clearly that words are used merely to drive the point home with a final punch. The layout or storyboard designer who consistently produces such graphic ideas is talented indeed. Consider, for example, the award-winning advertisement in Figure 13.6, and the simple, but highly effective, idea in Figure 13.7.

Other, perhaps less dramatic, examples include:

A hand-held dollar bill going up in flames, while the off-camera TV announcer advises: "Don't get burned by inflation."

A close-up picture of fingers twisting a thermostat dial with the headline: "Dialing for Dollars."

A Halloween ghost, wearing a graduation cap, asking the audience: "Haunted by questions about your education?"

An animated Hostess dessert cake, arm-in-arm with a lunch-pail-bearing child, with the accompanying line: "Take a Twinkie to lunch."

Of course, visual **symbols** can be used as relevant attention-getters and interest-holders, even though they don't by themselves form complete sales stories. For example, a handshake may symbolize friendship or success, and a pair of balanced scales indicates equality.

We must not forget, either, the selling value inherent in audience-participation advertisements. Psychologists have long maintained that involvement aids learning far more than passive reception of a message. And learning along with understanding leads not only to retention, but also to application of knowledge gained in the marketplace.[4] Ads and commercials, therefore, often ask audiences to "put yourself in this situation," or to "think what you would do (or say) if. . . ." The ad in Figure 13.8 calls for actual physical movement.

Or buy a Volkswagen.

Figure 13.6 When a graphic idea has as much impact as this one, lengthy copy blocks would only detract from it. [*Courtesy of Volkswagen of America, Inc.*]

Print: Photographs or Drawings?

Print illustrations can be produced by photography, drawing, or painting. The latter methods are referred to as art, but creative photographers are just as much artists as are their colleagues who work with pen or brush. A number of different drawing techniques are available to advertisers, and each has a distinctive character that recommends it for certain uses. Drawings done with pen and ink, crayon, or the dry-brush method result in clean, hard lines of solid black and white; printings can produce varying tonal gradations from black through shades of gray to white. Photographic art also contains depth of tonal values. Photos are printed using halftone reproduction techniques, and the end product is an illustration made up of tiny dots of different shades of black and gray which give the quality found in the original photograph.

In many cases, it is not easy to decide whether photographs or drawings will make the best illustrations. Photographs can usually be eliminated from consideration, of course, when the subject matter existed only in the past and was not photographed (or at least not adequately so.) While it may be physically possible to recreate the personality of Socrates or the stark drama of Valley Forge with photography, as motion pictures do, for printed advertising it is usually more effective and less expensive to rely on the artist's skill with brush or pen. The same applies to future events that may happen on manned space stations or on the moon.

In most circumstances, however, photographs can be secured quickly, easily, and economically. An amazing variety of stock photographs, catalogued by subject classifications, is available from news services, private collections, and libraries. The New York Public Library, for example, has a collection of more than 6 million photographs of every conceivable subject. The disadvantage of stock photos is that they are available to everyone, and are therefore often overused, although exclusive-use rights for a limited time may sometimes be purchased at extra cost. Therefore, an advertiser who might otherwise spend weeks and thousands of dollars getting on-the-scene shots of a volcanic eruption could probably find the exact pictures desired in library files or buy them from a commercial stock photo firm. These

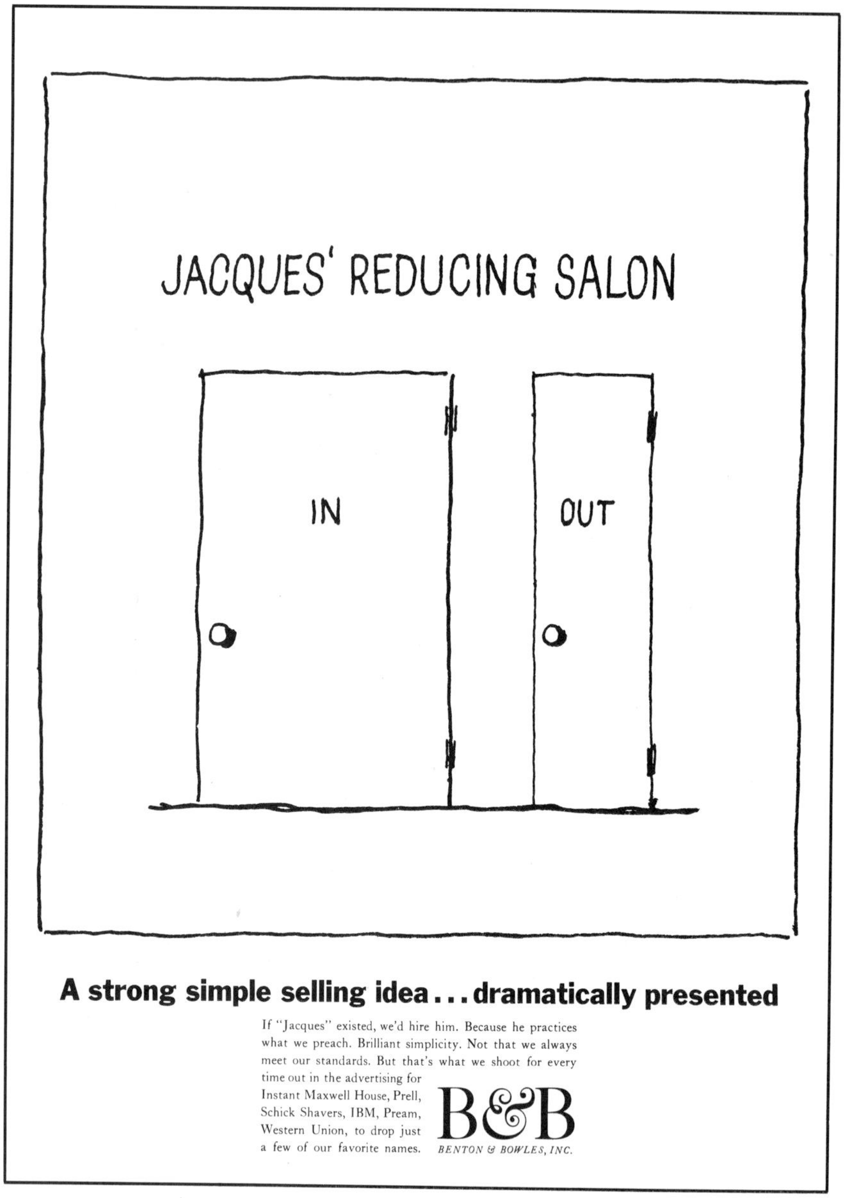

Figure 13.7 The importance of simplicity in advertising copy is the theme of this ad for a well-known advertising agency. [*Benton & Bowles, Inc.*]

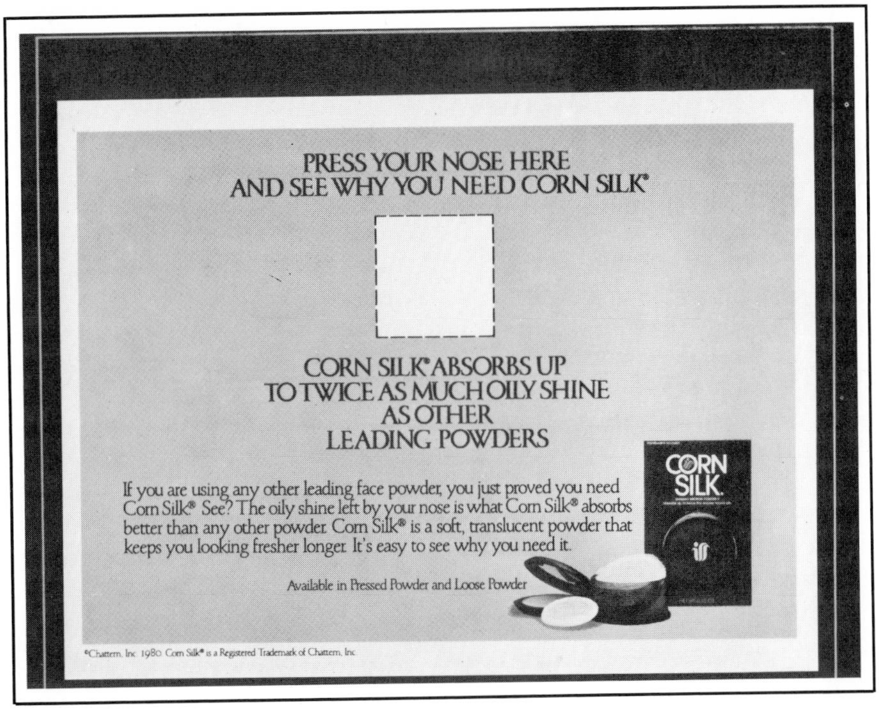

Figure 13.8 A fine example of an ad that calls for audience participation. [*Chattem, Inc.*]

particular shots might also be obtained, without cost, from the publicity departments of airlines or agencies promoting travel to areas with volcanic activity.

Many art directors feel that photography is something more than just another art technique. Although it is not accurate to say that the camera always tells the truth, there is an obvious realism to a photograph that adds to its impact. If a testimonial or case history is part of an advertisement, illustrating it with a photo provides an element of authenticity and believability that strengthens the entire message. There is also a sense of immediacy in photographic illustrations, so readers become personally involved. They can readily visualize, for example, how their families would react to advertised desserts or preserves. (Figure 13.9.)

We should remember, too, that people are accustomed to receiving news by means of photographs. Because news is one of the most important content elements of a headline idea, the photograph makes an ideal supplement. Finally, the camera can capture a unique situation or reaction. Special photographic techniques like superimposition of one photo over another or the use of time-lapse film can create "impossible" pictures that merge realism with the fantastic. This type of photography can give an ad more punch than a drawing.

We should not get the impression from this list of photographic advantages, however, that a skilled pen-and-brush technique is an inferior medium. Imaginative artists do not have to find the right models or settings for pictures, as the photographer must. They can see them in their minds, and then create the exact personalities, expressions, positions, and moods desired. The artist has more leeway to develop a distinctive atmosphere or a personal style than does the photographer, and this freedom can be quite important in gaining attention and building an advertiser's image.

Also, it is easier to emphasize or dramatize parts of a product or details of merchandise design or construction with drawings. Most photos in which structural detail is important are actually modified by retouching, a painstaking process. Finally, photographs cannot provide the degree of distortion or exaggeration so essential in cartoons and comic-strip characters. (See Figure 13.10.)

Television: Live Action or Animation?

Any moving picture in which living performers (human or animal) appear is generally thought of as "live action." On the other hand, animation consists

Figure 13.9 This ad shows both the realism which photographic art can convey and the value it can contribute to the overall sales message. [*Tracy Locke Advertising & Public Relations, Inc.*]

of drawings of characters and backgrounds that appear to move in a realistic manner—and may be presented in three basic ways. The first involves limited movement and is known as **limited animation;** it is a money-saver which can still be an effective creative tool.

The second involves very refined movement (often including lip movement) and is called **full animation;** it is often associated with Walt Disney productions. The third combines **animation and live action** in such a way that cartoon figures are superimposed over scenes with live talent. All three are excellent methods for presenting a product as the "star" of a commercial. Product identification is easy, and action is a natural. Further, clinical psychologists have found that the human eye is attracted to movement; animate both product and USP and it is not hard to hold viewer attention.

Usually, animation takes viewers into a kind of fantasyland—a world of beautiful maidens, knights in shining armor, and characters who are invulnerable to life's realities. But in fantasy commercials, the danger of "adiness" is tremendous while the task of creating credible, memorable brand differentiation is monumental. Still, fairy tales and dreamworld techniques may create genuine product enjoyment by association.

Of course, live-action demonstration is also a superb way to prove how and why claims are true—and, hence, to enhance both credibility and memorability. On the other hand, imagination can go too far in this area, too. Fairfax Cone, the late chairman of the board of Foote, Cone & Belding, put the matter in perspective when he said: "What I object to is foolishness in advertising: such as a woman rushing across a lawn into the face of a television camera and suddenly disappearing from view to act out the name 'Open Pit' barbecue sauce."[5] Here we have an excellent example of what might be called an advertising charade. It makes no promise, has no real signifi-

If you can put $1,500 a year away for retirement, and qualify, we can help you do it tax-free.
TAX FREE
New York Life's Personal-Pension Policies.
Until just recently, if you worked and your employer didn't set up a retirement plan for you, you probably wouldn't have one. There was no tax incentive for you to put money aside for later years.
But the new Federal pension law has changed all that.
Now you can put 15% of your annual income, up to a maximum of $1,500, into your own retirement plan—and deduct some or all of it on your Federal income tax return.
If your husband or wife has earned income and qualifies, he or she can start a separate plan. Together you may be able to put away $3,000 a year—and pay no tax on principal or interest until you retire.
All you need is a specially designed New York Life retirement annuity or endowment policy.
Unlike some retirement plans, a New York Life policy guarantees you and your spouse a monthly retirement income for as long as either of you lives. And you can even elect, in advance, to have *us* pay the premiums if you become disabled.
What's more, a New York Life endowment policy provides insurance protection for your family.
Personal pension. It's just one of the ways that your New York Life agent can help you protect your family and your future. See him or her soon.
We guarantee tomorrow today.
NEW YORK LIFE
New York Life Insurance Company, 51 Madison Avenue, New York, New York 10010. Life, Health, Disability Income, and Group Insurance, Annuities, Pension Plans.

Figure 13.10 It would be difficult, if not impossible, for photography to treat this ad's subject as distinctively as this drawing does. [*New York Life Insurance Company.*]

cance to consumer needs, and really does nothing whatsoever to demonstrate brand characteristics or superiority.

What Pictures Should Picture

Suppose the USP for a dishwashing detergent is: "Scrubbing power to make dishes sparkle with a skin conditioner to leave hands soft." Now, recall the four product-information categories discussed in Chapter 12. In each case, the graphic designer has a specific plan to follow.

The Background Setting

In a behind-the-scenes presentation in a magazine advertisement, an illustration of product composition might be most appropriate. Readers could see the actual ingredients in the detergent which result in clean dishes and smooth skin. The visual message in a TV commercial might feature development of the detergent's cleansing properties (in a test laboratory, for example), and the addition of skin-softening ingredients (perhaps right through the packaging process, so that viewers could see both elements combined in box or bottle).

The Functional Setting

The same USP in a product-in-use situation can be emphasized through a simple side-by-side comparison with a competitor's detergent, or through two separate pictures: one showing grease-cutting suds attacking dirty dishes, and the other showing the skin conditioner soothing a pair of hands. In television, cameras might take viewers underwater to examine firsthand the reason why the USP is true; while food stains took a beating, hands would not—and the audience might observe various emollients soaking into skin during the wash-and-rinse process.

The Result-of-Use Setting

Third, plans might call for a story of the results of product use—placing the same USP in still a different framework. Now the scene pictured would be "after-effects": soft hands for an evening's date after the dishes are done. Time-lapse photography in television might compare the same pair of hands over a period of days or weeks: dry, rough skin following use of harsh detergents, and smooth, soft skin thanks to the advertised brand.

The Incidentals Setting

Last, the "tough-on-stains-but-mild-on-skin" message can be told with reference to incidentals—the easy-to-handle container that holds the product, the variety of colors and fragrances available, or the selection of sizes and prices for a range of family needs.

Choosing the Right Graphic Approach

Decisions regarding picture content must be based on the same factors used in writing copy: the nature of the product and of competitive strategies, the audience to whom the message is aimed, the overall communication objective of the advertisement, and the medium used. Figure 13.11 shows an ad that capitalizes on the long columns of a full-sized newspaper. The product lends itself to vertical treatment, and the short, neatly spaced copy makes easy reading.

Readers of business publications, who are looking for information, will be attracted by nuts-and-bolts illustrations that would be skipped by a more casual consumer magazine reader bent primarily on entertainment, or by a homemaker shopping the pages of a local newspaper. When the objective of an advertisement is to complete the sale, as in mail-order advertising, the kind and number of illustrations may differ greatly from those used in an ad designed to create or reinforce a corporate image.

Probably the most important criterion to apply to advertising graphics is **relevance.** Every graphic display should be connected directly to the idea the advertisement attempts to deliver. A picture of a baby usually has high intrinsic attention value, but it is an irrelevant illustration if used over the headline: "This new cassette recorder comes with four rechargeable batteries."

On the other hand, an incongruous but relevant or offbeat illustration may provide an arresting effect

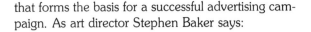

Parks Belk
Weekend Special
for only 3 days our entire stock* of rugs is on sale
25% off
That's right, our entire stock of floor coverings (except for bath rugs) is on sale. That means wools, wool blends, polyester blends, sizes from 3x5' to 9x12'. Even some orientals. What a choice, and what a chance. But you have to hurry.
*Bath rugs not included.
SALE ENDS SUNDAY, NOVEMBER 18
parks-belk bristol and kingsport
10 a.m.-9:30 p.m. mon.-sat. • sun. 1-6 p.m.

that forms the basis for a successful advertising campaign. As art director Stephen Baker says:

> The logical way of displaying merchandise is to show it where it belongs: the typewriter on the desk, the car on the highway. Put these objects where they are least expected and the result can be a stopper. The background need not be selected for its shock value alone; it can emphasize a sales point in a very real way. The office typewriter placed in the midst of a profusely blooming flower bed would underscore the headline: "The World's Most Beautiful Typewriter." A picture of an automobile parked *inside* a fancy hotel dining room might go nicely with the caption, "Distinguished people take their car wherever they go!"
>
> When handled photographically, the incongruity of a situation has even more impact. The realism of photography combined with the implausibility of the situation makes the reader look twice—or more often.[6]

Like anything else that promises greater return, the use of an incongruous illustration involves greater risk than does a more direct approach. It can fail miserably if not skillfully handled. But when it's well executed, it suggests to readers that "there must be a story about this picture," a story they want to find out more about.

Television pictures can provoke curiosity and suspense through carefully selected scene composition. Suppose, for example, that a commercial opens with a close-up shot of a person crying. Attention is aroused: Is someone hurt? Sick? Frightened? Then the camera pulls back slowly and we see the person is peeling onions. Or, a device as simple as a door may provide both intrigue and sales value if opened cautiously (over appropriate mood music or sound effects) to take viewers "through the door of investment opportunity" or "into the house of appliance bargains."

On the other hand, a careless use of visuals may lead to "vampire video"—scenes totally unrelated to

Figure 13.11 This ad makes fine use of the newspaper's columnar format. The product is easily displayed and takes on a certain kind of prestige because of the space it occupies. Notice that the illustration also serves as a pointing device toward the copy. [*Parks Belk Company.*]

the product or USP at hand. These are shots that literally feed on the commercial vehicle to serve purely selfish ends (usually artistic whims of copywriters or directors). Unfortunately, these same scenes are often brilliantly witty, highly memorable, and thoroughly enjoyed by audiences. At times, such commercials win creativity awards, too, and receive the praises of trade and lay persons alike. With no audience recall of product names, however, and no application of commercial content to any kind of selling message, *disciplined* creativity has gone out the window. And often, the campaign proves disastrous at the cash register.

Color versus Black and White

While very few television commercials are still produced in black and white, in the print media the color decision is an important one. Although basic principles of layout design and picture composition remain the same for both color and black and white, the decision to use color—and how much color—affects the development of copy and art and complicates the graphic arts processes required to reproduce the finished printed advertisement.

Except for such simple applications as printing in one color on paper stock of another color for a direct advertising piece, the addition of color to advertisements may materially increase costs. Periodicals charge a higher rate for color ads than for the same size ads in black and white. Art in color is more expensive than comparable black-and-white art, and mechanical production costs are also higher. Nevertheless, some advertisers are willing to pay the premium for color for a number of reasons.

First, color adds attention value. Second, it helps emphasize important elements in an ad. Third, it presents the product or situation with a sense of realism or atmosphere impossible in a black-and-white ad. Fourth, it provides a clear identification of product, brand name, and trademark. Finally, it endows the advertisement with a feeling of quality and prestige. For example, trying to convey the appetite appeal of catsup on a hamburger is extremely difficult in a black-and-white ad. Also, since readers have come to expect color in such instances, they are disappointed (or otherwise negatively impressed) when an ad fails to comply.

For some advertisers, however, the question is not so simple. The use of color may be hard to justify on the grounds of added attention value, since readership scores for black-and-white advertisements sometimes exceed those for color ads on a cost-ratio basis. The advertiser must decide whether, within the limits of a specific advertising budget, the extra cost for color is justified for the particular product involved, the advertising objectives, and the intended media.

Most of us would probably agree that food and travel advertisements, as well as ads for fabrics and fashions, can usually benefit greatly from color. On the other hand, messages designed to promote a particular brand of accident insurance or a new banking service may not demand color for effective communication. In fact, they might benefit from the feeling of stark realism (or the atmosphere of a news documentary) created through the use of black and white.

For specific examples of effective color advertisements, turn to the Color Plates.

Color in Newspaper Advertisements

Recall from Chapter 8 that advertisers can use color in newspapers in two ways. With the preprinted color-insert alternative, the advertiser furnishes the newspaper with rolls of the insert, and these are fed into the newspaper during the printing process along with the regular editorial and advertising copy. Hi-Fi color was discussed in Chapter 8 as one method used to produce preprinted inserts; here, advertisements appear in a manner similar to designs on wallpaper.

Spectacolor is the other form of preprinted color advertising in newspapers. While it eliminates the disadvantage of the continuous wallpaper effect and permits full-page ads to appear as separate units with their own margins, processing the preprinted rolls requires special equipment, which relatively few newspapers have. Newspaper magazine and Sunday comic sections, whether nationally or locally produced, also provide color advertising, but these supplements are more logically classed with magazines than with newspapers, as noted in Chapter 8.

The second opportunity for color advertising in newspapers is ROP, or run-of-paper, color. Its use has increased in recent years, probably because its added attention value helps justify its higher cost. Because most of both advertising and editorial content in newspapers appears in black and white, any additional color supplies an element of contrast and distinction that makes the message stand out from competition.

A typical surcharge or premium for one additional color in ROP newspaper advertising ranges from 15 to 25 percent, with a 1,000-line space unit the minimum acceptable. Two or three colors cost from 20 to 35 percent more than black and white, but may not be acceptable for ads that are less than a full page in size. (NOTE: An advertisement that is printed in black plus three colors is called a "four-color" or "full-color" ad because four different colored inks are used.)

An advertiser who can deliver a message effectively in a small space must decide whether the additional attention and prestige received from the use of color is worth the added cost of a full page of space. Department stores, among the largest users of newspaper space, still rely primarily on black-and-white advertisements except for special promotions.

Color in Magazine Advertisements

In magazines, especially national consumer publications, much of the editorial art and many of the advertisements are in color, and black-and-white space may be overwhelmed by color competition unless presented very dramatically. Furthermore, the quality of reproduction and the realism obtained from color in magazine space is considerably greater than is possible with the coarser screens and rougher paper stock used by newspapers. Finally, both brand identification and prestige are more frequent objectives for most national advertisers than for retail or local advertisers. Typical minimum space units for two-color magazine advertisements are 85 to 170 lines, and half-pages are a common minimum for full color. Surcharges for color vary widely. In some small-circulation magazines, the premium for four colors will run as much as 50 percent above the black-and-white rate. Currently, one multimillion-circulation consumer magazine charges 35 percent more for a four-color page than for a black-and-white one, while another charges only 10 percent more.

Color in Out-of-Home, Point-of-Purchase, and Direct-Mail Advertisements

In outdoor and transit advertising, there is no additional space cost for color, and the added costs of production in color are more than justified by increased attention and visibility in most cases. This is particularly true of outdoor, with its fixed position and moving audience. Point-of-purchase material and direct-mail advertising make wide use of color to attract initial attention, which is a very important objective. In both cases, the only added cost is in the printing process.

Color Characteristics and Dimensions

In addition to such specific advantages as increased attention value, realism, prestige, emphasis, and package, brand, or trademark identification, colors have a symbolism of their own which can contribute to the communication process. Blues and greens, perhaps from their association with the sky, sea, trees, and grass, are cool, restrained colors. Red and orange, at the other end of the color spectrum, are warm colors suggesting fire, passion, action, and excitement. Yellow is a bright, cheerful color, implying warmth without heat. Regardless of the symbolism or psychological impact of added color in advertisements, however, layout artists must consider its use in the same way they consider the use of additional illustrations. Color is another physical element of layouts and can be used effectively only if its dimensions are fully understood.

Without getting into the complexities of color theory, we can note that the primary pigment colors are red, blue, and yellow. From these the artist produces such secondary colors as purple by mixing red and blue, or orange by mixing yellow and red. A mixture of all three primary pigments neutralizes each of them, and tends to produce black if the primaries are equally strong and brilliant.

The artist identifies colors in terms of three qualities or, technically, measures color by three dimensions: hue, value, and chroma. **Hue** is the basic identity of color, the quality that distinguishes one color from another, such as blue from green, red from orange, or red-orange from red-purple. Pink, however, is not a hue, but only a tone or tint of red—a basic color neutralized by the addition of white. To change one hue into another, we must alter its fundamental nature, such as making blue into green by adding yellow.

Value is the lightness or darkness of a hue, the quality that distinguishes pink from red. We can increase the value of a hue by adding white and decrease the value by adding black without changing the hue. Adding white to blue results in a lighter tint and adding black produces a darker shade, but in neither case do we change the basic "blueness."

Chroma refers to the purity of a hue, its intensity in terms of saturation, or the strength or weakness of a color. When we change a color's value by adding black or white, we also change its intensity or chroma. The pink we make by adding white to red has a higher value than the original red, but it also has less chroma or intensity because its proportion of pure color is less.

Design Suggestions for Different Media

The principles of good composition apply to major print media. It may be helpful, however, to examine a few graphic concerns in terms of individual media characteristics.

Newspapers

To grasp the primary problem in the design of newspaper advertisements, we need only turn the pages of our local paper. The advertisements are stacked from the lower right corner to the upper right, and across to lower left. Here is competition for attention raised to the *n*th power—competition not only with other advertisers, but with the news of the day. The typical reader moves through this pandemonium of communications at a rapid pace, skipping from item to item and page to page while eating breakfast, riding the bus to or from work, or waiting for dinner.

Probably the most important design principle in newspaper ad layout is contrast. Large-size ads and ROP color are applications of this principle, but hardly the most economical ones for the majority of advertisers. A distinctive border (or a double border-within-a-border) may help an advertisement stand out from the mob, and so may the large, dark areas of photographs or good-sized illustrations of any type. The most effective attention-gaining contrast is the proper use of white space. A "white fence" can separate one property from all others on a page.

Magazines

With magazine advertisements, the designer can count on audiences reading at a more leisurely pace and also on their rereading. Unlike newspapers, magazines are rarely read in one sitting. Nor do magazine ads face the intense competition so typical of newspaper advertising. Magazine advertisements are not often "buried" by other ads above and alongside them; space as small as one column inch is almost always next to reading matter. Still, while bleeding an ad (running it to the edges of the page) can make the unit look larger, the smaller the ad is, the greater the need for a border.

Because better paper stock and finer reproduction processes are used in magazine production, the designer of magazine advertisements has more freedom in approach and technique, especially in the use of color, than does the designer of newspaper ads. The selective audience characteristic of most magazines enables layout artists to focus more directly on the moods and interests of a particular group. A sophisticated, high-style layout and art treatment that are out of place in a business publication or an outdoor magazine can be very effective in *Vogue* or *The New Yorker.*

Television

Effective television commercials use this medium's action capabilities and thereby provide viewers with great visual variety. After all, if a TV sales message is mainly in the audio channel over dull, repetitive shots, it might as well be a radio spot. Even when the visual material is vital, if it appears in relatively still form, it might as well be in a magazine. A good rule of thumb is: Let something move in every shot—the camera, the product, people, or special effects—because if *something* does not move, *viewers* will.

The demonstration technique is considered ideal for showing a specific product advantage, and animated demonstration can help simplify a complex procedure or deliver a distasteful story in a pleasant way. Slice-of-life presentations usually focus attention more on *users* than on *uses* of a product, but they can involve viewers in the selling message very effectively if they are handled believably.

Intricate features do not belong in television graphics because the TV camera cannot pick them up. A machine with 50 tiny moving parts is better demonstrated on the printed page. Also, visual sequences in television must flow naturally, logically, and believably throughout. If transitions are too abrupt, confusion often results. If they are drawn out too long, bored audiences tune out. Of course, there is a "willing suspension of disbelief" on the part of viewers; so a prepared cake mix can be popped into the oven in one scene and pulled out in ready-to-eat form in the next. Still, copywriters must take care not to exploit viewer trust through trick photography.

Outdoor Advertising

No medium relies more heavily on the pictorial method of communication than outdoor advertising. Here is advertising in its simplest and most direct form, without news or entertainment of any kind to attract initial attention and interest. Moreover, the audience is moving past the advertisement at a distance, and the message must be delivered clearly and completely in five seconds or less. The simplicity that is always desirable in layout becomes a vital principle with outdoor—simplicity not only in the number and arrangement of elements, but also in terms of the idea itself.

The Outdoor Advertising Committee of the Association of National Advertisers recommends that outdoor posters contain not more than three elements with *one* dominant one. Five or six words of copy are considered ideal, and eight or ten the maximum—exclusive of a trademark or logotype. The value of silhouette illustration, instead of a full-face view, is recognized by most poster designers, because the total illustration should stand out from its background and be readily identifiable from a distance.

Simplicity in outdoor design applies especially to typography. Although simple lettering, somewhat heavier than average in weight, is highly desirable, ornamental or script lettering should be avoided because of poor legibility. Bright, warm colors contrasting with cool ones provide good visibility, and the effective carrying power of a design may be increased with fluorescent ink or paint. Color visibility seems to depend less on contrasts in hue than on contrasts in value. Red and green combinations have poor visibility; blue or green and white have medium visibility. Combinations of yellow and black are the easiest to read at a distance and are used in many traffic safety signs.

Transit

The design problems of transit advertising are comparable to those of outdoor. Again we have a "pure" advertising medium, without news or entertainment to attract (or distract) readers. While the audience for car cards inside buses or trains is not an audience in motion, and the message can thus be longer than an effective outdoor message, each card faces tough competition from many other cards displayed close together. Therefore, simplicity should be a prime design objective. Because the audience for traveling displays on the outside of buses is usually in motion, as is the message itself, layout and copy should be even simpler and more easily visible than in the case of outdoor posters.

The Test of Effective Design

We have made the point that good advertising writing is tight writing—writing that contains no stuffing, no padding, no empty words or phrases. Every word works to tell the sales message. The same principle should be applied to advertising design. Nelson gives this advice to students:

> When you have arranged your elements into a good layout—when you have designed your ad—see whether you can remove any one of your elements without hurting the ad's balance, its proportion, its unity. If you find your ad doesn't suffer from having lost an element, you might well question its basic structure.[7]

The same line of reasoning applies to TV commercials: only scenes crucial to the unfolding of the USP should be included. A physically attractive presenter might win viewer attention, but that person's removal to an off-camera "voice-over" position might better focus that attention on the product and the selling message. Likewise, relevant action in a commercial helps speed development and comprehension of the advertiser's message; irrelevant gimmicks can result in viewer disgust and mental or physical tune-out.

Some experts even claim that an effective commercial is one that would be a disaster without the advertised brand. In other words, if a competitor's brand would fit in its place without changing the image the message creates, the commercial is a communication failure in terms of its USP. (The USP, of course, is supposed to give some kind of "unique personality" to one specific product.) As an example, consider the animated Raid insect spray can. A long series of TV commercials has featured insect "culprits" engaged in varying activities. Then, they are surprised by a Raid attack and, immediately thereafter, destroyed. If we tried to place a competing product, such as Black Flag, into Raid's role in the commercial, however, the message would fall apart. The personality *belongs* to Raid, and the play on the word "raid" clinches it.

The Importance of Creative Continuity

Regardless of the media used, designers should strive for a feeling of continuity, or resemblance, between advertisements in a given campaign series. Only then can messages produce a cumulative impression in consumers' minds, and thereby help attain the complete objective of the advertising campaign. Recall from Chapter 11 that repetition over time is a prime requisite for human learning.

Visual Similarities

Perhaps the most common type of continuity occurs in the form of visual similarities: (1) the same character or spokesperson (celebrity or otherwise) may appear repeatedly, and (2) a similar format may be used. Examples appearing in both magazines and TV include Charmin's "package squeezers" in the supermarket with Mr. Whipple, Bounty's "coffee-spillers" in Rosie's diner, and Jello's pudding-loving kids with Bill Cosby. A picture-caption technique or a distinctive border or type style may help tie ads together in newspaper campaigns.

Verbal Similarities

Verbal similarities give us a second kind of campaign tie. Slogans, both printed and spoken, come to mind immediately: "Nobody can do it like McDonald's can," "Get that great GM feeling with genuine GM parts," and "Like a good neighbor, State Farm is there." And, set to music, many of them become parts of radio and TV jingles. Another verbal approach is illustrated by advertisers such as H & R Block, whose advertisements and commercials all begin with a common line: "Here's reason number ____ for letting us prepare your income tax."

Similarities in Sound

A third technique uses sounds more than words: a doorbell, for "Avon Calling," an echo, for the Jolly Green Giant's ho-ho-hoing, or a familiar musical theme, like the instrumental version of McDonald's "Nobody can do it." In the first two of these examples, extensions are even made to the print media. The doorbell appears as the words "Ding-Dong," and the echo effect shows up as "Ho-Ho-Ho."

Similarities in Attitude

Finally, a similarity of attitude ties ads and commercials together in some campaigns. Kraft has become famous for its "Good food and good food ideas," and its "Good ideas keep popping up." Amateur photographers everywhere are often reminded to "Trust your story to Kodak film." And Sears, Roebuck continually reinforces its image as the store "Where America shops for value," whereas K mart is "The Saving Place."

Obviously, continuity should not be limited to advertisements in a single medium. Newspaper ads should have enough family resemblance to magazine, television, and other messages for each to aid the others in building a desired image. The same principle should be extended to include the design of packages, point-of-purchase materials, and even a company's letterhead, a store's delivery trucks, and uniforms worn by a sales staff.

Summary

Art directors are responsible for preparing physical advertising layouts and storyboards. Illustrations and layout design in print and moving pictures in television must work together with words to deliver advertisers' sales messages. Layout stages range from thumbnail sketches, through rough, actual-size layouts, to polished comprehensives. Basic layout elements include headlines, illustrations, body copy, and logotypes; they are arranged in accordance with five principles of design: balance, proportion, contrast, eye movement, and unity. In television, emphasis, motion, and unity are important aspects of commercial messages.

No layout, however, is an end in itself. Rather, it is prepared to achieve a specific communication task; and the overall impression created by the finished advertisement must be in harmony with the image of its product or firm. Similarly, TV commercials should involve viewers with the USP and take care to avoid irrelevant entertainment and distractions.

Print illustrations may include photographs, drawings, and paintings. TV commercials may use both live action and animation. The advertised products may appear in varied settings, depending on campaign objectives, the specific medium or media used, the audiences sought, and competitive efforts.

Nearly every television commercial on today's airwaves is produced in color, but many print ads commonly appear in black and white. The reasons for this are usually financial, though some advertisers justify added costs on the basis of extra attention value.

Different media offer designers different opportunities for using graphics effectively. Important graphic features are *contrast* in newspaper ads (especially in the use of white space); *selectivity* in magazine ads (especially in the use of colors and layout styles that create specific moods); *demonstration* in TV commercials; and *simplicity* in outdoor posters and transit ads.

Finally, regardless of the medium used or the visual techniques selected, we must strive for continuity throughout a campaign. Message themes across media may claim visual similarities, verbal similarities, audio (sound, music) similarities, and similarities in attitudes or moods created.

Questions for Discussion

1. What are the functions of an advertising layout? In what ways does the layout resemble an architect's blueprint?
2. Balance, contrast, and eye movement are three principles of design. Discuss three ways each of these may be achieved in layouts.
3. Select a product, a service, and a retail store. Explain how white space in a newspaper ad for each of them might be used for different purposes.
4. Describe (1) a current television advertising campaign that does a good job of stimulating audience involvement, and (2) a campaign that uses visual symbols well. Compare both campaigns with campaigns that do a poor job in each area.
5. What advantages do photographs offer as advertising illustrations? In what types of ads would you prefer to use drawings?
6. Discuss two advantages and two disadvantages of the use of animation in television commercials.
7. Name the four basic settings in which an advertised product may appear. Then find an example of each from either print or TV.
8. Color increases the cost as well as the attention value of ads. List three situations in which the added cost for color may be justified on grounds other than added attention.
9. Compare and contrast the need for simplicity in print ads, outdoor posters, and television commercials.
10. Name three ways advertisers may achieve creative continuity in campaigns. Find supportive examples for each in two or more media.

For Further Reference

Dorn, Raymond: *How to Design and Improve Magazine Layouts,* Brookwood Publications, Oakbrook, Ill., 1976.

Garland, Ken: *Graphics Handbook,* Reinhold Publishing Company, New York, 1974.

Latimer, Henry C: *Advertising Graphics: A Guide to New Creative Preparation and Production,* McGraw-Hill Book Company, New York, 1977.

Lem, Dean Phillip: *Graphics Master,* Dean Lem Associates, Los Angeles, 1977.

Nelson, Roy Paul: *The Design of Advertising,* 4th ed., Wm. C. Brown Company, Publishers, Dubuque, Iowa, 1981.

Schlemmer, Richard M: *Handbook of Advertising Art Production,* 2d ed., Prentice-Hall, Inc., Englewood Cliffs, N.J., 1976.

Turnbull, A. T.: *The Graphics of Communication: Typography, Layout, Design,* 3d ed., Holt, Rinehart and Winston, New York, 1975.

End Notes

[1] Draper Daniels, *Giants, Pigmies, and Other Advertising People,* Crain Communications, Inc., Chicago, 1974, pp. 253–254.

[2] Roy Paul Nelson, *The Design of Advertising,* 4th ed., Wm. C. Brown Company, Publishers, Dubuque, Iowa, 1981.

[3] Ibid.

[4] Steuart Henderson Britt, "How Advertising Can Use Psychology's Rules of Learning," *Printers' Ink,* Sept. 23, 1955, pp. 74–80.

[5] Fairfax Cone, *The Blue Streak,* Crain Communications, Inc., Chicago, 1973, p. 175.

[6] Stephen Baker, *Advertising Layout and Art Direction,* McGraw-Hill Book Company, New York, 1959, p. 175.

[7] Nelson, op. cit.

Chapter 14

Production of Print and Broadcast Advertising

● Before an advertiser's message can be delivered to prospects, both verbal and visual symbols must be processed or produced in forms that suit the mechanical or electronic requirements of the medium. The basic requirements of print and broadcast media are naturally quite different and will be considered separately in this chapter.

Mechanical Production in Print Media

Mechanical production is more than just a terminal procedure in the creation of a printed advertisement. If the possibilities and limitations of production methods are not considered early in the creative process, costs may be excessive and the effectiveness of the ad impaired. For example, a copywriter must tell a sales story in fewer words for a half-page than for a full-page ad, at least if the same relative emphasis is to be maintained between verbal and illustrative elements. If the advertisement is in color, the selling points and benefits developed may not be the same as those emphasized in a black-and-white ad. Then, too, the medium that will deliver the message and the printing process it uses can affect the choice of illustrations and layout design. Small photographs may be quite effective with high-quality magazine printing, but quite ineffective on the coarse paper generally used by newspapers.

Once a client has approved the copy, layout, and finished art for an ad, a series of graphic arts operations follows. If printing is to be done by the photographic process of offset lithography, the magazine or newspaper is usually supplied with a paste-up or what is often called "camera-ready copy." Line artwork and reproduction proofs of type are secured in place with rubber cement and photographed to get a line negative. Photos and other continuous-tone art are shot through a screen and then stripped into position with the line negatives. These stripped-in negatives are used to make the offset printing plates.

On the other hand, when printing is done by letterpress, the typographer sets the selected type to match layout specifications. Artwork is sent to the engraver, and proofs are assembled with the type, following the layout design. Finally, metal printing plates or mats (matrices) of the completed ad (instead of negatives) are delivered to the media.

Exact steps and sequences, of course, vary with the kind of advertisement and the printing facilities of specific newspapers and magazines. A local advertiser planning an all-type ad may send typewritten text and layout directly to the newspaper. No engraver is needed and the newspaper, functioning as typographer and compositor, supplies proofs to the advertiser for approval and makes the printing plates.

Basic Printing Methods

The four printing processes in common use by advertisers are offset (lithography), gravure, letterpress, and screen printing. Most newspapers and magazines today print by offset, and this process is also widely used for outdoor posters, point-of-purchase displays, and direct-mail advertising. Perhaps the most familiar examples of gravure printing are such newspaper magazine supplements as Sunday's *Parade* and magazine sections of the *New York Times.* Some national magazines also print by gravure; others use both gravure and letterpress in the same issue. Screening is used for small runs of posters, transit advertising, displays, and printing on cloth, metal, plastics, and other special surfaces.

Offset

The offset process is planographic printing, or printing from a flat surface. Ink from the printing plate is transferred to a rubber blanket or roller which, in turn, transfers (or offsets) it to the paper. This textbook and its cover were printed by offset.

Gravure

In both gravure and high-speed rotogravure printing, the design to be printed is cut or engraved into the plate. When the plate is inked and wiped clean, ink is retained in the depressions that form the image and is transferred from them to the paper.

Letterpress

The process used in letterpress is the reverse of gravure. The images or letters to be transferred are actually pressed into the paper by raised, or relief, surfaces which carry the printing ink.

How to Choose a Printing Method

Once a specific newspaper or magazine has been selected as an advertising medium, the advertiser is, of course, restricted to the printing process used by that publication. Still, it may be helpful to examine Table 14.1, which compares the three printing processes just described according to four basic criteria important to all advertisers. Then we shall consider screen printing.

Table 14.1
A Comparison of Characteristics of the Three Major Methods of Printing an Ad

	Offset	Gravure	Letterpress
Cost	Cost of metal plates lowest, but complete new plates must be made if corrections needed	Expensive copper cylinders; economical only in production of 100,000 or more	Metal plates cost more than offset, but less waste (no delay in obtaining water/ink balance)
Appearance	High quality: fine screen highlights even on rough surface	Rich effects, especially on cellophane, acetate, metallic foils	More body and brilliance; inks glossier; less problems with metallic inks
Paper stock	Sensitive to moisture changes; acute problems in paper curl and dimensional instabilities	May use softer paper than offset or letterpress but thereby fails to reproduce in sharp detail	Best-quality printing; works well with special stock; paper suitable for Bibles
Quantity	Small runs are ideal (low paper cost); even large jobs are reasonable, especially with *web* offset	Ideal for long runs on periodicals and catalogs, or package wraps	Almost no limits on number of impressions, but small, simple runs more expensive than offset

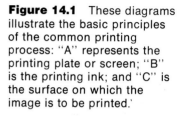

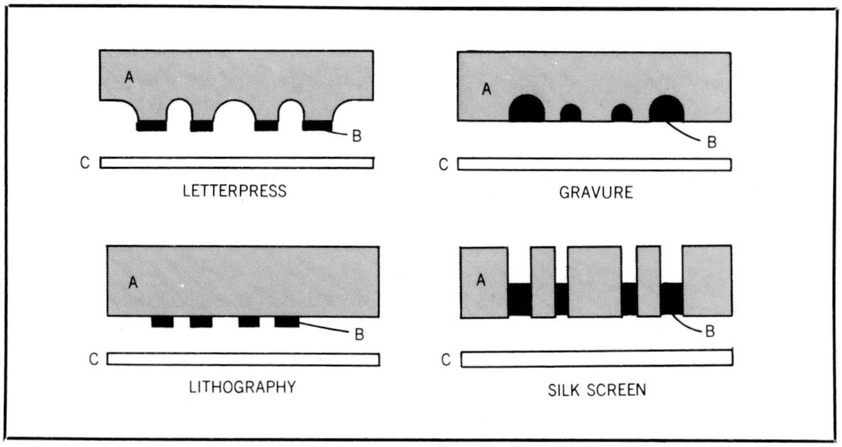

Figure 14.1 These diagrams illustrate the basic principles of the common printing process: "A" represents the printing plate or screen; "B" is the printing ink; and "C" is the surface on which the image is to be printed.

Screen Printing

In the screening procedure, or serigraphy, a special screen is placed over the surface on which the message is to be printed, and a stencil blocks out areas that are not part of the intended result. Rubber rollers, or squeegees, then force the printing ink through portions of the screen not covered by the stencil to reproduce the desired image. (NOTE: Printing stencils are generally made of nylon or stainless steel mesh. Formerly, they were made of silk, and the process was widely known as "silk screen.")

Since no printing plates are necessary, screening can be used economically in far smaller quantities than is true in other processes. Moreover, it will print on any surface of any thickness, from bottles and 55-gallon oil drums to sweatshirts. Figure 14.1 shows how inked images are transferred from one surface to another in each of the four printing processes.

The Art of Typography

Regardless of the printing process used, the words in the text of an advertisement must be either lettered by hand or set in type. Hand lettering is usually restricted to headlines and other display elements to create a special effect. The word "type" describes either a rectangular block of metal with a letter or character in relief on its upper surface or the image of these letters or characters printed on paper.

Typography is the art of selecting and arranging type in order to deliver a printed message effectively. In advertising, a selected type style must be inviting to the eye, easy to read, and appropriate to the message itself. Generally, readability is influenced by the spacing between words, lines, and paragraphs, and by type size and style. Type should never call attention to itself ("adiness"). Readers must be attracted *through* the type to the advertised product or service and to the sales message.

Of course, the design of type can convey meaning to a reader quite apart from the meaning of the words it forms. Some type styles look bold and heavy, whereas others are light and graceful. Still others say "new and modern," or "old-fashioned," or "bargains," almost as surely as if they spelled out the words. Delicate or antiquated type used in the headline below an action photo of a new, rugged earth-moving machine detracts from the impression created by the illustration.

How Type Is Set

Recent years have seen revolutionary developments in typesetting. Traditional machine-setting methods cast either individual letters or full lines of copy using molten metal to produce each letter. Then photocomposition, or **cold type,** with improved sharpness and clarity was developed, offering a greater choice of type sizes and faster output at lower cost. Machines (some very similar to electric typewriters) produced typographic composition on either film or sensitized paper.

Today's computer world has given us such digital typesetters as the one shown in Figure 14.2. Introduced in 1975, it claims speeds of over 4,000 lines per minute, and *stores* type "fonts" (complete assortments of capital and lowercase letters and figures in specific sizes and designs) as computer information

Figure 14.2 The APS Digital CRT Photosetter, by Autologic, one of the fastest typesetters available, has become an industry leader [*Autologic, manufacturer of high-speed digital CRT phototypesetters.*]

that is instantly accessible. The typesetting process involves "beaming" lines of type onto paper from a cathode ray tube (CRT).

Hundreds of these units are in use by large newspapers throughout the country as well as by commercial and financial printers and typographers. In addition, 1980 saw the introduction of high-quality CRT phototypesetting to small and medium-sized newspapers. Equipment similar to that shown in Figure 14.3 offers solid-state circuitry, along with operational simplicity and speeds of 1,250 lines per minute, in a middle-price range (around $50,000.)

We should also note here the increasing use of video terminals and computer storage in the writing of copy. In many newspapers and some agencies, the video terminal is replacing the typewriter. Copy is written and corrected on the terminal. Typesetting instructions are inserted and the copy is stored in a computer to await typesetting. Thus, some production decisions are now made directly by the copywriter.

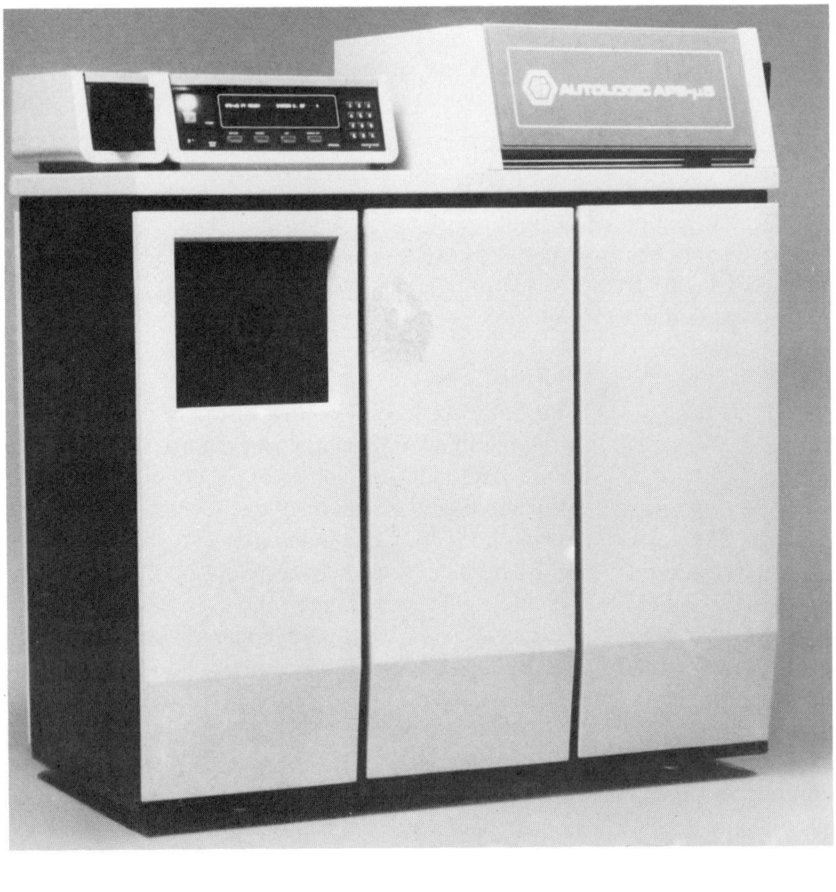

Figure 14.3 The APS-Micro 5 CRT Phototypesetter, by Autologic, is a highly reliable, compact digital typesetter used by small and mid-sized printing establishments. [*Autologic, manufacturer of high-speed digital CRT phototypesetters.*]

Type Structure and Measurement

As shown in Figure 14.4, type anatomy includes a face, a body, shoulders, and feet. The face is the design of the letter or figure, each of which is distinguished by its name and its size.

The point system of measuring type is different from our common way of measuring by inches, but no more difficult to grasp. The **point** is a measurement of type size (height and width), and for practical purposes 72 points equal 1 inch. Thus, 12 points equal 1/6 inch, 18 points equal 1/4 inch, 36 points equal 1/2 inch, and so on.

The point measurement does not reflect the size of a single letter, however. The point actually measures the height of a line of type, and it is the distance from the bottom of the descenders, or tails, of *g, j, p, q,* and *y* to the top of the ascenders of *b, d, f, h, k,* and *l.* As a result, a 72-point (pt.) capital letter *M* is slightly less than an inch in height, and a lowercase 72-point *m,* which has neither ascenders nor descenders, is considerably less than an inch high. On the other hand, a line of 72-point type—composed of a variety of letters—will measure 1 inch, and 6 lines of 72-point type will measure 6 inches in depth.

The width of a single letter of type depends on both the proportions of the letter and the design of that particular type face. In any design, for example, the letter *m* will obviously be wider than the letter *n.*

The unit of measurement for the width of lines or the depth of blocks of type is the **pica,** and it equals 1/6 inch. Printers also use the pica as a general unit of measurement for illustrations or other layout elements. Figure 14.4, for example, is 14½ picas deep. The total depth of a newspaper or magazine advertisement, however, is usually measured in agate lines or column inches, as explained in Chapter 8.

Lines of type would be too close together for easy reading or for a desired effect unless they were separated by space. The distance between lines of type is known as leading, pronounced like the name of the metal "lead." The following example shows lines of type of the same size (12 point) and design (Caledonia), set without leading ("set solid") and with 2-point leading (leading one-sixth the type size).

Chances are, when you bought your present washing machine, you expected it—like your car—to grow old and run down. There wasn't much you could do about it, so you thought. But today it's possible for your old washing machine

12 pt Caledonia

Chances are, when you bought your present washing machine, you expected it—like your car—to grow old and run down. There wasn't much you could do about it, so you thought. But today it's possible for your old washing machine

12 pt Caledonia, 2-point leaded

To provide the necessary space between words in a line or at the end of a paragraph, the compositor uses blank pieces of metal known as *quads* or *spaces.* It is also desirable at times to space between letters of type to produce a pleasing display effect. The example that follows shows a headline set with and without letter spacing.

HOME STYLE TOMATO JUICE

HOME STYLE TOMATO JUICE

The type you are reading at the moment, Souvenir, is 10/12 (read "10 on 12") which is a 10-point type with 2-point leading.

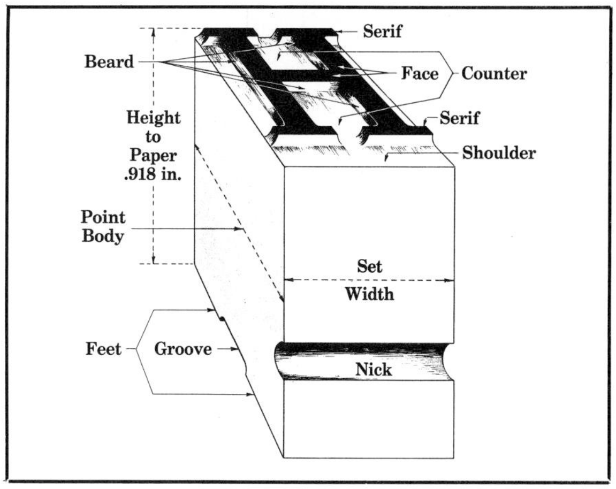

Figure 14.4 This piece of type, for the letter H, shows all parts of its anatomy, from its face and shoulders to its body and feet. [*American Type Founders Co., Inc.*]

Type Designs Classified

The character or personality of type results from its design, which also affects readability. *The Graphics Arts Production Yearbook* lists more than 1,000 different typefaces in common use today, and typographers continually develop new ones. Fortunately, they can all be classified into relatively simple groups.

The four "races" of type that are fundamental in modern typography are **roman, block letter, script,** and **ornamental,** and each has distinguishing features.

These words are set in roman.

This race is derived from the lettering chiseled into monuments during the days of the Roman Empire, and it probably includes a larger number of designs than any of the other three groups. The two most notable characteristics of roman letters are the small lines, or serifs, that cross the ends of the main strokes, and the variation in the thickness of strokes. Two of the main virtues of roman type are its versatility (providing contrasting effects without a basic design change), and its legibility, especially in small sizes.

These words are set in block letter.

The strokes forming the letters in this group do not vary, but remain a uniform thickness throughout. Also, they either lack serifs (sans serif), or the serifs have the same weight and thickness as the main strokes of the letters (square serif). Hence, many people feel that the block-letter group is harder to read than roman type, though its simple, clean lines give it a modern feel or tone that is effective in advertising. (NOTE: Most books, newspapers, and magazines use serif styles in type and sans serif in headlines.)

These words are set in script.

The script group includes a number of type designs that resemble handwriting; and, like much handwriting, script faces leave something to be desired in legibility. Script type should, therefore, be used with great care in advertising, even when an invitational or formal effect is an important typographic objective.

These words are set in ornamental type.

The last of the four basic races of type faces includes a large number of ornamental, decorative designs suggestive of other times and other cultures. They are used to create unusual, even "eccentric," effects. Figure 14.5 shows a font, design, and family of type, as well as the four basic races.

Fitting Copy and Type

Type, of course, must fit into the amount of space indicated for it in a layout. The larger the type size, the more space a given number of letters or words will require. But the number of characters that will fit in a line varies with different designs. For example, both lines below are the same length—15 picas, or 2½ inches—and both are set in 12-point type. The second line, set in the Century Bold Condensed "family" of type, however, accommodates seven more letters than the first line, which is set in Century Bold of the same point size.

The quick brown fox jumps over th

The quick brown fox jumps over the lazy dog.

The most accurate method of fitting type to layout is by means of type charts or tables that show the number of capital and lowercase characters per pica or per inch for different faces and sizes. For rough, preliminary fitting, though, we may simply count our total number of words, and divide it by the number of words per square inch that can be set in type of various sizes, according to guides like Table 14.2.

Table 14.2
Approximate Number of Words per Square Inch

Type Size	Words
6 pt., solid	47
6 pt., leaded 2 pt.	34
8 pt., solid	32
8 pt., leaded 2 pt.	23
10 pt., solid	21
10 pt., leaded 2 pt.	21
18 pt., solid	7
18 pt., leaded 2 pt.	6

A font of 6-pt. Century Expanded

ABCDEFGHIJKLMNOPQRSTUVWXYZabcdefghijklmnopqrstuvwxyz1234567890,.;:?¢@*&%$

Examples of sizes in the Caslon New type series

a a a a a a a a a a A A A A A A A A A A

Six variations of the Caslon family

Caslon	**Caslon Condensed**
Caslon Italic	**Caslon New**
Caslon Bold	Caslon Old Face

Examples of the four basic races of type

1. Roman.	
a. Old style	Caslon Old Face
b. Modern	Bodoni
2. Block letter.	
a. Sans-serif	**Spartan**
b. Square serif	**Stymie**
3. Script.	
a. True script	*Bank Script*
b. Cursive	*Coronet Light*
4. Ornamental	
a. Text	**Goudy Text**
b. Miscellaneous	P. T. Barnum, **Hobo**, **STENCIL**,

Figure 14.5 Examples of a font of type, different sizes in the same design, variations in a family of type, and the four basic races of type.

Although it is wise to leave the exact type specification to an expert, anyone who writes copy or evaluates advertisements should be familiar with a few fundamentals that affect readability and the appeal of type. **Italics**, for example, are harder to read in large quantity than vertical letters. Lines set all in capital letters are harder to read than capitals and lowercase letters, and italic caps are even more cumbersome than vertical ones. Lines of type that are either too long or too short make hard reading, but the larger the type size, the longer the line can be without becoming difficult (although hand-lettering is hard to read in quantity). A handy guide to maximum line length is 60 lowercase characters.

Also, we must be wary of *reverse* type (white letters on a black background), except in the case of especially large type, since the dark area tends to overwhelm the lighter letter. Unusual type *arrangements,* such as words in a circle or on a backward slant, can result in "adiness," too.

We should always strive for simplicity in type selection and should not use too many type faces in one advertisement. *One* in a small ad is probably a good rule, though several different type *sizes* may be used effectively. All the contrast and variety needed in most advertisements are readily available from a single family of the better type designs.

The Production of Graphic Elements

Basically, camera-and-chemical methods are used to reproduce graphic elements that are not composed (as some type is) of standard, movable units. Because hand-lettered headlines, for example, create an effect not easily obtainable with type, the words are executed as a piece of artwork and shot with a camera to make a negative. The offset negative is then stripped into the type and a plate is made. Finally, there is the transfer, by a photochemical process, to a suitable surface for printing.

Line and Halftone Engravings

Two different photoengraving processes are used in the preparation of artwork for letterpress printing. The first is the line engraving or line plate, which reproduces only two tones, solid black and solid white. If continuous tones from solid black through grays to white—like the varying tones of a photograph or wash drawing—are desired, the halftone-engraving process is used. Intermediate shades of gray result from breaking up tone values of a picture into tiny dots. When this engraving is used, each dot carries printing ink. Large dots form darker areas and small dots form lighter ones.

In the halftone process, original artwork is photographed through a screen with hundreds of parallel lines crossing one another at right angles. The more lines to the square inch, the finer the screen, and the sharper and clearer the details of the printed reproduction. Figure 14.6 shows one photograph shot through four different screens. (NOTE: Offset negatives of photos are created using the halftone process, too.)

Coarse screens are less expensive than fine ones, but the major factors determining the screen value chosen are the finish and weight of the paper on which the halftone will be printed. On coarse paper, a fine-screen halftone will smudge because the ink collects in the smaller spaces between the dots. The rough paper used by most newspapers restricts their use of halftones to 85-line screens or less. A magazine using a smooth, coated stock, however, will accept 110-line or even 150-line screens. Still finer screens are used for gravure and offset lithography, with satisfactory results on paper with a soft finish.

Color Reproduction of Print Advertisements

Normally, if an advertisement is to appear in color instead of black and white, a separate printing press operation is required for each color. In recent years, however, newspaper and magazine advertisers have had a choice of paper stock; the color green, for example, may be added to a black and white ad (through a separate printing process) or the black type and illustrations may appear on green paper.

Returning for a moment to letterpress printing and assuming plans call for an ad to appear in black and red, two different plates are required. One carries the black impression and the other the red. If the ad is printed by gravure or offset lithography, color-separated negatives are transferred to separate press plates or cylinders, each of which carries a different color of ink.

The advertisements or illustrations we see in complete natural color, or "full color," are usually printed from black and three primary pigment colors, as described in Chapter 13. These are called *process colors.* (It is also possible to print in other colors, but the ink needs to be specified.) The usual sequence is yellow first, red next, then blue, and black last. The black plate is called the key plate; it strengthens the depth and detail of the other plates, provides neutral shades of gray, and usually carries the text matter. See the inside cover of this text for an illustration of four-color printing.

To make four-color process plates, the engraver photographs the original full-color artwork four times, each time using a filter that eliminates all but

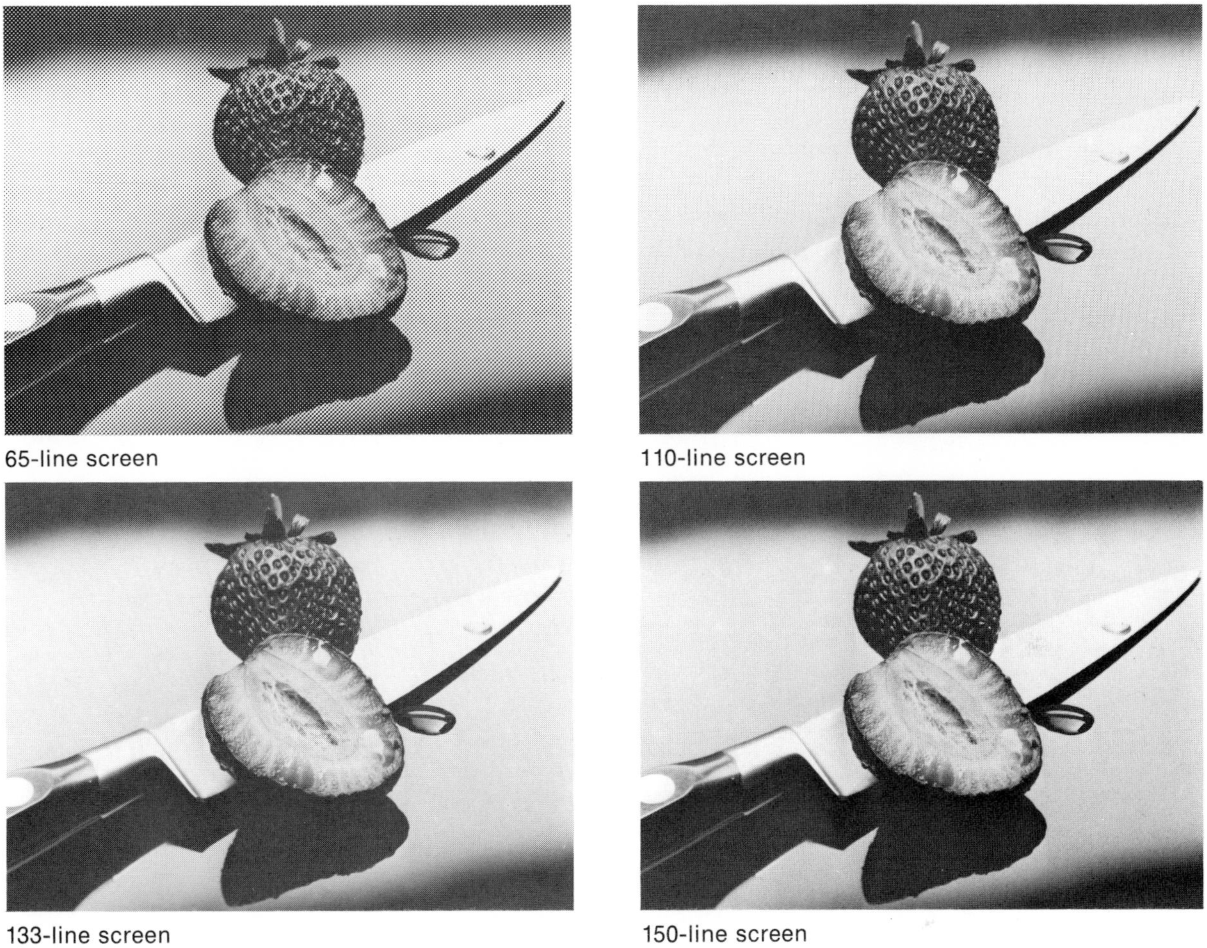

Figure 14.6 The more dots per square inch in a halftone, the finer the reproduction. The four sections of this illustration are reproduced from left to right in successively finer screens, from 65-line to 150-line. Refer to Figure 13.7 to see how this photo was used in an actual ad.

the desired color in the resulting negative. These are the color-separated negatives mentioned above. From each of the four negatives, the plates for offset lithography, gravure, or letterpress, or the stencils for screen printing, are made in the same way that a plate is made for black-and-white reproduction, although more hand finishing is required.

Broadcast Production

Radio and television productions include drama and the other performing arts. Their very nature makes them more susceptible to creative gimmicks than the operations encountered in getting ads into print. Unfortunately, the glamour and excitement often associated with broadcast production may sometimes overshadow the need for technical expertise and the attention to detail that we described in the sections on typography and printing.

Radio Commercial Production

Radio commercials are broadcast either live (adlibbed by deejays) or transcribed on tape or disk. In the latter case, music and sound effects can help create pictures in listeners' minds. Notice in Figure 14.7 that there are seven different types of effects, in addition to background music. Costs of an effective transcribed music-and-voice radio commercial can

Station: ROCK 104 - W I M Z / F M   Run: May 13-15, 1980

Account: SHIRTS ETC.   Length: :60

MUSIC: ESTABLISH, SLY STONE, "HOT FUN IN THE SUMMERTIME," AND UNDER THROUGHOUT

ANNCR: Shirts Etcetera, in the Suburban Shopping Center, has clothes to fit all of your hot-weather activities this summer. Swimwear, for splashing around in the pool...(SFX: SPLASHING)...or skiing one of East Tennessee's fine lakes...(SFX: MOTORBOAT). Cute little show-off shorts can help you become an ace tennis player, of course... (SFX: FOP/WHAP - "LOVE-40")...and Shirts Etcetera has neat jeans -- fit for sitting around the campfire with friends...(SFX: FIRE)... for motorcycling...(SFX: MOTORCYCLE)...or for enjoying outdoor entertainment...(SFX: LIVE CONCERT). Shirts Etcetera fits into your working life, too. You'll find attractive, comfortable skirts and dresses for the office...(SFX: TELEPHONES, CASH REGISTERS)... plus elegant attire, for warm summer nights -- and even warm-weather weddings! For all your clothing needs this summer, come to Shirts Etcetera. You'll love the fit -- and the price, too. Shirts Etcetera: in the Suburban Shopping Center.

Figure 14.7 A radio commercial with liberal use of sound effects (SFX) to help listeners visualize the message. [*WIMZ Radio.*]

be kept below $1,000, even with today's inflation. When station talent is used, costs may be zero, as they are when local or retail newspaper advertisements are created by the paper's display staff.

In radio, casting is crucial; inflection, vocal emphasis, and pacing are often as important as the actual words in communicating a sales message. Also, there is a quality of warmth and companionship in radio that wise copywriters use to full advantage. Friendly (and well-known) voices can enhance both the credibility and the memorability of a message.

Sometimes a musical jingle fills most or all of a commercial; sometimes a quieter musical background simply helps maintain the smooth flow of spoken copy. Libraries of such stock music (and also sound effects) are readily available in many cities, or original scores may be produced by recording studios.

Television Commercial Production

Live television commercials are very rare today, since so few programs are broadcast live. Rather, transcribed commercials appear on either film or videotape.

Film About 80 percent of commercial production on behalf of national advertisers is done on 35-millimeter film.[1] (For small stations that do not have 35-millimeter projection equipment, 16-millimeter prints may be prepared. Virtually all stations have videotape equipment, however, and usually prints are made on videotape instead of film, with better quality as a result.)

Film production lends itself to repeated telecasting, and to spot telecasting in a number of different markets. In can also be edited before airing, and performers, especially stars, prefer film commercials to anything done live because they can be produced at convenient times. Finally, film offers greater opportunities than videotape does for realism and action (through, for example, on-location shots and "chase sequences"), plus greater variety in sets and in camera and electronic effects. Figure 14.8 is an example of a filmed commercial.

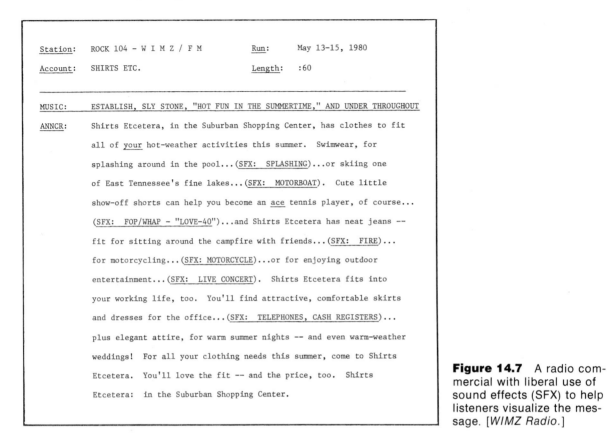

NEW
MIGHTY DOG®
from Carnation
"BRANDING IRON"

Pure beef.
Only new MIGHTY DOG . . .

from Carnation has it. All other canned dog foods contain by-products.

But New MIGHTY DOG is . . .

pure beef – no by-products.

No wonder it smells good.

And tastes better than any other dog food.

With vitamins and minerals for complete nourishment.

And single-serving cans that end left-overs.

Get new MIGHTY DOG.

Pure beef – no-by-products.

Figure 14.8 A 30-second TV commercial for nationally advertised Mighty Dog canned dog food. These still shots, taken from the actual filmed sequence, form what is called a photoboard. Each scene represents about three seconds of "moving picture" time. [*Carnation and Erwin Wasey, Inc.*]

Videotape Locally produced spots are almost all recorded on videotape.[2] This tape is a continuous plastic ribbon with magnetic particles, and it looks like audiotape enlarged about 8 times. Like film, it records both sound and video simultaneously, with the audio track running as a narrow strip on the edge of the wider video track. Both tracks can be erased and rerecorded separately, and the tape can be edited and spliced in the same manner as audiotape. It can record in color as well as monochrome.

Videotape offers the advertiser all the advantages of film transcription plus some that are unique. Tape transcriptions can be played back immediately without the time-consuming developing necessary with film. Both video and sound can be rerecorded while performers are still on the set, instead of requiring another shooting session. The production quality is superior to film, and on viewers' receiving sets it is virtually impossible to tell a videotape telecast from one that originates live. Last-minute changes in either audio or video can be made quickly because the tape is easily erased. The initial cost of tape is considerably less than film and film processing, and tape can be fully or partially erased and used again. Even more important, perhaps, are the savings in work-hours, both in shooting and in editing. With the development of compact, moderately priced recorders, the overall flexibility of tape and its lower costs make it possible for local advertisers to use the television medium with a creative potential impossible through either film or live telecast.

Figure 14.9 shows videotape equipment suitable for use in a television station. It is important to note, however, that this type of machinery has also become increasingly more *portable* in recent years; hence, it is a familiar sight on exterior shooting locations. Small cameras, monitors, and video recorders are easy to operate and are highly dependable. Bulky 2-inch recording tape has been replaced in many instances, too, with tape measuring just ¾ or ½ inch.

Of course, film and videotape may be combined in a single commercial. An example might be an in-studio videotaped message promoting a furniture sale with a filmed insert to take viewers on a trip through the furniture factory. In any case, at the local level advertisers often work from TV commercial *scripts* instead of the storyboards discussed in Chapter 13.

Figure 14.9 The RCA TR-800 video tape recorder is a full-feature, full studio console introduced to television stations in 1980. [*Compliments of RCA.*]

An example of a TV script appears in Figure 14.10. Instead of pictures, detailed video instructions are provided. These descriptions include some technical TV jargon related both to scene composition and to the transition between scenes. The terms describing composition are abbreviated LS, MS, MCU, CU, and ECU. They tell the TV director to shoot, respectively, a **long shot,** (LS, a wide-angle, all-inclusive picture), a **medium shot** (MS, showing performers from about the waist up), a **medium close-up** (MCU, showing performers at approximately shoulder level), a **close-up** (CU, showing just faces or product packages), and an **extreme close-up** (ECU, a very narrow, tight shot of a product name or, perhaps, a finger or set of teeth).

Transitions between scenes are accomplished in two ways. The first is physical. When a camera pivots from left to right, right to left, or up and down, the movement is called **panning.** A **zoom** is the movement of a camera lens in and out; the picture appears to shrink or grow accordingly. The second method is optical, or electronic, and includes the **cut** (an instantaneous switching between cameras), the **dissolve** (the gradual disappearance of one picture while another takes its place simultaneously), and the manipulation of **special effects** (objects and words that appear, disappear, and move as if by magic). Finally, a **super** is the superimposition of one thing over another, often words over pictorial material.

Production Techniques

Two basic techniques used in commercial production are live action and animation. Live action should not be confused with live broadcasting; a live-action commercial may be broadcast either live or on film or tape.

Live Action Live action means that real people are used as performers, and they convey both realism and credibility. Live action may use dialogue between on-screen performers who talk to one another or to the audience and is particularly adaptable to testimonials, dramatizations, and personality commercials. An alternative to dialogue is the narrative. It is usually less expensive than dialogue and is most frequently used with an off-screen voice over the demonstration of product uses and benefits.

Some commercial productions require rather elaborate sets. Consider the award-winning "Mean Joe Greene" commercials for Coca Cola: locker-room scenes in which a young fan trades his Coke for his football hero's jersey. The crew searched for a sta-

Agency: Kaylyn & Associates
Client: The Papaya Council
Title: Jim and Jenny

For Use: nationally
Length: :60 w/local tag
Date: 1/4/81

VIDEO	
FADE IN LATE NIGHT: JIM & JENNY IN BED. ZOOM LS TO MCU. HE TOSSES IN HIS SLEEP; SHE'S AWAKE, FRUSTRATED	JENNY: Jim? You've been tossing and turning all night! What's wrong?
ZOOM IN ON JIM	JIM: (MUMBLING IN SLEEP) Same old breakfast every morning: muffins-and-juice...muffins-and-juice...
CUT TO CU JENNY AS SHE SITS UP, NOW MUCH MORE ROMANTIC, ADDRESSING HIM AS IF HE WERE AWAKE	JENNY: Oh, Jim...I was going to surprise you tomorrow, but...
CUT TO CU JIM, STILL MUMBLING	JIM: ...same thing day after day...
CUT TO CU JENNY, ABSORBED IN HER THOUGHTS, OBLIVIOUS TO JIM	JENNY: ...well (HESITATINGLY), you see, I (EMBARRASSED) -- I bought a...papaya!
SLOW PAN RIGHT TO CU JIM	JIM: Juice-and-muffins...muice-and-juffins...
CUT TO CU JENNY FOR HER "STARTLED" LINE; THEN ZOOM BACK TO MS AS SHE CLIMBS OUT OF BED	JENNY: (STILL OBLIVIOUS) A real papaya, Jim. (ABRUPT CHANGE; SHE'S STARTLED BY HER IDEA) I'd better see if it's all right!
DISSOLVE TO KITCHEN SCENE NEXT MORNING: MS JIM AT TABLE & JENNY STANDS NEXT TO HIM HOLDING SOMETHING BEHIND HER BACK. (ONLY A CUP OF COFFEE AT HIS PLACE) ON CUE, SHE THRUSTS HALF-WRAPPED PACKAGE BEFORE HIM: PARTLY-VISIBLE FRUIT WITH "PAPAYA COUNCIL PAPAYA" SUPER	JIM: Good morning, Jenny, dear. (ABRUPT CHANGE) What's this? Papaya? But, how -- JENNY: It's a new breakfast idea, Jim: fresh fruit with a "tropical" taste. Zesty, really different.
JIM UNWRAPS GIFT, DIGS IN, LOOKS AT JENNY LOVINGLY. MOVE IN FULL ON JIM	JIM: Wow! That's got spunk! This isn't just breakfast, Jenny! It's a celebration!
CUT TO CU JENNY, YAWNING, DROWSY	JENNY: (ROMANTICALLY) Oh, Jim...if I...could only...stay...awake...
CUT TO ECU EMPTY PACKAGE WITH "PAPAYA COUNCIL PAPAYA" SUPERED; ADD EFFECTS: SEVERAL PAPAYAS "GROW" AROUND PACKAGE	ANNCR VO: Papaya. A refreshing change for your breakfast table. Try some tomorrow, and celebrate the good sleep you'll get tonight!
	(ADD LOCAL SUPERMARKET TAG LINE)

Figure 14.10 A script for a 60-second television commercial.

dium tunnel that looked dark and grungy, and one that was small enough to make Mean Joe look huge in contrast to his small co-star. (The one finally selected was in Mount Vernon, New York.) Special lighting effects created moody shadows, and the tunnel was even painted to create the desired atmosphere. Smoke was introduced to catch and hold the light, giving the overall film a bluish tint.

Postproduction activities, after all commercial scenes have been taped or filmed, include musical scoring, editing, and titling (adding of printed words). These tasks often require as much creative talent as the original writing and directing of scenes.

A typical 30-second spot, with seven scenes, takes an average of 3 hours to shoot. If an entire *group* of commercials is shot in the same location, and then edited into a package of separate messages, a set of six commercials can cost under $35,000. For example, a collection of different sports outfits worn by models might all be featured against a common golf-course backdrop. On the other hand, a celebrity may command $10,000 or more per day of commercial shooting, even if only one commercial is involved.

The popularity of movies with special effects (notably *Star Wars* and *Superman,* in the late 1970s) has attracted widespread interest among advertising production people. Major ad agencies are rapidly acquiring computer graphics systems that will enable them to produce an endless variety of special effects.

Animation In animated film or tape production for television, the position of inanimate objects is moved slightly while the transcribing camera is stopped. When the series of separate shots is projected at normal speeds, the result is the same sort of action delivered by the motion-picture camera.

Cartoons are perhaps the best-known form of animation and certainly one of the best-liked commercial techniques. They provide opportunities for fantasy that cannot be equaled with live-action production and, at the same time, offer a visual distinction that can be identified exclusively with an advertiser. But while cartoon commercials rate high in viewer interest and low in production cost compared with live action, they may easily lack credibility. Generally, they are most useful for impulse-purchase products. When combined with a live-action sequence, however, cartoons can be effective for more serious purchases.

Stop motion and photo animation are techniques used to bring products to life and make them walk, dance, grow, shrink, and so on. Refrigerator doors open and close, soft-drink bottles uncap, and packages unwrap to disclose their contents. Like cartoons, stop motion can both personalize products and lend an intriguing effect to demonstrations; for example, accessories may attach themselves dramatically to a vacuum cleaner without the aid of human hands. As is true with cartoons, however, supplemental live-action scenes are recommended if realism and believability are important message objectives.

There is some experimentation today using computerized animation on videotape. One such system describes desired shots on IBM punched cards and feeds them into a computer that is instructed to "move" objects in specific ways. Actions can be speeded up or slowed down and colors can be altered at will. In addition, items can grow, shrink, or undergo other transformations very creatively.

Combined Methods Some TV commercials are combinations of live action and animation. After a homemaker sprinkles cleanser on a stain, for instance, little animated "scrubber-helpers" might demonstrate to viewers just how and why a special formula removes the spot. At the retail level, photographic slides, rather than animated films or tapes, often accompany live-action presentations. They are relatively inexpensive, and may help provide continuity between newspaper and television campaigns by featuring identical pictures of merchandise or in-store displays.

Two Fundamentals of Advertising Production

Two vitally important rules of advertising production apply to all printing processes in both color and black and white, and to broadcast techniques as well. Though both are simple and nontechnical, they are often overlooked or ignored.

First, necessary corrections should be made before copy starts on its first step of mechanical or electronic production; desired changes should be completed while the text is in typewritten form, not after the words have been set in type or recorded. The later in the production process that alterations are requested, the more expensive they will be.

The same rule applies with even greater force to graphic elements. Major revisions in illustrative material cannot be achieved after the negative or engraving has been made. A photograph of a man pushing a lawn mower cannot become one of a woman pushing a baby carriage. All we can do is bring in the woman and the baby carriage and shoot a new picture. Minor changes can be made in finished art or even in engravings, but at a cost of both dollars and hours.

Taped and filmed commercials may be rerecorded or reshot, if changes are needed, but casts and crews must be recalled at additional cost and sometimes a special scene is next to impossible to reestablish. (Consider, for example, a concert, ballet, or circus performance.)

The second production rule is that on-going *communication* between copywriters and art directors or studio production specialists is essential. If a copywriter explains an idea fully to production experts, they may be able to suggest ways of improving the end result. Misunderstandings are more easily avoided, too, if wishes are stated in writing. Most advertising agencies have a firm policy that no production work begins until it is covered by a written order or memorandum.

When estimates for printing are prepared, we should be sure they include *all* costs. A common error occurs with folders or other direct-advertising pieces. Dummies and text copy are submitted to several printers for competitive bids, and the printers' bids are used as cost estimates for the job. It is regular practice, however, for printers to assume that they will be furnished complete artwork or engravings, and costs for such materials will not be included in estimates. When printers become responsible for artwork, costs can escalate.

Similarly, there is a big difference between using prerecorded, stock music in a radio or TV commercial and composing a brand-new background score or jingle. Also, characters are much more expensive when played by Hollywood stars than they are when played by unknown talent—though *residuals* (payments to acting talent for replays of the same commercial) are usually required in both cases.

Finally, on-location shooting usually costs more than in-studio work, and anything unusual (such as special lighting effects, elaborate stunts, or fancy sets or props) carries an extra price tag. The best practice is to use a standard production form that includes all possible items for job estimates. No individual project is likely to require every element listed, but checking off each one is a sure way to include all charges.

Law of the Unattainable Triad

The wise advertiser realizes that all advertising production is governed by the "Law of the Unattainable Triad." The goals of most production efforts are to produce top-quality ads, at low cost, in a hurry. (See Figure 14.11.) Because all three are impossible to achieve in a single production run, each advertiser must decide which point of the triad—time, price, or quality—is the most important for a particular campaign. The following illustrations will clarify this three-way conflict.

First, a tight advertising budget makes low cost the prime objective. So, the advertiser gets competitive bids from reliable suppliers or studios, or seeks out firms willing to do the work at less than standard rates. A supplier who charges a low rate, however, will often sacrifice quality and may require extra time to deliver the final product. Thus, a decision to save money often results in higher costs than are neces-

Figure 14.11 A graphic display of the Law of the Unattainable Triad.

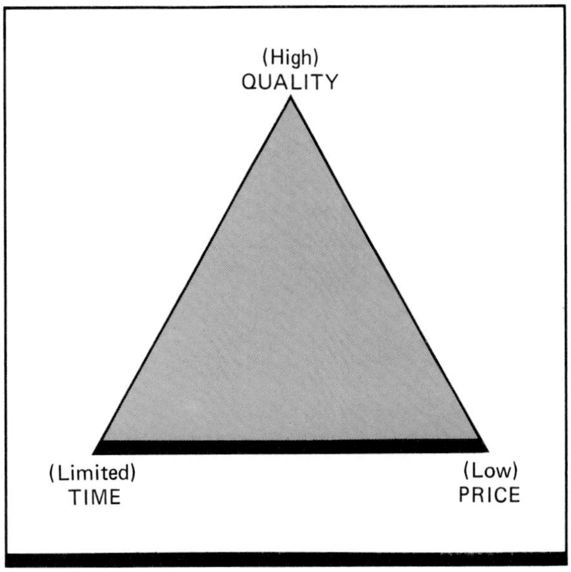

sary. Poor-quality ads can hurt a product's image and reduce sales revenue. In addition, the extra time needed to produce an ad might result in missed media deadlines.

Second, unanticipated but immediate competitive threats or marketing opportunities can make speed the most important requirement of production. If brand A launches a special merchandise offer in 14 key markets, it may be necessary for brand B to meet this threat with a new newspaper campaign. If the campaign is to be successful, mats must be shipped to newspapers in less than half the time normally allowed for their production, and that almost always means higher costs. Likewise, television film crews can work overtime to shoot a commercial ahead of schedule, but union wages may double.

Third, in many cases, fine-quality reproduction is the essential aim of advertising production. If a magazine advertisement is to present a prestigious image for a product or firm, the typography, engraving, and printing should be as high in quality as the copy and artwork. Anything less contradicts the advertising message that attempts to convey distinction. So does sloppy sound production in a radio commercial or music hastily composed or selected to meet a deadline.

A skilled production specialist may get top quality at a reasonably low price, but will almost certainly sacrifice speed. The only reason a quality printer, engraver, or radio sound specialist will cut prices is if the job can be done in spare time—and that means without being rushed. Or, we can shop for low price and fast delivery at a sacrifice of quality; but when fast delivery is combined with quality, bills are likely to be as much as 50 percent higher to cover overtime.

Everyone concerned directly or indirectly with the production of ads and commercials should remember the Law of the Unattainable Triad. In this business, as in many others, compromise is one of the keys to success; most campaigns represent a balance between reasonable cost, time, and quality demands, although one of the three is usually favored.

Summary

Mechanical and electronic production of advertisements and commercials require complex processes that are both time consuming and costly. Basic printing methods include offset, gravure, letterpress, and screen printing, and each has its advantages and limitations. Likewise, different styles of type have different personalities and are used to achieve distinct objectives.

Readability is affected by type size (measured in points and picas), by spacing, and by type style. Most modern typesetting is done using computer systems.

Ads appearing in full color are usually produced through the process of four-color printing. Primary yellow, red, and blue pigments can be mixed to form a range of secondary hues, and black is added to strengthen the depth and detail of other colors.

Radio and television commercials are broadcast live or (usually) on audiotape, videotape, or film. Music and sound effects may enhance a sales message, as can character voices, animated products or other elements, and celebrity presenters. Sometimes jingles are used to enhance product memorability, and televised scenes shot on location often increase credibility and the feeling of realism.

In live-action production, dialogue styles include testimonials, dramatizations, and personality commercials, whereas the narrative style is often combined with product demonstrations. Postproduction editing can be a very creative task, especially when a number of commercials are made from one filming or taping session. Animation can personalize products and bring them to life, but can also result in low levels of credibility.

A fundamental rule in communicating effectively with production experts is to give them complete information about requirements and objectives—and the best way is in writing. Sometimes standard forms or checklists for estimating production costs help make certain that nothing has been overlooked. Costs increase when ads or commercials must be redone to correct errors.

Regardless of its form, every production job is subject to the Law of the Unattainable Triad. Production specialists can combine fine quality with low cost, but not in a hurry. They can attain fine quality with rapid delivery if premium costs are no object. Or they can get production done in a hurry and at low cost, but quality is almost sure to be less than desired. Consequently, one of the most important decisions the advertiser must make about any production job is whether the prime objective is to keep down costs, get fine quality, or have the material delivered quickly.

Questions for Discussion

1 What are the fundamental differences between the four basic printing processes?
2 What considerations guide the selection and arrangement of type in an advertisement?
3 Explain the point and pica system for measuring type.
4 Name and compare two different photoengraving processes used in the preparation of advertising artwork for letterpress printing.
5 Consider the reproduction of color advertisements. Explain what we mean by "process colors" and "color-separated negatives."
6 What qualities should casting directors look for in choosing radio-commercial talent?
7 Name three advantages of videotape over film in the production of television commercials and three ways to cut costs in either filming or taping.
8 What is the difference between composition terms and transition terms in a TV commercial script?
9 Explain what we mean when we say that a live-action TV commercial does not have to be performed live. Then compare live action and animation.
10 Name the three objectives of the unattainable triad and explain why they cannot all be achieved simultaneously.

For Further Reference

Arnold, Edmund C: *Ink on Paper Two,* Harper & Row, Publishers, Inc., New York, 1972.

Herdeg, Walter: *Film and TV Graphics 2,* Hastings House, Publishers, Inc., New York, 1976.

Millerson, Gerald: *The Technique of Television Production,* 9th ed., Focal Press, Inc., New York, 1972.

Nelson, Roy Paul: *The Design of Advertising,* 4th ed., Wm. C. Brown Company, Publishers, Dubuque, Iowa, 1981.

Pocket Pal, A Graphic Arts Production Handbook, 12th ed., International Paper Company, New York, 1978.

Roman, Kenneth, and Jane Maas: *How to Advertise,* St. Martin's Press, Inc., New York, 1976.

Rosen, Ben: *Type and Typography,* Reinhold Publishing Corporation, New York, 1976.

Seiden, Hank: *Advertising Pure and Simple,* AMACOM, New York, 1977.

Turnbull, Arthur T: *The Graphics of Communication: Typography, Layout, Design,* 3d ed., Holt, Rinehart and Winston, Inc., New York, 1975.

Wilkie, Bernard: *Creating Special Effects for TV and Film,* Hastings House, Publishers, Inc., New York, 1977.

Zeigler, Sherilyn K., and Herbert H. Howard: *Broadcast Advertising,* Grid Publishing, Inc., Columbus, Ohio, 1978.

End Notes

[1] "Nat Eisenberg Tells Agencies: Videotape Commercials Merit More Consideration," *Advertising Age,* May 5, 1975.

[2] "Animation through Computer Offered as New Ad Technique," *Advertising Age,* March 17, 1975, p. 58.

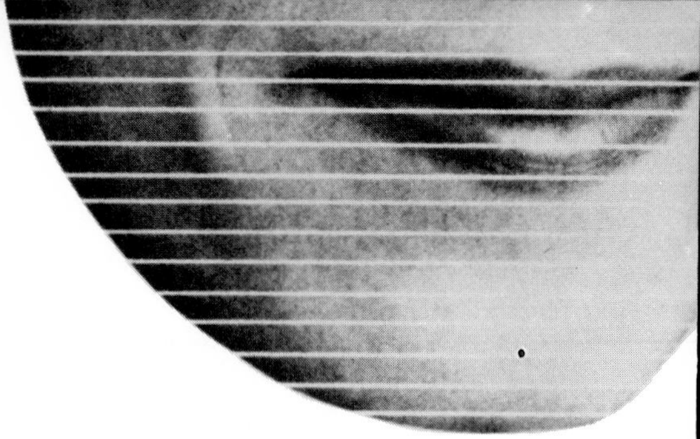

PART 5

Planning and Managing the Advertising Campaign

The tasks comprised in business management are commonly divided into three main groups: planning, organizing, and controlling. As a business activity, the management of advertising programs can be divided into the same groups. The essence of any advertising program is the advertising campaign, which evolves from a detailed plan for the promotion of a firm's product or service. The plan spells out the advertiser's policy for organizing the advertising resources in order to have the greatest impact on a target audience and includes the

evaluation of the advertising to see that the initial objectives are met.

Chapter 15 explains how campaign planning precedes action, while Chapter 16 highlights the importance of research in effective advertising planning. In Chapter 17 we learn how budgetary matters are handled, while Chapter 18 is devoted to the equally important media-selection decision. The need for careful coordination of advertising with other elements of the promotional mix is described in Chapter 19. Because all advertising decisions are influenced by laws and ethical considerations, Chapter 20 discusses those topics. Similarly, inasmuch as a great deal of advertising effort goes beyond the boundaries of a single country, we shall examine advertising management on the international scene in Chapter 21. We believe you will find that planning and managing the advertising function is a complex and challenging task.

Chapter 15

Advertising Planning

Advertising is a basic element in the marketing programs of most business firms. It is the communication arm for marketing organizations and advertising programs, whose planning, organizing, and controlling are important responsibilities of management, usually contain subparts known as **advertising campaigns.**

Underlying an effective advertising program, therefore, is sound marketing planning that establishes the interrelationship of all elements in the marketing mix. Basic marketing plans may remain effective for a period of years and provide a foundation for several advertising programs and a number of advertising campaigns.

The term "campaign" has long described battle maneuvers in warfare. Today the term is applied to many systematic efforts, including the election of political candidates, the raising of money for charities, and the persuasion of people to buy airline tickets, automobiles, records, or a myriad of other products and services. One definition of the term "campaign" is *a unit of effort to accomplish a set of objectives.* We define an advertising campaign as *a unit of product information distributed to accomplish a set of communication objectives.*

In a manner similar to the drawing out of the plan for the advertising program from the company's overall marketing plan, the plan for the advertising campaign evolves from the advertising plan. In this chapter we examine how the advertising campaign is both planned and carried out.

Seven Basic Steps in Campaign Planning

When an advertiser is planning an advertising campaign, seven essential steps are taken:

1. The advertising opportunity is appraised.
2. The market is analyzed.
3. Advertising objectives are determined.
4. The budget and necessary control systems are established.
5. Planning the strategy for:
   a. Selecting media
   b. Creating messages
6. Advertising is coordinated with other promotional and marketing systems.
7. Results are evaluated.

These steps are not individual activities. In practice, an advertiser will proceed with two or more steps at the same time or begin one step before the previous step has been concluded. For example, once the advertiser determines that the opportunity for advertising exists (step 1), the campaign plan is put into action. The market analysis (step 2) and determination of objectives (step 3) will be undertaken simultaneously because they are so interrelated. Advertising messages influence media choices, while the size of the budget can also affect media decisions (steps 4 and 5). Coordination efforts (step 6) are carried on parallel to advertising activities. Of course, results are measurable (step 7) only after the campaign has started and only if communication goals have been established.

A careful examination of Figure 15.1, which presents the planning and implementation cycle for the advertising campaign, should help you understand the flow of events that take place when an advertising campaign is being planned.

Appraising the Advertising Opportunity

Before an advertising campaign can be planned, the advertiser must determine whether advertising has a role to play in a particular marketing situation. Neil Borden, in his pioneering study of the economic effects of advertising, postulated that five conditions govern the opportunity for advertising. The presence of these conditions means that advertising, if well done, is likely to help meet the marketing objectives of the advertiser. On the other hand, if the conditions are absent or weak, advertising is likely to disappoint its sponsor. The five conditions leading to achieving maximum potential effectiveness for an advertising campaign are the following:[1]

1 *Presence of a favorable primary-demand trend.* If consumers are in a mood to purchase the basic product category, the manufacturer of a brand within that category is more likely to meet with market success. However, advertising a product of a type that is declining in consumer popularity is not likely to succeed. Advertising does not reverse adverse primary-demand trends; for example, it is difficult to sell big automobiles when the trend is toward compacts.

2 *Good chance for product differentiation.* Products, such as cabbage or light bulbs, which are

Figure 15.1 This chart shows how advertising decisions flow from the marketplace and eventually return there. [*Based in part on a chart devised by Kenneth Hollander, Atlanta.*]

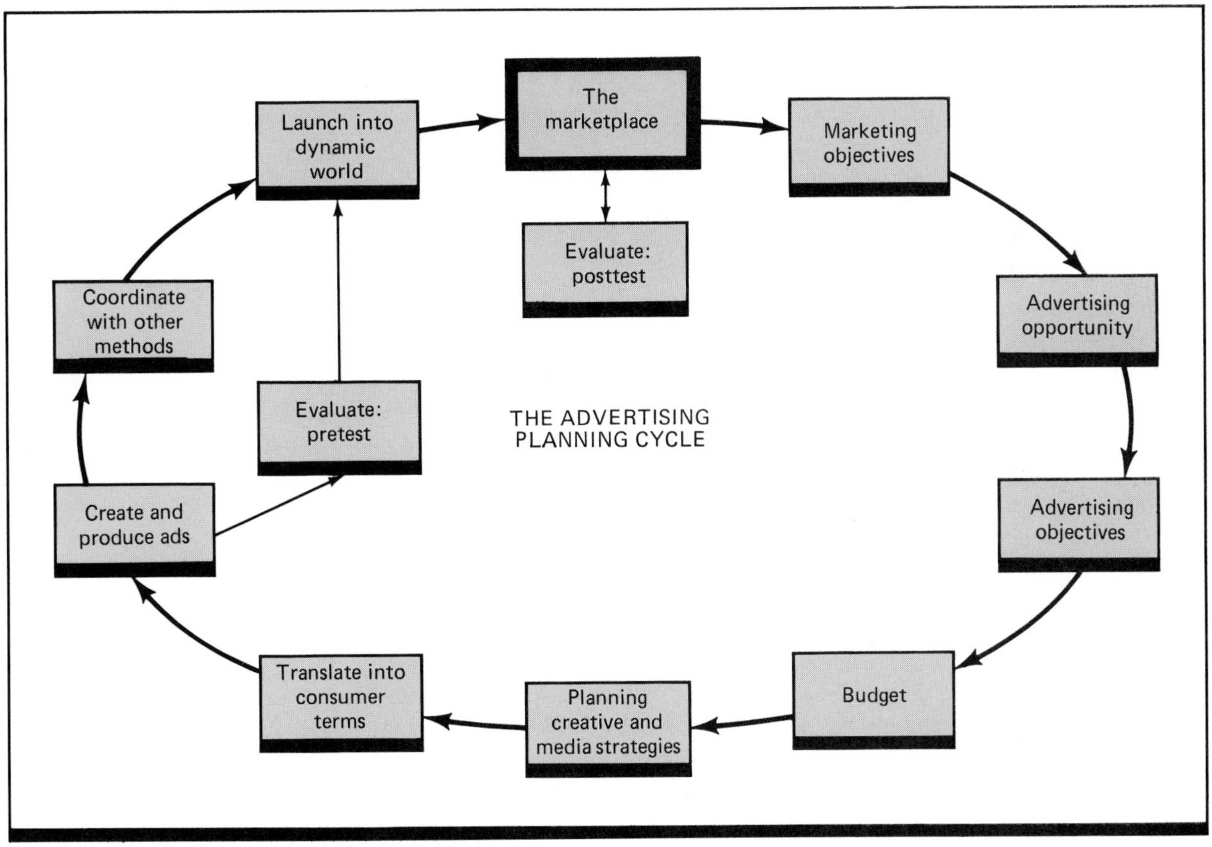

viewed as commodity, or parity, items by consumers, do not lend themselves to advertising. Product differentiation provides the opportunity for influencing consumers to prefer one brand over another by showing unique or exclusive qualities. Contrast the opportunity for advertising cosmetics or toothpaste, for example, with that presented by sugar or pencils.

3 *Presence of hidden qualities.* If the consumer can see the qualities the product possesses, the opportunity to advertise successfully is reduced. On the other hand, if the product's key virtues are hidden, advertising can help build mental associations regarding those characteristics. Dependability of various brands of mechanical products cannot be ascertained by looking at them on display in the dealer's showroom, yet it may be a fundamental concern in the buying decision. Washers and dryers are an example, and the Maytag Company recognizes this point and addresses it in its television commercials by emphasizing the loneliness of the Maytag repairman, whose services are never required. The physical characteristics of other products, even many of their innate attributes, are so apparent to the consumer—a bag of sugar or a box of toothpicks—that a strong case for the use of advertising in marketing efforts cannot be made.

4 *Presence of powerful emotional buying motives.* If advertising appeals can be made which strike right at the core of what is important to consumers, the advertisements are likely to be successful. Thus, oranges were marketed to the United States market in the early twentieth century by appealing to the desire of mothers to raise healthy children. Cosmetics can be promoted as providers of personal beauty and romance. It has been said that beauty aids are really "selling hope."

5 *Adequacy of funds.* Condition 1 in this list came out of the nature of the marketplace, while the next three conditions emerged from the product itself, or from consumers' perception of the product. The fifth condition springs from within the company itself. It is often said in the advertising business that "the greatest waste in advertising is to advertise too little." This means, of course, that some minimal amount of advertising must be done if sufficient impact on the target market is to be achieved. If the company lacks enough money to advertise at that level, the outlook for advertising success is dim. Chapter 17 contains a further discussion of this point.

A careful assessment of these five conditions may lead to the conclusion that the prospective advertiser should not use advertising in the pursuit of marketing objectives, or, more likely, that advertising will play a minor role in the marketing program of the company. We shall now proceed with our discussion of advertising planning, assuming that a case for the advertisability of the product has been established.

Analyzing the Market

A key step in the planning process is known as "analyzing the market." The analysis answers two important questions: "Where are we now?" and "Why are we there?" The most critical decision made when the market is analyzed is to define closely the **target market** for the product. Once the people for whom the product is made are known, an advertising campaign to reach those people can be designed. Marketing objectives are set that answer the questions: "Where do we want to be?" "Whom do we want to reach (who is the target market)?" And, "What response do we want?"

The advertiser's overall marketing plan provides the basis for a current analysis of the target market and a projection of market conditions when the campaign actually appears. Such information as the total industry volume over the past 10 years, the advertiser's share of industry sales as well as the shares of competitors, the legal constraints placed on the product category, and the role of foreign competition should be determined. These factors of demand, competitive response, and legal constraints are highly important in planning future action. Equally significant are conditions within the firm itself, including the firm's financial and production capabilities. If a company mounts a campaign that is successful, the factory may not be able to meet the demand for the product. Similarly, if there are not enough dollars available to make an impact in the national market, the plan may be structured to cover regional markets to the extent that funds will permit.

In 1971 Lever Brothers decided to develop a new toothpaste, which became its Aim brand. An analysis of the market at that time yielded some interesting data. The dentifrice category accounted for annual consumer sales of $460 million. Procter & Gamble products held a 45 percent share of that market, Colgate followed with 28 percent, Lever with 17 per-

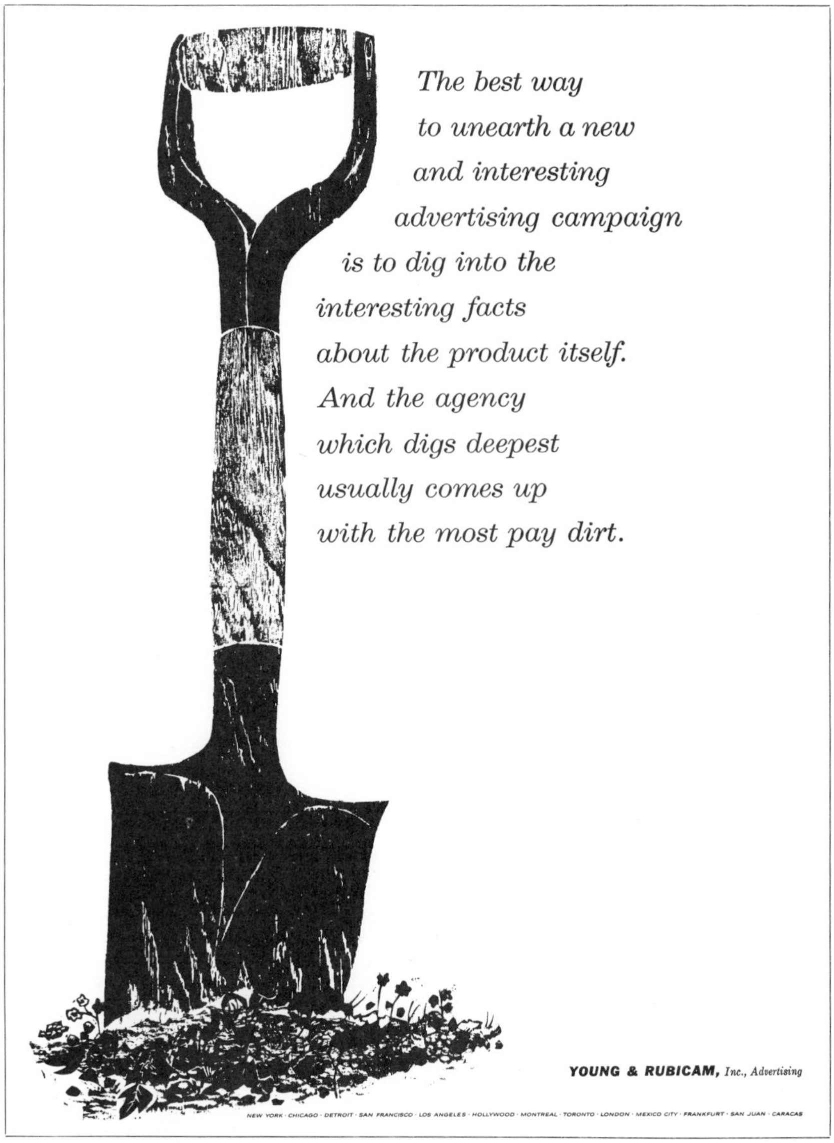

The best way
to unearth a new
and interesting
advertising campaign
is to dig into the
interesting facts
about the product itself.
And the agency
which digs deepest
usually comes up
with the most pay dirt.
YOUNG & RUBICAM, Inc., Advertising
NEW YORK · CHICAGO · DETROIT · SAN FRANCISCO · LOS ANGELES · HOLLYWOOD · MONTREAL · TORONTO · LONDON · MEXICO CITY · FRANKFURT · SAN JUAN · CARACAS

Figure 15.2 Planning an advertising campaign requires an analysis of the market, as this large advertising agency tells prospective clients.

cent, and all other brands, a little over 9 percent. When analyzed by advertising appeals, it was discovered that 64.9 percent of toothpaste was sold through a therapeutic appeal (cavity prevention) and 25.8 percent was sold through a cosmetic appeal (winning smile), with 9.3 percent using other approaches to the market. Procter & Gamble's two brands, Crest and Gleem, were both in the therapeutic section of the market, Colgate had a brand in each division—Colgate in the therapeutic segment and Ultra-Bright in the cosmetic area. Lever's two brands, Close-Up and Pepsodent, were both in the cosmetic portion. Obviously, the opportunity was for another entry into the therapeutic segment where 65 percent of sales resided, and Lever Brothers did not have an entry. The company formulated a new product which they believed to be superior to Crest, and then developed an advertising campaign designed to give consumers an alternative to Crest, as well as to diminish that brand's domination of the dentifrice market.[2]

Of course, the Lever Brother analysis of the dentrifice market was more thorough and in much greater detail than this short paragraph can relate.

DEWAR'S PROFILES
(Pronounced Do-ers "White Label")
RON BUCK
HOME: Malibu, California
AGE: 39
PROFESSION: Lawyer, writer, entrepreneur.
HOBBIES: Painting, writing screen plays.
LAST BOOK READ: 'A Lost King.
LAST ACCOMPLISHMENT: Brought The Factory into being, Hollywood's discothèque for the important people who like to swing.
QUOTE: "Frankly, I hate the snobbery and the pretense; it's how to lose friends and not influence people. But if you're going to be in the game you might as well play as best you can."
PROFILE: Confident, successful, but still struggling for an important way to express his feelings about a frail world and its people.
SCOTCH: Dewar's "White Label"
BLENDED SCOTCH WHISKY · 86.8 PROOF · © SCHENLEY IMPORTS CO., N.Y., N.Y.
Forty fine whiskies from the hills and glens of Scotland are blended into every drop of Dewar's "White Label."
Before blending, every one of the 40 is rested and matured in its own snug vat.
Then, one by one, they're brought together by the skilled hand of the master blender of Perth.
White Label
Dewar's never varies

(*a*)

Figure 15.3 One company's advertising program may contain more than one advertising campaign. Here a manufacturer of Scotch whisky seeks to tap two very different market segments. The "Profiles" campaign, illustrated by Figure 15.3(*a*) (above), is designed for younger consumers where Dewar's lacks market penetration. The "Authentic" campaign, Figure 15.3(*b*) (facing page), is aimed at an older group and seeks to reinforce an already established brand image. Dealing with two different mind sets means that one sales message will not do the communication job.

But the marketing plan created to introduce the new brand made advertising imperative as a communication medium, and its role self-evident to the success of the product.

Perhaps the most critical decision made when the market is analyzed is to define clearly the **target market** for the product. Essentially, this is an exercise in segmentation. Once it is known for whom the

(*b*)

product is intended, advertising campaigns can be built to reach these people. Of course, in some instances, conditions warrant a mass-market orientation which aims at nearly everyone. However, generally speaking, *the* market is broken up into several smaller segments or parts. Thus, Lever Brothers did not go after the entire dentifrice market with its new brand, Aim, but tried instead to reach the segment using toothpaste for therapeutic reasons. This is an example of segmentation by *benefit.* Obviously, that in itself was a heavy assignment; nevertheless, it was more likely to succeed than if the campaign had been aimed at the total toothpaste market. By 1975, Aim held a 10 percent share of the total market for toothpaste.

Aim eventually climbed to third position in the dentrifice market with a 12 percent-plus share. Then, along came Beecham's Aqua-fresh with a double-barreled appeal—cavity-fighting *and* breath-freshening capability—featured in twin-benefit advertisements. (See Figure 15.5.) By 1980, the new entry had moved to third position in the $650 million product category with a 13.5 percent share. Aim's share in that year dropped to 10 percent, and Crest stood at 36.2 percent share. P. & G launched "its first counterattack on 'those fancy stripes and gels' "[3]

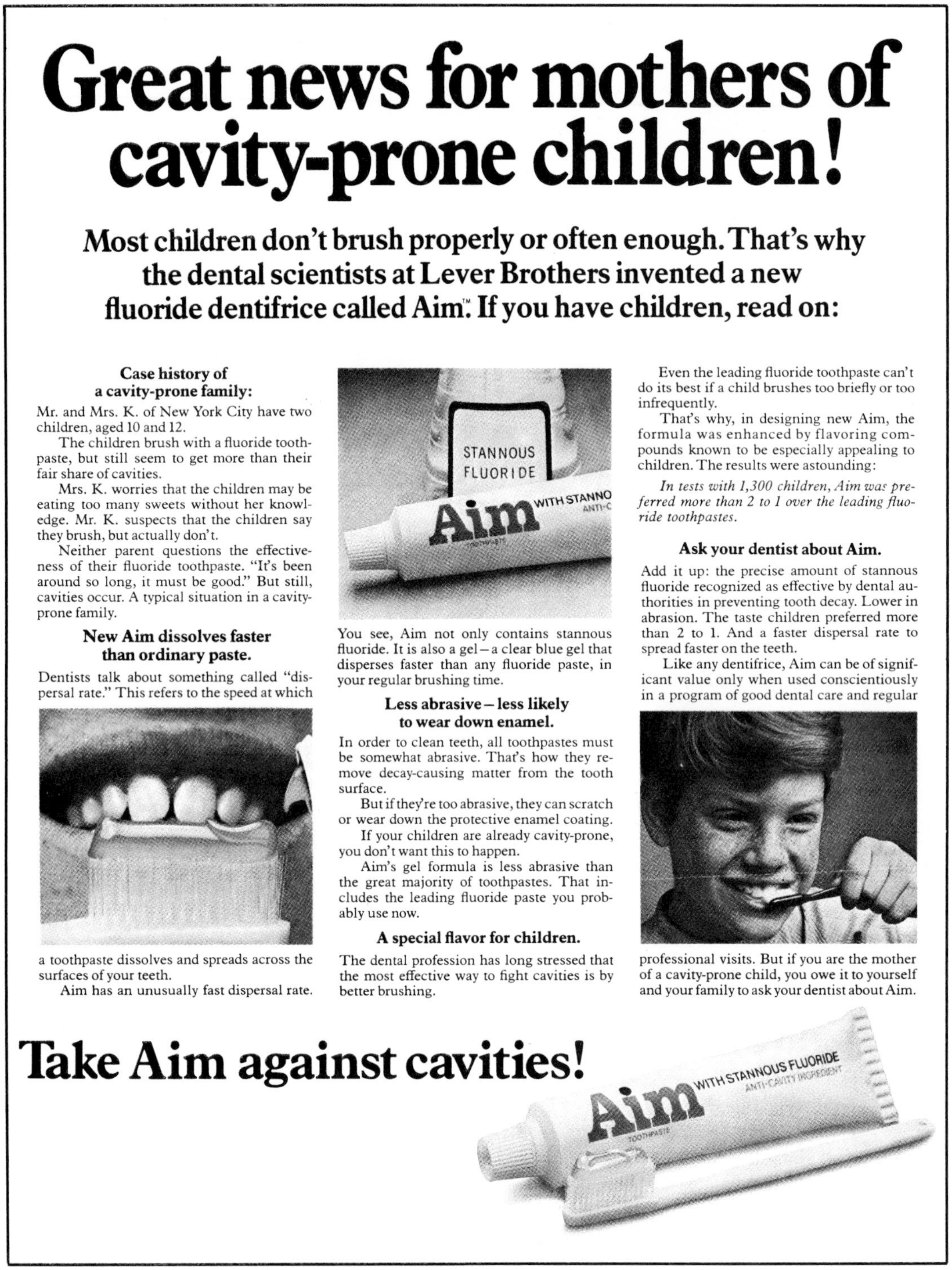
Great news for mothers of cavity-prone children!
Most children don't brush properly or often enough. That's why the dental scientists at Lever Brothers invented a new fluoride dentifrice called Aim™. If you have children, read on:
Case history of a cavity-prone family:
Mr. and Mrs. K. of New York City have two children, aged 10 and 12.
The children brush with a fluoride toothpaste, but still seem to get more than their fair share of cavities.
Mrs. K. worries that the children may be eating too many sweets without her knowledge. Mr. K. suspects that the children say they brush, but actually don't.
Neither parent questions the effectiveness of their fluoride toothpaste. "It's been around so long, it must be good." But still, cavities occur. A typical situation in a cavity-prone family.
New Aim dissolves faster than ordinary paste.
Dentists talk about something called "dispersal rate." This refers to the speed at which a toothpaste dissolves and spreads across the surfaces of your teeth.
Aim has an unusually fast dispersal rate.
STANNOUS FLUORIDE
Aim
WITH STANNO
You see, Aim not only contains stannous fluoride. It is also a gel—a clear blue gel that disperses faster than any fluoride paste, in your regular brushing time.
Less abrasive—less likely to wear down enamel.
In order to clean teeth, all toothpastes must be somewhat abrasive. That's how they remove decay-causing matter from the tooth surface.
But if they're too abrasive, they can scratch or wear down the protective enamel coating.
If your children are already cavity-prone, you don't want this to happen.
Aim's gel formula is less abrasive than the great majority of toothpastes. That includes the leading fluoride paste you probably use now.
A special flavor for children.
The dental profession has long stressed that the most effective way to fight cavities is by better brushing.
Even the leading fluoride toothpaste can't do its best if a child brushes too briefly or too infrequently.
That's why, in designing new Aim, the formula was enhanced by flavoring compounds known to be especially appealing to children. The results were astounding:
In tests with 1,300 children, Aim was preferred more than 2 to 1 over the leading fluoride toothpastes.
Ask your dentist about Aim.
Add it up: the precise amount of stannous fluoride recognized as effective by dental authorities in preventing tooth decay. Lower in abrasion. The taste children preferred more than 2 to 1. And a faster dispersal rate to spread faster on the teeth.
Like any dentifrice, Aim can be of significant value only when used conscientiously in a program of good dental care and regular professional visits. But if you are the mother of a cavity-prone child, you owe it to yourself and your family to ask your dentist about Aim.
Take Aim against cavities!
Aim
WITH STANNOUS FLUORIDE
ANTI-CAVITY INGREDIENT
TOOTHPASTE

Figure 15.4 The Aim brand was introduced with this ad which employs the therapeutic appeal.

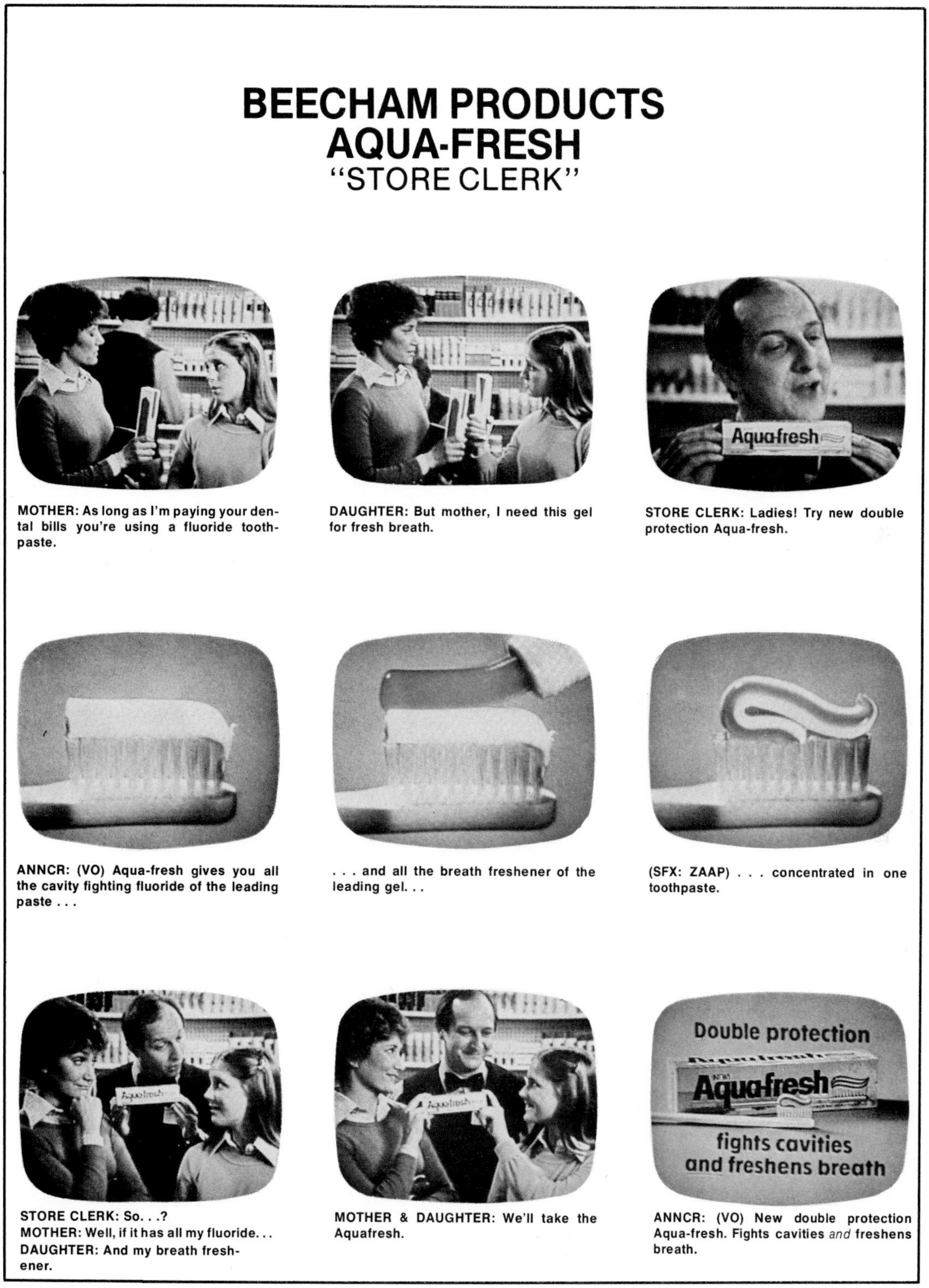

BEECHAM PRODUCTS
AQUA-FRESH
"STORE CLERK"
MOTHER: As long as I'm paying your dental bills you're using a fluoride toothpaste.
DAUGHTER: But mother, I need this gel for fresh breath.
Aquafresh
STORE CLERK: Ladies! Try new double protection Aqua-fresh.
ANNCR: (VO) Aqua-fresh gives you all the cavity fighting fluoride of the leading paste . . .
. . . and all the breath freshener of the leading gel. . .
(SFX: ZAAP) . . . concentrated in one toothpaste.
STORE CLERK: So. . .?
MOTHER: Well, if it has all my fluoride. . .
DAUGHTER: And my breath freshener.
MOTHER & DAUGHTER: We'll take the Aquafresh.
Double protection
Aquafresh
fights cavities
and freshens breath
ANNCR: (VO) New double protection Aqua-fresh. Fights cavities *and* freshens breath.

Figure 15.5 Aqua-Fresh uses a two-benefit appeal to promote its entry into the toothpaste market.

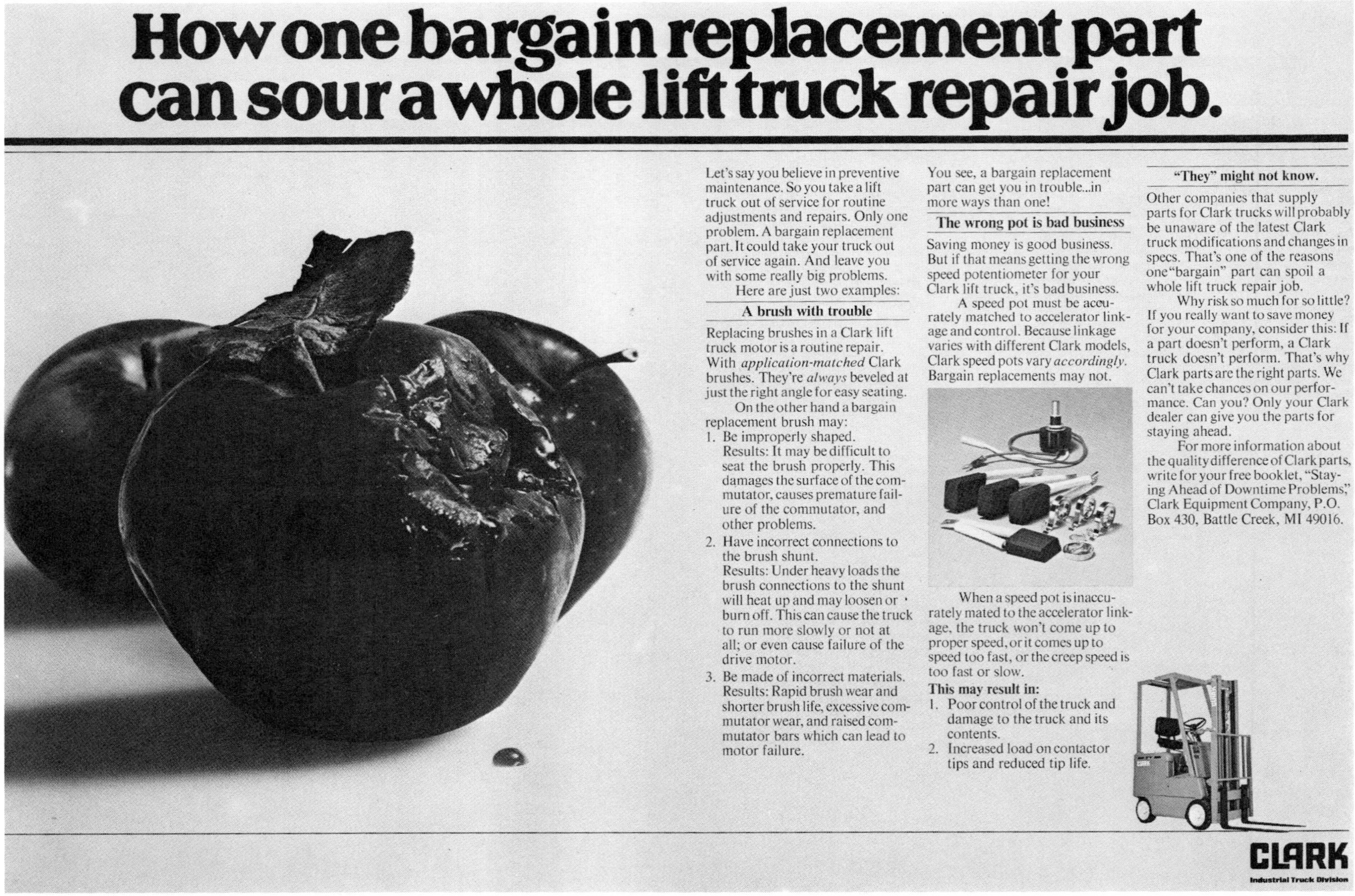

Figure 15.6 This industrial advertisement was recognized in the Objectives and Results competition sponsored by the American Business Press. The objective set was: "To achieve stocking and promotion of OEM parts by 80 percent of dealers." Results obtained were that 83 percent of the dealers participated in the program.

Determining Advertising Objectives

The communication role of advertising was discussed in Chapter 4 as a backdrop for understanding better how advertising functions. Because many advertising campaigns falter for lack of clearly defined objectives, the topic is emphasized here.

Planning any business activity starts with the setting of objectives by upper management. Broad corporate objectives are used to create objectives for each unit of the firm. In our discussion, they are considered the basis of marketing objectives, which in turn determine advertising objectives. Because of the "top down" method of objective setting, advertising objectives are phrased in terms of ultimate marketing goals, such as "increasing our share of the market." If the results of an advertising campaign are to be evaluated, however, advertising objectives must be clearly distinguished from marketing objectives. Moreover, because few advertising campaigns, and even fewer marketing plans, are restricted to the accomplishment of a single goal, the different advertising objectives should be carefully ranked by relative importance.

Some years ago, management consultant Russell H. Colley emphasized this point of separating marketing objectives, for which advertising is not the sole or even the primary cause, from advertising objectives. He further recommended that objectives—broad, long-range aims—be distinguished from goals—immediate, short-range objectives that are specific as to time and degree. These examples illustrate his point:

Objectives:
Marketing: To sell products
Advertising: To create brand preference for products

Goals:
Marketing: To achieve 12 percent of total industry sales in the product category in 1982
Advertising: To establish a 20 percent preference for brand A among Y million consumers in 1982.[4]

S. H. Britt made an in-depth study of "so-called successful advertising campaigns" and concluded that the designation was unwarranted in most instances because no clear-cut objectives were established for the campaigns at their inception. How can any endeavor be deemed a success when its purpose was not established at the beginning? Britt went on to advise that the statement of objectives for a new advertising campaign should contain four elements:

1 The basic *message* to be delivered
2 The *audience*
3 The intended *effect(s)*
4 The specific *criteria to measure* the success of the campaign later[5]

Two examples may be helpful. First, consider the case of American Motors when introducing its Buyer Protection Plan. The company might well have used the following objective: "To establish a reputation for product quality and service dependability for its automobiles." The related advertising goal would then be: "To register the name Buyer Protection Plan and its elements in the minds of at least 60 percent of all current Chevrolet, Ford, and Plymouth owners within 90 days after the program's introduction." This goal is specific, quantified, and measurable. It also provides the maker of the advertising message with a specific direction.[6]

Through consumer research, Tree Top, Inc., learned that consumer awareness of its new pear-apple juice product was at a level of only 20 percent. But, Tree Top also learned from this same research that over 50 percent of the consumers who were aware of the product were frequent purchasers. This appeared to be a clear-cut communication problem: to raise awareness of the product so that increased sales could be expected. The following advertising goal was established for seven test markets: To increase the awareness of women between the ages of 12 to 44 years regarding Tree Top Pear-Apple Juice from the present 20 percent level to 50 percent in a six-month period.

Six months later, after a heavy advertising program in the test markets, another round of research was conducted; it revealed awareness of the existence and store availability of the brand at levels running from 44 percent in one market to 61 percent in another. Sales volume increases were also evident in each market, roughly proportionate to the new awareness levels.

Before the advertising executive can develop any specific strategies for use in a current advertising campaign, objectives must be determined. The portion of the total marketing effort to be carried by advertising must be established, and these responsibilities for specific communication tasks or goals must be defined. Short-term communication goals should not be attained at the sacrifice of long-range objectives. For example, obnoxious advertising that might successfully "increase awareness of new product A among homemakers in 1982" could detract from the advertiser's long-range efforts to improve the brand or corporate image, thus seriously affecting accomplishment of long-range marketing objectives, or even the ultimate corporate objective of making a profit.

The ultimate responsibility for determining long-range advertising objectives and short-term goals rests with the management of the company doing the advertising. Such managerial personnel control the marketing organization charged with carrying out the defined objectives, as well as the budget which provides the funds for doing so. However, direct responsibility for developing advertising goals (and in some cases, even marketing goals when advertising is the principal element of the marketing mix) rests with the advertising management, whether that function be performed by market or product management or advertising manager. In practice, the advertising agency is usually assigned some portion of this responsibility as well.

Establishing the Budget and Necessary Control Systems

Once we know what advertising is expected to do (what the advertising objectives are), the funds to do the job must be provided. Because such large sums of money are spent for advertising by many business firms and because there has been a great deal of interest recently in "accountability" for these funds, it is important to budget advertising dollars carefully to be sure they are spent wisely. Although Chapter 17 is devoted entirely to the topic of budgeting and control, an overview is presented here, as it is an integral part of the advertising planning process, flowing naturally out of the objectives-setting step.

To control the use of funds in a large corporation, management assigns a specific amount of money to various departments. A budget is a plan that is used to allocate this amount to each department. Within the advertising appropriation (that amount allocated for all advertising costs), different products, different geographic or consumer markets, different media, and different time periods may each receive a share of the total. In order to determine the budget, estimates of the cost of each task are taken into consideration.

One should keep in mind that any budget is only a plan; an advertising budget is only a plan for financing certain future advertising operations. Even though budgets are established to cover a specific period of time, usually a year, they should be constantly reviewed in terms of changing marketing situations, just as the total marketing plan should be under constant review and evaluation. Shifts in distribution patterns, competition, changes in production capacity, and other elements in the marketing situation may require changes in advertising objectives and strategies, with consequent adjustments in the advertising budget. Flexibility is a key factor in a realistic budget. The establishment of a contingency fund within the budget is desirable, thus permitting rapid response to changed conditions.

Deciding how much to spend on advertising is one of the most perplexing problems faced by many corporate managers. It is difficult to measure what advertising does to profits, or even to sales volume, in most marketing situations. Therefore, the key factors in determining the optimum size of an advertising fund are the experience and judgment of management. This is a specialized kind of business creativity which is founded upon a philosophy toward advertising's role. Some managers think of advertising only as a current cost of doing business and as a cost that is more easily trimmed or eliminated than many others that appear on a firm's operating statement. This attitude tends to dilute the success of the advertising program, for almost any advertisement performs a dual purpose. It does help to produce immediate sales, and in this function, is rightly viewed as a current operating expense. But it also contributes to the image of the product or brand and the image of the advertiser, builds goodwill, creates acceptance for future products, and consequently serves as an investment toward future profits. When advertising is thought of as an investment, the likelihood of the company's mounting a carefully planned advertising program is greatly enhanced. Furthermore, the chances of advertising being made a scapegoat in periods of reentrenchment are lessened. Advertising is more than a stimulant to immediate sales. It should be looked on as a capital investment, just as an investment in a new piece of manufacturing equipment is regarded as a capital investment.

Developing the Strategy

Objectives describe the intent of the advertising; once they are laid down, it is time to develop appropriate strategies to accomplish them. Strategy issues arise in two major areas of advertising: (1) selecting media and (2) creating ads. Each area is discussed individually below, but first, what is meant by the term **advertising strategy**?

"Strategy," a military term, translates from the Greek literally to mean "generalship."[7] A specific strategem can be described as "an ingenious design for achieving an end." Thus, a strategy is oriented toward results. Furthermore, being "ingeniously designed," "it must go beyond a summation of facts and objectives to that *creative insight* leading to a more effective way to sell the product."[8] One additional quotation may help to illuminate this point:

> Advertising strategy is creativity applied to knowledge for the purpose of finding the most effective way of achieving an end. We believe that advertising strategy must encompass the totality of what a product or service is, and how it is sold to the consumer. It embodies the product's and service's reason for being; it is the product's most important property; it is the differentiating principle that the product embraces. Strategy welds all of the marketing factors into a cohesive unity that will achieve the end.[9]

In other words, creativity is applied to the advertising objective, and a design for achieving an end is developed.

Selecting Advertising Media

Identifying the members of a target market provides the essential information needed for the development of a media strategy. In a simplified way, the media-selection process can be described as matching the audience for a specific medium with the media habits of persons in the target-market group. Although media selection may use quantitative techniques and computers, a lot of art, or creativity, remains in the designing of an effective media plan.

The budgets established by advertising managers are spent for the use of media that have been recommended by the advertising agency. The costs of time and space in media absorb the major portion of money advertising budgets. Decisions on what types of media to use, and what specific media within these types, call for the kind of specialized skill and experience that are the backbone of agency service—the knowledge of how to create and deliver advertising messages efficiently.

What is sought in media selection is the delivery of effective advertising messages to the greatest number of prospects (people in the target market) at the lowest possible cost. That assignment is complicated by the many variables that affect the ability of any medium to communicate a particular advertising message, of which cost, coverage, merchandising possibilities, and the nature of the message are the most important. No one type of medium can be thought of as being better than all others, and few advertisers rely on a single type of medium. All types, and all specific media within these types, offer advantages and disadvantages. The media planner seeks to find the right combination for a particular advertiser at a particular time. Chapter 18 is devoted to the media-planning process.

Creating Advertising Messages

The importance of planning for the success of individual advertisements and commercials was discussed briefly in Chapter 12. We now amplify the ideas given there, for advertising messages are at the core of advertising planning.

The Association of National Advertisers holds that the value of an excellent advertising message may be 10 or more times greater than a mediocre message. This is true whether we are measuring consumer attitudes, preference for the product, or final sales results. In general, every advertiser pays the same amount for similar time or space in advertising media. Thus message content provides an opportunity area where dollar maximization can operate. Superior messages mean greater return on dollars spent for advertising.

The creation of the advertising message, like the selecting and scheduling of media, is one of the primary functions of the advertising agency. The two tasks must be closely interrelated, if not actually undertaken at the same time. Often the process of creating effective advertising is aided by devising a creative blueprint which can be derived from the answers to the following questions:

1 What business goals do we seek to accomplish?
2 What kind of people do we now sell to? What kind *should* we sell to?
3 How do those people now think, feel, and be-

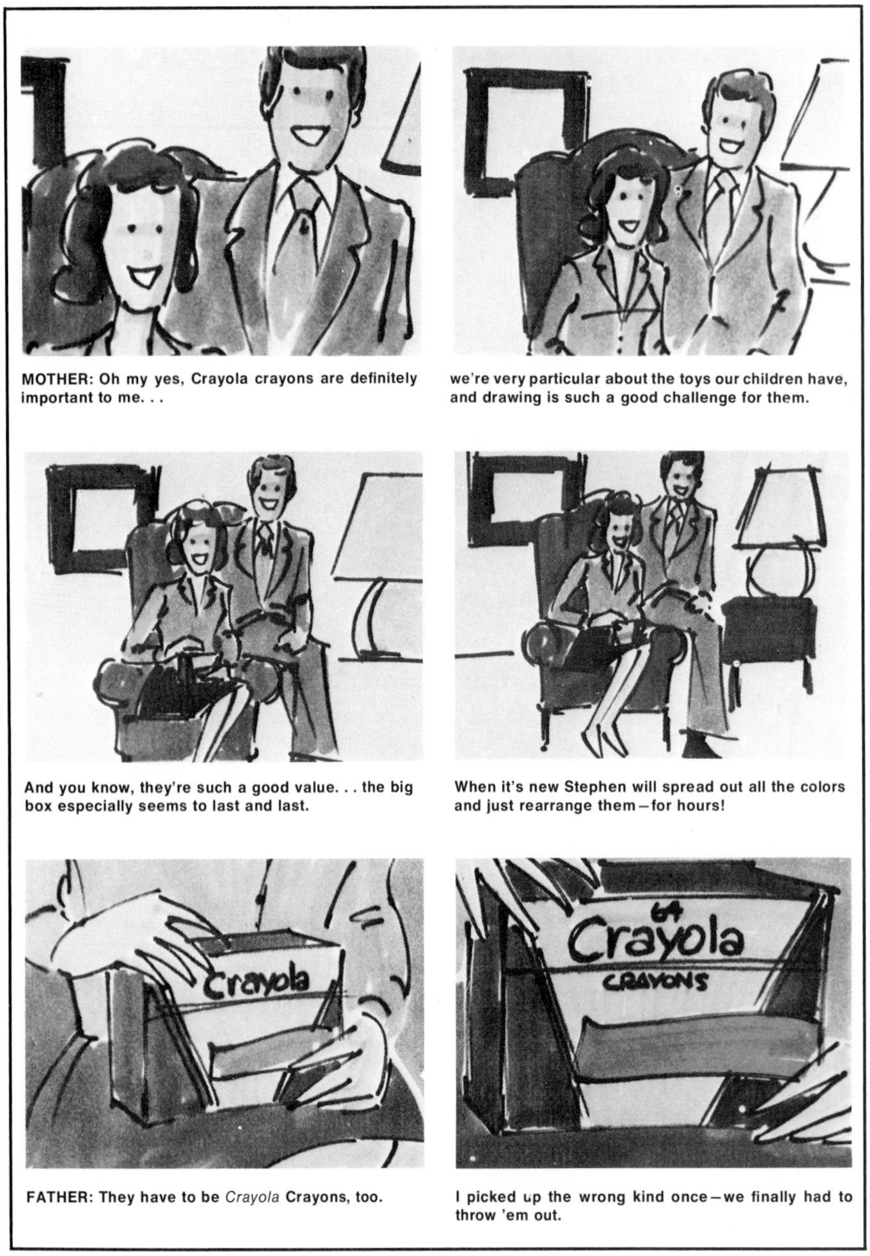

MOTHER: Oh my yes, Crayola crayons are definitely important to me. . .
we're very particular about the toys our children have, and drawing is such a good challenge for them.
And you know, they're such a good value. . . the big box especially seems to last and last.
When it's new Stephen will spread out all the colors and just rearrange them—for hours!
Crayola
FATHER: They have to be *Crayola* Crayons, too.
64
Crayola
CRAYONS
I picked up the wrong kind once—we finally had to throw 'em out.

(*a*)

Figure 15.7 Different appeals must be made when both children and adults are influential in the purchase of products. Figure 15.7(*a*) (at left) shows a television commercial aimed at parents, while children are the target of the message in Figure 15.7(*b*) (facing page).

lieve about our product, our company, and our competition?

4 What do we want those people to feel, think, and do?

5 What key thought can we put into those people's minds to make them think, feel, and believe or do that?

6 What tone of voice will get those people to hear and believe us?[10]

One of the important principles of copywriting is to emphasize or concentrate on a certain selling idea or theme. This principle deserves special attention in campaign planning.

The Campaign Theme Every advertising campaign should have a basic theme that reflects the campaign objective. This theme should appear in every advertisement, at least by implication. In this

BINNEY & SMITH
30 second TV commercial
"TWO-WAY TIP"
BSTV 7911
Crayola® Markers
Crayola Markers
It's fun to create with Crayola
You can use our two-way tip to draw things thick or thin
Like a paper space ship for. . .
A Martian and his twin
Crayola Markers
You can make a piggy bank . . .
or a butter fly
You can make a blue fish tank
A mask with one big eye
Cause it's fun to create with Crayola
VO: Crayola Markers come in eight rainbow colors.

(*b*)

way, each advertisement supports every other advertisement in achieving the desired results, just as each separate copy element supports the central sales idea of a single advertisement. The theme may or may not incorporate the whole Unique Selling Proposition (USP) as this concept was explained in Chapter 12. Without a basic theme to furnish continuity and focus, an advertising campaign becomes little more than a collection of unrelated messages. The advertising of Coca-Cola provides an excellent example of the use of the campaign theme. The firm changed to its theme "It's the real thing" in 1969 in order to make Coke advertising contemporary with the American scene at that time. The theme was used until 1976, when the "Coca-Cola Adds Life to . . " theme was introduced. Three years later, in 1979, the "Have a Coke and a Smile" slogan was introduced. The editors of *Advertising Age* speculated

We climbed above the clouds on Hawaii's "Volcano Island" to hide a case of Canadian Club.
And you can win a Hawaiian vacation to search for it.
"Watch out for Pele," the islanders warned us of their bad-tempered goddess. We'd come to the Volcano Island of Hawaii, where Pele's tantrums can send torrents of lava skyward, to hide a case of C.C.®
Lava hot enough to boil water.
"Want to see what Pele can do when she's angry?" friends asked. We did, so with our C.C. on a pack frame, we went searching for a hiding place on one of Hawaii's newest lava flows. The river of lava had been cooling for two full years, yet the heat of Pele's anger rose up hot enough to boil water in places.
The beach looked like shining coal.
Later, we cooled off while searching another of Pele's works. In a dark temper, the fire goddess had sent black lava coursing into the sea. But the surf had pounded it into a fine, coal-black sand to create one of the world's most beautiful beaches.
Climbing up to one of Hawaii's strangest sights.
Finally we packed our C.C. up 13,796-foot-high Mauna Kea volcano. A surprise awaited us at the peak. Snow! A sight we never expected in Hawaii! Along our trail up Mauna Kea, we buried a surprise for you, the case of Canadian Club. One clue: you don't need to reach the top of the world's highest island volcano (you won't even need to enter the state park) to find the world's finest tasting whisky. Be careful though, Pele thinks that C.C. is hers.
© 1979 · 6 YEARS OLD. IMPORTED

Figure 15.8 Once an advertiser develops a good communication vehicle it should be retained as long as results are being achieved. This ad appeared in the long running campaign for Canadian Club.

e Hawaiian C.C. on us.
to search for the C.C. on
waiian adventure vaca-
p down to your partici-
e store and pick up your
dian Club's "C.C. Hawaii"
or dial 800-223-1216, toll
s. (In Hawaii and Alaska,
850 and in New York, call
There's no purchase nec-
heless, you might want
ur offering to Pele while
ust say, "C.C., please."
Penn. or wherever prohibited by law.
Club
87 lands.
M WALKER IMPORTERS INC. DETROIT, MICH.
HISKY.
IMPORTED
Canadian Club
C.C.

that Coca-Cola might be guilty of making too frequent changes in its advertising theme. It was hypothesized that Coke's major competitor, Pepsi-Cola, which had been making market-share gains on the leader, had done so because the company has essentially stuck with its "Pepsi Generation" umbrella theme for more than 20 years, so people know why they should be drinking Pepsi.[11]

An interesting example of a long-running, successful advertising campaign is the "Hide-a-Case" program sponsored by Hiram Walker Incorporated for its Canadian Club brand whisky. In 1967, a case of Canadian Club was dropped by parachute in the neighborhood of Mount Kilimanjaro in Africa. Ads in leading magazines presented clues to help searchers pinpoint the location of the air drop. This effort generated so much interest that the campaign idea was continued, and in a little more than a decade, a total of 18 cases of the whisky were hidden in exotic and remote places around the world. Figure 15.8 presents one episode in the campaign. The campaign enhanced the brand with excitement and adventure, a theme that had been used in Canadian Club advertising since 1935 when Prohibition was ended in the United States. The campaign obviously lends itself to extensive publicity: first, when a case is hidden, and second, when one is discovered. Incidentally, 12 of the 18 cases had been located by 1979.[12] In 1981, another case was hidden somewhere along the Lewis and Clark Trail.

The importance of choosing the correct campaign theme is dramatized by the experience of Lever Brothers with its number one product in the heavy-duty liquid detergent category, Wisk.[13] In 1950, the company management concluded that the firm would not be able to make any impact on Tide's leadership in the detergent field with a powdered formulation. Research people were put to work developing a liquid laundry product which was launched in 1956 with $20 million of advertising support. When national distribution was completed in 1957, the product accomplished a conversion rate of 1 in 25 instead of the desired goal of getting 1 household in 8 to switch to the liquid detergent. Sales were disappointing. The advertising approach was something like "Try it, you'll like it." The consumer apparently didn't feel that was enough reason to change. Heavier rates of advertising yielded no significant increase in sales of the brand. Then, in 1967,

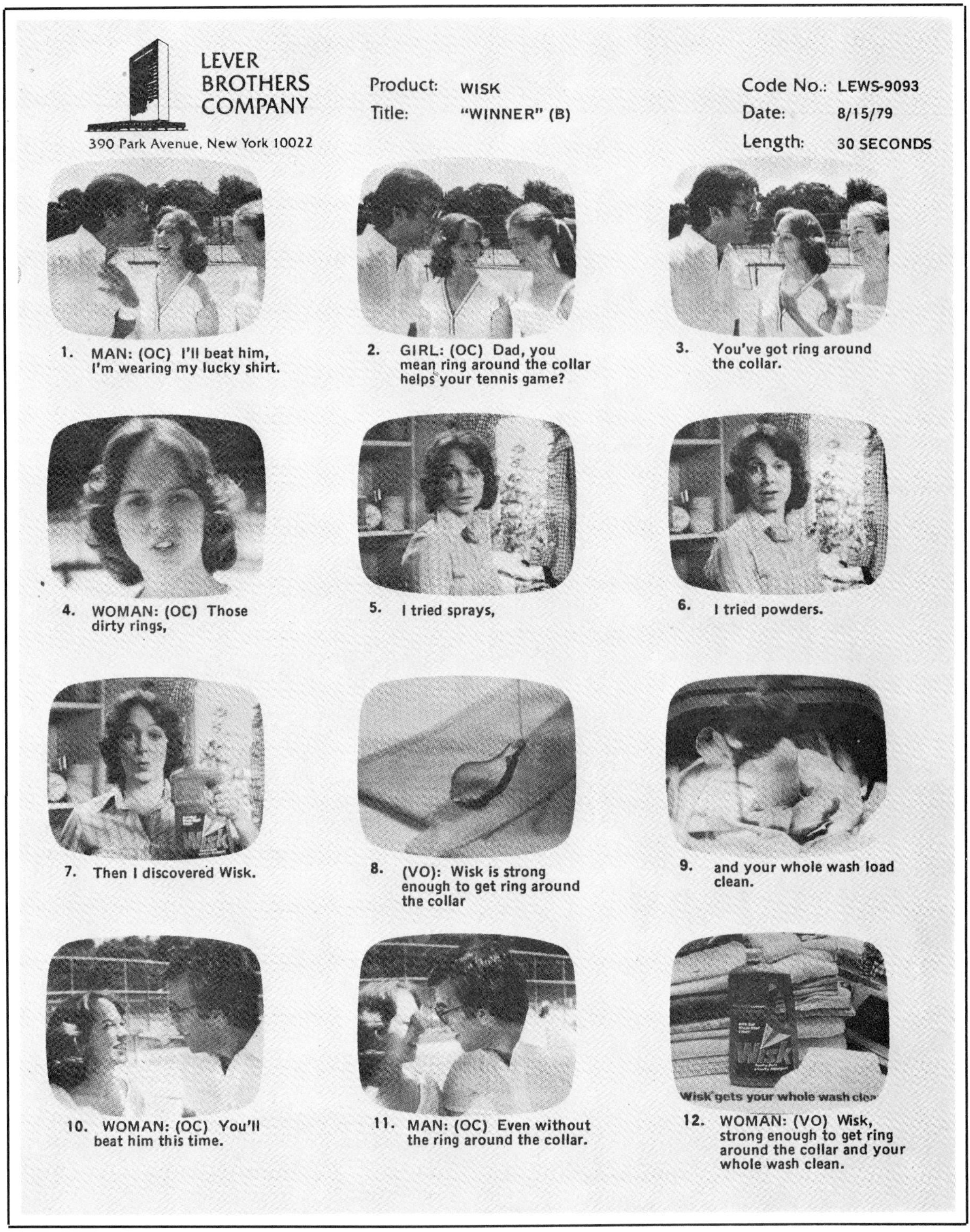

Figure 15.9 The "Ring Around the Collar" theme has been very successful for Wisk.

a copywriter at Batten, Barton, Durstine, & Osborn (BBDO), the agency for the Wisk brand, hit upon the "Ring around the Collar" copy execution. This theme exposed a need that the product satisfied well. The consumer need for stronger general cleaning was clearly addressed, and within eight years sales for the brand had tripled without any increase in advertising. Wisk is in third position in the total laundry detergent category and number one in the liquid detergent group. This success story is particularly dramatic when one realizes that the laundry detergent product category is a large, crowded, and mature market that grows only 2 percent per year.

Coordinating Advertising with Other Promotional and Marketing Methods

Advertising, to be fully effective, needs active support from the channels of distribution and from other nonadvertising components of the marketing organization. The responsibility for securing such cooperation rests with the advertiser. If the advertising program is to be successful, such elements as production, delivery, and inventory must be integrated with the advertising plan.

Personal selling by both the advertiser's own sales force and by intermediaries is an essential ingredient to total marketing success. What is sought in this area of advertising planning is to get maximum cooperation from distributors, dealers, and salespeople. The effort to get this cooperation is known as **merchandising the advertising.** This term means the process of selling the advertising program to the advertiser's own sales force and to dealers handling the products. The burden of that sales message is the story of how the advertising directed at prospects will make the job of these salespeople and dealers easier.

The ways in which advertising is merchandised to the sales force and to dealers are discussed more fully in Chapter 19, which contains information on how advertising is coordinated with all forms of promotion.

Evaluating Advertising Results

All previous steps in campaign planning must be in progress, at least partially, before the results of advertising can be evaluated. As soon as the campaign is underway, it can be subjected to testing within a simulated marketing environment. The results then are used to correct the format of the advertising message or to adjust expectations from the actual expenditures for the campaign. This process, called **pretesting,** is done before—and may influence—the buying of media and the creative steps yet to come. Pretesting is a research technique that determines the reaction to advertising by a representative sample of the target market before the advertiser makes full commitment to the campaign. The goal of pretesting is to eliminate errors or weaknesses before considerable sums of money are invested in the effort.

The other form of evaluation, **posttesting,** is done only after a full commitment to a creative approach and a schedule of media has been made. The objective is to ensure that future campaigns will be more effective. Underlying posttesting is the idea that we can learn from our past mistakes—and also from our successes.

Advertising testing can be isolated to the advertisement or any of its elements, such as the headline idea, basic theme, or illustrative treatment; such evaluation is usually called "copy testing." Furthermore, the underlying consumer benefit or "proposition" behind the advertising may be placed under the microscope. Similarly, the value of a particular kind of medium may be assessed. A whole series of research techniques, as explained in Chapter 16, are available when this step gets underway. Actual testing is carried out by the advertising agency or by an independent research organization. Advertising as a science has come a long way through these testing methods, but the methods are not a substitute for the creative skill that is the essence of good copywriting or imaginative media selection.

If the advertiser maintains a continuous watch over results while a campaign is in progress, a weakness in any phase of the planning—the campaign theme or the dealer program, for example—may soon become apparent. The campaign can then be strengthened quickly by making changes in the plan.

After the campaign has run its course, an attempt to see what returns have been received for the money spent should be made. Except in the case of the mail-order advertiser, determining the campaign's effect on sales is difficult. Even when relatively sophisticated experimental methods are employed to measure the effectiveness of advertising, the effect is seldom fully defined.

Profile

John G. Smale

Procter & Gamble is a corporation in which "its people are shaped as much by the organization as they shape the organization." It is also known for its promotion-from-within policy. Furthermore, as the biggest advertiser in the United States, P & G has required that executives destined to rise in the firm must obtain significant experience in the management of the advertising function as part of their training for company leadership. All these characteristics are beautifully illustrated by the career of John G. Smale, who was appointed chief executive officer in early 1981.

Smale, born August 1, 1927, in Ontario, Canada, graduated from Miami University (Ohio) in 1949. Prior to joining P & G, he worked in New York City for Vick Chemical Company and Bio-Research, joining the Cincinnati-based soap manufacturer in 1952 with the title of assistant brand manager. Six years later, in 1958, he became associate advertising manager and was later promoted to manager of the Advertising Department, Toilet Goods Division. By 1970, he had earned the title of vice president—group executive; three years later, John was elected to the position of executive vice president. After 22 years of service with the company, Smale became its president in 1974. His move to the position of chief executive officer (CEO) in 1981 presented him with the responsibility of running one of America's largest companies.

Many corporations today are headed by people with finance or production backgrounds. John G. Smale, however, is a prime example of a corporate leader whose training and expertise are centered in the fields of advertising and marketing. That Procter & Gamble finds its top leadership from those executives who have spent a considerable amount of their work-life managing advertising highlights the importance of the function to company success.

Execution of the Advertising Program

Planning the advertising program is the responsibility of the advertiser, who often delegates some of the task to the advertising agency. Execution of the plan, on the other hand, usually is performed by the agency, with the advertiser's role largely one of review and control. Execution of one phase is frequently in progress while planning for another is still being discussed. For instance, copy is prepared and submitted with rough layouts before specific media plans are approved. There is a need, therefore, to coordinate the planning and execution phases. The situation may call for adjustments when some execution decisions require a reexamination of earlier plans.

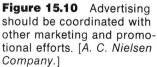

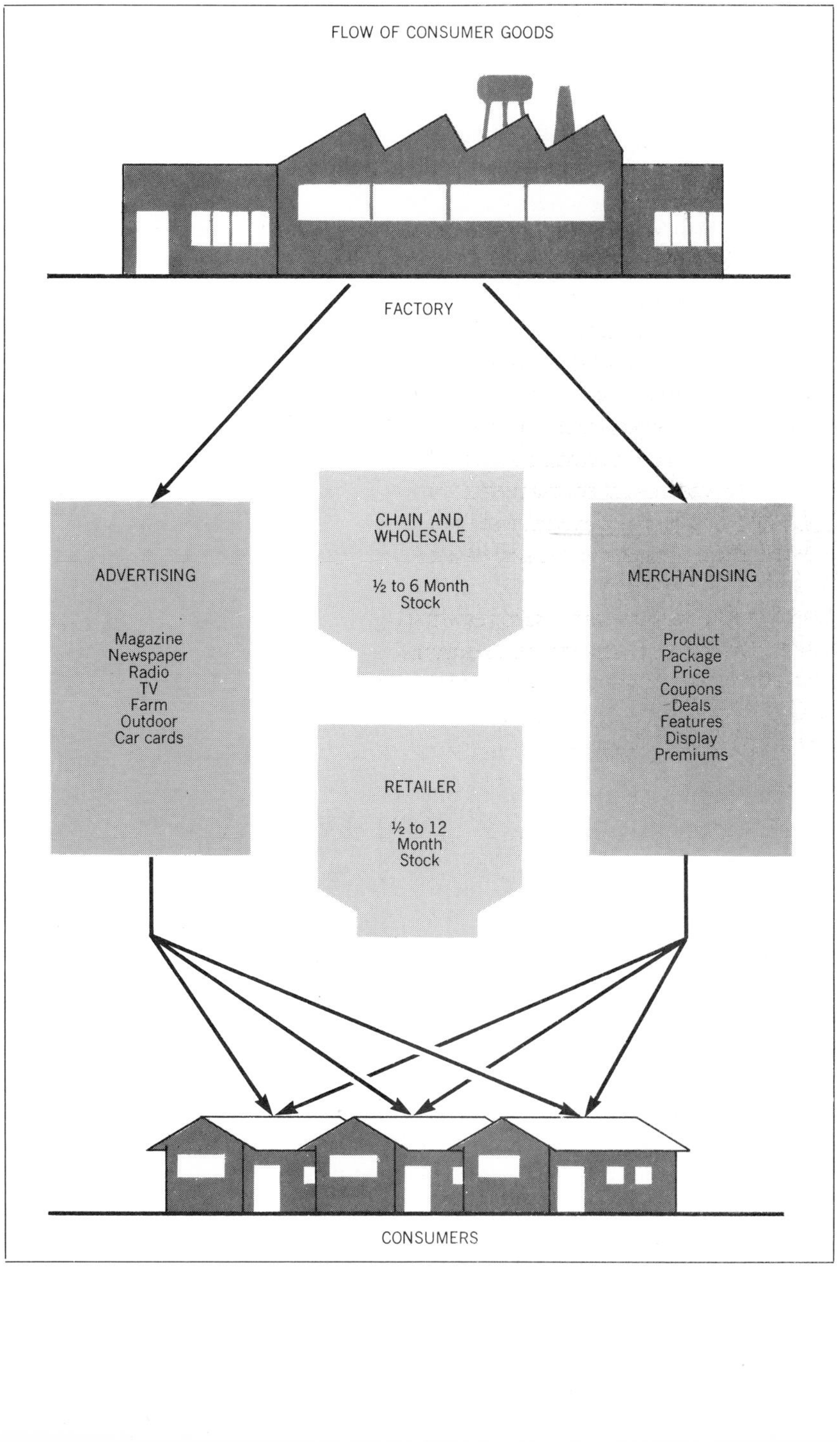

Figure 15.10 Advertising should be coordinated with other marketing and promotional efforts. [*A. C. Nielsen Company.*]

Summary

Effective advertising is built with sound advertising planning, which in turn depends upon a sound marketing plan. Seven steps are followed when an advertising campaign is being designed.

The first step is to determine whether advertising fits into the marketing needs of the company. If such an opportunity does exist, the remaining steps are taken as the advertising campaign is planned and implemented.

The second step is analyzing the market. Every advertising plan is the child of the marketing program for the firm, and knowledge of market conditions, competitive forces, legal restraints, and international considerations is vital to the advertising planning process. Defining the target market with which the advertising will strive to communicate is at the core of this step.

The third step involves establishing objectives for the campaign. Objectives should be specific, for a stated period of time, and set down in terms that can be measured after the campaign is finished. Once it is known what the advertising is to accomplish, the fourth step is deciding how much money will be needed to achieve the objectives. A budget is arrived at, and control methods are set up to ensure that the money is spent efficiently.

Two strategy issues constitute the fifth step in campaign planning. With the target market firmly in mind, two closely interrelated decisions are made: (1) the advertising media to be used, and (2) the creative approach to be employed. Media selection involves weighing the advantages and disadvantages of the various media against the objectives set and the budget available for the campaign. The creative blueprint is designed with the campaign theme at its core.

In the sixth step, advertising must be coordinated with other marketing and promotional activities to maximize the return from the effort and money expended on the advertising campaign.

Two forms of evaluation constitute the seventh step, pretesting the program's creative and media elements and posttesting the campaign after it has run.

Questions for Discussion

1. What are the major steps in planning an advertising campaign? Is there any set order in which these steps are to be taken? Explain.
2. List the main kinds of information needed for a complete analysis of the marketing situation.
3. What are three product categories where you feel the primary-demand trend is unfavorable? Do manufacturers in these product areas still advertise? Why? Discuss.
4. From current advertising campaigns, isolate specific ads where (*a*) hidden qualities exist in the product featured; (*b*) emotional appeals are employed; and (*c*) the chance for product differentiation is exploited. Write a short paragraph describing each of your choices.
5. Select a current advertising campaign and write objectives for it using the guidelines provided in this chapter. Obviously, you will have to make some assumptions, as you do not know the actual marketing situation for the campaign.
6. What is the present situation in the toothpaste market? Have additional brands recently entered the scene? Can you find out the present market shares held by the various brands? Write an appraisal of the current market.
7. Why is determining the advertising budget such a difficult task for management? Elaborate on your answer, showing that you understand the issues involved in the question.
8. What is the interrelationship between the size of the budget, the media schedule used for the advertising campaign, and the creative strategy for that campaign? Discuss.
9. How does coordination as an activity fit into the planning of advertising? Into the execution stage of advertising?
10. From current advertising campaigns, choose two themes that seem to be particularly effective and explain briefly why you think they are successful.

For Further Reference

Aaker, David A., and John G. Myers: *Advertising Management,* Prentice-Hall, Inc., Englewood Cliffs, N.J., 1975.

Anderson, Robert L., and Thomas E. Barry: *Advertising Management,* Charles E. Merrill Books, Inc., Columbus, Ohio, 1979.

Bogart, Leo: *Strategy in Advertising,* Harcourt, Brace & World, Inc., New York, 1967.

Britt, Steuart Henderson (ed.): *Marketing Manager's Handbook,* The Dartnell Corporation, Chicago, 1973.

Engel, James F., Martin R. Warshaw, and Thomas C. Kinnear: *Promotional Strategy,* 4th ed., Richard D. Irwin, Inc., Homewood, Ill., 1979.

Patti, Charles H., and John H. Murphy: *Advertising Management,* Grid, Inc., Columbus, Ohio, 1978.

Percy, Larry, and John R. Rossiter: *Advertising Strategy: A Communication Theory Approach,* Frederick A. Praeger, Inc., New York, 1980.

Quera, Leon: *Advertising Campaigns: Formulation & Tactics,* Grid, Inc., Columbus, Ohio, 1973.

Schultz, Don E., and Dennis G. Martin: *Strategic Advertising Campaigns,* Crain Books, Chicago, 1979.

Simon, Julian L.: *The Management of Advertising,* Prentice-Hall, Inc., Englewood Cliffs, N.J., 1971.

Stansfield, Richard H.: *Advertising Manager's Handbook,* 2d ed., The Dartnell Corporation, Chicago, 1977.

End Notes

[1] Neil Borden, *The Economic Effects of Advertising,* Richard D. Irwin, Inc., Chicago, 1942, pp. 424–427. Also see Charles H. Patti, "Evaluating the Role of Advertising," *Journal of Advertising,* Fall, 1977, pp. 30–35.

[2] This paragraph is based on a paper delivered before the Eastern Annual Conference of the American Association of Advertising Agencies, Nov. 19, 1974, by Charles Fredericks, Executive Vice-President, Oglivy & Mather, Inc.

[3] *Advertising Age,* Aug. 25, 1980, p. 21.

[4] Adapted from Russell H. Colley, *Defining Advertising Goals for Measured Advertising Results,* Association of National Advertisers, Inc., New York, 1961, p. 6.

[5] Adapted from: S. H. Britt, "Are So-Called Successful Advertising Campaigns Really Successful?" *Journal of Advertising Research,* June 1969, p. 5.

[6] John S. Wright and James R. Bostic, "The Advertising Message," in S. H. Britt (ed.), *Marketing Manager's Handbook,* The Dartnell Corporation, Chicago, 1973, p. 934.

[7] This paragraph is adapted from *White Paper I: A Point of View on Advertising Strategy,* McCann-Erickson, Inc., New York, 1972, pp. 2–4.

[8] Ibid., p. 2.

[9] Ibid., p. 3.

[10] Wright and Bostic, op. cit., p. 940.

[11] *Advertising Age,* Aug. 25, 1980, p. 20.

[12] Based on a press release, "A History of Canadian Club's Hide-A-Way Case Program," issued by R. C. Ardetta and Company, Inc., New York, undated.

[13] Based on "Packaged Goods: An Industry Profile," *Madison Avenue,* September 1975, pp. 19–20.

Chapter 16

The Role of Research in Advertising Campaign Planning

● Facts are the basis of sound planning, and the facts for advertising decision making are obtained through research. Many questions must be answered if an advertising campaign is to be effective. For example: Who are the prime prospects for our product? Are prospects aware of its existence? What media do prospects use in their search for information and entertainment? What appeal should be used to meet the needs and wants of prospects?

When advertising strategies are developed, information is needed to determine three important characteristics of consumers: (1) the nature of the *target market;* (2) their response to *advertising messages* for the product; and (3) the *media habits* of target groups. Chapter 15 covered the target market. In addition, behavioral science research techniques, as discussed in Chapter 11, are used to predict the consumption behavior of target groups. Chapter 18 explores the media planning process, and media research is explained there. The thrust of this chapter, therefore, is confined to explaining how research is used in (1) the development of the advertising strategy underlying the campaign, and (2) the measurement of the campaign's effectiveness. This area is generally known as **advertising research.** Before turning to that topic, however, we present an overview of the research process.

Research Overview

No need for advertising existed before the Industrial Revolution because sellers met face to face with buyers and, therefore, knew their customers intimately. Similarly, there was no real need for market research. Only after buyers and sellers became separated geographically were there a desire and need for market information. As business developed, the gap continued to widen, with even more intermediaries separating sellers and buyers. The information provided by market research became a valuable tool that enables sellers to satisfy the needs and wants of consumers.

The gathering of such information, now known as **market research,** went through an evolutionary process. When the census of the population of the United States began in 1790, it became the first source of information about the scattered American market. In 1890, a system of punched cards was developed which permitted more speedy tabulation of census data; more information could then be gathered by field interviewers. In the 1925–1940 period, the emphasis in market analysis shifted to the individual consumer, and rather sophisticated sampling techniques were developed to simplify the data-gathering process. In the 1940s, emphasis again shifted, and attention was given to the firm's impact on markets receiving attention in addition to the achievement of an understanding of the composition and operation of specific markets. The advent and growing availability of large-scale digital computers in the 1960s made the once burdensome manipulation of market data vastly quicker and more economical.[1]

Market Research and Advertising Research

The American Marketing Association defines market research as "the systematic gathering, recording, and analyzing of data about problems relating to the marketing of goods and services."[2] Such research is carried on "to guide managers in their analysis, planning, implementation, and control of programs to satisfy customer and organization goals."[3]

Most large business firms maintain a market research department as an integral part of the company's marketing organization. The research department assists the advertising manager through the gathering of market data and helps in sifting through and classifying the material, which is then fed to the advertising agency to use when discharging its functions of planning, creating, and placing advertising.

Information already existing within the company, **internal data,** such as sales figures and customer lists, are tapped first. However, available data in most situations are insufficient for accurate decision making; therefore, additional research is undertaken. **External data** can be added to the store of information necessary for thorough planning. **Secondary data,** the results of other researchers' efforts, should be brought together, assessed, and added to the company's inventory of marketing information.

If additional data are still needed, a program of original research is instigated. The overriding research constraints of time and money are felt most heavily at this point. The search for **primary data** can be conducted by the firm's own market research department, by the advertising agency's research people, or by special-service groups retained to perform such tasks.

Market research probes into all components of the marketing mix. When it is directed toward the advertising decision-making process, it is usually called **advertising research.** Advertising research is a subsystem of market research, which gathers information to be used by the advertiser and the advertising agency when engaged in campaign planning.

One business executive, Neil Holbert, describes advertising research as the "big apple" of the market research field.[4] For one reason, more money is spent for this part of the market research field than for any other area. Since advertising is the "primary interface between business and the public, . . . it is no wonder that business is so concerned with doing sensible advertising research."[5] Holbert also points out that advertising research is the final test of all the efforts to produce and market the product that have gone before. His thinking is expressed in these words:

> It is an absolute necessity to be thinking of the advertising, the advertisability, and the research on the advertising as the final product of all that is done in researching the product or service all along the way. The earlier that advertising (and advertising research) is integrated into the process of product and research planning, is regarded seriously, and is looked at in many early rough forms, the better the process will go. If it isn't, it may not go at all.[6]

Distinctions have been drawn between market research and advertising research. The first type of information describes and measures a particular market, whereas advertising research evaluates the impact of advertising messages on the market. By this distinction, a study of the days in the week when consumers purchase their groceries would be market research. A study of their readership of grocery advertisements in newspapers would be advertising research.

Rather than attempt to place market research and advertising research in two separate pigeonholes, a more practical approach for either the creation or the management of advertising is to think in terms of advertising *and* market research. Both types of information are needed, and the same basic techniques are used to collect and interpret both types of information. Advertising research, as is true for all forms of research, is based upon certain fundamental principles which are explained in the following survey.

Research Fundamentals

Through research, an investigator attempts to arrive at precise answers to precise questions. "Precise" is a relative term, and in areas involving human behavior the variables are more difficult to identify and to quantify than in the case of the physical and biological sciences. Research is used to reduce the risk to the point where one of several alternative courses of action can be chosen with confidence. All forms of marketing require selling something to people, an activity that is not nearly so predictable as manufacturing something or keeping accounts. Decisions based on market research are made, not with certainty, but with probability. Like many branches of science, market research attempts to quantify the unknown so that educated guesses can be made.

Market research employs several steps based upon the scientific method. In the following section we present a version of that procedure as used in market research. How good any piece or research actually is depends primarily on two criteria. First, is the researcher reliable—is his or her viewpoint objective, rational, and free from bias? Second, does the research employ the basic scientific procedures, such as the historical, experimental, or analytical methods and the generally accepted techniques developed in such relevant fields as statistics, psychology, and sociology?

Five Basic Steps in Research Procedure

Most marketing and advertising research authorities agree that a full-scale investigation includes these five steps:

1 Defining the problem
2 Collecting secondary, or available, data
3 Collecting primary, or original, data
4 Compiling and ordering data
5 Interpreting the findings

Defining the Problem The problems of advertising research are the problems of advertising itself, but searching for an answer to such a general question as "Why is brand X outselling our brand?" involves not one but several research projects.

Part of the answer may come from market research conducted at the retail level, which shows the distribution and movement of both brands in retail outlets, stock levels, relative shelf position and display, and other indications of what is happening to both products in distribution channels. But such a study tells us nothing at all about the people who are—or are not—purchasing our brand and brand X. This will require a separate research project, one designed to probe the habits and actions and, in some cases, even the ethnic orientation of the consumer rather than to focus on the retail outlets.

Part of the answer may also be found in studies of the effectiveness of advertising media used, in tests of advertising appeals, or in investigation of a number of other areas which exert positive influence on the sales curve. Just as the broad, general marketing objective "to increase sales" should be refined in terms of such specific advertising goals as "to establish 20 percent preference for brand A among Y million homemakers in 1983," so the broad, general questions posed as research problems should be rephrased as specific, workable hypotheses. Good answers are the replies to good questions, and if the problem is not clearly and specifically defined, research is off to a bad start.

One respected market researcher holds that defining problems can be more important than finding solutions:

> If we would represent ourselves more as problem-definers than as problem-solvers, the chances are we would solve more problems because if a researcher is only an order-taker and a client an order-giver, the research may well focus on the wrong problems.[7]

Collecting Secondary Data Gathering all information pertinent to the problem that is already available either from the internal records of the advertiser or from external sources is the second step in research procedure. Sales records, for example, should show the geographic distribution of buyers, seasonal fluctuations, high-volume outlets, and a wealth of other information that may have a bearing on the problem. Questions that confront a specific advertiser for the first time may have already been answered in published reports available from departments of federal or state government, advertising media, ad agencies, universities, foundations,

Metro Area Food Store Sales, Rank

January 1, 1979 to January 1, 1980

Rank		($000)
1	New York, NY-NJ	7,882,718
2	Los Angeles-Long Beach, CA	7,015,425
3	Chicago, IL	5,428,782
4	Philadelphia, PA-NJ	4,360,876
5	Detroit, MI	3,869,728
6	Boston-Lowell-Brockton-Lawrence-Haverhill, MA(1)	3,733,435
	Boston(2)	2,573,344
7	San Francisco-Oakland, CA	3,358,494

Rank		($000)
8	Houston, TX	3,043,280
9	Dallas-Fort Worth, TX	3,015,460
10	Washington, DC-MD-VA	2,838,788
11	Nassau-Suffolk, NY	2,776,091
12	St. Louis, MO-IL	2,107,706
13	Baltimore, MD	2,032,035
14	Newark, NJ	1,969,663
15	Pittsburgh, PA	1,901,115
16	Anaheim-Santa Ana-Garden Grove, CA	1,860,209
17	Minneapolis-St. Paul, MN	1,769,361
18	Cleveland, OH	1,749,179
19	Miami, FL	1,585,032
20	San Diego, CA	1,572,145
21	Seattle-Everett, WA	1,555,550
22	Riverside-San Bernardino-Ontario, CA	1,421,638
23	Atlanta, GA	1,381,664
24	Tampa-St. Petersburg, FL	1,376,741
25	Sacramento, CA	1,345,440
26	Denver-Boulder, CO	1,317,470
27	San Jose, CA	1,300,024
28	Phoenix, AZ	1,264,487
29	Kansas City, MO-KS	1,215,880
30	New Orleans, LA	1,204,274
31	Milwaukee, WI	1,190,720
32	Portland, OR-WA	1,177,483
33	Cincinnati, OH-KY-IN	1,134,254
34	Fort Lauderdale-Hollywood, FL	1,099,561
35	Buffalo, NY	1,019,470
36	San Antonio, TX	918,001
37	Indianapolis, IN	914,966
38	Columbus, OH	903,834
39	Rochester, NY	840,891
40	Hartford-New Britain-Bristol, CT(1)	820,379
	Hartford(2)	601,288
41	Memphis, TN-AR-MS	796,353
42	Louisville, KY-IN	777,717
43	Birmingham, AL	764,725
44	Bridgeport-Stamford-Norwalk-Danbury, CT(1)	755,697
	Bridgeport(2)	369,965
45	Nashville-Davidson, TN	747,436
46	Salt Lake City-Ogden, UT	715,190
47	Dayton, OH	706,750
48	Albany-Schenectady-Troy, NY	672,797
49	Greensboro-Winston-Salem-High Point, NC	664,450
50	Toledo, OH-MI	663,955
51	New Haven-Waterbury-Meriden, CT(1)	655,960
	New Haven-West Haven(2)	363,606
52	Oklahoma City, OK	650,095
53	New Brunswick-Perth Amboy-Sayreville, NJ	645,712
54	Providence-Warwick-Pawtucket, RI(1)	642,712
	Providence-Warwick-Pawtuckett(2)	696,883
55	Norwalk-Virginia Beach-Portsmouth, VA-NC	634,745
56	Worcester-Fitchburg-Leominster, MA(1)	628,324
	Worcester(2)	348,786
57	Jacksonville, FL	624,798
58	Grand Rapids, MI	615,897
59	Orlando, FL	605,806
60	Gary-Hammond-East Chicago, IN	603,251
61	West Palm Beach-Boca Raton, FL	598,015
62	Richmond, VA	593,055
63	Allentown-Bethlehem-Easton, PA-NJ	586,594
64	Charlotte-Gastonia, NC	580,989
65	Northeast Pennsylvania, PA	576,034
66	Long Branch-Asbury Park, NJ	575,649
67	Akron, OH	561,202
68	Syracuse, NY	548,817
69	San Juan, PR	536,165
70	Tulsa, OK	516,289
71	Austin, TX	512,319
72	Honolulu, HI	499,839
73	Paterson-Clifton-Passaic, NJ	498,146
74	Flint, MI	479,661
75	Oxnard-Simi Valley-Ventura, CA	472,289
76	Springfield-Chicopee-Holyoke, MA(1)	468,866
	Springfield-Chicopee-Holyoke(2)	453,270
77	Raleigh-Durham, NC	465,145
78	Las Vegas, NV	446,567
79	Tucson, AZ	445,175
80	Fresno, CA	443,928
81	Beaumont-Port Arthur-Orange, TX	443,255
82	Knoxville, TN	436,734
83	New Bedford-Fall River, MA(1)	431,723
	New Bedford(2)	137,191
84	Jersey City, NJ	430,586
85	Omaha, NE-IA	423,114
86	Chattanooga, TN-GA	421,782
87	Youngstown-Warren, OH	416,947
88	Baton Rouge, LA	404,197
89	Harrisburg, PA	398,992
90	Wilmington, DE-NJ-MD	393,754
91	Mobile, AL	392,098
92	El Paso, TX	382,603
93	Greenville-Spartanburg, SC	[illegible]
94	Albuquerque, NM	347,855
95	Corpus Christi, TX	346,430
96	Wichita, KS	342,073
97	Bakersfield, CA	336,794
98	Lansing-East Lansing, MI	327,876
99	Tacoma, WA	323,175
100	Johnson City-Kingsport-Bristol, TN-VA	323,019
101	Canton, OH	322,755
102	Des Moines, IA	317,619
103	Lakeland-Winter Haven, FL	316,939
104	Davenport-Rock Island-Moline, IA-IL	316,462
105	Newport News-Hampton, VA	315,730
106	Shreveport, LA	310,024
107	Santa Rosa, CA	307,489
107	Fort Wayne, IN	307,489
109	Trenton, NJ	303,929
110	Peoria, IL	303,810
111	Lancaster, PA	296,704
112	Vallejo-Fairfield-Napa, CA	288,472
113	York, PA	285,304
114	Little Rock-North Little Rock, AR	278,442
115	Huntington-Ashland, WV-KY-OH	278,335
116	Stockton, CA	277,522
117	Santa Barbara-Santa Maria-Lompoc, CA	277,404
118	Jackson, MS	276,267
119	Binghamton, NY-PA	275,583
120	Salinas-Seaside-Monterey, CA	273,743
121	Reading, PA	271,831
122	Madison, WI	271,162
123	Modesto, CA	266,266
124	Daytona Beach, FL	264,527
125	Spokane, WA	264,188
126	Pensacola, FL	261,969
127	Charleston, WV	258,264
128	Charleston-North Charleston, SC	257,621
129	Melbourne-Titusville-Cocoa, FL	257,166
130	Ann Arbor, MI	253,944
131	Lexington-Fayette, KY	253,724
132	Huntsville, AL	247,938
133	Kalamazoo-Portage, MI	244,642
134	Roanoke, VA	239,254
135	Manchester-Nashua, NH(1)	237,841
	Manchester(2)	96,411
136	Erie, PA	237,679
137	Utica-Rome, NY	235,671
138	Rockford, IL	233,204
139	Columbia, SC	232,789
140	Evansville, IN-KY	230,701
141	Visalia, CA	228,394
142	Reno, NV	227,138
143	Poughkeepsie, NY	226,738
144	Duluth-Superior, MN-WI	220,799
145	South Bend, IN	217,179
146	Johnstown, PA	216,688
147	Saginaw, MI	213,071
148	Montgomery, AL	212,781
149	Galveston-Texas City, TX	211,742
150	Eugene-Springfield, OR	211,083
151	Appleton-Oshkosh, WI	209,112
152	Sarasota, FL	208,975
153	Lorain-Elyria, OH	208,441
154	Lubbock, TX	207,465
155	Portland, ME(1)	206,706
	Portland(2)	180,127
156	Colorado Springs, CO	202,216
157	Augusta, GA-SC	200,759
158	Santa Cruz, CA	200,576
159	Atlantic City, NJ	200,132
160	Macon, GA	196,877
161	Hamilton-Middletown, OH	193,676
162	Amarillo, TX	187,768
163	Brownsville-Harlingen-San Benito, TX	187,411
164	Barnstable Town, MA	187,386
165	Savannah, GA	187,227
166	Waco, TX	184,921
167	Fort Myers-Cape Coral, FL	184,277
168	Salem, OR	182,068
169	Wheeling, WV-OH	179,711
170	Longview-Marshall, TX	178,603
171	Muskegon-Norton Shores-Muskegon Heights, MI	176,219
172	New London-Norwich, CT(1)	170,476
	New London-Norwich(2)	187,710
173	Springfield, MO	167,105
174	Lima, OH	161,845
175	Battle Creek, MI	161,022
176	McAllen-Pharr-Edinburg, TX	160,781
177	Springfield, IL	160,031
178	Killeen-Temple, TX	159,442
179	Asheville, NC	158,867
180	Racine, WI	156,274
181	Yakima, WA	156,204
182	Columbus, GA-AL	154,899
183	Topeka, KS	154,174
184	Biloxi-Gulfport, MS	152,877
185	Gainesville, FL	149,395
186	Bradenton, FL	146,896
187	Cedar Rapids, IA	145,248
188	Parkersburg-Marietta, WV-OH	144,443
189	Tallahassee, FL	143,804
190	Steubenville Weirton, OH-WV	143,721
191	Monroe, LA	142,907
192	Boise City, ID	141,924
193	Lynchburg, VA	141,665
194	Springfield, OH	139,566
195	Pittsfield, MA(1)	138,921
	Pittsfield(2)	106,384
196	Vineland-Millville-Bridgeton, NJ	138,733
197	Terre Haute, IN	138,221
198	Fort Smith, AR-OK	137,421
199	Green Bay, WI	136,563
200	Anchorage, AK	136,161
201	Wilmington, NC	135,394
202	Fayetteville-Springdale, AR	134,651
203	Lake Charles, LA	132,606
204	Tyler, TX	132,006
205	Petersburg-Colonial Heights-Hopewell, VA	131,985
206	Jackson, MI	130,295
207	San Luis Obispo, CA	126,089
208	Laredo, TX	123,077
209	Fayetteville, NC	123,023
210	Lafayette, LA	122,149
211	Altoona, PA	121,470
212	Odessa, TX	121,306
213	Pascagoula-Moss Point, MS	119,916
214	Janesville-Beloit, WI	119,510
215	Abilene, TX	118,347
216	Texarkana, TX-AR	117,330
217	Charlottesville, VA	117,329
218	Lincoln, NE	116,829
219	Tuscaloosa, AL	114,986
220	Pueblo, CO	114,709
221	St. Cloud, MN	113,548
222	Fargo-Moorhead, ND-MN	113,467
223	Wichita Falls, TX	112,460
224	Alexandria, LA	112,054
225	Waterloo-Cedar Falls, IA	111,905
226	Hagerstown, MD	111,453
227	Anderson, IN	111,311
228	Burlington, NC	110,670
229	Provo-Orem, UT	110,474
230	Mansfield, OH	110,310
231	Eureka, CA	109,314
232	Williamsport, PA	107,896
233	Clarksville-Hopkinsville, TN-KY	106,208
234	Kenosha, WI	105,471
235	Bay City, MI	105,396
236	Elkhart, IN	105,099
237	Florence, AL	104,155
238	Ocala, FL	103,263
239	Rocky Mount, NC	102,828
240	Bremerton, WA	102,175
241	Richland-Kennewick-Pasco, WA	102,021
242	Bangor, ME	101,777
243	Olympia, WA	100,474
244	Michigan City, IN	100,463
245	Champaign-Urbana-Rantoul, IL	99,079
246	Frederick, MD	98,638
247	Watertown, NY	97,640
248	Muncie, IN	97,214
249	Danville, VA	97,167
250	Fort Collins, CO	97,096
251	Eau Claire, WI	95,594
252	Hickory, NC	95,444
253	Sioux City, IA-NE	95,330
254	Decatur, IL	95,164
255	Bryan-College Station, TX	93,996
256	Ponce, PR	93,985
257	Cumberland, MD	93,294
258	Sherman-Denison, TX	93,045
259	Gadsden, AL	93,004
260	Lebanon, PA	92,243
261	Elmira, NY	90,841
262	Newark, OH	88,038
263	Lafayette-West Lafayette, IN	87,463
264	Merced, CA	87,318
265	Bellingham, WA	87,311
266	St. Joseph, MO	86,676
267	San Angelo, TX	85,817
268	Houma, LA	85,030
269	Albany, GA	84,309
270	Anniston, AL	84,041
271	New Castle, PA	83,059
272	Panama City, FL	82,781
273	Hilo, HI	82,612
274	Key West, FL	82,393
275	Anderson, SC	82,316
276	Yuma, AZ	82,292
277	Danville, IL	82,183
278	Fort Walton Beach, FL	82,126
279	Dubuque, IA	81,622
280	Billings, MT	81,570
281	Paducah, KY	80,945
282	Kokomo, IN	80,427
283	Sioux Falls, SD	80,252
284	Bloomington-Normal, IL	80,208
285	Greeley, CO	78,606
286	Lewiston-Auburn, ME(1)	78,123
	Lewiston-Auburn(2)	61,802
287	Wausau, WI	78,030
288	Owensboro, KY	77,492
289	Decatur, AL	77,214
290	Fond du Lac, WI	76,944
291	Greenville, NC	76,615
292	Fort Pierce, FL	76,336
293	Bloomington, IN	76,322
294	Florence, SC	76,312
295	Kankakee, IL	76,257
296	Columbia, MO	76,250
297	Hattiesburg, MS	75,755
298	Midland, TX	75,492
299	Joplin, MO	75,383
300	Greenville, MS	75,363
301	Sandusky, OH	75,339
302	Medford, OR	74,503
303	Grand Forks, ND	73,738
304	Victoria, TX	73,313
305	La Crosse, WI	72,867
306	Santa Fe, NM	71,621
307	Great Falls, MT	71,361
308	Flagstaff, AZ	71,310
309	Sheboygan, WI	71,307
310	Beckley, WV	70,459
311	Longview, WA	70,193
312	Concord, NH	69,930
313	Goldsboro, NC	69,229
314	Meridian, MS	68,195
315	Farmington, NM	67,335
316	Lufkin, TX	67,220
317	Rock Hill, SC	67,084
318	Iowa City, IA	66,804
319	Dover, DE	66,669
320	Pine Bluff, AR	66,249
321	Zanesville, OH	65,967
322	Dothan, AL	65,747
323	Missoula, MT	65,196
324	Bowling Green, KY	63,957
325	Idaho Falls, ID	63,943
326	Rochester, MN	62,424
327	Portsmouth, OH	62,406
328	Midland, MI	62,213
329	Richmond, IN	61,591
330	Rome, GA	61,540
331	Clinton, NH	61,522
332	Tupelo, MS	61,140
333	Bismarck, ND	61,047
334	Athens, GA	60,559
335	Jackson, TN	60,166
336	Grand Junction, CO	59,322
337	Lawrence, KS	58,842
338	Las Cruces, NM	58,158
339	Casper, WY	58,065
340	Caguas, PR	56,454
341	Cape Girardeau, MO	55,911
342	Marion, OH	55,777
343	Marion, IN	55,160
344	Hot Springs, AR	55,087
345	Lawton, OK	54,874
346	Hutchinson, KS	54,246
347	Quincy, IL	53,276
348	Valdosta, GA	53,264
349	Columbus, IN	53,008
350	Chillicothe, OH	51,457
351	Findlay, WV	50,977
352	Cleveland, TN	50,894
353	Grand Island, NE	50,838
354	Mason City, IA	50,622
355	Pocatello, ID	50,190
356	Ames, IA	49,369
357	Rapid City, SD	47,434
358	Columbus, MS	47,074
359	Roswell, NM	46,161
360	Jefferson City, MO	45,457
361	Enid, OK	44,796
362	Cheyenne, WY	44,150
363	Corvallis, OR	43,804
364	Salina, KS	42,996
365	Minot, ND	41,871
366	Fort Dodge, IA	41,811
367	Mankato, MN	39,782
368	Mayaguez, PR	39,064
	Total Metro Areas	154,317,832

(1) County Basis.
(2) Official S.M.S.A.

U. S. TOTAL FOOD STORE SALES—$194,675,011(000)

Figure 16.1 Secondary data are invaluable to advertisers. This page from Standard Rate & Data Service shows that more than $154 billion of the nation's $194-plus billion in food-store sales come from 368 metropolitan areas. Market share for each area is also given. [*Standard Rate & Data Service.*]

chambers of commerce, or trade associations.

Informal investigation—discussions with executives and salespeople for the company and talks with wholesalers and retailers—is useful in evaluating the importance of hypotheses developed for the preparation of the campaign.

Examination of available data and of the results of informal interviews with people who have some knowledge of the product and its market is sometimes referred to as the **situation analysis.** This step in research procedure takes place more or less concurrently with the first step—defining the problem. It helps redefine the problem, develops possible hypotheses, and provides a background for the planning of the next step—the collection of primary, or original, data. It may even show that planning original research can be an expensive and time-consuming procedure and that the chances of getting valid and reliable answers to a problem are sometimes slim indeed.

The usefulness of secondary data is definitely limited, of course, by two important factors. The first is possible bias. The study may be an effort to prove or document a particular point of view rather than an attempt to provide accurate, objective information. Both advertising agencies and advertising media perform research, and both have an obvious interest in how much is invested in advertising and where it is invested. The second factor is the possibility that the data are obsolete. Since markets are dynamic, a research report may be completely objective and still not reflect conditions applicable to today's problem.

Collecting Primary Data If existing information does not supply an adequate guide to decision making, the advertiser must look for answers elsewhere. Original research must be conducted. There are three standard or traditional methods of collecting primary data, and they may be used singly or in combination: (1) direct observation, (2) experimentation, and (3) the survey or questionnaire.

The **observational method** involves just what the label suggests: a person or a machine watching and recording an activity. The Nielsen Audimeter is a machine that uses the observational method to collect information on the viewing habits of television audiences.

The **experimentation method** requires some type of test operation. If the problem involves a new package design, the actual package may be distributed to stores in a test market, and its movement compared with that of the old design in a control market. A manufacturer who is considering a change in price or a premium offer may use the experimentation method to test the reaction to the price change or premium in restricted market areas before applying them in the total market.

The **survey** or **questionnaire method** is perhaps the best known and most popular method of securing original research data. It involves asking questions in order to get firsthand information from individual respondents—from a sample of consumers who use the product, retailers who sell it, or any other group which may play an important part in the success of an advertising campaign.

In all three methods, basing the research findings on a sample of the universe is a recognized practice. In research terminology, "universe," or "population group," applies to *all* the units under investigation, such as all black families living in Chicago, all persons holding American Express credit cards, or all independent druggists in California.

Compiling and Ordering Data Before conclusions can be drawn from original research, it is necessary to edit and tabulate the findings and critically compare their indications with those of existing data. Editing, or careful examination of the reports, serves two important purposes. First, it eliminates errors by either correcting or rejecting inaccurate or doubtful replies or records. In spite of careful planning, some respondents may have misinterpreted certain questions, or the mechanical recording devices may have made errors or failed to operate properly. Second, editing prepares field reports or questionnaires for tabulation by standardizing responses reported in a variety of ways. For example, in reply to the question "How long (in *months*) have you used product X?" some respondents may answer "One-and-a-half-years." Instead of discarding the answer as incorrect or doubtful, the field report editor will convert it into the standard units—18 months.

Compiling or tabulating the results involves counting and summarizing the statistical conclusions from all the reports not rejected. Tabulation may be done by computers, or if only a small amount of information is required, it may be done by hand, using standardized counting sheets. Regardless of the method of tabulation, statistical conclusions do not result automatically. A mere summary of the data, even when presented in neat tables or colorful charts, is likely to be meaningless. A good summary calls for both skill in statistics and imagination to establish significant relationships between different groups of facts and the objectives of the research.

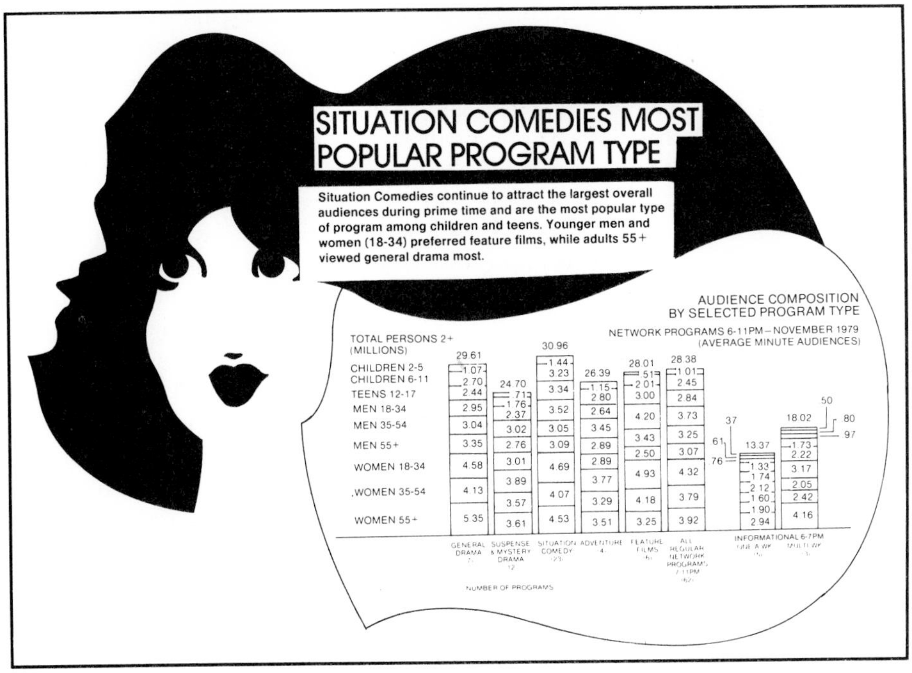

Figure 16.2 The results of research are easier to understand when presented in graphic fashion. This chart, derived from Nielsen data, shows the audience composition for situation comedies. [*A. C. Nielsen Company.*]

Interpreting the Findings The statistical findings reached in the data-compiling step are not the objective for which the research was undertaken, of course. They are merely evidence to be evaluated and interpreted in terms of alternative courses of action if the research is to aid the decision-making process. The computer's capacity for handling fantastic volumes of data with incredible speed has materially refined the decision-making process, but it has not eliminated the need for judgment and experience. A statistical summary is the end of the *inductive* process—the process of drawing general conclusions from a number of controlled experiments or investigations. The interpretation is *deductive* logic—the drawing of sound inferences from the statistical generalizations.

Straight thinking is necessary if the recommendations are to be both logical and practical. To be logical, they must, of course, be adequately supported by the statistical data. To be practical, logical recommendations must often be modified to suit a particular advertiser in a specific situation. A logical recommendation might call for the use of full-color ROP newspaper space in all markets, but if the advertiser does not have sufficient funds for such an investment, a practical recommendation might modify this to include only the dozen most important cities.

Additional Considerations Market research specialists, with an eye perhaps to the practical application of research projects, often add two other steps to the five just discussed: (6) presenting the results and (7) applying the conclusions, or follow-up.

Much of the effectiveness of a research project depends on the form in which recommendations are presented to management. This is a problem in communications rather than market or advertising research, and such basic principles as brevity, clarity, and consideration of the audience to which the recommendations are made are as important here as they are in the creation of advertising copy. Applying the conclusions drawn from research involves the management decision which the project itself was planned to aid.

Fundamentals of Primary Data Gathering: Quantitative Research

The third step in the research process possesses several elements which are hard for many people to understand. Therefore we expand our discussion at this point to cover these topics in detail.

Sampling Theory

Nearly every form of research employs sampling. When the medical doctor extracts a vial of blood from the patient's body, sampling is being done. The 2 or 3 ounces of blood that are analyzed represent the condition of all the blood, and this helps the doctor diagnose the patient's illness. The theory of sampling is derived from the mathematical theory of probability—the laws of chance—and it provides the researcher with a reliable means of getting the maximum amount of information for a minimum expenditure of time and money. If the sample is to be relied upon, however, it must meet two basic requirements: it should be representative and it should be adequate.

A sample is representative if it reflects the pertinent characteristics of the larger group, or population, from which it is drawn. If the particular population that is relevant to the specific problem is not carefully defined early in the project, the sample may be representative of the wrong population. Households—a single individual or any group of persons living together and pooling their resources—make up a population commonly sampled for studies of consumer spending. But if the study involves products like beer, soft drinks, or tobacco, bought in substantial quantities by such nonhousehold persons as members of the armed forces or students, households obviously do not provide a representative sample. In addition, the sampled population almost always differs from the total relevant population, merely because it is restricted to those willing to cooperate, and this may be important in evaluating the results.

If a sample is to be considered adequate, it must be large enough to give us confidence in the stability of the characteristics it reflects. The larger the sample, the less the probability of variation from the true nature of the universe. The question that must be answered is, "How accurate do we want to be?" Statisticians use the term "sampling error" or "sampling tolerance" to refer to the limits of accuracy in projecting sample figures or percentages to the total population. Formulas used to calculate sampling error have been determined, but they are too complicated for our discussion here.

Once an acceptable sampling error is established, then an adequate sample is the minimum size necessary to produce results within this range. But there are other sources of inaccuracy in research besides sampling error. No increase in sample size can compensate for inaccuracy that results from an unrepresentative sample or from faulty questionnaire design or poor interview methods.

Sampling Methods

The two most commonly used methods of sampling in marketing and advertising research are (1) probability sampling and (2) quota, or judgment, sampling.

Probability Sampling In the probability method, each unit of the universe has a known or equal chance of being selected, and the chance of any unit's being selected is unrelated to the subject or purpose of the study. Simple random sampling is one form of probability sampling. The most important characteristic of the probability method is that the variance between the characteristics of the sample and the true characteristics of the universe can be accurately estimated mathematically. Stratified sampling is often done when the probability sampling method is being employed. The total universe is first divided into two or more parts, or strata, and then a sample is drawn from each of the strata. For example, a total universe of 21,000 college students might be divided into four "subuniverses," consisting of 8,000 first-year students, 6,000 sophomores, 4,000 juniors, and 3,000 seniors. If 5 percent of the names from each of these four strata were selected at random, we would have a stratified probability sample of 1,050, proportionate in class standing to the total enrollment of 21,000. The sample would be representative.

Quota Sampling Quota sampling, which is sometimes called judgment sampling, is a method of sampling in which interviewers look for specific numbers of respondents with known characteristics. For example, suppose a marketer wishes to determine the attitudes of college undergraduates at Normal University before launching a new product. NU enrolls 10,000 undergraduates, including 4,000 first-year students, 3,000 sophomores, 2,000 juniors, and 1,000 seniors. To obtain a representative reading of this universe, a sample size of 1,000 students is set. Interviewers will talk with 400 first-year students, 300 sophomores, 200 juniors, and 100 seniors.

Within these quotas, considerable freedom is left to interviewers in the selection of respondents to fit these specifications.

The quota method is popular in market and advertising research as a means of getting the most from research dollars. It is likely to be both faster and less expensive than probability sampling. Also, in recent years, considerable attention has been given to ways of reducing the interviewer- or respondent-selection bias. Nor is it always practical to apply probability selection techniques to the problem under study. If considerable cooperation is required from individual respondents in order to complete interviews, probability sampling may be difficult if not impossible. Where speed and economy are more important than precision, quota sampling continues to be used with satisfactory results.

To sum up, haphazard or unsystematic sampling methods are to be avoided in any research project. In situations where the use of probability sampling techniques is impractical or where speed and economy are greater considerations than precision, quota sampling is the answer. But if a precise answer is required, along with an estimate of the extent of probable error, a probability sample is mandatory.

Methods of Getting Responses from the Sample Group

Most original information secured during market and advertising research is obtained (1) through questionnaires mailed to individuals or (2) by telephone or (3) by face-to-face interviews with consumers. The information-gathering phase is highly critical to the research process. Determining which data collection method to use is based on consideration of relative costs, sample size, type of respondent, nature of the information sought, time available, and desired accuracy. The advantages and limitations of each of the three major methods follow. The discussion assumes the need for an adequate and representative sample.

Mailed Questionnaires Mailed questionnaires are more economical than face-to-face interviewing, particularly when the respondents are widely dispersed geographically. People who are inaccessible to either personal or telephone interviews can be reached by mail. As the questionnaire can be filled out at the respondent's convenience, more time will likely be devoted to providing the information. The method is slow in generating responses, however, partially because of delays in mail service.

Many people are unable or unwilling to answer questionnaires without probing or stimulation from an interviewer. Extensive or complex questionnaires usually yield poor results when mailed. Furthermore, the respondent's interest in the subject under investigation has a direct effect on returns; thus mailed questionnaires are not usually an effective research tool for any but a highly selective group of respondents, such as college deans, ceramic engineers, or advertising managers of large companies. Most people receive large quantities of impersonal mail, and the mailed questionnaire competes for the receiver's attention. The number of completed questionnaires can be increased by a cover letter relating the study to the respondent's interests. An assurance that replies will be kept anonymous and the inclusion of a return-addressed postage-paid envelope also help enhance the response rate.

Telephone Interviews Large numbers of responses in a short time and at relatively low cost can be produced through telephone interviewing. Moreover, the method permits the reaching of respondents at specific times of the day; this is an important consideration in the study of radio and TV listening habits. Obtaining information on age, economic status, occupation, and other important respondent data by telephone is sometimes difficult. Securing cooperation through telephone inquiries is not easy, partly because the interview approach has been wrongly used as an entry approach for various selling schemes. The telephone method is often confined to studies involving rather simple questions and a relatively small amount of information. Another limitation to the method is that in many markets a significantly large number of telephones are unlisted in directories and thus are not likely to be included in the universe being sampled. The use of random digit dialing has tended to reduce this factor, however.

Personal Interviews The most reliable means of collecting the maximum amount of information from a representative sample is through the face-to-face or personal interview. The questionnaires can be longer and more complex. The interviewer can stimulate responses that are both complete and accurate by employing skilled observation and probing, by encouraging the respondent, and by repeating questions. Furthermore, the representativeness of the sample can be well controlled with personal interviews, and the researcher has a control over responses.

Face-to-face interviewing, of course, is more costly than other methods. Some respondents, such as high-level business executives, are difficult to contact. The personal bias of individual interviewers can affect results. The reliability of face-to-face interviewing depends on the skill and integrity of interviewers, which makes their selection, training, and super-

CONFIDENTIAL QUESTIONNAIRE

For a survey relating to the needs and purchases of Metropolitan Milwaukee families to be compiled by

THE MILWAUKEE JOURNAL

A VERY LARGE SHOPPING BAG FILLED WITH PACKAGES OF GROCERY ITEMS and other merchandise is yours **FREE** *for filling in this questionnaire.*

To get this bag of grocery products you must answer the questions herein and have your husband or the man of the house answer those questions regarding his purchases. Questionnaires will be accepted from single persons or widows who maintain households. All replies are confidential and names are not released for any purpose.

Your household address was selected at random as one of a few in your locality to give us household data representative of your community. Even if you live alone your reply is important. Answer any questions that apply. Without your questionnaire our survey will not be representative of your area.

You must be accurate in your answers and an adult member of the family must bring the questionnaire to the Survey Dept. of The Milwaukee Journal.

THE SURVEY DEPT. IS LOCATED AT **910 N. 4TH ST.**
IMMEDIATELY SOUTH OF THE JOURNAL BUILDING

The questionnaire must be returned BEFORE OR BY the due date specified below in red type.

Your co-operation will be appreciated and will help make possible publication of the nationally known "Consumer Analysis of the Metropolitan Milwaukee Market."

THE MILWAUKEE JOURNAL
SURVEY DEPARTMENT

INSTRUCTIONS

1. Each major question should be answered YES or NO with an "X" or other checkmark. Give brand names only for items which you have bought within SPECIFIED time periods. If your answer to the main question is NO, do not answer any of the subquestions.
2. PLEASE do not guess in answering this questionnaire. LOOK UP THE BRAND NAME if you don't remember it. In each case list the brand you, yourself, BOUGHT LAST.
3. IF YOU DO NOT KNOW THE BRAND NAME, AND CAN'T FIND OUT, WRITE "DON'T KNOW" ON BRAND LINE.
4. Some questions ask for quantity purchased. This should be the total quantity of this type of product you have bought within the SPECIFIED time period.
5. Please write plainly. Use ink or typewriter if possible.
6. Do not return this questionnaire by mail.
7. The completed questionnaire must be returned to the Survey Office of The Milwaukee Journal, IN PERSON, by an adult member of this household.

Name | Your Street Address | City, Town or Village | Zip | Telephone No.

You will receive a large shopping bag of grocery products if you fill in this questionnaire and bring it to The Journal Survey Dept. no later than **FRI., OCT. 10, 1980**

The Survey Office Hours Are 9 a.m. to 8 p.m., Monday Through Friday; 9 a.m. to 5 p.m., Saturday and Sunday

Figure 16.3 The probability method of sampling was used in this mailed questionnaire. Respondents were offered a reward for cooperating. The questionnaire was returned in person and checked by interviewers. [*The Milwaukee Journal.*]

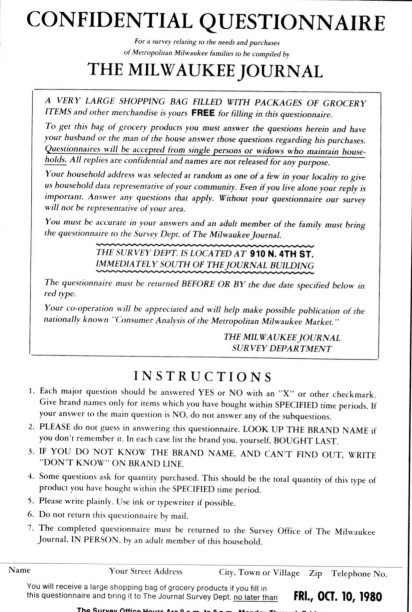

vision a significant factor. Personal interviewing of consumers in their homes has declined a great deal in recent years. It is difficult to get interviewers to do door-to-door interviewing, for one thing. Another factor is that many people are hesitant to answer their doorbells, and, of course, during daytime hours it is hard to find people at home, because many women now are working outside the home.

The **central-location interviewing technique** was developed to overcome this problem. Now researchers perform personal interviews where the people are: in shopping centers and malls. A common practice is for the shopping center management to grant exclusive interviewing privileges within the mall to a specific research company. This research organization may even take over store space and set up a research laboratory where interviews are conducted, or the firm may interrupt shoppers as they move from one store to another within the shopping center, asking them to be subjects for an interview. It is estimated that approximately half of advertising research is done using the personal interviewing method. Most of the remaining half is completed using the telephone method. Questioning through the mail is not very commonly used for testing advertising messages.

Questionnaire Design

The results of interviewing, regardless of the method employed, depend directly upon the questions asked. Designing a good questionnaire requires skill and great care, and the task is not subject to the statistical principles that guide sample design. Leading researchers claim the greatest errors in survey results are caused by the wording of questions. Asking the right question in the right way is an art more than a science.

Technically speaking, a questionnaire is a form which the respondent fills in, while a "schedule" is a series of questions used in face-to-face or telephone interviews wherein the answers are entered by the interviewer rather than by the respondent. In face-to-face interviewing, an "interview guide" may be employed. It consists of a list of topics to be covered. The interviewer possesses considerable freedom with respect to the order in which the questions are asked and the language used in posing them.

Questions on the schedule and the questionnaire are either "open" or "closed." Closed questionnaires are phrased in such a fashion that they permit only a relatively small number of alternative answers, which may be included in a checklist on the form. An example is: "Do you smoke cigarettes?" It has only two possible answers—"yes" or "no." Open-end questions—those to which the responses cannot be anticipated specifically—are also used extensively. A question like "Why do you buy X brand shaving cream?" does not, for instance, lend itself easily to an advance classification of answers.

Qualitative Research

Even when questions are so skillfully designed that there is no danger of misinterpretation by respondents, the research may not get valid answers simply because the respondent is either unable or unwilling to provide them. This is especially true when the questions are directed at explanations for a respondent's behavior, or the "why" of attitudes and actions. Because it may be even more important for the advertiser to know *why* consumers buy a given product than to know when or where it is bought, a variety of less structured methods of research is used in the attempt to answer the question "why" in market and advertising research. These methods are known collectively as **qualitative research.**

The survey research which we have been discussing up to this point was labeled as quantitative research, which can be described as "research which provides information to which numbers can be applied."[8] The following quotation describes qualitative research:

> Qualitative research is usually exploratory or diagnostic in nature. It involves small numbers of people who are not usually sampled on a probabilistic basis. . . . In qualitative research no attempt is made to draw hard and fast conclusions. It is impressionistic rather than definitive.[9]

Qualitative research methods generally fall into two categories: intensive and projective. Intensive techniques include depth and focus group interviews. Projective techniques include such devices as Thematic Apperception Tests (TAT), role playing, cartoon completion, and word association. The goal of

Figure 16.4 A trained interviewer meets with six women in a focus group session. Consumer attitudes toward household products are discussed. [*Wainwright, Spaeth & Wright, Inc., Chicago.*]

both types of technique is to probe beneath overt behavior and verbalized responses—to find answers to why-type questions.[10]

Intensive Techniques

Depth Interviews An unstructured conversation is the principal method used in this technique. The interviewer meets with the respondent on a one-to-one basis for an hour or more. The immediate goal is to get the consumer talking freely about attitudes toward the marketing situation under investigation. Ultimately, the goal is to interpret the underlying motivation involved in the buying process—"to get at 'true' rather than 'surface' answers to why-type questions."[11]

Depth interviews reveal more precisely the feelings of one individual to a larger extent than can be determined in a group interview. In other words, there may be a degree of more precision in the responses. Major limitations lie in the difficulty of getting skilled, qualified interviewers, who may be psychiatrists or psychologists, with the consequent expense that the method entails. Depth interviews are also very time-consuming in data gathering and in their interpretation; thus, in most instances, group approaches are employed.

Focus Group Interviews Research, like all human activity, has its fads and fashions. A popular research technique today is the focus group interview, sometimes called the group depth interview. Growing out of psychiatric group therapy, focus group interviews are:

based on the assumption that individuals who share a problem will be more willing to talk about it amid the security of others sharing the same problem. It offers a means of obtaining in-depth information on a specific topic through a discussion group atmosphere which allows an insight into the behavior and thinking of the individual group members. Rather than using a structured question-and-answer methodology, the procedure is to encourage a group to discuss feelings, attitudes, and perceptions about the topic being discussed."[12]

The procedure is rather simple. A small group of 8 to 12 homogeneous consumers, often homemakers, are brought together for a period of 1½ to 2 hours. Under the guidance of a moderator who is often a professionally trained psychologist, the participants are encouraged to engage in conversation about the topic under investigation. The technique has been employed in such decision areas as new-product prototype testing, package change, advertising strategy change, and advertising copy formulation.[13]

A whole body of guidelines concerning how the group should be chosen, who should participate, and so forth has developed in the field. It is generally agreed that the moderator's skill in leading the group is the critical factor for success when focus group interviewing is being conducted.

Projective Techniques

Projective techniques are another way to gather information that is difficult to secure by direct questioning. Projection, to the psychologist, is noncommunicative behavior, and a projective technique is any method of interpreting noncommunicative behavior, or of determining attitudes and needs people will not or cannot express. All the specific projective techniques operate on the principle of presenting the respondents with an ambiguous or vague stimulus—a picture, a sentence, a word that is abstract or incomplete. The respondents are asked to describe what the stimulus suggests to them, and their responses disclose to a skilled interpreter the information the respondents either cannot or will not supply in answer to direct questioning.

Among the projective techniques that have been used successfully in advertising and market research are word association, sentence completion, and picture response. **Word association** and **sentence completion** are accurately described by their names. In the first, individuals are given a series of words, one at a time, and asked to respond with the first word that comes to mind. In sentence completion, respondents are asked to complete a series of incomplete statements.

The **picture-response** technique is an adaptation of the Thematic Apperception Test and the Rosenzweig Picture-Frustration (P-F) Study, both used in clinical psychology. The individual is shown an illustration which may be interpreted in a number of ways and asked to tell a story about the picture or to interpret the feelings and actions of people in the picture. For example, when shown the illustration in Figure 16.5, women were asked to tell what they thought the woman in the picture was saying.

(1) *Imagine that this husband and wife have their choice of traveling by plane, automobile or train on their next vacation trip. What would he be saying about his preference? What would she be saying about her preference?*

Figure 16.5 This drawing is an example of the picture-response variety of the projective technique. It was used in a study of air travel and sought information by an indirect approach. [*Fawcett Publications, Inc., New York.*]

Another related questioning technique is the Rotter Internal-External Locus-of-Control test that accurately measures the extent to which a person feels in control of life events and thus is an active consumer, or whether the subject sees other persons and entities as controlling her or him. Results from the application of this technique have correlated strongly with several advertising criteria.

The use of projective techniques both requires a high level of cooperation from respondents and special skills in interpretation of responses, and poses difficult sampling problems. They are costly and time-consuming in comparison with direct approaches, and also are difficult to quantify. Though less publicized than they were a few years ago, they have proved valuable in uncovering hypotheses which in turn may be tested by more conventional, quantitative methods.

Research into the Creative Aspects of the Advertising Campaign[14]

Although other facets of advertising are often included in the sphere of advertising research, its very heart is what has been called **creative research.** This term is descriptive of "research as it applies to the development and evaluation of the agency's creative product, i.e., its ads and commercials."[15] Some people elect to call it "message research," and others limit it more by describing it as "copy research." Thus, we use the term "creative research" as it is applied to the creation of advertising. In other words, our focus is on the advertising message. Every advertising campaign can be thought of as having three distinctive stages in its life cycle, and research is done at each stage. The three stages of creative research are:

1 Developing copy strategy
2 Pretesting individual advertisements
3 Evaluating the cumulative effects of advertising campaigns

Developing Copy Strategy

The importance of choosing an appropriate copy theme and concept to serve as the foundation of the advertising campaign has been stressed earlier in this book. Many potential copy platforms are generated at the agency. Each idea is considered within the background of information about the product, the market, and the motivations of consumers. One specific idea must be chosen as the "right" copy strategy for the campaign.

Analysis of Competitive Appeals The first step is to look at the primary and secondary appeals that are being made for other brands in the product category. In some instances, investigation will reveal that a particular appeal is so strongly identified with a competitive brand that its use would only strengthen the position of the original user of that appeal. In other words, the appeal has been *preempted.* The hope is that a suitable appeal will be isolated which is not firmly identified with another brand and is thus available for adoption by the brand. The Ad-Files service of Starch INRA Hooper provides tear sheets of magazine ads which are grouped by product category and brand. Creative approaches used in the past and their relative success in regard to readership scores can be obtained from the service.

The techniques of qualitative research, including individual depth and focus group interviews, may be employed to learn consumer attitudes toward products, brands, and their advertising. Tentative creative strategies are developed; these hypotheses are called "selling propositions" or "copy concepts."

Selection of an Appeal Obviously, the list of alternatives must be narrowed to the one strategy believed most likely to accomplish the advertising objectives. The alternatives may be measured against previously established criteria, such as importance of features, believability of claim, exclusiveness, or informativeness.

In some way, the alternatives should also be brought before present or prospective customers to obtain their input into the evaluative process. A host of research techniques, including paired comparisons, simple rankings, semantic differential tests, ranking scales, and multivariate analysis, are available at this stage of research. In sum, there are many methods of testing copy concepts; each has its advocates, and each method can yield useful insights when a choice of creative strategy alternatives is to be made.

Pretesting Individual Advertisements

Once a creative strategy alternative is chosen, copywriters in the advertising agency start to translate the strategy into advertisements. Several alternative advertisements are developed stressing different Unique Selling Propositions (USPs) that fulfill the campaign strategy. Advertising research helps the advertiser select the copy slant that will eventually be used to communicate with consumers. There are various techniques that are used to evaluate the effectiveness of different advertisements. Our discussion is divided into two parts: one for print advertisements, the second for television commercials.

Print Advertising There are three major methods of pretesting print advertisements: consumer-jury tests, portfolio tests, and dummy magazine tests. In **consumer-jury tests,** respondents are shown various alternative ads and asked to rank the ads or to answer questions about the content of the advertisements. From this method, consumer preferences can be learned, as well as the believability, memorability, or comprehensibility of the various ads being scrutinized.

In the **portfolio test,** test ads are interspersed among other advertisements and editorial matter in a book something like a photo album. Groups of consumers are shown the portfolio, and respondents in a matching sample are shown the same portfolio without the test ad. Afterward, questions are asked to determine the recall of the advertisement being tested.

When **dummy magazines** are employed, an actual magazine is used in place of the portfolio. Test ads are stripped into the magazine, which is left with respondents for a period of time, after which they are questioned about the recall of advertising in the magazine. Two syndicated readership services, Gallup & Robinson and Starch INRA Hooper, provide pretest services for firms wishing to learn about their proposed magazine advertisements.

Television Advertising. Pretesting is more complex for commercials than for print advertisements. Production costs of television commercials are much higher than for most print advertising. If a finished commercial costs $50,000 and four different executions are to be tested, $200,000 will be spent before a choice among the four alternatives is made. For this reason, pretesting of television commercials relies on the use of prototypes, or unfinished "roughs." Three varieties of prototypes are in common use: animatics; photomatics; and videotapes of live action. **Animatics** is a series of photographs of storyboard drawings with a sound track attached. **Photomatics** is similar except that, instead of using drawings, a series of still pictures is photographed. In the third alternative, actors play out the story as their performance is videotaped. Whatever style is employed, the prototype is then shown to consumers.

This stage of pretesting is *diagnostic* because it permits the advertiser to try many elements of strategy without great expense. For example, when Paul Masson Wine was deciding whether to use actor Orson Welles as its presenter, the concept was tested by animatics, as shown in Figure 16.6.[16] When well done, these pretests yield results nearly as satisfactory as a finished commercial would.

Finished commercials are, of course, pretested. This stage might be called "postproduction" pretesting, as the money has already been spent for the making of the commercials. Before committing funds for airing the commercials, however, further testing is undertaken. We must realize that media charges consume a much greater share of the advertising budget than do production costs.

Regardless of whether finished or unfinished commercials are being tested, two different environmental situations are available for the testing. The first is under artificial or forced viewing conditions. Under these conditions, one approach is the **captive audience** method, wherein selected respondents are invited to a theater for the purpose of previewing a television show. Data are gathered at the beginning and the end of the show. Shifts in attitudes toward, or preference for, the brands featured on television commercials being tested during the showing provide the measuring stick for the commercials. High-scoring executions are then used in regular advertising schedules. One special-service group employing this technique is McCollum/Spielman Co. Audience Studies (ASI), also active in this field, measures audience reactions second by second during the entire showing.

Another approach is the **in-home projector,** or "black box," method. Test commercials are run on a 16-mm projector in the respondent's home with

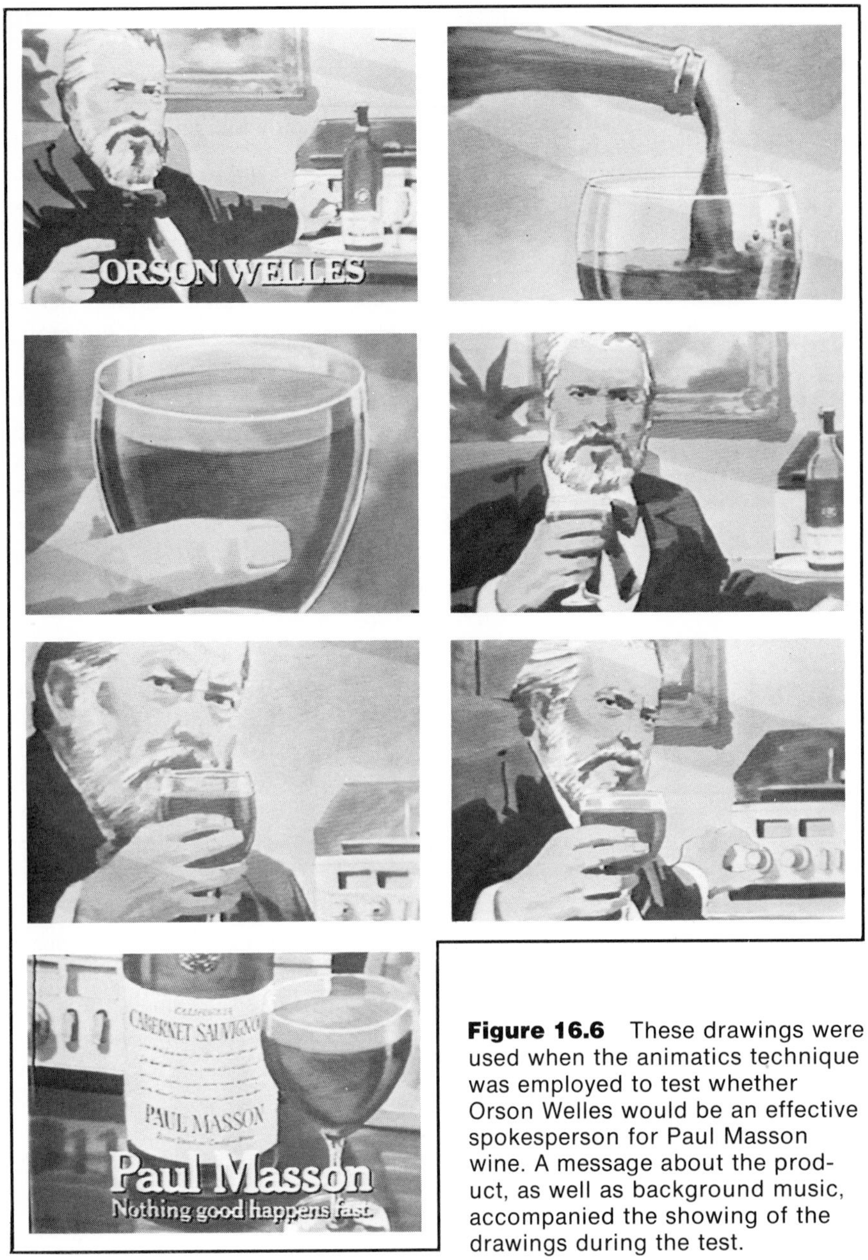

Figure 16.6 These drawings were used when the animatics technique was employed to test whether Orson Welles would be an effective spokesperson for Paul Masson wine. A message about the product, as well as background music, accompanied the showing of the drawings during the test.

questions asked before and after exposure to the commercials. The La Belle Courier is a similar device that uses an "endless loop" of film.

A third approach, the **recruited natural environment** method, is gaining popularity because, instead of measuring attitudes, it focuses on actual consumer behavior. Respondents are contacted in a real-life setting, such as a shopping mall, and asked to view commercials in a trailer set up like a theater. Respondents are asked questions about products, shown the commercials, and given a packet of coupons which can be used to purchase products featured on the commercials at price reductions. A matched sample of consumers who have not viewed the television commercials are given a similar packet of coupons. The differential in redemption rates between the two groups is attributed to the impact of the television commericals. Tele-Research, Inc., makes this method available to advertisers.

The second environmental situation available for the testing of television commercials is **exposure under normal viewing conditions.** Other names for this approach are "on-air" and "in-the-market" testing. In this test, the commercials being tested are substituted for regular commercials on established programming. While this may be done at the network level, it is more common to air these commercials in a local market. The commercial is "cut in" where another commercial would normally run, and later a sample of respondents is interviewed by telephone about the test commercial. Burke Marketing Research, Gallup & Robinson, and Mapes & Ross are well known in this field; however, a host of similar services is available for the advertiser wishing to test commercials under normal viewing conditions that do not have the artificiality of the forced exposure. The Qube innovation holds promise for future testing of commercials. Consumers are able to respond immediately (interact) to programming coming over their home television sets. Under the Qube system, consumers can order products through their television cable system immediately after viewing a commercial.

Evaluating Campaign Effectiveness after the Fact

Research can contribute to the evaluation of message effectiveness even after the advertising has been completed. The value in measuring effectiveness after the fact is that it can help make future advertising better. The money has been spent, the ad-

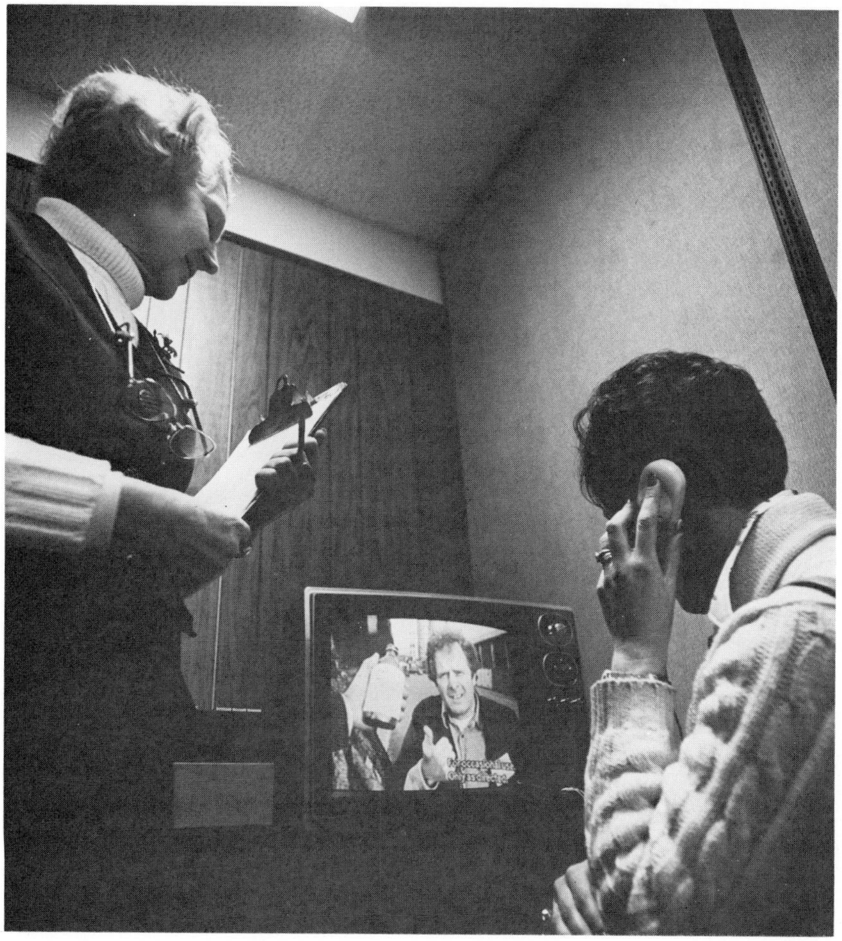

Figure 16.7 A television commerical is pretested in a research laboratory located in a shopping center. The respondent has a small speaker near her ear in order to avoid transmission of the audio part of the TV commercial from one interviewing station to another. [*Elrick & Lavidge.*]

vertising either did do its assigned job or failed to do so.

There are two ways that advertising can be assessed after it runs: (1) on an individual advertisement basis and (2) for an entire advertising campaign. **Posttesting** is the name given to the first type. It is discussed separately for print advertising and for television advertising, as was done for pretesting.

Posttesting of Print Advertising This facet of advertising research is characterized by two well-known syndicated readership services: *Starch Readership Reports* and *Gallup & Robinson Magazine Impact Studies.*

Starch is the most widely used syndicated research service found in advertising today. Magazine readers are classified into groups (expressed in percentages)

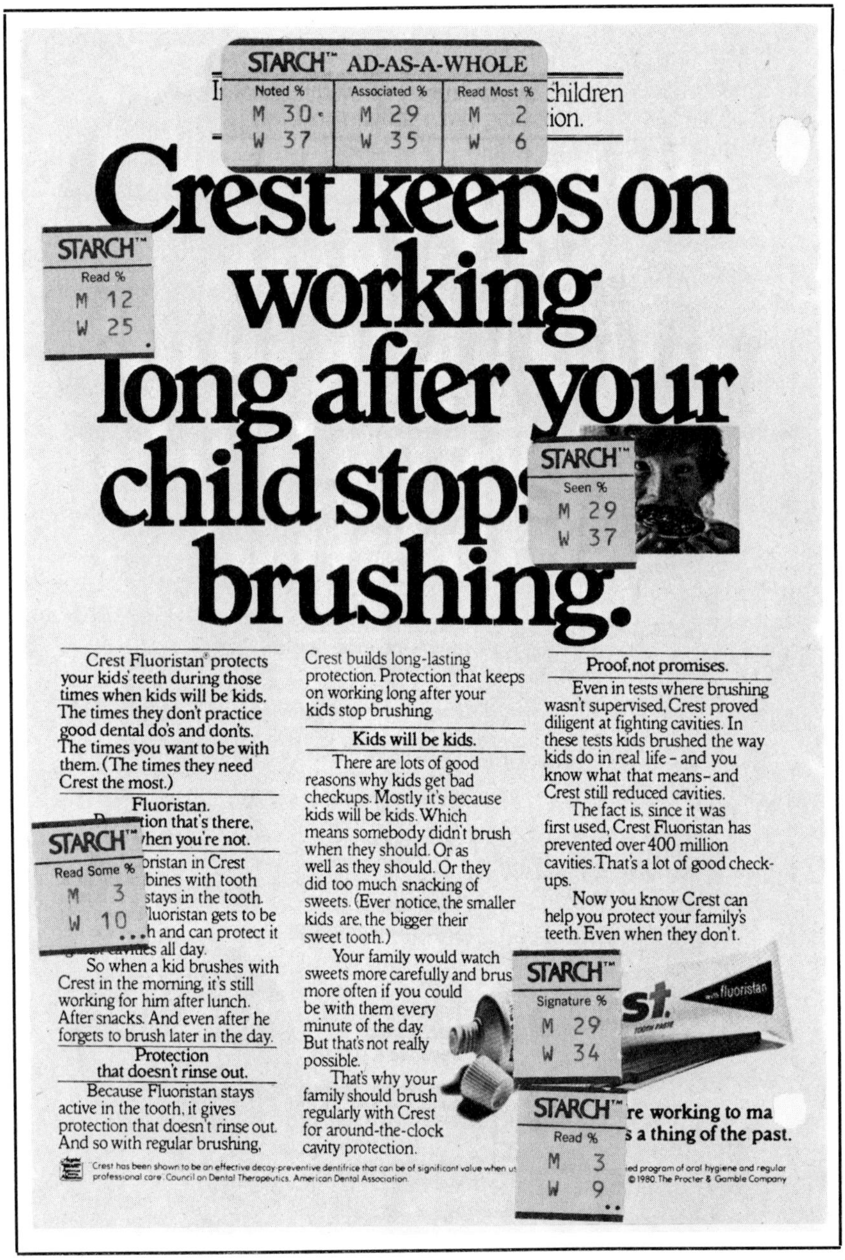

Figure 16.8 An advertisement for Crest toothpaste, which appeared in *Reader's Digest,* has been "Starched." The rating system's three scores of "Noted," "Associated," and "Read Most" are reported by sex. Five additional elements of the ad are also rated. This is an example of posttesting of print advertising. [*Starch INRA Hooper.*]

of those who remember seeing a particular advertisement, those who associated the sponsor's name with the advertisement, and those who read half or more of its copy. Starch labels these categories: "Noted," "Seen-Associated," and "Read Most." Figure 16.8 shows a magazine page with Starch scores indicated. This rating service is provided for most consumer magazines, for ads of a half-page or more in size. Research is also done for selected business and industrial publications. An added value of this service is that various advertising campaigns, yours and your competition's, can be compared over rather long periods. The company also can provide advertisers with qualitative data, gathered through depth interviews, from *Starch Reader Impression Studies.*

Starch's major competitor, Gallup & Robinson (G & R), uses a different, and probably more rigorous, method in gathering data from magazine readers. Where Starch interviewers turn magazine pages while asking respondents the questions about readership of ads, G & R interviewers first ask the respondent to recall and describe advertisements from the closed issue of the magazine. The advertiser's name is the only clue given to aid recall. Additional questions probe the respondent's memory of the sale message. Three levels of effectiveness are then indicated: "Proved Name Registration" (PNR) score, which gives the percentage of readers who remembered the ad and proved its recall by describing the ad; "Idea Playback Profile," a measure of sales message recall; and "Favorable Buying Attitude" score, which measures message persuasiveness along with the person's preresearch attitudes.

The magazine advertiser can get a good assessment of individual advertisements through these services. Furthermore, by careful analysis and tracking over periods of time, successive campaigns should improve in effectiveness. With many buyers of the service sharing the heavy costs of field interviewing involved, the information is available at a relatively reasonable cost. Thus, advertisers get information that would be too expensive for an individual firm to obtain by itself.

Posttesting of Television Advertising The services listed as providing pretesting of TV commercials are also engaged in their posttesting. Gallup & Robinson with its *Total Prime Time (TPT) Studies* is again active in this field of advertising research. A sample of television viewers is asked to trace their viewing pattern for the previous evening. Recall of commercials is probed as to sales points and persuasiveness. Two scores—"Commercial Recognition" (CR) and "Proved Commercial Registration" (PCR)—are reported for every commercial broadcast during prime viewing hours. Additional qualitative information is given to buyers of the service. Many other syndicated services are available in this field, and custom-made studies are also common.

Evaluating the Cumulative Effect of Advertising Campaigns

This stage of advertising research is less developed than the other stages; consequently, quantitative techniques are used less frequently. Because each advertising campaign is unique in its stated objectives, measuring the effectiveness of a given campaign must be done against those objectives. That is why we stressed earlier the importance of stating objectives in terms that are specific in time and character and that are expressed in measurable form. Sophisticated advertisers are increasingly engaging in ongoing campaign research in the form of **tracking studies.** Before an advertising campaign begins, the present market situation is compared with the objectives set for the campaign. Thereafter, the comparison is made on a regular basis, say, every three months. In other words, the progress of the campaign is tracked.

Ad-Tel is one source of economical syndicated research data that can be used at this stage of advertising research. Ad-Tel maintains a consumer panel whose members are subscribers to cable TV. The research firm can control the commercials reaching the consumers in the sample group; half the panel homes are beamed the message undergoing testing, while the others receive a different commercial on their sets. Panel members also keep a diary of the products purchased every week. Researchers can then determine whether seeing a particular television commercial had any impact on sales or not.

Expensive custom-made research is prevalent for advertisers seeking to measure the cumulative effect of their advertising. The usual research design employed is the **baseline,** or **benchmark,** study. An assessment of the variable to be influenced by advertising, such as awareness of the brand, is taken prior to

New Soft Look™ from Armstrong.
Fabric-covered ceilings for elegant settings.
CS-A-629-179 - ARCHITECTURAL RECORD, JAN.; AIA JOURNAL, JULY; PROGRESSIVE ARCHITECTURE, OCT., 1979

Figure 16.9 This business advertisement, which appeared in *Progressive Architecture,* was posttested by Readex, Inc. It was learned that 53 percent of the magazine's readers found the ad to be of interest to them. Continuous monitoring of such scores can help plan creative strategies for future ads in the campaign. [*Armstrong Cork Company.*]

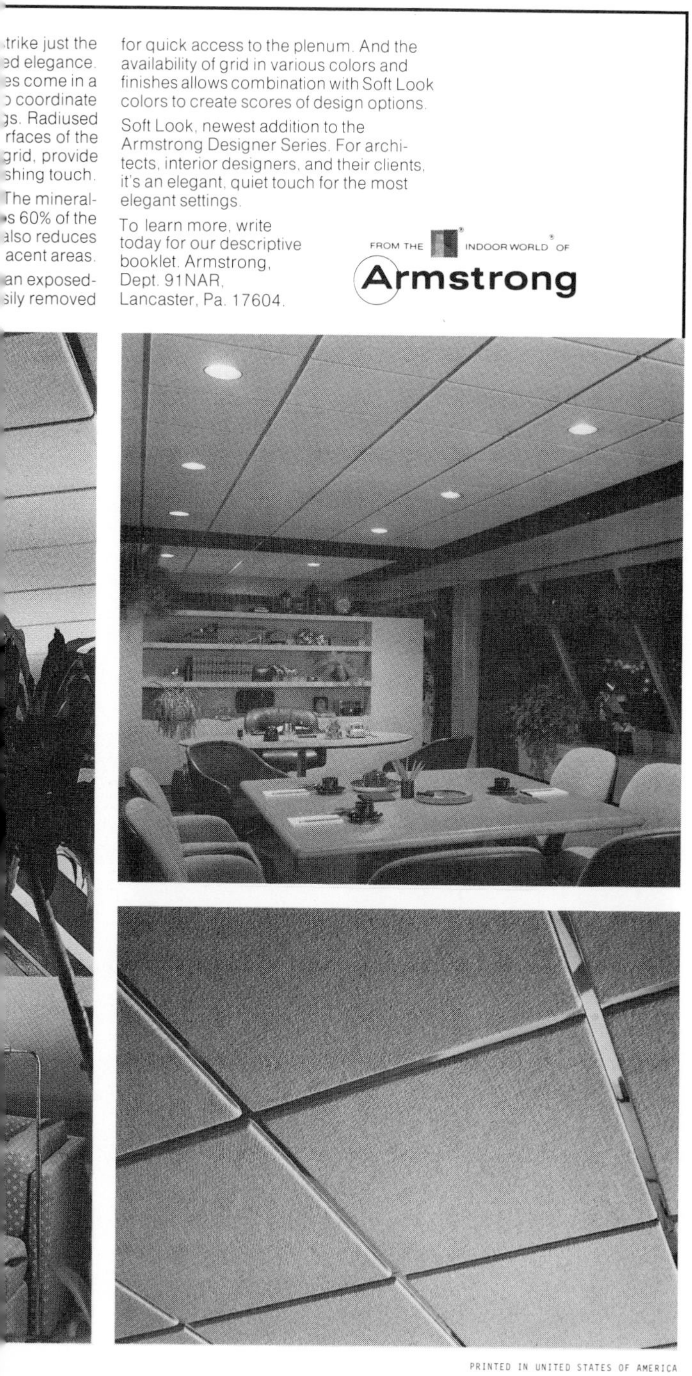

the campaign, and another is made at its conclusion. Probably the most commonly used measure is awareness, which has the advantage of being relatively simple to measure. Either people are aware of the brand or its benefits, or they are ignorant of it; research can disclose this condition. Other measures may include understanding, belief, interest, persuasion, and sale. Although the last condition is the ultimate goal of nearly every advertising campaign, it is hard to attribute a sale to an advertising campaign because of the difficulty in separating the multiple influences bearing on the purchase of a product. This stage of advertising research leaves many unanswered questions and presents an opportunity area for advertising researchers of the future. When better ways of determining whether an advertising campaign has worked as desired are developed, more efficient advertising should follow.

How Research Contributes to Business Success: The State Farm Insurance Company's Case[17]

Blair Vedder, chairman of the board of Needham, Harper and Steers (NHS) Advertising, related in a talk before the Advertising Research Foundation how advertising research was used over a 20-year period to guide a client's advertising. Although State Farm Insurance Company has been an NHS client since 1939, the story really begins in 1945 when American business emerged from World War II.

In the 1940s, State Farm became the leading auto insurance underwriter in the United States. Low rates was its primary consumer benefit. Allstate, a subsidiary of Sears, entered on the scene in the early 1950s and immediately became an effective competitor. Attitude research showed that State Farm was perceived as a rural company interested mainly in insuring farmers' cars. Sales projections made in 1953 showed that Allstate would overtake the company by 1957 or 1958. It was realized that a change in State Farm's advertising direction was in order.

A study of prospect attitudes made in 1954 revealed that State Farm was thought to provide inferior claim service and that it was too small, with insufficient resources to cover policyholder claims. A multipage insert was run in *Life* magazine telling the full story of the company's history, size, record with claims, and so forth. The company's share of market accelerated rapidly, and State Farm became a "true believer" in the value of consumer attitude research. A consumer probe conducted three years later showed there was no longer any doubt about the size of the company and its resources. Advertising had done its job.

The research did show, however, that people felt large companies are cold, impersonal, and insensitive to their customers. This finding posed a tough communications challenge, namely, how to show State Farm as a giant in its industry, selling insurance at low rates, yet as a company interested in its policyholders' well-being. Jack Benny, a well-known comedian of the era whose act revolved around his stinginess, was chosen as spokesman for the company. Benny presented the saving and service selling points with a light touch. Allstate struck back with its "Good Hands" theme delivered by Ed Reimers, a professional announcer, as spokesman. Significantly, Allstate was outspending State Farm in advertising by margins as high as 50 percent a year, a fact that added importance to the need for effective advertising by State Farm.

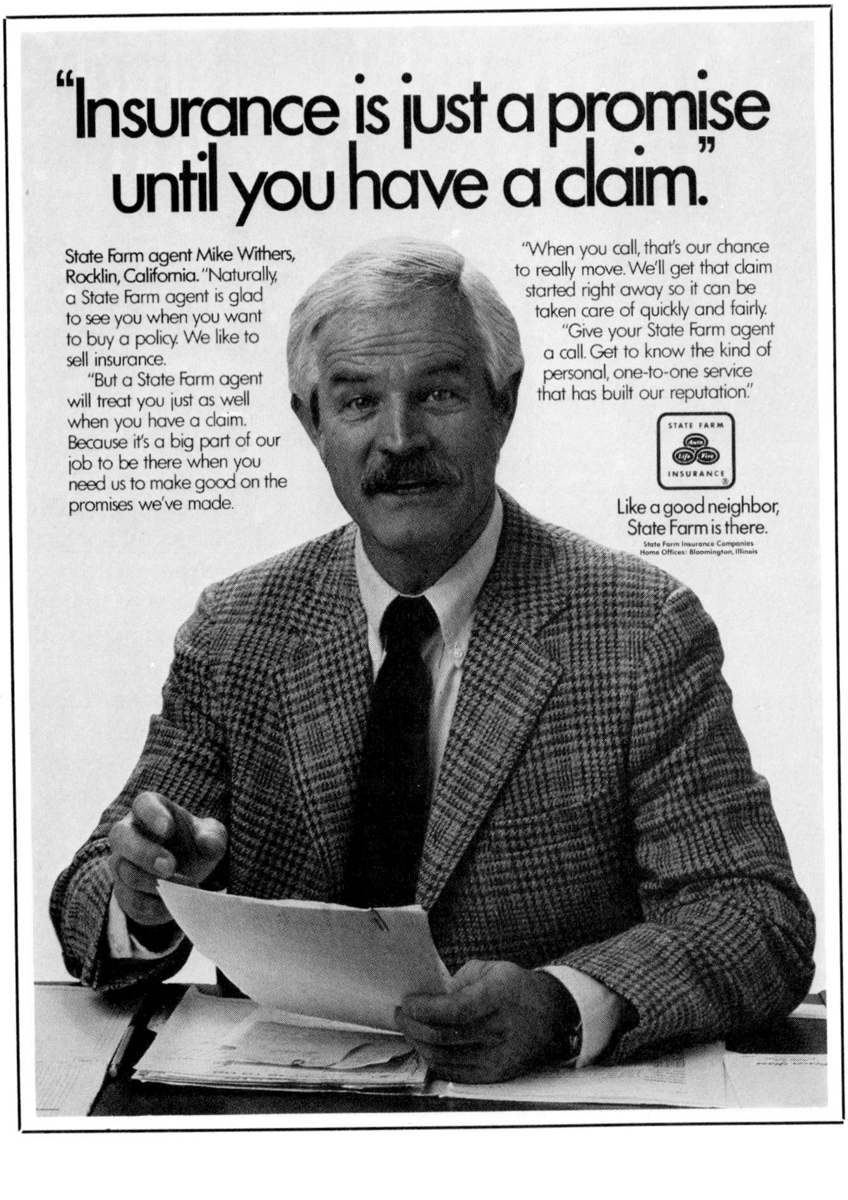

Figure 16.10 This print version of the State Farm campaign features company agents as a reason for patronizing the insurer. Television commercials are also used in the campaign, which was in its eighth year in 1981.

Profile

Rena Bartos

The important role played by women in the advertising research field is clearly shown by the career of Rena Bartos. Mrs. Bartos is senior vice-president and director of communications development at the J. Walter Thompson Company, a position she has held since 1975. Bartos was named Advertising Woman of the Year in 1980.

Rena's research efforts focus on the changing role of women in our society, especially as those changes affect consumption patterns and buying habits. She has also done research into the link between consumers and advertising messages. The combined results of her research have had considerable impact on the way modern advertisements and commercials are developed.

Mrs. Bartos is active in various advertising research organizations, having served as chairperson of the Research Committee of the American Association of Advertising Agencies, as a member of the board of directors for both the Advertising Research Foundation and the Travel Research Association, and as a member of the Copy Research Council. She is author of *The Future of the Advertising Agency Research Function* and *The Founding Fathers of Advertising Research;* both books are recommended reading for advertising research practitioners.

This energetic woman speaks frequently to professional groups. Her article "What Every Marketer Should Know about Women" was selected as a finalist in the 1979 National Magazine Award competition. Mrs. Bartos, who graduated from Rutgers University and pursued postgraduate work in sociology at Columbia University, serves on the board of advisers to the American Women's Economic Development Corporation. We can expect that her continued exploration of changing values will influence communication through advertising in the years ahead.

Further research at the time showed that the two competitors were confused in consumers' minds because of the name similarity between the firms. Therefore, State Farm changed its communications goal in order to minimize the confusion without losing the thrift theme, delivered in a warm and friendly tone.

In 1965, 10 years after the *Life* insert, State Farm led Allstate by $200 million in earned premiums, which was Allstate's total size when the battle began. In 1965, the automobile industry faced a new environment characterized by large underwriting losses. Obviously, the search for new business was halted, and the emphasis shifted to retaining the better policyholders already in the fold. Now the advertising objective became one of keeping the company name before these policyholders. Radio was selected as the vehicle, and again, comedians delivered the message.

Early in the 1970s, conditions changed again, and aggressive selling returned. The rate advantage previously held by State Farm had largely disappeared, and new research revealed that consumers were less interested in cost and more concerned with service from their insurer. One finding was that people's primary interest was in buying insurance from an agent who was *knowledgeable,* was *available,* and who could be *counted on* when help was needed. Inasmuch as State Farm has 10,000 agents, it was in a good position to meet these expectations. Thus, in 1971, the "Like a Good Neighbor, State Farm Is There" campaign was created. The promise was communicated first through film dramas and later by using a real-life agent as the star and spokesman of the message.

A decade later, the campaign theme remained the same, as is shown in the print version of the advertising run in 1981 (Figure 16.10). Monitoring of the campaign through various research approaches continued, and State Farm is the undisputed leader in car insurance today; the company is also the largest homeowners' insurance company and a fast-growing life insurance underwriter.

The State Farm case shows how research and advertising creativity interplay. People's concern over the various product attributes changes over time, and the continuous tracking of these shifts has permitted the company to continue to prosper because its communication with customers and prospects has had continued relevance for them.

Summary

Advertising campaign planning should be based on as many facts as possible. Pertinent information is sifted out of the marketplace using the tools of modern research. Advertising research is needed as the geographical distance between producers and consumers widens. Reliance is made upon data gathered by researchers within the company and from outside firms. Similarly, secondary and primary data are employed.

Market research covers investigations into all the many facets of the marketing process, while advertising research, a subsystem of market research, deals with the message and its dissemination. Creative research, the focus of this chapter, deals with the question of how to make advertisements, either singly or as part of campaigns, more effective.

Advertising research, as with all research, employs certain research fundamentals. The five basic steps used to gather data are defining the problem, collecting secondary data, collecting primary data, collating the data, and interpreting the data. A sample population is used in advertising research to save both time and money. The principal ways of sampling are the probability and the quota methods. The sample is chosen to represent the entire market. Respondents from members of the sample may be obtained through personal interviews, telephone queries, and mailed questionnaires. When motivational answers are desired, focus groups and projective techniques are brought in to supplement quantitative findings.

Creative research, which delves into the message itself, is conducted at three stages in the campaign: (1) when copy strategy is being formed, (2) when individual advertisements are pretested for relative effectiveness, and (3) when the effects of the whole campaign are assessed. The goal during the first stage is to isolate a copy theme around which to build a campaign. In the second stage, which is true copy testing, the execution of the strategy decided upon during the first stage is measured. Testing after the advertising has run, called posttesting, as well as evaluating the total effect of a specific campaign, is done during the third stage. In other words, advertising research can first help in deciding what to say and, through the creative research, even how to say it. Testing will tell if what was said was communicated and understood as planned. At each level, a number of syndicated services provide useful information at reasonable costs, although special-purpose studies may be also needed.

Questions for Discussion

1 Explain the difference between market research, advertising research, and creative research.
2 Have you ever participated as an interviewee in a market or advertising research project? If so, describe how you participated and your reactions to the experience.
3 List any secondary data that a videocassette player manufacturer might use to shape the firm's advertising campaign. Is this advertising research or market research?
4 What are the five basic steps in a full-scale "information-gathering" project? Explain how each step is used in marketing a product or service.
5 Do people answer questions truthfully? What implications does this tendency have on questionnaire and interview design? Do questions 1 through 4 imply the answer desired?
6 Why has the location for most personal interviewing shifted from the consumers' homes to the shopping center or mall? Is this trend likely to increase? Why?
7 Why is research into the communication value of print ads and TV commercials called "creative research"? Should other parts of the advertising process be included? Explain.
8 Explain why the pretesting of finished (postproduction) television commercials is declining. Does this change in research procedure pose any serious problem? Discuss.
9 What is a "tracking study"? What is its value in the advertising planning process?
10 Bring to class examples of magazine ads for State Farm, Allstate, and other automobile insurance companies. Write an analysis of what appear to be their copy themes.

For Further Reference

Aaker, David A., and John G. Myers: *Advertising Management,* Prentice-Hall, Inc., Englewood Cliffs, N.J., 1975.

Boyd, Harper W. Jr., Ralph Westfall, and Stanley Stasch: *Marketing Research: Text and Cases,* 4th ed., Richard D. Irwin, Inc., Homewood, Ill., 1977.

Churchill, Gilbert A., Jr.: *Marketing Research Methodological Foundations,* 2d ed., The Dryden Press, Hinsdale, Ill., 1979.

Engel, James F., Martin R. Warshaw, and Thomas C. Kinnear: *Promotional Strategy,* 4th ed., Richard D. Irwin, Inc., Homewood, Ill., 1979.

Erdos, Paul L.: *Professional Mail Surveys,* Prentice-Hall, Inc., Englewood Cliffs, N.J., 1976.

Fletcher, Alan D., and Thomas A. Bowers: *Fundamentals of Advertising Research,* Grid Publishing, Inc., Columbus, Ohio, 1979.

Green, Paul E., and Donald S. Tull: *Research for Marketing Decisions,* 4th ed., Prentice-Hall, Inc., Englewood Cliffs, N.J., 1978.

Holbert, Neil: *Advertising Research,* American Marketing Association, Chicago, 1975.

Lucas, Darrel B., and Steuart Henderson Britt: *Measuring Advertising Effectiveness,* McGraw-Hill Book Company, New York, 1963.

Luck, David J. et al.: *Marketing Research,* 5th ed., Prentice-Hall, Inc., Englewood Cliffs, N.J., 1978.

Percy, Larry, and John R. Rossiter: *Advertising Strategy: A Communication Theory Approach,* Frederick A. Praeger, Inc., New York, 1980.

Ramond, Charles: *The Art of Using Science in Marketing,* Harper & Row, Publishers, Inc., New York, 1974.

Schultz, Don E., and Dennis G. Martin: *Strategic Advertising Campaigns,* Crain Books, Chicago, 1979.

Simon, Julian L.: *The Management of Advertising,* Prentice-Hall, Inc., Englewood Cliffs, N.J., 1972.

Tolley, B. Stuart: *Advertising and Marketing Research: A New Methodology,* Nelson-Hall, Chicago, 1977.

Zaltman, Gerald, and Philip C. Burger: *Marketing Research: Fundamentals and Dynamics,* The Dryden Press, Hinsdale, Ill., 1975.

End Notes

[1] Based on Gerald Zaltman and Philip C. Burger, *Marketing Research,* The Dryden Press, Inc., Hinsdale, Ill., 1975, pp. 4–6.

[2] Committee on Definitions, Ralph S. Alexander, chairman, *Marketing Definitions,* American Marketing Association, Chicago, 1963, pp. 16–17.

[3] Zaltman and Burger, op. cit., p. 8.

[4] Neil Holbert, *Advertising Research,* American Marketing Association, Chicago, 1975, p. 1.

[5] Ibid.

[6] Ibid., p. 2.

[7] Emanuel H. Demby, *Marketing News,* June 6, 1975, p. 8.

[8] Danny N. Bellenger, Kenneth L. Bernhardt, and Jac L. Goldstucker, *Qualitative Research in Marketing,* American Marketing Association, Chicago, 1975, p. 2.

[9] Peter Sampson, "Qualitative Research and Motivational Research," in Robert M. Worcester (ed.), *Consumer Market Research Handbook,* McGraw-Hill Book Company, Ltd., London, 1972, p. 7.

[10] Paragraph based on Bellenger et al., op. cit., p. 2.

[11] Ibid., p. 30.

[12] Ibid., p. 7.

[13] Ibid., p. 8.

[14] The basic structure and some of the concepts discussed in this section were drawn from Daniel Lissance, ed., *The Advertising Man's Guide to Creative Research,* a professional publication of Richard K. Manoff, Inc., Advertising, New York, 1974.

[15] Ibid., p. 2.

[16] "The Value and Application of Diagnostic Measurements," McCollum-Spielman *TOPLINE,* Vol. 1, no. 7, October 1979, p. 1.

[17] Based on Blair Vedder, "Like a Good Neighbor, Research Was There," *1975 ARF Midyear Conference Proceedings,* pp. 39–41. Copyright by the Advertising Research Foundation.

Chapter 17

The Advertising Budget

Advertising costs money. Money pays for the research that underlies sound advertising programs. More important, it pays for the creative work that goes into the preparation of advertising messages and for the media costs incurred in getting those advertising messages before the target market.

An examination of Table 17.1 reveals that one advertiser alone annually spends well in excess of one-half billion dollars to convince consumers through advertising that they should buy its products. Out of every dollar in sales, Procter & Gamble spends 5.7 cents for advertising.

The advertising manager, therefore, needs to know how to determine the advertising budget. After deciding the how, when, and where of spending ad dollars, and after the campaign has run, the advertiser assesses how effectively these expenditures were invested to learn whether the company got its money worth.

We look at budget making for the advertising campaign in this chapter. Deciding the level of advertising support needed flows naturally from the process of setting advertising objectives. Budget decisions clearly affect strategy decisions. The size of the advertising appropriation often acts as a limiting factor when media choices are being made. Certain media are too costly for use in some advertising campaigns. Certain creative techniques, such as the use of four-color print ads or the use of elaborate settings or expensive talent in television commercials, may also be ruled out by budgetary constraints. On the other

Table 17.1
Leading National Advertisers in 1979

Company	Millions of dollars spent for advertising	Advertising to sales ratio
Procter & Gamble Co.	$614.9	5.7
General Foods Corp.	393.0	6.5
Sears, Roebuck & Co.	379.3	2.1
General Motors Corp.	323.4	0.5
Phillip Morris Inc.	291.2	3.5
K mart Corp.	287.1	2.3
R. J. Reynolds Industries	258.1	2.9
Warner-Lambert Co.	220.2	6.8
American Telephone & Telegraph Co.	219.8	0.4
Ford Motor Co.	215.0	0.5
Pepsi Co Inc.	212.0	4.2
Bristol Myers Co.	210.6	7.7
American Home Products	206.0	5.6
McDonald's Corp.	202.8	3.8
Gulf & Western Industries	191.5	2.9
General Mills	190.7	4.6
Esmark Inc.	170.5	2.5
Coca-Cola Co.	169.3	3.4
Seagram Co.	168.0	6.6
Mobil Corp.	165.8	0.3
Norton Simon Inc.	163.2	5.9
Anheuser-Busch	160.5	4.9
Unilever U.S. Inc.	160.0	7.5
RCA Corp.	158.6	2.1
Johnson & Johnson	157.7	6.6

Source: Reprinted with permission from the Sept. 11, 1980 issue of *Advertising Age*. Copyright © 1980 by Crain Communications, Inc.

"I had heard they were cutting their advertising budget."

Figure 17.1 One budgeting principle is that the amount of money available for advertising may determine the media that can be used. [*Reproduced by permission from Advertising Age.*]

hand, spending too little may mean that the impact on target audiences will be insufficient and the advertising investment unproductive. Advertising objectives or strategies may have to be modified to take budget constraints into account.

Advertising as an Investment

Two somewhat philosophical attitudes are important to the success of advertising programs. Management should, first of all, look at advertising from the prospective customer's point of view. Second, management must think of advertising as an investment because the expenditure of funds for advertising is likely to result in a greater return. Investment in a capital asset, such as a piece of industrial equipment, may cause more goods to be produced and sold. In the same sense, an effective advertising campaign may also increase sales.

The accountant lists advertising as a business expense, and the Internal Revenue Service accepts such handling for income tax purposes. Business managers are responsible for controlling expenses and cutting costs. Thus, when the income statement of a company is being reviewed, the chief executive may decide that advertising expenses should be reduced or even eliminated. This action, taken in the belief that good managerial initiative is being exercised, does not bode well for the role of advertising in the company's future, nor, quite possibly, for the future of the company itself. Viewing advertising only as a cost is a narrow attitude and not usually a sound one.

Joel Dean, a leading business economist, considers advertising as a capital investment rather than a current expense. He states that advertising is an investment that can be defined as "an outlay made today to achieve benefits in the future," whereas a current expense is "an outlay whose benefits are immediate." Therefore, it is reasonable to think of advertising as an investment just like a capital asset since both will provide larger returns in the future.

Regardless of bookkeeping practice or tax treatment, Dean states:

> Promotional investments do have unusual characteristics, different from many other investments that now fight for funds in the capital budget. However, these traits . . . do not destroy the essential investment character of the promotional outlays.[1]

We agree that advertising expenses, like all other expenses, should be carefully scrutinized for waste. A great deal needs to be known, however, about the results being derived, or failing to materialize, from advertising before a reduction or elimination is in order. Advertising expenditures must stand or fall on their own merits after a careful evaluation of income and expenditures and should not be made a scapegoat in periods of retrenchment for the firm. A cut in the advertising appropriation in periods of recession brings an inevitable trade-off in future sales.

Unsound or capricious treatment of advertising funds is not likely when the dollars spent for advertising are thought of as an investment in the creation of future customers as well as the retention of present ones. The tendency to consider advertising as a necessary evil begins to disappear, and the urge to spend funds quickly—so that "more important" business can be transacted—is curbed. Planned advertising expenditures result, and advertising is then looked upon as "building a consumer franchise" for the advertised brand in addition to being a source of direct returns. David Ogilvy once said, "Every advertisement is a long term investment in the image of a brand." When advertising's contribution to the long-term future of the firm is recognized and respected, effective advertising is more apt to emerge.

The Advertising Budget-Making Process[2]

Devising a budget—and the advertising budget is no exception—forces people to face realities and to plan. Neither task is pleasant for most of us, and yet the rewards from dealing with conditions realistically and from planning future action are great. Another reason advertising executives find the advertising budget troublesome is that it involves the financial side of the business; advertising managers must deal with accountants and controllers. And the two groups often hold different attitudes toward advertising and its role in the business and how company funds should be used. Furthermore, they speak different languages. Communication is difficult because both groups tend to use specialized terminology. Nevertheless, controllers and other company officers responsible for the firm's financial health must understand the presentation made on behalf of the advertising budget if they are to approve its provisions.

What Is a Budget?

A budget is "an expression in dollars and cents of the forward plan of any activity, and budgeting, in essence, is nothing more than planning." In fact, the terms "budget" and "plan" are often used interchangeably by advertising people. However, the concepts should be kept separate in our thinking. The following statement should help:

> The advertising plan typically includes a large body of information embracing sales goals, product facts, marketing information, competitive situation, creative platforms and rough examples of copy treatment. It sets forth marketing and advertising strategies, copy and media recommendations for implementing that strategy, and plans and schedules which define the timing of the campaign.
>
> The advertising budget is the translation of an advertising plan into dollars and cents—it is the "price tag." In its most elementary form, it states the amount of proposed advertising expenditures and informs company management of the anticipated cost of executing the advertising plan. It serves as a decision-making tool in the top-management process of allocating available funds to the various functions and activities of the company.

Anyone who develops an advertising budget must observe two fundamentals of budgeting. One, the budget must be constructed within the financial capabilities of the company. Two, it must contain specific details on the allocation of funds to specific operations. Only when this is done can the budget perform its "single most important purpose . . . as the cornerstone for an effective budgetary control system." The actual budgetary process consists of four steps: preparation, presentation, execution, and control.

Budget Preparation

Agency personnel often contribute much of the planning work. Chapter 16 outlines how research people provide information and insight for decisions dealing with target markets, products, packaging, advertising copy, new-product introductions, and media selection. Marketing research people, on the other hand, are seldom involved with the important issue of how much to spend for advertising.

Determining the size of the future advertising appropriation is the first step in preparing the advertising budget. Once this figure has been set through the use of the somewhat unsophisticated methods described in the next section of this chapter, budget specifics must be established. The total advertising pie is cut into slices, and the total budget is allocated among the various media and advertising functions. The budget must be allocated among different market segments, time periods, and geographic areas. Ideally, this is done on the basis of market potential within the segments, periods, or areas.

Presentation and Approval of the Budget

The presentation of the budget is a selling job. The advertising budget, as developed by the head of the advertising department in consultation with the agency, is subject first to approval either by the president, or chief executive officer, of the firm or by the vice president of marketing. The corporation's executive or financial committee may be involved in the final approval process. These executives act as a watchdog group over company funds; the prudent management of expenditures is one of their prime responsibilities. Every department of the company naturally feels its own activities are of major importance. But top management must allocate funds so they maximize the firm's profits, and many groups get less than they request in their budgets. Adjustments in advertising budget requests are common.

The final budget for advertising should be evaluated in conjunction with the sales forecast. Since advertising is employed to make sales, this budget must be compatible with sales goals. Although the advertising agency may provide the advertising manager with visual materials and moral support, getting the advertising budget approved is the advertising manager's responsibility and one important test of competence in that position.

Budget Execution

Each year the appropriation is used in execution of the advertising plan. Administration of advertising spending is a somewhat routine activity. Purchase of authorized advertising time and space is the primary task, and the advertising agency handles the job. The costs of advertising production, such as making television commercials, can also be significant elements in the overall expenditures for advertising; these are also incurred by the agency on behalf of the client. The advertising manager, therefore, should monitor these expenses to make certain that advertising dollars are spent in an economical manner. Constant surveillance and periodic checks to determine whether media discounts are being taken and special services are being purchased at competitive rates help to bring about this efficiency in the use of advertising funds.

An important duty of the advertising manager during the advertising program execution stage is to make sure that the marketing situation has remained unchanged. When critical changes do occur, it is vital that the budget have enough flexibility to permit program changes. One device that facilitates such action is the **contingency fund.** Many companies include a reserve for contingencies in their advertising budgets. When the practice is followed, some set part, such as 15 percent, of the budget as approved by management is set aside in a "service account." These dollars are then available for covering cost fluctuations such as media rate increases, and also for items not already worked into the planned advertising program because they were not anticipated at budget time.[3]

Control of the Budget

One important way the advertising manager controls the budget is to see whether advertising expenditures coincide with the schedule set down in the advertising budget. A procedure must be established which brings information about current expenditures to the attention of the advertising manager. These expenditures are then compared with the advertising plan. If the budget calls for expenditures of $100,000 during July, the advertising manager must be sure that no greater amount is actually spent. Planned expenditures and actual expenditures must run parallel if the budget is to serve as a control.

Protecting the budget from uses other than advertising is another vital responsibility of the advertising manager. Because advertising is closely related to many other business functions—personal selling, merchandising, sales promotion, packaging, sampling, and public relations—it is often difficult to state clearly which department should bear certain charges. For example, should the cost of free samples be charged to the advertising or the sales budget? Should a charitable gift be handled as an advertising or a public relations expense? Should production or advertising bear the cost of redesigning the product package? Department heads commonly fight to obtain larger budgets; almost all departments want more money to carry on their operations. If the argument for a larger budget is lost, there is another route to achieving the desired end, namely, to get other departments to pay expenses that are beneficial to the department escaping the charges. This process, whereby budgets are eaten up by outside forces, is sometimes called **budget attrition** and dramatizes the need for clarifying which budget is to be charged.

Making precise budget determinations is not always a simple matter. Certain expenses are obviously chargeable to the advertising budget: media charges, advertising department expenses, and advertising production costs. Some charges are almost universally excluded: annual reports, charitable donations, house organs, product research, coupon redemption costs, recruitment advertising, factory signs, product publicity, and premium handling costs. There exists, however, a gray area wherein certain charges may or may not be made against the advertising budget. This area includes advertising aids for salespeople, financial advertising, dealer-help literature, point-of-sale materials, catalogs for dealers, test-marketing programs, cost of contest entry blanks, mobile exhibits, packaging consultant fees, and consumer contest awards. In these instances, the decision is a matter of company policy or executive judgment. The advertising manager, acting as trustee of the advertising budget, must see that the advertising department does not bear the penalty of misdirected charges.

Specific Methods of Determining the Advertising Appropriation

Advertising appropriations are determined in a variety of ways. Adherents of each method fervently believe their own approach is best. The truth, however, is that no one method is ideal for all situations. Advertisers should therefore be aware of all major alternatives in their search for an appropriate budget decision model. Among national advertisers, three major methods predominate: (1) use of fixed guidelines, (2) the task method, and (3) subjective budgeting.[4]

Fixed Guidelines

A mathematical formula is used when the advertising appropriation is determined by the fixed guidelines method. Basically, there are three varieties available to users of this method. The percentage-of-sales approach is by far the most widely used. Some firms employ the unit-of-sales variation, while the third approach uses advertising expenditures of competitors as the guide.

Percentage-of-Sales Method The procedure in the percentage-of-sales method is to apply a stated percentage to the sales volume figure, and the advertising appropriation appears automatically. Nothing could be simpler. Management of the firm determines what percentage figure is to be used. It is usually based upon (1) the industry average or (2) what the company has spent in the past for its advertising. The chosen percentage is applied either to the sales volume achieved during the previous year (past year's sales approach) or to the sales level anticipated for the current year (planned sales approach).

The percentage-of-sales method has a major shortcoming: little attention is given to the specific advertising needs of the individual firm. The chosen percentage might be based upon industry averages, but the advertiser's situation may not be average. Companies vary a great deal in their relative share of market; some companies are dominant in their field whereas others are quite insignificant in the overall supply picture for the generic product. Moreover, firms employ different marketing systems to reach customers. Thus, an individual company may need to do more—or less—advertising than the average of the industry.

The same basic principle carries over when the firm's own experience is chosen as the measuring stick. Conditions change, and advertising expenditures should change with them. Moreover, there is the question whether the percentage should be applied to the previous year's sales or planned sales. The former method can lead to too little or too much advertising, depending on whether sales are increasing or declining. The latter method, while more logical, is complicated by problems of sales forecasting, among other things.

In essence, the philosophy underlying this method is faulty. It is based on the premise that advertising results from sales, while the converse—that sales result from advertising—is sounder thinking. Nevertheless, the percentage-of-sales method continues to be popular with many advertisers. Sheer force of habit provides one explanation for its use. Moreover, management may use the method because of its simplicity, and because it relates advertising expenditures directly to sales. When advertising changes from a fixed cost to a variable cost, management feels that advertising costs can be controlled more easily. If sales decline, advertising expenditures decline, and vice versa. However, the interaction between sales and advertising is ignored. Management is lulled into believing that it has this important problem under control when it does not. Use of this method is an indicator that money is budgeted by routine and probably spent in the same way.

Sometimes the percentage-of-sales method is used to bring a degree of stability to an industry. If all firms in the industry use the same percentage as their base, the volume of advertising done by each firm is directly proportional to its relative position in the industry. Thus, advertising loses some of its power to change share-of-the-market relationships. Of course, the creative selling power of competitors' advertising campaigns is still a means of bringing about such market changes.

The percentage-of-sales method can be used most effectively by companies that face the same conditions year after year. Some public utilities are in this situation; the companies operate in static industries where there is little reason—including product differentiation through advertising—for buyers to change from one seller to another. Few firms, however, are so situated. For this reason, the percentage-of-sales method should be supplanted or supplemented by a different method.

Unit-of-Sales Method A variant of the percentage-of-sales method is the unit-of-sales method, which is more precisely labeled the "fixed-dollar-unit-expense method." A specific dollars-and-cents amount is allocated to the advertising budget for each unit produced instead of applying a stated percentage of the sales figure to the advertising budget. Otherwise, the two methods are practically the same. The unit-of-sales method can be illustrated by looking at cooperative marketing organizations and their advertising budget procedures. For instance, members of the Washington State Apple Commission assessed themselves at the rate of 17 cents per hundredweight in 1980–1981; this figure is roughly 7.3 cents per box of apples. Application of this formula resulted in a budget of $3.1 million.

Often this budget method is called the assessment method. Among other users of the unit-of-sales method are the major car manufacturers. Each automobile produced results in an advertising allocation, and advertising programs are often revamped when sales are greater—or less—than planned. The unit-of-sales method has the same basic weakness as the percentage-of-sales approach to budgeting; the seller's *need* to advertise is not weighed carefully. Of course, the unit-of-sales method can be incorporated with some form of the task method, to make certain that funds are sufficient to meet the needs of advertising. The trouble is that often the amount of the assessment becomes habitual, and the advertising program is not designed to meet dynamic marketing problems.

Competitors'-Expenditures Method Advertisers base their advertising budgets on what competitors are doing may adopt one of two points of view. Some attempt to match competitive expenditures, while others strive to spend more than their competitors. In the first instance, advertising is viewed as a defensive device; the idea is to advertise only as much as competition requires. This defensive strategy is as poor in advertising as it is in war. The second attitude often springs from a deep-seated competitive spirit that tries to outdo competition on the basis of sheer volume of advertising.

Neither approach is sound, however, for the advertising task facing one firm is not the same as that of its competitors. Although the amount of competitive advertising may affect the market for an individual advertiser's products, matching or exceeding competitive expenditures is a poor way of developing a satisfactory advertising budget.[5]

The Task Method

The search for a budget method which would help develop more positive management attitudes toward advertising expenditures has been going on for a long time. Most budget methods fail to treat advertising as a vehicle for achieving business objectives. The task method, sometimes called the objective method, was developed with one purpose in mind: to use advertising to further the smooth functioning of the marketing process. Most major national advertisers claim to be users of the task approach. The task method involves four basic steps.

Defining the Task The first step taken in implementing the task method is to identify the objectives that advertising is to achieve. The number and variety of objectives that can be set down for advertising are practically endless, as discussed in Chapter 4. For example, some sellers use advertising primarily as a means of getting leads for their sales force or to arouse enough interest among prospects that they will be moved to send for additional information about the advertised product.

The sellers of encyclopedias often use advertising to stimulate inquiries. Let us assume that the Eureka Encyclopedia Publishing Company has a permanent sales force of 100 members. The company would like to see each salesperson sell—on an average—100 sets annually. Furthermore, let us assume that one call in five develops into a sale. If the only source of leads is inquiries from people who have been exposed to company advertising, 50,000 inquiries will be needed (100 salespeople × 100 sets sold annually = 10,000 sets; 10,000 sets × 5 inquiries per sale = 50,000 inquiries). The advertising objective is to secure 50,000 inquiries from consumers. The use of advertising to secure sales leads was also shown in the Medney Organization, Inc., case in Chapter 1.

A more typical task is the achievement of a specific level of brand awareness for the product among a group of consumers. The task is then expressed in communication terms. Other advertisers, such as those engaged in the direct-response business, may phrase the task in terms of actual sales. Advertising, of course, does not carry the entire burden in the achievement of most business objectives. For the moment, however, we shall put aside the real-life problem of specifying the relative role of advertising in the marketing mix and continue with our step-by-step explanation of the task method.

Determining the Type and Quantity of Advertising The truly difficult part of the task method lies in this step, for at this stage the most efficient and effective means of satisfying the objectives must be worked out. The problem is that there is no exact way to predict expected returns from advertising. An advertiser may decide that consumer magazines in general, and *Reader's Digest* in particular, are the best ways to reach the market for the advertised product. That media-selection decision is not easy in itself, as Chapter 18 will amplify, but the question of how much advertising is needed is much more complex. "How many full pages in four colors in *Reader's Digest* are needed to obtain 50,000 inquiries for the encyclopedia marketer?" is a hard question to answer with precision. While the task method is often considered the most scientific budget method, successfully determining the type and quantity of advertising depends largely on the practice of the art of advertising, although the techniques for evaluating advertising effectiveness can help the advertising decision maker. Clearly defined objectives, however, are vital to the measurement of advertising effectiveness.

Determining the Cost of the Advertising Program The third step in the task method is more mechanical than the first two steps. The addition of estimates of various costs, including media and production charges, is a matter of simple arithmetic.

Determining Whether the Program Is Affordable Once a cost figure is reached, management must decide whether the company is financially able to make such an expenditure for advertising. The totality of the costs is evaluated within the profit and loss structure of the brand and company. If the funds are not there, management can decide which objectives are to be sacrificed or modified in order to reduce the budget to reasonable dimensions. Research is needed when establishing advertising objectives and when deciding on the kind and quantity of advertising to use. The task method relies heavily on facts to complete these steps and to arrive at a final advertising budget. Moreover, in the task method, clearly stated objectives supplant prejudices and snap judgments in the budget-making process and demand conscious decisions.

Other Considerations The task method builds up the budget while most methods break it down. That is to say, in the task method the various needs for advertising and their costs are totaled and the advertising budget emerges. This is sometimes called **zero-base budgeting** in that the advertising manager, when building expenditures, must justify each step according to the specific objectives to be accomplished. In the breakdown method, a total is determined first and funds are then allocated to different advertising functions and media. Because the build-up approach forces management to set realistic objectives for advertising and fosters an attitude that regards advertising as a long-term investment, the task method has much to contribute when sound advertising budgets are being designed.

Subjective and Other Methods of Budgeting

Most advertisers probably use either one of the fixed-guidelines methods or the task method when setting budgets for advertising programs. At least, very few executives will admit that such an important decision is made on a subjective basis. Nevertheless, it is quite likely that the subjective method is used more than is admitted, especially by smaller firms.

Arbitrary Method When this method prevails, management states, "We will spend X dollars on advertising next year." The budget is arbitrarily set without any analysis of the tasks of advertising, the funds available, or any other considerations. The amount of the budget is set because it feels right to the decision maker.

What-Can-Be Afforded Method This method is better strategy than the arbitrary method, for at least some rational process is involved. The method, like the percentage-of-sales and the unit-of-sales methods, may emerge from a conservative advertising philosophy: the goal is to closely control advertising expenditures. The **what-can-be-afforded method** may, on the other hand, be used for the aggressive employment of advertising. This use of the method calls for advertising expenditures that are related either to company profits or to company assets. Management may decide to spend 20 percent of company earnings for advertising or to use 10 percent of the liquid assets for the advertising program. If management is too conservative, this approach may not yield enough to accomplish the advertising task. Inasmuch as the decision is left to the whim of management, general business psychology may be the ruling factor rather than the needs of the business.

Go-for-Broke Method A few advertisers feel that every cent they can get their hands on should go into advertising. The **go-for-broke-method** is essentially the what-can-be-afforded method taken to its optimistic extreme. The users of the method had sublime faith in the ability of advertising to sell products. For example, when the "halitosis" theme was first developed for Listerine around 1922, Gerard Lambert, who was general manager, sold the go-for-broke method to the Lambert Pharmacal Company management. The following quotation explains his program:

> At that time we were spending about $100,000 a year on advertising Listerine. I made the board a proposition. If they would let me spend $5,000 more each month, cumulatively—that is, $5,000, then $10,000, and so on—I would resign if I couldn't show an additional net profit for each month of at least $5,000. . . . By 1938 our expenditures for advertising were above $5 million a year.[6]

Radically different products with wide potential demand may be successfully advertised in this man-

Figure 17.2 In a classic campaign, Listerine's ability to "cure halitosis" was featured. The "go-for-broke" method was used to establish the advertising budget for the campaign.

ner. The shortcoming of the method, of course, is that it is risky. If this approach to the budget is used by unsophisticated advertisers, it is possible that advertising can become a great gambling adventure in which funds are spent willy-nilly. Moreover, early sales success, which seems to indicate an unlimited market for the product, may turn out to be merely a temporary fad or the prompt action of an interested—but small—market segment. This method of budget making should be employed only in rare circumstances—and then by persons who recognize that it is highly speculative.

Mail-Order Method With the **mail-order method,** the budget is set by the costs needed to obtain sales or inquiries through advertising. Once results are no longer paying for advertising charges, advertising is discontinued.

Profit-Planning Method The **profit-planning method** relates advertising expenditures to desired profits rather than to desired sales volume. The basic premise is that the results obtained from advertising can be precisely measured. Increased units of advertising are added to the advertising program until the marginal return from the last unit does not equal the marginal cost. This is fine in theory, but since advertising effectiveness cannot be isolated and measured precisely in most cases, the method is of limited practical use. One other limiting factor is that advertising is rarely used as the sole means of securing sales. Once marginal returns are weighed against marginal costs for several factors, the process becomes bogged down with complex mathematical calculations.

The Retail Advertising Budget

Retail store executives find the advertising budget as troublesome as do their manufacturer counterparts. The problems are basically the same and the procedures are similar. The retail store manager or department head, however, is often more intimately involved in budgetary matters of all kinds—including the advertising budget—because retail establishments are generally smaller in their scale of operations than manufacturing firms. Major executives in retailing are frequently called upon to make relatively minor advertising decisions, and advertising often plays a more important role in the overall sales pattern of retail establishments than of manufacturers. Thus, efficient handling of advertising funds often is more crucial to the success of retailers. This statement, of course, is a rather broad generalization; it applies to stores that rely heavily on advertising for traffic. Supermarkets and department stores, for example, use advertising as the primary sales-generating tool.

On the retail level, advertising is often treated as part of the publicity budget, just as in manufacturing it is a part of the marketing budget. This budget includes appropriations for all the nonpersonal selling activities of the store. Thus, it embraces advertising, display, and special-purpose publicity. The word "publicity" has a specialized meaning for retailers; when they speak of publicity, they may well be thinking of advertising.

Retail advertising can be divided into two types: **institutional advertising,** which is designed to establish the store as a place to shop, and **promotional advertising,** which appeals for direct action. Price is often an important element in promotional copy, whereas the institutional advertisement stresses services offered by the store, or the store's reputation for such things as wide assortments, style leadership, and quality merchandise. Every retailer must decide how the publicity budget is to be divided among advertising, display, and publicity expenditures, and between institutional and promotional advertising. Promotional advertising is the heart of retail advertising. The most important difference between national and retail budget-making processes is in the allocation of funds to various retail departments and to specific merchandise items.

The Retail Budget-Making Process

The American Newspaper Publishers Association (ANPA), through its Newspaper Advertising Bureau, has developed sound procedures for retail advertising budgets. Retailers are furnished with detailed guides to advertising planning. Although the motive behind the ANPA "total-selling" program is to convince retailers of the desirability of concentrating their advertising in newspapers, the basic plan can be used by most retailers regardless of the media employed in their advertising. The ANPA program recommends that budget making and planning be done coincidentally, emphasizing the interrelation of these processes. An advertiser follows four basic steps when the ANPA approach to retail advertising is used.[7]

Set a Sales Goal Defining objectives, or setting tasks for advertising, is the starting point for the program. Each task—or objective—is described in terms of sales volume, and the retailer is urged to start with the previous year's sales figures, broken down monthly department by department. These figures are then adjusted for changing conditions—store expansion, increased population, higher incomes, greater employment, competitive activities, and similar factors. The sales goal should be realistic and attainable, yet it should challenge employees to exert themselves to achieve the goal.

Decide How Much Advertising Experience again provides the starting point, for the retailer adjusts the previous year's expenditures for advertising to fit the sales goal, bearing in mind the level of competitive advertising. When a retailer arrives at a budget figure—expressed as a percentage of sales—the figure should be against industry averages. Whether a particular store's advertising appropriation should approximate average expenditures depends upon a number of factors: store location, length of time in the community, local reputation, competition, and other circumstances that may require more or less advertising.

Decide What to Promote The first two steps are essentially the task method applied to retailing. The third step brings in the allocation problem. The advertising budget must be divided among the departments of the store, if it is departmentalized. In addition allocations must be made to individual products stocked. The guiding principle behind the ANPA approach is that the retailer must be able to predict what customers will want item by item, month by month, and concentrate the advertising to coincide with consumer buying patterns. Each department and each merchandise item receives advertising funds in proportion to sales opportunities. The Newspaper Advertising Bureau has developed extensive data on buying patterns for major retail lines, as shown in Figure 17.3. These patterns are remarkably stable, year after year.

Schedule Ads Day by Day The fourth step is primarily concerned with the advertising plan rather than with the advertising budget. Timing of advertising now becomes the paramount consideration. To facilitate correct timing of advertisements, the ANPA has developed a monthly work sheet (Figure 17.4). Every retailer should develop a step-by-step advertising planning procedure similar to the work sheet, which provides for the allocation of funds at times when chances of success are greatest.

The Use of Computers and Quantitative Methods in the Budget Process

Computers play an important role in the budgeting of advertising, particularly in the area of control. Once the final budget is established, it is placed on the computer, and such items as invoices, costs, and commitments can be fed into the machine. Printouts that tell whether programs are progressing on target are then available to the advertising manager. Ready access to such information permits adjustment of the advertising program to changing conditions, provided such flexibility has been built into the budget.

Programmed with specially designed quantitative models, the computer is useful in the allocation process, especially in helping to decide which media to use. Chapter 18 covers the use of computer models in media selection. At this point in our discussion of the budgeting process, we shall describe the role of mathematical models in estimating how much money should be spent for advertising.

Using models of future economic and business conditions, the computer is better able to forecast future advertising needs than to evaluate current budgets. Several models have been developed thus far, but they have encountered two serious problems: (1) the information required for the forecasts is often unobtainable at reasonable cost; and (2) the models make budgetary recommendations based on the assumption that advertising is the only variable, and interdependencies within the marketing mix are ignored.[8]

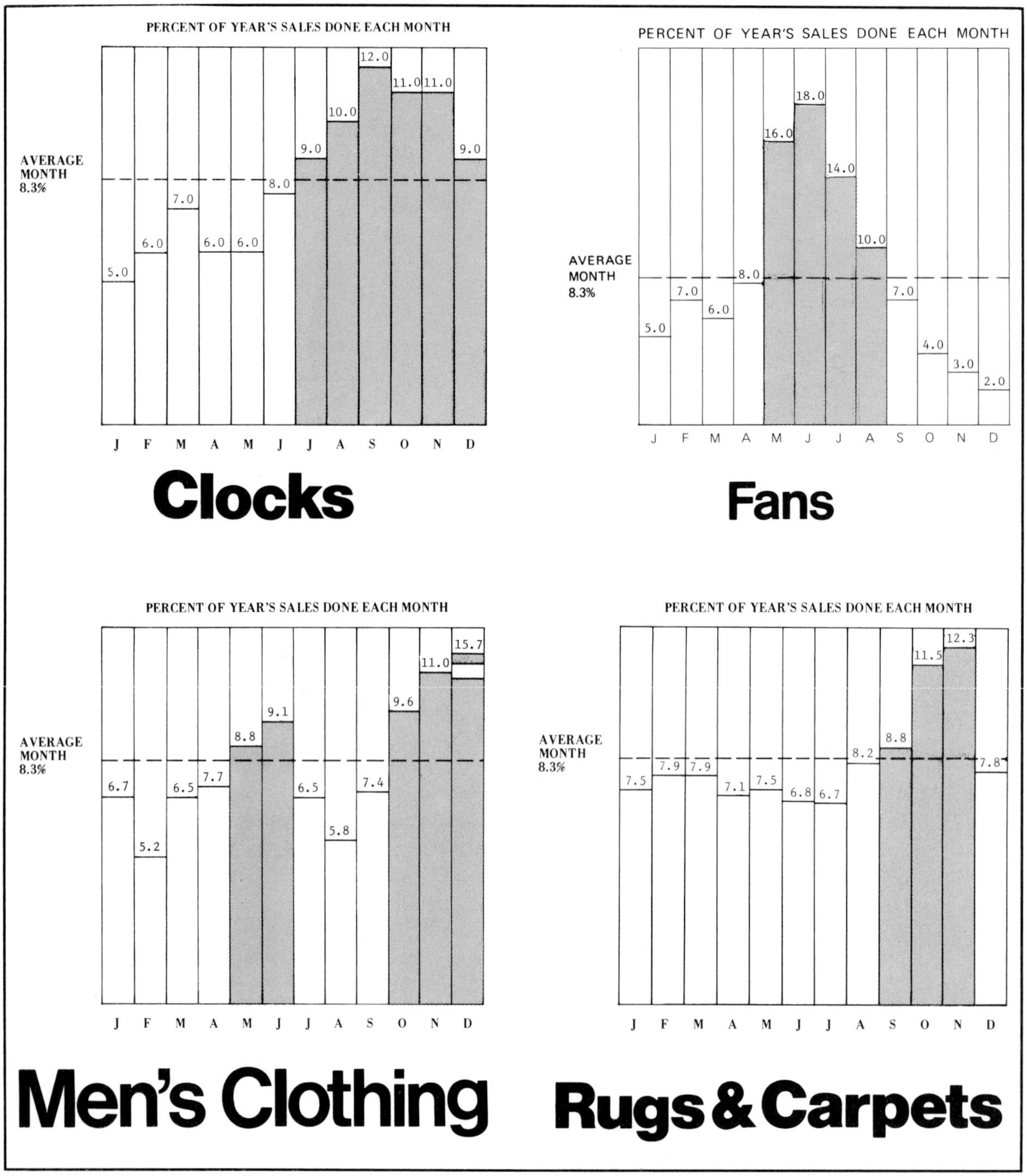

Figure 17.3 Different products experience different sales patterns, as these charts reveal. Retail advertisers want their advertising messages for clocks, fans, men's clothing, and rugs and carpets to coincide with the buying of such products by consumers. [*Newspaper Advertising Bureau, American Newspaper Publishers Association, Inc.*]

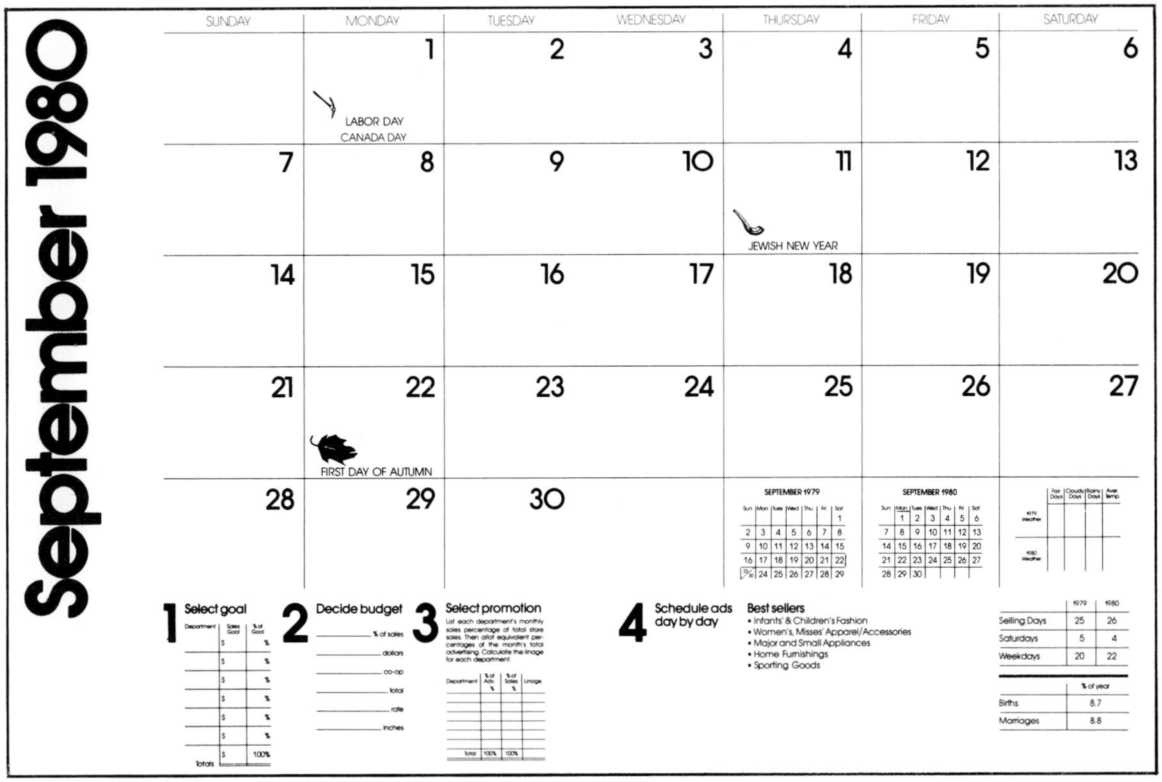

Figure 17.4 When the retail advertising manager is scheduling advertising, this work sheet is extremely useful. [*Newspaper Advertising Bureau, American Newspaper Publishers Association, Inc.*]

Because the bulk of the work is confidential, it is not available to other advertisers and students of advertising. The firm that finances the experimenting naturally keeps the information secret in order to enhance its competitive advantage. Fortunately, however, one advertiser, Anheuser-Busch, Inc., has released the results of 15 years of advertising research, part of it dealing with budgeting.[9] Two college professors were commissioned by the company to apply management science research procedures to the marketing division of the firm and to oversee the implementation of their recommendations. One prime area of attention was advertising expenditures.

Budweiser beer, the principal brand of Anheuser-Busch, was marketed in 198 geographic areas. The company president was constantly asked to provide increased advertising support for these markets on the premise that increased sales would follow. He asked the researchers to develop a model aimed at determining what amount should be spent on advertising. An interesting experiment was run in 1962. Eighteen areas were chosen randomly, and adequate control areas were selected. In six test areas, advertising expenditures were reduced 25 percent; in another six, the amount was unchanged; and in the third group of six markets, advertising was increased 50 percent. Two important marketing variables, the amount spent on sales effort (salespeople) and the amount spent on point-of-purchase sales displays and signs, were held constant in these areas. Price could not be controlled because of varying competitive pressures. Every month an observation was made in each market area.

The results of the experiment left Anheuser-Busch executives incredulous. They could easily believe that a 50 percent increase in advertising might well yield a 7 percent increase in sales, which it did for the relevant market areas. However, a 25 percent reduction of advertising produced a 14 percent increase in sale in the pertinent market areas. More elaborate tests were conducted in 1963 and 1964 with the results confirming those obtained in the first experiment. Advertising reductions of 15 percent were tried in many marketing areas. Later, the reduction was raised to 25 percent, and the number of markets involved was gradually increased. The advertising expenditure per barrel of beer was ultimately stabilized at 80 cents, whereas it stood at $1.89 when the research was initiated, a 58 percent reduction. Budweiser sales increased from approximately 7.5 million to 14.5 million barrels, and its market share increased from 8.14 to 12.94 percent in the years running from 1962 through 1968. We are conditioned to think that increased advertising expenditures automatically lead to increased sales and brand share. However, it is possible, as this case example illustrates, for an advertiser to be spending more than is necessary. Money saved from unnecessary advertising goes directly to company profits. Ackoff and Emshoff explored many other areas of the advertising decision making, including the timing of advertising, the effectiveness of various media, advertising message content, and beer-drinking behavior patterns. The lesson to be learned from this case is that the management sciences have much to offer the advertising decision maker, who should promote such experimentation.

Summary

As one of the six major steps in planning an advertising program, budgeting holds a unique place. On the one hand, no other steps can be taken—no other decisions can be made or implemented—without money being budgeted to them. On the other hand, the size of the budget depends largely on these other decisions; collectively, they add up to the funds required in the advertising appropriation.

Advertising is a cost of doing business and should be carefully scrutinized for waste; nevertheless, the expenditure should be thought of in broader, more fundamental terms—as an investment in the future of the enterprise. Immediate returns are important, but not nearly so important as payoff over the long term. Holding this philosophy leads to more intelligent advertising decisions.

Like all budgeting, advertising budgeting is a basic management technique for planning and controlling operations. It is a financial tool that is concerned with future operations. In its development, four stages are present. The first stage is its preparation, in which the advertising manager marshals the case for sufficient dollars to achieve objectives set down for the advertising program. The advertising manager then presents ("sells") the plan to higher levels of corporate management, whose approval is needed if implementation of the plan is to occur. This step involves considerable negotiations and adjustment among marketing and financial executives of the firm.

Once the budget is established, it is executed. In this third stage, the advertising agency has the primary responsibility, as it buys the media which are the major components of most advertising budgets. The advertising manager concurrently observes the firm's market to determine whether any changes are needed in the program. To facilitate such adjustments, every advertising budget should contain a contingency account which will permit flexibility in spending patterns. The fourth stage is concerned with control of the budget. The advertising manager watches to make certain that the monies are spent as planned and that purchases are made on an economical basis. Furthermore, the budget should be carefully guarded to see that its use for nonadvertising activities is prevented.

The size of the advertising budget can be determined in three basic ways: by the fixed guidelines method, by the task method, and by subjective methods. Fixed guidelines include the percentage-of-sales, unit-of-sales, and competitive-parity methods. All tend to overlook the specific task that advertising has to perform for a given company at a specific point of time; however, these methods are relatively simple to employ. The task method is oriented to objectives with the budget evolving from the job to be done by advertising. Its major stumbling blocks rest in the hard question of how much advertising is needed to accomplish a specific task. Subjective methods are least desirable, as they often possess little logic, being dependent upon the arbitrary opinion of the executive.

When the retail establishment makes its advertising budget, four steps are followed: (1) a sales goal is established; (2) the amount of advertising needed to obtain the goal is determined; (3) items to be promoted are selected; and (4) daily schedules of advertisements are set.

The computer is helpful in the routine management and control of the advertising budget. Management science now helps managers with the difficult question of how much to spend for advertising.

Questions for Discussion

1 How does the advertising budget-making process relate to (*a*) setting advertising objectives, (*b*) the media selection decision, (*c*) the creative strategy decision?

2 Will the budget decision become more demanding in the years to come? Why?

3 Compare the view that advertising is a long-term investment with an experience in your personal life. Outline this analogy.

4 What attitude should the advertising manager have toward the budgeting process? How can the right attitude help make this manager's job easier and more productive? Discuss.

5 What are the key problems encountered at each of the four steps in the advertising budget-making process? Are some more serious than others? Which, in your opinion, provides the most serious obstacle?

6 Explain "budget attrition."

7 What are the strengths and weaknesses of fixed guideline methods of advertising budgeting?

8 If the task method is so desirable, why is it not in universal use? What needs to be done before adoption of the method is likely?

9 From current professional or trade journals, find an article explaining the use of a model, similar to the Budweiser example, in advertising budgeting. Write a short summary of the article.

10 Interview a local retailer and find out how he or she decides how much to spend for advertising. Write a report of the interview and be prepared to discuss your findings in class.

For Further Reference

Aaker, David A., and John G. Myers: *Advertising Management,* Prentice-Hall, Inc., Englewood Cliffs, N.J., 1975.

Anderson, Robert L., and Thomas E. Barry: *Advertising Management,* Charles E. Merrill Company, Columbus, Ohio, 1979.

Bogart, Leo: *Strategy in Advertising,* Harcourt, Brace and World, Inc., New York, 1967.

Engel, James F., Martin R. Warshaw, and Thomas C. Kinnear: *Promotional Strategy,* 4th ed., Richard D. Irwin, Inc., Homewood, Ill., 1979.

Haight, William: *Retail Advertising,* Silver Burdett Company, Morristown, N.J., 1976.

Hurwood, David L., and James K. Brown: *Some Guidelines for Advertising Budgeting,* The Conference Board, New York, 1972.

McNiven, Malcolm A.: *How Much to Spend for Advertising,* Association of National Advertisers, Inc., New York, 1969.

Patti, Charles H., and John H. Murphy: *Advertising Management,* Grid, Inc., Columbus, Ohio, 1978.

Simon, Julian L.: *The Management of Advertising,* Prentice-Hall, Inc., Englewood Cliffs, N.J., 1971.

Wademan, Victor: *Risk-Free Advertising: How to Come Close to It,* John Wiley & Sons, New York, 1977.

End Notes

[1] Joel Dean, "Does Advertising Belong in the Capital Budget?" *Journal of Marketing,* October 1966, pp. 15–21.

[2] This section is based in part on Richard J. Kelly, *The Advertising Budget,* Association of National Advertisers, Inc., New York, 1967. Quoted material is from this source.

[3] See "Contingency Accounts," in Ovid Riso, *Advertising Cost Control Handbook,* Van Nostrand Reinhold Company, New York, 1973, pp. 22–23. For a different viewpoint, see Joseph Ostrow, "Reserves Revisted," in *Marketing & Media Decisions,* 1979, pp. 82–83.

[4] For a somewhat different treatment of this topic, see T. Kirk Parrish, "How Much to Spend for Advertising," *Journal of Advertising Research,* February 1974, pp. 9–11.

[5] Some of the complexities involved in securing data for this approach are discussed in Jeffrey A. Lowenhar and John L. Stanton, "Forecasting Competitive Advertising Expenditures," *Journal of Advertising Research,* April 1976, pp. 37–42.

[6] Gerard B. Lambert, "How I Sold Listerine," *Fortune,* September 1966, pp. 111, 196. (From *All Out of Step,* Copyright © 1956 by Gerard B. Lambert. Reprinted by permission of Doubleday & Company, Inc., New York.)

[7] Based on materials developed by the Newspaper Advertising Bureau, American Newspaper Publishers Association.

[8] James F. Engel, Martin R. Warshaw, and Thomas C. Kinnear: *Promotional Strategy,* 4th ed., Richard D. Irwin, Inc., Homewood, Ill., 1979, p. 264. See pp. 253–265 for a comprehensive discussion of the application of quantitative methods to the promotional budget.

[9] Russell L. Ackoff and James R. Emshoff: "Advertising Research at Anheuser-Busch, Inc. (1963–68)," *Sloan Management Review,* Winter 1975, pp. 1–15; also "Advertising Research at Anheuser-Busch, Inc. (1968–74)," ibid., Spring 1975, pp. 1–15.

Chapter 18

Developing the Media Plan and Media Strategy

Once the budget is established, another phase of campaign planning is undertaken. As we learned in Chapter 15, this step comprises selecting the right message for the advertising and the correct media in which to run it. Effective advertising is "saying the right thing in the right medium at the right time."[1] Creative strategy is the advertiser's chance to "say the right thing." This phase was discussed in Chapter 12 and will not be reviewed here. The media plan, the subject of this chapter, is the advertiser's opportunity to "use the right medium at the right time." The "where" decision is expressed in advertising terms as **media selection** and the "when" decision is called **media scheduling.** Media planning and media buying, when combined, determine the place ("where") and the time ("when") that should be used to place an advertising message before members of the target market.

Media Planning

Media planning is the process of designing a course of action that shows how advertising time and space will be used to contribute to the achievement of marketing and advertising objectives.[2] The media plan is created by the media planner from information about the market and prospective customers. Media decisions are based primarily on (1) the creative strategy established for the campaign, and (2) the characteristics of the target market.

The creative strategy for the advertising campaign may require that certain media be employed or, more likely, it may be influenced by the advertiser's having strong preference for certain kinds of advertising. Obviously, these factors must be taken into consideration when media are being selected.

Through market research, facts about the target market are accumulated and generalized into a **consumer profile.** This consumer profile, along with the basic copy strategy and copy requirements as modified by any need for seasonal or geographical emphasis and taking into account the size of the advertising budget, is then analyzed by the media planner. This analysis is followed by matching the audience characteristics of various media with the consumer profile and by evaluating the adaptability of the physical format of the media to the copy requirements. Finally, through the exercise of judgment concerning the dimensions of coverage, reach, frequency, continuity, and ad size, the media plan emerges.

As with all advertising decision making, the ultimate responsibility for choosing media rests with the advertising, or brand, manager in charge of the product. This executive is responsible for maintaining control over the advertising budget. In many instances, media planning is delegated to the advertising agency. The advertiser will, in most cases, review the media plan as developed by the agency and approve it before it is implemented. Recommendations for specific media are usually made by the advertising agency's media specialists.

Three decisions are made during the media selection process: (1) the general type of medium is chosen—newspapers, magazines, television, radio, or out-of-home; (2) classes within the chosen type are picked—network or spot television, women's magazines or shelter magazines; (3) a specific media "vehicle" within the chosen class of the preferred type is selected—*Family Circle,* or *McCall's,* or *Good Housekeeping.*

Key Factors Influencing Media Planning[3]

The media planner weighs three major forces when media decisions are being made: (1) marketing conditions facing the advertiser, (2) the level of competitive advertising efforts, and (3) specific media considerations.

Marketing Conditions

Marketing plans of the advertiser influence advertising plans, and media plans are likewise affected by what the firm hopes to achieve in the marketplace through the use of advertising. Brilliant creative strategy can fail because marketing conditions are not right. And, of course, the marketing plan determines the size of the budget available for media buys. Furthermore, the basic nature of the market—its size, its location, and its qualitative characteristics, such as sex, age, socioeconomic features, and educational background—does make an impact on the media plan. In addition, there are four other facets to consider when assessing marketing conditions: product characteristics, distribution channels, promotional strategy, and the nature of the advertising copy.

Product Characteristics Certain product characteristics may disqualify its advertiser from using a medium. For example, the television industry refuses liquor advertising, and legislation prevents the advertising of cigarettes on radio and television. In other instances, the presence of a product characteristic may virtually require that one advertising medium be employed as its status coincides, say, with the product's image. For example, ads for luxury jewelry are rarely placed in the broadcast media. Print media are used to convey the message. In other words, the media planner weighs the product characteristics carefully and matches them against the impressions conveyed by the various media.

Distribution Channels Most products can be promoted through any type of medium. The choice depends upon factors other than product characteristics. If the product is distributed locally or regionally, national media, in the absence of local or regional editions or networks, are inefficient. Advertisers of nationally distributed products, on the other hand, can choose between national media or a combination of local media.

Often overlooked are the reactions of middlemen toward various types of media. If the advertising is aired on television where the store manager can actually see the commercials in the role of viewer, the feeling that customers must be seeing the advertising is generated. Other retailers may believe that a "prestige" medium should be used to promote the product. Furthermore, such seemingly mundane matters as the size of the retail margin (markup) may affect the probability that the manufacturer can reasonably expect promotional support from channel members. The distribution system employed for the product can dictate whether the manufacturer must use a great deal of advertising or whether the promotional burden should logically rest with the retailer. The media planner, therefore, needs to be firmly grounded in the distribution patterns used in marketing the advertised product.

Promotional Strategy A synergism or interdependence should exist among the various parts of the promotional mix—personal selling, advertising, sales promotion, and public relations. Suppose an advertiser wishes to sponsor a contest to promote the sales of the product to consumers. Such sales-promotional devices must be advertised aggressively if they are to be successful. If the contest is devised in response to a sudden need for additional promotional effort, a flexible medium, such as newspapers or radio, which takes advertising copy on relatively short notice, may be the best choice. However, if the contest is part of a long-range program designed to enhance the prestige of the product, the ad may run in consumer magazines or on network TV.

In Chapter 3 we discussed the importance of "positioning the product" — obtaining a place for the product in the mind of the prospect — to marketing success. Media choices are important in product positioning because the use of one medium connotes one attitude about the product, whereas another medium presents a different view. Furthermore, a positioning strategy against the leading brand in the field may dictate the avoidance of the same media that the frontrunner is employing.

Nature of the Advertising Copy The advertising message itself provides the last major determining factor when media choices are made. Campaign themes may be designed for universal use, that is, they may be adaptable to almost every advertising medium. Or themes may be created to suit specific media. Slogan-type campaigns of soft-drink advertisers illustrate the universal approach, whereas animated-cartoon or demonstration themes of household cleaning aids are more effective on television.

Competitive Advertising Efforts

An important goal of most marketing programs is the improvement — or retention — of the seller's market share. Advertising, of course, is only one force used to achieve this goal, but it is a more apparent gauge of competitive activity than the work of a competitor's sales force or distributive organization. It is more difficult to find concrete information about these two areas of competitive activity. Thus, it is easy to attribute the success of a competitor to the advertising program employed, and competitors, therefore, watch one another's advertising expenditures closely.

The philosophy of matching a competitor's advertising may carry over into media planning. An advertiser may not want to spend the same amount of money as competitors, but may wish to spend it in the same media. If the industry leader is using television, other firms may adopt the medium but use fringe time instead of prime time, or advertise on sports programs instead of comedies. There is a considerable amount of fad and fashion in the use of advertising media. An advertising agency must recognize the influence of a major competitor's advertising program on its client when making media recommendations.

Many advertisers have personal media preferences and will impose these preferences when media decisions are being made. The advertiser's reasoning for copying a competitor's choice of media is that the market leader wouldn't be using a medium if it didn't produce results. This thinking is not only unscientific but ignores the individual needs of the advertiser. All firms in an industry do not have uniform advertising objectives. Following the leader changes an advertiser's efforts from investment in advertising to speculation.

Media Considerations

Advertising media possess certain dimensions that affect the media decision. When media objectives are being established, these factors have an impact: (1) size of the budget; (2) special requirements to be found in the media concepts of reach, frequency, continuity, and dominance; (3) discount structures of the various media; (4) cost-effectiveness of alternative forms of media; and (5) availability of media to advertisers.

Total Available Dollars Scientific media planning is aimed at expending advertising dollars where they will make the greatest possible impact. The smaller the advertising budget, the more crucial the media selection decision. Large-budget advertisers may be able to stand some waste in their advertising programs, but small-budget advertisers must wring every ounce of selling power from their advertising. A very small budget, however, makes this task difficult. The budget of every advertiser places an upper limit on the amount of advertising that can be created and used, and it prescribes what media the advertiser can afford. An advertiser with an advertising budget of $500,000 cannot buy a series of full-page advertisements monthly if the page rate in the chosen magazine is $80,000. A limited budget freezes out many media choices for the advertiser. The same principle, of course, applies to all advertisers in varying degrees.

Media Characteristics There are four characteristics inherent in advertising media that should be

How to spend $2 million on tv to remain practically anonymous.

The average tv viewer sees over 600 commercials in a 10 day period. Read how to catch his attention in the middle of it all.

Easy. Let's say you're the number 2 or 3 brand in your product category.

You may be sinking 2 million—or more—into an ingenious tv plan. Your commercials are dynamite. Yet the sales of brand number 1 go up, up, up—while you're lucky if you can hold your own.

What happened?

Brand misidentity is what happened. The Starch Atlanta Study, for instance, showed less than 32% of the viewers remembering commercials seen that very evening. (And of these, 25% *misidentified* the advertiser!)

Tv can be scarey for some advertisers.

People see a commercial for your Brand #2.

They may even remember it.

But they end up asking for Brand #1.

Today's utter avalanche of tv commercials (about 80% more on the air than 10 years ago) is what has created this problem.

And unless you're the guy with the biggest avalanche, it's *your* problem.

But we've got an answer.

It's two-fold.

First, when you advertise to the 43,000,000 adults who read The Digest every month, you're reinforcing your tv message with one out of every three adults in America. The very *best* adults, from a marketer's standpoint.

Second, well over one third of our readers (16,000,000) are light tv viewers. They watch an average of 27 minutes per day of prime time (Simmons). So even the biggest tv budget in the world is going to keep you all but anonymous to this huge, better-educated, better-able-to-buy group.

Use horse sense.

Obviously, tv's important to a lot of advertisers.

But equally as obvious, it just makes good sense to sock some of your tv money into The Digest.

Where you're in instant touch with our 16,000,000 light tv viewers . . . and reinforcing your message with another 27,000,000 Digest readers who do like tv.

Doesn't your product deserve the cleanest shot it can get?

Doesn't it deserve The Digest?

Reader's Digest
WORLD'S BEST SELLER

The visibility book.

Figure 18.1 Advertising media compete aggressively for advertising dollars, as this ad sponsored by a leading magazine shows. Note the media data included in the sales message.

taken into account when media objectives are developed. Two of these — the reach of the advertising and its frequency — are undoubtedly the most critical in media decision making. **Reach,** which is related to the concept of coverage, is the number of people who are exposed to the message at least one time during a stated period (usually four weeks). **Frequency** is the number of times the members of the target audience are exposed to the advertising message. When the advertiser wants a high rate of reach, many media vehicles are likely to be employed. When the orientation is toward frequency, a limited number of vehicles generally is used, with many repetitions of the message being the keystone of the plan.

Media scheduling attempts to balance the twin objectives of reach and frequency. The combination of these two characteristics has led to the concept of the **gross rating point** (GRP). GRP is "the sum of the percentages of TV households reached by a certain group of commercials; that is, the total of the rating points of each commercial in a specific group of commercials."[4]

The continuity of a medium is another factor to consider in media planning. **Continuity** of advertising can mean many things; for instance, it relates various advertisements in an advertising program to one another. This is important because isolated ads generally make little impact. It usually means the continuous scheduling of advertising during a month or a year. If a company advertises 365 days a year, its campain possesses *excellent* continuity. Creative continuity is brought about by the advertising theme, copy style, layout, etc. Continuity in media usage is also desirable. Audiences should be exposed to the message in a regular pattern over a period of time long enough to achieve the marketing objectives set for the campaign. At this point, we shall use continuity to evaluate the timing of the advertising.

A trade-off exists in the extent of the reach and frequency that an ad can attain. This is further complicated if continuity is a consideration in the media decision.[5] This trade-off is similar to the "unattainable triad" of advertising production that was discussed in Chapter 14. This quotation explains the implications of the trade-off:

> If the advertiser is willing to take a periodic hiatus during the campaign period, the budget will allow both reach and frequency to be enhanced during each flight of advertising. Conversely, since a steady flow of media dollars is needed to support continuous advertising, a continuous schedule limits the opportunity to maximize reach or frequency during any portion of the campaign period.[6]

A somewhat related media concept is that of **dominance.** Webster defined the word as "superior to all others." In the case of dominance in advertising, superiority is measured in many different ways. The concept is explained by Bogart as media's "third dimension," which he describes as the "size or length of the message unit."[7] Thus, full-page advertisements are considered more dominant than half-pages and usually serve as a determinant of true reach as opposed to potential reach.

As unit costs of advertising escalate, it becomes increasingly difficult for the advertiser to achieve dominance. One advertiser will seek it by concentrating commercials on a few television specials or in a few key selling time periods; others will move into less costly media. Along with dominance, an advertiser must establish the desired frequency, reach, and continuity for the advertisements in the campaign.

The designer of a media plan must weigh these various qualities, and when available funds are limited, the decision maker must decide where to cut corners. Should the advertiser reduce coverage and try to reach only a part of the potential market? Should advertising be done less frequently? Should the drive for dominance be curbed by abandoning full-page advertisements? The retailer has the special problem of weighing the need for frequent advertising against the principle of selling when customers are buying. Correct decisions are reached only after deliberation, experimentation, and constant study. Various combinations should be tried and carefully evaluated in order to develop better media combinations.

Media Discounts An advertiser may elect to concentrate advertising in a few media because of the discounts that are given to advertisers who use specific media frequently. Generally speaking, this factor in media selection is considered after the type and class of media have been chosen. Although few national advertisers use only one medium, let alone one class of media, we shall assume, for purposes of illustration, that such is the case. An advertiser has decided to use women's magazines as the prime advertising vehicle. Normally, the advertiser will then divide the media budget among several major publications in the field, say, *Family Circle, McCall's,* and *Good Housekeeping.* Advertisements may be scheduled in each magazine every other month throughout the entire year. The media buyer, after examining the rate cards, realizes that substantial savings will result if monthly insertions are placed in only one of the three publications. The money saved by this maneuver can be used to enhance readership through better-quality ads. For instance, color can replace black and white, or larger space units can be used. Dominance of the advertiser's message in one magazine is more likely. Continuity and frequency of advertising are increased. On the other hand, coverage or reach is lessened. And, although there is considerable duplication of readership among closely related media, this duplication actually increases the frequency of advertising impressions with the duplicated audience. Thus, the media buyer must weigh the possible gains and losses before final media selections are made. Examination of Figure 18.2 reveals the kind of mental juggling that goes into the media selection decision.

Figure 18.2 Media choices can increase media efficiency, as this chart indicates. In this example, *Cuisine* magazine is substituted for *Redbook* in a media schedule consisting of seven women's magazines. Total coverage was reduced by 114 readers, or .001 percent. Total cost, however, dropped by $25,180, or nearly 7.5 percent. [Madison Avenue Magazine, *October 1980, p. 84.*]

Better Homes & Gardens, Family Circle, Good Housekeeping, Ladies Home Journal, McCalls, ~~Redbook~~, Woman's Day, CUISINE

	7 Women's Books	6 Women's Books plus CUISINE	Change
Net Adult Women (000)	46,606	46,492	−114
Percent Coverage	57.5%	57.4%	−00.1%
4/c Page Cost	$337,295	$312,115	−$25,180
CPM	$7.24	$6.71	−$.53

Source: Simmons 1979/Telmar Simulation

Media Cost Efficiency Often advertisers attempt to reduce the media selection process to one simple question, "How much audience do I get for every dollar spent?" They compare the total audience with costs, and using the resulting figures as a base, choose the most efficient medium. They ignore qualitative factors and play a "numbers game." The marketers of some mass-consumed products may find this "cost-per-thousand" approach satisfactory, but audience characteristics are usually more important than sheer numbers. Cost effectiveness figures may be useful, however, when all other considerations seem to balance out. For example, if two radio stations appear to reach the same kind of people, the station that delivers the largest audience per dollar is obviously the better buy.

Media Availability The availability of time or space may determine media choices. This factor is extremely important in television. Often advertisers cannot use the medium because a suitable time slot is not available. Sometimes, advertisers who have not planned to use television in their current advertising program change their plans when a good time availability is presented to them. The same principle applies to other media. During hot political campaigns, for instance, candidates occasionally find that their opponents have already contracted for prime radio and television time and outdoor space. The built-in expansibility of publications makes availability a much less important factor in printed media than in broadcast or traffic media.

Media Decision Tools

Such information sources as Standard Rate & Data Service, Audit Bureau of Circulations, and the broadcast rating services are discussed in Part 2 of this book. We now look at those sources available to media planners that contain data on marketing conditions, competitive advertising efforts, and various media considerations. Several major sources of such information are discussed in this section. This list is not complete, for new services are constantly being developed, adding to or replacing existing sources. A comprehensive list is, therefore, not feasible, but this list will enable you to appreciate some of the more commonly used information-gathering firms.

Matching Media to Market

Before turning to these information sources, we need to examine how the media planner operates when carrying out his or her important duties. The media planner uses media information to isolate those media vehicles whose audiences most closely match the target market for the marketing and advertising campaign. Sometimes, the process is as simple as finding which media vehicles are exposed to heavy users of the product, and product usage data are the key factors in the decision. More often, knowledge of consumer demographics is necessary, either because product usage information is lacking or because the buying process is more complicated, with demographics affecting other elements in the marketing equation. Furthermore, there is often more than one target market to be taken into consideration, and attention may also be given to secondary as well as primary markets for the brand.

The media planner not only needs to be aware of the sources of needed information but must also be proficient in the interpretation and analysis of large amounts of varied data about the market and the media used to reach the market.

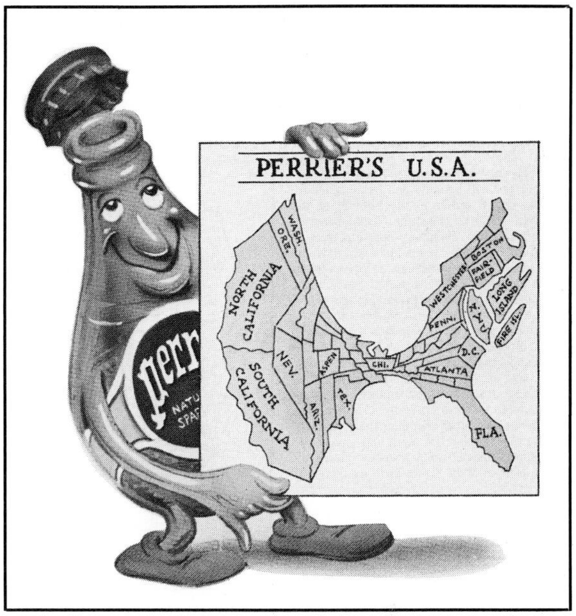

Figure 18.3 Markets for specific products are not uniformly spread throughout the nation. Here is how the map of the United States would look if the country were divided up proportionately with respect to the consumption of Perrier. [*Courtesy of* ADWEEK.]

Information about Market Conditions

Information on market conditions is closely guarded by business executives; therefore, easy-to-tap data are hard to come by. The federal government issues a wealth of pertinent statistics, such as census figures. However, by the time of publication they are often too old to be used in business planning. And there is a need for considerable sifting and analysis before decisions can be based upon such raw data. Thus, the advertiser's marketing research department and various independent marketing research firms may all be called upon to generate this kind of information —using available published data and the techniques of business intelligence to do so.

For the marketer of consumer products the *Survey of Buying Power,* published annually by *Sales & Marketing Management* magazine, is an invaluable tool. This volume of nearly 1,000 pages contains sections which give (1) data on county-city populations and incomes, plus data on farmers and their incomes; (2) data on county-city retail sales; (3) rankings and summaries by counties, cities, metropolitan areas, regions, and states; and (4) special Canadian data. Essentially, the publication gives important data about retail sales, population, and effective buying income. Every three months, *Sales & Marketing Management* also makes a quarterly retail sales forecast, and, periodically publishes other market data in its regular semimonthly issues. Advertisers who are trying to allocate their advertising dollars according to market potentials often find these data very useful.

The various editions of Standard Rate & Data Service (SRDS) provide similar data as reported in the *Survey of Buying Power.* Furthermore, the *Market Guide* issued by the trade publication *Editor and Publisher* is a source for the same kind of information in markets served by daily newspapers. For example, such detailed information as whether the local water supply is fluoridated or not is reported.[8]

Information about Competitive Advertising Efforts

The media planner needs to know how much competitors are spending for advertising. Equally important is information about where they are spending their advertising dollars. Just what are their respective media mixes? Such information would be impossible for the individual advertiser to gather. Fortunately, specialized services operate to furnish the data to advertisers wishing to purchase them from these collection agencies.

One important service, LNA (Leading National Advertisers), is perhaps the best known of the competitive data services. LNA analyzes every advertisement in 86 consumer magazines and 3 national newspaper supplements, as well as tear sheets from over 1,500 regional editions of magazines per year. It is estimated that the service monitors over 150,000 ads each year, recording space size, color, bleed, magazine, issue, brand advertised, and the division of the company doing the advertising. LNA supplies its data to the Publishers Information Bureau (PIB), which issues monthly and semiannual reports; the latter are entitled *Leading National Advertisers* and contain media expenditure data for all national advertisers investing $100,000 or more annually. LNA also provides data on competitive expenditures in the out-of-home medium.

BAR (Broadcast Advertisers Report) is active in the fields of network and spot television and network radio broadcasting. Broadcast material is collected on audiotape, from which information is transcribed into sequential listings of commercials by brand, station, time, length of commercial, and program. Computations are then made leading to estimates of expenditures for the respective media. LNA and BAR combine their data for quarterly and yearly *Multi-Media Reports.*

RER (Radio Expenditure Reports) traces the use of spot radio by brands; the compiled data are issued by the Radio Advertising Bureau on a quarterly basis. Data are obtained directly from stations using a sample of 800 stations, from which larger projections for the entire radio medium are made.

Media Records, Inc., gathers linage data by product classification and by name of advertiser for ads placed in 237 daily and Sunday newspapers located in 81 cities. Projections from these data lead to estimates of newspaper advertising expenditures in the top 125 markets. Competitive brand data for approximately three-fourths of all newspaper usage by national advertisers are made available to subscribers. The firm also issues the *Business Publication Report* on expenditures by 30,000 firms in 200 trade books.

ACB (Advertising Checking Bureau) is another source of competitive data on newspaper usage by national advertisers. The organization secures and measures every daily and Sunday newspaper and several hundred United States weeklies. Reports are tailor-made by client, or by product category. ACB is heavily involved in providing proof of performance to advertisers employing the cooperative advertising technique.

The A. C. Nielsen Retail Index furnishes measurable media expenditure data for major competitors in its bimonthly report to client subscribers.

These services do not provide all the information about advertising expenditures that a media planner might desire. Trade associations representing the various advertising media make estimates from time to time, and advertising media representatives offer guesses of competitors' advertising budgets. Little is known, however, about who spends what in such media as direct mail, business publications, or transit advertising.

Information about Media Audiences

The goal of media planning is finding media audiences that possess characteristics similar to the target-market groups that the advertiser wishes to reach. Total audience figures are important to the advertiser, but more information than mere numbers is needed. When one is attempting to match markets and media, there are three types of variables available for defining target markets: demographics, sociopsychographic composition, and product usage.

Every large advertising medium conducts studies which delineate its audience by demographic—and often sociopsychological—characteristics. The presence of this audience may be vital to the purchase or nonpurchase of certain products. Furthermore, the incidence of product use, such as by the heavy user, and exposure to a specific medium may be important when media decisions are to be made; therefore, many advertising media generate data on the subject. Moreover, media associations in the fields of newspaper, magazine, radio, television, outdoor, and transportation advertising make similar studies. Admittedly, these studies stress the value of the media types rather than individual publications, broadcast stations, or other media firms. Both sources of media information spew forth unbelievably large quantities of material that must be evaluated by media planners for possible bias, as stressed in Chapter 16.

To overcome this possible shortcoming, a number

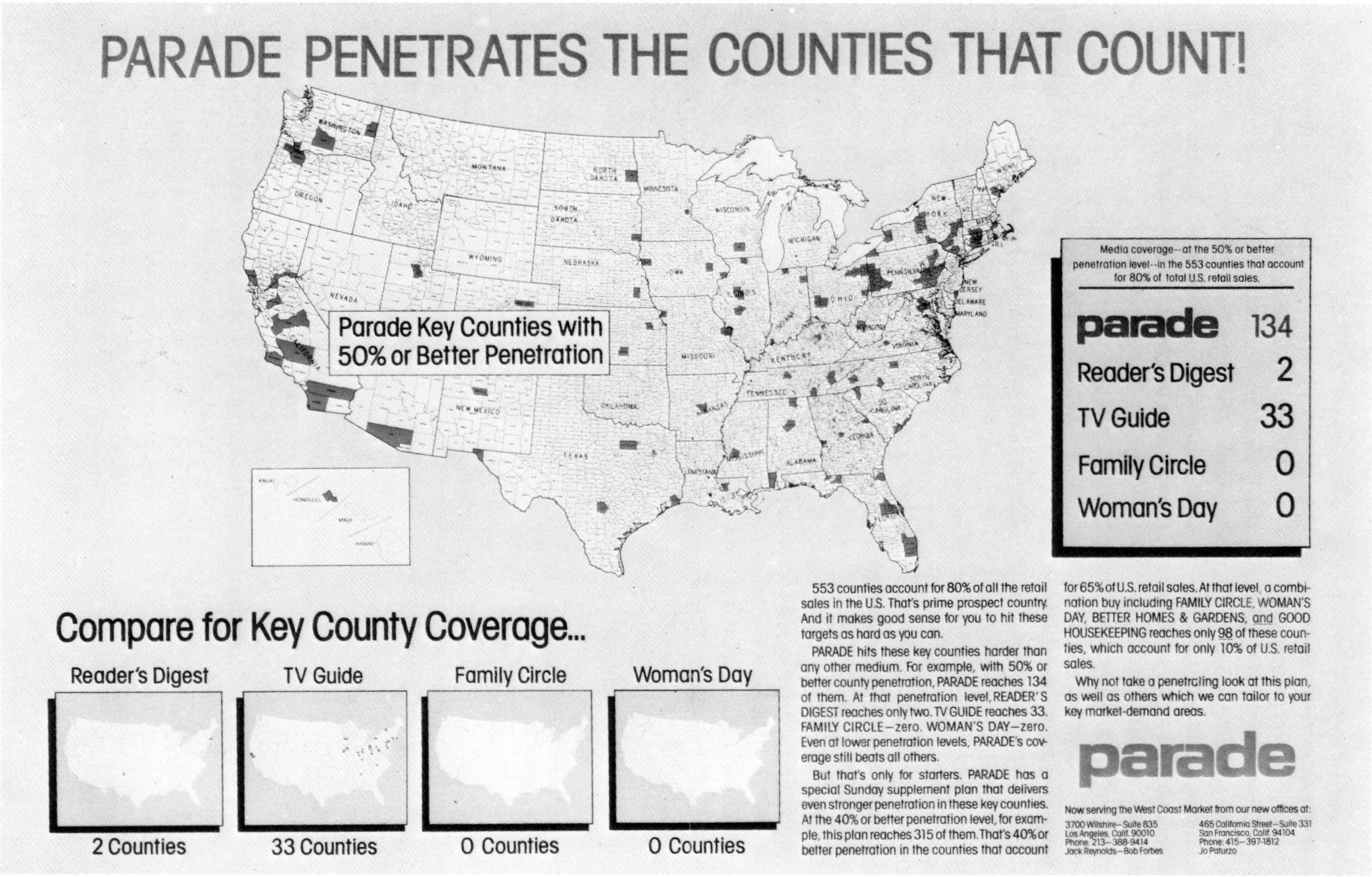
PARADE PENETRATES THE COUNTIES THAT COUNT!
Parade Key Counties with 50% or Better Penetration
Media coverage--at the 50% or better penetration level--in the 553 counties that account for 80% of total U.S. retail sales.
parade 134
Reader's Digest 2
TV Guide 33
Family Circle 0
Woman's Day 0
Compare for Key County Coverage...
Reader's Digest
2 Counties
TV Guide
33 Counties
Family Circle
0 Counties
Woman's Day
0 Counties
553 counties account for 80% of all the retail sales in the U.S. That's prime prospect country. And it makes good sense for you to hit these targets as hard as you can.
PARADE hits these key counties harder than any other medium. For example, with 50% or better county penetration, PARADE reaches 134 of them. At that penetration level, READER'S DIGEST reaches only two. TV GUIDE reaches 33. FAMILY CIRCLE—zero. WOMAN'S DAY—zero. Even at lower penetration levels, PARADE's coverage still beats all others.
But that's only for starters. PARADE has a special Sunday supplement plan that delivers even stronger penetration in these key counties. At the 40% or better penetration level, for example, this plan reaches 315 of them. That's 40% or better penetration in the counties that account for 65% of U.S. retail sales. At that level, a combination buy including FAMILY CIRCLE, WOMAN'S DAY, BETTER HOMES & GARDENS, and GOOD HOUSEKEEPING reaches only 98 of these counties, which account for only 10% of U.S. retail sales.
Why not take a penetrating look at this plan, as well as others which we can tailor to your key market-demand areas.
parade
Now serving the West Coast Market from our new offices at:
3700 Wilshire—Suite 835
Los Angeles, Calif. 90010
Phone: 213—388-9414
Jack Reynolds—Bob Forbes
465 California Street—Suite 331
San Francisco, Calif. 94104
Phone: 415—397-1812
Jo Paturzo

Figure 18.4 A newspaper supplement stresses that it reaches key markets better than some competitive vehicles.

of syndicated audience-measurement services have come into existence. Because these business firms are independent of the various media, their findings possess greater credibility. The A. C. Nielsen Company and the Arbitron rating service, for instance, furnish subscribers with data about people who watch television programs. Other research organizations gather radio listenership data.

For print media, measurement firms are particularly prominent in the magazine field. Circulation figures collected by the Audit Bureau of Circulations (ABC) receive high marks for credibility among media buyers. Nevertheless, audience research for print media does not have the general acceptance accorded to broadcast media, especially television. At the beginning of the 1980s, for instance, a controversy raged over the methods used to research readership. The two major syndicated services then operating in the field, Mediamark Research Inc. (MRI) and Simmons Market Research Bureau (SMRB), often came up with significantly different audience figures for the same magazines.

Simmons measures readership of 44 magazines using the **through-the-book** method. In this method, an interviewer sits down with a respondent with copies of magazines in hand and asks which had been read. Mediamark employs the **recent reading** method for 140 magazines in which the respondent is merely asked about his or her readership habits. The latter method yields much larger audience figures. This discrepancy in results is unfortunate because it casts shadows on the validity of magazine audience research, which has historically gathered valuable additional information, such as demographic breakdowns of audiences and the quantification of brand purchasing decisions for many products. These data permit a look at the role of media in actual product purchasing or intent-to-purchase patterns as well as the usage or ownership of products and services.

The Advertising Research Foundation (ARF), a nonprofit group established to foster independent research in advertising, is trying to resolve the conflict between the two competing data-gathering firms so that advertising decisions can be based upon sound information that is generally acceptable to all persons in the advertising business.

Recently, the Three Sigma Research organization announced the first syndicated newspaper readership study; it covers 240 newspapers in 34 major United States markets representing 57 percent of the nation's population and 50 percent of its purchasing power.[9]

You should realize that the syndicated research reports do not define markets for the advertiser. The planner still must isolate market segments appropriate to the firm's product and other strengths. The services are sources of input to media selection decisions; they are not a means of deciding to whom products should be marketed.

The Media Plan[10]

All this fact gathering, analyzing, evaluating, weighing, and thinking lead to the adoption of a media plan. Eight key factors need to be covered in a comprehensive media plan:

1 Creative requirements
2 Competitive pressures
3 Communications principles
4 Budget size
5 Dollar allocation: geographical, seasonal, prospects
6 Reach and frequency
7 Testing
8 Corporate policy[11]

Effective communication and persuasion constitute the goal of the media plan. Advertisements are the prime vehicles for this communication and persuasion. Certain messages are aimed at mass audiences, others at more selective groups; media selection accomplishes these objectives. Some messages need frequent repetition to do the assigned job; thus, frequency becomes crucial in the media plan.

Advertisers seek a "share of mind" for the brand from the target market. Competitive pressures—what other advertisers are doing—affect the chances of winning the struggle.

Media planners need to go beyond the potential exposure of the message, which comes from media circulation, and seek to ascertain whether actual communication takes place when a specific medium is employed. Chapter 11 contains a discussion of the communication process. Unfortunately, little is known about what media characteristics enhance communication of the advertising message; the area is in a state of development.

Radio TV Reports

41 East 42nd Street New York N.Y. 10017
(212) 697-5100

PRODUCT:	LUZIANNE TEA BAGS		G80-03472
PROGRAM:	DONAHUE	4/14/80	30 SEC.
	WAGA-TV	(ATLANTA)	9:57AM

1. BURL IVES: Folks, the big Iced Tea Taste Test is history

2. and the clear winner is Luzianne.

3. In Atlanta it's Luzianne over Lipton, 65 to 30.

4. In Birmingham, 67% prefer the great taste of Luzianne.

5. Luzianne's secret?

6. Luzianne just tastes a whole lot better.

7. See how satisfying iced tea can taste.

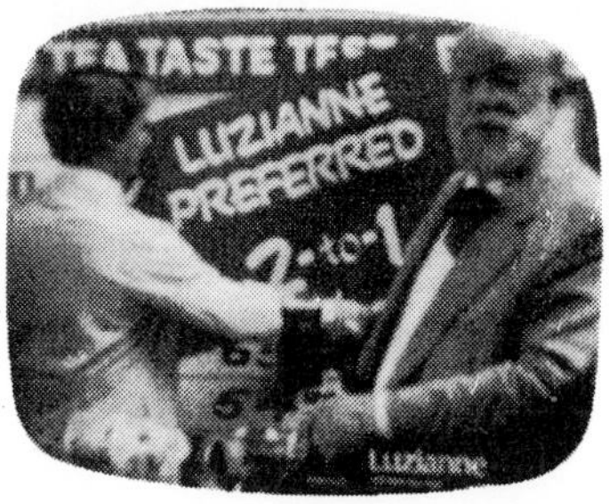

8. Final tally, Luzianne preferred 2 to 1.

9. It's the clear winner.

Figure 18.5 Advertising messages may be developed to take advantage of specific market conditions. A regional manufacturer of an iced-tea mix reveals research data showing that its product was preferred by residents of certain selected metropolitan areas.

YOUR DISPLAYS AND TIE-IN ADS CAN EARN STORE TAGS ON THESE TV SPOTS!

PEAR GINGERBREAD

With lemon sauce and a gingerbread square. You can get it all together with a fascinating

flair . . . Just add Canned Pears, you can buy them here, And enjoy yourself. . .

it's a Canned Pear Year

PEARS & CHICKEN

You'll like the roast chicken, tender and brown. Well to get it all together when you put the

Platter down . . . Just add Canned Pears, you can buy them here. And enjoy yourself . . .

it's a Canned Pear Year.

PEAR BREAKFAST

Like waffles in the morning. . . sausagey things? Then to get it all together in a way that

really sings. . . Just add Canned Pears, you can buy them here, And enjoy yourself. . .

it's a Canned Pear Year.

PEAR SALAD

You like lettuce, you like cottage cheese, Well to get it all together in a salad is

a breeze. . . Just add Canned Pears, you can buy them here, And enjoy yourself. . .

it's a Canned Pear Year.

SATURATION TV SCHEDULE
RETAIL TIE-IN TAGS COMBINE ADVERTISING AND DISPLAY FOR EXTRA SALES

MARKET	TELEVISION WEEKS OF	NEWSPAPER WEEKS OF
ATLANTA	Nov. 5, 12 & 26	Nov. 5, 12 & 26
BALTIMORE	Nov. 5, 12 & 26	Nov. 5, 12 & 26
BOSTON	Nov. 5, 12 & 26	Nov. 5, 12 & 26
CHICAGO	Nov. 5, 12, 26 & Dec. 3	Nov. 5, 12, 26 & Dec. 3
CINCINNATI	Nov. 5, 12 & 26	Nov. 5, 12 & 26
CLEVELAND	Nov. 5, 12 & 26	Nov. 5, 12 & 26
DALLAS-FT. WORTH	Nov. 5, 12 & 26	Nov. 5, 12 & 26
DENVER	Nov. 5, 12 & 26	Nov. 5, 12 & 26
DETROIT	Nov. 5, 12 & 26	Nov. 5, 12 & 26
HARTFORD-NEW HAVEN	Nov. 5, 12 & 26	Nov. 5, 12 & 26
JACKSONVILLE	Nov. 12, 26 & Dec. 3	Nov. 12, 26 & Dec. 3
KANSAS CITY	Nov. 5, 12 & 26	Nov. 5, 12 & 26
LOS ANGELES	Oct. 29, Nov. 5, 12, 26, Dec. 3 & 10	Oct. 29, Nov. 5, 12, 26, Dec. 3 & 10
MIAMI	Nov. 12, 26 & Dec. 3	Nov. 12, 26 & Dec. 3
MILWAUKEE	Nov. 5, 12 & 26	Nov. 5, 12 & 26
MINNEAPOLIS-ST. PAUL	Nov. 5, 12 & 26	Nov. 5, 12 & 26
NEW YORK	Nov. 5, 12, 26 & Dec. 3	Nov. 5, 12, 26 & Dec. 3
PHILADELPHIA	Nov. 5, 12 & 26	Nov. 5, 12 & 26
PHOENIX	Nov. 12 & 26	Nov. 12 & 26
PITTSBURGH	Nov. 5, 12 & 26	Nov. 5, 12 & 26
PORTLAND	Nov. 5, 12 & 26	Nov. 5, 12 & 26
SACRAMENTO-STOCKTON	Nov. 5, 12 & 26	Nov. 5, 12 & 26
SAN FRANCISCO	Nov. 5, 12. 26 & Dec. 3	Nov. 5, 12, 26 & Dec. 3
SEATTLE	Nov. 5, 12 & 26	Nov. 5, 12 & 26
ST. LOUIS	Nov. 5, 12 & 26	Nov. 5, 12 & 26
WASHINGTON, D. C.	Nov. 5, 12 & 26	Nov. 5, 12 & 26
YORK-LANCASTER	Nov. 12 & 26	Nov. 12 & 26

Figure 18.6 These two pages from a brochure designed for the grocery trade show (*left*) photoboards of TV commercials for the product and (*right*) the schedule for airing the commercials. The advertiser is clearly using the key-market strategy, concentrating the campaign in 27 markets. The black frame on the storyboard indicates where the cooperating retailer may place the store logo.

Dollar allocation deals with spending advertising dollars where the business is and takes into account such factors as geographic, seasonal, and prospect differences. Largely a matter of media strategy, the topic is explored in the next section.

Chapter 17 analyzed the budget question, and reach and frequency considerations were examined earlier in this chapter.

As in the case of advertising message development, where creative research is needed on a continuous basis, the media plan should be put up for review regularly. Media testing is that portion of the media plan that evaluates controlled projects to discover empirical criteria or to evaluate media objectives and strategy. The field of media research is a complex and highly specialized subset of the larger field of marketing and advertising research; it has been aided considerably by the development of the computer and by various mathematical models.

Media planners must recognize that their recommendations should be compatible with broader policy considerations laid down by the advertising firm. Furthermore, reasonable willingness to compromise is essential for long-term success in the media planning role.

Media Strategy

The media plan will employ one, or a combination, of three basic strategies. We call these strategies (1) the national plan, (2) the key-market plan, and (3) the skim plan. Other names are given to these plans by some advertising people, but the underlying principles are used by all advertisers.

The National Plan

Some advertisers have achieved nationwide distribution of their products and can advertise nationally. Here we mean nationally in the sense that people living in every corner of the nation are in the target market for the advertiser. The goal is to reach customers wherever they are located. Frequently, media choices for such advertisers will be those which are capable of reaching large numbers of consumers at low costs per impression. Under the national plan, an advertiser seeks a large number of impressions. Thus, the advertiser will probably concentrate the advertising in "mass" national magazines or on network television, although combinations of other media including newspapers, radio, and outdoor advertising may be chosen. The national plan is usually employed after one of the other approaches has been used successfully for a period of time to expand distribution to national levels.

The Key-Market Plan

Many advertisers do not go after the national market. Their strategy is to seek a substantial segment of it. The segment which the advertiser wants to reach may be selected on the basis of consumer characteristics or geographic units. A media strategy based on division of the market into geographic segments is called the key-market, or zone approach.

Advertisers who employ the key-market plan decide for one reason or another to concentrate their advertising upon certain selected marketing areas—a city, county, state, or region. Advertising efforts are not dissipated throughout the entire nation. If product distribution is only in certain areas, advertising is done in those areas. Creating buyer interest in products which are not readily available is pointless.

The funds available for advertising provide another limiting factor in media planning. The company may have national distribution; yet advertising in all markets may be uneconomic, or a significant portion of its distribution may be concentrated in a few key markets. For example, four metropolitan areas—New York, Los Angeles, Chicago, and Philadelphia—account for more than one-fifth of all food sales in the United States. In such instances, advertising will be concentrated in specific geograhic areas.

Key markets, however, may be chosen for a variety of other reasons. For example, one region may be the center of a peculiar competitive situation which the advertiser wishes to meet through advertising. Because of their isolation and population composition, other areas may be chosen to be test areas for the introduction of new products, different packages, or experimental advertising. These areas will not receive the same advertising treatment as other regions, even though the advertiser is a national advertiser in the sense previously discussed. National media are rarely used by the advertiser who adopts the key-market approach to company advertising. Instead, local media—newspapers, radio and television stations, and outdoor advertising—are chosen. The national plan, of course, is often the end result of a series of key-market campaigns.

The Skim Plan

An alternative way of approaching segmented markets is to aim at specific consumer groups, regardless of their geographic location. Market segmentation is usually based upon such factors as income, educational level, occupation, or social status. The advertiser's goal is to concentrate advertising upon those persons who are most likely to buy the product because they are in demographic or psychographic subgroups where possession or desired possession of

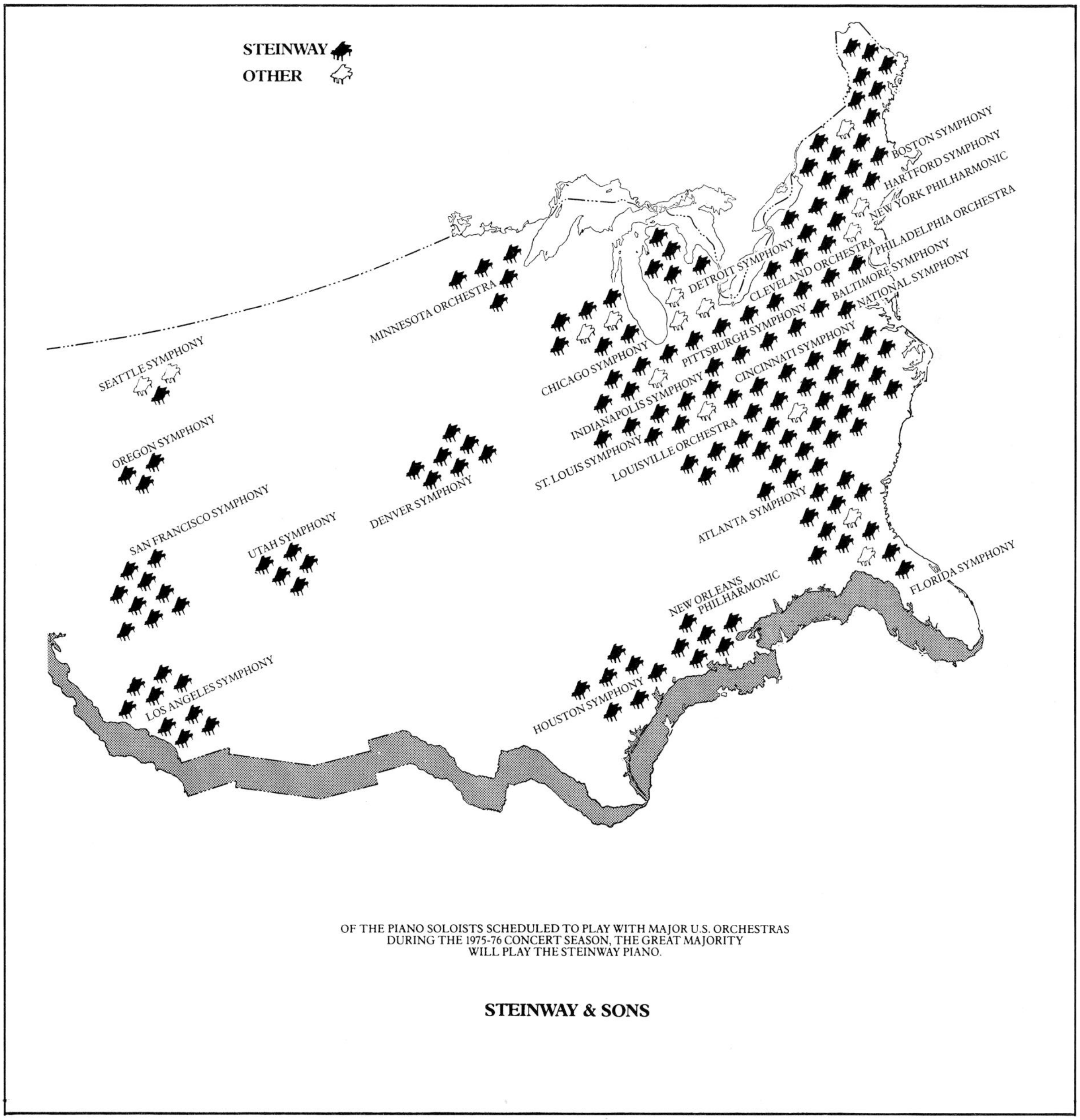

Figure 18.7 The "skim" strategy is used by a manufacturer of expensive pianos. This ad appeared in *Atlantic Monthly, Harper's, The New Yorker, Smithsonian,* and *Music Clubs Magazine,* whose audiences include the relatively few prospects for the product regardless of where they may live.

the product is likely. Once a segment has been tapped and its sales potential wrung out, a second group is chosen and the process is repeated. Often, it is hoped that interest in the product will trickle down the social ladder to the point where the product will be accepted by the mass market. In other cases, there is no hope that a product will be universally accepted, and the advertiser is satisfied to reach a limited market, as in the case of high-priced luxury goods such as Rolls Royces or Cadillacs.

Specialty goods frequently lend themselves to the skim approach. The media chosen are those which tap specialized audiences. Thus, the advertiser of sporting goods may employ special-interest publications such as *Outdoor Life* or *Surfer* magazine, instead of general magazines. Instead of network radio, advertising messages may be aired over a number of selected FM stations.

Advertisers do not limit themselves to only one of these basic media strategies in actual practice. They are often used in combination with one another. For example, many large food advertisers use the national approach to give "umbrella" coverage throughout the nation, and reinforce this with local media in the most important metropolitan market areas. Regardless of the strategy adopted, the goal is always the same. Advertising media are chosen and used in a manner that will yield the greatest return for the advertiser's dollar.

Once the analysis is completed, the essential media decisions are made, and the media plan is drawn up, steps must be taken to implement the plan—to execute it through actual placement of advertisements according to the plan.

Media Buying: Putting the Media Plan into Action

Once the media plan is established, the next step is to carry it out. This activity is called **media buying** and involves some routine and detailed procedures and also several scientific and complex processes. In the implementation state, advertisements are placed according to the media plan.

Scheduling Advertising

In factory management, scheduling is defined as "the determination of when each item of preparation and execution must be performed." Thus, a timetable is prepared and performance is checked against the schedule as a means of control. The term "scheduling" has two meanings in advertising. One use of the term is analogous to the factory situation. Procedures are established within the agency setup to make sure that creative work is done on time. The responsibility

Table 18.1
Normal Schedule for the Preparation of a Four-Color Print Advertisement

1 Agency account executive initiates copy request (5 working days).
2 Copy completed and layout checked (4 days).
3 Account group approves copy and layout (1 day).
4 Account executive sets up date with client (1 day).
5 Copy and layout submitted to client for approval, rejection, or revision—the first time the advertising manager sees the ad (2 days).
6 Approved copy is set in type and artwork prepared (15 or more days).
7 Art and type are physically put together in mechanical layout (2 days).
8 Mechanical layout is approved by account group (1 day).
9 Mechanical layout and finished art submitted to advertising manager for review and approval—the second time the advertising manager sees the ad (1 day).
10 Mechanical layout and art go into the production department or group, which supervises the making of plates by the engraver and the securing of proofs (25 days).
11 Proofs go to the advertising manager for final approval. If corrections are required at this point, there will doubtless be extra costs. This is the last time the advertising manager sees the ad before it is published (2 days).
12 Account executive returns approved proof to agency traffic department (1 day).
13 Agency traffic coordinator then forwards proofs and orders engraver to send plates to publication printer (1 day).
14 Agency traffic or forwarding department sends insertion order with a proof to the publication (same day).

for seeing that work flows smoothly through the agency is placed with the traffic department. At the heart of this kind of scheduling is the agency work order.

The traffic department issues work orders, or job memos, in order to keep creative work flowing smoothly through the various departments in the agency. The process starts from the closing dates set up by the various advertising media and works backward. Every medium sets a deadline; copy must reach the medium by the specified date, or the advertisement will not be run as scheduled.

Table 18.1 illustrates the step-by-step procedure followed in a normal schedule for preparing a four-color print advertisment. More than two months are involved, and of course, further delays are often possible, thus requiring even more time.

In its second meaning, the term "scheduling" is used to describe an activity closely related to the physical placement of advertisements with media. When all the thinking about which advertising media should be used is finally done, the mechanics of the media job remain. We shall not go into the routine procedures involved in placing advertisements, but we shall explain the use of a tool designed to facilitate the process—the **media schedule.** Although the forms of media schedules may vary greatly, every schedule contains four basic elements: (1) a list of media where the advertisement is to appear; (2) dates of insertion, airing, or posting; (3) space, time, or other units to be used; and (4) the cost. Circulation figures are sometimes given. Careful study of such schedules, either individually or in comparison with those used by other advertisers, tell a great deal about the campaign strategy being employed. Here the advertiser's thinking about such concepts as reach, continuity, frequency, and dominance is shown dramatically.

Scheduling Patterns The advertising effort needs to be allocated, as we have already mentioned, by target-market and geographic patterns. This process is called **media weighting** and is really a *matter of relative emphasis.*[12] Another dimension of the weighting activity is the timing of advertising. One pattern to be adopted, of course, is continual advertising, in which ads appear regularly throughout the time period covered on the media schedule. An alternative is to employ a policy of "flighting" or "pulsing" the advertising. These patterns involve heavy media usage for a while, followed by complete abstinence. In addition to budget constraints, which may dictate no advertising for periods of time, such factors as seasonal sales rates, product life cycle, repurchase patterns, and competitive advertising patterns may influence the choice of scheduling pattern.[13]

In publication advertising, four basic patterns are available. The *even* schedule calls for the placement of advertisements of equal size at regularly established intervals. Thus, a schedule may include 100-inch advertisements in the local newspaper every Friday morning or a series of full-page advertisements in *Playboy* magazine every month. Advertisers whose products are in demand throughout the time period, or whose campaigns are essentially institutional, may find the even schedule satisfactory.

The *alternating* or *staggered* schedule is a variation of the even strategy. Advertisements continue to appear at regular intervals, but their size alternates in a set manner. For example, a newspaper schedule may include 840-line advertisements on Wednesdays and full pages on Sundays. This schedule is often used as a budget stretcher. By reducing the size of some advertisements, the advertiser is able to keep the message before the potential customer, yet spend less money.

The staggered schedule may be used, of course, over a longer period of time than a week or a month. It may be used to take advantage of intermittent peaks in the demand pattern for such seasonal products as greeting cards. The bulk of the advertising by greeting-card firms, for instance, is scheduled to appear shortly before Christmas, Valentine's Day, and Mother's Day.

The other two scheduling patterns are direct opposites of each other. One schedule calls for starting the advertising campaign with relatively small advertisements. Each succeeding advertisement is somewhat larger than its predecessor until finally a large ad climaxes the campaign. This schedule is frequently used to introduce new models of automobiles and other new products. Initial advertisements are often "teasers," aimed at stimulating consumer interest in the forthcoming announcement by arousing curiosity. The opposite schedule starts with a large advertisement, which is followed by successively smaller ads. These patterns are called **step-up** and **step-down** schedules, respectively. The choice is a matter of strategy; the advertiser decides whether an initial smash or a gradual building of interest is desired.

Broadcast availabilities and the practice of selling network time for stated periods, such as 13 weeks, make it somewhat difficult to schedule step-up and step-down campaigns. Spot broadcasting, of course, can be employed if time availabilities can be secured. Broadcast campaigns involving many stations in scattered markets require intricate scheduling problems for the media buyer, although computerization has helped make the job considerably easier than it was for many years. Spot broadcasting can increase the advertiser's impact through the use of saturation schedules in chosen markets. For outdoor advertising, the 30-day selling period places a limitation on scheduling flexibility for advertisers wishing to use the medium.

The Media Schedule

The media schedule provides a work sheet against which the buyer charged with the responsibility of actually placing advertisements can check operations. The schedule is a handy device to show what the advertising program of the company contains. Moreover, it is an instrument of control over advertising expenditures. By totaling scheduled expenditures, one can determine whether the media budget is being exceeded. Finally, the schedule serves as a checklist against which media billing and proof of publication, airing, or posting can be compared. Figure 18.8 illustrates some of the steps followed in the media scheduling process.

Buying of Advertising Time and Space

With the media schedule firmly established, the final step in media plan implementation—the actual purchase of advertising—arrives. Three groups participate in buying media: (1) the advertising agency, (2) the advertiser, and (3) media buying services. Every advertising agency employs specialists skilled in buying broadcast time and publication space. Familiarity with media charges, discount structures, special buying opportunities, and other factors influencing the cost of advertising is the stock-in-trade for these individuals. They are performing one of the principal functions that the full-service agency renders to its clients—the *placement* of advertising messages. Advertising efficiency increases when the job is well done.

Retail advertisers traditionally deal directly with the media, buying time and space for advertisements created by store personnel. When advertising is placed by such advertisers, they are not usually given media commissions as national advertisers are. The house agency established by some national advertisers may also deal directly with media, with the commission received acting as a reduction in the cost of the advertising.

Some time ago, the dramatic rise in media costs, especially for spot television, led to the development of independent firms, known as **outside media buying services.** These buying services seek out special bargains that deviate from established advertising rates. Buying services purchase broadcast time for cash on the open market, with their profit coming from the differential between the price they pay to the station and what they charge an advertiser. Often the net price to the advertiser is lower than the advertising agency can obtain from the stations; thus the advertiser can save money when the buying service is used. Some advertising agencies have reacted by strengthening their own buying operations, while others welcomed relief from the burden of buying radio and TV time for clients. Media buying services have shown that broadcast time costs are negotiable, and their influence in the advertising industry has led to improvement in the overall efficiency of time buying, regardless of who actually does the job.

The Computer and Media Decisions

The computer is a useful tool for both media planning and media buying. There has been a vast explosion of information about markets and media in recent years. In the past, a media planner could rely upon intuition when media were being chosen, but this is increasingly risky in the economy of the 1980s. When a large number of calculations are to be made, such as in reach and frequency computations, the computer can perform these operations quickly and

M&F ADVERTISING

MELDRUM AND FEWSMITH, INC. 1220 HURON ROAD, CLEVELAND, OHIO 44115 TELEPHONE 216-241-2141
26011 EVERGREEN ROAD, SOUTHFIELD, MICHIGAN 48076 TELEPHONE 313-358-5300
200 EAST RANDOLPH DRIVE, 76TH FLOOR, CHICAGO, ILLINOIS 60601 TELEPHONE 312-861-0006

PRINT MEDIA ESTIMATE

Originating Office
☒ CLEVELAND ☐ SOUTHFIELD
☐ CHICAGO

CLIENT GLIDDEN DIV. OF SCM CORPORATION
Division: Glidden C&R Architectural & Maintenance
Product: Fiscal 1980-81

DATE November 14, 1980
Est. No. Rev. 2

Publication	Description and Unit Rate		Total Cost
BUILDING & ARCHITECTURAL MARKETS			
BUILDING DESIGN & CONSTRUCTION (M) 6x 58,104	1 - 1 Page, 4 Color, Bleed	$3,830.*	$ 3,830.
CONSULTING ENGINEER (M) 6x 33,185	2 - 1 Page, 4 Color, Bleed 4 - 1 Page, 4 Color, Bleed	2,445. 2,695.	15,670.
ENGINEERING NEWS-RECORD'S BUILDING CONTRACTOR DEMO (M) 6x 27,905	3 - 1 Page, 4 Color, Bleed 3 - 1 Page, 4 Color, Bleed	2,075. 2,260.	13,005.
F. W. DODGE CONSTRUCTION NEWS ALL AIA/CSI EDITIONS (4 Ed.) Comb rate 89,272	4 - 1 Tab Page, 4 Color, Bleed (Inside Front Cover)	3,850.	3,850.
NAHB BUILDER (M) 1x 135,330	1 - 1 Page, 4 Color, Bleed	5,140.	5,140.
MULTI-HOUSING NEWS (M) 1x 43,516	1 - Tab Page, 4 Color, Bleed	4,400.	4,400.
PROFESSIONAL BUILDER (M) 6x 107,836	6 - 1 Page, 4 Color, Bleed	5,005.	30,030.
PROGRESSIVE ARCHITECTURE (M) 6x 71,949	1 - 1 Page, 4 Color, Bleed 5 - 1 Page, 4 Color, Bleed	3,530.* 4,060.	23,830.
THE CONSTRUCTION SPECIFIER (M) 6x 12,411	6 - 1 Page, 4 Color, Bleed	1,920.	11,520.
QUALIFIED REMODELER (10-T) 1x 35,573	1 - 1 Page, 4 Color, Bleed	3,305.	3,305.
	SUB-TOTAL BUILDING & ARCHITECTURAL MARKETS:		$114,580.

*Cost based on 1979 fiscal earned rate.

Approved ____________________

MF 221

(*a*)

Figure 18.8 How an advertising agency implements a media plan is shown in these forms developed by its media department. (*a*) This estimate shows how the advertiser will spend its $115,000 budget during the fiscal year. [*Courtesy of Meldrum and Fewsmith, Cleveland, Ohio.*]

PAGE ONE

M&F ADVERTISING

Client: GLIDDEN DIV. OF SCM CORPORATION
Division: C&R - Architectural & Maintenance

Period: Fiscal 1980-81
Date: November 14, 1980 (Revised)

MEDIA	JUL'80	AUG	SEP	OCT	NOV	DEC	JAN'81	FEB	MAR	APR	MAY	JUN
BUILDING & ARCHITECTURAL MARKET												
BUILDING DESIGN & CONSTRUCTION Monthly 6x rate 58,104	1P4CB* A-6769Rev. GLID- WALL											
CONSULTING ENGINEER Monthly 6x rate 33,185			1P4CB A-1581 CORROSIVE WORLDS		1P4CB A-5361 ALL WORLDS		1P4CB*	1P4CB	1P4CB*		1P4CB*	
ENGINEERING NEWS RECORD'S BUILDING CONTRACTOR DEMO Monthly 6x rate 27,905	10/ 1P4CB A-3183 CONCRETE WORLDS		11/ 1P4CB A-5361 ALL WORLDS		13/ 1P4CB A-1581Rev. CORROSIVE WORLDS		8/ 1P4CB		12/ 1P4CB		7/ 1P4CB	
F. W. DODGE CONSTRUCTION NEWS ALL AIA/CSI ED. 4 Editions Comb. rate 89,272	1981 17/ Tab4CB CSI RECAP									24/ Tab4CB AIA PROGRAM	29/ Tab4CB CSI PROGRAM	12/ Tab4CB AIA RECAP
NAHB BUILDER Monthly 1x rate 135,330							1P4CB NAHB SHOW					

*Readership Studied

(*b*)

Figure 18.8 (*Cont.*) (*b*) A plot sheet is used to indicate how the advertising campaign is scheduled by publication and by month.

MF 206 Rev. 3

James K. Millhouse
919 N. Michigan Ave.
Chicago, Ill. 60611

312/642-6625

M&F ADVERTISING

MELDRUM AND FEWSMITH, INC., 1220 HURON ROAD, CLEVELAND, OHIO 44115 TELEPHONE 216-241-2141
26011 EVERGREEN ROAD, SOUTHFIELD, MICHIGAN 48076 TELEPHONE 313-358-5300

SPACE RESERVATION

Originating Office
☒ CLEVELAND ☐ SOUTHFIELD

TO PUBLISHER OF BUILDING DESIGN & CONSTRUCTION
5 South Wabash Ave.
Chicago, Illinois 60603

RESERVATION NO. F 42114

DATE December 10, 1980

PLEASE PUBLISH ADVERTISING OF (advertiser) GLIDDEN/ARCHITECTURAL & MAINTENANCE #289
FOR (product) 1980-81 SCM Corporation

DATES OF INSERTION	SPACE	RATE
September 1980	1P4CB	3830
November		
January 1981	1P4CB	3830
March		
April		
May		

POSITION

RATE BASE 6 Time

AGENCY COMMISSION 15 PER CENT ON GROSS | CASH DISCOUNT --0- PER CENT ON NET

IMPORTANT: **No insertions are to be made against this space reservation without specific instructions covering each insertion.**

PER Lillian Jones/jh

SUBJECT TO STANDARD CONDITIONS ON BACK HEREOF WITH EXCEPTION THAT COMPLETE CHECKING COPIES ARE REQUIRED FOR EACH INSERTION WHETHER NATIONAL OR REGIONAL.

Member of
AMERICAN ASSOCIATION OF ADVERTISING AGENCIES

PUBLISHER

(*c*)

Figure 18.8 (*Cont.*) (*c*) Once the estimate and schedule are approved by the client, a space reservation form is issued. This form alerts the publication to possible dates and frequencies and establishes the billing rate for the advertisements. This is not an authorization to run an ad, however.

M&F ADVERTISING

Client: GLIDDEN/ARCHITECTURAL & MAINTENANCE #289
Division: SCM Corporation

Period: 1980-81 Program
Date: 11/26/80

MEDIA	JUL	AUG	SEP	OCT	NOV	DEC	JAN	FEB	MAR	APR	MAY	JUN
BUILDING DESIGN & CONSTRUCTION	80						81					
(M) 13,832			1P4CB		1P4CB		1P4CB		1P4CB	1P4CB	1P4CB	
ISSUE: Monthly												
			3830*		3830		3830*		3830	3830	3830	
CLOSE: 15th of 2nd prior mo.												
TERMS: 15-0												
RATE BASE: 6x												
* Readership Study												
							TOTAL:	$ 22,980.00				

(*d*)

Figure 18.8 (*Cont.*) (*d*) Publication from form (*b*) is now entered on individual schedule sheet. Details regarding circulation frequency, closing dates, rate base, and mechanical specifications are included in the form.

MF 204 Rev. 3

ADVERTISING

MELDRUM AND FEWSMITH, INC., 1220 HURON ROAD, CLEVELAND, OHIO 44115 TELEPHONE 216-241-2141
26011 EVERGREEN ROAD, SOUTHFIELD, MICHIGAN 48076 TELEPHONE 313-358-5300
200 EAST RANDOLPH DRIVE, 76TH FLOOR, CHICAGO, ILLINOIS 60601 TELEPHONE 312-861-0006

INSERTION ORDER

Originating Office
☒ CLEVELAND ☐ SOUTHFIELD
☐ CHICAGO

TO PUBLISHER OF BUILDING DESIGN
& CONSTRUCTION
5 South Wabash Avenue
Chicago, IL 60603

ORDER NO. G 2993

DATE December 18, 1980

PLEASE PUBLISH ADVERTISING OF (advertiser) GLIDDEN/ARCHITECTURAL & MAINTENANCE #289
FOR (product) 1980-81 SCM Corporation

DATES OF INSERTION	AD NO. AND CAPTION	SPACE	RATE
July, 1980	A-6769-Rev. "INTRODUCING GLID-WALL. A NEW, LOW COST WALL SURFACE RENOVATION SYSTEM FROM GLIDDEN..."	1 Page, 4 Color, Bleed	$3,830.00

POSITION | CONTRACT YEAR

RATE BASE 6 Time

AGENCY COMMISSION 15 PER CENT ON GROSS | CASH DISCOUNT 2% PER CENT ON NET

Subject to standard conditions on back hereof.

THIS IS A REPEAT OF March, 1980 issue. YOU HAVE MATERIAL.

PER J. Hennessy/jh

WE ARE FURNISHING SEPARATELY (WITH A DUPLICATE OF THIS ORDER) THE FOLLOWING MATERIAL:

PUB HAS MATERIALS. AD IS REPEAT OF MARCH, 1980 ISSUE.

NOTE: All invoices to be sent to Cleveland. Checking copies of advertisements MUST be sent to office(s) indicated.

☒ CLEVELAND
☐ SOUTHFIELD
☐ CHICAGO

SUBJECT TO STANDARD CONDITIONS ON BACK HEREOF WITH EXCEPTION THAT COMPLETE CHECKING COPIES ARE REQUIRED FOR ALL PUBLICATION ADVERTISING WHETHER NATIONAL OR REGIONAL. TEARSHEETS ARE ACCEPTABLE FOR NEWSPAPER ADVERTISING.

Member of
AMERICAN ASSOCIATION OF ADVERTISING AGENCIES

PUBLISHER

(*e*)

Figure 18.8 (*Cont.*) (*e*) Upon approval of the reproduction materials by the client, the insertion order is prepared. It is sent to the publication with the production material attached. This serves as an order to run the ad.

efficiently, manipulating raw data into useful information. The computer, by processing sales information that shows where or when demand or distribution is the greatest, can aid in the allocation of the advertising budget to regions or to seasons of the year. Advertising can be directed to more dynamic markets or to certain seasons. Similarly, when such factors as market conditions, competitive advertising efforts, and media considerations are analyzed prior to the selection of media, vast quantities of data are involved. This point is highlighted by this quotation:

> As an example of the potential complexity of the media decision . . . in the simplest circumstances, a media buyer selecting 3 media from a group of 6 has 20 potential different choices. The same media buyer selecting 10 media from a group of 100, has 17,310,000,000,000 different alternatives available to him. If he could analyze 1 alternative per second, 24 hours a day, 7 days a week, he could cover all of his choices [in] one-half million years![14]

On-line Media Computer Services

At one time, both linear programming and simulation were used extensively in media decision making. Now media buyers rely on systems of mathematical equations that are used to estimate reach and frequency distributions and to generate optimal media mixes.

Figure 18.9 The computer is extremely useful in the interpretation of vast quantities of data. Here, through the "computer mapping" technique, *Time* magazine can see how it has penetrated the Boston market by zip code areas. [*Courtesy of Demographic Research Company and Time, Inc.*]

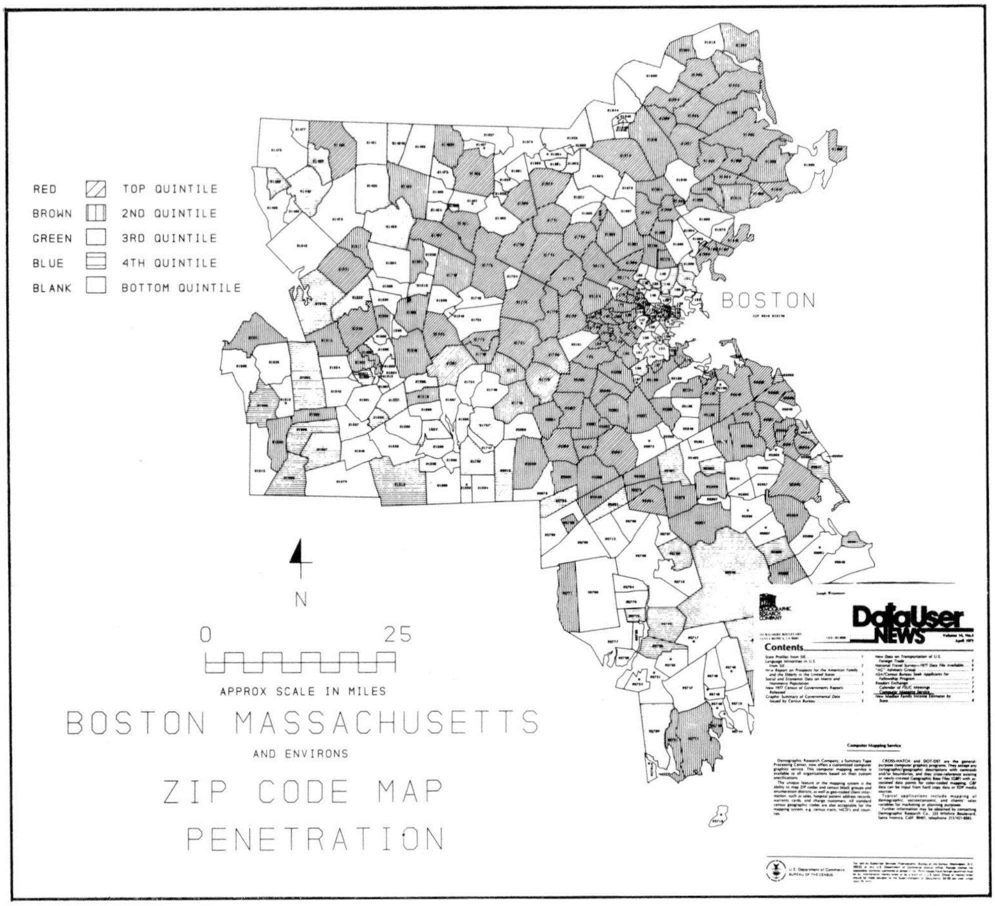

Profile

R. E. (Ted) Turner

Ted Turner, proclaimed to be the "Mouth of the South," was born in Cincinnati, Ohio, on November 19, 1938. He is best known for rebuilding his father's failing billboard company into a multimillion-dollar radio, television, and cable network conglomerate, along with owning the Atlanta Braves and the Atlanta Hawks. His activity in television broadcasting is at the core of the "demassification movement" in advertising.

At the age of nine, Ted moved to Savannah, Georgia, where his father had recently purchased an outdoor advertising company. During his summer vacations, Ted worked for the firm. Upon his father's death in 1963, Ted stopped the sellout of Turner Advertising and began to rebuild the overburdened company.

Expansion commenced in 1970 with the purchase of radio station WTCG (now WTBS) in Atlanta. This acquisition soon enabled Ted to corner the sports, movie rerun, and situation comedy markets by capturing a 16 percent audience share in the Atlanta area.

In 1975, two major events occurred that shaped Turner Broadcasting's future. First, the Federal Communications Commission relaxed its restriction on cable television. Second, RCA launched the SATCOM 1 satellite, enabling WTBS to beam its signal to cable systems around the country on a full-time basis. As a result, Turner is attracting a greater share of national advertising dollars.

Turner began the operation of Cable News Network (CNN) on June 1, 1980. News is fed into Atlanta from 20 full-time reporters located in the United States, London, and Rome. Topics covered during the 24-hour news broadcasts are economics and finance, personalities, psychology, exercise, pet care, skiing conditions, home repairs, real estate, health, and farm news. This programming is then available for airing over the nation's cable systems, reaching more than 20 percent of all homes in the United States.

Figure 18.10 The media calculator, which costs around $500, allows the user to evaluate media schedules in seven seconds or less. The system is supported by Telmar, which provides media analysis software for use in this portable system.

This work can be done by an advertising agency's media department, but it is more likely to be farmed out to on-line media computer services. These special service organizations, such as TELMAR and IMS (Interactive Market Systems, Inc.), can provide the media planner with vast quantities of data along with analysis of the data. For example, the media planner who wishes to make a buying decision about spot television needs to know a great deal of information about many local markets. The media computer services are capable of providing such information almost instantaneously through computer hardware similar to that shown in Figure 18.10. The software programs available from these services permit the media planner to have enormous calculating power for less than $1,000. The information is purchased as it is needed, a fact tending to even out the differential advantage of the large organization which, in the past, was financially able to generate the needed data, whereas smaller agencies and clients were not. The use of minicomputers, of course, is advantageous to larger organization, too, as it is much more efficient in providing information and calculations than older methods.

Increasing use of computers to process essential information will lead to better media decisions in the advertising world of the future. The computer is only a tool and will not replace judgment, art, or even intuition. The human factor will remain as the key to media decision making. But the human being, however, must be better trained in order to succeed in the task.

Summary

The goals of media planning are to select media and place advertisements where they will have the greatest impact on the target audience. Before media selection and media buying can take place, the media planner must evaluate (1) market conditions, (2) competitive efforts, and (3) media considerations. There are several sources of available information that media planners can use in evaluating each factor, and the data must be used imaginatively when devising a strong media plan.

Once a formal media plan is drafted, the advertiser adopts one of three strategies: (1) the national plan, (2) the key-market plan, or (3) the skim plan. The next step in the media planning process is to adopt a media schedule that gives detailed information on when and where advertising messages are to appear.

Implementation of the media plan takes place through the media buying process. This step is more mechanical than the planning phase and includes the scheduling and timing of advertising. Scheduling patterns can be even over time, or they can employ the flighting technique.

The actual buying of advertising time or space is usually performed by the ad agency on behalf of the client. Recently, some advertisers have been performing the time buying themselves (inhouse), and others have employed independent media buying services. The goal in all cases is to achieve maximum advertising exposure for dollars spent.

The computer has simplified the complex job of analyzing the quantities of data that need to be examined when media decisions are made. On-line media computer services are available to provide needed information for quick and accurate media decision making and to reduce the time needed to make calculations and to analyze data.

Questions for Discussion

1 Why is a sound media plan important to advertising success? Explain.

2 What is involved in media planning? In media selection?

3 What kinds of information are needed before good media planning can be performed? Elaborate with examples.

4 How do the advertising efforts of competitors affect media decisions of the advertiser?

5 Clearly explain how the media concepts of reach, frequency, continuity, and dominance interact within the media decision process.

6 What information sources would you use when seeking data on marketing conditions? On competitive advertising efforts? On media characteristics?

7 Exactly what is involved in the media-market matching process?

8 What are the three main forms of media strategies that are available to the media planner? Describe each briefly.

9 What are the major scheduling patterns available to the media buyer? Provide examples of each pattern.

10 How can the computer help in media planning? In media buying? Explain.

For Further Reference

Aaker, David A., and John G. Myers: *Advertising Management,* Prentice-Hall, Inc., Englewood Cliffs, N.J., 1975.

Barban, Arnold M., Stephen M. Cristol, and Frank J. Kopec: *Essentials of Media Planning,* Crain Books, Chicago, 1976.

Heighton, Elizabeth J., and Don R. Cunningham: *Advertising on the Broadcast Media,* Wadsworth Publishing Company, Inc., Belmont, Calif., 1976.

Jugenheimer, Donald W., and Peter B. Turk: *Advertising Media,* Grid Publishing Inc., Columbus, Ohio, 1980.

McGann, Anthony F., and J. Thomas Russell: *Advertising Media: The Managerial Approach,* Richard D. Irwin, Inc., Homewood, Ill., 1981.

Naples, Michael J.: *Effective Frequency: The Relationship Between Frequency and Advertising Effectiveness,* Association of National Advertisers, New York, 1979.

Percy, Larry, and John R. Rossiter: *Advertising Strategy: A Communication Approach,* Frederick A. Praeger, Inc., New York, 1980.

Roth, Paul M.: *How to Plan Media,* Time & Space Labs Incorporated, Chicago, 1968.

Sissors, Jack Z., and E. Reynold Petry: *Advertising Media Planning,* Crain Books, Chicago, 1976.

Surmanek, Jim: *Media Planning: A Quick and Easy Guide,* Crain Books, Chicago, 1980.

Toffler, Alvin: *The Third Wave,* William Morrow & Company, New York, 1980.

End Notes

[1] Donald G. Hileman, "Changes in the Buying and Selection of Advertising Media," *Journalism Quarterly,* Summer 1968, p. 279.

[2] Arnold Barban, Stephen M. Cristol, and Frank J. Kopec, *Essentials of Media Planning,* Crain Books, Chicago, 1975, p. 1. Credit was given by these authors to Roger Barton, *Media in Advertising,* McGraw-Hill Book Company, New York, 1964, p. 19.

[3] Based upon a combination of Lyndon O. Brown, Richard S. Lessler, and William M. Weilbacher, *Advertising Media,* The Ronald Press Company, New York, 1957, pp. 283–354, and Barban et al., op. cit., pp. 5–27.

[4] *Ayer Glossary of Advertising and Related Terms,* 2d ed., Ayer Press, Philadelphia, 1977, p. 122.

[5] Barban et al., op. cit., p. 51.

[6] Ibid., pp. 51–52.

[7] Leo Bogart, *Strategy in Advertising,* Harcourt, Brace & World, Inc., New York, 1967, p. 145.

[8] Donald W. Jugenheimer and Peter B. Turk, *Advertising Media,* Grid Publishing, Inc., Columbus, Ohio, 1980, p. 34.

[9] *Advertising Age,* Sept. 8, 1980, p. 78.

[10] Drawn in part from Paul M. Roth, *How to Plan Media,* Time Space Labs Incorporated, Chicago, 1968.

[11] Ibid.

[12] Barban et al., op. cit., p. 66.

[13] Ibid., p. 68.

[14] Joseph St. Georges, "How Practical Is the Media Model," *Journal of Marketing,* pp. 31-32, July 1963.

Chapter 19

Advertising Coordination

An important duty for any manager is coordinating diverse activities. In business, coordination consists of integrating and relating all activities of the firm from sales, production, and finance to purchasing and mail distribution. A leading management expert defines coordination as "the orderly arrangement of group effort to provide unity of action in the pursuit of a common purpose."[1] In most businesses the coordination of diverse functions is achieved by a formally structured organization. A winning football team is an example of a well-coordinated organization. Each player on the team has two responsibilities. First, to learn the movements and skills required to play his position and, second, to coordinate his movements with the other players on the team into the harmonious joint action called *teamwork*.

Every player must know the team's plays, strategies, and signals; otherwise, all are not moving toward the ultimate goal of winning the championship and may even get into one another's way. The *coach*, the coordinator, relates the functions of each player into an organized unit working toward the objectives of winning the game and the goal of winning the championship.

In this chapter, we discuss the interaction of advertising with a number of other activities that are vitally important to marketing success and to the achievement of business management's ultimate goal—long-range profit maximization combined with consumer welfare.

Coordination in Advertising

In order to be effective, a firm's advertising program must be coordinated with internal groups within the firm, with its advertising agency, and also with external organizations engaged in the marketing and distribution of the firm's products.

Internal Coordination

Internal coordination is analogous to the first responsibility of the football player described above. All the muscles of the athlete must work together and the player must coordinate every movement to perform effectively on the field. In the same manner, the advertising program must fit together. The advertising message must be appropriate to the medium employed; advertisements must be created and prepared for delivery to the medium far enough in advance to meet deadlines. When many media are used, continuity is strongly needed in all creative efforts so that the total campaign is saying the same thing to prospects at every stage of the promotional effort. No advertising program can succeed if its elements are not coordinated for the right action at the right time.

External Coordination

External coordination in advertising is equivalent to the teamwork of the winning football team. A team may have an extremely talented quarterback, but without the support of the other players it cannot possibly win a game. External coordination is one element that contributes to the firm's overall success. Marketing success usually depends on a desirable product, proper distribution channels, correct pricing, and effective personal selling and advertising.

Advertising can take different positions on different marketing teams. Sometimes it bears the primary burden of selling products. At other times, it is a support function for the sales staff. Regardless of its function in any specific marketing system, the advertising must be coordinated with all other marketing activities if sales goals are to be met. Moreover, since advertising is so closely related to certain other business activities, such as sales promotion and public relations, this coordination is especially important. In addition, external coordination not only involves the integration of advertising and other elements of the marketing system or other company functions, but also requires coordination of company efforts with those of outside organizations, especially middlemen.

Advertising and Personal Selling

Few products are sold by advertising alone. Most marketing organizations employ varying amounts of personal selling. Because both have the same general objective—the making of sales—it is logical that advertising and personal selling require a high degree of coordination. The interrelationship differs, however, for consumer goods and for industrial products.

Consumer Goods

Securing and maintaining proper levels of product distribution are among the most important selling tasks for the manufacturer of consumer items. Wholesalers and retailers need to be persuaded to stock and promote the advertiser's product, or consumer advertising is largely wasted. If consumers are unable to locate the product after advertising has stimulated their interest, the advertising expenditure has accomplished nothing. Most manufacturers of consumer products therefore maintain sales force to call upon wholesalers and retailers.

Trade advertising is used to assist the salesperson in the field by persuading middlemen of the advantages of stocking the manufacturer's products. A favorable climate has already been established before the sales representative calls. The salesperson may even wish to start off the sales conversation with a reference to the advertising, such as "Did you see our advertisement in the latest issue of *Progressive Grocer*?" The ice has been broken by advertising, assuming that it is creatively effective and properly placed in the right media.

Many salespeople, unfortunately, carry on their selling activities completely independent of the company's trade advertising. It is imperative that salespersons know what sales themes are being featured in the firm's trade advertising and that they be encouraged to incorporate these themes in their sales presentations.

Consumer advertising for the product also assists the field salesperson. When the company advertises extensively to consumers, that very fact may be used as another reason why retailers should stock and promote the brand. They know that consumers are aware of the product features and benefits. This kind of promotion of consumer advertising, often called "merchandising the advertising," is discussed later in this chapter.

Industrial Goods

Manufacturers of industrial products also maintain sales forces. The primary task of these industrial salespeople is to sell products directly to industrial users. Industrial advertising campaigns may often have as their objective the familiarization of the manufacturer's name with potential buyers. More likely, the goal is to obtain leads for the sales force. When an inquiry comes into the home office in response to an industrial advertisement, the inquiry should be passed along to the sales department promptly. Furthermore, the salesperson should follow up the lead before competitors do. When the salesperson knows which advertisement evoked the prospect's interest, the correct buying motive can then be used in the sales presentation. More than magazine advertising is available to industrial salespersons. One survey indicated that advertising handouts (specialties), product literature, direct-mail advertising, and product publicity are of more value in making industrial sales.[2] It is obvious, therefore, that an integrated and

Figure 19.1 When a special price offer is made, its availability needs to be promoted. This newspaper ad was part of a complete advertising campaign that included television, radio, and point-of-purchase advertising.

coordinated promotional program is needed in industrial-product areas as well as for consumer goods.

Organizing for Coordination

Whether salespeople know about the company's advertising programs depends largely upon the internal organization of the firm. When advertising and selling are departments under the same marketing executive, chances for communication are greatly improved. Regardless of common leadership, however, interdepartmental communication does not happen automatically. Steps must be taken to brief the sales force on the advertising program. The advertising department should take the initiative in this situation. Time should be allotted to explain the advertising program at major sales meetings.

The advertising manager, in other words, must be a salesperson who convinces sales managers that their subordinates should know and use the company's advertising program. The advertising manager should stand ready to convince the sales force of the importance of advertising to the success of the company and to the personal success of the salesperson. Conversely, the advertising manager can receive real help in developing the advertising program from feedback from the sales force.

Salespeople have contact with wholesalers and retailers who, in turn, deal daily with consumers and their problems. Thus, in many firms regional sales managers help in such activities as media selection, determination of advertising budgets, and on some occasions, the choice of advertising themes. Participation in the planning of advertising programs, of course, makes sales-force personnel more favorably disposed toward the coordination of advertising and selling activities. If the jobs outlined in this section are conscientiously performed, satisfactory coordination between advertising and personal selling will exist in the manufacturing firm. The first essential of external advertising coordination will have been achieved.

National Advertisers and the Retailer

Consumer products usually are purchased in retail stores. Consumers buy most products in one of two ways: (1) through salespeople in the retail outlet, or

(2) through self-service. Advertising plays an important role regardless of which method is operating. Therefore advertising should be coordinated with retail selling and self-service distribution. Products are purchased, or not purchased, at least partially because of consumer familiarity with the brands offered for sale in the retail store. But dealers must also give aggressive support to the product if maximum sales are to be achieved.

Techniques for Achieving Brand Sales in Retail Stores

There are three major techniques for speeding the rate of sales of selected brands in retail stores. First, retail salespeople may be tutored in product characteristics and selling points and urged to push particular brands. Sometimes an additional incentive is given to the salesperson in the form of "prize money" or "push money" (pm's) or "spiffs." These incentives are bonuses for the sale of specified items and may be paid by the retailer or the manufacturer. Second, the retailer may display chosen brands advantageously and may use manufacturers' point-of-purchase materials in the store. Third, the dealer may promote sales by advertising the product over the name of the store.

Advertising can do little directly to stimulate the use of the first technique. If retail salespeople are to be trained to promote a particular brand, the manufacturer's sales representative must convince the retailer of the value of the idea. The retailer or a representative of the manufacturer will then do the actual training. Sales manuals, training films, and other aids may be prepared to help in such sales training. These materials are not advertising in the true sense, but they should be related to current advertising themes. In other words, retail salespeople should know as much as possible about the advertising program for reasons similar to those discussed for the manufacturer's representative. Of course, trade advertising can assist in selling the dealer on the advantages of this type of sales-training program.

Preferential shelf space for the manufacturer's products and the use of point-of-purchase materials can increase sales tremendously (up to 1000 percent in a few instances), but the retailer must be sold on their value to the store. Once again, trade advertising can do part of the sales job, but the personal sales representative usually must do most of it. The primary obstacle the salesperson faces is the intense competition for these special treatments, and strong consumer advertising may influence a retailer to provide preferential shelf space and point-of-purchase displays for one manufacturer rather than for another.

Nearly every manufacturer of consumer products is bidding for the favor of the retailer. Sometimes dealer allowances are used to convince retailers to display the product prominently. The retailer may be paid in this situation, a display allowance—usually a discount on price—in exchange for agreeing to display merchandise or POP advertising in a prescribed manner. Advertising allowances are controlled by the provisions of the Robinson-Patman Act, which states that such allowances must be made on a proportionately equal basis to all competing buyers, or the practice will be ruled discriminatory, thus illegal.

The third technique—getting dealers to advertise the manufacturer's brand over their own store name—also involves personal selling. One procedure, cooperative advertising, has been thoroughly developed and generally used by national advertisers; therefore, the following section is devoted exclusively to a discussion of securing dealer support.

Coordination in the Retail Store

Two other points should be mentioned, however, before we pass on to a discussion of cooperative advertising. First, advertising and retail selling efforts require coordination. Products should be on dealers' shelves prior to the appearance of an advertising campaign featuring the products. This warning is especially important when new products are introduced, when established products are featured in a special promotion, or when the product is one of seasonal use. The absence of merchandise from dealers' shelves results not only in lost sales, but in ill feeling toward the brand and the manufacturer. Therefore, the sales force must contact retailers far enough in advance to permit delivery of the advertised products. Moreover, production must be geared to possible expansion in demand patterns caused by the advertising program. Usually, advertising cannot be completely efficient if distribution of the product does not precede the appearance of the advertisement. If distribution takes place too far in advance, however, retailers may logically conclude that the product is unsalable. *Timing is vital.*

Second, coordination is needed between retail advertising and the stock of goods available for sale (inventory). Over the past few years, retail advertising has been rapidly increasing, with an ever-changing variety of products. The retail salesperson may have difficulty keeping track of items in stock. Since retail advertising calls primarily for direct action and consumers come into the store seeking the advertised product, uninformed salespeople can hinder sales. It is frustrating and annoying to receive a blank look from the salesperson when we ask for an item featured in the morning newspaper, or to be informed that the item is out of stock. Therefore, the retail advertiser should first ensure that no item is advertised unless sufficient quantities are on hand to meet reasonable demand for the merchandise. Short supplies or a limited variety of sizes or models should be clearly stated in the advertisement if such conditions are known at the time the advertisement is run.

Salespeople must be informed about featured merchandise. Department heads recommend the items and are responsible for educating their sales staff. The advertising manager can assist, however, by supplying advance proofs of the store's advertisements to be displayed where employees can examine them before coming on the sales floor. Often a discussion of the items featured in current advertising is held at the daily departmental sales meeting. Professional shoppers employed by the store can check salespeople's familiarity with store advertising, and rewards can be given to those who are up to date.

Cooperative Advertising

The term **cooperative advertising** is used in two entirely different ways by advertising executives. One way, sometimes called **horizontal cooperative advertising,** describes joint sponsorship by competitors of an advertising program designed to stimulate primary demand in the industry. For example, the egg industry sponsors national consumer advertising to promote the economical cost and food value of eggs. Similarly, the nation's dairies, while vigorously continuing to compete locally, have joined to produce national and regional advertising campaigns to convince consumers of the natural wholesomeness of milk and butter. They are attempting to increase the size of the pie they divide among themselves. Figure 19.2 presents an example of this kind of cooperative advertising.

Manufacturer's Cooperative Advertising

Our main interest, however, is in the second form of cooperative advertising, called **vertical** cooperative advertising, **dealer** cooperative advertising, or **manufacturer's cooperative advertising.** Although each term accurately describes the technique in part, we prefer the third name because the initiative for the establishment of such programs comes from the producer rather than the middleman.

How Cooperative Advertising Works

The manufacturer and the retailer selling the brand reach an agreement in which the manufacturer promises to refund all or a portion of the retailer's advertising costs for those advertisements featuring the manufacturer's products. Frequently, the parties agree to split the advertising costs on a 50-50 basis.

In order to illustrate the procedure, let us assume that a cooperative advertising agreement exists between Day Department Store and Night Manufacturing, and the refund rate is established at 50 percent. When the newspaper bills Day for $850, its regular page rate for retail advertisers, the bill is sent, along with a tear sheet as proof of publication, to Night Manufacturing. Night then sends a check or credit memo for $425 ($850 × 50 percent) to Day, and the two parties have thus advertised under a cooperative advertising agreement. This type of cooperative advertising may be used when a manufacturer's product is featured in multiple-item advertisements, such as those run by supermarkets. The food store is reimbursed on a proportionate basis for the space devoted to the brand. This arrangement gives the retailer twice as much advertising per advertising dollar. Moreover, because the rate differential paid by the national advertiser is often as much as 50 percent in some media, the manufacturer actually receives 4 times as much advertising space as would be received if the messages were placed directly with the medium over the corporate name.

In the last five years, the amount spent for manufacturer co-op plans has increased to over $5 billion, and retailers are changing their merchandise mix heavily toward brand names supported by profes-

Raising kids costs so much, we're glad we could make your life insurance cost less.
Here's one of life's necessities that costs less to buy today than it did twenty years ago. Life Insurance. How do we do it? We keep a sharp eye on operating costs, and work constantly to hold them down. We invest the money entrusted to us, and the earnings on those investments help keep the price of life insurance down. And you, our customers, have helped too—by living a little longer. For more information about life insurance write to the Institute of Life Insurance, 277 Park Avenue, New York, N.Y. 10017.
America's 900,000 life and health insurance people.
What we're doing makes a difference.
One in a series from the Life and Health Insurance Companies of America.

Figure 19.2 This print advertisement promotes life and health insurance as generic services. It is an example of horizontal cooperative advertising.

Curlee
Clothes for men who dress for women.
WOMAN: When I meet a man, I notice his clothes.
Every woman does.
That's why I'm telling you about Curlee.
Curlee makes men's clothes
I not only notice, I like.
You wear Curlee Clothes
They don't wear you.
I could spend a lot of time with a man who dresses that way.
Curlee
Store Name
SUPER: Curlee. For men who dress for women STORE NAME

Figure 19.3 This storyboard shows a television commerical used as part of a manufacturer's cooperative advertising program.

sional, comprehensive, and budget-stretching cooperative advertising programs. There is another $1 billion available for co-op advertising, however, which is not being used because of certain disadvantages in the arrangement. An example of this type of cooperative advertising is presented in Figure 19.3.

Problems in Cooperative Advertising

The manufacturer incurs additional costs when cooperative advertising is used. These costs may cover the preparation of the advertisement and reproduction materials and the additional paperwork required to see that advertisements are run according to instructions, as well as the auditing and paying of media bills. Abuses can occur, such as the practice of **double billing.** A bill for advertising space or time used is prepared by the local advertising medium for a higher sum of money than the retailer actually pays the medium. The manufacturer then ends up paying more than expected under the terms of the agreement.

Wasted circulation is another potential cost in cooperative advertising. Retailers may choose media

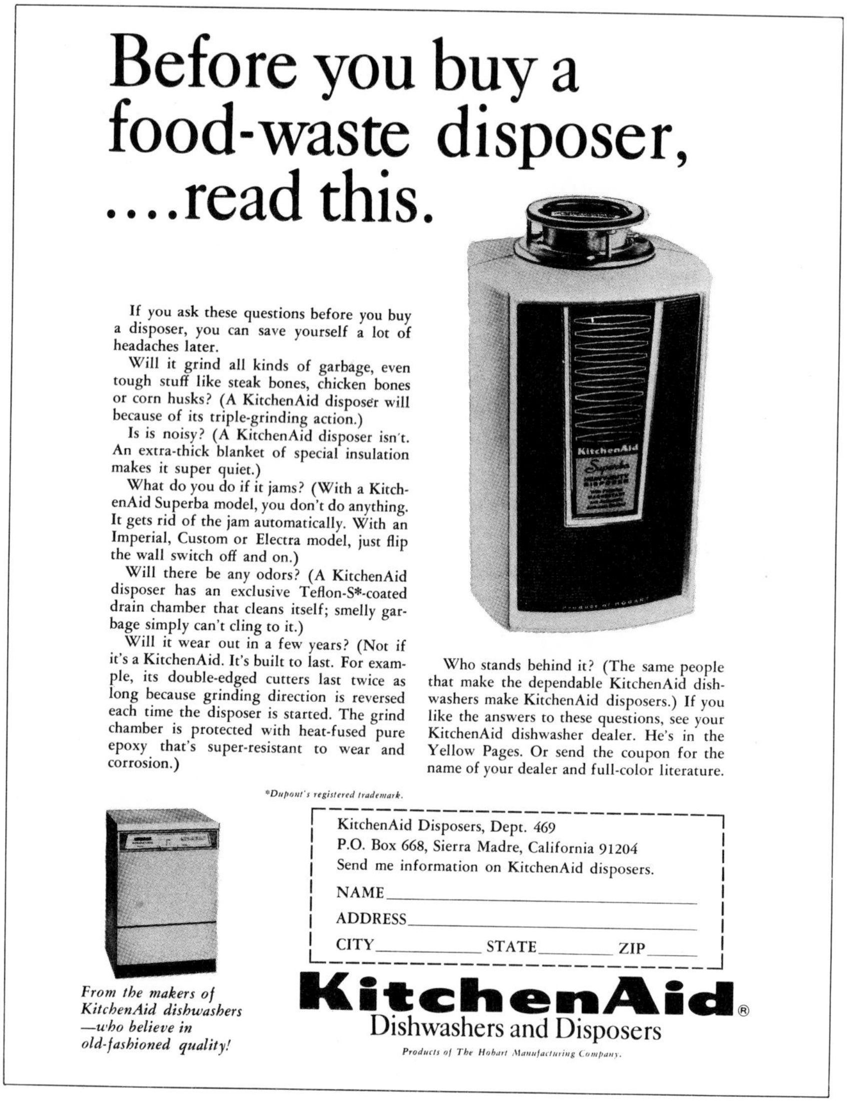
Before you buy a food-waste disposer, ...read this.
If you ask these questions before you buy a disposer, you can save yourself a lot of headaches later.
Will it grind all kinds of garbage, even tough stuff like steak bones, chicken bones or corn husks? (A KitchenAid disposer will because of its triple-grinding action.)
Is is noisy? (A KitchenAid disposer isn't. An extra-thick blanket of special insulation makes it super quiet.)
What do you do if it jams? (With a KitchenAid Superba model, you don't do anything. It gets rid of the jam automatically. With an Imperial, Custom or Electra model, just flip the wall switch off and on.)
Will there be any odors? (A KitchenAid disposer has an exclusive Teflon-S*-coated drain chamber that cleans itself; smelly garbage simply can't cling to it.)
Will it wear out in a few years? (Not if it's a KitchenAid. It's built to last. For example, its double-edged cutters last twice as long because grinding direction is reversed each time the disposer is started. The grind chamber is protected with heat-fused pure epoxy that's super-resistant to wear and corrosion.)
Who stands behind it? (The same people that make the dependable KitchenAid dishwashers make KitchenAid disposers.) If you like the answers to these questions, see your KitchenAid dishwasher dealer. He's in the Yellow Pages. Or send the coupon for the name of your dealer and full-color literature.
*Dupont's registered trademark.
KitchenAid
Superba
KitchenAid Disposers, Dept. 469
P.O. Box 668, Sierra Madre, California 91204
Send me information on KitchenAid disposers.
NAME
ADDRESS
CITY STATE ZIP
From the makers of KitchenAid dishwashers —who believe in old-fashioned quality!
KitchenAid®
Dishwashers and Disposers
Products of The Hobart Manufacturing Company.

Figure 19.4 Manufacturers often offer to send literature and dealers' names to interested prospects. This ad also suggests that yellow pages advertising in the telephone directory be consulted.

that are not good vehicles for advertising the manufacturer's product. That shortcoming can be controlled, however, by the terms of the agreement.

Presently, most cooperative advertising is run in newspapers, with direct mail second in importance. However, the broadcast media are agressively seeking more participation. Many radio and television stations employ specialists whose job is to expedite the placement of cooperative advertising in other stations.

Benefits of Cooperative Advertising

Retailers fail to engage in cooperative advertising arrangements with manufacturers because of (1) inertia, (2) a feeling that they do not contribute to their profits, or (3) the paperwork involved. Despite the disadvantages, retailers can benefit from cooperative advertising. With media costs escalating and a greater emphasis on localized marketing, a retailer can advertise effectively on a small budget. Media localization (zoned newspapers, local broadcasting, and the like) fits beautifully with market-by-market cooperative advertising, and there are synergistic benefits for retailer and manufacturer in the arrangement. The following paragraphs describe how manufacturers can incorporate cooperative advertising into their promotional mix with good results.

When to Use Cooperative Advertising

Manufacturers use cooperative advertising when operating through the exclusive or selective methods of distribution. The manufacturer's brand is sold in one—or a few—retail outlets in a marketing area. It is important, therefore, for the consumer to know where the product can be purchased. National advertising may stimulate initial interest in the brand, but identification of the local retail outlet is essential if such interest is to be translated into buying action. For this reason, telephone directory advertising is high on the approved media lists of most manufacturers engaging in cooperative advertising.

Current statistics show that most merchants selling popular retail categories, such as clothing, appliances, foods and drugs, and general merchandise, receive from 35 to 55 percent of their locally placed advertising budgets from manufacturer cooperative

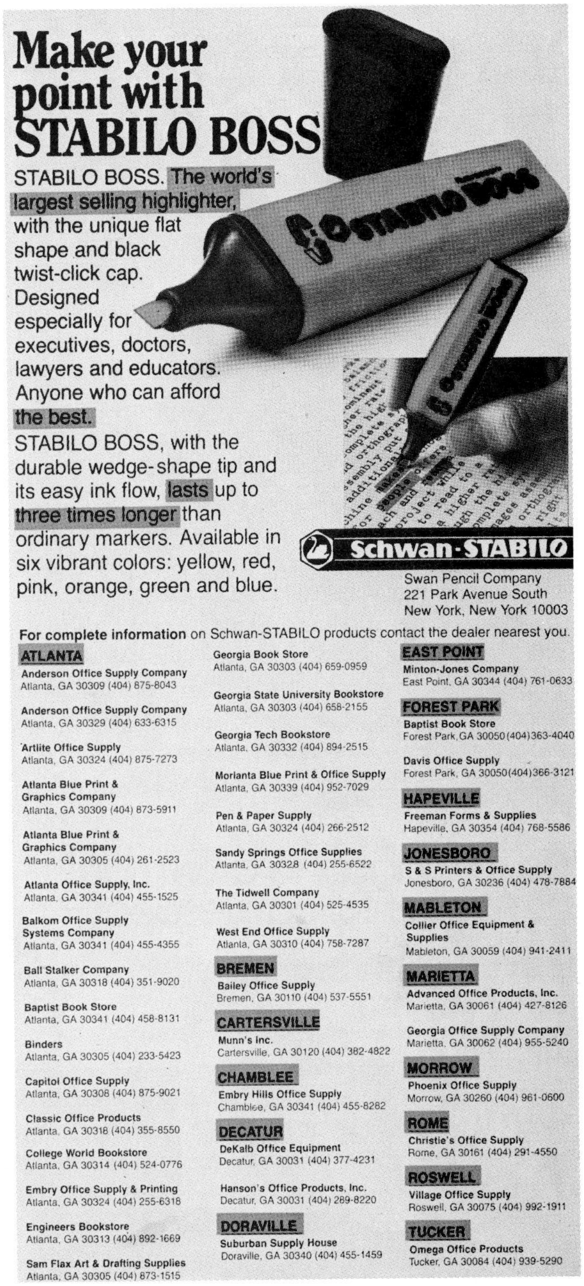

Figure 19.5 This two-thirds page ad appeared in a regional edition of *Time* magazine. The manufacturer lets consumers know where the product can be purchased. It is not known whether retailers were asked to contribute to the cost of the advertising; most likely, they were required to stock a certain level of the product in order to be listed.

funds.[3] The trade media are heavily involved in cooperative advertising. Associations such as the Newspaper Advertising Bureau, the Radio Advertising Bureau, and the Television Bureau of Advertising provide consultation and promotional aid to their members.

Cooperative advertising rarely can be used successfully to introduce a new product or to help move a small-volume item. In such cases, the retailer wants to know whether the product can be sold at all. The retailer believes the manufacturer has the responsibility of building demand. After the product has been established at satisfactory levels of volume, cooperative advertising is probably more advantageous for both the manufacturer and the retailer.

Convenience products, such as food, soap, and drugs, are also given cooperative advertising support. The reason, more than likely, is to give the retailer a price discount. In other words, cooperative advertising is not used as an inducement for the retailer to advertise the brand. Instead advertising allowances and cooperative advertising are used as a means of obtaining distribution for products. Such inducements may be given in a discriminatory fashion despite the Robinson-Patman Act provision that advertising allowances must be made proportionately available to all competing buyers.

Merchandising the Advertising

"Merchandising" is a term that has many meanings in the language of marketing. For our purposes here, "merchandising" is a synonym for "selling," and "merchandising the advertising" means "selling the advertising program." The manufacturer using this technique hopes to arouse enthusiasm and support for the advertising program where so many dollars are invested. According to its advocates, merchandising the advertising can double the value of the firm's investment in advertising.

The two most important groups to be influenced are the manufacturer's own sales force and middlemen, particularly the retailers handling the brands. The manufacturer wants both groups to feel that the advertising program is a positive force, designed to make their respective tasks easier and to increase their sales volume.

Merchandising to the Sales Force

Manufacturer's salespeople are told how the new consumer advertising will make it easier to convince retailers of the benefits of stocking the manufacturer's product. They are also briefed on how the retail trade advertising program provides another inducement for retailers to buy and promote the brand. Generally, the manufacturer's sales force receives such motivation from ad department personnel, and also from agency and sales executives and direct-mail promotion. The sales force is an important resource both for providing advertising ideas and for helping to accomplish the objectives of advertising.

Merchandising to the Retailers

If retailers can be convinced that the manufacturer's consumer advertising program will produce an increasing demand for the product, facilitating a rapid stock turnover, they will stock the brand. In addition, they may promote the product in the various ways previously discussed—preferential shelf space, special merchandise displays, use of point-of-purchase materials, advertising the manufacturer's brand over the retailer's name, and dealer tie-ins.

In his autobiography, *How to Make $100,000,000 in a Hurry,* Jeno Paulucci attests to the value of merchandising the advertising in the success of the Chun King Corp. When his company was in its infancy, a four-color, full-page ad was run in *Life* to launch a new 3-pound package of Chinese food. With the ad scheduled to run in February, Chun King sales representatives started to show millions of preprints to the trade as early as the previous June. The advertisement cost $30,000, a staggering drain on company resources at the time, but it lent prestige to the company and its product and aided in securing wide distribution in retail stores.[4]

Organizing for Merchandising the Advertising

Placing the responsibility for the program of merchandising company advertising is a difficult task. Surely the advertising department must bear a heavy share of the burden, for its personnel are in the best position to know the details of the advertising program. Moreover, advertising people should have the most enthusiasm for the company's advertising program since they develop it. On the other hand, the

Figure 19.6 This trade ad, which appeared in *Progressive Grocer,* tells retailers about the advertising support being given to the product by the manufacturer. It will help the salesperson when merchandising the advertising to retailers.

sales department is largely the instrument for transmitting such information to both retailers and the sales force. When a separate sales promotion department is maintained within the organizational structure of the firm, this department often carries out the assignment.

The philosophy behind the technique of merchandising the advertising is well expressed in this short quotation: "Many people are so busy getting out the next ad that they haven't time to do a good job in 'putting over' the ad they just got out."

Another Dimension of Merchandising the Advertising

Merchandising the advertising can also affect another group—the company's employees. If, for example, the advertising message states that "We try harder," the employees should know what is expected of them, for the customers are also likely to expect the employees to "try harder."[5] An exceptional advertising campaign is a source of pride to employees. They appreciate being associated with the firm and may even perform their jobs better. Alternatively, if the company's advertisements depict it as a concerned, socially responsible organization when the employees know it is not, cynicism, not pride, results.

Advertising and Product Management

To be effective, the advertising program must coordinate with product innovation, packaging, pricing, and other components making up the total product. The advertising department should be aware of the development of new products. Research and development people will brief advertising executives on activities far enough in advance for creative personnel to have time to develop good sales themes to be used in product promotion. Moreover, since lags exist in the process, time must be allowed for the mechanical production and media placement of advertisements. The product development department cannot suddenly announce a new discovery and expect the advertising department to release an outstanding campaign designed to introduce the product to the market. For one thing, some forms of advertising media must be contracted for months in advance. This area of coordination, however, is often overlooked even in well-managed firms. The desire for secrecy furnishes a partial explanation. The commercial researcher wishes to keep news of activities away from competitive organizations. The greater the number of people in on a secret, the greater the chance of an information leak. Employment mobility of sales and advertising executives, particularly agency personnel, intensifies this problem. When people move, secrets may go with them.

Coordination, between the production and advertising departments may be viewed from another perspective: Advertising executives should inform production officials of changes that advertising is expected to stimulate in the marketplace. It is important to have merchandise on retailers' shelves at the time an advertising campaign is launched, so adequate time must be allowed to produce the items and get them into distribution pipelines. Production schedules must be adjusted to fit anticipated demand for products. A failure to coordinate the two resulted in significant problems for General Motors when a big advertising campaign was designed to stimulate sales for the Chevrolet 4-cylinder Nova. The production department had decided to deemphasize this car, and by the time the advertisements began to appear, the plant machinery had already been converted to produce some other model.

Often, advertising executives decide whether price will be stressed as a buying appeal in company advertising and thus are in a position to know a great deal about prevailing pricing conditions. Their opinions should be considered along with those of other company officials involved in pricing. Any anticipated price change should be made known to advertising executives far enough in advance to permit inclusion of any necessary shifts in advertising.

Advertising and Sales Promotion

Our discussion to this point has dealt with the need for the coordination of advertising with other elements of the marketing mix: the product, its distribution channels, its price, and also with personal selling. We now look at how advertising relates to two other promotional tools: sales promotion and public relations.

The Nature of Sales Promotion

The marketing activity known as **sales promotion** is an elusive one to define. One writer does so in these words:

> Sales promotion, as the conjunction of the two words implies, lies halfway between the two functions of face-to-face selling and the promotion of a product or service through media advertising; it could perhaps be described as the adhesive which bonds the two together. Its main application is in marketing situations where there are intermediaries between the producer and the consumer—agents, distributors, wholesalers, retailers—situations more typical of consumer than industrial marketing.[6]

Sales promotion is neither personal selling nor advertising, but it possesses characteristics of both as well as of publicity. Occupying a sort of middle-ground position between personal selling and advertising, it helps make each activity more effective. Frey distinguishes sales promotion from advertising on the basis of media used by each activity. He observes that advertising messages appear in media owned and controlled primarily by persons other than the advertiser, while "sales promotion . . . 'educates' and arouses the enthusiasm of salesmen, middlemen, consumers, and perhaps others through a variety of materials, tools, and devices that the company itself controls."[7] In other words, the basic tools of sales promotion are internally created and distributed, whereas advertising relies upon outside media to disseminate messages created by persons external to the company's personnel. There is, of course, a gray area where the media of advertising and the media of sales promotion touch. A very succinct definition of sales promotion is : "a short-term incentive to the trade or consumer to induce purchase of the product."[8]

Sales promotion is basically a motivation activity. Its efforts are aimed principally at three groups: company salespeople, middlemen, and consumers. The general principles involved in merchandising the advertising apply also to sales promotional devices directed at company salespersons and intermediaries. The motivation of these two groups is crucial to company success in marketing products; consequently, the products are promoted to them through demonstrations, exhibits, training films, sales manuals, catalogs, and a number of other ways.

Rather surprisingly, the importance of sales promotion has only recently received the attention of marketers. Yet, since 1969, more money has been spent on sales promotion than on advertising. It has been estimated that in 1979, sales promotion accounted for 58.5 percent of total promotional dollar allowances, compared with 41.5 percent for media advertising, meaning over $60 billion was spent on consumer and trade sales promotion.[9] Specialized sales promotion agencies are prospering, and in recent years the most popular workshops sponsored by the Association of National Advertisers have taught techniques to manage the sales promotional activities of advertising firms.

Consumer-Directed Sales Promotion

The various kinds of consumer-directed sales promotion are familiar to all of us in our roles as consumers. Advertisements in the daily newspaper tell us of special deals being offered on products through cents-off coupons; from magazine ads and direct mail we learn of prizes to be won in manufacturer-sponsored contests; cereal boxes illustrate premiums to be had in exchange for box tops; even television and radio now inform us of special coupon offers available in newspapers and magazines.

Consumer-directed sales promotion is sometimes called either "quick action stimuli" or "forcing methods." Whereas national advertising is primarily indirect action in its appeal, sales promotion is a direct-action appeal. Behind most national advertisements is the goal of implanting favorable attitudes in the minds of consumers, a strategy to cause the consumer to consider or favor the advertised brand when making a purchase. Sales promotion, on the other hand, is a tactic that hedges long-term advertising bets by moving buyers to immediate action.

Luick and Ziegler classify consumer-product sales promotion devices into two groups according to the manufacturer's objective: (1) to increase the purchase of established products and (2) to stimulate purchases of new products.[10] In many highly competitive consumer-product fields, such as cereals, soaps, and toiletries, sales promotion devices have become standard. The reason is that trial is often the only way a consumer can be induced to switch brands, and a sales promotion device can stimulate trial. For example, such a device may persuade a skeptical consumer to try a new shampoo, whereas mere claims of product superiority would not. To increase the purchase of established products, the manufacturer may offer a premium for a certain number of proofs of purchase. Therefore, instead of buying a variety of cereals, for example, a homemaker may buy only that manufacturer's brand until enough proofs of purchase (box tops or whatever) are accumulated to obtain a set of stainless steel flatware.

In either case, the sales promotion method is relatively short-lived. Yet, the offerer of the special inducement to consumer action is still interested in more than immediate sales. If the forcing method is employed to induce sampling of a new product, the underlying hope is that the consumer will like the product and include it on future shopping lists. The goal is to reinforce a buying pattern favoring the promoted brand. The belief supporting this strategy is that consumers are creatures of habit who tend to buy the same brand time after time unless a strong reason for changing brands is offered.

Quick-action stimuli must be appropriate for the product whose purchase is being encouraged. This condition limits the use of some, or all, sales promotion devices for some prestige products. The aura of quality surrounding a product can be dissipated if the product is sold by means of a something-for-nothing appeal. Also, too frequent use of promotions may tend to diminish a product's image in the public's mind and result in artificial sales increases followed by lower than normal repeat sales. The typical home medicine cabinet is full of products that were purchased primarily because of some sort of special offer, yet the purchaser has not continued to buy the product.

The Advertising/Sales Promotion Relationship

Before looking at the most common methods of stimulating consumer action, we should establish their relationship to advertising. At the outset, we should note that the success of any promotional device depends on consumer awareness of its existence. Advertising is the primary method of informing the public of the details of specific sales promotion efforts; therefore, many people think that advertising and forcing methods are the same thing. Others think that they are substitutes for each other. Neither point of view is correct. In fact, the decision to use forcing methods almost always results in an increased need for advertising. The stimulation behind the special promotion is usually additional advertising. The reason is simple: The typical advertisement announcing the manufacturer's current sales promotion device has very little to say about the product itself. Therefore, regular indirect-action advertising must be continued or the reputation of the product in the minds of consumers will gradually decline. The

Figure 19.7 A major oil company used this sales promotional program to help solve a public relations problem that all oil refiners faced as America's energy crisis intensified. By 1981 this series contained 27 different titles and was instrumental in enhancing the reputation of Shell as a responsible citizen.

primary objective of advertisements featuring quick-action stimuli is to make some sort of special offer, whereas the objective of most regular advertising is to sell the product through a dramatization of its consumer benefits. These objectives are not the same, and their achievement calls for different strategies and copy approaches.

Advertising featuring sales promotion devices can help "merchandise the promotion" to salespeople, building enthusiasm and perhaps increasing sales. It may also strengthen the overall reputation of the brand because increased mention of the product name in mass media generally increases consumer familiarity with the product.

One of the most successful sales promotions of the last decade was introduced by Shell Oil Company and its advertising agency, Ogilvy & Mather. "Come to Shell for Answers" is a series of eight-page "answer books" developed to give consumers useful and tangible information about automobile products, driving techniques, and the safe and proper care of their automobiles. The answer books are distributed through national magazines and Shell service stations, and were supported by network television and other media advertising. Volume 27 of the series appeared in August 1981.

Research showed that as a result of the promotional program, consumer awareness of and attitudes toward Shell grew favorably. In a period when consumer attitudes toward oil companies as a whole were decidedly negative, this was an outstanding accomplishment. Shell received many requests from consumers for the series plus many complimentary letters from government officials and other influential consumers.[11]

Sales Promotion Planning and Strategy

Careful planning is as essential to sales promotion programs as it is to advertising programs. Objectives should be set and strategies developed for their attainment. Sales promotion should be part of the total promotional program, not just a sudden, hastily instigated bid for a sales surge. The manufacturer seeking to lead consumers into buying action has a bewildering array of promotion devices to consider. This decision is complicated by the patterns of fad and fashion that are common in sales promotion. For instance, contests requiring participants to write jingles or statements "in 25 words or less" were extremely popular at one time. This approach is seldom seen today. On the other hand, coupon offers and rebates are quite popular in recessionary periods. The choice should be in tune with the moment. In 1979, coupons were the most important consumer promotional tool, followed by price-off offers and cash refunds. Premium offers grew in importance while sweepstakes and contests fell. Sampling increased for established brands and declined for new brands.[12]

In other years, different patterns of sales promotional usage could be expected. The primary goal in promotion is to find a fresh approach—not too unusual a one—to put a fresh twist on a time-tested method. Only a few of the thousands of different promotions launched annually are overwhelmingly successful. Many fail completely.

Major Consumer-Directed Sales Promotion Alternatives

In this section we will discuss the basic nature, advantages and disadvantages, and possible uses of the major alternatives available to the sales promotion decision maker. When new products are being introduced, three major kinds of sales promotion may be used: (1) consumer sampling, (2) couponing, and (3) money-refund offers. On the other hand, when the objective is to increase the use of established products, the major alternatives are (1) price-off promotions, (2) premiums, and (3) consumer contests and sweepstakes.[13] The core group of sales promotion devices consists of four kinds of promotion: deals, coupons, premiums, and contests. Each type is now examined.

Deals

There are basically two different kinds of special offer: the money refund for products in the introductory stage, and the price-off promotion for established products. The term "deal" is commonly used to describe these promotional devices, which are promotions essentially price-oriented in appeal. Outright price reduction is avoided, as the price is reduced for a limited time and that fact is made clear to the consumer. When the promotion is over, the consumer should be willing to pay the regular price for the item. The deal promotion can be implemented in two ways through (1) special prices and sales and (2) combination offers.

Special Price Offers The special price is sometimes used to introduce a new product, but this approach has a built-in danger. Consumers may come to think of the special price as the regular charge for the item. Raising the price later then becomes difficult. The money-refund offer reduces this hazard. The customer is required to furnish proof of purchase to the manufacturer in order to receive the price reduction. For instance, the package label must be mailed in to the company, which then sends the stipulated amount of money to the buyer. The short-run limit of the offer must be stressed, and the consumer must be furnished a reasonable explanation why the price is temporarily reduced.

Special offers by manufacturers are frequently expressed in terms of "cents-off" specials. Such cents-off promotions have been popular for supermarket items in recent years. The level of price reduction is highly important in the success of a particular promotion of this type. If brand share is to be influenced at all, the reduction should be at least 11 to 12 percent of the regular sales price. Moreover, the advantage is only for a short time. Of course, the stimulation of immediate sales is an important motivating factor, but the establishment of the habit of using the featured brand is still a goal to be attained. Most of that task, however, must remain in the advertising program and in the quality of the product itself. The deal merely gets the consumer to try the product one time.

The special price is used not only for low-priced items, and many durable consumer products are offered in this manner. A classic example was the "rebate" offers made by automobile makers in 1980. Faced with huge inventories of unsold new, "gas-guzzling" cars and a new model year approaching, the manufacturers offered rebates ranging from $400 to $1,000 to consumers who would buy one of their cars. The offers were not very successful because consumers wanted fuel-efficient vehicles. The example illustrates an important point: Promotions will not move unwanted merchandise. Too-frequent use of the special price or the special sales event may create skepticism in consumers' minds.

Special prices and sales are used in industrial as well as consumer selling. Furthermore, "trade deals" are extensively employed to get middlemen to stock particular brands. In a trade deal, a reduced price is given to the retailer instead of the ultimate consumer. The retailer then has the option to pass along the saving to the customer or to retain it as additional profit.

Figure 19.8 Through most of the 1970s, the use of coupons increased. This chart shows that between 1974 and 1980 the number of coupons distributed more than tripled. The values shown for each year are billions of coupons distributed. [The Nielsen Researcher, *no. 4, p. 9, 1979.*]

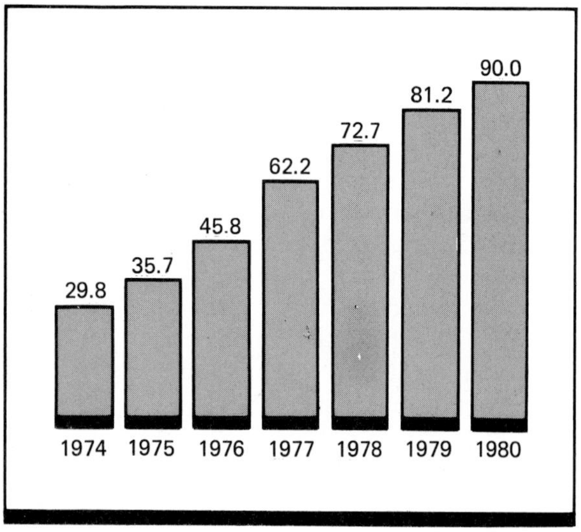

Combination Offers A combination offer brings two or more products together at a price less than consumers would have to pay if the items were purchased separately. For example, toothpaste manufacturers may combine their brand with a toothbrush, and razor makers offer a razor along with blades and shaving foam. The purchaser pays slightly more for the combination than for the host item alone, if the deal promotion is well-designed. These two examples illustrate an important principle of creating good combination offers. The items in a combination offer should be interrelated in consumer use. The offer may be used to introduce new products, and the unknown item is then tied to a well-established product. The consumer who is planning to buy the old product is persuaded to pay a little bit more—or maybe no more—to get an additional new product. "What have I got to lose?" is the prevailing attitude, and the consumer is "forced" into trying the new product.

Combination offers also are useful in switching brand loyalities in highly competitive fields. Obviously the retailer's support is necessary to the success of a consumer deal; otherwise, consumers will not be able to find the featured products.

Coupon Offers

The coupon is an extension or variation of the consumer deal strategy, serving to implement cents-off deals. Each coupon offers a price reduction on a specific item in the manufacturer's product line. When these coupons are presented at the grocery store at the time of purchase of the featured item, the amount specified on the face of the coupon is deducted from the regular price.

Coupon use has been very popular in recent years. (See Figure 19.8.) It is estimated that the typical American family received more than 1,200 coupons in 1980, and 80 percent of those household use coupons as part of their buying behavior.

The advantage of coupons over special prices is that the product is never marked at a price lower than the established one. Psychologically, the coupon carries the idea of urgency and a temporary opportunity better than special prices. Many coupons have expiration dates that accentuate these characteristics. The average face value of coupons in 1979 was 17 cents. The two most important uses of coupons are (1) to maintain market share of established products, and (2) to help introduce new items. Coupons have also been described as tie-breakers in an era of parity products. The coupon is sometimes the only discriminating factor when choosing between products.

One important management problem is selecting the method of distribution for getting the coupon to potential users. Six popular methods along with the percentages of use in 1977 and 1978 are shown in Figure 19.9.

Coupons delivered by direct mail have the highest redemption rates. The free-standing insert, described as "that part of the Sunday paper that falls either on the floor or on your lap as you open the paper," also has a high redemption rate. Like the in-ad technique, it appears in a medium regarded highly by the retail trade.

Each of the methods has its own advantages and limitations. Therefore the manufacturer using coupons needs to become knowledgeable in the various distribution alternatives.

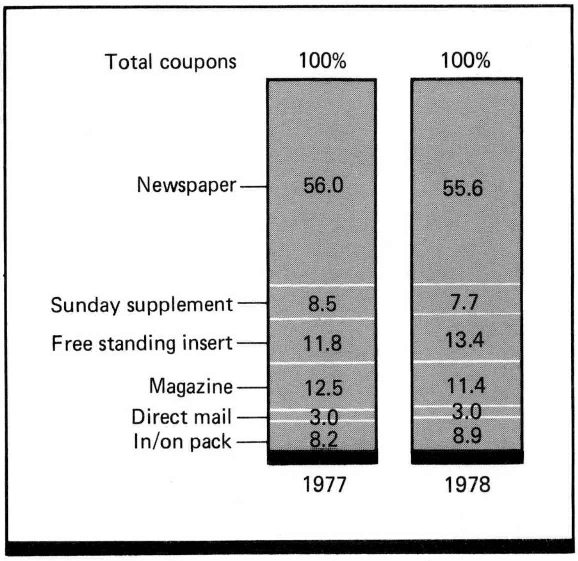

Figure 19.9 Companies using coupons search constantly for the most efficient method of distributing their offers. The shift taking place between 1977 and 1978 is illustrated in this chart. The values shown are the percent of coupons distributed by each medium. [The Nielsen Researcher, *no. 4, p.11, 1979.*]

Retailer cooperation is essential when coupons are redeemed in the store. One of the controversial points in the manufacturer-retailer relationship arises over this process. Retailers claim that redeeming coupons slows up the sales transaction procedure without providing a compensating advantage. Manufacturers answer that such offers speed the rate of stock turnover; retailers counter that coupon offers cause consumers merely to switch brands without any increase in total sales in the product category. Retailers do receive a nominal payment of 7 cents each for redeeming and handling coupons for the manufacturer. The manufacturer often makes arrangements with coupon-redemption specialists such as A. C. Nielsen to handle the flow of coupons from retailers. These services may be expensive, but they do relieve the advertiser of many headaches.

A troublesome abuse is **misredemption,** the intentional or accidentally improper use of coupons, as when a customer presents coupons at the supermarket checkout stand for products not purchased and receives the cash deduction because the supermarket employee does not bother to match coupons

Figure 19.10 This newspaper ad not only informs consumers about the product's advantages but contains an attractive coupon offer.

with actual purchases. In 1979, misredemption accounted for $1.7 billion, and it is estimated that 33 percent of all redeemed coupons are misredeemed.[14] In 1977, federal authorities, working with manufacturers, placed a bogus coupon for 25 cents off a fictitious detergent named Breen in a Sunday cooperative free-standing insert of three New York area newspapers. Within a few weeks, more than 70,000 Breen coupons were redeemed. Federal authorities identified over 1,600 individual accounts that redeemed the coupons; some were individuals who "gang-cut" the coupons (stacked several inserts together and cut the coupon area) in their own homes. Over 150 indictments resulted, with some prosecutions for larceny, mail fraud, and conspiracy.[15] Once the Universal Product Code (UPC) operates in all retail stores, it will be easier to accommodate proper redemptions. The coupon will carry the same marking as the product being offered at "cents-off," and the computer will automatically make the proper deduction from the register total.

Premiums

Premiums often are confused with advertising specialties, low-cost items that are advertising media in themselves since the giver's name is imprinted on the items. Premiums, however, do not carry, ordinarily, such marks of giver identification. The fundamental distinction between these two sales promotion devices is that the advertising specialty is given in anticipation of future business, while the premium is tied to current sales. If there is no sale, no premium is given.

The premium is offered to the customer as a reason for buying a particular product. If the customer buys the item, the premium comes as a gift. Thus, cereal manufacturers give toys in exchange for box tops, and soap manufacturers give household aids for soap wrappers. For Coca-Cola bottle caps, a consumer received an extended 3-minute recording of the original 60-second commercial jingle, "I'd Like to Teach the World to Sing," which had skyrocketed onto pop music charts in the mid-1970s. Of course, the all-time favorite premium is the prize found in boxes of Cracker Jack.

The premium and the product which it promotes are not usually interrelated in use, as in the case of the combination offer. The premium is chosen for its uniqueness or desirability to the person who might want the item but does not wish to spend money for its purchase. Premium offers are based on the assumption that most people have the "something-for-nothing" motivation in their personality makeup.

Often a more attractive premium can be featured through the use of the **self-liquidating technique.** The consumer not only sends proof of purchase but a specified amount of money. The amount often approximates the cost of the premium to the manufacturer who buys in large quantities, and the offer pays for itself as consumer money comes in. The buyer does not suffer, for the cost is usually less than the cost for the item in local stores. The manufacturer still must pay for the promotion and handling of the offer. The average value of self-liquidators has been increasing in recent times, and some of the featured items are relatively expensive. For instance, in 1973 Kool Cigarettes redeemed over 20,000 sailboats at $88 plus 10 empty packages as proof of purchase.[16]

Distribution of the premiums poses a managerial challenge. Common methods of distribution include mailings, placement in the package, and attachments to the package. When the request comes to the manufacturer through the mail, a system for premium fulfillment must be established to ensure that consumers obtain the premium within a reasonable time after sending in for it; otherwise, dissatisfaction with the company results. Special fulfillment houses provide this kind of service for many manufacturers.

The promotional possibilities inherent in premium offers are dramatized by the self-liquidating offers made by Texaco, Inc., in the 1960s. For many years, a toy fire engine was featured at $3.98. More than 1 million units were distributed annually, and estimates placed the number of new customers generated by the offer at 150,000 per year.

How a premium offer may outperform a price

Figure 19.11 A soft-drink manufacturer uses a cooler for the product as a self-liquidating premium. Sports personalities in the same age range as the target market are featured. Sunday supplements were used as the medium. Total estimated circulation was 51 million people.

reduction is described in this statement by Herman W. Lay, then president of the Frito-Lay Company, manufacturers of potato chips and other snack foods:

> You can't give a customer a price reduction of less than 10¢ to 15¢ and have it mean anything. But we have been highly successful in forcing sales of our Corn Fritos and Potato Chips by using premiums that cost six-tenths of a cent on the average. We're using recipe booklets, flower packets, plastic roses and orchids, and miniature plastic dinosaurs, particularly in our Twin-Paks. We're violently opposed to off-price promotions, but these premiums do an outstanding job for us.[17]

Premiums also are used to stimulate industrial and trade buying, although the practice causes problems when the gift is viewed as a form of commercial bribery. In the field of sales management, gift incentives—especially glamorous vacation trips—are a very popular and effective form of motivation for sales personnel and middlemen.

Trading Stamps

The concept behind trading stamps is to reward retail-store customers for their shopping loyalty with tangible, valuable incentives, rather than to motivate them, using quick-action stimuli, to purchase specific brands. The trading stamp is proof that the holder spent a small amount of money, usually 10 cents, at a store sponsoring a particular stamp plan. The stamps, which are collected by an estimated one-third of all American households, are accumulated until a sufficient quantity is available to exchange for merchandise of considerable monetary value.

Trading-stamp programs are long-term promotions and must be aggressively pushed by the retailer. Every customer should be encouraged to save the featured stamp if customer loyalty to the store is to be built by the technique.

The energy crisis of the 1970s brought hard times to the trading-stamp industry. Between May 1973 and February 1974, Sperry and Hutchinson Company, whose Green Stamps dominate the field, lost 90 percent of its business with service stations. Many food stores also stopped issuing the promotional devices as consumers became more price-conscious as the national rate of inflation increased.

As with all promotional tools, trading stamps experience periods of popularity and then seem to go into an eclipse only to return again when circumstances warrant a different strategy. Whether trading stamps will appear soon at food stores and at filling stations is difficult to predict. Selected retailers have elected to retain the trading stamp as a means of reaching those customers who remain loyal to this means of getting merchandise without a direct cash outlay.

Contests

There are two kinds of contests: those of skill and those of chance.

Contests of Skill When skill is required in the contest, the participating consumer is asked to do something that will be judged, and prizes are awarded for superior performances. Devising a new brand name, writing an essay, composing a limerick, and thinking up a slogan about the sponsor's product are examples of the kind of creative effort required.

Another approach is to require the consumer to use the manufacturer's product in its normal way and have the end product judged. The Pillsbury Bake-Off Contest is a classic example of this kind of skill contest. Another skill contest as promoted through advertising is shown in Figure 19.12.

Sweepstakes When the chance, or sweepstakes, approach is employed, the consumer's name is pooled with the names of all entrants. The winner is selected at random. Therefore, all entrants have an equal chance of winning. Obviously, the number of people likely to enter is much higher than in the case of contests of skill. One sweepstakes contest operated by Lever Brothers pulled over 10.5 million entries, and in 1968 more than 6.8 million consumers won prizes in sweepstakes contests. The recession year of 1975 saw sweepstakes contests still in use. For instance, Pepsi-Cola offered 65,000 prizes ranging from $1 to $50 worth of groceries, and Eveready batteries offered " a trip to the Super Bowl and a $10,000 trip to the supermarket (of your choice)." Kraft's "Family Reunion" sweepstakes tied in with the twenty-fifth anniversary of Disneyland, offering a free vacation for family members. These prizes, vacations and "Food Money," had a practical flavor: They are cash or look like cash.

Sweepstakes offer broad merchandising opportu-

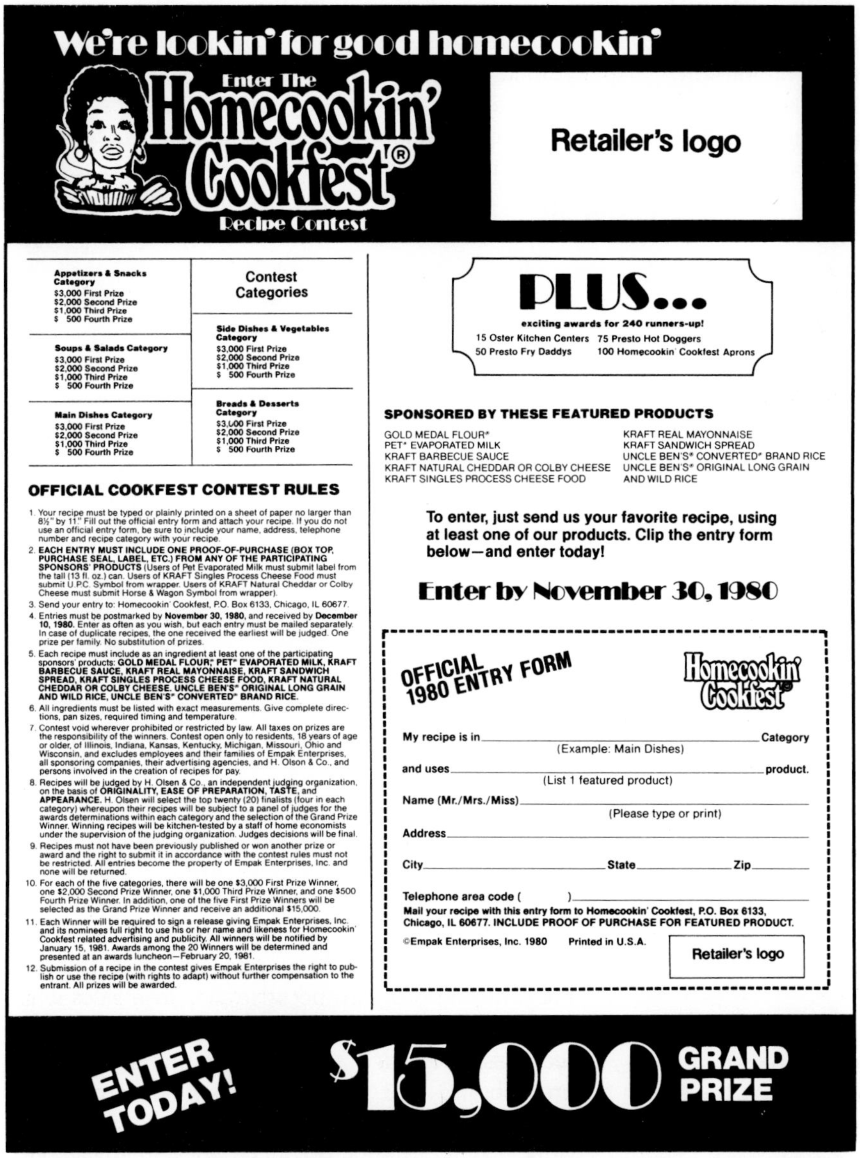

Figure 19.12 This advertisement urged black women living in the metropolitan Chicago area to enter a skill contest. Recipes employing the sponsors' products were called for, and over 1,200 were submitted in the first year's contest. The event now occurs annually and is spreading to additional markets.

nity for the product, reinforce product image, provide a reason for point-of-purchase displays, and generate a high level of consumer and trade interest and involvement. In addition, the cost is low compared with other sales promotion devices. Premium offers and skill contests require individual handling of all entries; with a sweepstakes, there is no handling of entries except the drawing. Sweepstakes contests are ideal for the mass marketer who wishes to reach women twenty-five to forty-five years of age with one to three children, since three-quarters of all participants are from this demographic group.

Each entry in the typical contest requires the purchase of one unit of the sponsor's product, and a contest in which every entrant has an equal chance to win carries considerable attraction when the top prizes are expensive. One problem in the contest of chance is that it must be legal. Lotteries are often outlawed as a form of gambling. Illegal lotteries involve the payment of money—"consideration" in legal jargon—by participants. As a general rule, the purchase of merchandise is not ruled to be sufficient consideration to classify the contest as a lottery. Furthermore, contestants are offered an opportunity to do something different from purchasing the product —to draw a facsimile of the label or print the product name, for instance, to qualify as an entrant.

The sweepstakes contest, particularly the game variety, went through difficult times in the late 1960s, and the promotional device went out of favor. Guidelines, established by the Federal Trade Commission, overcame the major criticism of contests that not all prizes were awarded, so that consumers distrusted the contest practices. Now all prizes must be awarded and often the odds of winning are given. Even if the odds are 784,152 to 1 of winning, though, people's interest and imagination are captured. With the legal problems clarified, sweepstakes are in the midst of a revival.

Topical contest themes, such as baseball, football, or politics in their respective seasons, are used to arouse customer interest. With the increase of regional marketing, local promotions are becoming quite popular. These programs are directly related to the interests of the consumers of a specific market and tie in with the local baseball team, amusement park, or events like raft contests and road races.

Appropriateness of the contest and of its prizes to the product is an important consideration. For some products the contest approach may cheapen the brand image. Generally speaking, contests are used in the promotion of frequently purchased merchandise, because the contest offer must coincide with demand for the generic product if many consumers are going to be moved to action by the forcing method.

As with other promotional methods, the success of a contest depends to a large degree upon how well consumers are informed of its existence. Advertising can do a great deal to engender public interest in a consumer contest. A feature of the contest is that this form of promotional effort often contains suitable material for publicity campaigns, and thereby increases the sponsor's return from the contest.

Product Sampling

"A good product promotes itself" is a recognized marketing axiom, and distributing a small sample of the product to potential customers is an important way of promoting a product. Many sellers feel that sampling is the best way to promote their products. Although sampling does not require the aggressive promotion that other devices need, sampling programs should be coordinated with advertising programs for maximum effectiveness. If both sampling and advertising are in the promotional mix, consumers should receive samples shortly after exposure to advertising messages about the product's benefits. The combination is somewhat like the one-two punch in boxing. Sampling, however, is costly; to the expense of the give-away item itself must be added those incurred in getting the sample to the consumer.

The physical distribution of the sample is an important operational problem when this technique is employed. When sampling is defined as including "any method possible to get an actual product into the consumer's hands," the following methods are alternatives.[18]

1 Mail
2 House-to-house delivery
3 Point-of-purchase areas in stores
4 Newspaper or magazine offer
5 Offer included in another product
6 Refund offer
7 Cents-off coupon

Another perplexing decision concerns the size of the sample. Should it be trial size or actual size? Enough of the product must be provided to let the consumer give it a satisfactory test; yet the supply should not be so large that the consumer will be kept out of the market for a long period.

Where the size given away is the size most consumers normally purchase, retailers often object to the sampling program because they lose sales while the sample is being used. For instance, a major coffee roaster decided to send 1-pound cans of the firm's brand to 1 million homes in a certain geographic section of the United States. As far as retail stores in the area were concerned, coffee sales declined 1 million pounds. Retailers naturally prefer promotional methods that bring sales volume to their outlets, as consumer deals do.

Mass sampling involves its own peculiar form of promotional waste. It is estimated that 20 percent of all products given away as samples are wasted. Some recipients are not interested in the product, such as the nonsmoker who gets a sample packet of cigarettes. Or the receiver may already be a user of the item.

Product sampling, however, is becoming highly selective, due in part to increased efficiency in planning and execution and in part to the use of computers. It is now possible to send samples to specific demographic markets and to identify nonusers of the product. This enhances the program's effectiveness, measured in terms of how many recipients bought the product again, because building sales is the purpose of sampling, as it is for all forms of sales promotion.

Advertising and Public Relations

Public relations, like sales promotion, means different things to different people. One definition is:

> Public relations is the management function which evaluates public attitudes, identifies the policies and procedures of an organization with the public interest, and executes a program of action and communication to earn public understanding and acceptance.[19]

Public relations, as with advertising, is carried on with target groups. Engel, Warshaw, and Kinnear, who are marketing communications experts, believe that there are five significant targets for public relations efforts: consumers; company employees; suppliers; stockholders; and the community at large.[20] Obviously, other groups exist with which an organization might wish to communicate, but these five are certainly important groups for most business firms. Engel, Warshaw, and Kinnear go on to point out that the communication can be internal (to employees) or external. The latter form "is designed to enhance the image of the organization in the minds of its various publics."[21] In their view, the external campaign con-

Figure 19.13 An important audience for many corporations consists of investors. Here a large consumer goods manufacturer uses corporate advertising to communicate with potential investors. [*Courtesy of Nabisco, Inc.*]

tains four important ingredients: (1) organizational symbols; (2) corporate advertising; (3) customer relations programs; and (4) publicity.[22] Corporate symbols were discussed in Chapter 3 and corporate advertising in Chapter 4. We feel that customer relations programs are outside the scope of this book. Publicity, however, deserves our attention as it is a close kin to advertising and needs to be coordinated with the advertising program.

Publicity

The American Marketing Association defines publicity as "any form of nonpaid commercially significant news or editorial comment about ideas, products, or institutions."[23] You will recall that in Chapter 1 we distinguished publicity from advertising by describing it as "unpaid-for advertising." Unlike advertising, which is paid for and controlled by the company, publicity is issued by a third party, such as a newspaper or broadcast station, that controls its delivery. Publicity, therefore, implies this third-party endorsement and substantiates advertising claims, unifying the long-range objectives of both forms of promotion —advertising and publicity—to establish a favorable product image.

The marketing departments of many companies maintain, therefore, a product publicity function, apart from the organization's public relations department. This group generates news stories about the company's products and seeks to place them in the trade press as well as in consumer publications. The need for coordination is clear-cut. Publicity can build customer enthusiasm in advance of advertising, making it a "highly effective and cost-efficient tool for creating awareness of and generating sales for new products, both consumer and industrial."[24]

Merchandising the publicity is similar to merchandising the advertising. Salespeople can include reprints of favorable feature stories or reviews in their presentation folders. Such material can be presented at sales meetings and be a significant motivating factor for salespeople. In fact, favorable publicity for a company increases the morale for all employees. Such news stories and features create pride in present employees and have a positive influence on recruitment, since outsiders will be attracted to the company.

Coordination with Other Facets of the Public Relations Effort

The firm's public relations department is not part of the marketing organization. Usually positioned in the executive offices of the company, it deals with many broad-ranging problems including governmental relations. Press releases, other than product publicity, are issued concerning company activities and policies on public issues.

Special public relations firms serve corporate clients in a fashion very similar to that provided by advertising agencies. Each organization. of course, specializes in its own form of communication, advertisements in the case of ad agencies, and press releases and position statements by the public relations firm.

The advertising messages of the firm must be consistent with the public relations posture of the organization. The importance of this kind of coordination is illustrated by the total communications approach being adopted by many companies. This trend is reflected in the merging of public relations firms and advertising agencies into "super agencies" designed to handle all forms of communication with the public.

Marsteller, Inc., a prominent advertising agency, long had under its wing a public relations subsidiary, Burson-Marsteller. By the time Marsteller merged with Young & Rubicam in 1979 (to make Young & Rubicam the largest agency in the world), Burson-Marsteller was the second largest public relations firm in the United States. In 1980, Hill and Knowlton, the national's largest PR firm, was acquired by J. Walter Thompson. These moves highlight the close relationship between advertising and public relations activities.

Summary

Coordination of activities is an essential business function. The goal is to achieve maximum efficiency in business operations. Advertising activities are no exception; they must be coordinated both internally and externally if maximum returns are to be derived. Internal coordination of advertising includes meshing the various parts of the advertising program together into a smoothly functioning system. Timing and scheduling are both critical in this kind of coordination.

External coordination of advertising is accomplished at two levels. It must be coordinated with other elements that compose the balance of the promotional mix, and it must be coordinated with the product and distribution subsystems to produce an efficient, integrated marketing system. Advertising is an effective selling tool for the manufacturer's sales force and for middlemen. Selling time can be reduced if customers have been made aware of the product and its benefits through advertising. This is true whether the customers are consumers, industrial buyers, or middlemen. Furthermore, consumer advertising can persuade retailers to stock and display the manufacturer's products, and it is important for the manufacturer to get active promotional support from middlemen. Cooperative advertising programs have been developed to encourage such dealer support. The advertising programs of many manufacturers are aggressively sold to their own sales force and to retailers through a process called merchandising the advertising. The objective is to see that the advertising program is understood and used as a sales tool by both groups.

Advertising must be coordinated with sales promotion, public relations, and publicity, as well as with personal selling. It is particularly important to see that the use of such quick-action promotional devices as premiums, deals, coupons, and contests is properly related to the advertising which is necessary to inform both intermediaries and customers of the special offer.

Public relations, in a broad sense, includes any activity that may affect the attitudes of a number of different target groups toward the company. These groups, or "publics," include not only customers for the company's products, but also employees, suppliers, stockholders, legislators, and residents of the communities where the company has production or distribution facilities. Publicity is the activity most closely associated with public relations. Inasmuch as the underlying purpose of publicity and advertising is the same—to inform the public of the company and its products—the information that both present should be consistent. Of course, advertising should be coordinated with the overall public relations program for the same reason.

Questions for Discussion

1 Distinguish clearly between "internal" and "external" coordination as these terms apply to advertising.
2 How can consumer ads in *Reader's Digest* or television commercials explaining the product's advantages to consumers be useful to the manufacturer's salespeople as they work in the field?
3 What are the three ways of speeding up the rate of sale for a brand in retail stores?
4 How is coordination of advertising carried out in the retail store?
5 What are the two forms of cooperative advertising? When is each form used? Bring in tear sheets of print ads that are examples of each form.
6 How is advertising merchandised? To whom? Explain.
7 What is the fundamental difference between advertising and sales promotion? Does an increase of one preclude the employment of the other? Discuss.
8 Why do we see the various forms of consumer-directed sales promotion come into popularity and then later decline in use? What forms are most popular today? Be prepared to cite specific examples.
9 Is product sampling the "best" form of promotion? Does such a program pose any problems to the manufacturer who decides to use sampling?
10 Discuss the interrelationship that exists between advertising publicity, and public relations.

For Further Reference

Chevalier, Michel, and Ronald Curhan: *Sales Promotion,* Marketing Science Institute, Cambridge, Mass., 1975.

Clayton, Alden: *The Relationship between Advertising and Promotion,* Marketing Science Institute, Cambridge, Mass., 1975.

Crimmins, Edward C.: *A Management Guide to Cooperative Advertising,* Association of National Advertisers, Inc., New York, 1970.

Cutlip, Scott M., and Allen H. Center: *Effective Public Relations,* 5th ed., Prentice-Hall, Inc., Englewood Cliffs, N.J., 1978.

Engel, James F., Martin R. Warshaw, and Thomas C. Kinnear: *Promotional Strategy,* 4th ed., Richard D. Irwin, Inc., Homewood, Ill., 1979.

Hart, Norman, *Industrial Advertising and Publicity,* John Wiley & Sons, Inc., New York, 1978.

Hurwood, David L., and Earl L. Bailey: *Advertising, Sales Promotion and Public Relations—Organizational Alternatives,* The National Industrial Conference Board, Inc., New York, 1968.

Luick, John F., and William Lee Ziegler: *Sales Promotion and Modern Merchandising,* McGraw-Hill Book Company, New York, 1968.

McNutt, George L.: *Business/Industrial Marketing and Communications: Key to More Productive Selling,* Crain Books, Chicago, 1978.

Moore, H. Frazier, and Bertrand R. Canfield: *Public Relations: Principles, Cases, and Problems,* 8th ed., Richard D. Irwin, Inc., Homewood, Ill., 1981.

Morton, Walker: *Advertising and Promoting the Professional Practice,* Hawthorn Books, Inc., New York, 1979.

Riso, Ovid (ed.): *Sales Promotion Handbook,* 7th ed., The Dartnell Corporation, Chicago, 1979.

Sales Promotion Techniques: A Basic Guidebook, American Association of Advertising Agencies, New York, 1978.

Smith, Gary R.: *Display and Promotion,* 2d ed., McGraw-Hill Book Company, New York, 1978.

Stanley, Richard E.: *Promotion: Advertising, Publicity, Personal Selling, Sales Promotion,* Prentice Hall, Inc., Englewood Cliffs, N.J., 1977.

Steinberg, Charles S.: *The Creation of Consent: Public Relations in Practice,* Hastings House, Publishers, Inc., New York, 1975.

Strang, Roger A.: *The Promotional Planning Process,* Frederick A. Praeger, Inc., New York, 1980.

End Notes

[1] James Mooney, "The Coordinative Principle, in Joseph A. Litterer (ed.), *Organization: Structure and Behavior,* vol. 1, John Wiley & Sons, Inc., New York, 1963, p. 39.

[2] John M. Trytten, "Ads Are More than Just a Way to Introduce Your Salesman," *Sales Management,* June 26, 1972, p. 36.

[3] George Donahue, "Grass Roots Coop," *Marketing Communication,* March 1980, p. 66.

[4] *Advertising Age,* June 9, 1969, p. 78.

[5] See Franklin Acito and Jeffrey D. Ford, "How Advertising Affects Employees," *Business Horizons,* February 1980, for a good discussion of this subject.

[6] Colin McIver, *Marketing for Managers,* Longmans Group, Ltd., London, 1972, p. 139.

[7] Albert W. Frey, *The Roles of Sales Promotion,* Dartmouth University, Tuck School, Hanover, N.H., 1957, p. 4.

[8] *The Tools of Promotion,* Association of National Advertisers, Inc., New York, 1975, p. 1.

[9] *Advertising Age,* May 5, 1980, p. 51.

[10] John F. Luick and William Lee Ziegler, *Sales Promotion and Modern Merchandising,* McGraw-Hill Book Company, New York, 1968, pp. 37, 65.

[11] Ogilvy & Mather, New York, "Come to Shell for Answers: Summary Report," Sept. 4, 1978.

[12] *Advertising Age,* Dec. 24, 1979, p. 20.

[13] Luick and Ziegler, loc. cit.

[14] *Advertising Age,* Dec. 24, 1979, p. 20.

[15] H. R. Wientzen, "Identifying and Controlling Coupon Misredemption," Association of National Advertisers, New York, 1979, pp. 7–8.

[16] *The Tools of Promotion,* loc. cit., p. 9.

[17] *Sales Management,* Aug. 7, 1964, p. 67.

[18] *The Tools of Promotion,* loc. cit., p. 1.

[19] John E. Marston, *Modern Public Relations,* McGraw-Hill Book Company, New York, 1979, p. 6.

[20] James F. Engel, Martin R. Warshaw, and Thomas C. Kinnear, *Promotional Strategy,* 4th ed., Richard D. Irwin, Inc., Homewood, Ill., 1979, p. 587.

[21] Ibid., p. 588.

[22] Ibid., pp. 588-595.

[23] Marketing Definitions, American Marketing Association, Chicago, 1960.

[24] Gerald S. Schwartz, "Viewpoint: Product Publicity as a Marketing Tool," *Marketing News,* vol. 12, no. 6, Sept. 22, 1978, p. 3.

Chapter 20

Advertising and the Law

All business in the United States is subject to some type of governmental regulation, and interest by government in how businesses are run has increased appreciably over the past few decades. Governmental rules and regulations state how firms are to prepare their financial records; they limit the ability of a business to borrow money; and, often, through regulatory commissions, they specify the way a firm can conduct its profit-making activities.

Because advertising is such an integral part of modern life and its persuasive abilities have a large impact on society, the business of advertising and advertising messages are scrutinized by many government agencies. Many people feel that the advertising industry should demonstrate more social responsibility and that advertising is manipulative and undesirable. We do not believe this view of advertising is a fair one, as we explained in Chapter 2 and will show again in this chapter.

Abuses in advertising can, obviously, have unfortunate effects on consumers, ranging from misspent money on an item that did not live up to the expectations developed in the advertising to hazardous accidents resulting from the misrepresentation of faulty goods. Three major groups exist to protect consumers against misleading or fraudulent advertising: (1) governmental agencies enforcing laws against offenders; (2) advertising industry associations and media groups that impose self-regulation upon members and advertisers; and (3) advertisers themselves, acting through enlightened self-interest and a sense of social responsibility.

Advertising is self-publicizing. The content of the advertising message is a matter of public record, unlike personal sales appeals or telephone solicitations. Consumers and competitors are in a good position, therefore, to expose dishonest advertising. Most advertisers depend on repeat business in order to remain in business. Truthful advertising, leading to consumer satisfaction, is the only successful long-range strategy to follow, inasmuch as false or misleading ads bring customer disenchantment and indignation. Developing loyal customers through misleading ads is difficult, if not impossible. Therefore, enlightened companies establish guidelines designed to ensure that their advertising does not violate the general rules of honesty and fair play. This philosophy may appear idealistic, but the company that follows this plan in its advertising finds itself with fewer entanglements.

That most advertising people behave decently because they are decent people should be stressed. Such people have to face themselves in the mirror every day. If what they are doing in pursuit of their careers in the advertising business is not up to the standards of our society, their lives will contain undesirable frustration. Therefore, not only is honesty in advertising good business practice but it is vital to the sound mental health of advertising practitioners.

This chapter is devoted, first, to the legal restrictions placed on advertising, then to a discussion of the ways that self-regulation is implemented by advertising associations and media groups and by the promotion of professional standards for the industry.

Legal Restrictions on Advertising Practice

For generations, advertising was controlled under the common law practice of caveat emptor (the Latin expression for "let the buyer beware"). This meant that sellers had no liability for damages resulting from their advertising claims unless they were either (1) warrentied by the advertiser or (2) represented fraudulently. Late in the nineteenth century, there was a decided shift in public opinion toward business. The policy of laissez-faire, the tenet that the public benefits to the greatest extent in an environment that lets the forces of free competition operate without restriction, shifted toward one that permitted certain business activities to be controlled by government commissions.

Our federal government became interested in the control of certain advertising practices as early as 1914 when the Federal Trade Commission (FTC) was established. The FTC regulated such business practices as pricing, selling below cost, quantity discounting, terms of sale, trademarking, labeling, and advertising. The policing of these activities collectively is known as **trade regulation.** In addition, many states passed similar legislation to regulate advertising practices that were not covered by federal law.

The amount and extent of government regulations of advertising have varied since 1914 when the first laws were enacted to limit various business practices. For example, the consumer movement of the 1960s and 1970s resulted in many new laws and commissions aimed at further regulating the practices of advertisers and their advertising messages. The climate of the 1980s eased many of these policies because many voters felt that government had become too pervasive and the cost of the programs was greater than their social value. Nevertheless, anyone involved in advertising must know about the legal restrictions imposed by government agencies. The most severe penalties for ignoring these restrictions are fines and jail terms. More likely, the highest price of ignorance of legal edicts is paid by the advertising executive who spends more time on legal problems than on creating effective and useful advertising.

Making you an expert on advertising law is not our aim in this chapter. Rather, this survey of twentieth-century advertising law will emphasize the need to consult a well-qualified lawyer when questions arise. You will be better able to appreciate the impact of regulations upon the advertising industry if you know more than the specific nature of the restrictions. The thinking and events leading to the passage of the various laws we shall discuss should help you to understand the reasons for their passage. Thus, the content of several important laws and their background are presented in this chapter. Our aim at this point is to show briefly how advertising currently is affected by various laws.[1]

Figure 20.1 Before advertising was regulated, the lack of truthfulness in claims made for products was common, as this ad reveals.

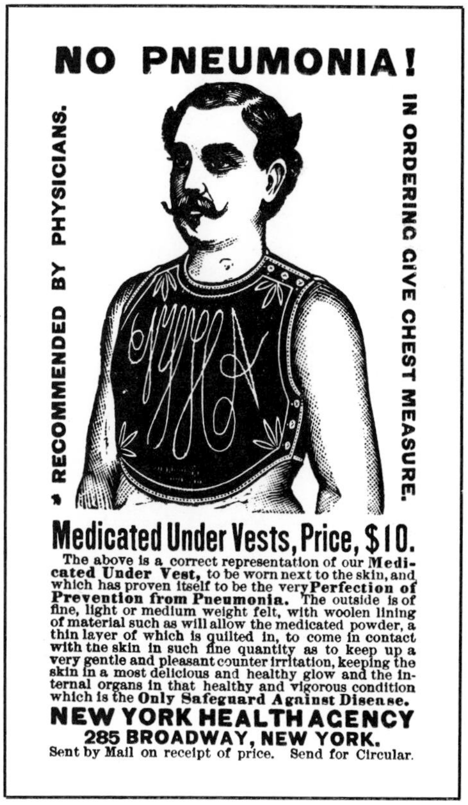

Regulation of False and Deceptive Advertising

False claims about products, when made in advertisements, destroy public faith in all advertising. So do statements which, although not technically false, mislead buyers. Thus, the area of false and misleading advertising is highly important to any discussion of advertising regulation, and it is important to be familiar with the types of legislation that have been enacted to control this abuse of the privilege of advertising one's wares to the public. Two legislative bodies regulate advertising: the federal and state governments.

Figure 20.2 Even under regulation, modern-day advertising can be untruthful. This firm's advertising and personal selling methods were found to be deceptive and unfair competition by the Federal Trade Commission. [FTC Docket 8690.]

Federal Trade Commission Act The Sherman Act was passed by Congress in 1890 and amended by the Clayton Act in 1914. These two acts were designed to cover more effectively such business behavior as price discrimination, exclusive dealing and tie-ins, acquisition of stock, and interlocking directorates. It was felt that those practices led to monopoly and should be attacked at their roots. Another bill passed in 1914, the Federal Trade Commission Act, provided for additional control of business activity.[2]

The Federal Trade Commission Act created the Federal Trade Commission and defined its powers and duties. In time the FTC was to become the "policeman of advertising." Its power evolved from the provisions contained in Section 5 of the act:

> Be it enacted . . . that unfair methods of competition in commerce are hereby declared unlawful.
>
> The Commission is hereby empowered and directed to prevent persons, partnerships, or corporations, except banks and common carriers subject to the Acts to regulate commerce, from using unfair methods of competition in commerce.

This section continues with a detailed description of the cease-and-desist-order procedure to be followed by the FTC and the recourse to judicial action available to the commission and to the defendants in a particular case.

Uncertainty about whether false advertising could be treated as an unfair method of competition existed for many years. This point was apparently settled by a Supreme Court decision in 1922.[3] The power of the commission over the content of advertisements, however, was still considered to be somewhat weak. Strengthening legislation was passed later.

Wheeler-Lea Act Congress passed the Wheeler-Lea Act in 1938, substantially amending the Federal Trade Commission Act.[4] Among other things, the important Section 5 was rewritten to read:

> (a) Unfair methods of competition in commerce, and unfair or deceptive acts or practices in commerce, are hereby declared to be unlawful.

"Has this truth in advertising hurt your business any?"

Figure 20.3 The truth-in-advertising issue is humorously treated by a cartoonist. The cartoon appeared in a weekly newspaper serving the advertising business. [*Reprinted from* Advertising Age *by special permission.*]

With the addition of the phrase "unfair or deceptive acts or practices," it was no longer necessary for the FTC to show that competition had been injured in a case under scrutiny. If the act was unfair or deceptive, a prima facie action was established against the defendant.

Congress also placed a specific responsibility upon the shoulders of the Federal Trade Commission to guard against the false advertising of food, drugs, and cosmetics. While the Food and Drug Administration (FDA) retained control over the contents and labeling of products in these categories, the FTC became active in controlling advertising of them. As a matter of fact, the work of the commission in the advertising-regulation area has tended to concentrate on the advertising of food, drug, and cosmetic products mentioned specifically in the 1938 amendment.

Section 15 of the Wheeler-Lea Act defined false advertising in these words:

The term "false advertisement" means an advertisement, other than labeling, which is misleading in a material respect; and in determining whether any advertisement is misleading, there shall be taken into account (among other things) not only representations made or suggested by statement, word, design, device, sound, or any combination thereof, but also the extent to which the advertisement fails to reveal facts material in the light of such representations or material with respect to consequences which may result from the use of the commodity to which the advertisement relates under the conditions prescribed in said advertisement, or under such conditions as are customary or usual.

Magnuson-Moss Warranty-Federal Trade Commission Improvement Act This act, passed by Congress early in 1975, contains two parts or "titles."[5] The first deals with consumer product warranties and reflects consumer pressure for clearer warranties. Its provisions are, of course, vitally important to any marketer whose total product package includes a warranty. Our interest, however, is in the second part of the act, which is headed "Title II—Federal Trade Commission Improvements."

Section 201 broadened the jurisdiction of the FTC by providing that Section 5 of the Federal Trade Commission Act be amended by striking out "in commerce" and substituting the phrase "in or affecting commerce." Furthermore, the administrative body's rule-making authority was extended by the insertion of a new section:

Sect. 18. (a) (1) The Commission may prescribe—(A) interpretive rules and general statements of policy with respect to unfair or deceptive acts or practices in or affecting commerce. . . . and (B) rules which define with specificity acts or practices which are unfair or deceptive acts or practices in or affecting commerce. . . . Rules under this subparagraph may include requirements prescribed for the purpose of preventing such acts or practices.

The act continues with detailed provisions dealing with hearing procedures, rules of evidence, judicial review, and so forth.

Soon after these changes were enacted by Congress, the Carter administration appointed new FTC members, and the commission became active in using these rule-making powers. Advertisers of both food and over-the-counter drug products did not adapt easily to the proposed restrictions on their advertising efforts. In addition, other industry leaders from various businesses objected to the expansion of FTC's powers. The commission seemed to overstep its bounds in the area of television advertising to children, risking its very existence over the controversial issue. In a Trade Regulation Rule (TRR) proposed by the FTC in February 1978, three regulations were set down:

(1) All advertising to children under eight years of age is banned.
(2) All advertising of sugared products, likely to cause tooth decay in children under twelve years of age, is also banned.
(3) Dental health and nutritional advertisements, paid for by the food industry, are required.

These regulations were felt by many business people to be excessively broad in their restrictions on the advertising of legal products. The regulations were presented without documented proof on the ill effects of television advertising on children. This action by the FTC served as a rallying point for many groups who were dissatisfied with the governmental agency for whatever reason, and a lobbying effort against the FTC was launched. Passage of the FTC Improvement Act of 1980 was the end result.

The FTC Improvement Act of 1980[6] From 1978 to 1980, Congress refused to approve a formal budget for the Federal Trade Commission, using limitation of funds to control FTC actions and believing that approving funds for the agency would be viewed as favoring the commission's recent regulations. The arrangement became difficult for both Congress and the FTC, however, because the other work of the commission was stopped or delayed by these budgetary restrictions. Finally, Congress passed a new improvement act in 1980 and authorized a budget through 1982. In doing so, Congress established procedures by which it could review actions taken by the FTC. Congress also clarified the procedure by which the FTC could impose rules and regulations.

The most meaningful change brought about by the Improvement Act of 1980 was the removal of the agency's use of unfairness as a criterion for industrywide trade rules against advertising. A record of deception must now be present when such rules are being written. The issue of whether advertising to children is unfair (and therefore not to be allowed) was not resolved because the act was to be in effect only through 1982. Whether power granted to the FTC will be increased or diminished in future years is a political question that all persons engaged in advertising will want to monitor.

Regulation of the Use of Advertising Allowances

Clayton Act When the Clayton Act[7] was passed by Congress in 1914, its goal was to strengthen the Sherman Act in a number of ways. The most significant way, to us, was control of the practice of price discrimination among competitive buyers, particularly retailers. Price discrimination was an important means of bringing about the establishment of monopolies. Thus Section 2 of the Clayton Act provided that "it shall be unlawful . . . to discriminate in price between different purchasers . . . where the effect of such discrimination may be to substantially lessen competition or to tend to create a monopoly." Provisions were made for price variation when products of different quality, grade, or quantity were sold; and a differential in price was permitted when the costs of selling or transportation varied among competing buyers.

Many ways were found to circumvent the Clayton Act. The advertising allowance was one loophole. Some favored middlemen were given an allowance for promotion of the manufacturer's products; others were not. While many buyers may have actually used these funds for this purpose, some took the allowance as a form of price discrimination or discount. During the 1930s there was considerable feeling in our country against the chain store as a business institution. People felt chains, because of their bigness, were driving small independent merchants out of business. An appeal was made to Congress, and the Robinson-Patman Act was passed in 1936.[8]

Robinson-Patman Act Essentially designed to put teeth into the price-discrimination provisions of the Clayton Act, the Robinson-Patman Act strengthened the wording of Section 2 of the parent act so that the manufacturer must treat all retailers equally when giving advertising allowances. The manufacturer can elect to grant such allowances; but once granted, every competing reseller must be afforded the privilege on "proportionate terms." A 1968 case held that a supplier is required to make available on proportionally equal terms promotional allowances to retailers who buy from wholesalers and who compete with a favored direct-buying retailer.[9] These provisions of the Robinson-Patman Act have had considerable influence on the use of such devices as manufacturers' cooperative advertising programs and in-store display allowances. Some of the economies of scale of large buyers have been taken away by the act. Certainly some sellers have avoided the use of advertising allowances because of the problems that can result when they are used.

Legal Protection of Trademarks

The use of trademarks is tied in closely with a firm's advertising. An advertisement usually contains a reproduction of the featured product's trademark, for the trademark is one means of assuring buyers that they are getting the specific product they want. Their desire for the product may well have been stimulated by exposure to advertisements. While the intricacies of trademark law cannot be explained in a few paragraphs, this treatment will provide you with an understanding of the rudiments of legislation designed to protect trademarks.

Lanham Act For nearly a century, the only protection of trademarks in the United States was to be found in the common law. In 1881 and in 1905, Congress passed laws setting forth more specifically the rights of persons who possess certain trademarks. In 1946, Congress again examined this area and decided that new legislation was needed. The Trademark Law of 1946, commonly known as the Lanham Act, was enacted.[10]

Basically, the Lanham Act set up registration procedures to be followed by persons and business firms wishing to protect their trademarks. Two registers, the Principal Register and the Supplemental Register, were established. If a trademark qualified for placement on one of the registers, its owner was entitled to certain rights, and legal recourse was provided in case these rights were violated by other parties.

Other sections of the Lanham Act permit the registration of service, collective, and certification marks in the same manner as trademarks. Section 45 defines these terms in the following way:

Trade-mark. The term "trade-mark" includes any word, name, symbol, or device or any combination thereof adopted and used by a manufacturer or merchant to identify his goods and distinguish them from those manufactured or sold by others.

Service mark. The term "service mark" means a mark used in the sale or advertising of services to identify the services of one person and distinguish them from the services of others and includes without limitation the marks, names, symbols, titles, designations, slogans, character names, and distinctive features of radio or other advertising used in commerce.

Certification mark. The term "certification mark" means a mark used upon or in connection with the products or services of one or more persons other than the owner of the mark to certify regional or other origin, material, mode of manufacture, quality, accuracy or other characteristics of such goods or services or that the work or labor on the goods or services was performed by members of a union or other organization.

Collective mark. The term "collective mark" means a trademark or service mark used by the members of a cooperative, an association or other collective group or organization and includes marks used to indicate membership in a union, an association or other organization.

The marks used by laundries, dry cleaners, restaurants, hotels, and other service establishments are examples of service marks. Certification marks are used by Underwriters' Laboratories, *Parent's Magazine,* American Dental Association, and other organizations that rate, recommend, or approve products. The "Sunkist" mark used by the Sunkist Growers, Inc., is an example of a collective mark.

There are two main advantages in registration on the Principal Register. First, such registration gives "constructive notice" of the registrant's claim of ownership. Other parties cannot start using the mark after the date of registration, even if done in good faith or without knowledge of the registrant's use of the mark. Second, after five years on the Principal Register, a mark may become incontestable, and the registrant then has exclusive right to its use even though another party may have used the mark prior to its registration by the registrant.

Detailed statements of remedies for infringements are contained in other sections of the act, which contains a total of 50 sections.

Legislation Respecting the Content and Dissemination of Advertising Messages

Advertising copy is governed by the laws of defamation, libel, and slander. No untrue statements may be made about anyone, nor may a person be held up to contempt. Moreover, the use of an individual's name, picture, or statement without his or her consent is an invasion of the right of privacy and ground for action for damages. As a result, careful procedure to obtain legal releases from persons pictured or mentioned in an advertisement is standard practice. But if the advertisement exposes the person to ridicule or contempt, or is otherwise defamatory, the publisher, the advertiser, and the agency are all liable even though standard releases have been obtained.

Various governmental bodies are also interested in the content of advertisements. Fraudulent advertising, as well as obscene materials, is denied the use of the mails by the U.S. Postal Service. This agency is also concerned, along with various state governments, with the control of lotteries. The lottery laws of the different states vary greatly in content and interpretation. Basically, a lottery exists if a prize, some form of consideration, and chance are present. Advertisements promoting lotteries may be ruled illegal. The Securities and Exchange Commission controls misrepresentation in the offering of securities to the public. The Federal Communications Commission works closely with the Federal Trade Commission to control false or misleading advertising that reaches the public through radio or television.

Congress enacted in 1965 legislation prohibiting the placement of billboards and other signs within 660 feet of the Interstate Highway System and the Primary Road System. The Public Health Cigarette Smoking Act was passed by Congress in 1970.[11] Probably the most far-reaching legislation affecting advertising, the law restricts the advertising of cigarettes. All advertising for cigarettes was banned from the broadcast media, effective January 2, 1971, and after July 1, 1971, the FTC was given authority to require cigarette advertising in print media to contain health warnings similar to those that were required to be placed on packages containing cigarettes.

Interpretation of Laws Regulating Advertising

The mandate given to the Federal Trade Commission is a broad one: to ensure fairness within the economic system. One area under the FTC's jurisdiction is the structure of different industries and the effect of that structure on competition. The second which is our interest here is upon marketing practices involving consumers. This activity is sometimes called "consumer protection."

In discharging its obligations, the FTC has experimented with many different approaches to regulation. Probably the most significant ones taken in the 1970s were advertising substantiation and corrective advertising. Every student and practitioner of advertising needs to understand these two concepts, which are discussed along with several other approaches developed by the commission.

Advertising Substantiation

Since 1971, the Federal Trade Commission has maintained a policy of **advertising substantiation.** If requested by the FTC, an advertiser must supply documentation supporting any and all claims made in the firm's advertisements. The advertiser also must show that the documentation was used when preparing the advertisement. In other words, it is not sufficient that the claims made are truthful; the advertiser must have had proof of these claims before creating the advertising message. The reason for the advertising substantiation program is that the advertiser, knowing that the FTC may require proof for any claims, is not likely to make unfounded claims.[12]

The FTC's policy of advertising substantiation has raised many questions about the type of proof statements that are needed as a basis for an advertisement. Often technical questions arise about the type of research methods used. The FTC will scrutinize test results based on the types of testing procedures commonly used for a product category, and it will try to determine the extent to which consumers are likely to evaluate an advertising claim when purchasing the product. The commission relies heavily on advertising substantiation when determining the truthfulness of an ad or a campaign, and this policy has certainly affected the creation of advertising. The result among advertisers is a much more cautious, legalistic approach to advertising creativity. One lawyer who serves the advertising community summarizes the situation in this pithy remark:

> It's clear then, before you make a claim, assemble your objective data, prepare a report relating it to the ad claim, and you're on the air.[13]

Corrective Advertising

Corrective advertising is advertising run by an advertiser to remove misimpressions resulting from earlier ads produced by that advertiser. The rationale for corrective advertising is that the ads will:

1 Dispel the "residual effects" of such deceptive advertising
2 Restore competition to the stage that prevailed before the unfair practice
3 Deprive firms of falsely obtained gains to which advertising may have contributed

The first case we discuss to illustrate corrective advertising is Profile bread. The brand was advertised as having fewer calories than competitive brands. The FTC claimed that the advertising was false because Profile bread had the same number of calories as any bread and was not useful to people who wished to limit their caloric intake. The bread company agreed to an order (called a "consent decree") that required it to devote at least 25 percent of each advertisement published in 1972 to a clear disclosure of the dietetic properties of Profile. The corrective advertisement stated that Profile slices were cut thinner than other breads, which was the only reason they contained fewer calories.

Another major case arose in late 1975 when the Warner-Lambert Company was claiming that its brand of mouthwash, Listerine, prevented colds and sore throats or lessened their severity. The FTC charged that this assertion was untrue and required that corrective advertisements be aired to dispel the deception. The new commercials, which cost the advertiser $10.2 million, were to state that "Contrary to prior advertising, Listerine will not prevent colds or sore throats or lessen their severity." Warner-Lambert tested the right of the FTC to order it to spend its own money in a manner that would be detrimental to the promotion of its product. The company lost the case, but the presiding judge permitted the removal of the phrase "Contrary to prior advertising," thus making Warner-Lambert's action appear to be voluntary.

In 1980, the FTC decided against the issuance of a trade regulation rule "that would have required *automatic* corrective advertising whenever an ad campaign of a year's duration on health, safety, or nutritional products was found to be misleading."[14] Each case would be reviewed individually to determine whether corrective advertising was needed.

Another interesting use of corrective advertising involved the Ford Motor Company. The FTC claimed that Ford failed to inform all Ford buyers that the company would make certain repairs without charge after the normal warranty period. Ford agreed to a $4 million media plan for ads conveying the information about its new repair-service program. In an agreement with the FTC, Ford would run ads over an eight-year period commencing in 1981. The agreement was unique in prescribing the media plan for the corrective advertising being undertaken: Five insertions of the ad ran in *Newsweek, People, Sports Illustrated, Time,* and *U.S. News & World Report,* three insertions in each magazine during the second year, and at least one insertion in each annually during the six remaining years of the agreement.[15]

Affirmative and Full Disclosure of Information

Based upon the premise that consumers should have sufficient information to make valid comparisions between purchasing alternatives, laws have been passed and regulatory commission rulings issued to require that specific kinds of information be provided to them. The Food and Drug Administration (FDA), for instance, set up a program in 1975 requiring that the labels on packages of processed food list the nutritional value of the contents. The Federal Trade Commission also was considering at the time requiring that nutritional information appear in all food advertising. Advertisers have resisted this potential rule, largely because they think that the impact of advertisements such as 30-second television commercials would be lost if they became a mere recitation of nutritional facts about the featured product.

Affirmative disclosure is a concept that would require advertisers to tell not only the positive story about their products, but also to describe any important negative features. Thus, in addition to any full disclosure of information about the product that might be required, advertisers would have to tell about product deficiencies and limitations. The mak-

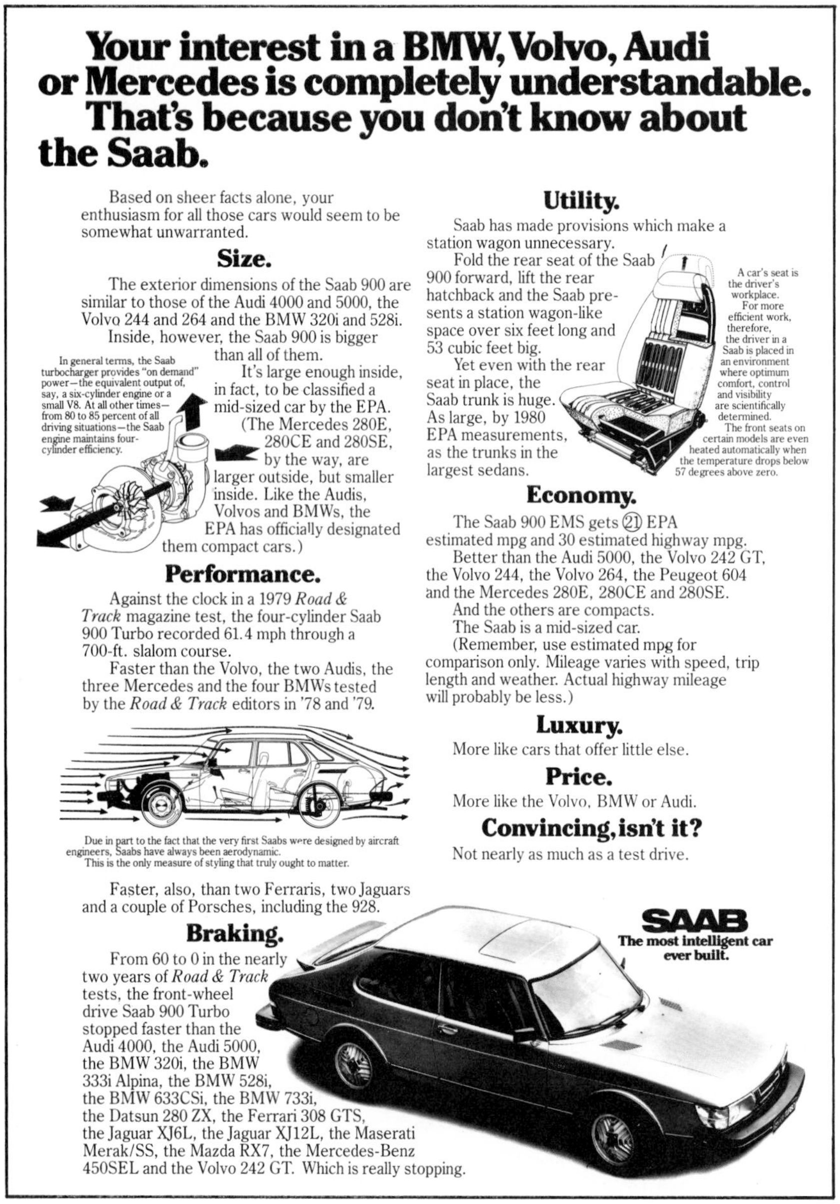
Your interest in a BMW, Volvo, Audi or Mercedes is completely understandable. That's because you don't know about the Saab.
Based on sheer facts alone, your enthusiasm for all those cars would seem to be somewhat unwarranted.
Size.
The exterior dimensions of the Saab 900 are similar to those of the Audi 4000 and 5000, the Volvo 244 and 264 and the BMW 320i and 528i.
Inside, however, the Saab 900 is bigger than all of them.
It's large enough inside, in fact, to be classified a mid-sized car by the EPA.
(The Mercedes 280E, 280CE and 280SE, by the way, are larger outside, but smaller inside. Like the Audis, Volvos and BMWs, the EPA has officially designated them compact cars.)
In general terms, the Saab turbocharger provides "on demand" power—the equivalent output of, say, a six-cylinder engine or a small V8. At all other times—from 80 to 85 percent of all driving situations—the Saab engine maintains four-cylinder efficiency.
Performance.
Against the clock in a 1979 *Road & Track* magazine test, the four-cylinder Saab 900 Turbo recorded 61.4 mph through a 700-ft. slalom course.
Faster than the Volvo, the two Audis, the three Mercedes and the four BMWs tested by the *Road & Track* editors in '78 and '79.
Due in part to the fact that the very first Saabs were designed by aircraft engineers, Saabs have always been aerodynamic.
This is the only measure of styling that truly ought to matter.
Faster, also, than two Ferraris, two Jaguars and a couple of Porsches, including the 928.
Braking.
From 60 to 0 in the nearly two years of *Road & Track* tests, the front-wheel drive Saab 900 Turbo stopped faster than the Audi 4000, the Audi 5000, the BMW 320i, the BMW 333i Alpina, the BMW 528i, the BMW 633CSi, the BMW 733i, the Datsun 280 ZX, the Ferrari 308 GTS, the Jaguar XJ6L, the Jaguar XJ12L, the Maserati Merak/SS, the Mazda RX7, the Mercedes-Benz 450SEL and the Volvo 242 GT. Which is really stopping.
Utility.
Saab has made provisions which make a station wagon unnecessary.
Fold the rear seat of the Saab 900 forward, lift the rear hatchback and the Saab presents a station wagon-like space over six feet long and 53 cubic feet big.
Yet even with the rear seat in place, the Saab trunk is huge. As large, by 1980 EPA measurements, as the trunks in the largest sedans.
A car's seat is the driver's workplace.
For more efficient work, therefore, the driver in a Saab is placed in an environment where optimum comfort, control and visibility are scientifically determined.
The front seats on certain models are even heated automatically when the temperature drops below 57 degrees above zero.
Economy.
The Saab 900 EMS gets (21) EPA estimated mpg and 30 estimated highway mpg.
Better than the Audi 5000, the Volvo 242 GT, the Volvo 244, the Volvo 264, the Peugeot 604 and the Mercedes 280E, 280CE and 280SE.
And the others are compacts.
The Saab is a mid-sized car.
(Remember, use estimated mpg for comparison only. Mileage varies with speed, trip length and weather. Actual highway mileage will probably be less.)
Luxury.
More like cars that offer little else.
Price.
More like the Volvo, BMW or Audi.
Convincing, isn't it?
Not nearly as much as a test drive.
SAAB
The most intelligent car ever built.

Figure 20.4 Car advertisers are frequent users of the comparative advertising technique. Here the SAAB automobile is compared directly with four other imports. [*Courtesy of Saab-Scania of America.*]

ers of Geritol, for instance, have been required to disclose in their ads that the "great majority of people who experience symptoms of tiredness do not experience them because of vitamin deficiency." And in a more specific example, a consent order for Forever Young, a chemical designed for use in the removal of wrinkles and skin blemishes, prescribes that at least 15 percent of all advertising for the product must disclose the dangers inherent in the use of the product.

These issues were not actively pursued at the beginning of the 1980s. The FTC was busy with the question of unfairness in advertising. It is always possible that a program advocating disclosure will become a priority for the FTC in the future.

Comparative Advertising

One advertising technique that became popular in the 1970s was **comparative advertising** (also known as **comparison advertising**). Comparative advertising:

1 Compares two or more specifically named or recognizably presented brands of the same generic product or service class
2 Makes such a comparison in terms of one or more specific product or service attributes.

Examples include the classic Plymouth advertising of the 1930s, when the relatively unknown brand of automobile asked consumers to "Look at All Three," and the Avis campaign of the 1960s, in which a comparison was made to Hertz—because Avis was number two in the rent-a-car business, the claim that its employees "tried harder" was given as a reason for doing business with the firm.[16] In the 1970s Datril, an over-the-counter headache relief medicine, made direct comparisons with Tylenol, which was dominant in the product category at the time; here the message was that the competitive product was just as effective, yet was being sold at much lower prices.

In the battle for leadership in the soft-drink market, Pepsi-Cola compared its cola drink to Coca-Cola in its "Pepsi Challenge" commercials. Pepsi ran taste tests in selected markets, then advertised the findings that in blindfold tests, consumers—even those who stated a preference for "Coke"—preferred Pepsi over Coca-Cola. Coca-Cola was faced with a decision on how to answer this comparative advertising. After several false starts using differing approaches to the challenge by the number two competitor, the company apparently adopted the strategy of ignoring Pepsi insofar as the comparative ads were concerned. Coca-Cola's position was that such advertising tends to destroy consumer confidence in all the brands involved. Advertising strategists in the soft-drink field differ on whether the comparative advertising technique is effective in the long run.

Use of comparative advertising is encouraged by the FTC and consumer groups because they feel that such messages provide consumers with needed additional information upon which to base purchasing decisions. When advertisers use comparative advertising, they must be sure the message does not disparage competitors or the product. If the ad is libelous, the competitor can sue the advertiser for damages. There is no conclusive evidence to show that comparative advertising is effective in persuading consumers to the advertiser's point of view. One major advertising agency, Ogilvy & Mather, has studied the technique in detail and recommends against its use by clients:

> Our study of television commercials that name names suggests that there is little to be gained from this type of advertising for the advertising industry, the advertiser, or the consumer. The only one who may benefit is the competitor who is named in the advertising. It must be remembered, however, that these findings may be limited to 30-second television commercials for packaged goods. Different effects may be found for other media, such as print.[17]

Thus, more research is needed. In the meantime, the Federal Trade Commission, in a policy statement issued in August 1979, continued to encourage the use of comparative ads by stating that "brand comparisons, when done clearly and accurately, serve as sources of information in assisting consumers in their purchasing decisions," and furthermore, that "brand comparisons encourage product improvement, innovation, and lower prices."[18] Although the results of comparative advertising are controversial, this technique is likely to be used in the future because of its popularity with some advertisers, consumers, and regulatory agencies.

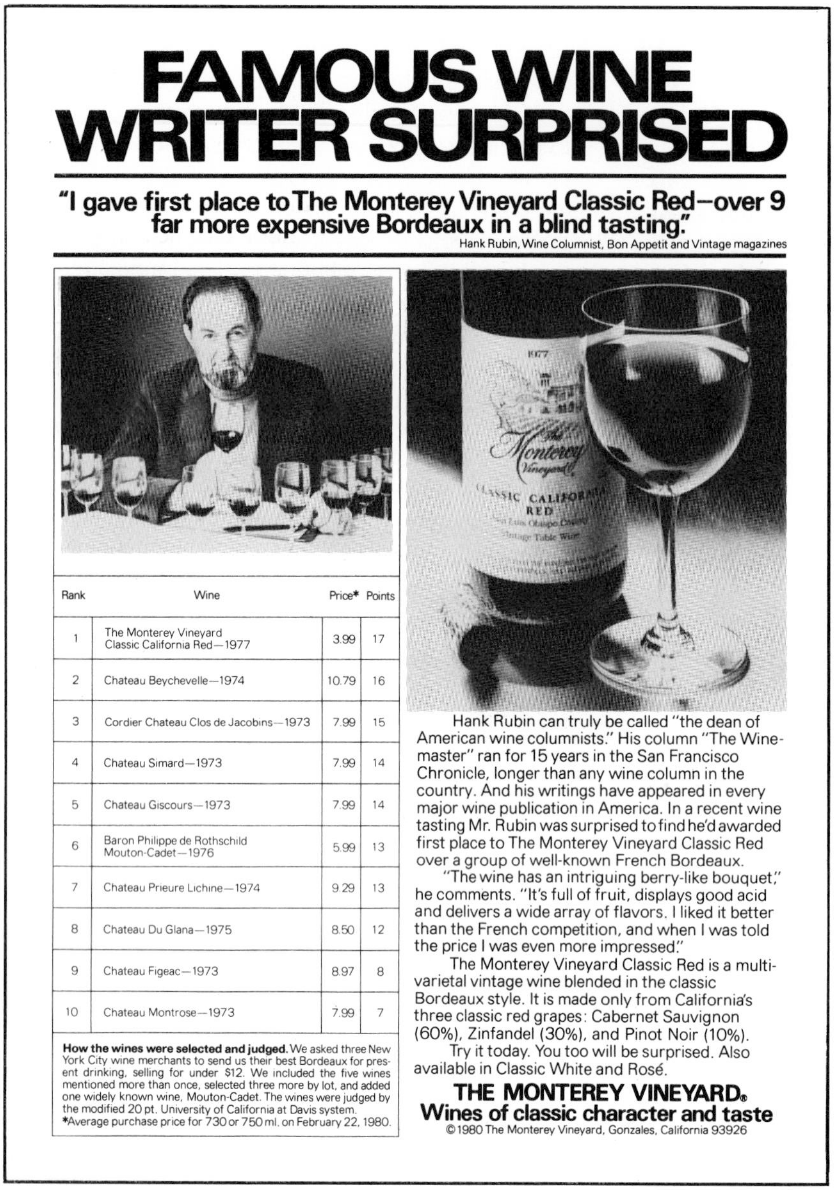
FAMOUS WINE WRITER SURPRISED
"I gave first place to The Monterey Vineyard Classic Red—over 9 far more expensive Bordeaux in a blind tasting."
Hank Rubin, Wine Columnist, Bon Appetit and Vintage magazines

Rank	Wine	Price*	Points
1	The Monterey Vineyard Classic California Red—1977	3.99	17
2	Chateau Beychevelle—1974	10.79	16
3	Cordier Chateau Clos de Jacobins—1973	7.99	15
4	Chateau Simard—1973	7.99	14
5	Chateau Giscours—1973	7.99	14
6	Baron Philippe de Rothschild Mouton-Cadet—1976	5.99	13
7	Chateau Prieure Lichine—1974	9.29	13
8	Chateau Du Glana—1975	8.50	12
9	Chateau Figeac—1973	8.97	8
10	Chateau Montrose—1973	7.99	7

How the wines were selected and judged. We asked three New York City wine merchants to send us their best Bordeaux for present drinking, selling for under $12. We included the five wines mentioned more than once, selected three more by lot, and added one widely known wine, Mouton-Cadet. The wines were judged by the modified 20 pt. University of California at Davis system.
*Average purchase price for 730 or 750 ml. on February 22, 1980.
Hank Rubin can truly be called "the dean of American wine columnists." His column "The Winemaster" ran for 15 years in the San Francisco Chronicle, longer than any wine column in the country. And his writings have appeared in every major wine publication in America. In a recent wine tasting Mr. Rubin was surprised to find he'd awarded first place to The Monterey Vineyard Classic Red over a group of well-known French Bordeaux.
"The wine has an intriguing berry-like bouquet," he comments. "It's full of fruit, displays good acid and delivers a wide array of flavors. I liked it better than the French competition, and when I was told the price I was even more impressed."
The Monterey Vineyard Classic Red is a multi-varietal vintage wine blended in the classic Bordeaux style. It is made only from California's three classic red grapes: Cabernet Sauvignon (60%), Zinfandel (30%), and Pinot Noir (10%).
Try it today. You too will be surprised. Also available in Classic White and Rosé.
THE MONTEREY VINEYARD®
Wines of classic character and taste
©1980 The Monterey Vineyard, Gonzales, California 93926

Figure 20.5 When the Coca-Cola Company entered the wine industry, packaged-goods marketing techniques were introduced to the product category for the first time. One technique employed was comparative advertising, as this magazine advertisement shows. [*Courtesy of* The Wine Spectrum.]

Endorsements and Testimonials

Since the late nineteenth century, advertisers have used endorsements, or testimonials (the terms are interchangeable), as integral parts of their advertisements. Consumers are persuaded to purchase the product because some well-known personality placed his or her stamp of approval on it. The principles of **emulation, association,** and **reassurance** are employed. Sometimes endorsements are abused, and consumers are misled. If claims are untrue, consumers may lose faith in the credibility of testimonial advertising. The FTC issued in 1975 a set of guidelines covering the use of endorsements in advertisements. Revised in 1980, the guidelines contain three key provisions.

1 Endorsers must actually use the product, if the ads state that they do, and advertisers must have "good reason to believe" the endorser continues to use the product so long as the endorsement is used.

2 When consumer endorsements are used, advertisers must either be able to show that the

average person can expect comparable performance, "clearly and conspicuously" disclose what performance generally can be expected, or disclose that the endorsement has limited applicability.

3 Consumers' endorsements of drugs must be consistent with any determinations about the drug made by the Food and Drugs Administration.[19]

The guides do not have the force of law but do advise the advertising industry on how the commission will interpret the law. Under these new guidelines, endorsers need not be celebrities or experts but may be ordinary citizens.

Bait-and-Switch Advertising

This type of consumer deception is not new; however, the FTC has recently shown increased interest in the sharp practice. As is humorously shown in the accompanying cartoon (Figure 20.6), the retailer advertises an enticingly low price for a consumer item; when the consumer goes to the store, he or she hears that (1) the item is not in stock, or (2) it is inferior in quality. The salesperson then attempts to switch the prospect's interest in another (higher-priced) model.

One of the nation's largest retailers brought consumers to its outlets with an advertisement featuring an attractive sewing machine at an unusually low price. According to an FTC complaint issued in 1974, salespeople downgraded the item with statements including: "(1) The advertised sewing machines are noisy, and are not guaranteed for as long a period of time as the firm's more expensive models; (2) certain of them will not sew straight stitch, zig zag stitch, or in reverse; (3) none of the advertised sewing machines is available for sale and, if ordered, there will be long delays in delivery."[20] It was further alleged that rates of compensation of salespersons were greater when higher-priced models were sold.

The FTC is not, of course, the only regulatory body interested in bait-and-switch advertising abuses. When, for instance, in 1980 the manufacturer of a Japanese-built automobile offered Toyota Corolla Tercels for $3,698, the consumer protection officials in several southeastern states got involved. When consumers came to showrooms to purchase the advertised automobile, they found that the cars were available only on special order. Instead of the advertised auto, the salesperson offered these potential buyers Tercels equipped with an "optional protection package" which cost $650 more.[21] The ad-

Figure 20.6 Several years ago a cartoonist spoofed the bait-and-switch advertising technique. Although prices have gone up since the cartoon first appeared in the nation's newspapers, the practice, unfortunately, is still employed by some retailers. [*King Features Syndicate, Inc.*]

vertiser was persuaded to withdraw the controversial commercials after being contacted by state officials.

The Role of FTC Rules and Guides

The Federal Trade Commission has the power to enforce the statutes it administers. To facilitate this process, the FTC informs and guides business people about the requirements of such statutes. It aids sellers and advertisers by issuing two kinds of documents: *Industry Guides* and *Trade Regulation Rules.*

Industry Guides are designed to clarify regulations affecting single-industry problems, such as cigarette advertising, tire advertising, and shoe labeling. Other guides discuss practices that cut across industry lines —deceptive pricing and bait advertising are examples. These guides are essentially statements on how the FTC would interpret the law should an actual case arise. They alert the industries involved and help educate consumers and protect them from being victimized by improper sales practices.

Trade Regulation Rules (TRR) present the conclusions of the commission about the legality of certain business practices. A given rule may apply nationally, or it may be limited to certain markets or geographic areas. The rules have the full force and effect of law; violation of a TRR is equivalent to violation of the FTC Act. Industry cooperation is sought when the guides and rules are being written. They are designed to remove uncertainty in situations where matters are not perfectly clear. The advertising of pet food, claims of broadcast audience ratings, the granting of advertising allowances, premium offers to children, and the use of endorsements in advertising are examples of this kind of FTC consideration.

Enforcement of Laws Affecting Advertising: Some Important Cases

Many legal cases have become landmarks in the development of advertising law. Obviously, in an introductory survey we cannot discuss all of them. Instead we will mention briefly several important cases so that you may better understand the complexity of advertising legislation, its interpretation, and its enforcement. Some cases involve court decisions; others are concerned with rulings by the Federal Trade Commission and may be tested in the courts when challenged by advertisers.

The "Mock-up" Cases

As television became the dominant advertising medium for many products, the need for firm ground rules on the use of demonstrations in commercials became apparent. Television demonstrations were attacked in the early 1960s on two points: (1) nonexistence of a claimed superiority, and (2) failure of the demonstration to prove what it purported to prove. A new legal concept was involved in the second case.

The so-called White Jacket case appeared before the 1960s. Actors wearing medical clothing were used to present medical and dental products; these commercials were ruled misleading because the viewer might believe that medical doctors and dentists were in fact urging use of the advertised product. Commercials claiming to show the ability of one brand of aluminum foil to preserve food better than competitive brands, an auto wax's resistance to heat and cold, a cigarette filter's ability to absorb tar and nicotine, the moisture content of margarine, and the comparative safety of a razor came under FTC scrutiny and were ordered stopped.

In these early cases, the advertisers consented to stop the demonstrations; therefore, court decisions were not needed to test the legality of the FTC's decisions. It wasn't until the "Rapid Shave" case reached the courts that a legal decision on television commercials was made. The commercial in question presented the moisturizing qualities of the advertised shaving cream by apparently removing the sand from sandpaper with one stroke of a safety razor immediately following application of the cream. Sandpaper was not used, however, in the demonstration; instead the commercial showed a simulated mock-up of sand on Plexiglas, which can, of course, be easily shaven clean. The advertiser claimed that the substitution was made because of the technical limitation inherent in the television medium. Although the use of mock-ups in television was not ruled illegal per se, the case established that tests performed on television must be performed as the advertiser states they are. In other words, the undisclosed use and substitution of mock-ups or props in demonstrations showing proof of product claims are an illegal misrepresentation. This case finally reached the Supreme Court in 1965, when the FTC position was upheld.

The Campbell Soup Company Case

In 1970, FTC action against the Campbell Soup Company was resolved by a consent order prohibiting the company from using false advertising to sell soup or any other food product.[22] Campbell had placed marbles at the bottom of a bowl of soup, which was then pictured in television commercials and in magazine advertisements. The marbles raised the solid ingredients to the top, thereby giving the illusion of more meat and vegetables in the soup than were really present. Without the marbles, the soup picture understates the case, for it shows no meat or vegetables. With the marbles, it shows the solid ingredients but implies so many vegetables that they rise above the broth surface. Since meat and vegetables settle to the bottom of a bowl of soup, Campbell contended that there is no way to show these ingredients without some kind of contrived situation. The creative answer was, however, that the contents could be shown being spooned or poured to prove their presence.

A group of law student activists originally pressed this case against Campbell. Heinz, a leading competitor in the soup market, also was interested in the outcome. Consumer leaders objected strenuously to the consent order, as they advocated that Campbell be required to disclose the practice in future advertising in order to overcome and dissipate any residual deception resulting from the company's advertising of soup through the use of marbles. This recommendation was rejected by the FTC majority. The seeds for corrective advertising, however, were planted.

The ITT Continental Baking Company Case

The FTC claimed in 1971 that the advertising for Wonder bread, Hostess snacks, and Profile bread was false, and cease-and-desist orders were issued. The Profile case has already been discussed. The FTC claimed that the advertising for Wonder Bread exploited children's aspirations for rapid and healthy growth by showing the product as an extraordinary food, whereas it was no different from competitive breads. Furthermore, it was claimed that the advertising for both the bread and Hostess snacks tended to exploit parents' concern for children's healthy growth and the nutritional effects of children's snacks. It resisted these claims and the cease-and-desist orders.

An administrative law judge dismissed the proceedings against both products in late 1972. Appeal to the commission led to the dismissal of charges alleging false advertising of Hostess snack cakes. A second cease-and-desist order requiring the company to stop advertising Wonder bread as more nutritious than other foods was issued in 1973.[23] At the many hearings over these matters, exhaustive consumer surveys and expert witness testimony were employed by both sides of the case, which served as an important breakthrough for the use of behavioral science concepts in settling legal matters. In the end, the FTC decided not to use the corrective advertising remedy.

This case had an important impact on advertising agencies as well as on advertisers. It was ruled that since advertising agencies are expert in communication, their executives cannot claim that they did not know that a particular claim was conveyed in an ad. In other words, advertising agencies are just as responsible as advertisers for the dissemination of deceptive claims.

The Dry Ban Case

An administrative law judge found in 1975 that Bristol Myers, the manufacturer of Dry Ban deodorant, and its advertising agency, Ogilvy & Mather, used false demonstrations in television commercials promoting the product. The FTC claimed that false representation was used to show that the product was a dry spray, was not wet when applied to the body, left no residue, and was superior to competing products for these reasons. The commissioners who reviewed the ads found that they represented the product's dryness only as compared to a leading competitive spray; there was no claim in the commercial that Dry Ban was absolutely dry.[24] In other words, it was held that relative rather than absolute claims were made in the commercial. Inasmuch as the FTC case was based upon the doctrine of absolute claim, its position failed for lack of proof.

In its dismissal statement, the FTC noted the circumstances under which such charges would be ruled to be not in the public interest. The presence of the following factors is the key:

> Those persons affected do not constitute a particularly vulnerable group; there are no health or safety considerations that might legitimately demand further expenditure of public funds; there was no significant economic harm to a consumer who purchased the product (Dry Ban) and found it 'less dry' than anticipated; the advertising in question was terminated over four years earlier; there was no indication on the record that competition was adversely affected by whatever deception might be proved; nor was the case dealing with intentional wrongdoers.[25]

These criteria thus provide guidelines of reason when the FTC is contemplating action against an advertiser. When the potential harm to the consumer's physical or economic well-being is trivial, action is not warranted. Resources for prosecution of cases are limited and should be reserved, according to this line of reasoning, for more serious offenses. As the membership of the FTC changes, we may anticipate various degrees of adherence to this philosophy. Pursuit of some blatantly false ads, even though they are trivial in health, safety, or economic dimensions, is likely.

F-310 Additive: Standard Oil Company of California and Batten, Barton, Durstine & Osborn, Inc.[26]

This case, which was begun in 1970 and finally was settled in 1978, highlights two important points: (1) the advertiser, when making an essentially true product claim, must be careful not to be guilty of "fatal overbreadth"—of claiming more than is deliverable; (2) the advertising agency may be held liable for misleading advertising.

In early 1970, Standard Oil broadcast three television commercials featuring its gasoline additive, F-310. The commercials showed transparent balloons attached to exhaust systems of various automobiles. Clear emissions resulted when the additive was used in the vehicle, whereas a black cloud appeared in the balloons attached to vehicles without F-310.

The FTC objected to the commercials because they implied that the use of the product would result in a complete elimination of air pollutants, whereas there was merely an 80 percent reduction of pollution with F-310. Cease-and-desist orders were issued against Standard Oil Co. of California and its advertising agency, BBDO. Upon appeal, the court determined that the commercials misrepresented that the absence of black smoke from the exhaust meant there was no pollutant, for most pollutants are colorless. The agency was shown to have been sufficiently involved in the development of the advertising to be held responsible for the misrepresentation, along with the advertiser.

The Kroger Co. Case[27]

The Kroger Co. operates a chain of 1200 retail food stores. As a promotional tool, the company developed its "Kroger Price Patrol," a group of store shoppers who gathered data on food prices for 150 items in the major food stores in the market area. The results were advertised via television commercials, as a form of comparative advertising, to prove that "Shopping at Kroger will enable you to spend less for your food than at any other store."

Although it has acknowledged that comparative advertising has potential value for consumers, the FTC in this case makes clear that such advertising must be supervised. The regulatory body ruled that the advertisements were unfair and deceptive because they were based on methodologically unsound surveys and failed to disclose that meat products, produce, and house brands were not included in the surveys. The cease-and-desist order issued against the Kroger Co. did not specifically prohibit the continued use of the Price Patrol; instead, it set down requirements that the public be informed of items not included in the survey. Furthermore, comparisons in the future must be of "identical or substantially similar" products. The company soon discontinued this advertising program.

Implications and Conclusions

What implications and conclusions can be drawn from this brief discussion of cases and policies involving the interpretation and enforcement of laws affecting advertising? For one thing, it should be clear that

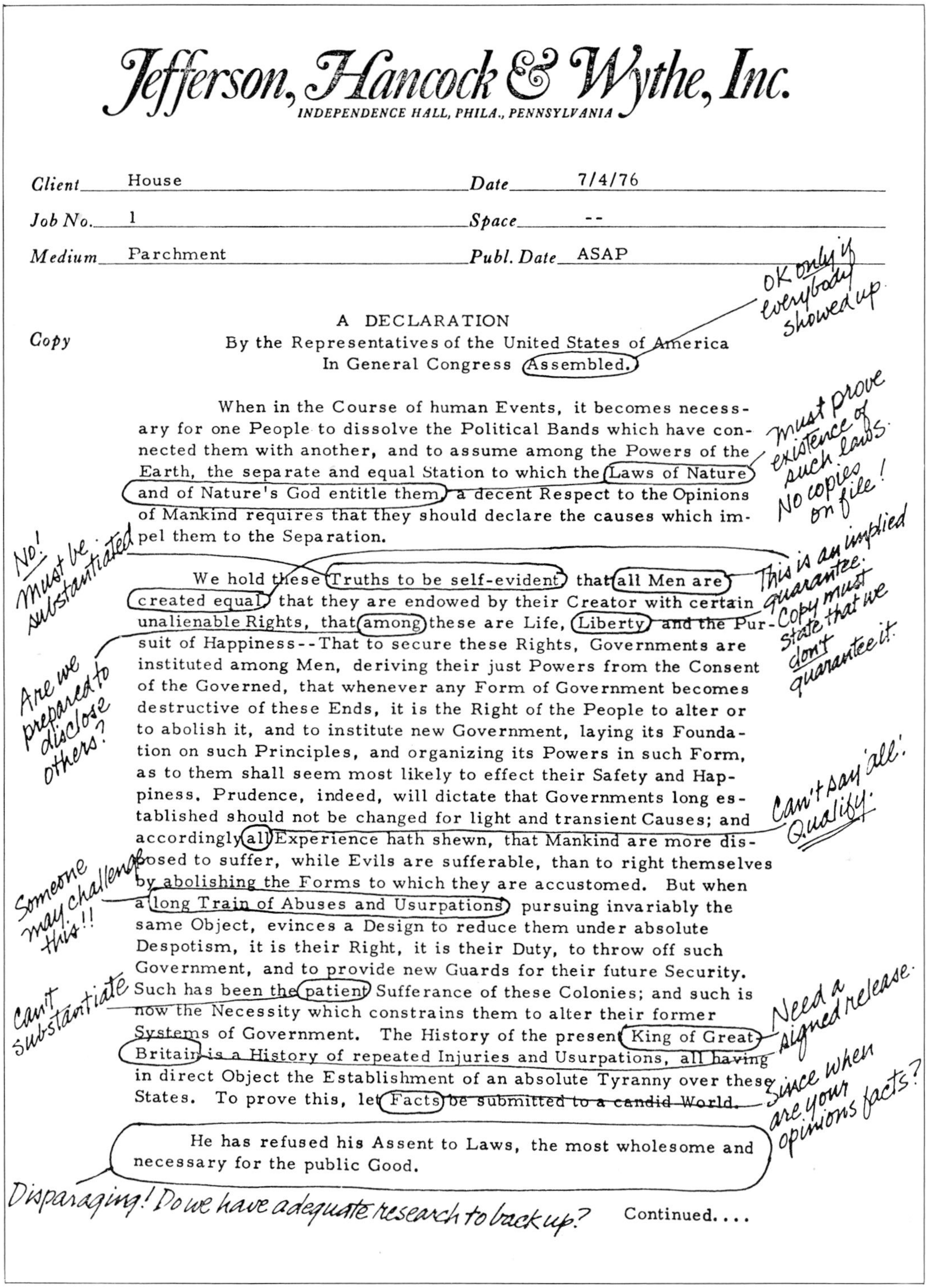

Jefferson, Hancock & Wythe, Inc.
INDEPENDENCE HALL, PHILA., PENNSYLVANIA

Client House *Date* 7/4/76
Job No. 1 *Space* --
Medium Parchment *Publ. Date* ASAP

Copy

A DECLARATION
By the Representatives of the United States of America
In General Congress Assembled.

When in the Course of human Events, it becomes necessary for one People to dissolve the Political Bands which have connected them with another, and to assume among the Powers of the Earth, the separate and equal Station to which the Laws of Nature and of Nature's God entitle them, a decent Respect to the Opinions of Mankind requires that they should declare the causes which impel them to the Separation.

We hold these Truths to be self-evident, that all Men are created equal, that they are endowed by their Creator with certain unalienable Rights, that among these are Life, Liberty and the Pursuit of Happiness--That to secure these Rights, Governments are instituted among Men, deriving their just Powers from the Consent of the Governed, that whenever any Form of Government becomes destructive of these Ends, it is the Right of the People to alter or to abolish it, and to institute new Government, laying its Foundation on such Principles, and organizing its Powers in such Form, as to them shall seem most likely to effect their Safety and Happiness. Prudence, indeed, will dictate that Governments long established should not be changed for light and transient Causes; and accordingly all Experience hath shewn, that Mankind are more disposed to suffer, while Evils are sufferable, than to right themselves by abolishing the Forms to which they are accustomed. But when a long Train of Abuses and Usurpations, pursuing invariably the same Object, evinces a Design to reduce them under absolute Despotism, it is their Right, it is their Duty, to throw off such Government, and to provide new Guards for their future Security. Such has been the patient Sufferance of these Colonies; and such is now the Necessity which constrains them to alter their former Systems of Government. The History of the present King of Great Britain is a History of repeated Injuries and Usurpations, all having in direct Object the Establishment of an absolute Tyranny over these States. To prove this, let Facts be submitted to a candid World.

He has refused his Assent to Laws, the most wholesome and necessary for the public Good.

Continued....

OK only if everybody showed up.
Must prove existence of such laws. No copies on file!
No! must be substantiated
This is an implied guarantee. Copy must state that we don't guarantee it.
Are we prepared to disclose others?
Can't say 'all'. Qualify.
Someone may challenge this!!
Can't substantiate
Need a signed release.
Since when are your opinions facts?
Disparaging! Do we have adequate research to back up?

Figure 20.7 If current rules and regulations facing copywriters had been applied when the Declaration of Independence was being written, here is how its beginning would have appeared. The changes indicated would come from lawyers when they reviewed the copy. [*Edward A. McCabe, Scali, McCabe, Sloves Advertising.*]

the legal restrictions on advertising are becoming more numerous and complex, and consumers are becoming more critical. No decision about advertising strategy can be made safely without weighing its legal consequences. Advertising men and women are frequently heard to say in their day-to-day deliberations, "Let's legal it." Translated, this expression means to check out the matter with an attorney.

Many of these legal restrictions have tended to hamstring the creative side of the advertising business. In an effort to avoid legal pitfalls, messages are often written with extreme caution, for truth always puts some limits on everything, including creativity. Resulting ads tend to be bland compared with ads where creative license with truth is freely taken. How one advertising man believes the Declaration of Independence would have to be written today, if it were to avoid being labeled as deceptive, is shown in Figure 20.7.

At several places in our survey of advertising laws, we have highlighted the need for additional research. Present laws and policies of regulatory bodies are based upon assumptions respecting the effects of advertising messages on consumers; these assumptions may or may not be valid. It would appear that behavioral science concepts and research methodology are of potential value as the theories underlying advertising regulation are being tested. Substantial research is being performed by the advertising industry and academic people to discover the correctness of these assumptions.

There is no doubt that deceptive advertising does exist. What is deceptive is sometimes hard to define, and how to redress its effects on consumers and prevent its reoccurrence are truly troublesome matters. The FTC is a political body whose membership changes with the passage of time and administrations. These changes bring shifts in emphasis and philosophy. There was evidence that the commission was moving in the 1970s from its former role perception as the preventer of false, misleading, or deceptive advertising to one of establishing standards based on its concept of what is good for the consumer. This trend appeared to be stopped when the Reagan administration took office. The advertising practitioner and the student of advertising must, therefore, continually study its actions, and those of other regulatory bodies, closely. The activities of legislative bodies similarly need to be monitored regularly in order to see that new laws affecting advertising are passed only after advertising's point of view has had a hearing. Good laws and good regulation should be welcomed by professionals in the advertising business. The reverse—bad laws and poor regulation—should be resisted.

Advertising and the First Amendment[28]

Recent interpretations of the First Amendment to the United States Constitution have resulted in an emerging body of law affecting the field of advertising. In these reinterpretations, advertising regulators cannot be so strict that the "free flow" of truthful information is stopped.

The First Amendment states that "Congress shall make no laws . . . abridging the freedom of speech, or of the press . . . ." The framers of the Constitution believed that citizens in a democratic society should be free to express their views without censorship by the government.

For a long time, First Amendment protection was not applied to "commercial speech," which included advertising. The Supreme Court held in 1942 that an ordinance prohibiting the distribution of advertising handbills was legal, and that advertising was not an exercise of free speech under the protection of the Constitution.[29] In other words, commercial speech was not deemed worthy of protection.

It was not until 1975 that a significant change occurred. In that year the Supreme Court ruled that an advertisement for an abortion service could be run by a Virginia newspaper whose editor had been charged with a misdemeanor for violating a state statute on the encouragement of abortion.[30] The decision was based on the principle that commercial advertising, when mixed with public interest, may overbalance state interests and gain First Amendment protection.

This small wedge was the start of considerable change during the remainder of the 1970s. Consumer activists in Virginia filed a suit against the Virginia Board of Pharmacy, which had established a rule that advertising the prices of prescription drugs by a licensed pharmacist was unprofessional behavior. The Supreme Court of the United States agreed that such a rule is in violation of the First Amendment, for commercial advertising is entitled to protection.[31] The Supreme Court held that the free flow of commercial information is needed if the free enterprise system is to operate effectively. The Court's rules permitted the advertising of contraceptives, and the advertising of legal services soon followed.

Advertising by Professionals

Codes of ethics for such professional groups as medical doctors and lawyers had prohibited advertising by their members for generations. A formal announcement that an office location had been changed, a new partner added, or a practice established was the only advertising allowed.

This situation has changed. In a case involving the State Bar of Arizona, the Supreme Court has ruled that certain restrictions on advertising by lawyers were in violation of the First Amendment.[32] In that case, lawyers were given the right to advertise prices charged for routine legal services. Now local newspapers throughout the nation carry ads reading "Uncontested Divorces $89" and "Simple Bankruptcy $150." It is quite likely that the content of advertising by legal firms will gradually be broadened to include descriptions of the services that a firm offers and reasons why the featured firm should be patronized. It should be noted, however, that these new rulings are merely permissive; no law firm is forced to advertise and most law firms still refrain from doing so.

Accounting firms, including the top ("Big Eight") CPA organizations, as well as dentists, architects, and other professional groups, are following the lead of lawyers and are using advertising. Recently, the FTC waged an aggressive campaign against a provision in the code of ethics of the American Medical Association (AMA) against advertising by its members. In the summer of 1980 the AMA suddenly dropped the clause from its code. Thus, the First Amendment has become the vehicle for permitting advertising by doctors so that potential patients will be better informed about the services and prices that are available to them.

Self-Regulation of Advertising

Advertising people have long been committed to the idea of self-regulation. The foundation for state laws against deceptive advertising came from an advertising trade publication, *Printer's Ink*, which developed a model statute in 1911; this legislation was passed by state legislatures largely through the lobbying efforts of advertising clubs throughout the nation. We now turn to the non-legislative efforts of the advertising industry in its efforts to keep its own house clean.

Better Business Bureaus

The Better Business Bureau (BBB) idea was first developed by the Advertising Club of Cleveland, Ohio. Today, over 240 of these bureaus operate at both local and national levels to fight illegal advertising and to raise the standards of advertising practice. Advertisers, advertising agencies, and advertising media work together to stamp out deceptive advertising through the BBB approach. Each bureau acts as a watchdog within its community. When a firm is accused of engaging in fraudulent advertising and this is called to the attention of bureau personnel, an investigation is made. If the advertising appears to be deceptive, the advertiser is contacted and the BBB attempts to persuade the advertiser to stop the practice. The bureau has no legal power, although it may work with local law enforcement officials to help prosecute fraudulent advertisers and those guilty of other sharp practices. Moreover, the bureau maintains a file of consumer complaints about operators in the community. Consumers, in turn, may call the bureau, which will report the number and nature of complaints on file with them. There is, of course, no claim that the complaints are justified; however, normally a high level of them on file should be fair warning to the inquirer.

The effectiveness of BBBs varies greatly from city to city. This is due, in part, to the quality of leadership operating local units. Another factor is the amount of financial and other support provided the bureaus. Each bureau depends solely on the voluntary contributions of advertisers, media, and agencies; this support can vary greatly. BBBs are not funded by taxes.

BBBs are interested in people operating within the local area, primarily retailers and service establishments. A great deal of the BBB caseload centers on the one-shot huckster with a scheme to fleece the unwary public. This situation contributes to a frequently held attitude that the bureaus are not overly successful in achieving their worthwhile objectives; the end of one unsavory practice seems to be followed only by another equally undesirable one. Without its BBB, however, the local marketplace

Figure 20.8 A firm of certified public accountants takes advantage of the new opportunity permitting professionals to advertise their services. Note the "reason-why" copy approach.

would be far more hazardous for consumers in many communities.

National Advertising Review Board

For many years the National Association of Better Business Bureaus expended some effort on the self-regulation of national advertising, while the local bureaus concentrated on local and retail advertising. A reorganization took place in the early 1970s when the Council of Better Business Bureaus (CBBB) was established; the new group became much more involved in national advertising regulation. The CBBB set up a policy-making group known as the National Advertising Review Council, which consists of eight members drawn from the chairpersons and presidents of the four leading professional associations serving the field of advertising—American Association of Advertising Agencies, Association of National Advertisers, American Advertising Federation, and the CBBB.

The National Advertising Review Board (NARB) was then established. The board has 50 members; 40 are advertising professionals and 10 are public members. The NARB acts as the supreme court of the self-regulation system of advertising and is broken up into "panels" of five members, or "judges."

Another part of the self-regulation mechanism is the National Advertising Division (NAD) of the CBBB, which is also staffed by advertising professionals. Complaints about national advertising go first to the NAD. This body investigates and often settles complaints at the staff level through suggestions made to the offending advertiser.

When the advertiser will not agree to cease or modify the advertising found to be misleading by the NAD, the matter is referred to a NARB panel for consideration. The panel can agree with the decision by the NAD or can find the complaint without merit and rule for the advertiser. How the review system operates is shown by the flowchart presented in Figure 20.9.

How NAD actually works may be better understood by looking at its workload during a typical month. The review board handled 10 cases in July 1980. Seven advertisers, including American Home Products, Avis, Inc., Champion Spark Plug Company, Ektelon, Grand Union Company, Reevest International, and Remington Rand Corporation, agreed either to modify or to discontinue claims following challenges by the NAD. One of the cases was described in *Advertising Age* thus:

Champion Spark Plug Co., in tv spots for its Champion spark plugs, stated, "If your engine isn't starting on cue, put in a fresh set of Champion spark plugs at least once a year." NAD was concerned that those not familiar with auto mechanics might think that if their engine has trouble starting, spark plugs are inevitably the problem. Champion agreed to modify the claim to suggest a more comprehensive rationale for changing spark plugs.[33]

Three advertisers were able to substantiate their challenged claims: Hoover Company ("It offers cleaning efficiency no other upright can"), Norton Norwich Products ("In a medical study, adults chose Chloraseptic three to one over the other leading lozenge. For quick temporary relief of minor sore throat pain"), and Procter & Gamble ("I can do almost three times the dishes with Joy. Joy's the better bargain" when compared with the "average bargain liquid").

The value of the activity is shown by a statement from Thomas Rosch, director of the FTC's Bureau of Consumer Protection, that the "NARB helps relieve us (FTC) of much of the burden in the regulatory area."[34] Advertisers escape the adverse publicity which often springs from FTC action against them, and issues are settled much more expeditiously. Review boards have now been established in many communities with the goal of solving similar disagreements about possibly misleading advertising at the local level through this quasi-arbitration approach.

Another product of the joint effort for self-policing was the development of a code for consumer advertising, as shown in Table 20.1. The statement provides a useful guideline when self-regulation of advertising abuses is undertaken. Surely every advertiser should have the code in mind when evaluating advertising messages about to be released to the media for dissemination.

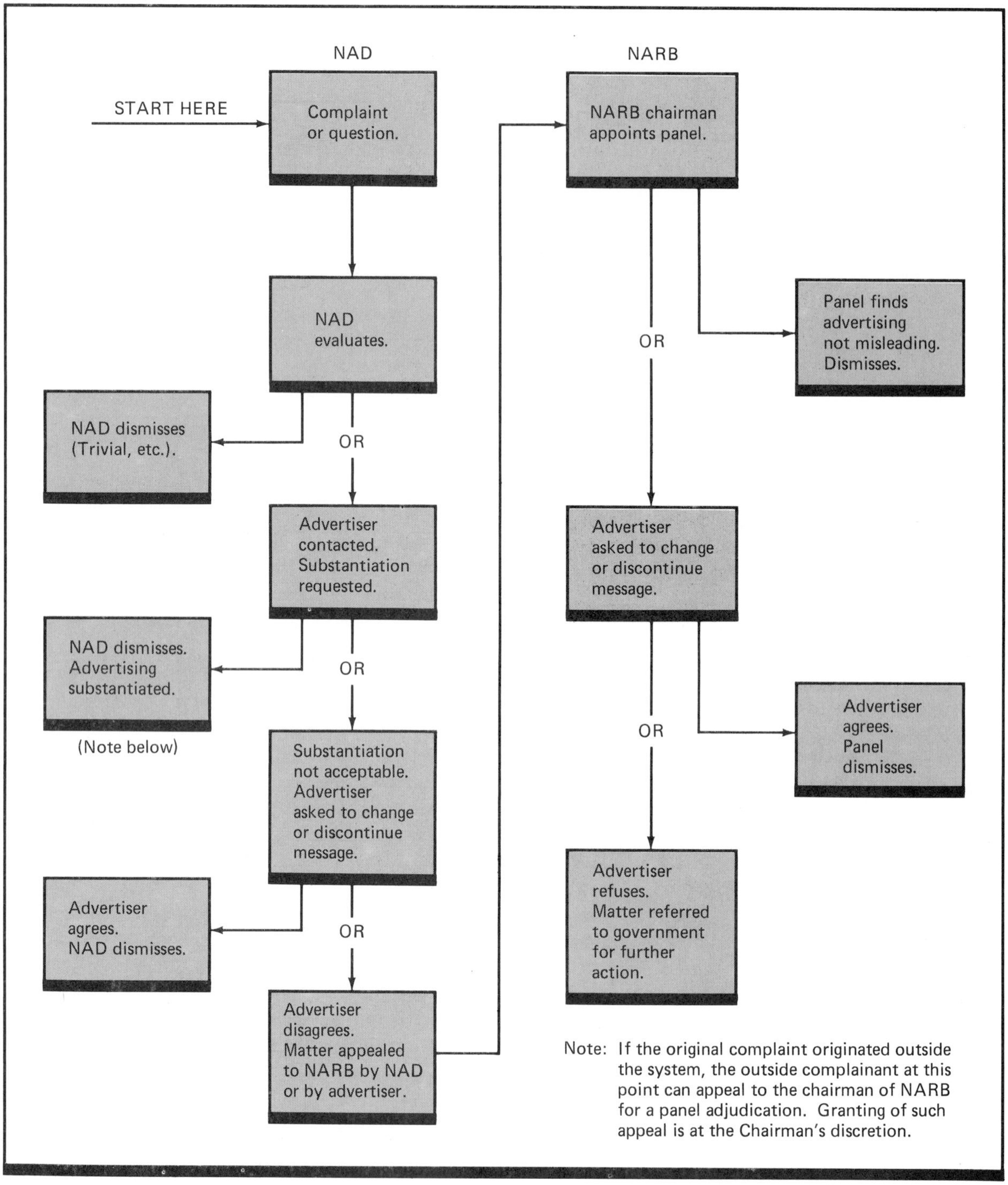

Figure 20.9 This flow chart traces the steps followed when a complaint against an advertiser is lodged for handling through the self-regulatory procedures established by the advertising industry. [*The National Advertising Review Board.*]

TABLE 20.1
The Advertising Code of American Business

I	*Truth.* Advertising shall tell the truth, and shall reveal significant facts, the concealment of which would mislead the public.
II	*Responsibility.* Advertising agencies and advertisers shall be willing to provide substantiation of claims made.
III	*Taste and decency.* Advertising shall be free of statements, illustrations or implications which are offensive to good taste or public decency.
IV	*Disparagement.* Advertising shall offer merchandise or service on its merits, and refrain from attacking competitors unfairly or disparaging their products, services or methods of doing business.
V	*Bait advertising.* Advertising shall offer only merchandise or services which are readily available for purchase at the advertised price.
VI	*Guarantees and warranties.* Advertising of guarantees and warranties shall be explicit. Advertising of any guarantee or warranty shall clearly and conspicuously disclose its nature and extent, the manner in which the guarantor or warrantor will perform and the identity of the guarantor or warrantor.
VII	*Price claims.* Advertising shall avoid price or savings claims which are false or misleading, or which do not offer provable bargains or savings.
VIII	*Unprovable claims.* Advertising shall avoid the use of exaggerated or unprovable claims.
IX	*Testimonials.* Advertising containing testimonials shall be limited to those of competent witnesses who are reflecting a real and honest choice.

Explanatory note: This code was part of a program of industry self-regulation pertaining to national consumer advertising announced jointly on September 28, 1971, by the American Advertising Federation, the American Association of Advertising Agencies, the Association of National Advertisers, and the Council of Better Business Bureaus, Inc.

Self-Regulation by Advertising Media

All advertising media reserve the right to reject any advertising submitted if it is considered objectionable to their readers, listeners, or viewers, even if it is not misleading. *Sunset* magazine, for instance, has banned any advertising for products containing dangerous insecticides since 1969. At the time the decision was made, the magazine carried more advertising for insecticides than any other nonfarm magazine.

In the area of broadcast advertising, the National Association of Broadcasters (NAB) through the operation of its Code Authority has established extensive sets of guidelines for advertisers wishing to use radio and television in their media mixes. Of particular interest has been advertising directed primarily to children. Self-regulation has zeroed in on such specific instances of selling to children as host selling, toy advertising, and premium offers. Futhermore, the guidelines have caused the creative approaches used by many advertisers to be changed materially. In some instances, it was decided to exclude children from designated target audiences for advertising messages.

The advertising of alcoholic beverages is either prohibited or carefully controlled by the Radio Code and the Television Code. Moreover, how personal products, such as sanitary napkins and tampons, are advertised is prescribed. The objective, of course, is to forestall governmental regulation of advertising over the airwaves.

We have already shown how professional groups control their members' advertising in the section "Advertising and the First Amendment."

Conclusion of Self-Regulation

The self-regulation of any industry practice faces hard sledding. For one thing, there is an ever-present skepticism concerning such efforts which the outside observer may view as self-serving, even collusive, and designed to circumvent the law. There is a serious limitation, furthermore, in the ability of professional groups to enforce their decisions. The policy body usually has no real power to force compliance with its rulings. When the issue cannot be satisfactorily settled at the self-regulation level, persuasion and pressure from other members of the industry group are relied upon. The implicit threat that the matter will go to the FTC or the local district attorney may be in the background. If a significant number of industry members decide not to participate in the self-regulatory effort, compliance is difficult to accomplish. All broadcasters, for example, do not subscribe to the Radio and Television Codes; such nonsubscribers often violate code guidelines.

Enlightened self-interest, however, should encourage advertisers to support such self-regulation efforts with vigor and enthusiasm. Progressive firms, like Giant Food Co. and Kraft, Inc., find that tasteful, informative, appealing ads bring about positive consumer response. Advertising is being judged today by the public on more than the criterion of "Does it sell?" If governmental regulation and control are forestalled or avoided, the advertising business will benefit, and the interest of consumers will be protected at a lower net cost and probably more readily than through the legal process.

Summary

Deceptive advertising and other forms of unethical behavior do occur in the field of advertising. Protection is available in three forms: law, industry self-regulation, and enlightened self-interest on the part of advertisers. Many legal restrictions have been placed upon advertisers in order to control the unethical behavior of those who fail to invoke the self-interest philosophy. False and deceptive advertising is one of the concerns of the Federal Trade Commission. When businesses are found to be dealing deceptively with consumers, the FTC issues cease-and-desist orders and accepts consent decrees from violators. The use of advertising allowances is regulated by the FTC. What is said in advertising messages and where they may appear are also subject to legal control in several ways.

Interpreting and enforcing laws affecting advertising is a complex task. Over time, an extensive body of law has developed which is based on a series of landmark cases. The rules of law set down in these cases provide guidelines to persons who create advertising messages, sometimes, it is believed, to the detriment of creativity. The FTC, moreover, in its efforts to protect consumers adopts policies which affect how advertising can be carried out in the United States. Policies of current interest and possible concern are advertising substantiation, affirmative disclosure, bait-and-switch advertising, comparative advertising, and corrective advertising.

Self-regulation by the advertising industry itself may help to forestall additional regulation of promotional activities.

Questions for Discussion

1 Why is an attitude of enlightened self-interest so vitally important to the development of a sound advertising program? Explain.

2 Briefly describe the provisions of the Federal Trade Commission Act as it affects advertising. How was the power of the FTC over advertising affected by the Wheeler-Lea Act? The Magnunson-Moss Act? The FTC Improvement Act of 1980?

3 What does the Robinson-Patman Act have to do with advertising? The Lanham Act? The First Amendment?

4 What was the key issue in the so-called mock-up, Campbell Soup Company, and F-310 cases? What is your personal opinion about this matter?

5 Why was the Dry Ban case considered to be so important to the future of advertising? Explain.

6 Briefly define each of the following FTC policies: (*a*) advertising substantiation, (*b*) affirmative disclosure, (*c*) comparative advertising, and (*d*) corrective advertising.

7 Have you ever been a target for what appeared to be a bait-and-switch scheme? Describe how it

operated and how you reacted to the situation.

8 In your college library, locate a recent FTC *Industry Guide* and a *Trade Regulation Rule* that affect advertising. Summarize each and bring them to class; be ready to discuss and debate the suitability of the guide and the rule.

9 From the pages of a recent issue of *Advertising Age* or some other periodical, locate a recent decision by the NARB. Bring a summary of the ruling to class for discussion; if possible, bring a copy of the advertisement involved.

10 Can self-regulation lessen the need for the control of advertising by governmental agencies? Explain.

For Further Reference

Howard, Marshall C.: *Legal Aspects of Marketing,* McGraw-Hill Book Company, New York, 1964.

Kintner, Earl W.: *A Primer on the Law of Deceptive Practices,* The Macmillan Company, New York, 1971.

Leff, Arthur Allen: *Swindling and Selling,* Free Press, New York, 1976.

Preston, Ivan L.: *The Great American Blow-up: Puffery in Advertising and Selling,* The University of Wisconsin Press, Madison, 1975.

Rosden, George, and Peter Rosden: *The Law of Advertising,* Matthew Bender, New York, 1974 (updated periodically).

Welch, Joe L.: *Marketing Law,* Petroleum Publishing Company, Tulsa, Okla., 1980.

Wright, John S., and John E. Mertes: *Advertising's Role in Society,* West Publishing Company, St. Paul, Minn., 1974.

End Notes

[1] The best source of reference material on the subject is Joe L. Welch, *Marketing Law* (Petroleum Publishing Co., Tulsa, Okla., 1980), especially chap. 5, "Unfair and Deceptive Promotional Strategy." Also useful is Marshal C. Howard, *Legal Aspects of Marketing* (McGraw-Hill Book Company, New York, 1964), especially chap. 5, "Advertising and Labeling."

[2] Public Law 203, approved Sept. 26, 1914, 2d Sess., 63d Cong., U.S. Stat. L., vol. 38, pp. 717–724.

[3] Federal Trade Commission v. Winsted Hosiery Co., 258 U.S. 483, 42 S. Ct., 384, 66 L. Ed. 729 (1922).

[4] Public Law 447, approved March 21, 1938, 3d Sess., 75th Cong., U.S. Stat. L., vol. 52.

[5] Public Law 93–637, 93d Cong., S. 356 (Jan. 4, 1975).

[6] Public Law 96–252, May 28, 1980.

[7] Public Law 212, 2d Sess., 63d Cong., U.S. Stat. L., vol. 38, pp. 730–740.

[8] Public Law 692, 2d Sess., 74th Cong., U.S. Stat. L., vol. 49, p. 1526.

[9] Federal Trade Commission v. Fred Meyer, Inc., 390 U.S. 341 (1968).

[10] Public Law 489, 79th Cong., 60 Stat. 427.

[11] Public Law 91-222, House Res. 6543.

[12] Pfizer, Inc., 3 Trade Reg. Rep., 20,056 (FTC, July 11, 1972).

[13] David H. Carlin, "An 'un-burning' issue in FTC regulation," *Marketing Communications,* May 1980, p. 6.

[14] *Marketing News,* June 13, 1980, p. 16.

[15] *Advertising Age,* March 31, 1980, p. 16.

[16] William L. Wilkie and Paul W. Farris, "Comparison Advertising: Problems and Potential," *Journal of Marketing,* October 1975, p. 7.

[17] Philip Levine, "Commercials that Name Competing Brands," *Journal of Advertising Research,* December 1976, p. 14.

[18] Marianne M. Jennings, "New FTC Policy Statement Encourages Comparative Ads," *Marketing News,* Oct. 19, 1979, p. 8.

[19] *FTC New Summary,* Jan. 19, 1980, p. 1.

[20] *Journal of Marketing,* January 1975, p. 101.

[21] *Advertising Age,* June 23, 1980, p. 34S.

[22] FTC Dkt. C-1741, CCH 19.261 (May 1970).

[23] FTC Dkt. 8860, CCH 20.464 (October 1973).

[24] FTC Dkt. 8897, CCH 20.900 (April 1975).

[25] *Journal of Advertising,* January 1976, p. 92.

[26] Based in part on "Legal Developments in Marketing," *Journal of Marketing,* Spring 1979, pp. 111–112.

[27] Loc. cit., Winter 1980, pp. 86–87.

[28] This section draws heavily from Dorothy Cohen, "Advertising and the First Amendment," *Journal of Marketing,* July 1978, pp. 59–67, and Peter B. Turk, "The First Amendment: An Emerging Defense for Commercial Expression," Annual Conference of the American Academy of Advertising, Austin, Texas, April 3–6, 1976.

[29] Valentine v. Christensen (316 U.S. 52, 1942).

[30] Bigelow v. Commonwealth of Virginia (U.S. 44 L.Ed. 2d 600, 1975).

[31] Virginia State Board of Pharmacy v. Virginia Citizens Consumer Counsel, (U.S. 96 S.Ct. 1817, 1976).

[32] Bates v. State Bar of Arizona, U.S. Sup. Ct., CCH Newsletter 287, Part II, BNA ATRR No. 820 (June 30, 1977).

[33] *Advertising Age,* Aug. 18, 1980, p. 10. All material on NAD cases from this source.

[34] *Advertising Age,* June 6, 1975, p. 66.

Chapter 21

International Advertising

The Prologue introduced international advertising as a major force in modern advertising. Our emphasis throughout this book, however, has been on domestic advertising produced for United States markets. Advertising as a marketing tool and method of communication is used throughout the world. Paraphrasing the orange juice commercial, "advertising isn't just for the United States anymore." In this chapter, we turn to the topic of **international advertising,** or **transnational advertising,** as it is sometimes called, to see how the techniques used in domestic situations apply to the larger markets of the world.

For most American business firms, success in foreign markets is crucial to continued growth and profitability. To market American goods and services to foreign audiences requires an understanding of how advertising works in other nations. What messages will be received most positively? Will the same campaign theme work in all nations? What media will have the greatest impact on potential customers? Do local customs or laws bar the use of certain advertising strategies? This chapter describes the conditions facing international advertisers and the people creating international advertising programs. It will illustrate how advertising is used to communicate with consumers in an international market.

Advertising in Other Countries

Advertising did not originate in the United States, but conditions for its growth and development made it essential for the marketing of goods and services in our economy. Among the most important factors contributing to the need for advertising were the industrialization of the United States economy along with a surplus of goods, a viable transportation system, and the presence of media to carry advertisements. Thus, by 1979 the United States spent more than $49 billion for advertising. On an international scale, many other industrialized nations with smaller economies than ours devoted substantial sums to advertising their products and services also. Table 21.1 (page 468) lists 12 other industrialized countries that had advertising expenditures in excess of $1 billion. Furthermore, as more and more developing nations expand their economies and become industrialized in a manner quite similar to the stages of development experienced by the United States, their advertising commitments should increase as well.

Another way of assessing the relative importance of advertising in a nation's economy is illustrated by Table 21.2 (page 468). As can be seen, 2 percent of the U.S. gross national product is devoted to adver-

1. GO BACK & CLEAN YOUR ROOM
2. RAKE UP LEAVES.
3. MOW THE LAWN.
NOW! LOVE, MOM
P.S. BE HOME FOR SUPPER

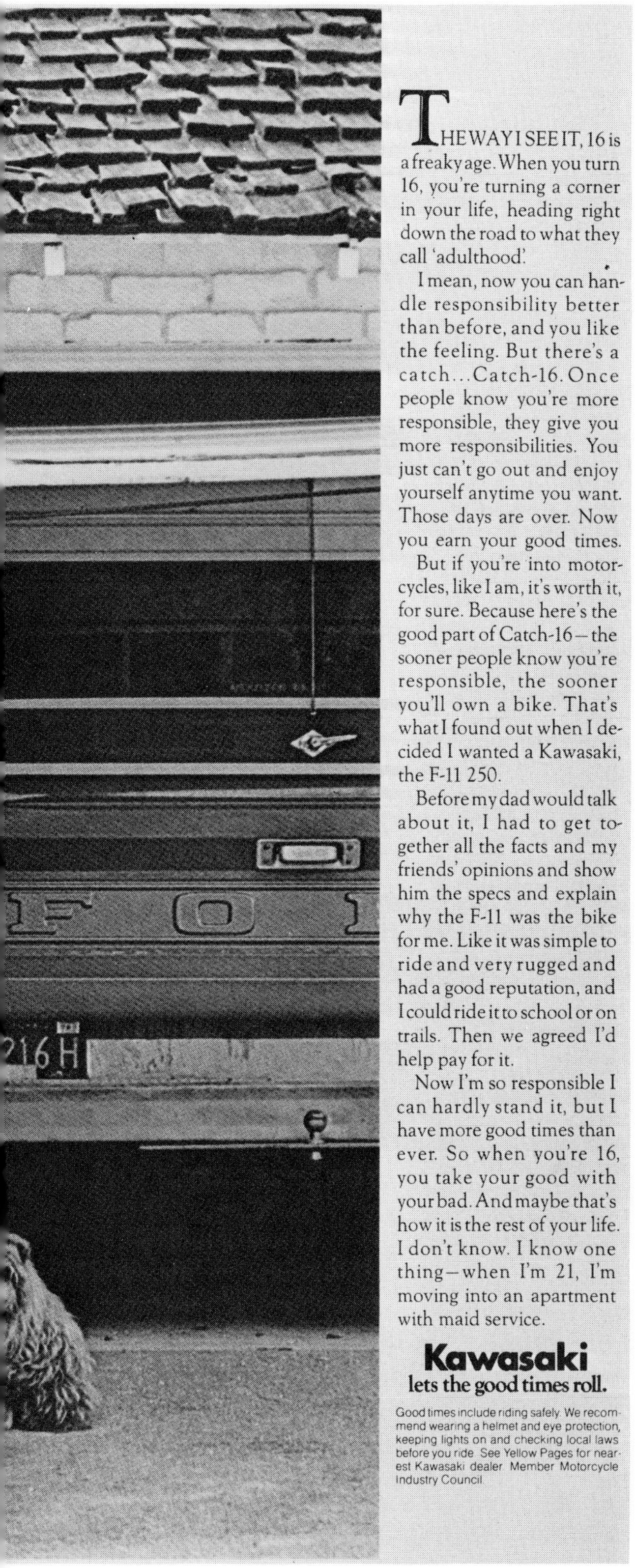

THE WAY I SEE IT, 16 is a freaky age. When you turn 16, you're turning a corner in your life, heading right down the road to what they call 'adulthood'.
I mean, now you can handle responsibility better than before, and you like the feeling. But there's a catch...Catch-16. Once people know you're more responsible, they give you more responsibilities. You just can't go out and enjoy yourself anytime you want. Those days are over. Now you earn your good times.
But if you're into motorcycles, like I am, it's worth it, for sure. Because here's the good part of Catch-16—the sooner people know you're responsible, the sooner you'll own a bike. That's what I found out when I decided I wanted a Kawasaki, the F-11 250.
Before my dad would talk about it, I had to get together all the facts and my friends' opinions and show him the specs and explain why the F-11 was the bike for me. Like it was simple to ride and very rugged and had a good reputation, and I could ride it to school or on trails. Then we agreed I'd help pay for it.
Now I'm so responsible I can hardly stand it, but I have more good times than ever. So when you're 16, you take your good with your bad. And maybe that's how it is the rest of your life. I don't know. I know one thing—when I'm 21, I'm moving into an apartment with maid service.
Kawasaki
lets the good times roll.
Good times include riding safely. We recommend wearing a helmet and eye protection, keeping lights on and checking local laws before you ride. See Yellow Pages for nearest Kawasaki dealer. Member Motorcycle Industry Council.

Figure 21.1 The foreign manufacturer of a widely used consumer good uses American advertising strategies to tap the United States market. The art form employed is similar to that made famous by Norman Rockwell.

tising. In 23 other countries, somewhere between 1 and 2 percent of the GNP is spent for advertising. Per capita expenditures for advertising are listed in Table 21.3 (page 469). Twenty-seven countries spent more than $25 per capita for media advertising in 1979. The lowest per capita expenditures (not shown) were those in the less developed nations of Africa and Asia. Less than $1 per capita was spent during 1979 in Ethiopia ($0.06), Nepal ($0.07), India ($0.37), Ghana ($0.68), and Liberia ($0.71).[1]

Robert J. Coen, a specialist in tracking advertising expenditures, points out that the dominance of the United States is slowly diminishing.[2] In 1960, when $18 billion were spent for advertising throughout the world, two-thirds ($12 billion) was accounted for by the United States. By 1970, the total reached $35 billion; the United States share, $20 billion, was approximately 57 percent of the total. In 1980, the United States and the rest of the world each spent $55 billion. Coen predicts total world advertising expenditures will reach $780 billion in the year 2000. The United States share of the total will then be approximately 40 percent.

In nations where advertising is emerging as an important economic force, United States advertising practices and methods are used as models. Despite the dominance of U.S. advertising over the years, American advertisers are beginning to learn new techniques from foreign advertisers, particularly in the area of advertising graphics.

Advertising in Controlled Economies

The nations described in the preceding section have mixed economies. The market system, with its laws of supply and demand, is allowed to work freely in distributing goods and services among consumers. The government, however, does regulate the economy to some degree in each nation to provide a more equitable distribution of goods and services to all consumers. On the other hand, there are many nations of the world that are founded on the Marxian philosophy of economics, which includes the view that any marketing operation other than simple retailing is parasitic and of no social value. In these communist nations, the economy is controlled by the government. An interesting question is whether advertising can play a role in such controlled economies. In fact, advertising for consumer goods is employed in a relatively unsophisticated way in communist nations, a fact that seems to explain its universality once the conditions for its use are present.

Figure 21.2 An American product is sold in Japan through advertising. (Note the American models.) The Wrangler brand was propelled from an unknown status to the number one selling brand in less than three years. The copy block on the left-hand side of the ad is translated:

THE WIND FROM THE COTTONFIELDS

Clear days are when I go out to the field,
to tend my cabbage crop.
But on a rainy day,
I stay home
and leaf through
Ray Bradbury's
short shorts.
But rain or shine,
always in my
Wrangler Jeans.

Wrangler Jeans are made from U.S. cotton grown by abundant sunshine and the crystal air of America's Deep South. Wrangler Jeans, the best U.S. brand.

Table 21.1
Advertising Expenditures in Thirteen Countries Spending More than $1 Billion in 1979

Country	(in billions of U.S. dollars)
United States	$49.720
Japan	8.851
West Germany	6.271
United Kingdom	5.136
France	4.350
Canada	2.892
Netherlands	2.206
Sweden	1.673
Brazil	1.650
Australia	1.647
Switzerland	1.265
Spain	1.259
Italy	1.077

SOURCE: *World Advertising Expenditures, 1980,* Starch INRA Hooper, Mamaroneck, N.Y., 1980, p. 6.

In this section, we review the status of advertising in the Soviet Union and in China. The Soviet view of advertising is changing, and the present growth of advertising in the Soviet Union and the eastern European nations supports our view that advertising is a productive force in economic life. China opened its doors to the West in the late 1970s, enabling us to see how advertising has been used since Mao's cultural revolution.

The Soviet Union The Soviet Union provides a dramatic example of advertising in a controlled economy—an economy founded on the Marxian philosophy. The traditional communist view of advertising has been that it is a total social waste and forces unwanted goods on consumers.

For centuries Russia was in the primary stage of economic development. Its population was largely agricultural, the standard of living was very low, and a seller's market for consumer goods prevailed. In the late 1950s, the U.S.S.R. entered into a secondary stage of economic development. Supplies of certain consumer goods exceeded demand, and an increasing number of citizens possessed some discretionary income for the purchase of more than the bare necessities of life. In this secondary stage, the social ideal of a planned balance between production and consumption still appeared far away.

The managers of the Soviet economy, therefore, started to adopt methods of distribution that resemble those employed in capitalist economies. In 1958, the Ministry of Trade was reorganized, and a state-controlled advertising agency, *Torgreklama,* was established with branches in most Soviet cities. Advertising is playing an increasingly important role in both export and domestic marketing. The state advertising agency prepares advertising, for a commission, to be placed in a full array of media, which includes newspapers, magazines, outdoor posters, radio, and television, all of which are state-owned.

The Russian government publishes and distributes an English-language magazine, *Soviet Life,* in the United States. This quality publication compares favorably with other class magazines and shows the competent employment of Western techniques in the Soviet's efforts to communicate with the American public and business community.

Table 21.2
Advertising Expenditures as a Percentage of Gross National Product

Country	Percentage of gross national product, 1979
United States	2.02
Sweden	1.88
New Zealand	1.79
Bermuda	1.78
Netherlands	1.77
United Kingdom	1.74
Puerto Rico	1.59
Switzerland	1.59
Finland	1.47
Dominican Republic	1.38
Australia	1.37
Norway	1.37
Canada	1.32
Denmark	1.31
Austria	1.29
Argentina	1.27
South Africa	1.20
Taiwan	1.15
Bahamas	1.10
Jamaica	1.05
Egypt	1.02
Ireland	1.02
Singapore	1.00
West Germany	1.00

SOURCE: *World Advertising Expenditures, 1980,* Starch INRA Hooper, Mamaroneck, N.Y., 1980, p. 11.

Table 21.3
Per Capita Advertising Expenditures in Selected Areas

Country	Expenditures in 1979 (in U.S. dollars)
United States	$224.37
Sweden	201.59
Switzerland	200.79
Norway	159.93
Netherlands	158.77
Denmark	138.31
Canada	122.04
Bermuda	118.33
Australia	115.17
Finland	105.88
West Germany	102.14
Austria	97.99
United Kingdom	91.87
New Zealand	87.09
France	81.31
Japan	76.37
Belgium	57.82
Iceland	56.00
Bahamas	55.00
Luxembourg	51.00
Puerto Rico	46.32
Netherlands Antilles	42.33
Singapore	37.96
Ireland	37.90
Spain	33.31
Israel	33.08
Argentina	25.25

SOURCE: *World Advertising Expenditures, 1980,* Starch INRA Hooper, Mamaroneck, N.Y., 1980, p. 7.

More significant, however, is the increased use of advertising domestically—within Russia itself—for the purpose of communicating with the citizenry of the country. Several uses for advertising include the sale of unacceptably large inventories of obsolescent goods and of perishable goods. Some advertising is used to support new brands or services and design changes in old brands. Noteworthy is the advertising aimed at building store patronage for specific retail outlets. Classified advertising for services and secondhand goods flourishes, and there is a great deal of public service advertising.[3] Anastas I. Mikoyan, an important U.S.S.R. political leader, stated the governmental view as:

> The task of Soviet advertising is to give people exact information about the goods that are on sale, to help to create new demands, to cultivate new tastes and requirements, to promote the sale of new kinds of goods and to explain their uses to the consumer.[4]

One additional quotation, this from a Soviet executive, should be sufficient to show that advertising is being recognized in the Soviet Union as an important institution:

> It is incorrect to think of advertising as solely a directional, local tactic to provide information on goods and services. Every year it is becoming more and more an effective way to promote our life style and achievements. To a certain extent, therefore, it performs a social function. . . .
>
> Good advertising not only creates favorable conditions for a product or service, but also molds rational needs on the part of the consumer.[5]

Figure 21.3 Shoes are advertised thus in a Hungarian magazine. The graphics used there parallel those appearing in Western publications.

Figure 21.4 These three outdoor signs appeared in Peking, China. Note that two of the billboards feature consumer products—men's shirts and shoe polish—and the third promotes an industrial good. [*Courtesy of Stanley Cohen.*]

China American travelers are now able to observe economic life in the People's Republic of China after many years when diplomatic relations and trade between our two nations did not exist. This communist nation of 970 million people was visited in 1980 by Stanley E. Cohen, Washington editor of *Advertising Age.* From his perspective as a long-time observer of American advertising, Cohen offered many interesting observations on how advertising operates in China.[6] Obviously, the advertising structure and its output are quite primitive. A big surprise was Cohen's discovery that outdoor advertising is used extensively in China's major cities. Figure 21.4 shows three outdoor posters featuring both consumer and industrial products. Use of broadcast advertising, especially television, is limited by the shortage of receiving sets. Most news is disseminated by pages posted on display cases located in high traffic locations in the cities, instead of by newspapers. The stage of economic development in mainland China obviously has not reached the point where demand stimulation for consumer goods is greatly needed.

The Nature and Significance of International Advertising

Whether advertising is domestic or international, its goal is to communicate product information to a target audience or to persuade potential customers to buy the product. International advertising is defined as "advertising sponsored by a producer of a product or service who is located in one nation but whose advertising message is aimed at potential buyers residing in one or more countries foreign to the advertiser's homeland."

The world truly is getting smaller every day. The development of very rapid means of transportation (e.g., supersonic jet aircraft) and sophisticated systems of worldwide communication (e.g., satellite relay stations for television programming) have brought all parts of the globe closer together. Furthermore, national economies are increasingly interdependent: a single nation cannot realistically aspire to self-sufficiency.

International trade has grown tremendously since 1945 when World War II ended. Dollar volume of world trade has doubled each decade since then and stood at $2,198.4 billion at the end of 1979.[7] In the United States alone, there are at least 15,000 multinational companies. A multinational firm is one that has substantial investment, sales, and profits from foreign markets. For example, the Coca-Cola Company, based in Atlanta, Georgia, sells more than 250 million servings of its soft drink every day of the year in 135 countries spread throughout the world. Moreover, the corporation achieves 63 percent of its sales and more than one-half its profits from countries other than the United States, where it is the leading seller of soft drinks.

The United States dependence on international trade is illustrated in Figure 21.5. About 25 percent of our gross national product is derived from foreign trade. This staggering sum not only is the result of American products being purchased in international markets, but it includes sales of foreign products in our markets. You need only think of such familiar brand names as Toyota, Datsun, Honda, Volkswagen, Mercedes-Benz, Sony, Panasonic, Sharp, Minolta, and Seiko to realize that our standard of living is increased by the availability of foreign products. To achieve the maximum benefits from international trade, countries must import goods that they cannot produce efficiently and to export those that they do. At the start of the 1980s, half the watches bought in America were imports, 42 percent of the cameras sold in the United States were not made

Figure 21.5 Trends in foreign trade, as a part of the gross national product of the United States, 1970–1980, are shown in this chart. [*U.S. Department of Commerce.*]

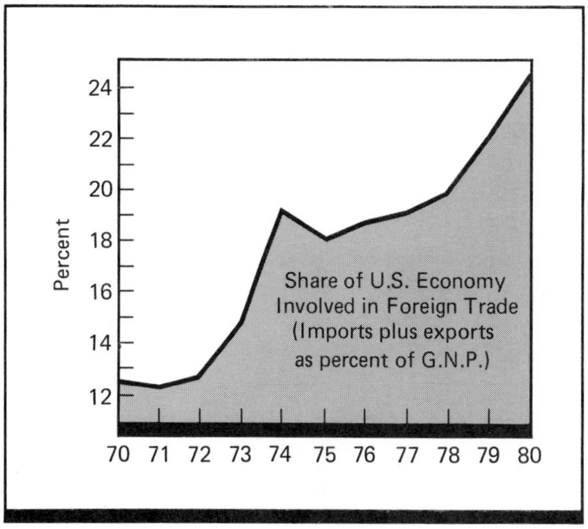

here, more than 35 percent of all television receivers selling domestically bore foreign names, and nearly 30 percent of all passenger cars sold were foreign-made.[8]

Because international trade is so important for the economic health of all nations and for raising the standard of living of their citizens, international advertising has grown as well to spread information and increase each nation's world markets. The role of international advertising will increase as trade between nations grows. Larger markets of course, permit, greater economies of scale, thus allowing more people to obtain lower-priced goods.[9] The advertising executive of the future, therefore, needs to learn about the intricacies and pitfalls of advertising on the international level.

International Advertising Decisions

International advertising managers face the same decisions as executives responsible for domestic advertising programs. Some aspects of international advertising present special problems, which are discussed in this section. These special situations are grouped into three main decision areas:

1 Selecting the agency
2 Designing the advertising message
3 Selecting the media

Selecting the Agency

Deciding whether to use an American agency or a foreign one is the first step taken by the United States seller wishing to advertise in another country. The world's agency structure, as will be discussed shortly, has been dominated by American-based organizations. Most United States advertisers have tended to employ agencies headquartered in this country. However, in recent years foreign agencies have expanded their capabilities and services, and United States companies are using more foreign-based agencies for their overseas marketing. Nationalism is a major factor in some countries (for example, in Canada) and the international advertiser may be well advised to engage a local agency if goodwill of the population is desired. Sometimes governmental regulations require that local agencies be used. The overruling consideration, of course, should be, "Who can do the best job for the client?"

The International Advertising Agency When American packaged goods were first extensively introduced to foreign markets following World War II, the need for international advertising by American firms increased appreciably. One study showed that 72 percent of American companies selling products in foreign markets employ advertising in their marketing mixes. Major United States agencies expanded their international operations to represent their American clients internationally and also to develop new profit potential for themselves.

In 1979, advertising agencies in 68 countries, not including the United States, posted billings of $20.8 billion compared with $20.3 billion in United States markets.[10] Increased advertising budgets overseas and the appreciation of foreign currencies against the dollar helped to bring about the slight dominance of foreing-based agencies. Dentsu, Inc., a Japanese agency with billings of $2.437 billion bas been the world's leading advertising agency since 1973 when it first surpassed J. Walter Thompson Company in total billings. Thompson, now second largest, posted $1.693 billion for 1979. The next eight largest agencies were McCann-Erickson; Young & Rubicam; Ogilvy & Mather; Ted Bates; SSC&B; BBDO; Leo Burnett; and Foote, Cone & Belding.[11]

J. Walter Thompson and McCann-Erickson were the first United States agencies with international offices. They established branch offices in the major cities of the world. Later entrants into the international field purchased existing local agencies, as with the Leo Burnett acquisition of the London Press Exchange. Many agencies chose to expand their international business through the formation of partnerships. Typically, the American agency entered into a joint ownership arrangement with a strong foreign agency and provided it with a highly developed system for the coordination of advertising activities. Uniform standards for planning and developing market strategy and creative execution resulted in a stronger agency. The partnership approach was adopted, for example, by Grey Advertising, Inc., which has partners in Argentina, Australia, Austria, Belgium, Canada, France, Germany, Holland, Italy,

Japan, South Africa, Spain, Sweden, the United Kingdom, and Venezuela. The international partnership is advantageous when a foreign nation restricts United States ownership of business firms within its country.

The International Advertising Message

Another critical problem for the international advertising decision-maker is creating the advertising message itself. The **ethnic approach**—creating a specific message for each market with the consumer of that country in mind—is one way to solve this problem. To communicate accurately with consumers, the international advertiser should have a proper understanding of words, phrases, and sentence structure as used in a particular culture, or risk that the message will not be properly received. Since advertising is one-way communication, lack of feedback makes it difficult to evaluate the consumer's reaction to any advertising message. When language and cultural barriers exist, the problem is intensified. The ethnic approach, which often entails using local agencies or personnel, attempts to overcome these communication barriers.

The **standardized approach** is just the opposite of the ethnic route. Advertisers using it believe that the needs and desires of people throughout the world are basically the same. It is the people's methods of satisfying their needs and wants that vary, yet certain market segments in different nations are culturally similar. Thus, the same message aimed at college students could persuade them to purchase denim jeans no matter the country in which it was published. Figure 21.2 illustrates this point.

With the standardized approach, the emphasis is on common denominators, not differences. The philosophy held by Coca-Cola, for example, is for advertising to possess "one sight, one sound, one sell." The same commercial depicting a drummer in a rock band enjoying Coca-Cola was shown both in Europe and Latin America. One obvious advantage to the standardized approach, therefore, is cost savings. It is certainly less expensive, in terms of commercial product costs, to use the same film with different sound tracks.

Another important advantage in the standardized approach to international advertising is the control afforded the advertiser. Coordination and communication can be more effective and efficient, and preparation of campaigns is easier. Also, if the company wishes to present one worldwide image, this approach is useful. For those many consumers who travel in several countries, the uniform advertising may provide confidence in and preference for the brand.

Several factors influence the appropriateness of a standardized advertising appeal. One is whether the product is judged mainly by objective, physical characteristics (as tractors, tires, and razor blades are), or on a more psychological basis (as food and drugs are). Another factor is whether the product is consumed similarly across markets. The success of Coca-Cola's standardized international approach may be because the product meets similar needs or wants everywhere: it quenches thirst with a taste found agreeable by many people in many nations.

Literal translations of advertising messages are to be carefully appraised before using the same words in different countries, because the sense of some words varies across borders. Some humorous, embarrassing, and sometimes disastrous mistakes have occurred when advertisers failed to account for local customs, preferences, or attitudes. For example, "Body by Fisher" became "Corpse by Fisher" in Flemish.[12] Certain colors have different meanings in different countries and must be used carefully. Yellow is considered an imperial color and is used in religious contexts in China. Therefore an advertiser will not want to use it in a derogatory manner ("cleans dingy yellow floors"). White is the color of mourning in Japan. Knowledge of the significance of symbols is important, then, to proper understanding of consumer behavior in international markets. Cultural differences in customs, religions, traditions, and beliefs can create problems for the international advertiser if the message unintentionally offends the audience or if it fails to convey the proper meaning. Esso Oil Company's "Put A Tiger in Your Tank" slogan, although successfully translated for some foreign markets, failed in Thailand because the Thais do not consider the tiger a symbol of power.[13]

Certain illustrations seem to have universal appeal. Thus, a company can adapt copy to the same picture for all countries. Airlines use pictures with worldwide significance. An advertisement featuring a tropical sunset can be understood by people in any nation as representing any number of faraway vacation spots.

(*a*)

Figure 21.6 A familiar product is presented (*a*) to English-language residents of Hong Kong and (*b*) to Chinese-language residents.

Owing to cultural differences again, some illustrations would not be appropriate. The use of animals in animation to represent human behavior does not appeal to people of Islamic faith.

Apparently, the best approach to international advertising is a compromise between complete control and total decentralization of advertising tasks. Ideally, there should be a high degree of uniformity with

(*b*)

careful consideration of local marketing research to allow local adaption of advertisements. The centralization should be in advertising planning and strategy, and the decentralization, in the execution of advertising campaigns. Thus, the best of both worlds—the central control of strategy and planning, and the customizing of actual execution—can be achieved.

Figure 21.7 American industrial goods are advertised in an Arabic language business magazine. [*Courtesy of B-R-M International Division, Bozell & Jacobs, Inc.*]

International Advertising Media

The number, type, availability, characteristics, and effectiveness of media vary widely throughout the world. A country's stage of economic development, its social and political climate, and its legal environment determine the media structure an advertiser will choose. Television does not reach consumers in some nations at all, and low literacy rates reduce the effectiveness of print media. Print has maintained its position as the most important worldwide advertising medium, with 43 percent of the total 1979 advertising expenditures made in newspapers and magazines. Television was second, with 20 percent, and radio was third, with 6 percent. The remaining expenditure was divided among various other advertising media: outdoor, direct mail, transit, and film shown in movie theaters.[14]

The movie theater provides an important advertising vehicle in many countries. Like television, cinema advertising is especially useful when the product requires demonstration or the use of color. Unlike television, however, it has the added benefit of a captive audience, undisturbed by the normal distractions of the typical advertising environment, and reach can be more accurately assessed.

In most European countries, radio and television stations are owned by the government, and advertising is not permitted or is greatly restricted. Many areas of the world have low literacy rates, such as Latin America and Asia, and radio is used extensively in these areas to disseminate advertising messages.

Until recently, the one advertising medium in Saudi Arabia was the newspaper, which reaches only 42 percent of the country's population.[15] Outdoor billboards are now permitted, thus expanding the advertiser's reach there.

The international advertiser places all media into two broad categories: (1) international media, or those that circulate or are seen or heard in more than one country; and (2) foreign media, those that are local in scope. Magazines like *Time, Newsweek,* and *Reader's Digest,* are international media, as are many European publications. Many technical publications for scientists and engineers are international, as are specialized business publications on such subjects as management, agriculture, petroleum, and transportation.

Foreign media, however, get the major share of the advertising budget of most international advertisers. There is significant regional variation in the media mixes employed. For instance, in Europe and in Australia and New Zealand, the proportion of advertising expenditures spent in print media is high (55 percent and 49 percent, respectively), while in Latin America it is low (28 percent).[16] On the other hand, television expenditures account for a large percentage of all advertising in Latin America (38 percent) and Asia (34 percent), but only a small amount in Europe (12 percent) because many European TV stations do not allow advertising.[17] Radio advertising is also limited in Europe, accounting for only 3 percent of all advertising expenditures, while it is strongest in Latin America (16 percent).[18] The United States and Japan led the world in television advertising in 1977; their combined expenditures accounted for almost 70 percent of the total world television advertising expenditures.[19]

International Advertising in Action

Several foreign firms made significant inroads into the American market, assisted by aggressive advertising campaigns. One of the all-time great success stories is that of Volkswagen, the German car manufacturer that fulfilled the desire of a segment of American motorists for an economical compact automobile not available from Detroit car makers. The advertising created to promote the "Bug," as done by Doyle Dane Bernbach, won many plaudits for its creativity and also sold millions of Volkswagen cars. Later on, Japanese autos—Datsun, Toyota, Honda, and other brands—were equally successful, again aided by advertising designed by American ad agencies. Similarly, Japanese motorcycles became outstanding marketing successes. Nations of the world advertise themselves as desirable tourist attractions. (See Color Plate 7 for an outstanding example.)

In the 1970s, United States business firms became increasingly aware of the need to engage in overseas marketing and advertising. The accelerating prices for oil extracted by OPEC placed the United States in an unfavorable trade balance relationship with other nations. Our nation was importing more goods and services than it was exporting. One reason for this unfavorable balance of trade was the high prices of American goods. Our merchandise often was priced

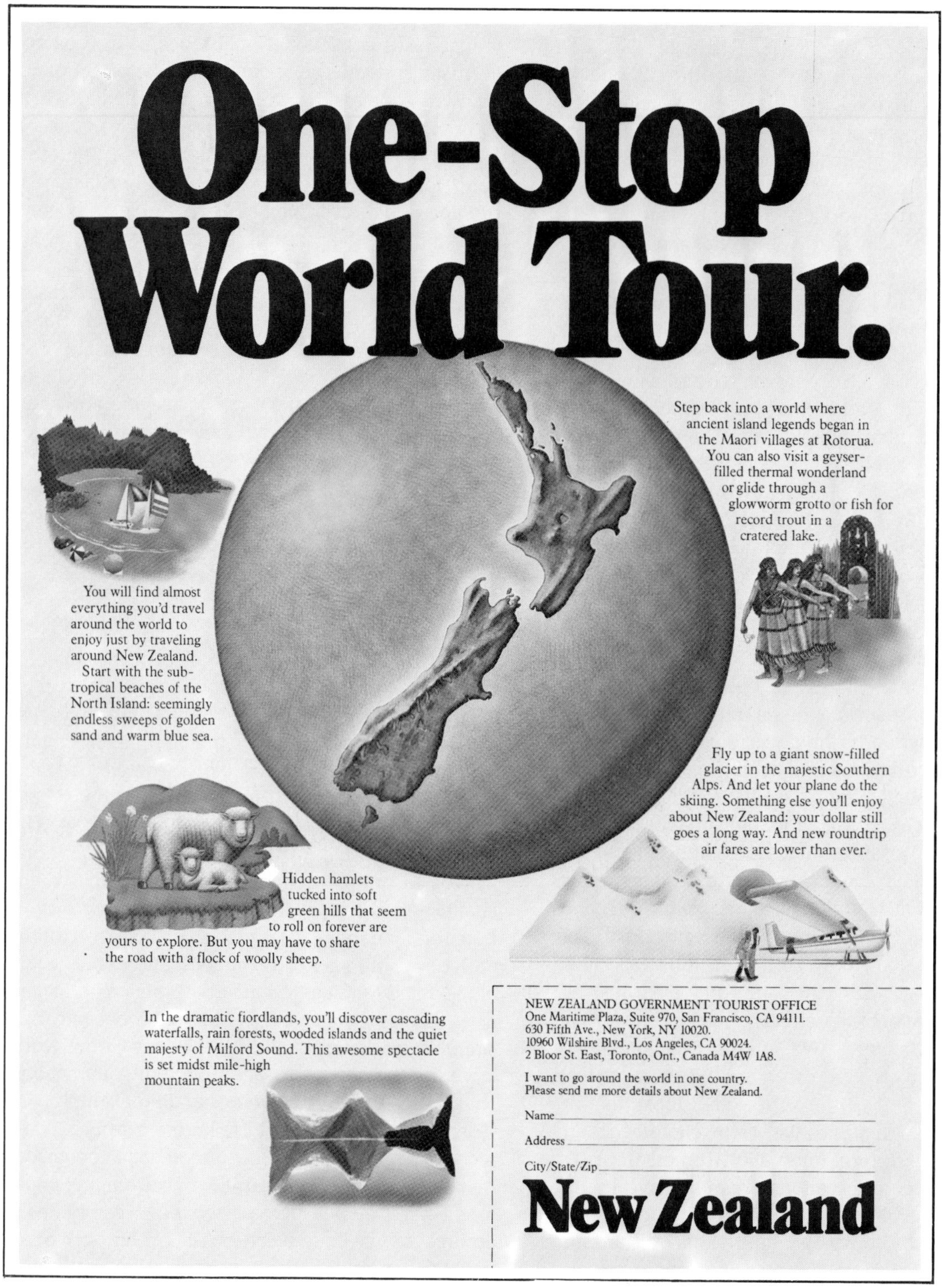

One-Stop World Tour.
Step back into a world where ancient island legends began in the Maori villages at Rotorua. You can also visit a geyser-filled thermal wonderland or glide through a glowworm grotto or fish for record trout in a cratered lake.
You will find almost everything you'd travel around the world to enjoy just by traveling around New Zealand.
Start with the sub-tropical beaches of the North Island: seemingly endless sweeps of golden sand and warm blue sea.
Fly up to a giant snow-filled glacier in the majestic Southern Alps. And let your plane do the skiing. Something else you'll enjoy about New Zealand: your dollar still goes a long way. And new roundtrip air fares are lower than ever.
Hidden hamlets tucked into soft green hills that seem to roll on forever are yours to explore. But you may have to share the road with a flock of woolly sheep.
In the dramatic fiordlands, you'll discover cascading waterfalls, rain forests, wooded islands and the quiet majesty of Milford Sound. This awesome spectacle is set midst mile-high mountain peaks.
NEW ZEALAND GOVERNMENT TOURIST OFFICE
One Maritime Plaza, Suite 970, San Francisco, CA 94111.
630 Fifth Ave., New York, NY 10020.
10960 Wilshire Blvd., Los Angeles, CA 90024.
2 Bloor St. East, Toronto, Ont., Canada M4W 1A8.
I want to go around the world in one country.
Please send me more details about New Zealand.
Name
Address
City/State/Zip
New Zealand

Figure 21.8 This print ad is typical of those in the United States to persuade Americans to visit foreign countries as tourists.

higher than the output of other nations, in part because of the higher wages paid workers in our country. The United States, however, does have a comparative advantage in the production of many goods and services. When this is the case, a mechanism is needed to bring that advantage to the attention of the people of other nations so that we can make sales and help to adjust the balance of trade. Advertising is that mechanism. Two areas where the United States possesses a comparative advantage are (1) in the production of food and (2) as a travel destination.

Food Products The richness of our soil and its vast acreage, coupled with highly sophisticated machinery and scientific farming methods, gives our nation outstanding farm productivity. We are the "breadbasket of the world" in a sense, and students of the future (futurists) predict that as world population grows, food will become as scarce as oil is today. In the meantime, our comparative advantage in food production should be exploited to enhance our economic stability. We must learn to promote the consumption of our food throughout the developed and developing nations of the world in order to maintain a favorable balance of trade.

Branded food items, such as Sunkist citrus fruit, are in great demand in countries like Japan. However, much of the food that we do export is in the form of commodities: grains, meat, and canned fruits and vegetables. Commodities can be promoted successfully by our nation. The purpose of the federal government's Foreign Agriculture Service (FAS) is to do just that; over the past decade, FAS has helped to push our exports of agricultural products from $7 billion to $35 billion.[20] The campaign developed to promote soybeans to European countries, as illustrated in Figure 21.9, has stimulated a primary demand in Germany to the point that 25 percent of all cooking oil used there is derived from soybeans grown in the United States. Similar campaigns for other kinds of food can and should be mounted in the future.

Figure 21.9 Educational messages, such as the one in this ad, helped to win over German consumers to the idea that soybean oil is an acceptable substitute for cooking oil. The message reads:

> What do many mayonnaises, fish cans, baking fats, and salad sauces have in common?
>
> SOY OIL
>
> The most important vegetable fat in the world. (Soy oil's share of the total consumption of all edible vegetable fats and oils in the Federal Republic of West Germany totals 40 percent because soy oil is absolutely without specific taste, contains a high percentate of essential polyunsaturated fatty acids, and is favorable in price.)

Tourism For a long time, United States citizens formed the target market for advertisers promoting foreign tourist attractions. Ads featuring vacations in Europe, the Caribbean, Mexico, Central America, and many more exotic places were aimed at the United States population. Less developed nations saw American tourists as a source of dollars, and tourism was an industry capable of providing jobs for their unskilled workers. Although our government established its U.S. Travel Service to promote American vacations to foreign tourists, the agency was never adequately financed and did not achieve its goal.

As the value of the dollar declined during the

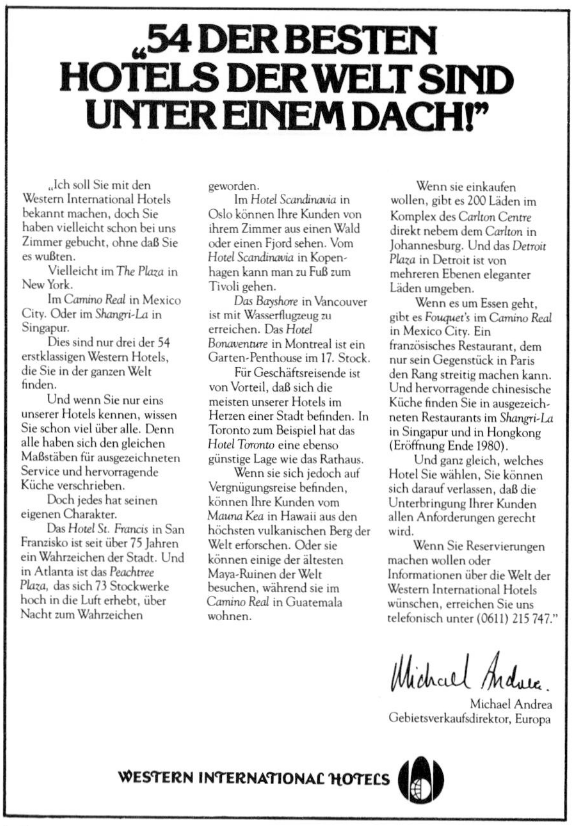
„54 DER BESTEN HOTELS DER WELT SIND UNTER EINEM DACH!"
„Ich soll Sie mit den Western International Hotels bekannt machen, doch Sie haben vielleicht schon bei uns Zimmer gebucht, ohne daß Sie es wußten.
Vielleicht im *The Plaza* in New York.
Im *Camino Real* in Mexico City. Oder im *Shangri-La* in Singapur.
Dies sind nur drei der 54 erstklassigen Western Hotels, die Sie in der ganzen Welt finden.
Und wenn Sie nur eins unserer Hotels kennen, wissen Sie schon viel über alle. Denn alle haben sich den gleichen Maßstäben für ausgezeichneten Service und hervorragende Küche verschrieben.
Doch jedes hat seinen eigenen Charakter.
Das *Hotel St. Francis* in San Franzisko ist seit über 75 Jahren ein Wahrzeichen der Stadt. Und in Atlanta ist das *Peachtree Plaza,* das sich 73 Stockwerke hoch in die Luft erhebt, über Nacht zum Wahrzeichen geworden.
Im *Hotel Scandinavia* in Oslo können Ihre Kunden von ihrem Zimmer aus einen Wald oder einen Fjord sehen. Vom *Hotel Scandinavia* in Kopenhagen kann man zu Fuß zum Tivoli gehen.
Das Bayshore in Vancouver ist mit Wasserflugzeug zu erreichen. Das *Hotel Bonaventure* in Montreal ist ein Garten-Penthouse im 17. Stock.
Für Geschäftsreisende ist von Vorteil, daß sich die meisten unserer Hotels im Herzen einer Stadt befinden. In Toronto zum Beispiel hat das *Hotel Toronto* eine ebenso günstige Lage wie das Rathaus.
Wenn sie sich jedoch auf Vergnügungsreise befinden, können Ihre Kunden vom *Mauna Kea* in Hawaii aus den höchsten vulkanischen Berg der Welt erforschen. Oder sie können einige der ältesten Maya-Ruinen der Welt besuchen, während sie im *Camino Real* in Guatemala wohnen.
Wenn sie einkaufen wollen, gibt es 200 Läden im Komplex des *Carlton Centre* direkt nebem dem *Carlton* in Johannesburg. Und das *Detroit Plaza* in Detroit ist von mehreren Ebenen eleganter Läden umgeben.
Wenn es um Essen geht, gibt es *Fouquet's* im *Camino Real* in Mexico City. Ein französisches Restaurant, dem nur sein Gegenstück in Paris den Rang streitig machen kann. Und hervorragende chinesische Küche finden Sie in ausgezeichneten Restaurants im *Shangri-La* in Singapur und in Hongkong (Eröffnung Ende 1980).
Und ganz gleich, welches Hotel Sie wählen, Sie können sich darauf verlassen, daß die Unterbringung Ihrer Kunden allen Anforderungen gerecht wird.
Wenn Sie Reservierungen machen wollen oder Informationen über die Welt der Western International Hotels wünschen, erreichen Sie uns telefonisch unter (0611) 215 747."
Michael Andrea
Gebietsverkaufsdirektor, Europa
WESTERN INTERNATIONAL HOTELS

(*a*)

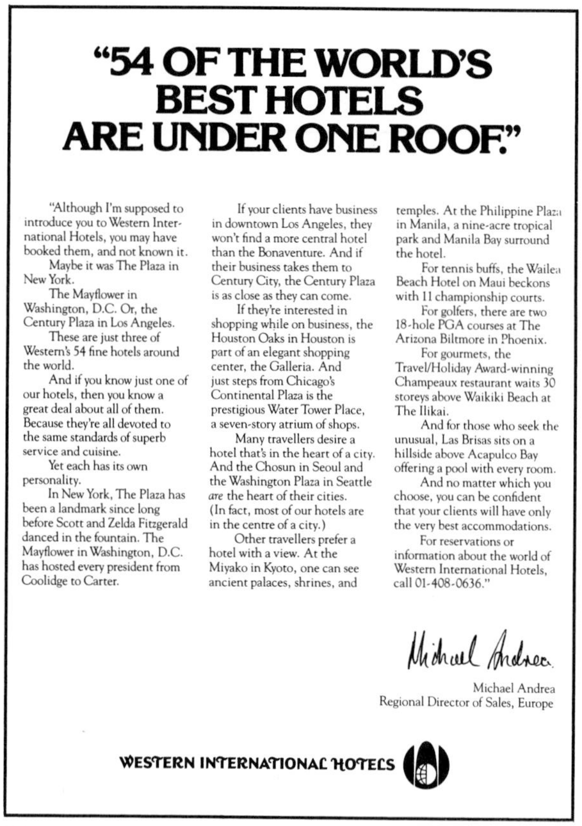
"54 OF THE WORLD'S BEST HOTELS ARE UNDER ONE ROOF."
"Although I'm supposed to introduce you to Western International Hotels, you may have booked them, and not known it.
Maybe it was The Plaza in New York.
The Mayflower in Washington, D.C. Or, the Century Plaza in Los Angeles.
These are just three of Western's 54 fine hotels around the world.
And if you know just one of our hotels, then you know a great deal about all of them. Because they're all devoted to the same standards of superb service and cuisine.
Yet each has its own personality.
In New York, The Plaza has been a landmark since long before Scott and Zelda Fitzgerald danced in the fountain. The Mayflower in Washington, D.C. has hosted every president from Coolidge to Carter.
If your clients have business in downtown Los Angeles, they won't find a more central hotel than the Bonaventure. And if their business takes them to Century City, the Century Plaza is as close as they can come.
If they're interested in shopping while on business, the Houston Oaks in Houston is part of an elegant shopping center, the Galleria. And just steps from Chicago's Continental Plaza is the prestigious Water Tower Place, a seven-story atrium of shops.
Many travellers desire a hotel that's in the heart of a city. And the Chosun in Seoul and the Washington Plaza in Seattle *are* the heart of their cities. (In fact, most of our hotels are in the centre of a city.)
Other travellers prefer a hotel with a view. At the Miyako in Kyoto, one can see ancient palaces, shrines, and temples. At the Philippine Plaza in Manila, a nine-acre tropical park and Manila Bay surround the hotel.
For tennis buffs, the Wailea Beach Hotel on Maui beckons with 11 championship courts.
For golfers, there are two 18-hole PGA courses at The Arizona Biltmore in Phoenix.
For gourmets, the Travel/Holiday Award-winning Champeaux restaurant waits 30 storeys above Waikiki Beach at The Ilikai.
And for those who seek the unusual, Las Brisas sits on a hillside above Acapulco Bay offering a pool with every room.
And no matter which you choose, you can be confident that your clients will have only the very best accommodations.
For reservations or information about the world of Western International Hotels, call 01-408-0636."
Michael Andrea
Regional Director of Sales, Europe
WESTERN INTERNATIONAL HOTELS

(*b*)

Figure 21.10 (*a*) This is one page from a six-page insert placed in a German travel magazine whose readers are travel agents. The other pages were in color, and each featured one of the hotels in the chain. (*b*) The same ad was aimed at British travel agents. [*Courtesy of Western International Hotels, now named Westin Hotels.*]

1970s, the United States became more attractive to vacationing Europeans, Japanese, and Australians. Miami, Florida, became popular with affluent South Americans as well as with many British tourists who visited our country on inexpensive package tours. Tourist destinations throughout the nation now cater to foreign travelers. Over 22 million foreigners visited the United States in 1980. An example of advertising aimed at foreign travelers is shown in Figure 21.10. The Western International Hotel chain's message tries to interest travelers in visiting the United States and in patronizing its hotels when doing so.

Naturally, our attempts to market our consumer and industrial goods and services throughout the world will continue. Employment of imaginative advertising will help us to do this with success. We must also look for other products and services to feature in our international marketing efforts so that we can retain our national economic vitality. One cannot overestimate the importance of effective international advertising to the achievement of our nation's economic survival.

Legal and Social Environment for International Advertising

An additional problem facing international advertisers, similar to that facing domestic advertisers, is the existence of laws and regulations that limit the advertising message that can be printed or broadcast and the kind of media that can be used in an advertising campaign. For example, no foreign good is advertised on television in the Soviet Union, nor are com-

Profile

Alexander Brody

Alexander Brody serves as president of Young & Rubicam, International, a subsidiary of Young & Rubicam, Inc. This assignment places Brody in charge of 39 offices located throughout the world to serve transnational advertisers. He also serves as executive vice president of the parent firm, having held both posts since 1970.

Born in Budapest, Hungary, in 1933, Brody earned his B.A. degree at Princeton University. Later, he attended the Woodrow Wilson School of Public and International Affairs. He is fluent in five languages and conversant in several others, including mandarin Chinese.

Brody joined Y & R's New York office in 1953 and worked in both the Television and Account Management Departments. His first exposure to international advertising work began with an assignment to the agency's Frankfurt, Germany, office in 1959. In 1964, he was named executive director of the Brussels office.

Between 1967 and 1970, Brody opened seven international offices for Young & Rubicam, International. After only 17 years with the agency, he gained his present position. Underlying his phenomenal success in international advertising is his philosophy: He believes that the exchange of creative people among agencies is "absolutely central to the success of an international agency." Therefore, Y & R, International, rotates creative people to new environments on a regular basis. This practice means that the international client gets an agency recommendation which represents marketing reality and not a parochial point of view. The agency that Alex Brody heads is a leader in the international advertising field.

mercials for liquor or cigarettes permitted. Some countries forbid comparative advertising and the use of superlatives in the advertising message. Products whose international advertising is widely regulated are food, drugs, and cosmetics.

West Germany's advertising legislation is the world's strictest and most specific. Even the objective truth of the message can be questioned; truth is determined not merely by the facts but by the possibility that the ad may mislead the consumer. A phrase like "world's most popular" cannot be used since it might imply that the product is Germany's most popular, when it is not.

Several countries tax advertising billings or the agencies or the media. In drafting the advertising budget in these areas, the taxes must be included in figuring the total cost of the campaign.

Many nations control their advertising media. In some countries, an advertiser must obtain permission to use certain media. Others, like India and the United Kingdom, have tried to restrict the amount of advertising expenditures by companies. Advertising to children is an issue throughout the world. Although most nations allow advertising to children, this is a sensitive area and one that is most likely to be regulated by government.

International advertisers must understand social conditions in each foreign market. Consumers in many countries feel that foreign corporate power threatens their nationalism, and they prefer to place economic power in the hands of their own governments.[21] In countries with strict regulations on foreign corporations and foreign advertising, advertisers must construct their marketing and advertising plans with great care. Clearly, offending consumers in foreign markets will result only in lost sales. An advertiser's best policy is to create tasteful, informative ads that fulfill the requirements of local laws and that conform to the social customs of the foreign nation.

We have seen that foreign markets are important sources of revenue for many United States firms. Those companies doing business with foreign consumers must be aware of the customs and laws in foreign nations to maximize their sales and to get the greatest benefit from the advertising dollars spent to reach these markets.

Summary

About one-half the world's advertising originates in the United States. Our country, leader in advertising for over a century, provides expertise around the world through its highly developed system of advertising agencies.

Advertising increases in importance when economies become developed. Such developed countries as Japan and West Germany employ American-style advertising in their own nations and when seeking sales overseas. Even such controlled economies as the Soviet Union and China use advertising to a small degree. Countries with varying levels of economic development find advertising helpful in achieving their national economic goals.

Because the economic survival of the United States depends upon foreign trade, American producers need to understand the opportunities and problems that advertising abroad entails. Several key decisions face the firm desiring to advertise in other than domestic markets. First, the advertiser must decide whether to use an American-based advertising agency that operates internationally, or to retain a local agency in the country where the advertising will be run.

Creating advertising suitable for foreign markets presents an advertiser with the greatest challenge. Here, the core choice is between the ethnic message, which is designed specially for the particular foreign market, and the standardized message, which is the same for all countries except for translation into the appropriate language. Many blunders can occur at this stage of the advertising process if cultural differences of the audience are not fully understood.

Management of the international advertising program is further complicated by the question of media choice. Each country presents its own array of suitable vehicles. Advertisers must match media and audiences using the media available to them in a geograhic area. Another factor influencing the international advertising decision that is beyond the control of the advertiser consists of the local regulations imposed on advertising.

Questions for Discussion

1 Explain why American advertisers should become more knowledgeable in the strategies and tactics of international advertising.

2 Describe the two major approaches available when designing an advertising message for foreign markets. Which would you use for such

products as soft drinks, toothpaste, and cigarettes? Which would you be likely to use when perfume, women's ready-to-wear clothes, and contraceptives were being promoted?

3 Why does the media mix employed by the international advertiser vary from country to country? When would the advertiser use (*a*) print media; (*b*) radio; (*c*) television; (*d*) outdoor?

4 Go to the "International Advertising" section of a recent issue of *Advertising Age*. Choose one article which you found interesting and write a short summary of its contents. Be ready to discuss the information in the article before your class.

5 Find two examples of magazine advertisements that illustrate how a foreign manufacturer is using American advertising techniques to obtain sales in the United States. Explain the techniques you believe are being used.

For Further Reference

Cateora, Philip R., and John M. Hess: *International Marketing*, 4th ed., Richard D. Irwin, Homewood, Ill., 1979.

Dunn, S. Watson, and E. S. Lorimor: *International Advertising and Marketing*, Grid Publishing, Inc., Columbus, Ohio, 1979.

Fayerweather, John: *International Marketing*, Prentice-Hall, Inc., Englewood Cliffs, N.J., 1970.

Greer, Thomas V.: *Marketing in the Soviet Union*, Frederick A. Praeger, Inc., New York, 1973.

Keegan, Warren J.: *Multinational Marketing Management*, 2d ed., Prentice-Hall, Inc., Englewood Cliffs, N.J., 1980.

Miracle, Gordon E., and Gerald S. Albaum: *International Marketing Management*, Richard D. Irwin, Inc., Homewood, Ill., 1970.

Ricks, David, Marilyn Y. C. Fu, and Jeffrey S. Arpan: *International Business Blunders*, Grid, Inc., Columbus, Ohio, 1974.

Terpstra, Vern: *International Marketing*, 2d ed., The Dryden Press, Inc., Hinsdale, Ill., 1978.

Thorelli, H. B. (ed.): *International Marketing Strategy*, Penguin Books, Inc., Baltimore, Md., 1973.

End Notes

[1] *World Advertising Expenditures*, Starch INRA Hooper, Mamaroneck, New York, 1980, pp. 8–9.

[2] Paragraph drawn from "Vast U.S. and Worldwide Ad Expenditures Expected," by Robert J. Coen, *Advertising Age*, Nov. 13, 1980, p. 10.

[3] Thomas V. Greer, *Marketing in the Soviet Union*, Frederick A. Praeger, Inc., New York, 1973, pp. 96–97.

[4] Quoted in David Ogilvy, *Confessions of an Advertising Man*, Atheneum Publishers, New York, 1963, p. 150.

[5] Ye. Kanevsky, "The Effect of Advertising," *Pravda*, April 1, 1972, p. 3 CDSP, 24(April 26, 1972), p. 32, as quoted in Greer, op. cit., p. 100. Also see "The Socialist Countries," by Robert S. Trebus, in S. Watson Dunn and E. S. Lorimor, *International Advertising and Marketing*, Columbus, Ohio, Grid Publishing, Inc., 1979, pp. 349–360.

[6] *Advertising Age*, Sept. 8, 1980, pp. 43–44, and Sept. 15, 1980, pp. 45, 48, 50.

[7] *Directory of Trade*, International Monetary Fund, Washington, D.C., May 1980, pp. 4–5.

[8] *Advertising Age*, Dec. 8, 1980, pp. 55.

[9] Paraphrased from James Killough, "Improved Payoff from Transnational Advertising," *Harvard Business Review*, July–August 1978.

[10] *Advertising Age*, April 14, 1980, p. S-1.

[11] Loc. cit.

[12] David Ricks, Marilyn Y. C. Fu, and Jeffrey S. Arpan, *International Business Blunders*, Grid Publishing, Inc., Columbus, Ohio, 1974.

[13] John Ryans, "A Tiger in Every Tank?" *Columbia World Business Review*, March–April 1969, pp. 69–75.

[14] *World Advertising Expenditures*, op. cit., pp. 15–17.

[15] *Advertising Age*, Oct. 22, 1979, p. S-11.

[16] *World Advertising Expenditures*, op. cit., pp. 16–17.

[17] Ibid., p. 27.

[18] Ibid., p. 31.

[19] *Advertising Age*, March 12, 1979, p. S-11.

[20] Martin Mayer, "Our Butter-and-Egg Men Are Winning Big Abroad," *Fortune*, May 19, 1980, pp. 146–154.

[21] *Advertising Age*, May 14, 1979, p. 58.

PART 6

Advertising and the Future

Throughout this book, we have stressed the changes made in advertising to correspond both to the needs and desires of modern consumers and to dynamic market conditions. Advertising is not static; it is dynamic. Many new demands will present advertisers and the people who create advertising with challenges in the future. In this part of the book, we examine some of the factors that will shape the course of advertising as we approach the year 2000. It is not possible, of course,

to predict the future with certainty, but trends in current markets, advertising technology, and the economy do provide clues to advertising's future role. As a business person or as an advertising professional, you must be aware of these changes and adapt to them in order to be successful.

Chapter 22 examines the role of advertising in the marketplace and as a mode of communication, anticipating some of the changes that are likely to occur in coming years. We shall look at recent developments in the economy, in technology, in society, and in politics and attempt to extend these trends to the future. The use of advertising for nonbusiness purposes is also explained.

Finally, in Chapter 23, we shall discuss the future of advertising in your own career plans. This chapter reviews jobs in advertising and provides guidance for those persons wishing to enter the business of advertising.

Chapter 22

Where Is Advertising Headed?

● During the late 1960s and throughout the 1970s, the pace of American lives increased dramatically. Advances in communications speeded up long-distance phone calls and the transmission of written communications, the time required for news reporting, and the dissemination of information through print and broadcast media. Changes in transportation reduced the time needed to go across the country or around the world. The explosion of computers and the widespread availability of computer systems enabled tedious tasks to be done more quickly and expanded the banks of information available to business people, scientists, and other individuals. The list of changes is endless, and the speed of change has been the hallmark of our modern age.

Several books appeared in the 1970s that described some of the effects of rapid change on our society. *Future Shock,* by Alvin Toffler, and *The Greening of America,* by Charles Reich, highlighted the impact of rapid change on our lives and provided guidelines for marketing and advertising planners as they tried to understand the needs of consumers and to adjust their strategies to our changing society. Toffler published a sequel in 1980 called *The Third Wave;* it predicted even more cataclysmic changes in this decade.

In the 1970s, we experienced change in the availability of oil and other natural resources, limiting some of the growth that we had experienced in the decades following World War II and creating several problems in our economy. *The Limits to Growth,* a study made in 1972 by a socioeconomic group called the Club of Rome, provided a timetable for the reduction of economic growth that would result from a shortage of resources. Although this timetable has been revised, since depletion did not occur as rapidly as predicted, society realized that there are limits to technological progress if we continue to rely on the same natural resources for our economic well-being.

The pattern of the 1970s set the stage for the last portion of the twentieth century. One can safely conclude that rapid change will continue despite the limits imposed by natural resources, and society will look for other energy sources and raw materials to maintain its standard of living.

In response to economic and social conditions, marketers and marketing organizations must assume that changes will take place at an even faster pace. They must rely on strategic plans to provide information so that action can be adjusted to changes as they arise. The ability to cope with change will be essential to the survival of organizations and individuals. Business executives, whatever their specialty, must become students of the future. The new discipline of **futurism** undoubtedly will become popular and flourish. What is the role for advertising in this age of change? Let's look into our crystal ball to see where advertising is headed and to isolate some of the changes that will influence its practice as we approach A.D. 2000.

The Future of Advertising in the Marketplace

Advertising is not created in a vacuum. Forces operating to change our society affect advertising messages, the media used to disseminate those messages, and the amount of advertising that a firm uses in its marketing mix. The forces having the greatest influence on advertising are economic, social, technological, and political. As you can imagine, these areas are volatile, and the future of advertising as a force in the marketplace is influenced strongly by trends in each of these areas. To be successful in the markets of the future, an advertiser must be aware of the trends and changes, and alter the firm's advertising in reaction to significant changes in the economy, lifestyles, technological advances, and political pressures.

Figure 22-1 Advertising is used to inform prospective buyers of the availability of new products. Here a manufacturer tells the features possessed by one brand of personal computers. [*Courtesy of Atari.*]

Economic Forces

Advertising is used by manufacturers and other producers of goods and services to inform consumers of the availability and benefits of their products and to persuade them to purchase those goods and services. In this role, advertising aids the firm's marketing efforts. Advertising developed as a marketing force during the Industrial Revolution when the factors of production (land, labor, and capital) became geographically separated from the markets in which those goods and services were consumed. The Industrial Revolution spawned and nourished the concept of **mass production.** The tasks used to produce goods were separated, and the employment of assembly lines enabled manufacturers to produce goods more cheaply than they could be produced by individual handcrafters. These mass-produced goods had to reach consumers, and advertising to the masses permitted our **mass-consumption society,** along with the economies of Western Europe, Japan, and other industrialized nations, to develop. In this economic environment, "not a few individuals, or a thin upper class, but the majority of families now have discretionary purchasing power and constantly replace and enlarge their stock of consumer goods."[1]

It is not likely that there will be major changes in the way that goods are mass-produced and mass-consumed in the future, and advertising's traditional role as a communication vehicle for producers should remain unchanged. There are factors operating in the market, however, that will alter the manner in which advertising is employed. A **market,** as you learned in Chapter 3, consists of (1) people, with (2) money, and (3) willingness to spend. Advertising reaches people and persuades them to spend their money on the advertiser's product, and in this manner it has a strong effect on the market and on the economy as a whole.

The people or audiences for advertising messages have changed in the 1970s and are likely to change even more in the future. **Population shifts** alter the advertiser's target market and the format of advertising messages.

Changes in the economic climate alter the amount of money people have to spend on goods and services and also affect advertising goals and messages. **Income trends,** too, will undergo tremendous change, and advertisers must create advertising campaigns and messages that will enable them to maintain or increase their market shares if they are to be successful in coming decades.

Population Trends In 1980 the population of the United States was more than 226.5 million, having increased from 204.9 million in 1970. The Census Bureau predicted a total growth rate for the 1980s of 9.6 percent, with a 1990 population estimate of 243.5 million.

More significant to marketing and advertising is the changing composition of our population. In the decade from 1980 to 1990, the fastest growing population segment will be the group between 35 and 54 years of age, which will experience a 28 percent increase. People over age 65 will increase by 20 percent. The young adult category (ages 20 to 34) will grow a mere 3 percent, while the 55- to 64-year category will decline by 2 percent. The most dramatic change will be in teenagers (ages 13 to 19), with a 17 percent decline.[2]

Advertisers must adjust their sights when creating target markets for the future based on these trends. For example, the number of people in the household-formation stage (usually considered to be persons in their twenties) is declining. Therefore, manufacturers of consumer durables, such as furniture and household applicances, can predict a smaller market for these goods. One strategy which they might adopt would be to convince persons aged 35 to 54 to upgrade their furniture and electrical appliances instead of sticking with those items purchased during the family-formation stage. Other advertisers can expect increases in the number of people interested in their goods and services. The group beyond the child-rearing age will be free from the responsibility for the care and education of children and will provide an excellent market for leisure goods and services.

Advertisers should beware of placing too much reliance on population data. History has proved that many of these estimates have been wrong. Montesquieu, the French philosopher, stated in 1743 that "the population of the earth decreases every day, and, if this continues, in another 10 centuries the earth will be nothing but a desert." And not too many years ago, demographers predicted a great expansion in the United States population. Attitudes on child-bearing and family formation changed dramatically, negating their predictions. Advertisers who placed great faith in these predictions of population growth were sorely disappointed. For example, baby-food manufacturers saw their market decline from 4.258 million children born in 1960 to 3.144 million born in 1975. Since they projected demand on population growth estimates, the companies faced a decline in sales. Some of them made an effort to convert the elderly into users of their products.

The size of the market is an important factor for any advertiser, and demographic data are valuable aids in projecting future demand. Needless to say, advertising strategies of the future must be aimed at the largest potential group of consumers, and information about this group is essential in preparing plans and campaigns.

Family Income Trends Persistent inflation throughout the late 1970s and early 1980s ended the long-term trend of increasing family income that followed World War II. Although personal income figures have been rising, once these figures are adjusted for inflation, the average American family finds itself with barely any increase in purchasing power. If this trend continues, as seems likely, the United States will remain affluent but growth in consumer spending will be stagnant. Advertisers can no longer rely on increased purchasing power to maintain their market position, and they will find themselves in fierce competition for a fairly constant pool of consumer dollars. This situation bodes well for increased levels of advertising. It probably will also mean that advertising messages will become more value-oriented than in the past.

One significant group is expected to experience increased affluence in the 1980s: households with more than one wage-earner. Economists predicted that in the 1980s, "the number of households with incomes of $25,000 or more, measured in constant dollars, will increase 70%, or 3½ times as rapidly as total households."[3] Furthermore, roughly one of every three households will have more than one wage-earner by 1990, and these households will then be earning nearly 60 percent of the nation's personal income.[4] By 1990, households with $50,000 or more in annual income will have 18 percent of the total spending power in the United States. The resulting two-level segmentation of the population, when viewed on the basis of family income, means that advertisers of expensive consumer durables will still have a sizable market for their products. Obviously, messages directed to such consumers will contain very different appeals from those directed at population segments existing at a mere survival level.

Willingness to Spend The third economic factor contributing to making a market is the willingness of consumers to spend their money for goods and services. For consumers to be willing to part with their money is largely a factor of consumer optimism. For many years, advertisers contributed to this mood through the use of persuasive messages. However, consumers living in times of inflation and declining real incomes are harder to persuade by older, more familiar appeals.

Although faced with declining markets and large segments of the population with reduced purchasing power, advertisers do have tools available to them which will help improve the efficiency of their advertising campaigns in these changed times. Advertising, as we point out at many places in this book, is quite sophisticated and quantitative these days. The proliferation of minicomputers aids in creating consumer profiles, isolating the real target market for products, and in correct product positioning. Furthermore, advances in the understanding of consumers through the discoveries of the science of consumer behavior also help to reduce waste in advertising and permit the reaching of the right people with the correct message. One interesting development in these pressing times is the tendency of many consumers to seek expensive but durable items instead of less costly products that might need frequent replacement. There undoubtedly will be many other changes in consumption patterns in the years ahead. Advertisers can arouse the willingness to buy if they have the key to consumer psychology.

The Competitive Environment Changes in the composition of the market, as we have just discussed, is obviously not the only economic force affecting marketing and advertising in the 1980s. Marketers will live in a tough competitive environment, fighting for fewer consumer dollars. This condition must be taken into account when advertising strategies are planned. Higher advertising-to-sales ratios may be anticipated. There will probably be more use of comparative advertising. Greater emphasis on "hard-sell" advertising copy is expected.

Late in the 1970s, supermarket retailing experienced a development that may affect advertising expenditures in the 1980s. **Generic products,** which are essentially non-branded merchandise offered as a lower-priced alternative to nationally advertised products, became quite popular. Instead of purchasing Bounty, the national market leader in the paper towel category, the consumer could now choose a package simply labeled "Paper Towels," In 1980, the share of category sales garnered by generics was significant. For example, bleach accounted for 27 percent; canned pineapple, for 25 percent; coffee creamers, for 31 percent; facial tissue, for 21 percent; paper towels, for 16 percent; plastic bags, for 25 percent; toilet tissue, for 13 percent; and tomato juice, for 25 percent.[5]

The immediate impact of the introduction of generic products was a decline of network television and women's magazine advertising for food and household products. In its place the manufacturers substituted various kinds of price promotions. Some brand manufacturers are enhancing the quality of their products in an effort to convince consumers that it pays to buy branded merchandise, even though higher-priced. Some observers predict that the trend toward the generic brands will have a major adverse effect on those brands that are not in first or second place in the product category, leaving a situation where the brand front-runners will remain to compete against the generic brands. This development bears close watching over the next decade.

Social Forces

Changes in social values and lifestyles among the American population pose both problems and opportunities for advertising. Changing attitudes have influenced the rate of population growth, as women (and their spouses) view the ideal family as having fewer members than in past generations. The development of improved methods of birth control has, of course, made it much easier to limit family size. Similarly, income size for many American households has increased because so many women have entered the work force and created the two-income family. The working woman was once the exception, but now the nonworking woman is fast becoming unusual. The traditional family, a working father, a housewife mother, and two or three children living together in one home, now accounts for less than 20 percent of all households in this country.

Households Another major change in American society that is likely to continue is the increase in the number of households. In 1980 there were approximately 80 million households in the United States. A 23 percent increase is estimated by 1990, bringing the total number of households to 99 million. (A more conservative projection estimates a 16 percent increase, which still results in a figure of 92.4 million households.)[6] The increase has occurred because people are postponing marriage and living as singles for longer periods, because the increase in the divorce rate is creating many one-parent families, and because more and more widows and divorced people are living alone. Food advertisers have attempted to meet the needs of this new market by changing package sizes for their products and advertising them on the merits of convenience. These households are using media in a considerably different way from that of traditional homes; therefore, media selection becomes critical when trying to reach such persons.

Education Citizens of the United States, regardless of their socioeconomic or ethnic background, have greater opportunities for formal education than did previous generations. By 1980, more than 10 million Americans were enrolled in some form of higher education. In that year for the first time in history, more entering students were women than men. Between 1980 and 1990, there will be a 42 percent increase in college-educated adults, contrasted with a 10 percent increase in population. More education generally means greater earning capacity. Furthermore, education creates different tastes for products and changing levels of aspiration. Advertising aimed at this group illustrates the value systems of an improved lifestyle. Education makes people more sophisticated; advertising appeals therefore need to be geared to this group's level of accomplishment. More education and high income levels among consumers means that markets are more fragmented than they were when the population was closer together in education and income levels. In other words, mass-market advertising is less likely to be successful. Advertisers have begun to structure their campaigns at specific market segments grouped together by interests or educational levels.

Mobility In any five-year period, one-half the people of the United States change their places of residence. Persons in their late twenties are even more mobile; 8 out of 10 move in the same period of time. Within the nation, the movement is to the West and the South—the Sunbelt. Such states as Florida, Arizona, Colorado, Nevada, Alaska, Utah, Idaho, New Mexico, Texas, and Wyoming are projected to gain 15 or more percent in population between 1980 and 1990.[7] Previous trends which saw people moving from the inner city and rural communities to suburban areas are expected to continue. People entering any new area look for new retail sources and therefore are open to new and useful information. Advertising becomes the newcomer's guide to the new environment. Advertisements provide clues about whether a particular store is the place where he or she wants to shop. New patterns of product preference are created through the relocation process. The national advertiser also must be aware of geographic switches so that correct media vehicles will be chosen to reach prospects where they now live.

Working Women In addition to contributing to two-income households, working women have changed society in other ways. Approximately 39 percent of all women aged 16 years or older were working in 1965. By 1970, the figure approached 43 percent, climbed to 48 percent in 1977, and hit the 50 percent level before the turn of 1980. However, in 1977, actually "only 38 percent of all women in our country were full-time housewives; 10 percent more women are working out of the house than staying home and keeping house. The others are out of the mainstream—either still in school, or retired and/or disabled."[8]

This change was brought about by new attitudes concerning the role of women in our society. Legislation helped women gain greater economic status by opening up new employment opportunities to them. The woman's traditional role as the household purchasing agent has been altered. More responsibility for family shopping is placed on the husband and the family's children, thus requiring different advertising strategies to reach these buyers. When the woman still performs the shopping function, she does so in a much different manner—less leisurely, more businesslike, and involving less frequent comparison of product offerings in several stores. Advertising is relied upon more heavily as a source of information about products and prices in order to save shopping time. Product reputation, created in part by advertising, is more important to the busy shopper. The advertiser needs to take a new look at the media used to reach such shoppers. J. Walter Thompson Company, a large advertising agency, describes this consumer as the "moving target" and highlights the importance of knowing about her with these words, "The way to hit your target is to aim at where it's going and not at where it's been."[9] Old advertising strategies will not work with America's liberated women.

The increase in the number of women workers has also expanded the market for prepackaged, prepared foods and for devices for quick food preparation, such as microwave ovens. Advertising has the job of explaining these products and their availability to working women.

Leisure Another important trend is greater participation in leisure activities and interest in personal well-being. Changes in dietary habits and regimens of exercise are fast becoming an integral part of lifestyle in the United States. Most people receive longer vacations than were usual in years past, and vacation homes in the mountains or on the water have become part of the normal pattern of life for many middle-income Americans. Others indulge in extensive travel throughout the world. Do-it-yourself hobbies are stimulated in part by more free time. Many people are encouraged to learn practical skills because of the scarcity and cost of house painters, carpenters, and other craftworkers. Advertising acts as a stimulus to this trend by showing how the various tasks can be performed by amateurs. Participants in active sports and various creative hobbies, including oil painting and woodworking, are also part of the leisure market at which future advertising will be aimed. With so many options available to consumers in their search for personal fulfillment, time itself has become the critical scarce resource in many people's lives. Advertisers can help individuals improve their personal time allocation by saving them from time-consuming shopping and by providing information quickly and completely about options available in the marketplace.

When people reach retirement, their leisure time increases. This market had only begun to be tapped by advertisers in the 1970s. It will be an important source of revenue for advertisers in the future.

Voluntary Simplicity Our population today contains a group that is known as the "voluntary simplicity" segment.[10] Estimated at 10 percent of all Americans, this group holds five core values: material simplicity, humanism, self-determinism, ecological awareness, and personal growth. People in this group often work at jobs below personal skill levels so that they will have time and energy for avocational pursuits. They have lower family incomes and show a more modest consumption of goods and services. However, the goods they purchase are usually of high quality and often handcrafted. Whether this segment will become a trend-setter or not is something that marketers will want to watch.

Conclusion In sum, effective advertising of the future must be relevant to the needs and desires of those persons with whom the seller wishes to communicate. Advertisers, therefore, must be keen observers of the changing American scene, if their messages are to be deemed relevant to potential consumers of their goods and services.

Technological Forces

Recently, the United States has lost some of its predominance in technological innovation. Other developed countries, notably Japan and West Germany, have challenged our competitive edge in many product categories. Nevertheless, our research and development laboratories continue to operate, and a revived emphasis on technology seems likely as we realize the critical importance of superior products as we expand into foreign markets.

The development of new products is one activity where technology and advertising intertwine. New products are vital to the survival of many businesses. As they are developed, advertising is needed to inform potential buyers of their availability. Today's consumers do not beat a path to the better mousetrap inventor's doorstep, regardless of Emerson's axiom. Thus, when Minnetonka, Inc., introduced a new product concept to serve the billion-dollar soap market in April 1980, it advertised "Softsoap" so effectively that the company captured a 7 percent share of the market in less than one year.[11]

In a similar fashion, Smoky Mountain Enterprises, of Asheville, North Carolina, promoted an old, somewhat neglected product (shown in Figure 2.8 on page 46) as a solution to one of today's household problems. Many homes are coping with the energy crisis through the use of old-fashioned wood-burning stoves. Other energy-efficient applicances will be popular with consumers of the future as well.

Two technological revolutions taking place in the fields of computers and communications affect the practice of advertising. We explained how the computer aids in conducting advertising research and in the development and control of the advertising budget. But we have only hinted at the impact that new communications technology is making on the field of advertising.

If the 1960s can be characterized as advertising's "age of creativity," and the 1970s as its "age of positioning," then the 1980s should be called the "age of media." Tidal waves of change are taking place in advertising media because of technological changes, particularly in television. Such innovations as video recording, satellite transmission of television signals, cable television systems, and interactive television are combining to accomplish what Toffler calls the "demassification of the media." Toffler says:

> Today, instead of masses of people all receiving the same messages, smaller demassified groups receive and send large amounts of their own imagery to one another. As the entire society shifts toward Third Wave diversity, the new media reflect and accelerate the process.[12]

What Toffler means is that the mass audience being reached by the television medium today is being broken into many smaller groups because technology is now available to reach these segments efficiently. Media selection will now become very precise. For example, the advertiser of garden seeds will be able to place the sales message in a television program of interest only to gardeners. The possibilities for targeting markets are endless. Furthemore, the job of advertising copywriting will be greatly simplified, as the message can be specific to the needs of the target group, and the need to compete for viewer attention will decrease as audiences become able to preselect programs appealing to their specific interest. Although network programs that appeal to general audiences are likely to remain for a long time, television viewers will have more options, as is already the case for magazine readers. Television is likely to become an even more important medium for advertising, but it will become much more diffused, thus making expertise in its management increasingly essential in the future.

The Technology-Creativity Interface As advertising practitioners use more scientific methods in their day-to-day operations, some advertising professionals fear that messages may become less creative —mechanical, stereotyped. However, the solution of advertising problems is becoming both more scientific and more imaginative. One reason for this paradox is that a feeling exists in the advertising community that creativity is something that can be learned. Alex Osborn pioneered this concept and maintained that everyone possesses creative ability to a degree. Its lack results from failure to use and develop a capacity that is originally almost universal. He made a strong case for the idea that creativity not only can be developed or learned, but can also be taught. Osborn's book, *Applied Imagination,*[13] presents guiding principles around which this theory is developed.

The greater dissemination of scientific research about advertising and the increased recognition of the importance of scientific methods in the application of advertising to marketing and social problems promise new opportunities for a variety of skills in the advertising field. At the same time, the need for people with highly developed creative and communicative abilities is as great as—or greater than—ever before. Leo Burnett, one of advertising's creative geniuses, put it this way:

> If people could tell you in advance what they want, there would never have been a wheel, a lever, much less an automobile, an electric refrigerator or a TV set. There would never have been a Barnum and Bailey circus, a *South Pacific* or a modern magazine. Somebody with the urge, the inspiration and the drive had to think it up and push it through. That goes for new advertising ideas, too. Somebody has to think them up and push them through. And somebody has to have imagination and guts enough to buy them.[14]

Another creative giant, William Bernbach, believes that for communicators to satisfy all people and to reconcile the tremendous diversity of opinion in the world, science is not the answer.[15] He states that ". . . it is insight into human nature that is the key to a communicator's skill. For whereas the writer is concerned with what he puts into his writing, the communicator is concerned not just with what he puts into a piece of writing but with what the reader gets out of it. He therefore becomes a student of *how* people read or listen."[16] Advertising is truly a skillful blend of science and art.

Political Forces

Television now permits candidates to address large numbers of people at one time and allows millions of voters to see as well as hear candidates through ads, talk shows, and debates. Dwight Eisenhower's successful campaign for the presidency in 1952 was aided by short commercials that caused the opposition to state that "the presidency is being sold like a bar of soap." Many political experts believe John F. Kennedy won the presidency in 1960 because of his ability to project youthfulness and vigor over television. Being photogenic on television has become a decided plus for any aspirant for political office.

The role of media and political advertising has grown substantially since the 1960s. Media consultants are important members of any campaign team, and campaign slogans are created as carefully as the most effective copy themes for consumer products. The 1980 presidential election illustrates the power that a media personality exerts on voters. Ronald Reagan, who for many years earned his living as a media personality, projected a controlled image of a very capable candidate for the presidency.

The importance of advertising in political campaigns is further illustrated by the size of the advertising budgets employed. In the 1980 election, President Carter and candidate Reagan each received $28 million in federal funds to run their post-convention campaigns, and additional dollars earmarked for advertising were contributed by supporters of both men. As in the past, the Democratic and Republican parties supplemented these funds as well.

The emphasis on broadcast advertising (particularly TV advertising) has trickled down to elections for state and local candidates. Television allows candidates to reach more people, more often, at lower cost per impression, than old-fashioned platform appearances could.

Use of media and media advertising in our political processes enable people to become involved more easily in political affairs and to be more sophisticated about the choices available to them. The role of media advertising will certainly become more important in future political campaigns, as more and more candidates become skilled in addressing their constituents via broadcast media and in presenting their views on controversial issues. The high cost incurred by modern political campaigns are disturbing to some observers because they feel that only persons of financial means, or those capable of finding supporters with sufficient cash, will be able to seek and win political office.

Another dimension of the political force upon advertising in the future is, of course, how the institution will be regulated by the government. This particular question is discussed fully in Chapter 20. Suffice it to say that when advertising steps out of bounds, the public is likely to ask its elected officials to take action to curb its undesirable activities. With the inauguration of Ronald Reagan, the political climate in the United States shifted. Most voters and newly elected officials favor less governmental regulation. If business seizes this opportunity and maintains a clean house through the practices of enlightened self-interest and self-regulation by combined industry efforts, we may not see a return to close control of advertising practices.

Figure 22.2 This print ad was developed by the Heart Fund. It is run gratis by publishers of newspapers and magazines. The social cause advertising message is to encourage good health habits, thus reducing the risk of heart attack.

Extending Advertising to Nonbusiness Areas

Advertising developed from the need for businesses to communicate with their customers, and it became a powerful economic and social force. People in nonbusiness areas have begun to use advertising to persuade others to act in certain ways, and the techniques that were derived and developed by businesses have proved adaptable to numerous nonbusiness settings. The growth in this type of advertising increased during the 1970s, and an estimate has been made that 10 percent of all advertising is performed by nonprofit organizations. Looking ahead, one can only project more and more uses for nonbusiness advertising, given the successes of social advertising campaigns in the 1970s.

Social Advertising

Many nonprofit organizations engage in advertising to raise their stature in the public eye. Advertising takes on some of the prestige of the activity it promotes. At least such use of advertising leads to its being looked at from a different point of view. If an advertising critic's favorite cause—say, the Sierra Club—successfully employs advertising to promote membership or sales of its books, he or she will naturally look at advertising differently.

Kotler calls these efforts **social advertising,** which he divides into five subgroups: political advertising, social cause advertising, philanthropic organization advertising, government organization advertising, and private nonprofit organization advertising.[17]

Political Advertising This topic has been discussed in the previous section of this chapter.

Social Cause Advertising Many public interest causes employ advertising to reach the public with their messages. Thus, we see the Planned Parenthood League, NOW, and similar groups among those employing advertising for social purposes.

Social causes advertising has been aided by the

VD is for everybody.
If you need help, see a doctor.
A Public Service of Transit Advertising & The Advertising Council
Ad Council
American Social Health Association

Figure 22.3 This transportation car card is a very simple social cause message. The ad is representative of the work done through the Advertising Council.

1980 CENSUS
"Not another PSA!"
With every good cause in town asking for free air time, it's easy to see why broadcasters feel over taxed. But here's a PSA with a payoff *for the broadcaster:* the 1980 Census. It's *not* just another PSA.
Read how airing Census spots will actually help your station.
How the Census works for you.
Both Nielsen and Arbitron use Census data to compile profiles of audience demographics. The accuracy of the Census determines the accuracy of the demographics. The stronger the response, the more accurate the national rating services will be with demographic information.
By broadcasting the 1980 Census commercials and encouraging your local community to correctly fill out and return their forms, you *directly* contribute to the reliability of information about *your broadcast area.*
And what it does for America.
The 1980 Census is more than a head count. It assures Americans of equal representation in Congress. And it shows where funds are needed for jobs, health care and new schools.
"Marketing Radar"– A.C. Nielsen
A.C. Nielsen, Jr., President, A.C. Nielsen Company, the nation's leading marketing research firm, said this about the value of the Census: "All marketers need various types of information to sharpen their appeals and deliver their message, with the right features at the right time. Census information is marketing radar. It's an *essential tool* in modern marketing research...essential, too, for service companies."
For the broadcaster, that means knowing how to identify and reach your target audience. For specific demographic groups, there is census data on such characteristics as age, range of income and general educational background.
Your part is easy.
Here are just a few suggestions for encouraging people to answer the Census:
• saturate public service time slots
• produce a "Special" presentation showing the benefits of census data to the community
• insert news and editorial items into regular programming
• arrange for endorsements and interviews with local celebrities.
Work for the PSA that works for you. Convince your audience to answer the Census; it's good for them, and it's good for you.
Get America to answer the Census. We're counting on you.
CENSUS '80
A Public Service of This Magazine & The Advertising Council
Ad Council

Figure 22.4 The Advertising Council not only develops social advertising but also promotes its use by the media, as this advertisement shows. The media are flooded with public service announcements and must choose those they will air on a complimentary basis.

work of the Advertising Council, which was started during World War II as a means of securing public support for such causes as the purchase of war bonds, donation of blood, and the enlistment of women into the armed services. Advertising agencies and advertising departments volunteer the skills of their employees to develop advertising programs for those causes selected for promotion under the sponsorship of the Advertising Council. The finished ads are then published or broadcast by media either as a free public service or in return for the payment of media charges by the sponsoring advertiser. Social causes received $562,531,751 of advertising in 1979 through the operation of the Advertising Council.

Philanthropic Organization Advertising The intent of social cause advertising is primarily pro-

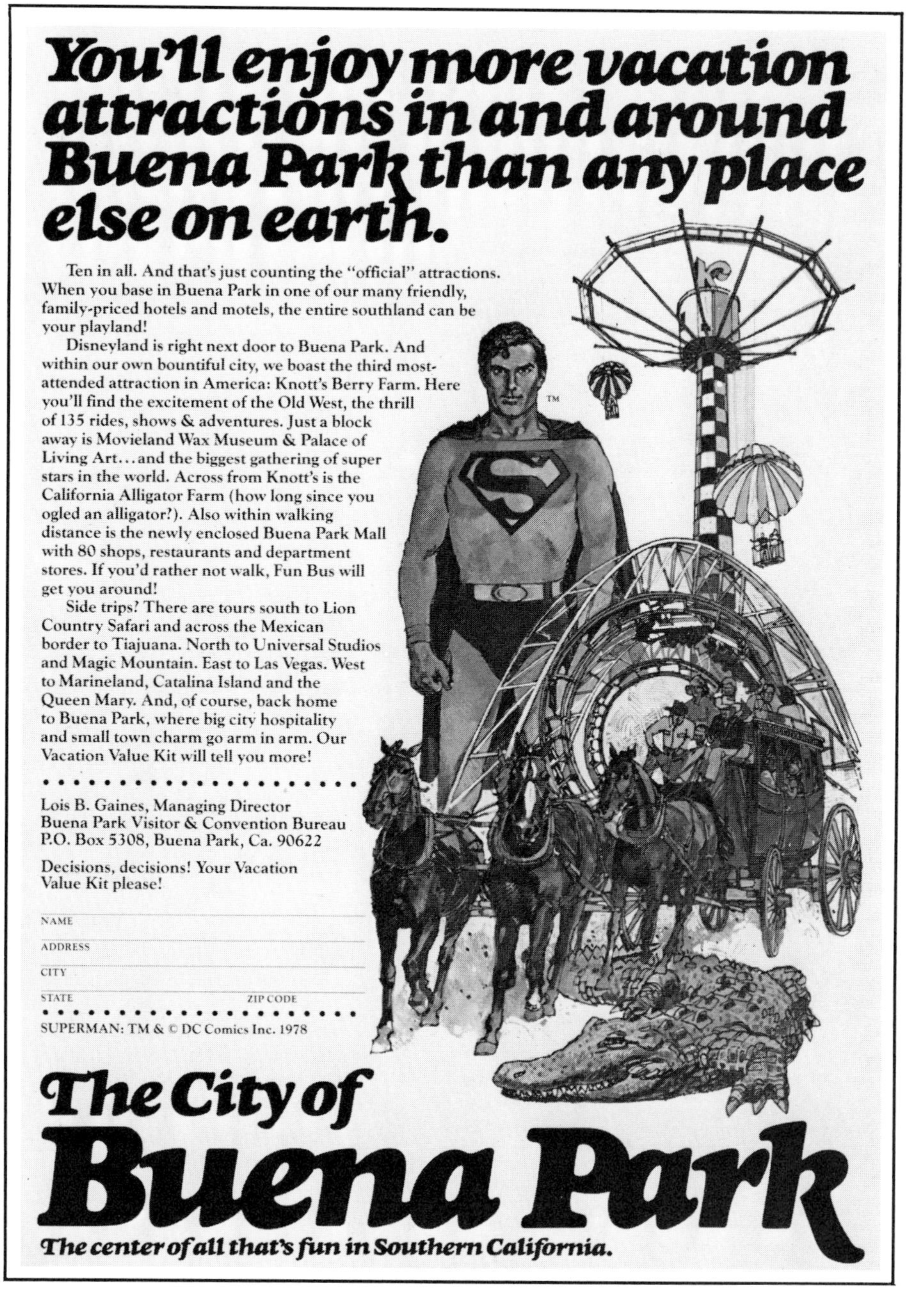

Figure 22.5 Here a relatively small city government uses media advertising to promote its community as a tourist destination.

pagandistic in intent; it aims to persuade the public to adopt a particular point of view. Philanthropic advertising focuses on fund raising for worthwhile causes. Mass appeals are made to encourage people to contribute to the United Fund campaign in many cities, as well as to obtain financial assistance for the Red Cross, Christmas Seals, Easter Seals, and so forth. Philanthropic organizations often spend a considerable portion of the monies raised for the very advertising designed to raise funds. Direct mail is frequently used in these efforts.

Government Organization Advertising Many state governments and some municipalities employ advertising to attract tourists and new industries to their areas. Similarly, units of local government, such as park commissions and police departments, dis-

Why our students actually have an advantage over those at Harvard, Columbia and Princeton.
All great universities promise to make their students fluent in liberal arts.
But the liberal arts graduate who doesn't know how to make a living in the real world is not a happy person. Neither are the parents who had to foot the bill ($25,000? $40,000?).
The mission of the University of Bridgeport is to prevent this kind of casualty. And another kind just as painful, i.e., the skilled engineering graduate who discovers later in life that she/he has just been passed over in favor of another engineer who is not more competent, but more "persuasive."
The University of Bridgeport unflinchingly orients its students towards the real world.
We believe a student's earning power is determined within the few short years of higher education.
We believe these same few years affect a person's confidence in his own individuality in the future.
We believe many students don't yet know what they want to do with their lives and therefore deserve a chance to taste the real world ahead of time, to "find" themselves and, if necessary, to change career direction before committing a lifetime to the wrong career.
"You can earn $12,000, even $16,000 while "finding" yourself at UB."
Because of these beliefs, the University of Bridgeport is neither vaguely "liberal arts" nor narrowly technical.
We are, in fact, one of the few Universities anywhere to offer our students the combined advantages of a 5-pronged preparation for the real world:
1. An unusually wide range of nationally accredited professional and liberal arts programs. But we don't stop there.
2. Real jobs, real pay, in the real world, through optional, alternate semester co-operative education programs with major corporations such as GE, Xerox, Sikorsky. But we don't stop there.
3. Career Management Program: the real-world strategies of job advancement, long after graduation. But we don't stop there.
4. Mandatory liberal arts Core Curriculum to arm each student with the key cultural, analytical, verbal and motivational skills that frankly separate the technical drone from the leader. But we don't stop there.
5. Finally, we infuse students with a global perspective through exposure to a multi-national student body (representing 60 nations).
Few other universities fuse these academic and real-world advantages so deliberately.
The University of Bridgeport is nothing less than a dress rehearsal for reality.
That's why our graduates help shape public policy, become bank presidents, revolutionize space medicine and head up major technology projects and government agencies.
The statistics are impressive. 70% of recent graduates of UB are now earning their living doing exactly what they want to be doing. And in the field of choice they settled on at UB.
UB students can be a proven success before graduating. Because they are deliberately given the means of entering the real world ahead of time. Unlike those at Harvard, Columbia and Princeton.
LELAND MILES
PRESIDENT
UNIVERSITY OF BRIDGEPORT
Boston is nice, but...
The New York Times recently reported a great surge of interest among students wanting to go to college in Boston. Any college. Not just Harvard or Boston University.
Curiously, the reason given over and over and over again for choosing Boston institutions was not prestige, not campus life, not glamour, but an interest in getting ahead in the real world.
I commend these students (and their parents) on their sense of realism.
But I must point out one little thing: the University of Bridgeport, more than any University I know, offers its students a unique combination of more professional choices, more real job, real world, real pay internships, plus a 4-year Career Management program designed to enhance financial progress in the real world years after graduation.
Am I biased in favor of Bridgeport? Yes, I am. For good reasons. Including this: the complaint Boston students have about Boston is that they can't find that many jobs in Boston after graduation.
Bridgeport, on the other hand, is in the front yard of America's major corporations. And a city called New York, the medical, financial, publishing, advertising, fashion and legal capital of the world, is in our backyard.
Warren Cooper
Vice President,
Student Services
P.S. Incidentally, I graduated from Harvard.
The University of Bridgeport.
The competitive advantage of reality.
For admissions bulletin, call (203) 576-4552 (local calls only)
or 1-800-972-9488 (from other Connecticut locations) or 1-800-243-9496 (from Mass., R.I., N.H., N.Y., N.J.)

Figure 22.6 Here a university employs advertising to help achieve its marketing objectives. The ad was designed to: (1) increase public awareness of UB; (2) establish a distinctive UB position in the student marketplace; and (3) proclaim several documentable advantages students obtain by enrolling at UB. Applications for freshman admissions ran 26 percent ahead of the previous year in spite of the fact that the college age population in the Northeast had declined by 5 percent. The rate of increase experienced by UB was triple that of private institutions in the region. [*Courtesy of the University of Bridgeport.*]

patch advertising messages containing information about recreational opportunities, local events, and safety tips to residents of the community. Since abolition of the military draft, the armed services of the United States government have become major advertisers, spending $144,300,000 in 1980, in their efforts to sign up volunteers.

Private Nonprofit Organization Advertising Colleges and universities, particularly those that are privately financed, use advertising to encourage students to enroll in their particular institutions. Kotler reminds us that "museums, symphonies, hospitals, and religious organizations all have strong communication responsibilities and are involved in preparing annual reports, direct mailings, classified ads, broadcast messages, and other forms of advertising."[18]

Greater use of advertising for nonbusiness purposes is anticipated in future years. Charities always seem to have difficulty raising needed funds; personal solicitation is both costly and time-consuming. With the movement of women entering the work force, the pool of volunteers, who formerly did much of the soliciting for charities, has dried up. Any device that materially reduces such costs is welcomed. Political candidates will look more and more to the communication techniques of advertising to accomplish their communication goals. Governmental agencies seek to communicate their goals to the public in order to be more effective with their programs. Religious organizations are turning to advertising as a way of promoting membership. Such activities increase not only the pervasiveness of advertising, but also its recognition as an important institution in modern society. The advertising profession has a challenging opportunity to employ its innovative skills to facilitate the dissemination of new thoughts, as well as information about new products.

Advocacy Advertising

The various forms of social advertising are not alone in the public interest area. Many corporations carry on institutional or corporate advertising programs. Many of these campaigns are devoted to public service themes quite similar to those carried in social advertising. There is one variety of corporate advertising, however, that needs to be discussed separately: **advocacy advertising.** It is similar to social advertising in that its focus is upon ideas. These ideas are important to the corporation that is attempting to disseminate them through advertising. Advocacy advertising is

> any kind of paid public communication or message from an identified source and in a conventional medium of public advertising, which presents information or a point of view bearing on a publicly recognized controversial issue.[19]

Starting in the mid-1970s, the energy crisis spawned many advertisements addressed to the problem's solution. Over time, the Mobil Oil Corporation came to be the most visible user of the technique with its editorial-like advertisements placed frequently in newspapers and magazines. Corporations engage in advocacy advertising when they believe that the established media are not presenting both sides of the issue. In effect, the ads are paid editorials that appear in the media in the form of advertisements. Figure 22.7 is an example of advocacy advertising. Although the effectiveness of the technique is debated, its users are likely to continue the practice. One proponent, when asked about the effectiveness of advocacy advertising, said "I don't know, but you see that the senators and congressmen who opposed the oil industry all lost their seats."[20]

Summary

Advertising will continue as an important factor in the marketplace of the future. Successful advertisers must realize that underlying the need for advertising are several forces that influence its effective functioning. Changing trends in the operation of these forces must be monitored constantly if advertising plans are to be adjusted properly to changing circumstances. There are four types of forces that need watching: economic, social, technological, and political.

Such economic factors as the increased concentration of production in the hands of fewer and larger manufacturers, coupled with greater mobility of the population, separate producers and buyers even more, thus necessitating more advertising. Similarly, the development of new products requires that potential users be informed of the product's availability and benefits. Although inflation may reduce consumer funds available for products, businesses will increase their advertising in the struggle over the remaining share. Changing patterns in population distribution and family income need to be studied so that marketing and advertising strategies can be adjusted appropriately. Advertisers will continue to study buyer psychology in order to keep consumers' willingness to buy at satisfactory levels.

Many social forces will affect advertising plans. As more women enter the work force, not only will average family income increase, but traditional shopping patterns will break down. Both conditions will be favorable to the increased use of advertising. As more of our population is better educated, people's income will increase as well as their levels of sophis-

Mother Nature is lucky her products don't need labels.
All foods, even natural ones, are made up of chemicals.
But natural foods don't have to list their ingredients. So it's often assumed they're chemical-free. In fact, the ordinary orange is a miniature chemical factory. And the good old potato contains arsenic among its more than 150 ingredients.
This doesn't mean natural foods are dangerous. If they were, they wouldn't be on the market. The same is true of man-made foods.
All man-made foods are tested for safety. And they often provide more nutrition, at a lower cost, than natural foods. They even use many of the same chemical ingredients.
So you see, there really isn't much difference between foods made by Mother Nature and those made by man. What's artificial is the line drawn between them.
© Monsanto Company 1980
For a free booklet explaining the risks and benefits of chemicals, mail to: Monsanto, 800 Lindbergh Blvd., St. Louis, Mo. 63166. Dept. A3NA
Name
Address
City & state
Zip
Monsanto
Without chemicals, life itself would be impossible.

Figure 22.7 A large manufacturer of chemicals engages in advocacy advertising. The principal target audience consisted of college-educated adults. *[Reprinted by permission of the Monsanto Company.]*

tication and expectations. Increased leisure will also be important on the American scene. All these changes call for adaptive behavior on the part of advertisers.

Technological forces, particularly in communication media, will lead to many adjustments in advertising. Greater segmentation of markets will take place as television becomes capable of reaching smaller, more specialized audiences. The computer will assist in many facets of advertising planning, thus making that process more scientific. At the same time, efforts need to be taken to ensure that creativity in advertising is not stifled by technology.

Advertising will continue to be important in politics. Its techniques are increasingly employed by candidates for political office. Dissatisfaction with advertising practices may lead to action through the political process aimed at the passage of restrictive legislation regarding advertising.

The years ahead will see greater use of advertising for nonbusiness purposes. Social advertising will be employed by a vast number of nonprofit organizations ranging from colleges and universities through charities to governmental agencies. Corporations, in their attempts to influence public opinion on controversial issues, will use advocacy advertising to press their case. All in all, the future for advertising appears bright indeed.

Questions for Discussion

1 Go to the library and obtain 1980 census data. Isolate five demographic changes that you think are significant for advertising strategies during the 1980s. Do the trends you indicate lead to a demand for more advertising? Less advertising? A change in advertising approach? Discuss.

2 If the United States population continues to grow quite slowly, how will advertising change? What if the real income of consumers fails to rise substantially? If it declines? Do you think these are realistic possibilities? Explain your answer.

3 Write a short essay, based on research in the library, showing how technological changes in communications have affected advertising in this country.

4 What is social advertising? Explain each of its five subtypes. Bring print advertisements to class as examples of each type.

5 What is advocacy advertising? Clip a magazine or newspaper ad that you think is a good example of this form of advertising.

6 What changes in social values and lifestyles in your own college environment do you believe may well change the way in which advertising is carried on in the United States? Give specific examples of the changes you discuss and show how they apply to advertising strategy.

For Further Reference

Kotler, Philip: *Marketing for Nonprofit Organizations,* Prentice-Hall, Inc., Englewood Cliffs, N.J., 1975.

"The Shape of Things to Come: The Next 20 Years in Advertising and Marketing," Special Issue of *Advertising Age,* Crain Communications, Inc., Chicago, Ill., Nov. 13, 1980.

Toffler, Alvin: *The Third Wave,* William Morrow & Co., Inc., New York, 1980.

"Twentieth Century Advertising and the Economy of Abundance," Special Issue of *Advertising Age,* Crain Communications, Inc., Chicago, Ill., April 30, 1980.

End Notes

[1] George Katona, *The Mass Consumption Society,* McGraw-Hill Book Company, New York, 1964.

[2] *The Wall Street Journal,* June 26, 1980, p. 26.

[3] Op. cit., June 27, 1980, p. 27.

[4] Ibid.

[5] Material drawn from *Business Week,* March 23, 1981, pp. 70–73, 76, 80.

[6] *The Wall Street Journal,* July 1, 1980, p. 26.

[7] Op. cit., July 2, 1980, p. 17.

[8] *The Moving Target,* J. Walter Thompson Co., New York, 1979, p. 3.

[9] Ibid., p. 1.

[10] This paragraph drawn from Abraham Shama, "How Marketers Can Cater to 'Voluntary Simplicity' Seg-

ment," *Marketing News,* March 21, 1980, pp. 1, 3.

[11] "Minnetonka Credits 'Thinking,' Not Research, for Success of Softsoap," *Marketing News,* Dec. 26, 1980, p. 1.

[12] Alvin Toffler, *The Third Wave,* William Morrow & Co., Inc., New York, 1980, p. 181.

[13] Alex F. Osborn, *Applied Imagination,* rev. ed., Charles Scribner's Sons, New York, 1963.

[14] Leo Burnett, *Communication of an Advertising Man,* privately printed, Chicago, 1961, pp. 78–79.

[15] AAAA Newsletter, June 1980, p. 1, from an address before the American Association of Advertising Agencies, Annual Meeting, 1980.

[16] Ibid.

[17] See Philip Kotler, *Marketing for Nonprofit Organizations,* Prentice-Hall, Inc., Englewood Cliffs, N.J., 1975, pp. 202–203.

[18] Ibid., p. 203.

[19] Stephen A. Kliment, "Advocacy Advertising by U.S. Corporations: Can Money Buy Friends?" *Madison Avenue,* February, 1981, p. 29.

[20] Ibid.

Chapter 23

Your Future in Advertising

● Throughout this text we have presented advertising as a dynamic, challenging, multifaceted business. Media, agencies, supplier groups, and advertisers, the four basic components of the advertising business, offer jobs in management and research, in the creative area, and in the sale and analysis of media space and time. As advertising's prestige and expenditure levels increase throughout most of the world, its role in both business and nonbusiness activities grows in importance. But is it the field for *you?* In this chapter we will try to answer some of the questions most frequently asked by those considering careers in advertising:

1 What kinds of work are included in different jobs, and how many jobs are available?
2 What specific background and abilities do I need?
3 How do I apply for an advertising job and whom do I contact?
4 What possibilities exist for advancement and how much money can I expect to make?

Additional information is available from references listed at the end of this chapter and from conversations you may have with men and women already engaged in this field.

Size and Scope of the Advertising Business

The United States today has approximately 5 million business firms, all of which either advertise or are affected by the advertising of competitors. In addition, there are probably between 6,000 and 9,000 advertising agencies of all sizes.

A conservative estimate is that more than 100,000 men and women are employed in professional advertising jobs or hold other positions requiring specific advertising skills. Somewhere in the neighborhood of 7,500 to 10,000 new positions develop annually because of deaths, retirements, people changing career fields, and new business needs. Advertisers and media have a greater number of personnel slots to fill than do advertising agencies (year in and year out), and they usually place a lower premium on past experience. Newcomers to advertising may find more job opportunities and a better chance for initial employment with these organizations than they will find with agencies.

Peter Allport, president of the Association of National Advertisers, once stated that the advertising business needs 10 different groups of professionals: (1) writers; (2) artists; (3) dramatists or theatrical producers; (4) salespeople; (5) marketers and decision makers; (6) psychologists; (7) statisticians; (8) media analysts; (9) financial managers; and (10) people managers, project managers, and entrepreneurs.[1]

Most people in advertising work in sales. Media organizations must sell space and time if their business enterprises are to succeed. Special-service groups must also sell what they have to offer. In a different sense, the advertising agency must sell its services, too—first, in getting accounts, and later, in keeping clients happy with agency performance. There is a pressing need for selling talent in advertising, as James Webb Young emphasizes in his concise book *How to Become an Advertising Man.*[2]

All advertising organizations, however, are businesses. As such, they must do more than sell to survive; they must be managed. People must be hired and fired, work assignments must be made, payrolls must be met, and many other managerial tasks must be performed. Most advertising executives reach managerial positions by moving up the ladder from other positions. The creative person may eventually perform business administration tasks instead of, or sometimes in addition to, writing copy. In Figure 23.1, several different members of an agency account group try out their client's cosmetic products. Firsthand product knowledge is helpful both in developing and in evaluating advertising appeals.

Another talent sought by advertising organizations is analytical ability—and a knowledge of computers. People working in research and media selection must be able to wrestle with problems, tackling them in a logical manner. And whoever is responsible for the advertising budget must know how to analyze figures and come up with meaningful answers. In fact, most advertising jobs require all four abilities—creative, selling, managerial, and analytical—with different emphases placed on each depending on the specific assignment. No person is likely to be equally endowed with all four talents. So, each must analyze his or her

Figure 23.1 Job opportunities in advertising are varied. This account group at Bozell & Jacobs, Inc., Dallas, is personally trying out a client's cosmetic products.

Figure 23.2 The art director and the senior creative director at Marsteller, Inc., Chicago, work on creative approaches for their client. [*Marsteller, Inc.*]

own strengths and weaknesses to determine where the greatest opportunities for success lie.

Agency-Produced Campaigns

Successful advertising results from a combination of efforts. The Chicago office of the Marsteller advertising agency provides us with an excellent example of teamwork in action. Gould, one of Marsteller's clients, is a manufacturer of electric and electronic equipment that faced a big repositioning problem. Research confirmed that consumers still thought of Gould as the "battery company" it was in its earliest days. How could Gould make people aware of a recent expansion into electrical and electronic markets and position the company as a leader in the field of technology?

The solution was developed in stages. First, Gould managers identified eight products that demonstrated significant milestones in company development. Then, Marsteller's art director and senior creative director, shown in Figure 23.2, came up with four different creative approaches. All were pretested to determine which one would elicit the greatest company interest among prospective customers. The winning idea was then converted into a series of ads, all of which were approved by Marsteller's creative board and by the client.

After media objectives were clearly defined, the agency's media programmer, shown in Figure 23.3, started ordering advertising space. Meanwhile, the creative production cycle began. When ad proofs came back to the agency, they were checked carefully for quality and accuracy and then shipped to scheduled publications—among them *The Wall Street Journal, Business Week, Barron's, Forbes,* and *Fortune.*

Gould's advertising communication problem was solved effectively and efficiently. Creative appeals successfully repositioned the company's products in the minds of potential customers, and ultimately, sales enjoyed a healthy increase.

Public Service Campaigns

We noted earlier that many nonprofit organizations owe a large part of their success to advertising. The "Keep America Beautiful" campaign discussed in Chapter 1 benefits from the time and talents of Advertising Council members who also work with numerous educational groups and organizations responsible for public safety. But let's look now at

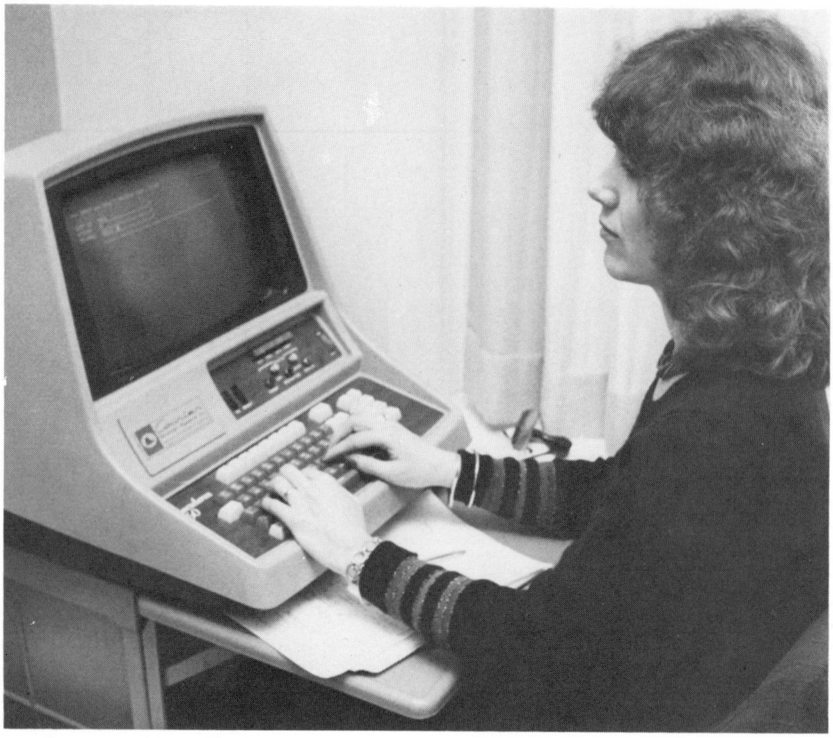

Figure 23.3 Placement of ads in the media is handled electronically by a member of Marsteller's media department. [*Marsteller, Inc.*]

some advertising-related jobs in *local* public service campaigns. Whether you work for a manufacturer or a retail store, an advertising agency or a supplier group (especially a graphic arts firm or TV production company), you may be asked occasionally to work for charity.

The free concert advertised in Figure 23.4 was sponsored by the United States Marine Corps at its Hawaiian air base not far from Honolulu. The purpose of the show was twofold: (1) to further an understanding among civilians of the input made by military services to Hawaii's economy, and (2) to develop solid communication channels between these two groups. Although military and civilian personnel had lived in Hawaii for many decades, it was thought that members of each group tended to socialize only with their peers.

Months of work preceded the concert, and the following are some of the positions and responsibilities that were involved. Notice, first, how they are in keeping with Peter Allport's list of advertising jobs and, second, how they may relate to experiences you have had—even if you thought you had no preparatory background for a job in advertising:

1 Program directors booked acts for the show, arranged for on-location security and police escorts, and wrote official thank-you letters in the days following the program. These were the theatrical producers and dramatists who had to decide (*a*) what types of performances would best suit the intended audience, and (*b*) whether the performers' drawing powers justified the time and effort required in obtaining them. Similarly, TV commercial planners and those who supply ideas and materials for client sales presentations must weigh the anticipated effects of elaborate staging and production activities against their costs.

2 Promotional writers prepared media news releases. Even though they cannot technically be classified as ads, these pieces contained a great deal of persuasive communication. They required the collection and analysis of much factual material and the translation of that material into a format of consumer (concert spectator) benefits.

3 Artists and printers prepared publicity posters, along with VIP and concert-participant passes for access to the staging area, dressing rooms, and parking facilities. The talents and efforts involved here differ very little from those involved in the preparation of an advertising or sales promotion campaign.

4 Media coordinators made sure the concert was well publicized both before and after the day of presentation:

a On radio and TV: promotional messages and talk-show discussions (interviews with the concert star and military director)
b In newspapers: articles in Honolulu's morning and evening dailies, as well as a local weekly and several tourist and military papers
c In magazines: listings in two local coming-events publications
d Through posters: dozens of announcements displayed in stores and service establishments
e On a follow-up TV talk-show the week after the concert
f In follow-up newspaper stories

These coordinators were both media analysts (who selected the appropriate media) and experts in creativity (who adapted press-release information into hard-hitting sales communications). Part of their time was spent working with the promotional writers and program directors.

5 Set-construction crews built and decorated the stage and installed attractive ramps for easy handling

Figure 23.4 At the entrance to the Marine Corps base, the entertainment benefit is advertised. It is meant for viewing by both military and civilian personnel.

Figure 23.5 When he's not performing, concert star Danny Kaleikini helps handle equipment (the same kind used for on-location production of many commercials). He must make certain that these two musical performers are heard by the 5,000-member audience. [*U.S. Marine Corps.*]

of equipment and musical instruments during the show. Again, dramatic flair was needed, as it often is for setups for TV commercials filmed on location. (Consider, for example, the outdoor setting for a floral-scented skin-cream commercial. How much foliage should be used? And where should it appear in relation to the product and the performers? If an ideal setting is not naturally available, it may be created through proper placement of plants and shrubbery.)

6 Technical crews planned and implemented the elaborate sound system required. Singers and musicians had to be heard above the wind and crowd noises, and microphones had to be portable. (See Figure 23.5.) The work involved here was supervised by a project manager—in this case, an electronics specialist. A background in this field would benefit (*a*) the commercial production employee in an advertising agency or production firm, (*b*) any advertising team member of an electronics account, or (*c*) copywriters for any product or service whose image and positioning might benefit from analogies to high-quality amplification and reproduction.

7 Photographers captured scenes such as the one in Figure 23.5 for post-concert publicity and preserved crowd reactions on videotape for later inclusion in TV newscasts. Figure 23.6 shows the TV camera crew in action. Once more, artistic abilities are called for in this line of work, since a picture's depth

Figure 23.6 The development of portable videotape equipment permits on-the-spot recording and immediate or delayed playback. [*U.S. Marine Corps.*]

and perspective can affect viewer reactions significantly. Think, for example, of the different associations you might have for a pictured product shot from *above* (so it looks small, even inferior) and one shot from *below* (so it looks powerful or majestic).

Was the military concert worth all the effort? The measure of success here was the same as it is for any advertising campaign. Since the program fulfilled the goals established at the outset, it was deemed effective. Concert promoters, participants, and spectators believed the show enhanced favorable relations between Hawaii's civilian and military communities.

Advertising Job Qualifications and Preparation

An understanding of human behavior, of the art and science of mass communication, and of the principles of marketing is fundamental in any area of advertising. Creativity can be developed through practice. The ability to state ideas clearly and concisely must be cultivated. Advertising artists need formal training in the techniques and methods of commercial design, and an appreciation for graphic as well as verbal communication is helpful in any creative advertising position.

Analytical ability is developed through the study of mathematics, statistics, logic, computer programming, and the natural and social sciences. Managers need to know something about accounting and office management and must be able to work well with people. Even if an employee is sometimes temperamental, a good manager can keep him or her productive. Selling abilities are developed largely through practice, although an understanding of buyer behavior and communications principles is important.

Most of these talents can be enhanced through formal education. There are successful advertising people, especially in creative areas, who do not have college degrees, but today the noncollege person has difficulty getting started in advertising. Most employers require a college degree as one of their minimum standards of employment. A survey of 1,800 advertising managers and advertising agency executives found that slightly over 80 percent believed "a college education is helpful because it gives a general intellectual background, maturity, and improves the ability to think."[3] Further, in some large advertising agencies an M.B.A. degree is required for any account executive position.

Three basic educational programs are available to college students interested in advertising: a major in liberal arts, one in business administration, or one in communications or journalism. Employers who advocate the liberal arts approach feel that graduates can learn the techniques of advertising on the job and will perform better in the long run because of the breadth of their education. Persons with a knowledge of history and literature, art and science, economics and math, and psychology and political science are believed ideally suited to the tasks of synthesizing information presented to them on the job. And, it is felt they can readily apply relevant theoretical concepts to practical assignments.

Other employers prefer the beginner who is already prepared in the fundamentals of advertising. Here, it is believed that the job candidate offers a strong career motivation, a knowledge of basic advertising terminology and technical procedures, and a sense of the disciplines required for success in this highly competitive field of business. In business schools, the emphasis is more on selling, merchandising, and marketing research—on how advertising is used in marketing programs. In journalism and communications schools, priorities are placed on the planning, creation, and placement of advertising. A major in one area and a minor in the other is recognized by most employers as an excellent background for an advertising career.[4] Figures 23.7 and 23.8 show advertising students developing and analyzing projects during class sessions.

Today, nearly 100 institutions of higher learning award bachelor's or master's degrees with a major in advertising. Approximately 20 percent of these degrees are offered in schools of business, with the remainder in schools of journalism or communications.[5] Hundreds of other schools offer one or more advertising courses within marketing and communications programs or in schools of art and design, and there are now thousands of "ad grads" every year across the country. Because economic recessions often result in advertising job cutbacks (especially at the agency level), the competition for available positions remains keen.

Regardless of your major field of study, however, if you're interested in an advertising career, you can profit from the advice of recent graduates, academic faculty, and advertising practitioners. They overwhelmingly support the value of good *written com-*

Figure 23.7 An advertising professor explains the fine points of typography to a student in an advertising production class. [*The University of Tennessee, Department of Advertising.*]

Figure 23.8 The importance of demographic data is explained to an advertising class. [*The University of Tennessee, Department of Advertising.*]

munication skills and *problem-solving abilities.* They strongly encourage participation in campus and community advertising clubs and industry internship programs, and advocate part-time jobs with college newspapers or broadcast stations.

Many also endorse the intercollegiate competitions set up by such organizations as the American Advertising Federation, Datsun/13-30, General Motors, and Philip Morris. Each year students in advertising and marketing programs throughout the nation prepare advertising messages and campaigns for designated products. Presentations are later made to representatives of the companies involved. Colleges and universities compete by districts, and regional winners participate in annual national competitions. Many participating students wind up with job offers, and schools gain academic and industry recognition. Sometimes, winning ads are actually published or broadcast, and every participant agrees that the learning that occurs is priceless.

Beyond the Classroom

Some aspects of advertising cannot be learned completely in a classroom, of course. Practical knowledge often spells the difference between success and failure in the advertising world. The first requirement on the list of many practitioners is the absolute necessity for meeting deadlines. The copywriting student who turns in a late radio commercial, presenting what he feels is a legitimate medical or other personal excuse, is not preparing himself for the job market. If that commercial were scheduled for one airing only, say on Monday at noon, its arrival even one minute late would mean lost business.

A second advertising job requisite is the ability to accept and apply constructive criticism. Students have been known to complain bitterly over failing scores and negative comments received on course assignments. Some resign themselves to low grades and stop trying. Such behavior, however, is not greeted with sympathy in advertising circles, where the adage "Quitters never win and winners never quit" is a way of life.

Third, successful advertising personnel know how to cope with the often bewildering demands of clients, coworkers, and superiors: conflicting instructions for creative treatment of ads, requests for unavailable media time or space, or strong disagreements over advertising goals and budgetary allowances. Frustrations are a very real part of the advertising business, and there is never enough time or money to achieve perfection. Many people thrive on this kind of atmosphere, though, and really do their best work under pressure.

Self-Development

Looking at the matter a little differently, we find that formal education is only one facet of vocational preparation. For a prospective career in advertising, various work experiences can also provide worthwhile insights. Selling, whether it is from door to door or in retail establishments where customers need and expect sales assistance, is extremely helpful. Since both marketing and advertising are aimed at consumers, time spent serving customers can deepen an understanding of what motivates them toward buying action. Any activity that brings you close to people in their everyday living furnishes a storehouse of such information.

Advertising accomplishments depend in part on an applicant's powers of observation and imagination. Remember that prospective employers try to decide whether applicants have the potentials for success in a field where precise job specifications are difficult to set down. Whatever you can do to broaden your perspective will help you gain, and later maintain, career success in advertising.

Applying and Interviewing for an Advertising Job

Numerous manufacturers and retail stores, along with some advertising agencies and a few supplier groups, conduct on-campus recruiting programs. In most cases, however, these interview sessions are followed by meetings between prospective employees and employers in the employers' own offices. Frequently, too, job seekers (1) send letters of application to a series of firms, (2) call a selected few on the telephone, and (3) personally visit others.

Opinions on the effectiveness of these and other job-hunting activities vary greatly. (But if you are uncertain as to how to write an effective business letter, consult one of the many fine textbooks on this topic.) There *is* almost universal agreement that a neat, concise personal resumé is your number one selling tool in the advertising job market. Many forms are acceptable. The resumé illustrated in Figure 23.9 is a popular format.

Portfolios

If you are applying for a job in the creative area of advertising, you probably should also have a portfolio. Often called your "book," this collection of samples of your creative work (primarily in copywriting, art, or print and broadcast production) may be the main screening device used by potential employers on your behalf. For most purposes, 12 to 18 examples will suffice.

If your sole experience has been in a classroom, you have only speculative pieces to show—material that has never been published or broadcast. (But don't discount the value of posters done for campus events, mailers designed for club membership drives, etc.) On the other hand, even if you do include professional work in your portfolio, don't be afraid to supplement it with some examples of original thinking done on your own time. Choose material that reveals as many of your best advertising skills as possible. Go beyond your copy and layout talents to organizational abilities as demonstrated, perhaps, in creative strategy statements and copy platforms.

Ideally, you should include examples of multimedia campaigns, a cross section of work done for products, services, and stores, and maybe something in the area of public relations or public service. Be sure to include with each example a statement of the objectives the project was designed to fulfill and, if available, some proven results. Finally, if you come up short in terms of both class and on-the-job assignments, select a few ads currently running in print or broadcast media. Include ad tearsheets or transcribed commercials with your personal re-dos. Explain what you would change and why, in order to improve each message, and then prepare rough layouts, radio scripts, and TV storyboards, as appropriate. (*Note:* Direct mail offers a wealth of opportunities here, too.) In every case, make sure all entries are neat, and check them carefully for proper spelling and grammar.

Job Interviews

Now we return to that all-important job interview. Again, many articles, and even entire books, have been written on this subject. We will confine ourselves, however, to a few words of advice in four areas: (1) your interview preparation, (2) your appearance, (3) your responses to questions asked, and (4) your own inquiries.

Preparation First, know something about your interviewer's company. Look it up in the *Standard Directory of Advertisers,* the *Standard Directory of Ad-*

Lee Courtney Howard

6443 College Road
Anytown, U.S.A.

PHONE: (251) 555-7611

Career Objective

Copywriter on household products accounts in a medium-sized agency; advancement to creative supervisor within five years. Available in June, 1982. Willing to relocate.

Education

1978-1982: Academic University, Anytown, U.S.A. B.S. in Communications, June, 1982
MAJOR: Advertising and Journalism
MINOR: Marketing
Dean's List 4 semesters; communications scholarship 2 years

Honors and Affiliations

Member, Alpha Lambda Delta, freshman honorary society
Outstanding Student Intern Award, WXXX Radio
Business Manager, Alpha Delta Sigma, national advertising fraternity
Social Chairman, Panhellenic Council
Vice President, Academic University's Creative Writing Club

Professional Experience

1981-1982: Advertising Manager, Academic University Daily News
1980-1981: Assistant Producer and Writer, WXXX Radio, Anytown, U.S.A.
1978-1980: Household product sales, Main Department Store, New Town, U.S.A. (summer work)

References

Dr. Louise Roderick, Head
Department of Advertising
Academic University
Anytown, U.S.A.

Dean Walter Martin
College of Business
Academic University
Anytown, U.S.A.

Mr. Arthur Gordon, Manager
WXXX Radio
6565 Fence Lane
Anytown, U.S.A.

Figure 23.9 A concise personal resume is a definite asset to any candidate seeking a job in advertising.

vertising Agencies, Broadcasting Yearbook, Editor & Publisher Yearbook, Leading National Advertisers, or other publications recommended by your academic faculty or librarian. Know the company's clients and accounts, the nature of its work, and the size of its staff and budget, along with its media involvements. In addition, the firm may have been discussed in a trade magazine, such as *Advertising Age,* in connection with a particular campaign, award, or research study, a response made to a legal inquiry, or a recent change in management, philosophy, or locale. One question you are likely to be asked in a job interview is why you are interested in working for that particular firm. You will feel a lot more at ease if you can answer this question intelligently.

Be familiar with current ads running in all major media, too. Other popular interview questions are, "What's the best, or worst, ad you've seen lately? And why do you regard it that way?" Since you are applying for an advertising job, you will naturally be expected to be aware of what is going on in the field.

Appearance This comment may seem obvious, but good grooming and proper dress make a tremendous impact on prospective employers, and first impressions are not easily forgotten. Conservative outfits are generally most appropriate, although there is some leeway here as long as you are clean and neat, with a smile on your face and enthusiasm in your manner and approach. Make sure you are prompt, too. Since the advertising business literally runs on time, you will make a poor impression if you show up late for your interview.

Responses Most employers agree that they like job candidates to be themselves during interviews. If you are an optimistic, curious, active individual, let these qualities show. If you thrive on hard work, enjoy challenges, and appreciate the fact that much of advertising is a team effort, don't keep it a secret. Answer questions as honestly and specifically as you can, but always remember that you are trying to make a sale. Your goal should be to present your qualifications in the most appealing way possible—one that is both appropriate to the job at hand and striking enough that it will stand out in your interviewer's mind days and weeks later when hiring decisions are made.

Finally, be prepared to track the significant portions of your life, to identify your own strongest and weakest traits, and to reveal what you would like to be doing five or ten years in the future.

Perhaps we should add a word here for the interviewee who is changing jobs. The question in your case, of course, is "Why do you wish to move?" "To make more money" is not the most respected answer, even if it may be the most frequent (and, we admit, the most truthful). Consider the value of new and more important responsibilities, and the challenge of working with different people, accounts, and media. You may foresee greater opportunities with a firm larger or smaller than your present one. If you are looking for a job that is exclusively creative or only involves media, you will aim for a fairly large agency. On the other hand, if you want to wear several different hats, a relatively small operation may be your ideal.

There is no formula we can give you to predict how long you should stay with a job before deciding to move on. Advertising practitioners offer frequent advice, however, through the pages of their trade paper, *Advertising Age.* Between two and three years is considered a minimum stay, especially on your first job. Some feel three to five years is a better span.

Questions from You Many job interviews end with the question, "Do *you* have any questions?" If, as noted earlier, you have done your homework, you can come up with some queries that reflect your newly gained insight. For example, you might ask: "Is your new branch office proving successful?" "Did you hire new employees to handle your new account?" "Was your political campaign account more difficult to handle than others?"

Feel free to talk about salary, too, if you haven't already been asked for your financial demands. Be alert to what the going rate is in the job marketplace. We will discuss some industry figures in the next section of this chapter, but we can note here that as the nation's economic picture improves, salaries may increase significantly. In the early 1980s, advertising and marketing jobs involving major consumer package goods were paying an average of $40,000 to persons with four or five years of experience. And, according to *Advertising Age,* a good rule of thumb is to aim for a 20 percent increase in real income within your first eight years of employment.[6]

Profiles

Peter Finn

"Outstanding Advertising Agency of 1979" was the title granted by *Advertising Age* to the Henderson Agency of Greenville, South Carolina—Peter Finn, President.

Mr. Finn, a native Bostonian, began his advertising career at J. Walter Thompson, the largest United States advertising agency, as a market research trainee in 1962. With a bachelor's degree from Holy Cross and an M.B.A. from George Washington University, Peter moved quickly up the rungs of the professional ladder. After only two years at Thompson, Peter joined Foote, Cone & Belding, and later moved to Doyle Dane Bernbach.

In the next seven-year period, Finn was employed at F. William Free as senior vice president. Then, in 1974, Henderson tapped him as its new president. His quest for advancement never seemed to be satisfied, for Peter Finn became president of Bozell & Jacobs/Southwest in 1980. Each move offered more responsibility over increasingly larger companies. In moving to Bozell, Finn increased his reign of control from $40 million in billings at Henderson to $100 million at his new agency.

This profile portrays the rapid advance of one person's career. Our major emphasis, however, is not on how fast one person has changed but on how fast the dynamics of an entire industry are changing, and furthermore, on the mobility the advertising field offers to prospective professionals.

Advertising Promotions and Salaries

Job advancement can be quite rapid in advertising. It is a field where initiative is encouraged and there are few rules of seniority. Happily, it is also a business with an increasingly impressive record for hiring youth, women, and members of minorities. A 1980 Radio Advertising Bureau survey found that 68 percent of all radio salespeople are under 35 years of age, and 36 percent are women.[7] These groups often prove invaluable in helping to position products and select media schedules for their respective peer groups.

Though there is no such thing as an average advertising salary, any more than there is an average amount of job satisfaction or frustration, we can examine some salary ranges that may prove enlightening. It is generally accepted that the pay is highest in major markets such as New York and Los Angeles, but living costs are also high there. Large companies and agencies ranked near the top in terms of billings pay higher salaries than do smaller firms. Finally, although creative personnel may rise to a much higher income bracket than management personnel, the latter usually begin at a higher level. One university in a middle-sized market recently ran a business school's recruiting ad headlined: "By 1990, staying a bachelor is going to cost a fortune." The copy pointed out that five years after graduation, most persons with M.B.A.s after their names have doubled their starting salaries.[8]

Major-market, middle-sized advertising agencies have pay tables approximating the following (based on 1980 salary scales):

0 to 2 yrs. of experience: $10,000–20,000 per year

3 to 4 yrs. of experience: $15,000–30,000 per year

5 to 10 yrs. of experience: $25,000–50,000 per year[9]

Current regional help-wanted ads in the field of advertising offer:

$20,000–35,000 for media and research employees

$20,000–40,000 for managerial employees (account executives and advertising managers—the middle-management level)

$25,000–50,000 for copywriters and creative supervisors

$25,000–60,000 for artists and art directors

Requirements are, among others, talent, ambition, and experience (we assume three to five years).

But what about the "big money" often associated with the field of advertising? Experts tend to agree that it takes anywhere from 10 to 15 years for talented people in the creative branch of the business to make salaries of $50,000 to $75,000 and more. People earning such salaries consistently create and develop good ads. They have keen powers of observation and an insatiable appetite for new experiences and acquaintances.

Advertising practitioners who make $100,000 or more per year total about 5 percent of the field. These are top-level management positions in broadcast stations and advertiser firms, whereas managers in supplier organizations make somewhat less. Major advertising agency presidents and board chairmen make $300,000 to $500,000, and a select few reach salaries of seven figures. High-ranking media executives, including newspaper-group publishers and heads of TV networks, also frequently make from $300,000 to well over $1 million per year.

Summary

The advertising business needs many different types of employees, from writers and artists to statisticians. They work for media, agencies, supplier groups, and advertisers of all sizes. Advertising people possess creative, selling, managerial, and analytical abilities in varying combinations. Public service organizations and campaigns draw on advertising-related skills, too, in technical production areas as well as in planning and writing.

Most of the talents required in advertising jobs can be developed through formal education courses in business, communication, and liberal arts. These should be supplemented, however, by participation in advertising clubs and internship programs, and through advertising-related jobs.

Many people believe that the importance of meeting deadlines, the ability to take constructive criticism, and the wherewithal to produce under pressure cannot be learned completely in a classroom. In these cases, there is no substitute for on-the-job experience.

Before applying for a job in advertising, candidates need a personal resumé and, if they're interested in creative areas of the business, a portfolio as well.

Prior to any interview, prospective employees should learn something about the company, since they are apt to be asked why they are interested in joining a particular firm. Attention should be paid to personal grooming and promptness. Interviewees should always remember that they are selling themselves. Their qualifications, therefore, should be presented in as positive and favorable a light as possible.

Job advancement is often rapid in advertising, since there are few rules of seniority. Large companies in large markets tend to pay the highest salaries, but there are wide variations depending on the type of job involved. Typically, managerial positions pay more at the outset than do creative positions, but persons in the latter category often earn more after a few years on the job.

Questions for Discussion

1 What four talents should you cultivate if you are interested in an advertising executive position?

2 Name five behind-the-scenes jobs in local public service campaigns. Then, briefly describe the kind of work each job entails.

3 Discuss the arguments in favor of (1) a liberal arts education and (2) an advertising-based education for the prospective advertising employee.

4 What are three important advertising job requisites that can't be learned completely in college classrooms?

5 Describe at least five different items that belong in a job-oriented personal resumé.

6 Explain what we mean by a job candidate's portfolio. Then, list some things that should be included in it.

7 How would you find out about a company you would like to work for—before talking with that company's interviewer? What types of information might you discover?

8 Assume a prospective employer asks, "Why do you think our company should hire you?" How would you respond?

9 List three questions you would ask a prospective employer during an interview for a media sales job. Then do the same thing for a job in the creative department of an advertising agency.

10 Explain precisely why you feel you can be successful in an advertising career.

For Further Reference

Bikkie, James A: *Careers in Marketing,* McGraw-Hill Book Company, New York, 1978.

Boothe, Anna: *Job Hunting That Works,* Creative Arts Book Company, Berkeley, Calif., 1978.

Bostwick, Burdette E: *Resumé Writing,* John Wiley & Sons, Inc., New York, 1976.

Donaho, Melvin W: *How to Get the Job You Want,* Prentice-Hall, Inc., Englewood Cliffs, N.J., 1976.

Groome, Harry Connelly: *Opportunities in Advertising Careers,* Vocational Guidance Manuals, Louisville, Ky., 1976.

Haldane, Bernard: *Job Power Now,* Acropolis Books, Washington, D.C., 1976.

Holbert, Neil: *Careers in Marketing,* American Marketing Association, Chicago, Ill., 1976.

Komar, John J: *The Interview Game: Winning Strategies for the Job Seeker,* Follett Publishing Company, Chicago, Ill., 1979.

Nutter, Carolyn F: *The Resumé Workbook,* Carroll Press, Cranston, R.I., 1978.

Paetro, Maxine: *How to Put Your Book Together and Get a Job in Advertising,* Executive Communications, Inc., New York, 1979.

Salmon, Richard D: *The Job Hunter's Guide to Eight Great American Cities,* Brattle Publications, Cambridge, Mass., 1978.

End Notes

[1] Peter W. Allport, "Professionalism in Advertising," *Journal of Advertising,* vol. 3, no. 4, 1974, p. 19.

[2] James Webb Young, *How to Become an Advertising Man,* Advertising Publications, Inc., Chicago, Ill., 1963, pp. 9–11.

[3] William A. Cather, "What It Takes to Become an Adman —as Admen See It," *Advertising Age,* Dec. 23, 1974, p. 17.

[4] John S. Wright, "Our Working Adpeople and Educators Must Agree on a Basic Ad Curriculum," *Advertising Age,* Nov. 13, 1980, p. 78.

[5] Donald G. Hileman and Billy I. Ross, *Where Shall I Go to College to Study Advertising?* Advertising Education Publications, Lubbock, Texas, 1980.

[6] "Job Hunting and Recruitment," *Advertising Age,* Section 2, Jan. 1, 1979.

[7] *Broadcasting,* Feb. 9, 1981, p. 38.

[8] From a local advertisement for Chaminade University, Honolulu, Hawaii.

[9] *Advertising Age,* March 31, 1980, p. 48.

Glossary

AAA (American Academy of Advertising) A professional organization of college teachers of advertising and practitioners interested in furthering advertising education.

AAAA (4A's) (American Association of Advertising Agencies) An organization of leading United States advertising agencies.

AAF (American Advertising Federation) An association of advertising clubs, advertisers, agencies, media, and allied companies, with the objective of making advertising more effective for business and more useful to the public.

ABC (Audit Bureau of Circulations) An organization sponsored by publishers, agencies, and advertisers to validate the circulation statements of magazines and newspapers.

ABP (American Business Press) An organization of technical, professional, industrial, and other business publications formed by merger of the Associated Business Publications and National Business Publications groups.

AFTRA (American Federation of Television and Radio Artists) A guild of broadcast announcers and performers.

AM Amplitude modulation. The standard radio broadcasting method, with tone modulation governed by variations in the height of waves rather than by their frequency.

AMA (American Marketing Association) A professional organization of marketing teachers, marketing research practitioners, and marketing executives.

ANA (Association of National Advertisers) A national organization of advertisers, with larger manufacturers constituting the majority of the members.

ANPA (American Newspaper Publishers Association) An organization of publishers of daily newspapers in the United States and Canada.

APA (Agricultural Publishers Association) An association of farm magazine and farm newspaper publishers.

ARB (American Research Bureau) A broadcast program rating service for television only; it uses both the viewer diary method and an electronic recording and tabulating system known as *Arbitron*.

ARF (Advertising Research Foundation) A nonprofit organization of advertisers, agencies, and media, with colleges and universities as academic members, to promote greater effectiveness in advertising and marketing through impartial, objective research.

ASCAP (American Society of Composers, Authors, and Publishers) An organization that administers the licensing of, and collection of fees from, networks and stations for music and other program material.

Absolute cost The charge for a certain amount of time or space in an advertising medium.

Account An advertiser. The client of an advertising agency or to a firm placing advertising direct with media.

Account executive The member of an advertising agency who supervises the planning and preparation of advertising for one or more clients, and who is responsible for the primary liaison between agency and advertiser. Sometimes called *account supervisor* or *contact person.*

Adjacencies Programs immediately preceding or following a specific commercial time period or program.

Advertising (a) As defined by the AMA, any paid form of nonpersonal presentation and promotion of ideas, goods, and services by an identified sponsor to a group.

Advertising (b) From the communications viewpoint, controlled, identifiable information and persuasion by means of mass communications media.

Advertising Council A nonprofit organization of advertisers, agencies, and media formed to plan, create, and distribute public service advertising programs. Founded as the War Advertising Council in 1941.

Advertising registers Directories of national advertisers or advertising agencies, published annually in separate editions.

Advertising Research Foundation (ARF) See *ARF.*

Advertising specialties A form of direct advertising. Products bearing the name and address or slogan of a business firm are given away free by the advertiser to present or prospective customers. Sometimes called *remembrance advertising.*

Advertising substantiation Documentation supporting advertising claims, and proof of having relied on that documentation when preparing the advertising. Advertisers must be able to supply the Federal Trade Commission with such documentation and show their dependence on it when creating their advertising.

Affiliate A broadcast station belonging to, or carrying the programs of a specific network.

Affirmative disclosure A procedure which would require advertisers to tell not only the positive story about their products, but also the negative side.

Agate line A unit of measurement for advertising space, one column wide and one-fourteenth inch deep.

Agent One who represents or handles business contacts for artists, actors, musicians, or writers. Also an owner or partner in an advertising agency.

Agricultural Publishers Association (APA) See *APA.*

Aided recall A research technique used to measure the impression made by an advertisement or other communication, and in which the interviewer shows the respondent an advertisement, program log, or other aid to memory.

American Academy of Advertising (AAA) See *AAA.*

American Advertising Federation (AAF) See *AAF.*

American Association of Advertising Agencies (AAAA, 4A's) See *AAAA.*

American Business Press (ABP) See *ABP.*

American Federation of Television and Radio Artists (AFTRA) See *AFTRA.*

American Marketing Association (AMA) See *AMA.*

American Newspaper Publishers Association (ANPA) See *ANPA.*

American Research Bureau (ARB) See *ARB.*

American Society of Composers, Authors, and Publishers (ASCAP) See *ASCAP)*

Animation Movement added to static objects. Usually applied to cartoon drawings filmed for television, or to POP material or outdoor advertisements with moving parts.

Arbitron An instantaneous system for obtaining television program ratings by means of electronic devices placed in homes and wired to a central tabulating headquarters. See *ARB.*

Area sampling A probability sampling technique which divides the total geographical area under study into a number of smaller areas and then uses random selection to determine the specific areas or specific respondents to be interviewed.

Association of National Advertisers (ANA) See *ANA.*

Audience The total number of people who *may* receive an advertising message delivered by a medium or combination of media.

Audience composition The proportion of various types of people, classified by characteristics—demographic or psychographic—reached by an advertising medium or message.

Audience flow The gain or loss in audience during a broadcast program, or from one program channel to another.

Audimeter An electromechanical device used by A. C. Nielsen Company to record station tuning of TV receivers by a sample of viewers.

Audio Sound or pertaining to sound. In television, the transmission or reception of sound as opposed to the picture portion, or video.

Audiotape Tape used for radio broadcasting to record sound only, in contrast to videotape, which records both sound and visual portions of telecasts.

Availability Broadcast time offered to an advertiser for sponsorship.

BBB (Better Business Bureau) Local organizations supported by business firms to discourage false or misleading advertising.

BMI (Broadcast Music Incorporated) A music copyright organization formed by stations and networks to perform functions similar to ASCAP.

BPA (Business Publications Audit of Circulations) An auditing organization for business publications primarily concerned with controlled circulation.

BPAA (Business and Professional Advertisers Association) A professional organization of marketing and advertising executives in the business products field. Formerly the Association of Industrial Advertisers.

Bait advertising Advertising that features exceptional prices or terms for a product in order to attract prospects to a store, where they find it difficult or impossible to buy the product as advertised.

Bartering In broadcasting, the trading of advertiser-produced programs for free advertising time within them; also, the exchange of merchandise for commercial air time.

Better Business Bureau (BBB) See *BBB*.

Billing The total amount of money charged to clients by an advertising agency, including media bills, production costs, and service charges.

Bleed Printing to the very edge of the page, leaving no margin.

Body copy Main copy block or blocks of an advertisement, as distinguished from headline, subheads, coupon copy, etc.

Body type Type used for body copy in an advertisement, in contrast to display type used for headlines and subheads.

Boldface Type that is heavier in strokes than other designs of the same type family, or heavier than the text type with which it is used.

Boutique A form of limited-service advertising agency, usually performing only the creative function for a fee.

Box-top offer An offer of a premium based on the return of the box top from a package or other proof of purchase.

Brand label A label that informs the buyer of the product's brand name and its manufacturer.

Broadcast Music Incorporated (BMI) See *BMI*.

Broadside A giant folder, often sent as a self-mailer, used especially in direct-mail advertising to the trade.

Brochure An elaborate or impressive booklet.

Broker A manufacturer's sales representative who receives commissions on sales made to wholesalers or retailers in a specified territory.

Budget attrition The process whereby the advertising budget is used up for nonadvertising activities.

Bulk discount A discount for quantity purchases.

Bulk mailing Third-class mail delivered to the post office in bundles, sorted by states and cities.

Bulk sales Large quantities of a publication bought for redistribution.

Business advertising A collective word to describe all forms of advertising designed to sell goods and services for purposes other than personal satisfaction.

Business Publications Audit of Circulations (BPA) See *BPA*.

Business and Professional Advertisers Association (BPAA) See *BPAA*.

CU (Close-up) A camera shot to show a single object or part of it at close range.

Cable TV A system of distributing televised messages to homes connected to a transmitter by means of physical cables; these homes pay subscription fees for the service.

Caps In typography, capital, or uppercase, letters in contrast to small, or lowercase, letters.

Caption Explanatory text accompanying an illustration. Also, the heading of a chapter, page, or section.

Center spread A single sheet of paper that forms the two facing pages in the center of a publication and permits printing across the fold, or gutter.

Channel The frequency in the broadcast spectrum assigned to a station for its transmissions.

Character An individual letter, figure, or other unit of type.

Checking copy Copy of a publication delivered to an agency or advertiser to verify insertion of an advertisement as ordered.

Chroma In color, the dimension of strength or intensity. Two other dimensions are required in color measurement: *hue*, the quality that distinguishes one color from another, and *value*, or depth, the degree of lightness or darkness.

Circular An inexpensive form of direct advertising consisting of small sheets of paper printed on one or both sides for delivery by mail or by hand, and frequently distributed as inserts with letters, statements, or catalogs. Also called *leaflets*.

Circulation The number of copies of a publication distributed. Used loosely to refer to the number of homes regularly tuned to a broadcast station.

City zone The portion of a newspaper's coverage area that includes the corporate city plus adjacent areas which have the characteristics of the city.

Classified advertising Advertising arranged according to the product or service advertised, and usually restricted in size, illustration, and format. *Display classified* permits illustrations and greater variety in size and format. See *display advertisement.*

Class selectivity A medium's ability to reach a specific demographic or psychographic group with its messages.

Clear channel station A radio station with interference-free broadcasting rights on a particular frequency and broadcasting power up to 50,000 watts.

Client An agency or media term referring to an advertiser with whom business is done.

Closing date The final date on which advertising must be delivered to a medium in order to appear in a specific issue or time slot.

Cognitive psychology A theory focusing on the human's desire to know. The underlying notion is that behavior is a function of cognitions (knowings) which are nothing other than ideas, bits of knowledge, values, and beliefs held by the individual.

Coincidental survey A method of checking viewers or listeners of a broadcast program while it is on the air. Usually conducted by telephone.

Collateral In advertising, the non-commissionable media used in a campaign.

Color separation In full-color advertisements, either a black-and-white negative of one primary color in the full-color original or the process of breaking down full-color copy into its primary-color components.

Column inch A unit of publication space one column wide and one inch deep.

Combination rate A special rate for advertising in two or more publications under the same ownership.

Company magazine A publication issued regularly by a business firm for its employees, dealers, prospects, or other groups. A house organ.

Comparative advertising Advertising which contrasts two or more specifically named brands of the same generic product class and makes such a comparison in terms of one or more specific product attributes. **(Also known as comparison advertising.)**

Competitive advertising An approach designed to convince consumers that the advertised product is superior to other products of similar type.

Composition Setting type and assembling it with engravings.

Comprehensive A layout prepared to resemble the finished advertisement as closely as possible. Often called *comp.*

Consumer behavior In advertising, those activities dealing with the buying of products and the reasons for such action.

Consumer jury A method of pretesting products or advertisements by exposing them to potential purchasers or users.

Contest A form of sales promotion whereby potential consumers of the featured product may win prizes either through skill or by chance. Designed to stimulate quick buying action.

Continuity in advertising Repetition of the same basic theme, layout, or commercial format. Continuity in media refers to the regularity with which messages appear in advertising media.

Continuous tone A screened photographic image which contains gradient tones from black to white.

Controlled circulation The circulation of business publications delivered free, or largely free, to individuals selected by job category or other relevant criteria. To meet BPA standards, the publication must be issued quarterly or oftener and must contain no less than 25 percent editorial material. See *qualified circulation.*

Convenience goods Those items that are frequently purchased, are low in cost, and are bought at the most accessible retail outlet shortly after a need for the product is felt.

Cooperative advertising Most commonly used to refer to advertising paid for jointly by a national advertiser and its wholesalers or retailers; sometimes called a *dealer's, manufacturer's, or vertical* cooperative. Also applied in advertising sponsored by several national advertisers or several local advertisers, and classed as a *horizontal* cooperative.

Copy Broadly, all elements, both verbal and visual, which will be included in the finished advertisement. In a narrow sense, the verbal elements only, or the material to be set by a compositor.

Copy casting See *copy fitting.*

Copy chief Head of a copy group in an agency or advertising department.

Copy fitting Counting the number of characters or words in a piece of copy in order to determine how much space it will require if set in a specified type face and size. The same procedure is used to determine the amount of copy needed to fill a fixed amount of space. Also called *copy casting.*

Copy platform See *creative strategy statement.*

Copyright Legal protection granted an artist or author against the reprinting, use, or sale of an original work without express consent.

Copy testing Measuring the effectiveness of an advertising campaign, an advertisement, or elements of an advertisement.

Corporate advertising Advertising that stresses the resources, skill, or character of the advertising firm rather than promoting a product or a brand. See *institutional advertising.*

Corrective advertising Advertising run by a sponsor to correct misimpressions resulting from earlier advertising. Done at the request or order of the FTC.

Cost per inquiry The cost of producing one inquiry about the product from an advertisement or an advertising campaign.

Cost per thousand The cost to the advertiser for the delivery of a message to 1,000 readers, viewers, etc. May be applied to a variety of bases, such as *cost per thousand homes,* cost per thousand *circulation,* or cost per thousand prospects.

Counter card Point-of-purchase material with an easel on the back, to be placed on the counter or near the product.

Coupon A form of sales promotion whereby consumers can exchange the coupon for a reduction in price or refund when purchasing the featured product.

Coverage The percentage of households or individuals who are exposed to a specific advertising medium in a given area.

Coverage map A map showing the geographical area reached by transmission from a broadcast station. Usually divided into primary and secondary coverage areas for both day and night.

Creative research Research applied to the development and evaluation of the creative product—advertisements and commercials.

Creative strategy statement or **copy platform** The starting point for every ad and commercial; a statement that includes discussion of a proposed message's objective, target audience, basic creative promise, and style of presentation.

Crop To remove portions of an illustration by trimming the edges, either to eliminate undesirable content or to change illustration proportions.

CU See *close-up*.

Cumulative audience The total number of persons or homes reached by a number of successive issues of a publication or successive broadcasts. In broadcasting, sometimes referred to as *cumulative reach*.

Cumulative reach See *cumulative audience*.

DMMA (Direct Mail Marketing Association) An organization of producers and users of direct advertising materials.

Dealer imprint A dealer's name and address, or other identification, placed on material produced by a national advertiser.

Dealer's cooperative See *cooperative advertising*.

Delayed broadcast A repeat broadcast of a program by tape or film. Frequently used to compensate for time differences between station locations in network operations.

Demarketing A state in which demand exceeds the level at which the marketer feels able or motivated to supply it.

Demographics The statistical description of a market or other population group based upon such facts as age, sex, marital status, education, etc. See also *psychographics*.

Depth interview A research method based on the use of open-end questions and stimulation of the respondent to talk freely and at length about the subject.

Direct advertising Printed advertising delivered to prospects by mail, salespeople, dealers, or canvassers, in contrast to advertising delivered by publications or by broadcast or position media.

Direct Mail Marketing Association (DMMA) See *DMMA*.

Direct-mail advertising Direct advertising delivered to prospects through the mail.

Direct marketing The consummation of a sale of a product by mail, without aid of intermediaries or personal, face-to-face selling. Similar to mail-order advertising.

Director In broadcasting, the person responsible for on-the-air production of a program. See *producer*.

Directory advertising Advertising in printed directories, such as telephone, industrial, and city directories.

Display advertisement In publications, advertisements using attention-attracting elements, such as illustrations, typographical variety, white space, or color, in contrast to classified advertising.

Display type Type used for headline or other emphasized elements; also, any type larger than 14-point.

Dissolve In television or film production, the technique of bringing one scene into full focus as a previous one fades or is wiped out.

Double-page spread An advertisement appearing on two facing pages.

Drive time The peak period for radio listenership, when people are driving to and from work.

Dubbing In broadcasting, adding pictures or sound after the original recording has been made. Also, making duplicate recordings of original material.

Dummy In direct advertising, a model indicating the size, shape, and layout of the finished printed product. In periodicals, a facsimile of the proposed issue.

Duplication Two or more advertising media reaching the same individual or household.

ECU (Extreme close-up) In television, a very close camera shot to show maximum detail.

EDP (Electronic data processing) The storing, retrieving, and analyzing of masses of data by use of computers and other electronic equipment.

Earned rate The rate an advertiser pays for space or time actually used within a specific time period.

Editorial matter The news, educational, or entertainment portion of a publication or broadcast, as distinguished from the advertising.

Electric spectacular An outdoor advertisement using electric lights to form words and designs, and usually animated.

Engraving An original printing plate. Also, a method of reproducing a design for printing by cutting or etching metal plates.

Envelope stuffer Direct-mail advertising inserted in mailings of statements or other correspondence.

Experience goods Products whose quality is not obvious through inspection but which must be purchased and used in order to determine product quality.

FCC (Federal Communications Commission) The government agency that licenses broadcast stations and regulates broadcasting.

FDA (Food and Drug Administration) The government agency responsible for enforcement of the Food, Drug and Cosmetics Act, which forbids interstate commerce in such products if misbranded or adulterated. Also regulates advertising of these product categories.

FM (Frequency modulation) A method of modulating tone in broadcasting by frequency of waves rather than their amplitude. More limited in coverage area than AM, but less affected by static. See *AM.*

FTC (Federal Trade Commission) A government agency concerned with the regulation of interstate commerce, including interstate advertising.

Face The style or design of type. Also, the printing surface of a type character or engraving.

Fact sheet An outline of key product facts supplied to copywriters, or to broadcast announcers who use it as a basis for ad-libbed, rather than prepared, commercials.

Fair trade Laws which restrain retailers from selling products at prices less than those established by agreement between manufacturer and retailer. More properly called *resale price maintenance.*

Family of type One design of type in a complete range of sizes and variations, as Caslon Bold, Caslon Bold Condensed, Caslon Bold Italic, Caslon New, Caslon Old Style, etc.

Federal Communications Commission (FCC) See *FCC.*

Federal Trade Commission (FTC) See *FTC.*

Feed To transmit a broadcast from one station or location to another.

Feedback The response or reaction to a communication which tells the sender how his or her message is being interpreted.

Field intensity In broadcasting, the measurement of station signal strength at different locations. Field intensity contour maps indicate station coverage patterns. See *coverage map.*

Fifteen and two The standard discounts to advertising agencies allowed by most media. The agency retains 15 percent of the gross bill as its commission; 2 percent of the net bill is a cash discount normally passed on to the advertiser.

Flat rate A uniform rate for advertising space or time, with no discounts for volume or frequency.

Flexibility In media, a scheduling capability related to the lead time required between the receipt of ads for publication or broadcast and their actual appearance in print or on the air; the shorter the lead time, the greater the flexibility from the advertiser's point of view.

Flight saturation Maximum concentration of spot commercials in a short time period.

Flush Printed matter set even with other material or with the edge of the page.

Focus-group interview A form of qualitative research involving a joint depth interview with several respondents selected because of their similarities.

Font A complete assortment of type characters in one face and size, including numbers, punctuation marks, etc.

Food and Drug Administration (FDA) See *FDA.*

Format The size, shape, style, and appearance of a publication, printed page, or advertisement. In broadcasting, the organization of each element in a program

Four-color process A printing process that reproduces a full range of colors by overprinting red, yellow, blue, and black.

Frequency The number of times an advertising message is delivered within a set period of time. Also, the number of impulses per second sent out by a broadcast transmitter.

Frequency discount A reduction in advertising rates based on the number of insertions or commercials used in a given period.

Frequency modulation See *FM.*

Fringe time Time periods in which normal customary broadcast audiences are unavailable.

Full color See *four-color process.*

Full disclosure The requirement that manufacturers of specified products disclose specific kinds of information about them; for example, processed food makers must list the nutritional value of their products on labels and in advertisements.

Full position A special preferred position for newspaper advertisements, either next to and following reading matter or at the top of the column next to reading matter.

Full showing In transit advertising, a message on each bus or other unit of the system. Also used loosely to refer to a 100 showing of outdoor advertising.

GNP See *gross national product.*

GRP See *gross rating point.*

Gallup-Robinson A research organization, best known for impact studies of TV and magazine advertisements.

General advertising National or nonlocal advertising in newspapers.

Generic name A name used to describe a product category rather than a specific brand.

Geographical selectivity A medium's ability to reach a specific geographical area with its messages.

Gimmick Any clever idea or device.

Government organization advertising A form of social advertising sponsored by government agencies to get the public to join the armed services, travel in a certain area, and so forth.

Grade A coverage The primary coverage area of a television station.

Grade B coverage The secondary coverage area of a television station.

Gravure A printing process which transfers image to paper with ink retained in depressions in the plate. See *intaglio.*

Gross national product (GNP) The

value of all goods and services produced in a nation in one year.

Gross rating point (GRP) A measurement of the saturation for a given media effort. One gross rating point equals 1 percent of the TV homes in a given market. Computed by multiplying the rating figure by the frequency number. Used in buying television coverage.

Group discount In broadcasting, a special discount for the use of a group of stations simultaneously.

Gutter The two inside margins of facing pages in a newspaper or magazine.

Half showing In transit advertising, a card in every other vehicle of the system. Loosely used for a 50 showing of outdoor advertising.

Halftone An engraving made by photographing through a screen which breaks up the subject into small dots of varying size, reproducing continuous shades or tones.

Handbill A small form of direct advertising distributed by hand.

Head-on position An outdoor advertising location directly facing traffic, as distinguished from either an angled or a parallel position.

Heaviside layer A region of ionized air beginning about 65 miles above the earth's surface. At night it reflects AM broadcast signals back to earth, but does not affect FM transmissions.

Hidden offer A special offer buried in the body copy of a print advertisement as a test of readership.

Hi-Fi Color In newspaper advertising, preprinted color ads which feed into the press like wallpaper so that the paper may be cut at any point without damaging the effect of the ad.

Holdover audience In broadcasting, the audience that is retained from a previous program over the same network or station.

Homes using television (HUT); homes using radio (HUR) The percentage of all TV or radio homes in an area with sets turned on during a particular measurement period. (*Note:* Sometimes the term *Sets in use* is used for radio.)

Horizontal cooperative See *cooperative advertising.*

Horizontal publication A business publication edited for readers employed in similar job categories in different industries, such as *Product Engineering, Purchasing,* and *Journal of Accountancy.*

House agency An advertising agency controlled by a single advertiser.

House organ A publication issued regularly by a business firm for its employees, dealers, prospects, or other groups.

Hue In color, the dimension that distinguishes one color from another, as red from yellow.

ID Identification announcement. A broadcast term for a brief commercial between programs and preceding the station identification announcement.

IOA (Institute of Outdoor Advertising) An educational and promotional organization of the outdoor advertising field.

Impulse purchase Unpremeditated purchase of consumer goods.

Industrial advertising Advertising goods or services to businesses for use in the production or distribution of other goods and services.

In-house agency An advertiser firm that performs agency functions for itself instead of engaging an advertising agency. See *house agency.*

Inquiry test A method of testing advertisements or media by comparing the number of inquiries received from readers, listeners, or viewers.

Insert A special page printed by the advertiser and forwarded to a publisher who binds it into the publication. Also, an advertising tabloid placed inside a newspaper.

Insertion order Written authorization for a publication to print an advertisement of a specified size in a particular issue at a stated rate.

Institute of Outdoor Advertising (IOA) *See IOA.*

Institutional advertising Advertising created primarily to build long-range goodwill or prestige for the advertiser, rather than to stimulate immediate product purchase. See *corporate advertising.*

Island display A store display centered in an aisle or other open space.

Island position A newspaper advertisement position entirely surrounded by editorial matter or page margin; rarely available.

Jingle A musical commercial.

Judgment sampling See *quota sampling.*

Junior unit A unit of space that permits an advertiser to use the same plates for large- and small-page magazines. Plates prepared for full-page space in the smaller magazine appear in the larger one with editorial material on two or more sides.

Justify type To arrange type so that letters are properly spaced and lines are of even length. Machine-set type is justified automatically.

Keying an advertisement Putting a code number or letter in a coupon or in the advertiser's address so that the particular advertisement or medium producing an inquiry can be identified. See *inquiry test.*

Key plate In color-process printing, the plate with maximum detail to which other plates must be registered.

Lanham Act The federal statute governing registration of trademarks and the other identifying symbols on products sold in interstate commerce.

Layout The arrangement of creative elements on a printed page: headlines, copy blocks, illustrations, logotypes, and other items which serve as a blueprint for the finished ad.

Leading The insertion of metal strips, or leads, between lines of type to provide greater space and improve readability and appearance. (Pronounced *ledding.*)

Letterpress printing method of printing in which the ink is carried on a raised, or relief, surface.

Licensee In broadcasting, the owner of a station.

Lifestyle A distinctive mode of living, focusing on how people go about their daily routines.

Lightface A type design that has thin, light lines, in contrast to *boldface.*

Linage Any amount of advertising space measured in agate lines.

Line A unit for measuring the depth of advertising space. See *agate line.*

Line charges In broadcasting, the cost for microwave relay, coaxial cable, or telephone lines to transmit a network or remote program to a radio or TV station. See *remote.*

Line cut (plate) An engraving made without a screen; reproduces only solid lines or areas, without intermediate shades or tones. See *halftone.*

Line drawing A brush or pen drawing consisting of solid lines or masses without continuous tonal gradations.

Line-of-sight signal In broadcasting, the FM signal, which cannot be received at any significant distance from the point where it becomes tangent to the earth's surface.

Lip sync In television, the synchronization of an actor's lip movements with separately recorded spoken lines.

List broker A commission agent who rents direct-mail lists to advertisers.

Listener diary In broadcasting, a method of research in which respondents maintain a continuing record of listening or viewing.

List price The manufacturer's or wholesaler's recommended retail price.

Lithography The process of printing from a flat surface on which the ink for the image is retained by a greasy or albuminous deposit; planographic printing.

Live program Simultaneous performance and broadcasting, in contrast to broadcasting from magnetic tape or film.

Local advertising Advertising that is placed by a local entrepreneur, in contrast to national or general advertising.

Log In broadcasting, an hourly chronological record of all programs and commercials aired by a station.

Logotype The signature or standard name plate of an advertiser.

Loss leader A product offered at cost or below to attract store traffic.

Lowercase Small letters, in contrast to capital (uppercase) letters.

MAB (Magazine Advertising Bureau) A bureau within the MPA to promote the sale of advertising space in consumer magazines. See *MPA.*

MPA (Magazine Publishers Association) An organization of consumer magazine publishers.

Magnuson-Moss Warranty-Federal Trade Commission (FTC) Improvement Act An amendment to the FTC Act, passed in 1975, broadening the scope of the FTC.

Mail-order advertising Advertising designed to produce orders direct from prospects by mail; any type of medium may be used to deliver the advertising message.

Make good Repeating an advertisement without charge, or refunding space or time charges, as compensation for an advertisement's having been omitted or containing a significant error.

Manufacturers cooperative advertising See *cooperative advertising.*

Market People who have the ability and inclination to buy, or prospects for a product or service. Also, a geographical area which includes a significant number of prospects.

Market profile Facts about the prospects, or an analysis by age, sex, income, possessions, etc., of people who constitute the market for a product or service. See *demographics* and *psychographics.*

Market segmentation Dividing the market for a product into homogeneous subsections in order that each segment may be treated in the most appropriate manner.

Market share One firm's share of the industry's total sales volume.

Marketing A total system of interacting business activities designed to plan, price, promote, and distribute want-satisfying products and services to present and potential customers.

Marketing concept A unifying approach marshaling and directing the total resources of the business firm toward the determination and satisfaction of customer and consumer wants and needs in a way planned to enhance the firm's overall profit performance.

Marketing mix The blending of product, price, distribution channels, personal selling, and advertising into a suitable marketing program for the firm.

Mass communication The delivery of large numbers of identical messages simultaneously by communication organizations or media, in contrast to personal or individual communication.

Mat service A commercial organization supplying advertisers, publications, and printers with ready-made mats and illustrations through a subscription service.

Media characteristics The various dimensions by which advertising media may be compared, including selectivity, coverage, flexibility, cost, editorial environment, production quality, permanence, trade acceptability, and merchandising cooperation.

Media director An agency executive responsible for the selection and scheduling of advertising media.

Media planning The process of designing a course of action that shows how advertising time and space will be used to contribute to the achievement of marketing objectives.

Media Records, Inc. An organization that publishes records of the space used by different advertisers in newspapers that subscribe to the service.

Media representative A firm that represents noncompetitive media in a given market in the sale of advertising time or space.

Mediamark Research, Inc. (MRI) A syndicated service providing advertisers and agencies with information on the characteristics of selected media audiences.

Medium Any vehicle used to convey an advertising message, such as television, magazines, or direct mail. Also, the method and tools used by an artist, such as pen and ink, crayon, or photography.

Merchandising Any activity to stimulate trade interest in moving the product or service to the prospect.

Merchandising the advertising The promotion of a consumer advertising program to members of the advertiser's sales force and to the trade.

Microwave relay A method of relaying television signals by use of ultra high frequency relay stations at high topographic locations or in mobile equipment.

Milline rate A theoretical unit for comparison of newspaper advertising rates in relation to circulation; the cost of one agate line for one million circulation.

Mixing In broadcasting, mixing different audio effects, as music and voice, or leveling the volume from scene to scene.

Mobile billboards Billboard announcements attached to moving vehicles whose owners are paid to circulate in specified areas.

Mock-up A facsimile of products or packages used in television.

Monitor To listen to or view a broadcast program. Also, a television receiver in the control room or studio used by production personnel or performers to follow the action of a program.

Motivation research (MR) Research which attempts to relate behavior to underlying desires, emotions, and intentions, in contrast to research which merely enumerates behavior or describes a situation; it relies heavily on the use of techniques adapted from psychology and other social sciences.

Moving shot In television, following the action with a camera.

Multiplexing In broadcasting, the use of special equipment to transmit more than one program service from the same station, such as an FM station "storecasting" music and commercials to supermarkets and broadcasting regular programs to home listeners.

NAB (National Association of Broadcasters) An organization of radio and television stations and networks.

NAD (National Advertising Division of the Council of Better Business Bureaus) The entry gate for complaints registered against national advertisers as part of the advertising industry's self-regulation procedure. The complaint moves up to NARB if not resolved at this level.

NARB (National Advertising Review Board) The final arbiter of complaints registered against national advertisers as part of the advertising industry's self-regulatory machinery. Uses moral suasion to get undesirable practices stopped.

NOAB (National Outdoor Advertising Bureau) A cooperative organization for placement and inspection of outdoor advertising, owned and used by advertising agencies.

NSAD (National Society of Art Directors) A professional organization of art directors for agencies, media, advertisers, and advertising suppliers.

National advertising The advertising of a manufacturer or wholesaler, in contrast to the advertising of a retailer or local advertiser. Also, any advertising in media with nationwide circulation.

National Advertising Bureau, Inc. An agency promoting the use of daily newspapers as advertising media. Sponsored by the American Newspaper Publishers Association (ANPA).

National brand A brand distributed widely through many different outlets, in contrast to a *private brand* or *private label* owned by a distributor or retailer.

Net audience An unduplicated number of homes, or of readers, viewers, or listeners, reached over a period of time, or by a combination of different media.

Net profit Profit after payment of all costs of operation. *Net before taxes* is profit after payment of all operating costs except taxes.

Net rate A medium's published rate less agency commission.

Network In broadcasting, a group of stations affiliated by contract and usually interconnected for simultaneous broadcast of the same programs.

Network affiliate One of the stations in a broadcasting network.

Next to reading matter (NR) An advertisement position immediately adjacent to reading matter or editorial content.

Nielsen Drug (Food) Index Reports on the market movement of products, by type and brand, through panels of drugstores and food stores.

Nielsen rating In broadcasting, the percentage of TV homes in a given area tuned to a given television program, as reported by the A. C. Nielsen Company.

OAAA (Outdoor Advertising Association of America) An association of plant owners operating standardized outdoor advertising facilities.

O and O station A broadcast station owned and operated by a network.

Off camera In television, action or sound outside camera range and not visible to the audience.

Off mike In broadcasting, voice or sound away from microphone.

Offset A lithographic printing process in which the image is first transferred to a rubber roller, or blanket, which in turn makes the impression on the paper.

On camera In television, action or sound within camera range and visible to the audience.

On mike In broadcasting, any sound that can be clearly heard via the microphone.

One-time rate The rate paid by an advertiser who does not use enough space or time to earn volume discounts. The same as *transient rate.*

Open rate An advertising rate subject to discounts for volume or frequency.

Operations research An interdisciplinary approach to marketing and advertising research using physical or mathematical models which are subjected to possible courses of action.

Outdoor advertising Signs placed alongside highways and streets which meet the standards established by the OAAA. Includes posters and painted bulletins.

Outdoor Advertising Association of America (OAAA) *See OAAA.*

Out-of-home advertising A collective term to describe advertising media that depend upon people or traffic passing the location of the medium. Includes outdoor advertising, nonstandardized signs, and transit advertising. Sometimes called *traffic* or *position media.*

Overrun The number of pieces of printed material in excess of the specified quantity. An advertiser usually accepts up to 10 percent overrun at pro rata cost.

PIB Publishers Information Bureau. An organization which furnishes periodic reports on the expenditures of national advertisers in magazines and network television.

POP Point-of-purchase, or point-of-sale, advertising; any displays or advertising material used in or around a retail store.

POPAI (Point-of-Purchase Advertising Institute) An organization of advertisers, agencies, and producers of point-of-purchase advertising material.

Package insert Advertising material packed with a product, usually to advertise a different product.

Package program In broadcasting, a complete program, including all elements except commercials, sold as a unit; may be either live or transcribed, or on film or tape.

Packaging Institute An organization of manufacturers and users of packing materials, machinery, and services.

Page proof A proof of type and illustrations in page form as they will finally appear, usually pulled after *galley proofs* have been corrected.

Painted bulletin An outdoor advertisement that is painted on a panel, in contrast to one of printed paper pasted on.

Pan or **panning** In television, to move the camera up and down or from left to right, in contrast to moving it to or from the subject.

Panel A group of respondents used repeatedly to supply data in marketing or advertising research. Also, the portion of an outdoor board on which printed paper is pasted.

Paper See *poster.*

Participation program A regularly scheduled network or station program on which advertisers may place spot announcements without any responsibility for program content.

Pass-along reader A person who reads a publication not purchased by anyone in that person's household.

Paste-up A layout in which illustration and type material are combined on one sheet for reproduction as a single engraving.

Pay TV A plan which allows TV viewers to receive special programs after payment of a specific fee.

Penetration The ability of an advertising medium to reach a certain percentage of homes or prospects in a given geographical area. See *coverage.*

Philanthropic organization advertising A form of social advertising designed to raise funds for worthwhile causes.

Photocomposition A photographic method of setting type, rapidly gaining favor in newspaper and other printing production. Cold type.

Photoengraving A relief printing plate made by a photochemical process. Also, a print made from such a plate, or the process itself.

Photostat A rapid and inexpensive process for copying text or illustrations. Also, the copies so made, often called *stats.*

Pica A unit of measurement for type or other printed material; six picas equal one inch.

Piggyback Two broadcast commercials aired one after the other featuring two different products of the same advertiser.

Pilot program In broadcasting, a representative program from a series, produced either for the purpose of pretesting audience reaction or as a sample for prospective sponsors.

Pioneering advertising Advertising aimed at building acceptance for a previously unknown product.

Planographic printing Lithography, whether direct or offset.

Plate A term loosely applied to any material used to make a printed impression by letterpress, gravure, or lithography.

Point A unit of vertical type measurement equal to $1/72$ inch.

Point-of-purchase advertising See *POP.*

Political advertising A form of social advertising used to support the candidacy of individuals in election campaigns.

Portfolio test A method of pretesting advertisements by interspersing them among editorial matter in a book similar to a photo album.

Positioning See *product positioning*.

Poster An advertising message printed on large sheets of paper and pasted on boards or panels.

Poster panel A standard structure on which posters are pasted.

Poster plant The local organization that builds and maintains standard outdoor advertising facilities.

Predate issue An edition of a publication that is released before the date it actually bears.

Preemption In broadcasting, the appropriation of time from regularly scheduled programs to permit broadcast of special programs of higher priority, such as a presidential speech.

Preferred position Any advertisement position in publications for which the advertiser must pay a premium when specifically ordered.

Premium An offer of merchandise, either free or at nominal cost, as an immediate inducement to purchase a product.

Preprint A reproduction of an advertisement prior to publication.

Press run The printing of a specific job. Also, the number of copies printed.

Primary colors In printing, red, yellow, and blue.

Primary coverage The area in which the reception of a radio station is consistently good to excellent. Corresponds to *grade A coverage* in television.

Primary demand In economics, the demand for a type of product without regard to a specific brand.

Private-label goods Goods produced for exclusive labeling by distributors, retailers, or other intermediaries.

Private nonprofit organization advertising A form of social advertising sponsored by nonprofit organizations to "sell" such goods and services as symphony tickets, college tuition, church attendance, and the like.

Probability sampling A method of sampling in which each unit of the universe has a known or equal chance of selection. See *quota sampling*.

Process plates Printing plates to reproduce the message in two, three, or four colors.

Process printing Printing in which one color is printed over another with transparent inks to produce different hues.

Producer In broadcasting, the person responsible for program production. The producer is primarily concerned with overall administration rather than on-the-air production. See *director*.

Product A set of tangible and intangible attributes, including packaging, color, price, manufacturer's prestige, and manufacturer's and retailer's services, which the buyer may accept as offering satisfaction of wants and needs.

Product positioning A marketing strategy which takes into consideration how consumers perceive a product relative to competitive offerings.

Product reputation advertising Advertising which highlights product features as reason for purchase of the product.

Production department In an advertising agency or advertising department, those persons responsible for the conversion of copy and artwork into printed advertising material. In broadcasting, those responsible for the production and presentation of a program.

Professional advertising Advertising aimed at such professional persons as doctors, dentists, and architects for the purpose of getting them to recommend the featured product to clients. Also may describe advertising by such professionals as doctors, dentists, CPAs.

Program rating The percentage of a sample of radio or TV homes tuned to a specific program at a particular time.

Progressive proofs A set of engraver's proofs used in color process printing, showing each color plate separately and in combination.

Projective techniques Motivational research methods, including thematic apperception tests, used to discover why individuals behave as they do.

Psychographics The statistical description of a market or other population group based upon psychological criteria such as interests, innovativeness, lifestyle, sophistication, etc. See *demographics*.

Public relations A program to build public goodwill toward a company or product.

Publicity A story or message about a product or a company prepared as editorial rather than advertising material and published or broadcast without cost to the originating source.

Publisher's representative An independent organization or individual that sells advertising space for a publication or group of them.

Publisher's statement The statement of circulation issued by a publisher.

Puffery A legal concept which recognizes that someone with something to sell tries to put the item in the best possible light. Such puffery is to be expected and is not actionable under the common law.

Pull advertising Advertising that is used to stimulate consumer demand to a sufficient degree that retailers are forced to stock the brand in order to please their customers.

Push advertising Advertising aimed at middlemen with the goal of getting them to aggressively promote the manufacturer's brand to consumers.

Qualified circulation A term now preferred by BPA to *controlled circulation*.

Qualitative research A variety of indirect methods of research attempting to answer the "why" question in marketing and advertising.

Quarter showing In transit advertising, a message in every fourth unit of the system. Loosely used for a 25 showing in outdoor.

Quota A specific sales goal, in terms of units or dollars, which is established in advance.

Quota sampling A method of sampling in which interviewers look for specific numbers of respondents with known characteristics. Each unit in the universe does not have a known or equal chance of selection. Also called *judgment sampling.* See *probability sampling.*

RAB (Radio Advertising Bureau) An organization of representatives, stations, and networks to promote radio as an advertising medium.

ROP (Run-of-paper) A term that indicates the position of an advertisement will be at the publisher's discretion. See *preferred position.*

Random sampling A form of probability sampling in which each unit of the universe has an equal chance of selection. See *quota sampling.*

Rate card A card or folder issued by an advertising medium listing rates for space or time and providing mechanical requirements and other data usually required by advertisers when preparing ads.

Rate holder The minimum-size advertisement that must appear in a medium during a specified period if the advertiser is to earn a frequency discount rate.

Rating In broadcasting, the same as *program rating.*

Reach The numbers of different homes, people, or prospects reached by one or a group of commercials or advertisements. In broadcasting, a synonym for *cumulative net audience.*

Readership The percentage of audience who recall a specific advertisement or editorial item in a given issue of a publication.

Recall test A method for testing advertising in which respondents are provided with clues and then asked to recall particular ads and the various elements of those ads.

Recognition The acceptance by a medium or a media association of an advertising agency as one entitled to receive standard agency commissions.

Recognition test A method for testing advertising copy in which respondents are shown an ad and asked whether they saw it, read the copy, noted the illustration, etc.

Relative cost The absolute cost of time or space compared to, or spread over, the size of audience delivered by a medium (expressed in terms of homes, people, or demographic groups).

Relay stations See *microwave relay.*

Release A signed statement by a person quoted or photographed which authorizes use of the statement or photograph for advertising purposes. Also, authorization to a medium for the insertion of an advertisement.

Relief printing Printing from a raised surface; letterpress, in contrast to gravure, planographic, or silk-screen printing.

Remembrance advertising Another name for *advertising specialties.*

Remote A broadcast originating outside the regular station or network studios, such as a football game or a convention. Also called *remote pickup.*

Rep Representative. See *publisher's representative and media representative.*

Repro proof Reproduction proof. A clean, sharp proof of type used for reproduction by photoengraving or offset or gravure printing.

Resizing The production of an advertisement in various sizes for different units of space.

Respondent The individual interviewed or subjected to test in marketing and advertising research.

Retail advertising Advertising designed to attract people to the retail outlet to purchase merchandise in stock.

Retail trading zone The area lying outside the city zone, the residents of which patronize city retailers to an important degree. See *city zone.*

Retouching Correcting or improving photographs or other artwork prior to the production of printing plates.

Robinson-Patman Act Federal legislation restricting price or promotional discrimination between customers in interstate commerce.

Roman type A race of type distinguished by variation in the weight of strokes and the inclusion of serifs. Also, all type faces that are not italic.

Rotation Repeating a series of advertisements in the order in which they first appeared.

Rotogravure High-speed gravure printing on rotary presses.

Rough A preliminary sketch submitted for approval before the finished illustration or layout is completed.

Run-of-paper See *ROP.*

SAG (Screen Actors Guild) An organization of film talent which negotiates collective bargaining agreements with motion-picture and television producers.

S.C. The typographical abbreviation for small capital letters.

SRDS (Standard Rate & Data Services, Inc.) An organization which publishes current information on advertising rates, mechanical requirements, closing dates, and similar data on publication, broadcast, and transit media. Accepted as the standard source of advertising media information.

Sales promotion Any sales activity that supplements or coordinates personal selling and advertising, but which cannot be strictly classified as either.

Sampling In research, selecting a

representative portion of the universe. Also, the distribution of miniature or full-size trial packages of a product to introduce it or promote its use.

Sans serif A type face that has no cross strokes, or serifs, at the top or bottom of the characters.

Satellite station A television station that carries little or no local programming, but tends to restrict its broadcasting to duplicating programs of a parent station.

Saturation campaign The intense use of broadcast media in a market, such as 20 TV or 100 radio commercials a week over a single station; usually purchased at special low rates.

Schedule A listing or proposed advertisements, by specific media, with dates of appearance, amount of space or time, etc.

Screening A method of printing based on the stencil principle; ink is squeezed through a screen upon which the design to be printed is imposed.

Script A face of type that resembles handwriting. Also, in broadcasting, the written material used to produce a program or commercial.

Search goods Items whose quality can be obtained less expensively by physical inspection of the product than through actual use. See *experience goods.*

Secondary coverage The area in which the reception of a radio station is generally fair, but subject to variation. Corresponds to *grade B coverage* in television.

Selective demand In economics, the demand for a particular brand of product. See *primary demand.*

Self-mailer A direct-mail piece that can be mailed without a wrapper or envelope.

Semantic differentaial A method of measuring the meaning of words or concepts, which employs bipolar scales separated by an odd number of equal intervals.

Serifs The short cross strokes at the top and bottom of the characters in certain designs of type, especially those of the roman race.

Sets in use A term used to designate the percentage or number of television or radio homes in a given area with sets turned on at a specific time. See *homes using radio.*

Set solid To set lines of type without leading.

Share of audience In broadcasting, the percentage of homes with sets in use tuned to a particular program or station.

Share of market The ratio of an advertiser's sales to total industry sales on either an actual or a potential basis.

Shopping goods Products purchased after careful consideration of quality, price, and suitability. Such a product is infrequently purchased and has a high unit price. It is considered to be a major purchase.

Short rate The higher rate an advertiser must pay when failing to use the amount of space or time specified in the contract.

Shoulder of type The portions of a unit of type which extend above and below the type character, and which do not print.

Signature The advertiser's name in an advertisement. Also, a single sheet of paper which, when folded, will form four, or multiples of four, pages. In broadcasting, a sound effect or music that identifies a program or commercial.

Signs In outdoor advertising, nonstandardized posters and painted bulletins which do not meet the specifications of OAAA. See *outdoor advertising.*

Simmons Market Research Bureau (SMRB) A syndicated service providing advertisers and agencies with information on the characteristics of selected media audiences.

Simulcast A program broadcast simultaneously over radio and television, or over AM and FM radio.

Social advertising Advertising for nonbusiness reasons by nonprofit organizations.

Social cause advertising A form of social advertising used to bring public interest causes to public attention, primarily propagandistic in intent.

Sound on film (SOF) In broadcasting, film footage with a sound track, usually recorded simultaneously.

Space buyer An advertising agency employee who helps plan printed advertising campaigns, and who selects and buys space in publication, outdoor, and transit media. See *time buyer.*

Specialties See *advertising specialties.*

Specialty goods Brand products, with a high unit price, that are purchased infrequently but which the consumer is convinced are superior to all competitive brands. Substitutes will not be accepted if the preferred brand is not in stock.

Spectacolor A more sophisticated version of *Hi-Fi Color* in which preprinted ads are fed into the press, but the point at which the paper is cut is critical to the sense of the ad.

Spectacular A large outdoor electric sign, usually animated. Also, in broadcasting, an elaborate special program irregularly scheduled, usually an hour or more in length.

Speculative presentation A demonstration by an agency to a prospective client showing how it would handle the account if awarded the business. A "pitch."

Split run Two or more advertisements of the same size in the same position in different copies of the same issue of a publication. Used to test different versions of an advertisement, or to feature different products in the regional editions of a national magazine.

Sponsor A radio or television advertiser. In a strict sense, one who pays for program time as distinguished from an advertiser who pays only for an announcement or for commercial time.

Spot announcement A short commercial, one minute or less in length, inserted between radio or television programs, or included in participating programs.

Spot broadcasting An approach to national broadcast advertising, by which the advertiser selects specific markets and specific stations. The opposite of network broadcasting.

Spread Two facing pages in a publication.

Starch A research organization best known for readership studies of magazine advertisements.

Stat See *photo stat.*

Station break The identification or call letters of a radio or television station, or the allowable time between two programs for this identification. Also referred to as *station identification.*

Station identification See *station break.*

Station representative An individual or organization selling spot broadcasting time on a specific station or group of them. See *publisher's representative.*

Still In television, a photograph or similar material inserted into a program or commercial.

Stimulus response model A model attempting to explain how humans behave in their role as consumers and holding that the consumer can be manipulated at the will of the seller.

Stop motion A photographic technique for animating inanimate objects.

Storecasting Broadcasting at the point-of-purchase, usually offering music and news as well as commercials.

Storyboard A series of sketches, with accompanying copy, providing in parallel sequence the video and audio portions of a TV program or commercial. A "layout" for television.

Stripping In broadcasting, a programming strategy that runs episodes of the same series at the same time 5 or 6 days a week.

Super or **superimposition** In television, the imposition of the image from one camera over the image from another; usually refers to a name, trademark, or slogan.

Superstation A television station that sends its signal to cable-equipped homes by means of satellite.

Supplement A special feature section, often in magazine format, distributed with a newspaper.

Sustaining program An unsponsored broadcast program on a commercial station.

Syndication The practice of rerunning a series of successful network television programs on local stations in hours not covered by network programming. Programming, in addition to former network programs, can be specially created for syndication.

Systems approach An orderly discipline for dealing with complex problems under uncertainty.

TAA (Transit Advertising Association) An organization of firms selling transit advertising.

TAB (Traffic Audit Bureau) An organization that furnishes uniform, impartial data on outdoor advertising circulation.

TvB (Television Bureau of Advertising) An organization of networks, stations, and representatives to improve and promote the use of TV as an advertising medium.

Tabloid A newspaper that is usually about one-half the standard size.

Tabloid insert An advertising section prepared by retailers and other sellers for inclusion in newspapers. Usually presented in a tabloid format.

Tag In broadcasting, an addition to a commercial, such as a voice-over message following a transcribed message, or an announcement or musical bit that serves as a finale.

Talent In broadcasting, actors, musicians, announcers, talk-show hosts, or other performers.

Tape In broadcasting, either audiotape or videotape used to record programs or commercials.

Target market A group of the population which is believed to hold the greatest sales potential for the product. The advertiser tries to isolate media which reach the target market and designs messages which communicate with its members.

Tear sheet A page containing an advertisement, clipped from a publication and sent to the advertiser for checking purposes.

Teaser Any advertisement designed to stimulate curiosity by withholding identification of the advertiser or product, but promising more information in future messages.

Theme The central idea of an advertisement, campaign, or program. Also, in broadcasting, the musical identification of a program or commercial.

Thirty sheet A 30-sheet outdoor poster. Uses the same poster panel as the 24-sheet, but provides a copy area 11 inches higher and 25 inches wider.

Three sheet A vertically proportioned outdoor poster, pasted on a panel approximately 8½ feet high and 5 feet wide. The panels are usually located near retail outlets or public transportation stations and are designed to reach pedestrian rather than vehicular traffic.

Thumbnail A rough layout in miniature.

Time buyer An advertising agency employee who helps plan campaigns in broadcast media, and who selects and purchases radio and television time. See *space buyer.*

Time clearance The process of making a specific program period available on particular stations, as when certain affiliated stations have been ordered as part of a network.

Trade advertising Advertising directed at wholesalers or retailers.

Trade character An animate being or animated object designed to identify and personify a product or an advertiser.

Trademark A word or symbol attached to merchandise or its package to identify the maker or origin. See *trade name.*

Trade name The name under which a firm does business, or by which the firm or its products or services are usually identified. Also called *brand name.* See *trademark.*

Traffic department In an advertising agency, the department that schedules the work of other departments and is responsible for its completion according to schedule. In broadcasting, the department responsible for the scheduling of all programs and announcements to be aired.

Traffic media See *out-of-home advertising.*

Transient rate The flat or one-time rate for advertising, without quantity or frequency discounts.

Transit advertising A form of out-of-home media; depends upon consumer usage of commercial transportation facilities—buses, airlines, and subway and commuter trains—and upon pedestrians viewing the advertising from the streets. Also called *transportation advertising.*

Translator station A television station that rebroadcasts programs from another station on another channel, but has no local studio and is not permitted to originate programs or commercials locally.

Transportation advertising See *transit advertising.*

Traveling display An exhibit of point-of-purchase material which is the property of the advertiser and is moved from one dealer or one location to another. Also, transit advertising on the outside of vehicles.

Triple spotting Broadcasting three commercials in succession, without intervening news or entertainment.

Twenty-four sheet A 24-sheet outdoor poster, 104 inches by 234 inches. Originally it required 24 separate sheets of paper, but now it may be produced with 10. See *thirty sheet.*

Type family A group of type faces of the same basic design, but with variations in width of characters, boldness or lightness of strokes, and the like. For example, Bodoni, Bodoni Bold, Bodoni Bold Italic, Bodoni Book, etc.

UHF Ultrahigh frequency, or television channels 14 through 84.

UPC (Universal Product Code) A voluntary system wherein manufacturers place on all package labels a series of linear bars and a 10-digit number which describes the particular product. This permits speed and record-keeping at the supermarket checkout.

Unaided recall A research technique in which respondents must answer questions without any aids to memory. See *aided recall.*

Unique selling proposition (USP) The central selling idea for an ad or commercial; a selling point matched with a consumer benefit, expressed in a unique way.

Uppercase Capital letters.

Use payment In broadcasting, fees paid talent for use of commercials in which they appear; established by SAG or AFTRA codes.

VHF Very high frequency, or television channels 2 through 13.

VTR (Videotape recording) See *videotape.*

Value The quality, or depth, of a color by which it is seen as light or dark. See *hue* and *chroma.*

Vehicular advertising See *mobile billboards.*

Vertical cooperative See *cooperative advertising.*

Vertical publication A business publication edited for persons in a particular industry or profession, regardless of specific job categories, in contrast to a *horizontal* publication.

Video Loosely used as a synonym for television; more accurately, the visual portion of a television broadcast.

Videotape An electronic unit that simultaneously records both audio and video on the same tape, and permits immediate playback and rapid editing.

Visualization The process of picturing in the mind how an ad will look before it is produced. Also used to denote a rough layout or storyboard.

Voice-over (VO) In television, narration with the narrator not visible on the screen.

Wash drawing A drawing similar to watercolor, executed with brush in varying shades of gray and black; reproduced by halftone engraving.

Waste circulation Advertising in a geographical area where the advertiser has no distribution for the advertised product. Also, that portion of the circulation of a medium which cannot be considered to reach logical prospects for a product because they are unable to use it or unable to pay for it.

Weight of type The relative blackness of a particular type face.

Wheeler-Lea Act An amendment to the Federal Trade Commission Act, enacted in 1938, designed to protect the consumer against unfair trade practices in interstate commerce, and especially against false or misleading advertising of food, drugs, and cosmetics.

Wipe In television, a rapid transition shot replacing one image on the screen with another.

Zero-base budgeting A business policy wherein the advertising manager must justify each step when building expenditures according to the specific objectives to be accomplished.

Zoom In television, a rapid change of perspective which makes the image grow larger ("zoom in") or smaller ("zoom out"). Done with a special lens.

Index

blue (cyan) +
yellow

yellow + red
(magenta)